Second Edition

THE ECONOMICS OF THE MIDDLE EAST AND NORTH AFRICA (MENA)

Joseph Pelzman

George Washington University, USA

NEW JERSEY • LONDON • SINGAPORE • BEIJING • SHANGHAI • HONG KONG • TAIPEI • CHENNAI • TOKYO

Published by

World Scientific Publishing Co. Pte. Ltd.
5 Toh Tuck Link, Singapore 596224
USA office: 27 Warren Street, Suite 401-402, Hackensack, NJ 07601
UK office: 57 Shelton Street, Covent Garden, London WC2H 9HE

Library of Congress Cataloging-in-Publication Data
Names: Pelzman, Joseph, author.
Title: The economics of the Middle East and North Africa (MENA) / Joseph Pelzman.
Description: 2nd edition. | New Jersey : World Scientific, 2018. |
Includes bibliographical references and index.
Identifiers: LCCN 2018026884 | ISBN 9789813203976
Subjects: LCSH: Middle East--Economic conditions. | Middle East--Economic policy. |
Africa, North--Economic conditions. | Africa, North--Economic policy.
Classification: LCC HC415.15 .P45 2018 | DDC 330.956--dc23
LC record available at https://lccn.loc.gov/2018026884

British Library Cataloguing-in-Publication Data
A catalogue record for this book is available from the British Library.

For any available supplementary material, please visit
https://www.worldscientific.com/worldscibooks/10.1142/10352#t=suppl

Desk Editor: Shreya Gopi

Typeset by Stallion Press
Email: enquiries@stallionpress.com

Printed in Singapore

Dedication

I wish to express my gratitude to my mother and father, Zina (ז"ל) and Abraham (ז"ל) who taught me innumerable lessons, both in their words as well as by the model of their own lives, that it is our responsibility to rise above xenophobia; to my wife Linda, a philosopher, who has to put up with an economist; and to my children Sarah-Felicia, Philip Michael, Amos, Ilana and Jacob David who never fail to keep me in stitches, and make our home cozy, interesting and lively.

Contents

List of Tables xi

List of Figures xvii

List of Acronyms and Abbreviations xix

About the Author xxiii

Chapter 1. Introduction **1**

Chapter 2. Survey of Main Economic Outcomes **21**

2.1 GDP Sector Divisions 21
2.2 Labor in MENA 32
2.3 Education and Human Capital in MENA 40
2.4 Health Expenditure in MENA 52
2.5 Growth and Capital Formation in MENA 65
2.6 Decomposition of MENA International Trade "Openness" 83
2.7 Impediments to Business Activity within MENA 123

Chapter 3. Islamic Economics: The Role of Interest-Free Finance in MENA's Development **163**

3.1 Basic Principles of Islamic Law Applicable to a Loan Agreement: Prohibition of Interest (*Riba*) and Risk/Uncertainty (*Gharar*) 168
3.2 Contractual Modes of Financing under Islamic Law 171
3.2.1 Partnerships (Musharaka and Mudharaba) 171

3.2.2 Lease (Ijara and "Ijara va iqtina") 172
3.2.3 Mark-Up Sale (Murabaha) 173
3.2.4 Commissioned Manufacturing (Istisna') 173
3.2.5 Empirical Evidence: Is Islamic Banking Interest-Free? 174

Chapter 4. Investment in Human Capital **179**

4.1 A Simplified Endogenous Growth Model 179
4.2 Human Capital Acquisition in MENA 183
4.2.1 The Demand Side 185
4.2.2 The Supply Side 209

Chapter 5. Labor Market in MENA **231**

5.1 Human Capital and Economic Growth 232
5.2 Measuring Aggregate Productivity 271
5.3 Labor Market Structure 276
5.3.1 Static Efficiency 277

Chapter 6. Oil Money and the 'Dutch Disease' **333**

6.1 The Basic Model of a Resource Curse 337
6.2 The Empirical Evidence on the Resource Curse 340

Chapter 7. Science, Technology and Innovation in MENA **369**

7.1 The Output of Science, Technology and Innovation in MENA 372
7.2 The Innovation Process within MENA 398

Chapter 8. International Trade in MENA **409**

8.1 The Formal Model of the Value-Added Chain in International Trade 419
8.2 The Value-Added Chain in MENA's International Trade: Looking Backward and Forward 424
8.3 Protectionism in MENA 432
8.4 MENA Country International Trade Competitiveness: An Assessment Based on Revealed Comparative Advantage (RCA) and Constant Market Share (CMS) Indexes 439

8.4.1 Competitiveness Based on RCA and Herfindahl Indexes 445
8.4.2 Competitiveness Based on CMS Decompositions 448
8.5 Regional Trade Agreements and MENA 460

Chapter 9. Conclusions and Prospects for MENA **465**

Data Appendix **467**

References **493**

Index **507**

List of Tables

1.1 Per Capita GDP for Individual MENA Countries (1970–2015) (Constant 2010 US Dollars) 4
1.2 Control of Corruption 5
1.3 Government Effectiveness 7
1.4 Political Stability and Absence of Violence/Terrorism 8
1.5 Regulatory Quality 9
1.6 Rule of Law 10
1.7 Voice and Accountability 12
1.8 2016 Index of Democracy by Category (Ranked, Overall and by MENA Countries) 13
1.9 The Washington Consensus: Lowest Common Denominator of Policy Reform to Promote Economic Growth and Practitioners' Augmentation 15
1.10 Ideal Representation of the Washington Consensus 16

2.1 Broad Sources of MENA Country Gross Domestic Product (Broad Sectors' Value Added as Percent of GDP and Natural Resource Rents as Percent of GDP) 22
2.2 Public Sector Remuneration for 2015 within MENA (% of GDP) 34
2.3 Profile of MENA Labor Force Participation, 2014 and Population, 2015 35
2.4 International Human Development Indicators — Education index for MENA 41
2.5 Education Achievements in MENA 2005–2015 43
2.6 Government Expenditure on Education and Per Student in Tertiary, Secondary and Primary Education in MENA . . . 46

2.7 MENA Country Expenditure on Research and Development and Internet Users . . . 53
2.8 Health Expenditure — Total, Public and Private and Per Capita in MENA Percent of GDP and PPP Constant 2011 International $ . . . 57
2.9 Hospital Beds (Per 10,000 Population) . . . 65
2.10 Physicians (Per 1,000 People) . . . 66
2.11 Life Expectancy at Birth and Healthy Life Expectancy at Birth, 2015 . . . 67
2.12 Capital Formation and Financing in MENA . . . 69
2.13 MENA Country International Trade Exposure . . . 85
2.14 Commodity Composition of MENA Merchandise Trade . . . 98
2.15 Commodity Composition of MENA's Major Components of Service Trade . . . 108
2.16 Commodity Composition of MENA High-Technology Exports and Tourism Trade . . . 116
2.17 Ease of Doing Business Index in MENA (2015–2016) . . . 125
2.18 Complexity and Bureaucracy of Starting a Business in MENA . . . 127
2.19 Dealing with Construction Permits in MENA, 2016 . . . 141
2.20 Registering Property in MENA, 2016 . . . 143
2.21 Ease of Getting Credit in MENA, 2016 . . . 146
2.22 Protecting Minority Investors in MENA, 2016 . . . 149
2.23 Paying Taxes in MENA, 2016 . . . 151
2.24 Cost of Trading Across Borders in MENA, 2016 . . . 155
2.25 Enforcing Contracts in MENA, 2016 . . . 159
2.26 Resolving Insolvency in MENA, 2016 . . . 161

4.1 Availability of Information and Communication Technologies (ICT) . . . 187
4.2 Ranking Information and Communication Technologies (ICTs) Infrastructure in MENA, 2016 . . . 207
4.3 Various Knowledge Economy Indices, Weighted by Population for MENA . . . 211
4.4 International Benchmark of Mathematics and Science Achievement in MENA . . . 216

5.1 Trends of Educational Attainment of Total MENA Population Aged 15 and Over. . . . 233

5.2 Trends of Educational Attainment of the MENA's Female Population Aged 15 and Over. 250
5.3 TFP Estimates Under Various Assumptions of Elasticity of Output with Respect to Physical Capital. 275
5.4 Employment by Sex and Economic Activity, Thousands, (ISIC-Rev.4). 278
5.5 Employment by Skill Level ISIC Rev 4 in Thousands and Percent. 308
5.6 Unemployment Distribution by Aggregate Education Levels (By Sex and Age) (Percent). 328

6.1 Basic Data on MENA Oil Producing Countries (2000–2016) 336
6.2 Oil — Total Proven Reserves for MENA 337
6.3 Outcome Variables for the Private Sector in MENA (2007–2017) 343
6.4 Global Perceptions of the Public Sector and the Rule of Law in MENA 350

7.1 Breakdown of Sources of Growth in a Number of MENA Economies, 1970–2000 373
7.2 Patents with Foreign Co-Inventors, 2000–2013 376
7.3 Foreign Ownership of Domestic Inventions 381
7.4 Number of Science & Engineering Articles in All Fields (Per Million Population) 384
7.5 Number of Science & Engineering Articles in Agricultural Sciences (Per Million Population) 386
7.6 Number of Science & Engineering Articles in Astronomy Sciences (Per Million Population) 387
7.7 Number of Science & Engineering Articles in Biological Sciences (Per Million Population) 388
7.8 Number of Science & Engineering Articles in Chemistry (Per Million Population) 389
7.9 Number of Science & Engineering Articles in Computer Sciences (Per Million Population) 391
7.10 Number of Science & Engineering Articles in Engineering (Per Million Population) 392
7.11 Number of Science & Engineering Articles in Geosciences (Per Million Population) 393

7.12 Number of Science & Engineering Articles in Mathematics (Per Million Population) 394

7.13 Number of Science & Engineering Articles in Medical Sciences (Per Million Population) 395

7.14 Number of Science & Engineering Articles in Other Life Sciences (Per Million Population) 396

7.15 Number of Science & Engineering Articles in Physics (Per Million Population) 397

7.16 Number of Science & Engineering Articles in Psychology (Per Million Population) 399

7.17 Number of Science & Engineering Articles in Social Sciences (Per Million Population) 400

7.18 Research and Development Expenditure in MENA (% GDP) 403

7.19 Triadic Patent Families in MENA 406

8.1 MENA Country Exports to the World (Million US Dollars and Percent). 410

8.2 MENA Country Imports from the World (Million US Dollars and Percent). 413

8.3 Intra — MENA Country Exports (Million US Dollars and Percent). 415

8.4 Intra — MENA Country Imports (Million US Dollars and Percent). 417

8.5 Foreign Value-Added Content of MENA's Exports by Major Categories as a Percent of Total Exports to the World (2000–2011). 425

8.6 Backward Participation: Origin of MENA Country Foreign Value-Added Content of Its Exports, 2000–2011 (Percent). 428

8.7 Forward Participation in GVCs-Domestic MENA VA Embodied in Foreign Exports, as Percent of Total Gross Exports of the Source Country. (Percent). 430

8.8 Fraser Institute Index for Freedom to Trade Internationally for MENA (1 = Most Restrictive, 10 = Least Restrictive). 434

8.9 Revealed Comparative Advantage (RCA) for MENA Country Exports by Major Product Group (2009–2015). 446
8.10 Herfindahl Market Concentration Index (2000–2016). 449
8.11 Decomposition of Changes in MENA Country Exports into CMS Components (2012–2016 and Percent). 450
8.12 Leading Regional Trading Agreements. 462

List of Figures

2.1 The Difference between the Share of Women and Men who are Either Employed or Looking for Work as a Percentage of their Respective Population 38
2.2 The Difference between the Share of Women and Men who Would Like to Work but are Unable to Find Jobs as a Share of their Respective Population 39

List of Acronyms and Abbreviations

CPI	Consumer price index
DC	Developed country
EU	European Union
FDI	Foreign direct investment
GATT	General Agreement on Tariffs and Trade
GCC	Gulf Cooperation Council
GDI	Gross domestic investment
GDP	Gross domestic product
GNI	Gross national income
GNP	Gross national product
GOIEC	General Organization for Import and Export Control
GSM	Global system for mobile communication
GTAP	Global Trade Analysis Project
HIC	High-income countries
ICT	Information and communication technology
IIT	Intra-Industry Trade Index
ILO	International Labor Organization
IMF	International Monetary Fund
ISIC	International standard industrial classification
IT	Information technology
LDC	Less Developed Country
MENA	Middle East and North Africa
NIC	Newly Industrialized Country
ODA	Official Development Assistance
OECD	Organization for Economic Co-operation and Development
OPEC	Organization of Petroleum-Exporting Countries
PAFTA	Pan-Arab Free Trade Area

PPP	Purchasing power parity
QIZs	Qualifying industrial zones (Jordan)
RIAs	Regional integration agreements
SITC	Standard Industry Trade Classification
SSA	Sub-Saharan Africa
UAE	United Arab Emirates
UEA-GCC	Unified Economic Agreement between the Countries of the Gulf Cooperation Council
UNCTAD	United Nations Conference on Trade and Development
UNDP	United Nations Development Programme
UNESCWA	United Nations Economic and Social Commission for West Africa
UNIFEM	United Nations Development Fund for Women
VAT	Value added tax
WDI	World Development Indicators
WTO	World Trade Organization

North Africa and the Middle East

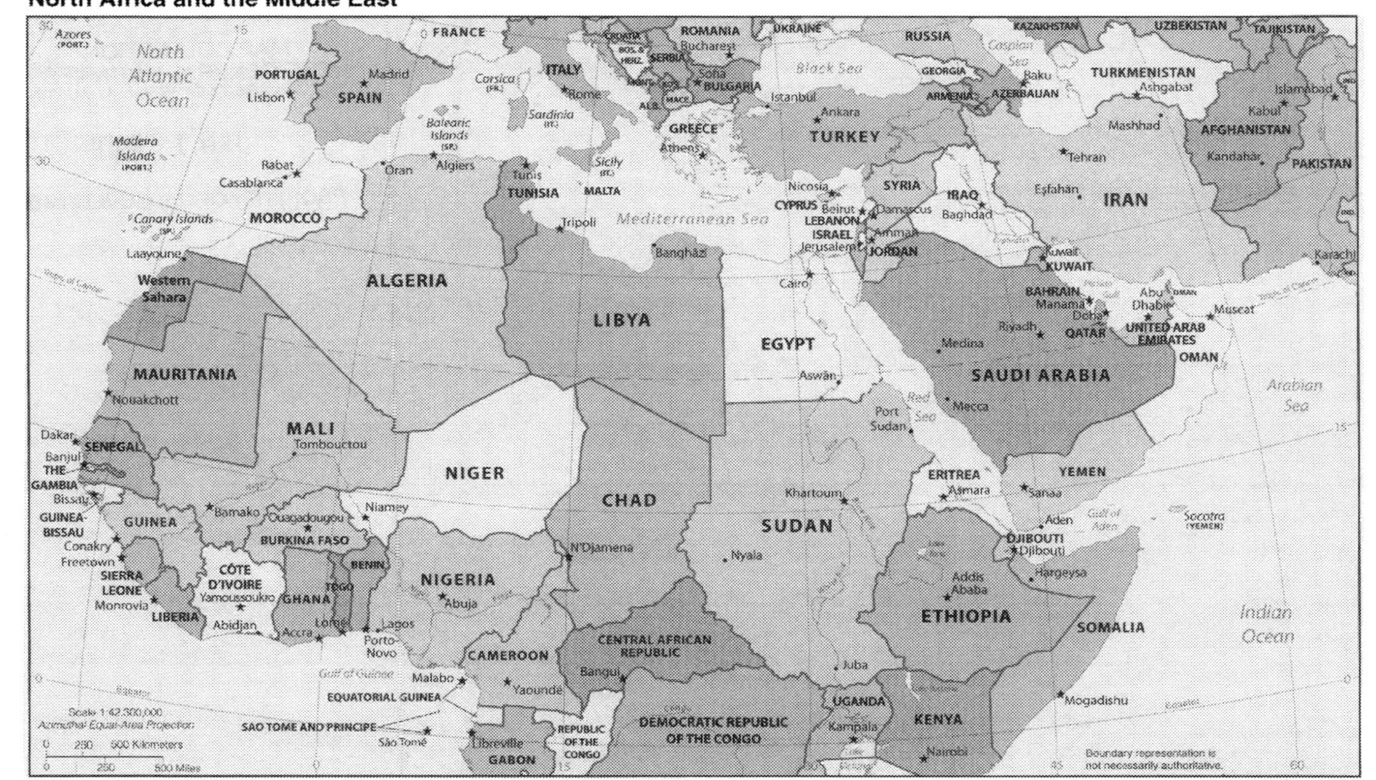

Source: http://www.lib.utexas.edu/maps/africa/n_africa_mid_east_pol_2009.jpg.

About the Author

Professor Joseph Pelzman is an internationally recognized authority and author on US and WTO international trade policy, the economics of international trade law, contemporary international trade policies affecting the PRC, with a strong interest in the Transition economies in Europe and in Asia.

Before joining the faculty at George Washington in 1980, he was a Brookings Institution Economic Policy Fellow. Prior to that he was a faculty member at the University of South Carolina (1976–79). He has held appointments at Renmin University, School of Economics, Beijing, (PRC) as a Fulbright Senior Scholar (2012–13); at Ben Gurion University of the Negev (Israel) as Fulbright Senior Scholar (1995–96); Visiting Professor of Law and Economics at Catholic University Law School (2001–05); Visiting Professor of Law at the Radzyner School Of Law, The Interdisciplinary Center, Herzliya, Israel (2001); Research Associate, The Maurice Falk Institute for Economic Research in Israel, The Hebrew University of Jerusalem, Jerusalem, Israel (1988–97); Visiting Scholar and Fellow, The Russian Research Center, Harvard University (1991–92); and Visiting Professor of Economics and Lady Davis Fellow, Department of Economics and Soviet and East European Research Center, The Hebrew University of Jerusalem (1984–85).

As part of his outreach program, he served as the founding Chair of the International Academic Board of the International School of Economics at Tbilisi State University (ISET), Tbilisi Georgia, (2006–08); and as a Member of International Advisory Board at the Kyiv School of Economics,

Ukraine, (2002–17). He also serves as a Member of the Board of Directors of the Trade, Aid and Security Coalition (TASC), Global Works Foundation, Washington DC. (2006–present);

Professor Pelzman is the current Managing Editor of the *Global Economy Journal* and President of the International Trade and Finance Association. He is also a frequent contributor to the international media, and has been a consultant to various governments, research institutions, foundations, and private corporations.

Professor Pelzman is a prolific author, having published articles in a number of leading economics journals, including the *American Economic Review*, *Journal of Political Economy*, *European Economic Review*, *Southern Economic Journal* and more recently published a number of books.

Chapter 1

Introduction

Today there is no unifying description of the group of countries that make up the Middle East and North Africa (MENA). Historically, there were dozens of nomadic tribes occupying this area. If we look at the historical references in the Torah (Hebrew Bible), we can identify two distinct nomadic tribes in the area which remain to this day differentiated by language and religious customs. In the Torah, however, they are distinguished not by language or religion but rather by location and living style. The first group, העברי or Hebrew (Yibri)[1] refers to Abraham and his descendants as those who had traveled from the other side of the Euphrates River. The second group, the הָעַרְבִי[2] or Arabs, are described as one of the nomadic tribes in the area who were "tent dwellers."

The continuous animosity between these two major groups within MENA — the Hebrews (modern-day Israel) and the Arabs — is based on a long-standing division in economic and humanistic principles which sets them apart. Modern-day Israel is the only democracy in MENA with full access to the global economy and a dedication to investment in the human capital of its citizens. The Arab members of MENA are struggling with the concept of democracy, as was obvious from the discontent of the Arab Spring, and therefore are very cautious about the advantages of investing in the human capital of their citizens. These countries are still being governed by non-representative agents that rely on hate and xenophobia to control the lives of their populations.[3] Despite the long-standing animosity

[1] העברי: שבא מעבר הנהר. The Hebrew: (הָעִבְרִי) because he came from the other side (מֵעֵבֶר) of the [Euphrates] river (Bereishit–Genesis — Chapter 14:13 and Rabbah 42:8).

[2] "A tent dweller, who is always found outside in the deserts, and because of this, he is called ערבי since he dwells in the ערבה, the plain." Jeremiah Chapter 3:2.

[3] Despite the fact that Arabs and Hebrews (Israel) lived in the area for over 4,000 years, the exclusion of Israel from being considered part of MENA can only be explained by

between these two groups, and the acquiescence by the IMF, UN and World Bank to exclude Israel from MENA, this volume includes Israel as part of MENA. We do not, however, address the economic issue of the territories Israel captured or liberated in the 1967 war with Jordan. The question of who is a Palestinian — Hebrew or Arab — is relegated to the political arena, along with the legitimacy of the post WWI geographic division of the ערבה into the current Arab states.[4]

A significant number of countries within MENA have historically avoided many of the necessary economic reforms that would take them out of the development trap. With the end of a century and a millennium many within MENA began a major period of stocktaking about their development experiences and started to discuss an agenda for the future. This

---

Arab hatred and xenophobia which currently is expressed via attempts to delegitimize Israel and treat it as a "special case" or as a Western outsider. A more reasonable explanation for this behavior is the difficulty that Arab leaders have in explaining to their local populations why a small economy with no natural resources and a heavy defense burden can manage to maintain a democracy with complete gender equality, variety of political expression, a democratic succession process and outperform their regional neighbors without exception.

[4] A derivative of the name **Palestine** first appears in Greek literature in the 5th century BCE (Before the common era) when the historian Herodotus called the area **Palaistin** (Greek — **Παλαιστινη**). In the 2nd century CE (common era), the Romans crushed the revolt of Shimon Bar Kokhba (132 CE), during which Jerusalem and Judea were regained, and the area of Judea was renamed **Palaestina** in an attempt to minimize Jewish identification with the land of Israel. Under the Ottoman Empire (1517–1917), the term **Palestine** was used as a general term to describe the land south of Syria; it was not an official designation. In fact, many Ottomans and Arabs who lived in Palestine during this time period referred to the area as Southern Syria and not as Palestine. After World War I, the name Palestine was applied to the territory that was placed under British Mandate; this area included not only present-day Israel but also present-day Jordan. Leading up to Israel's independence in 1948, it was common for the international press to label Jews, not Arabs, living in the mandate as Palestinians. It was not until years after Israeli independence that the Arabs living in the West Bank and Gaza Strip were called Palestinians. The word Palestine or Filastin does not appear in the Qur'an. It does appear in the Torah no fewer than 250 times. See *The History of Herodotus* by Herodotus (written 440 B.C.E and translated by George Rawlinson). In 1937, a local Arab leader, Auni Bey Abdul-Hadi, told the Peel Commission, which ultimately suggested the partition of Palestine: "There is no such country [as Palestine]! 'Palestine' is a term the Zionists invented! There is no Palestine in the Bible. Our country was for centuries part of Syria." The representative of the Arab Higher Committee to the United Nations submitted a statement to the General Assembly in May 1947 that said "Palestine was part of the Province of Syria" and that, "politically, the Arabs of Palestine were not independent in the sense of forming a separate political entity." A few years later, Ahmed Shuqeiri, later the chairman of the PLO, told the Security Council: "It is common knowledge that Palestine is nothing but southern Syria."

developed a series of World Bank studies along with the first edition of this book. Overwhelmingly, sustained economic growth remained the fundamental answer for reducing poverty. Furthermore, the development record in Asia and Latin America confirmed the effectiveness of investing more — and more efficiently — in education and health, reducing barriers to trade and investment, dismantling domestic price controls in agriculture and industry and reducing fiscal deficits. The participation in a global production network and in a global research and development network, despite temporary dislocations, could not call into question the fundamental efficacy of "globalization."

Economic development generally begins with a discussion of higher per capita income. In Table 1.1 we present a snapshot of the per capita GDP for the members of MENA, for 1970, 1980, 1990, 2000, 2010 and 2015. It is not surprising to find that for most of the MENA countries, there has not been a major uptick in real per capita income over this period. The exceptions include, Cyprus, Iraq, Israel, Morocco, Tunisia and Turkey. All of these countries undertook significant structural economic reforms along the lines of the "Washington Consensus," which outlined a policy prescription for liberalizing markets.

The outcome of an effective economic development program involves much more than raising real per capita GDP. It involves a restructured educational system which can develop skilled workers for meaningful job opportunities. It involves an effective plan to provide full gender equality. It involves more efficient health and nutrition services. It involves a cleaner, more sustainable natural environment. It involves a transparent and impartial judicial and legal system. It involves civil and political freedoms without corruption.

As real per capita incomes rise, some of these other outcome variables are expected to improve. Within MENA, the old stakeholders have placed limits on these other outcome variables, which continue to have a devastating impact on political stability within their states and in the region in general. Without change in the qualitative dimensions of development, some of the current MENA leaders will find themselves overthrown by a popular grassroots apprising.

In order to address these other qualitative dimensions of economic development which can be used to characterize these MENA countries, we present the six summary variables developed by the Worldwide Governance Indicators project. (www.govindicators.org.). In Table 1.2 we present the aggregate indicators of Control of Corruption from 2006 to 2015 with

Table 1.1. Per Capita GDP for Individual MENA Countries (1970–2015) (Constant 2010 US Dollars)

Country	1970	1980	1990	2000	2010	2015	Growth
Algeria	2,693	3,622	3,551	3,541	4,473	4,794	1%
Bahrain	—	21,184	17,934	22,878	20,386	22,348	0%
Cyprus	—	13,165	21,157	27,318	30,818	27,788	2%
Djibouti	—	—	1,566	1,065	1,358	1,650	0%
Egypt	798	1,213	1,588	1,996	2,668	2,707	3%
Iran	5,679	4,270	3,659	4,281	6,300	—	0%
Iraq	1,466	3,346	4,077	4,310	4,487	5,119	3%
Israel	12,908	17,220	20,469	27,026	30,662	33,117	3%
Jordan	—	3,129	2,587	3,006	4,054	3,976	1%
Kuwait	—	—	—	38,042	37,725	35,889	0%
Lebanon	—	—	4,231	6,748	8,764	7,045	1%
Libya	—	—	—	8,998	11,934	—	1%
Morocco	1,017	1,346	1,716	1,966	2,858	3,240	3%
Oman	9,239	9,907	14,903	18,937	19,921	15,966	1%
Qatar	—	—	—	60,737	70,870	74,687	0%
Saudi Arabia	15,134	26,419	14,980	14,980	18,754	21,313	1%
Syria	—	—	—	—	—	—	—
Tunisia	1,238	2,024	2,249	3,051	4,177	4,329	3%
Turkey	4,059	4,788	6,486	7,909	10,111	11,523	2%
UAE	—	115,003	68,508	64,133	34,342	39,313	−2%
Yemen	—	—	980	1,143	1,310	774	−1%
MENA	3,678	5,288	4,656	5,478	7,116	7,543	2%
USA	23,310	28,734	36,312	45,056	48,374	51,638	2%
OECD	16,909	21,570	27,249	32,758	35,658	37,457	2%

Source: World Bank — GDP per capita is gross domestic product divided by midyear population.
GDP is the sum of gross value added by all resident producers in the economy plus any product taxes and minus any subsidies not included in the value of the products. It is calculated without making deductions for depreciation of fabricated assets or for depletion and degradation of natural resources.
Data are in constant 2010 U.S. dollars.

a calculated slope to measures improvements or departures in the measure. Control of Corruption captures perceptions of the extent to which public power is exercised for private gain, including both petty and grand forms of corruption, as well as "capture" of the state by elites and private interests. The reported estimates provide the country's score on the aggregate indicator, in units of a standard normal distribution, i.e., ranging from approximately −2.5 to 2.5. Positive measures equate with control of corruption. Several of the MENA countries exhibited positive improvements in controlling corruption as measured by the perception data. They included: Bahrain, Egypt, Iraq, Morocco, Saudi Arabia and the UAE. Having said

Table 1.2. Control of Corruption

Country	2006	2007	2008	2009	2010	2011	2012	2013	2014	2015	SLOPE
Algeria	−0.480	−0.510	−0.561	−0.547	−0.488	−0.495	−0.474	−0.471	−0.615	−0.682	−21.509
Bahrain	0.244	0.252	0.249	0.241	0.249	0.237	0.399	0.458	0.299	0.173	9.260
Cyprus	1.094	1.078	1.242	0.933	1.005	0.887	1.254	1.248	1.066	0.981	−0.690
Djibouti	−0.597	−0.445	−0.180	−0.289	−0.318	−0.306	−0.341	−0.424	−0.492	−0.575	−4.663
Egypt	−0.663	−0.679	−0.707	−0.418	−0.549	−0.657	−0.588	−0.604	−0.593	−0.559	11.502
Iran	−0.450	−0.500	−0.743	−0.861	−0.991	−0.924	−0.817	−0.680	−0.570	−0.609	−2.345
Iraq	−1.566	−1.580	−1.571	−1.394	−1.310	−1.205	−1.247	−1.263	−1.338	−1.371	15.411
Israel	1.003	0.814	0.839	0.750	0.668	0.713	0.837	0.850	0.825	0.894	−3.352
Jordan	0.312	0.317	0.413	0.183	0.042	0.096	0.080	0.097	0.155	0.260	−12.460
Kuwait	0.544	0.491	0.539	0.415	0.400	0.130	−0.158	−0.151	−0.263	−0.218	−8.431
Lebanon	−0.965	−0.908	−0.845	−0.828	−0.859	−0.886	−0.870	−0.930	−1.063	−0.878	−10.265
Libya	−1.028	−0.962	−0.860	−1.167	−1.258	−1.293	−1.403	−1.524	−1.610	−1.695	−10.284
Morocco	−0.402	−0.327	−0.377	−0.308	−0.175	−0.400	−0.435	−0.363	−0.260	−0.249	10.833
Oman	0.186	0.267	0.455	0.288	0.284	−0.001	0.084	0.082	0.251	0.200	−8.937
Qatar	1.092	0.810	1.112	1.723	1.569	1.083	1.197	1.246	1.093	0.984	−0.295
Saudi Arabia	−0.246	−0.180	−0.028	−0.011	0.057	−0.375	−0.059	−0.005	0.097	0.064	10.289
Syria	−0.998	−1.026	−1.081	−1.068	−1.080	−1.044	−1.179	−1.218	−1.549	−1.533	−12.793
Tunisia	−0.070	−0.105	−0.179	−0.109	−0.149	−0.168	−0.141	−0.135	−0.093	−0.111	−8.450
Turkey	0.011	0.092	0.086	0.075	0.030	0.055	0.173	0.117	−0.122	−0.115	−13.331
UAE	0.949	1.079	1.131	0.955	0.929	1.073	1.185	1.303	1.233	1.124	15.302
Yemen	−0.686	−0.681	−0.683	−1.018	−1.159	−1.184	−1.230	−1.211	−1.551	−1.448	−9.128
USA	1.317	1.342	1.410	1.263	1.260	1.265	1.387	1.293	1.323	1.379	3.852

Source: Kaufmann *et al.* (2010).
Notes: Control of Corruption captures perceptions of the extent to which public power is exercised for private gain, including both petty and grand forms of corruption, as well as "capture" of the state by elites and private interests. Estimate gives the country's score on the aggregate indicator, in units of a standard normal distribution, i.e., ranging from approximately −2.5 to 2.5.

that, most of the MENA countries experienced a loss of control of corruption throughout the 2006–2015 period.

Table 1.3 presents the aggregate indicators for Government Effectiveness which captures perceptions of the quality of public services, the quality of the civil service and the degree of its independence from political pressures, the quality of policy formulation and implementation, and the credibility of the government's commitment to such policies. The reported estimates provide the country's score on the aggregate indicator, in units of a standard normal distribution, i.e., ranging from approximately −2.5 to 2.5. Several of the MENA countries exhibited positive improvements in government effectiveness as measured by the perception data. They included: Bahrain, Iraq, Israel, Morocco, Qatar, Saudi Arabia, Turkey and the UAE. Despite the improvements in government effectiveness for these MENA countries, the majority of MENA countries did not experience an effective government throughout the 2006–2015 period.

Table 1.4 presents the aggregate indicators for Political Stability and Absence of Violence/Terrorism measures perceptions of the likelihood of political and/or politically motivated violence, including terrorism. The reported estimates provide the country's score on the aggregate indicator, in units of a standard normal distribution, i.e., ranging from approximately −2.5 to 2.5. Unfortunately, the historic perception of political stability for most countries within MENA is very pessimistic. While there were some minor improvements in perception concerning violence and terrorism, all the observations were in the unstable range. Observations for Morocco and Israel showed the greatest level of optimism.

Table 1.5 presents the aggregate indicators for Regulatory Quality which captures perceptions of the ability of the government to formulate and implement sound policies and regulations that permit and promote private sector development. The reported estimates provide the country's score on the aggregate indicator, in units of a standard normal distribution, i.e., ranging from approximately −2.5 to 2.5. The historic perception of regulatory quality in favor the development of a private sector various across the spectrum for most countries within MENA. On the optimistic side stands Israel, Qatar, Turkey and the UAE, where there have been major efforts to bring back the market economy with limited State intervention. In the balance of MENA countries, the role and importance of the State still dominates economic activity for most of the population.

Table 1.6 presents the aggregate indicators for Rule of Law which captures perceptions of the extent to which agents have confidence in and abide

Table 1.3. Government Effectiveness

Country	2006	2007	2008	2009	2010	2011	2012	2013	2014	2015	SLOPE
Algeria	−0.472	−0.556	−0.613	−0.578	−0.476	−0.575	−0.539	−0.539	−0.483	−0.506	14.251
Bahrain	0.405	0.424	0.407	0.496	0.484	0.546	0.550	0.595	0.591	0.574	37.971
Cyprus	1.316	1.427	1.521	1.431	1.528	1.565	1.389	1.363	1.136	1.036	−10.356
Djibouti	−0.911	−0.876	−0.883	−0.909	−0.990	−0.965	−1.074	−0.971	−0.983	−0.956	−32.393
Egypt	−0.481	−0.373	−0.351	−0.273	−0.376	−0.571	−0.818	−0.889	−0.840	−0.762	−10.461
Iran	−0.565	−0.606	−0.628	−0.574	−0.475	−0.441	−0.534	−0.687	−0.411	−0.202	13.001
Iraq	−1.770	−1.592	−1.258	−1.202	−1.222	−1.154	−1.125	−1.116	−1.133	−1.269	10.003
Israel	1.246	1.243	1.334	1.260	1.367	1.330	1.263	1.229	1.159	1.375	0.137
Jordan	0.184	0.224	0.233	0.260	0.116	0.094	0.000	−0.042	0.135	0.136	−18.540
Kuwait	0.241	0.106	0.007	0.214	0.178	0.020	−0.068	−0.063	−0.148	−0.024	−17.575
Lebanon	−0.290	−0.324	−0.402	−0.488	−0.275	−0.257	−0.345	−0.396	−0.375	−0.471	−13.433
Libya	−1.113	−1.198	−1.157	−1.077	−1.101	−1.356	−1.484	−1.488	−1.715	−1.697	−11.064
Morocco	−0.135	−0.164	−0.170	−0.132	−0.090	−0.153	−0.052	−0.033	−0.066	−0.061	47.395
Oman	0.268	0.352	0.438	0.412	0.416	0.268	0.272	0.222	0.287	0.094	−18.480
Qatar	0.555	0.444	0.613	0.997	0.891	0.777	0.956	1.082	0.992	0.996	11.282
Saudi Arabia	−0.226	−0.109	−0.074	−0.065	0.031	−0.323	0.035	0.071	0.225	0.210	12.664
Syria	−0.959	−0.785	−0.637	−0.586	−0.602	−0.498	−1.174	−1.432	−1.441	−1.634	−5.200
Tunisia	0.583	0.471	0.321	0.403	0.239	0.029	−0.044	−0.070	−0.118	−0.104	−11.061
Turkey	0.170	0.312	0.272	0.289	0.309	0.364	0.415	0.386	0.381	0.233	19.759
UAE	0.917	0.925	0.882	1.025	0.907	1.059	1.149	1.179	1.477	1.537	11.506
Yemen	−0.923	−0.879	−0.880	−1.078	−1.022	−1.133	−1.259	−1.208	−1.405	−1.641	−11.505
USA	1.604	1.648	1.603	1.504	1.549	1.513	1.523	1.514	1.457	1.462	−42.515

Source: Kaufmann *et al.* (2010).

Notes: Government Effectiveness captures perceptions of the quality of public services, the quality of the civil service and the degree of its independence from political pressures, the quality of policy formulation and implementation, and the credibility of the government's commitment to such policies. Estimate gives the country's score on the aggregate indicator, in units of a standard normal distribution, i.e., ranging from approximately −2.5 to 2.5.

Table 1.4. Political Stability and Absence of Violence/Terrorism

Country	2006	2007	2008	2009	2010	2011	2012	2013	2014	2015	SLOPE
Algeria	−1.118	−1.124	−1.091	−1.215	−1.261	−1.362	−1.319	−1.184	−1.166	−1.046	−2.876
Bahrain	−0.390	−0.242	−0.236	−0.163	−0.506	−0.959	−1.137	−1.345	−0.931	−1.078	−5.803
Cyprus	0.516	0.534	0.641	0.379	0.443	0.596	0.618	0.550	0.556	0.543	7.253
Djibouti	−0.224	−0.057	0.303	0.501	0.262	0.180	0.165	−0.121	−0.743	−0.448	−3.889
Egypt	−0.864	−0.592	−0.521	−0.619	−0.907	−1.445	−1.465	−1.648	−1.608	−1.343	−5.635
Iran	−1.079	−0.985	−0.979	−1.552	−1.617	−1.420	−1.328	−1.257	−0.906	−0.905	1.229
Iraq	−2.820	−2.788	−2.479	−2.186	−2.251	−1.839	−1.934	−2.019	−2.488	−2.287	5.100
Israel	−1.274	−1.264	−1.333	−1.623	−1.320	−1.191	−1.069	−1.089	−1.045	−1.118	11.000
Jordan	−0.768	−0.313	−0.365	−0.356	−0.310	−0.516	−0.521	−0.616	−0.547	−0.576	−4.604
Kuwait	0.362	0.559	0.458	0.337	0.436	0.293	0.176	0.140	0.130	−0.109	−13.586
Lebanon	−1.843	−2.130	−1.891	−1.578	−1.629	−1.556	−1.660	−1.695	−1.691	−1.719	9.288
Libya	0.346	0.730	0.804	0.814	−0.029	−1.283	−1.544	−1.809	−2.346	−2.198	−2.143
Morocco	−0.475	−0.511	−0.600	−0.410	−0.383	−0.395	−0.462	−0.485	−0.432	−0.336	21.870
Oman	0.814	0.902	0.916	0.799	0.586	0.417	0.451	0.450	0.707	0.695	−9.314
Qatar	0.902	0.941	1.098	1.209	1.115	1.164	1.211	1.190	0.976	0.977	5.677
Saudi Arabia	−0.538	−0.503	−0.373	−0.507	−0.224	−0.460	−0.451	−0.408	−0.281	−0.544	5.919
Syria	−0.276	−0.298	−0.305	−0.493	−0.810	−2.008	−2.692	−2.684	−2.757	−2.938	−2.418
Tunisia	0.238	0.188	0.120	0.058	−0.040	−0.369	−0.742	−0.931	−0.853	−0.867	−5.943
Turkey	−0.603	−0.818	−0.844	−1.032	−0.920	−0.954	−1.194	−1.201	−1.068	−1.276	−13.213
UAE	0.907	0.970	0.700	0.915	0.784	0.908	0.868	0.892	0.761	0.755	−13.285
Yemen	−1.344	−1.561	−1.991	−2.320	−2.417	−2.413	−2.410	−2.351	−2.632	−2.632	−6.110
USA	0.486	0.372	0.558	0.427	0.433	0.595	0.632	0.635	0.575	0.699	21.917

Source: Kaufmann *et al.* (2010).

Notes: Political Stability and Absence of Violence/Terrorism measures perceptions of the likelihood of political and/or politically motivated violence, including terrorism.

Estimate gives the country's score on the aggregate indicator, in units of a standard normal distribution, i.e., ranging from approximately −2.5 to 2.5.

Table 1.5. Regulatory Quality

Country	2006	2007	2008	2009	2010	2011	2012	2013	2014	2015	SLOPE
Algeria	−0.565	−0.610	−0.795	−1.070	−1.166	−1.189	−1.281	−1.168	−1.284	−1.170	−9.615
Bahrain	0.702	0.792	0.724	0.714	0.732	0.743	0.698	0.612	0.695	0.828	−2.360
Cyprus	1.283	1.333	1.386	1.374	1.432	1.237	1.133	0.922	1.095	1.060	−13.783
Djibouti	−0.751	−0.704	−0.670	−0.614	−0.624	−0.529	−0.425	−0.520	−0.514	−0.689	17.109
Egypt	−0.433	−0.282	−0.174	−0.187	−0.157	−0.325	−0.471	−0.638	−0.742	−0.796	−9.680
Iran	−1.484	−1.616	−1.631	−1.730	−1.695	−1.507	−1.415	−1.488	−1.463	−1.280	14.016
Iraq	−1.404	−1.323	−1.147	−1.006	−1.051	−1.092	−1.249	−1.239	−1.247	−1.233	3.035
Israel	1.021	1.112	1.181	1.112	1.225	1.325	1.165	1.159	1.209	1.270	22.895
Jordan	0.349	0.322	0.333	0.283	0.230	0.303	0.194	0.131	0.080	0.048	−25.959
Kuwait	0.299	0.276	0.181	0.158	0.169	0.091	−0.037	−0.075	−0.131	−0.156	−17.868
Lebanon	−0.209	−0.255	−0.236	−0.031	0.078	−0.038	−0.109	−0.069	−0.221	−0.277	0.412
Libya	−1.461	−1.078	−0.880	−1.128	−1.183	−1.539	−1.649	−1.859	−2.111	−2.237	−5.620
Morocco	−0.171	−0.200	−0.179	−0.048	−0.067	−0.105	−0.077	−0.114	−0.124	−0.172	14.294
Oman	0.586	0.624	0.712	0.537	0.458	0.336	0.483	0.482	0.690	0.582	−4.313
Qatar	0.341	0.427	0.663	0.689	0.606	0.492	0.809	0.754	0.567	0.692	12.250
Saudi Arabia	−0.061	0.042	0.147	0.180	0.183	0.029	0.113	0.088	−0.007	0.030	−1.452
Syria	−1.386	−1.290	−1.123	−0.952	−0.890	−0.928	−1.538	−1.553	−1.674	−1.633	−5.282
Tunisia	0.116	0.053	0.074	0.003	−0.019	−0.191	−0.192	−0.331	−0.386	−0.394	−14.981
Turkey	0.302	0.328	0.274	0.296	0.311	0.382	0.427	0.436	0.408	0.330	33.562
UAE	0.645	0.639	0.600	0.467	0.336	0.469	0.689	0.793	0.977	1.133	8.128
Yemen	−0.776	−0.671	−0.711	−0.624	−0.596	−0.808	−0.675	−0.716	−0.845	−1.101	−11.903
USA	1.648	1.499	1.544	1.397	1.436	1.449	1.293	1.263	1.272	1.298	−21.205

Source: Kaufmann *et al.* (2010).
Notes: Regulatory Quality captures perceptions of the ability of the government to formulate and implement sound policies and regulations that permit and promote private sector development.
Estimate gives the country's score on the aggregate indicator, in units of a standard normal distribution, i.e., ranging from approximately −2.5 to 2.5.

Table 1.6. Rule of Law

Country	2006	2007	2008	2009	2010	2011	2012	2013	2014	2015	SLOPE
Algeria	−0.658	−0.726	−0.706	−0.758	−0.749	−0.776	−0.746	−0.658	−0.734	−0.831	−27.974
Bahrain	0.422	0.574	0.567	0.553	0.480	0.392	0.285	0.361	0.449	0.460	−15.334
Cyprus	1.075	1.082	1.190	1.191	1.196	1.053	1.079	1.008	1.059	1.012	−22.619
Djibouti	−0.822	−0.696	−0.584	−0.649	−0.714	−0.794	−0.769	−0.752	−0.852	−0.899	−18.717
Egypt	−0.207	−0.191	−0.084	−0.058	−0.115	−0.407	−0.455	−0.597	−0.602	−0.503	−11.660
Iran	−0.903	−0.933	−0.868	−0.944	−0.984	−0.941	−0.893	−0.976	−1.033	−0.954	−36.219
Iraq	−1.794	−1.928	−1.843	−1.771	−1.615	−1.519	−1.496	−1.481	−1.364	−1.459	14.529
Israel	0.888	0.811	0.827	0.823	0.899	0.999	0.927	0.962	1.105	1.168	21.632
Jordan	0.380	0.452	0.461	0.297	0.224	0.259	0.385	0.404	0.482	0.462	6.357
Kuwait	0.577	0.647	0.624	0.613	0.603	0.545	0.394	0.397	0.050	0.035	−11.295
Lebanon	−0.637	−0.711	−0.678	−0.689	−0.690	−0.666	−0.745	−0.775	−0.759	−0.786	−50.981
Libya	−0.992	−0.814	−0.704	−0.847	−0.939	−1.177	−1.141	−1.357	−1.532	−1.688	−8.315
Morocco	−0.254	−0.266	−0.286	−0.192	−0.157	−0.223	−0.203	−0.242	−0.052	−0.077	28.815
Oman	0.374	0.510	0.709	0.657	0.639	0.542	0.594	0.565	0.579	0.462	1.670
Qatar	0.723	0.635	0.788	1.011	0.946	0.842	1.042	1.054	0.986	0.885	14.311
Saudi Arabia	0.109	0.187	0.189	0.160	0.260	0.135	0.251	0.274	0.269	0.254	37.317
Syria	−0.865	−0.697	−0.596	−0.485	−0.505	−0.693	−1.102	−1.406	−1.339	−1.431	−6.145
Tunisia	0.197	0.170	0.142	0.200	0.122	−0.136	−0.147	−0.208	−0.133	−0.053	−15.190
Turkey	0.043	0.018	0.083	0.103	0.118	0.079	0.043	0.084	0.037	−0.060	−21.209
UAE	0.372	0.359	0.486	0.463	0.365	0.531	0.569	0.652	0.711	0.708	20.260
Yemen	−1.033	−0.973	−0.982	−1.085	−1.065	−1.273	−1.263	−1.166	−1.171	−1.238	−21.314
USA	1.575	1.579	1.613	1.575	1.630	1.605	1.615	1.547	1.615	1.604	23.163

Source: Kaufmann *et al.* (2010).
Notes: Rule of Law captures perceptions of the extent to which agents have confidence in and abide by the rules of society, and in particular the quality of contract enforcement, property rights, the police, and the courts, as well as the likelihood of crime and violence.
Estimate gives the country's score on the aggregate indicator, in units of a standard normal distribution, i.e., ranging from approximately −2.5 to 2.5.

by the rules of society, and in particular the quality of contract enforcement, property rights, the police, and the courts, as well as the likelihood of crime and violence. The reported estimates provide the country's score on the aggregate indicator, in units of a standard normal distribution, i.e., ranging from approximately −2.5 to 2.5. The perception for a positive set of norms called Rule of Law exists in Bahrain, Cyprus, Israel, Jordan, Oman, Qatar, Saudi Arabia, and the UAE. The biggest improvements for the perception of Rule of Law were for Israel, Qatar, Saudi Arabia and the UAE. For the balance of countries within MENA, the perception of a positive expectation for Rule of Law was non-existent and sadly deteriorating.

Table 1.7 presents the aggregate indicators for Voice and Accountability which captures perceptions of the extent to which a country's citizens are able to participate in selecting their government, as well as freedom of expression, freedom of association, and a free media. The reported estimates provide the country's score on the aggregate indicator, in units of a standard normal distribution, i.e., ranging from approximately −2.5 to 2.5. The perception for a positive voice and accountability in the MENA region does not exist, with the exception of Cyprus and Israel. The biggest improvements, from large negative observations, for the perception of Voice and Accountability were in Egypt, Iraq, Libya, and Tunisia.

From the data in Tables 1.2–1.7 we can conclude that the local perceptions within the MENA region is that they are inhabitants in countries that are undergoing structural changes in governance, at varying speeds. Overall there are a number of MENA countries which have decided to tackle the governance issue more forcefully than their neighbors. They include Israel, Qatar, Saudi Arabia and the UAE. For the balance of countries within MENA, the perception of positive results from governance reforms is still not present.

In political terms these economies run the gamut from authoritarian rule by cliques and juntas to monarchies and tribal fiefdoms in Arab MENA to the only experienced Western democracy, Israel. Table 1.8 presents the ranking of MENA countries by democratic institutions as developed by *The Economist.* As is commonly expected, there is a big gap between the non-Arab and Arab MENA with respect to these indices. These huge disparities between the various member states in MENA raise a whole set of questions about what variables play an important part in determining the large differences in economic development and growth within MENA. The current paradigm starts with an investigation of the role of democratic

Table 1.7. Voice and Accountability

Country	2006	2007	2008	2009	2010	2011	2012	2013	2014	2015	SLOPE
Algeria	−0.920	−0.996	−0.989	−1.057	−1.027	−1.001	−0.897	−0.893	−0.824	−0.853	25.042
Bahrain	−0.908	−0.862	−0.875	−0.799	−0.972	−1.223	−1.326	−1.322	−1.320	−1.321	−11.856
Cyprus	1.050	1.068	1.089	1.078	1.022	1.053	1.014	0.975	1.037	1.043	−50.246
Djibouti	−1.096	−1.180	−1.179	−1.183	−1.248	−1.402	−1.417	−1.465	−1.425	−1.402	−20.556
Egypt	−1.156	−1.125	−1.174	−1.122	−1.147	−1.134	−0.765	−1.039	−1.143	−1.096	8.364
Iran	−1.475	−1.532	−1.539	−1.553	−1.575	−1.551	−1.585	−1.603	−1.572	−1.538	−54.879
Iraq	−1.402	−1.231	−1.198	−1.100	−1.056	−1.136	−1.122	−1.096	−1.223	−1.194	13.006
Israel	0.764	0.724	0.701	0.549	0.563	0.645	0.631	0.638	0.728	0.744	−1.403
Jordan	−0.688	−0.654	−0.716	−0.780	−0.798	−0.796	−0.734	−0.816	−0.770	−0.779	−39.335
Kuwait	−0.553	−0.519	−0.523	−0.460	−0.506	−0.539	−0.629	−0.648	−0.650	−0.654	−33.167
Lebanon	−0.411	−0.500	−0.455	−0.377	−0.354	−0.419	−0.415	−0.437	−0.464	−0.481	−12.359
Libya	−1.936	−1.896	−1.884	−1.862	−1.890	−1.560	−0.938	−1.010	−1.129	−1.366	6.106
Morocco	−0.730	−0.736	−0.787	−0.778	−0.728	−0.742	−0.632	−0.730	−0.737	−0.660	33.034
Oman	−1.119	−1.006	−1.018	−1.030	−0.997	−1.017	−0.984	−1.002	−1.053	−1.029	25.863
Qatar	−0.662	−0.906	−0.877	−0.888	−0.894	−0.964	−0.799	−0.862	−0.991	−1.012	−18.943
Saudi Arabia	−1.705	−1.623	−1.645	−1.775	−1.736	−1.863	−1.815	−1.827	−1.798	−1.759	−26.001
Syria	−1.705	−1.726	−1.664	−1.639	−1.640	−1.751	−1.797	−1.782	−1.800	−1.849	−31.296
Tunisia	−1.232	−1.321	−1.288	−1.314	−1.374	−0.393	−0.214	−0.121	0.158	0.192	4.117
Turkey	−0.102	−0.093	−0.079	−0.086	−0.117	−0.161	−0.227	−0.261	−0.331	−0.374	−25.834
UAE	−1.003	−0.914	−0.918	−0.843	−0.913	−0.908	−1.013	−1.030	−1.064	−1.067	−25.102
Yemen	−1.193	−1.114	−1.225	−1.281	−1.343	−1.412	−1.388	−1.355	−1.306	−1.494	−22.402
USA	1.079	1.088	1.120	1.086	1.122	1.113	1.143	1.085	1.062	1.075	−19.520

Source: Kaufmann *et al.* (2010).

Notes: Voice and Accountability captures perceptions of the extent to which a country's citizens are able to participate in selecting their government, as well as freedom of expression, freedom of association, and a free media.

Estimate gives the country's score on the aggregate indicator, in units of a standard normal distribution, i.e., ranging from approximately −2.5 to 2.5.

Table 1.8. 2016 Index of Democracy by Category (Ranked, Overall and by MENA Countries)

Country	Overall score	Overall rank	Regional rank	Category Scores: I Electoral process and pluralism	II Functioning of government	III Political participation	IV Political culture	V Civil liberties	Regime type
Israel	7.85	29	1	9.17	7.50	8.89	7.50	6.18	Democracy
Cyprus	7.65	36	—	9.17	6.43	6.67	6.88	9.12	Democracy
Tunisia	6.40	69	2	6.00	6.07	7.78	6.25	5.88	Democracy
Turkey	5.04	97	—	5.83	6.07	5.00	5.63	2.65	Hybrid
Lebanon	4.86	102	3	4.42	2.14	7.78	4.38	5.59	Hybrid
Morocco	4.77	105	4	4.75	4.64	4.44	5.63	4.41	Hybrid
Iraq	4.08	114	6	4.33	0.07	7.22	4.38	4.41	Hybrid
Jordan	3.96	117	7	4.00	4.29	3.89	4.38	3.24	Authoritarian
Kuwait	3.85	121	8	3.17	4.29	3.89	4.38	3.53	Authoritarian
Algeria	3.56	126	9	2.58	2.21	3.89	5.00	4.12	Authoritarian
Egypt	3.31	133	10	2.58	3.93	3.33	3.75	2.94	Authoritarian
Qatar	3.18	135	11	0.00	3.93	2.22	5.63	4.12	Authoritarian
Oman	3.04	141	12	0.00	3.93	2.78	4.38	4.12	Authoritarian
Djibouti	2.83	145	—	0.42	2.14	3.33	5.63	2.65	Authoritarian
Bahrain	2.79	146	13	1.25	3.21	2.78	4.38	2.35	Authoritarian
UAE	2.75	147	14	0.00	3.57	2.22	5.00	2.94	Authoritarian
Sudan	2.37	151	15	0.00	1.79	3.89	5.00	1.18	Authoritarian
Iran	2.34	154	16	0.00	3.21	3.89	3.13	1.47	Authoritarian
Libya	2.25	155	17	1.00	0.00	1.67	5.63	2.94	Authoritarian
Yemen	2.07	156	18	0.00	0.00	4.44	5.00	0.88	Authoritarian
Saudi Arabia	1.93	159	19	0.00	2.86	2.22	3.13	1.47	Authoritarian
Syria	1.43	166	20	0.00	0.00	2.78	4.38	0.00	Authoritarian

Source: *The Economist Intelligence Unit's Index of Democracy 2016.*
Note: Total pool is 167 countries. Regimes considered authoritarian begin with country ranking of 117. *The Economist's* index of democracy is based on the rating of 60 indicators grouped into five categories: Electoral process and pluralism, Functioning of government, Political participation, Political culture and Civil liberties. Each category has a rating on a 0 to 10 scale, and the overall index of democracy is the simple average of the five category indexes.

versus non-democratic institutions, the process by which scarce resources are allocated to the various economic agents, and whether or not economic decision-making was simply incompetent or short-sighted.

The purpose of this book is not to provide a country-by-country study but rather to deal with general themes found in Arab MENA and Israel, such as problems associated with growth and structural change, the role of 'State' intervention and the development of oligarchies in the country specific local markets, labor market imperfections driven by gender bias, technology gaps and endogenous growth, capital market development in a restricted financial model based on religious constraints, savings and investment behavior in a model of state subsidization and intervention designed to control local development, and the role of state-induced -bottom-up corruption. This approach helps us to raise general questions about the growth experience of the region as a whole and at the same time to focus on key sector issues, such as the relevance of Islamic banking to capital formation and the role for international trade and investment. This volume serves as both a textbook and a summary of the very large literature on MENA. Data sources used in the volume include country-specific data, and international data from the World Bank, UN, IMF and OECD data sources.

Consequently, the best generalizations in terms of economically sound "growth strategies" are those focusing on the large picture strategies, namely trade liberalization, liberalized factor markets, improved refinement of the human capital delivery systems and human capital acquisition, liberalization of credit instruments and financial markets, and a return to an incentive-based market system.

The consensus of the neoclassical growth literature is that in order to sustain economic growth, one must ensure some basic economic principles — protection of property rights, contract enforcement, market-based competition rules, transparent financial markets, and appropriate incentives. These "first principles" are dependent on the development of appropriate institutions and rules by which they function. There is no single unique approach that delivers these first-order principles.

Easterly (2001) provides an insightful historical account of the evolution of thinking on economic development from the post-war period to the latest accepted paradigm known as the "Washington Consensus." The path to success evolved from the "big push" and import substitution as the magic bullets in the 1950s and 1960s to the export promotion and reliance on market signals as the medium of success in the 1970s to Williamson's "Washington Consensus" of the 1980s and 1990s (Williamson, 1990). The

Table 1.9. The Washington Consensus: Lowest Common Denominator of Policy Reform to Promote Economic Growth and Practitioners' Augmentation

Original Washington Consensus Top 10
1. Fiscal discipline
2. Reorientation of public expenditures
3. Tax reform
4. Interest rate liberalization
5. Unified and competitive exchange rates
6. Trade liberalization
7. Openness to Direct Foreign Investment
8. Privatization
9. Deregulation
10. Secure property rights
Augmented by development practitioners
11. Corporate governance
12. Anti-corruption
13. Flexible labor markets
14. Adherence to WTO disciplines
15. "Prudent" capital-account opening
16. Non-intermediate exchange rate regimes
17. Independent central banks/inflation targeting
18. Social safety nets
19. Targeted poverty reduction

Source: Williamson (1990); Stiglitz (1998); World Bank (1998); Naim (2000); Birdsall and de la Torre (2001); Kaufmann (2002); Kuczynski and Williamson (2003); and Rodrik (2005).

basic elements of this Consensus plus the augmentations that were developed by countless practitioners are presented in Table 1.9.

The rationale for augmenting the "Washington Consensus" was developed because it became obvious that the "Victorian virtues in economic policy" as characterized by Krugman (1995) were inadequate. Market-oriented reforms short of substantial institutional transformation in the cost of doing business; to labor market reforms eliminating gender biases, were inadequate. With all due respect to the power of trade liberalization, labor market restrictions based on 16th century prohibitions against women would eliminate the benefits of increased competition and factor market flexibility. Consequently, the focus was augmented to include central bank independence, adherence to international standards in the labor market and financial codes and standards. How well-suited are the targets

Table 1.10. Ideal Representation of the Washington Consensus

Institutional Changes	Ideal Changes
Property rights	Private, enforced by rule of law
Corporate governance	Shareholder control, protection of shareholder rights
Business-government relations	Arms' length, rule-based
Industrial organization	Decentralized, competitive markets, with tough anti-trust enforcement
Financial system	Deregulated, securities-based, with free entry; prudent supervision through regulatory oversight
Labor markets	Decentralized, de-institutionalized, "flexible" labor markets
International capital flows	Free
Public ownership	None in productive sector

Source: Rodrik (2005).

listed in Table 1.9 to MENA? Could this list of "best practices" represent the dividing line between Arab and non-Arab MENA?

How can policymakers translate these "best practices" into concrete institutional changes? Rodrik (2005) suggests a number of policy changes that would represent the institutional changes suggested by the Washington Consensus. Table 1.10 lists his ideal market institutional requirements to achieve the "best practices" listed in the Washington Consensus. Can one hypothesize that not following this suggested list of ideal changes would lead to poorer performance? Can one further hypothesize that the big divide between Arab and non-Arab MENA is represented by these Western norms which have been advertised as "best practices"?

Are these "ideal scenarios" too unrealistic or do they represent a distinction between the "Western" paradigm and the rest of the world (i.e., cultural differences)? In this volume it will become clear that much of the explanation of the poor performance of Arab MENA can be explained by their aversion to this Western paradigm. That is, the key characteristic which sets Arab MENA apart from other developing countries in Latin America and Asia, and which accounts for their lackluster performance, is their long history of intense and generally adversarial interaction with Europe and everything European. In that prism, Israel, who is a member of MENA, is considered "the" representation of Europe.

Along these lines, a common thread is the view that many of the economic and social problems confronting most MENA countries stem from their failure to become more integrated into the global economy.

The term "globalization" is not well-defined. In the advanced industrial countries and in Israel it is often largely viewed in economic terms — the free movement of goods, services, labor and capital across borders. It is often seen as the inexorable integration of markets, nations and technologies to a degree never witnessed before in a way that is enabling individuals and corporations to reach around the world further, faster, deeper and more economically than ever before.

In the Arab MENA, "globalization" is viewed in largely ideological terms. It has been seen as a new version of imperialism. Critics have pointed to a number of related dangers, all of which they see as part of a real or potential threat to their political, economic and cultural independence. Consequently, the Arab MENA region remains one of the most un-globalized regions in the world. The region receives only one-third the foreign direct investment (FDI) expected for its economic size (and most is concentrated in enclave sectors of a handful of countries), while portfolio investment is virtually non-existent because equity markets are underdeveloped.

As a recent International Monetary Fund study observed (Abed and Davoodi, 2003):

- "Global financial integration lags behind that in other regions; less than half of MENA countries have meaningful access to financial markets.
- Trade performance is below that of other regions: while oil exports continue to be a substantial source of foreign exchange earnings for oil producers, the relative importance (until the recent price increases) of such exports has declined since 1985.
- The growth of non-oil exports varied during this period, but on the whole, was slower than for developing countries as a group.
- As a result, the MENA region's share of the world export market fell by more than half between 1980 and 2000 (the results are the same including or excluding oil exports), whereas the developing countries' share rose slightly during this same period.
- The region's information and technology links are among the weakest in the world — the number of internet user per capita, for example, is low compared with other regions."

The Arab MENA region as a whole did as well or better than Latin America and even Asia in the first post-war decades, but has declined steadily over the last 30 years despite the dramatic rise in the price of oil — as its failure to integrate with the world economy has become glaringly obvious (Noland and Pack, 2007). This is a testament to the fact that it is easier to initiate a growth process rather than to sustain it. Over the past 20–25 years, most of the region has essentially "de-globalized" at a time when its population was doubling.

Bergsten (2004) lists the following indicators as indicative of the de-globalization of the MENA countries as opposed to the rest of the world:

- "The Middle East share of world trade has dropped by 75 percent in the last 25 years;
- Half of the Arab League's 22 members have not even joined the World Trade Organization (WTO);
- The 22 nations of the Arab League, with a population of 260 million, receive half as much FDI as Sweden, with a population of 9 million;
- The ratio of FDI to gross domestic product (GDP) in the Middle East countries is at least three to four times lower than found in other developing economies;
- Tariff rates in the region remain very high — ranging from more than 40 percent or higher in nations such as Egypt, Syria and Saudi Arabia;
- While regional economic integration has become a top priority throughout Asia, Latin America and even Africa, conflicts, boycotts and sanctions limit the possibility in the Middle East;
- Foreign equity investment in the entire region roughly equals that of Indonesia, suggesting a very undeveloped capital market and poor allocation of the very limited savings pool it has to draw upon;
- The Middle East countries together spend about half as much per year tapping international technology as does Brazil."

In this volume, the economic realities of the region are examined and compared across the MENA economies (in varying degrees of depth): technology gap and comparative development; the value of education and human capital development; water and food security; the economics and politics of oil; population growth, role of gender and labor mobility; the role of the state as economic actor; the economic value of democracy; and the prospects for regional integration.

Chapter 2 presents a snapshot of the current situation in MENA in terms of composition of GDP by broad sectors, level of education and human capital, expenditure on education, health care, capital formation and its impact on growth, decomposition of MENA trade, and the current impediments for business activity within MENA. Chapter 3 presents a discussion of the impact of the key Islamic institutional constraint — prohibition of interest and undue risk on growth and development in MENA. Current research on Islamic banking in Malaysia is presented to show that if we allow competition in the banking industry, then there are no differences between Islamic and non-Islamic banking in terms of the riskiness of their portfolios or in terms of interest charged. Chapter 4 presents a simplified endogenous growth model and draws attention to the need for investment in human capital in order to expand economic growth in MENA. A discussion of the demand for human capital as well as the supply constraints in Arab MENA is compared and contrasted with that in non-Arab MENA. The chapter uses the Knowledge Economy Index, the Knowledge Index and its components, prepared by the World Bank, to argue that if growth is the objective function of the individual MENA countries, then there are no alternatives to a major structural reform in their education system. As evidence of the latter we look at the international benchmark data in mathematics and science achievements in MENA for 2007, 2011 and 2015, as compared to the rest of the world. Continuing the focus on the implications of the endogenous growth model, the discussion in Chapter 5 is on the labor supply problems within MENA. The misallocation of labor and capital resources in the 1960s resulted in a major reduction of total factor productivity (TFP) within Arab MENA until the end of the 1990s. Without a major revision in the institutional constraints in Arab MENA with respect to gender and age, the labor market will not be able to compete in the 21st century. The unemployment problem combined with the age profile of Arab MENA is a ticking bomb for each country's leadership and for the Western world at large.

Chapter 6 focuses on the resource curse hypothesis which posits that dependence on natural resources rather than on human capital will misdirect a country's comparative advantage and become a "curse." The economic literature cited suggests a number of reasons why the natural resource "curse" is indeed real. The major reason for this conclusion is that in natural resource economies, the incentives for rent-seeking have a negative effect on economic development. Consequently, the necessary and sufficient condition to eliminate the negative effects of the resource "curse" is an effective and relatively corruption-free state apparatus.

Chapter 7 addresses the basic question for R&D expenditure — are investments in the knowledge economy a necessary and sufficient condition for sustained creation, adoption, adaptation and use of "knowledge" in domestic economic production? Will this lead to increased probability of economic success, and hence economic development, in the globalized world economy? The latest data for 2016 on the number of patents generated and the number of research publications per million people presents a disturbing picture concerning the lack of Arab MENA's participation in the global economy. The poor performance of the majority of MENA countries in this area is linked to the knowledge-unfriendly institutional environment and the aversion to globalization in terms of the free and unhindered flow of knowledge. Despite attempts by the oil-rich MENA countries to alter these domestic policies, their attempts may be too little, too late in a 21st century world where innovation is moving faster than their attempts to build sequestered science and research institutions in the desert.

Chapter 8 continues the basic theme of the book, that participating in the global economy and taking full advantage of its potential is the only way that Arab MENA can resolve its greatest economic challenge — job creation for its large and rapidly growing labor force. Expanding trade and investment offers the best hope for generating the requisite growth and jobs that are required to maintain local stability. The performance record for Arab MENA with respect to their utilization of the global trade and investment network is abysmal.

Chapter 9 summarizes the arguments made in the first eight chapters and presents a number of different policy outcomes based on individual MENA country adoption of critical institutional overhauls or in the alternative a "muddling" through program.

Chapter 2

Survey of Main Economic Outcomes

The countries that compose the MENA region are diverse in all of the basic outcome variables including size, geography, per capita GDP, natural resource endowments, economic structure, investment in human capital, role of women in the economy, role of the state in the economy and the existence of democratic institutions.

2.1. GDP Sector Divisions

We begin the survey of main economic outcomes within MENA by beginning with the most frequently used indicator in the national accounts — the Gross Domestic Product (GDP) and its major sector divisions. By focusing on the value added our single figure avoids the pitfalls of double counting. All the production is carried out by all the firms, non-profit institutions, government bodies and households in a given MENA country during the 2007–2015 period, regardless of the type of goods and services produced, provided that the production takes place within the country's economic territory. For our purposes GDP is defined as being equal to the sum of the value added of each firm, government institution and producing household in a given country:

$$GDP = \sum value\ added + taxes - subsidies$$

The four major sector divisions, Agriculture, Industry, Manufacturing and Services, in terms of value added as a percent of GDP for the MENA countries for the period 2007–2015 are presented in Table 2.1. In order to incorporate the significance of natural resources within MENA, we present

Table 2.1. Broad Sources of MENA Country Gross Domestic Product (Broad Sectors' Value Added as Percent of GDP and Natural Resource Rents as Percent of GDP)

(2007–2015)

Country Name	Series Name	2007	2008	2009	2010	2011	2012	2013	2014	2015	SLOPE
Algeria	Agriculture	7.7	6.7	10.1	9.0	8.6	9.4	10.6	11.1	13.1	1.3
Algeria	Industry	58.6	59.5	51.6	53.9	52.7	51.3	47.8	45.7	39.0	−0.4
Algeria	Manufacturing	—	—	—	—	—	—	—	—	—	—
Algeria	Services	33.7	33.9	38.3	37.1	38.7	39.3	41.6	43.3	47.9	0.6
Algeria	Total natural resources	25.0	27.0	19.0	20.0	23.6	23.0	21.3	19.3	11.8	−0.4
Algeria	Natural gas	3.1	3.3	3.4	2.0	2.9	3.9	3.7	3.3	2.6	0.2
Algeria	Oil	21.7	23.2	15.3	17.7	20.4	18.8	17.4	15.7	9.0	−0.5
Bahrain	Agriculture	—	—	—	0.3	0.3	0.3	0.3	0.3	0.3	0.0
Bahrain	Industry	—	—	—	45.0	49.5	47.5	47.9	46.5	40.3	−0.3
Bahrain	Manufacturing	—	—	—	14.5	15.0	14.9	14.8	14.9	17.3	1.3
Bahrain	Services	—	—	—	54.7	50.2	52.2	51.8	53.2	59.4	0.3
Bahrain	Total natural resources	5.9	6.7	5.3	4.8	7.6	8.7	8.6	8.2	4.9	0.6
Bahrain	Natural gas	2.4	2.9	2.9	1.9	3.1	3.9	4.1	3.7	2.4	1.5
Bahrain	Oil	3.5	3.8	2.4	3.0	4.5	4.8	4.5	4.5	2.6	0.6
Cyprus	Agriculture	2.3	2.4	2.3	2.4	2.5	2.2	2.3	2.1	2.3	−13.6
Cyprus	Industry	21.1	20.7	18.1	16.7	14.3	12.8	11.3	10.7	10.6	−0.6
Cyprus	Manufacturing	6.7	6.3	6.1	5.8	5.2	4.7	4.3	4.7	4.8	−3.0
Cyprus	Services	76.6	76.9	79.6	80.9	83.2	84.9	86.5	87.2	87.2	0.6
Cyprus	Total natural resources	0.0	0.0	0.0	0.1	0.1	0.1	0.1	0.1	0.1	0.0
Cyprus	Natural gas	0.0	0.0	0.0	0.0	0.0	0.0	0.0	0.0	0.0	0.0
Cyprus	Oil	0.0	0.0	0.0	0.0	0.0	0.0	0.0	0.0	0.0	0.0

Djibouti	Agriculture	3.9	—	—	—	—	—	—	—	—	—
Djibouti	Industry	16.9	—	—	—	—	—	—	—	—	—
Djibouti	Manufacturing	2.5	—	—	—	—	—	—	—	—	—
Djibouti	Services	79.3	—	—	—	—	—	—	—	—	—
Djibouti	Total natural resources	0.5	0.8	0.7	0.8	0.9	0.8	0.7	1.1	0.9	13.3
Djibouti	Natural gas	—	—	—	—	—	—	—	—	—	—
Djibouti	Oil	—	—	—	—	—	—	—	—	—	—
Egypt	Agriculture	14.1	13.2	13.6	14.0	14.5	11.1	11.0	11.1	11.2	−1.4
Egypt	Industry	36.8	37.9	37.6	37.5	37.6	38.8	38.9	39.0	36.3	0.8
Egypt	Manufacturing	16.1	16.3	16.6	16.9	16.5	16.0	16.2	16.4	16.6	1.1
Egypt	Services	49.2	48.9	48.8	48.5	47.9	50.1	50.1	49.9	52.5	1.4
Egypt	Total natural resources	13.0	15.7	8.2	8.7	12.0	10.8	9.5	8.0	3.9	−0.6
Egypt	Natural gas	2.1	2.4	1.8	1.0	1.6	1.8	1.8	1.6	0.8	−3.4
Egypt	Oil	10.6	12.2	5.9	7.3	9.6	8.3	7.0	5.9	2.6	−0.7
Iran	Agriculture	7.4	6.4	7.3	6.9	5.9	7.9	9.0	9.3	—	1.4
Iran	Industry	46.0	45.2	40.6	41.4	46.5	41.4	40.2	38.2	—	−0.6
Iran	Manufacturing	11.8	11.9	12.4	12.0	11.0	12.6	11.7	11.8	—	−0.3
Iran	Services	46.6	48.4	52.1	51.7	47.6	50.8	50.8	52.4	—	0.7
Iran	Total natural resources	29.7	33.6	19.6	22.6	26.2	20.4	22.5	24.3	—	−0.3
Iran	Natural gas	1.7	2.0	1.9	1.2	1.8	2.6	3.0	3.5	—	2.5
Iran	Oil	26.7	30.2	17.0	20.2	23.0	16.9	18.4	20.0	—	−0.3
Israel	Agriculture	2.5	2.4	2.8	2.4	2.5	2.4	2.2	2.0	1.9	−8.2
Israel	Industry	14.5	15.1	15.3	15.9	15.7	15.0	15.6	15.3	15.4	3.0
Israel	Manufacturing	21.5	21.1	20.2	21.7	20.3	20.3	19.2	18.8	18.7	−2.2
Israel	Services	61.9	61.6	61.8	60.0	61.5	62.2	62.5	63.3	63.8	1.7
Israel	Total natural resources	0.1	0.5	0.2	0.1	0.3	0.3	0.3	0.3	0.2	3.2
Israel	Natural gas	0.1	0.1	0.1	0.1	0.1	0.1	0.2	0.2	0.1	0.0
Israel	Oil	0.0	0.0	0.0	0.0	0.0	0.0	0.0	0.0	0.0	0.0

(Continued)

Table 2.1. (*Continued*)

Country Name	Series Name	2007	2008	2009	2010	2011	2012	2013	2014	2015	SLOPE
		(2007–2015)									
Iraq	Agriculture	6.1	4.8	4.8	5.2	5.6	4.6	4.8	4.7	3.4	−2.8
Iraq	Industry	54.7	56.8	56.5	55.8	55.6	56.5	57.3	58.6	62.3	1.0
Iraq	Manufacturing	1.8	1.7	2.3	2.3	2.2	1.9	1.7	1.3	1.0	−3.8
Iraq	Services	39.6	38.1	38.5	39.0	38.9	38.8	37.5	36.0	32.5	−1.0
Iraq	Total natural resources	50.6	51.4	36.3	40.9	50.0	47.2	42.5	41.3	28.6	−0.2
Iraq	Natural gas	0.1	0.1	0.1	0.0	0.0	0.0	0.0	0.0	0.0	0.0
Iraq	Oil	50.5	51.3	36.3	40.8	49.9	47.2	42.4	41.2	28.6	−0.2
Jordan	Agriculture	2.8	2.7	3.1	3.4	3.3	3.1	3.4	3.8	4.2	5.4
Jordan	Industry	31.6	33.8	32.1	30.7	31.1	30.1	29.7	29.8	29.6	−1.6
Jordan	Manufacturing	21.2	21.0	20.1	19.2	19.4	18.8	19.4	19.0	18.5	−2.5
Jordan	Services	65.5	63.5	64.9	65.9	65.6	66.8	66.9	66.4	66.2	1.8
Jordan	Total natural resources	0.6	8.3	1.5	1.7	3.3	2.6	1.5	1.1	1.2	−0.4
Jordan	Natural gas	0.1	0.1	0.0	0.0	0.0	0.0	0.0	0.0	0.0	0.0
Jordan	Oil	0.0	0.0	0.0	0.0	0.0	0.0	0.0	0.0	0.0	0.0
Kuwait	Agriculture	—	—	—	0.4	0.4	0.3	0.3	0.4	0.6	9.0
Kuwait	Industry	—	—	—	61.0	67.4	69.1	67.9	64.6	51.1	−0.1
Kuwait	Manufacturing	—	—	—	5.5	5.2	5.5	5.5	5.1	6.2	2.0
Kuwait	Services	—	—	—	38.5	32.2	30.6	31.8	35.0	48.3	0.1
Kuwait	Total natural resources	49.8	54.7	37.4	48.4	60.8	60.6	57.0	54.2	39.1	0.0
Kuwait	Natural gas	0.5	0.5	0.6	0.4	0.6	0.8	0.9	0.8	0.6	0.0
Kuwait	Oil	49.3	54.2	36.8	48.0	60.2	59.8	56.1	53.4	38.5	0.0

Lebanon	Agriculture	5.3	4.8	4.4	4.3	4.1	4.5	4.8	4.9	4.8	−0.9
Lebanon	Industry	16.5	16.9	17.0	14.9	16.1	15.2	15.5	16.9	16.6	−0.5
Lebanon	Manufacturing	7.5	8.5	8.6	8.3	8.2	8.4	8.6	9.3	9.1	4.2
Lebanon	Services	78.1	78.3	78.5	80.8	79.7	80.3	79.6	78.2	78.6	0.0
Lebanon	Total natural resources	0.0	0.0	0.0	0.0	0.0	0.0	0.0	0.0	0.0	0.0
Lebanon	Natural gas	0.0	0.0	0.0	0.0	0.0	0.0	0.0	0.0	0.0	0.0
Lebanon	Oil	0.0	0.0	0.0	0.0	0.0	0.0	0.0	0.0	0.0	0.0
Libya	Agriculture	2.1	1.9	—	—	—	—	—	—	—	—
Libya	Industry	76.4	78.2	—	—	—	—	—	—	—	—
Libya	Manufacturing	4.5	4.5	—	—	—	—	—	—	—	—
Libya	Services	21.5	19.9	—	—	—	—	—	—	—	—
Libya	Total natural resources	59.3	61.4	45.8	55.0	50.9	—	—	—	—	—
Libya	Natural gas	1.0	1.1	1.4	0.8	1.5	—	—	—	—	—
Libya	Oil	58.3	60.2	44.4	54.1	49.2	—	—	—	—	—
Morocco	Agriculture	12.2	13.3	14.7	14.4	14.2	13.4	14.7	13.0	14.5	1.1
Morocco	Industry	27.7	29.8	27.3	28.6	28.9	28.6	28.7	29.4	29.2	1.6
Morocco	Manufacturing	17.0	16.8	17.5	17.4	16.8	16.5	17.0	18.3	18.0	2.5
Morocco	Services	60.1	57.0	58.0	56.9	56.9	58.0	56.6	57.6	56.3	−1.4
Morocco	Total natural resources	1.5	8.3	1.9	2.7	4.3	4.3	2.9	2.2	2.6	−0.3
Morocco	Natural gas	0.0	0.0	0.0	0.0	0.0	0.0	0.0	0.0	0.0	0.0
Morocco	Oil	0.0	0.0	0.0	0.0	0.0	0.0	0.0	0.0	0.0	0.0
Oman	Agriculture	1.4	1.1	1.5	1.4	1.3	1.2	1.3	1.3	1.6	4.4
Oman	Industry	61.1	66.9	59.6	64.1	71.6	70.1	67.5	64.0	53.9	−0.1
Oman	Manufacturing	10.8	10.5	11.6	10.6	11.4	10.7	10.8	9.7	9.7	−2.4
Oman	Services	37.5	31.9	38.9	36.6	32.2	33.2	35.8	39.0	47.4	0.3
Oman	Total natural resources	39.9	39.7	31.9	37.2	48.6	45.8	44.0	38.7	22.9	−0.1
Oman	Natural gas	2.8	2.6	3.0	1.8	3.1	3.8	4.1	3.4	2.5	1.3
Oman	Oil	37.1	37.1	28.9	35.3	45.5	41.9	39.9	35.3	20.5	−0.1

(Continued)

Table 2.1. (*Continued*)

		(2007–2015)									
Country Name	Series Name	2007	2008	2009	2010	2011	2012	2013	2014	2015	SLOPE
Qatar	Agriculture	0.1	0.1	0.1	0.1	0.1	0.1	0.1	0.1	0.2	0.0
Qatar	Industry	90.6	76.1	96.6	94.8	73.2	73.5	71.8	69.8	58.5	−0.2
Qatar	Manufacturing	12.4	10.2	13.6	12.5	9.5	10.5	10.2	10.1	9.7	−1.1
Qatar	Services	36.8	27.6	40.2	33.2	26.7	26.4	28.1	30.1	41.3	0.0
Qatar	Total natural resources	25.5	25.9	17.8	17.9	21.2	21.4	20.4	17.4	11.3	−0.5
Qatar	Natural gas	3.6	4.1	4.9	3.8	5.9	7.7	8.2	7.0	5.4	1.1
Qatar	Oil	21.8	21.8	12.9	14.0	15.3	13.7	12.2	10.4	5.9	−0.5
Saudi Arabia	Agriculture	2.8	2.3	2.9	2.4	1.9	1.8	1.9	1.9	2.3	−4.7
Saudi Arabia	Industry	63.0	66.8	55.0	58.5	63.8	62.9	60.0	57.4	45.9	−0.3
Saudi Arabia	Manufacturing	9.9	9.0	10.9	11.0	10.0	9.8	10.0	10.8	12.3	1.6
Saudi Arabia	Services	34.2	30.9	42.1	39.1	34.2	35.3	38.1	40.7	51.8	0.3
Saudi Arabia	Total natural resources	48.6	55.9	35.5	42.3	50.0	47.6	44.2	40.1	23.4	−0.2
Saudi Arabia	Natural gas	0.8	0.9	1.0	0.6	0.9	1.2	1.2	1.1	0.8	4.7
Saudi Arabia	Oil	47.8	54.9	34.5	41.6	49.0	46.3	42.9	38.9	22.5	−0.2
Syria	Agriculture	17.9	—	—	—	—	—	—	—	—	—
Syria	Industry	33.0	—	—	—	—	—	—	—	—	—
Syria	Manufacturing	—	—	—	—	—	—	—	—	—	—
Syria	Services	49.1	—	—	—	—	—	—	—	—	—
Syria	Total natural resources	20.8	—	—	—	—	—	—	—	—	—
Syria	Natural gas	0.7	—	—	—	—	—	—	—	—	—
Syria	Oil	20.1	—	—	—	—	—	—	—	—	—

Tunisia	Agriculture	9.4	8.5	9.1	8.2	9.0	9.5	9.4	9.7	10.4	2.8
Tunisia	Industry	31.2	33.9	30.3	31.5	31.5	31.1	30.2	29.3	28.2	−1.3
Tunisia	Manufacturing	18.1	19.5	18.4	18.0	17.5	17.0	16.7	16.8	16.9	−2.5
Tunisia	Services	59.4	57.7	60.6	60.3	59.5	59.4	60.3	61.0	61.4	1.7
Tunisia	Total natural resources	6.1	11.2	4.8	5.9	6.6	6.9	5.9	4.7	3.0	−0.7
Tunisia	Natural gas	0.2	0.4	0.3	0.3	0.5	0.6	0.6	0.5	0.3	10.2
Tunisia	Oil	5.4	5.8	3.3	4.2	5.2	5.2	4.4	3.4	1.8	−1.4
Turkey	Agriculture	8.5	8.5	9.1	9.5	9.0	8.8	8.3	8.0	8.5	−2.2
Turkey	Industry	27.7	27.2	25.3	26.4	27.5	26.7	26.6	27.1	26.5	−0.5
Turkey	Manufacturing	18.6	17.8	16.6	17.4	18.2	17.4	17.3	17.8	17.6	−1.1
Turkey	Services	63.7	64.4	65.6	64.2	63.5	64.5	65.1	64.9	65.0	1.6
Turkey	Total natural resources	0.4	0.7	0.4	0.6	0.8	0.6	0.5	0.5	0.4	−4.8
Turkey	Natural gas	0.0	0.0	0.0	0.0	0.0	0.0	0.0	0.0	0.0	0.0
Turkey	Oil	0.1	0.1	0.1	0.1	0.1	0.1	0.1	0.1	0.0	0.0
UAE	Agriculture	1.1	0.9	1.0	0.9	0.8	0.7	0.7	0.7	0.7	−18.1
UAE	Industry	55.4	55.2	54.4	54.9	55.1	55.3	53.9	53.8	54.1	−3.1
UAE	Manufacturing	9.2	9.8	8.9	9.0	9.4	9.3	8.4	8.5	8.5	−4.1
UAE	Services	43.5	43.9	44.7	44.3	44.1	44.0	45.4	45.5	45.2	3.1
UAE	Total natural resources	22.1	25.2	16.8	20.8	25.9	26.2	25.3	22.5	11.9	−0.1
UAE	Natural gas	0.9	1.0	1.0	0.7	1.0	1.3	1.3	1.1	0.7	2.5
UAE	Oil	21.2	24.2	15.8	20.2	24.8	24.8	24.0	21.4	11.2	−0.2
Yemen	Agriculture	9.9	8.7	10.0	8.2	8.5	8.4	7.9	7.8	9.5	−1.5
Yemen	Industry	48.7	44.2	52.0	43.1	45.8	45.8	43.2	43.4	53.1	0.0
Yemen	Manufacturing	8.2	7.8	9.4	8.0	8.7	8.8	8.4	8.6	10.6	1.8
Yemen	Services	32.2	29.0	34.0	28.1	29.7	29.7	27.9	28.0	34.2	−0.1
Yemen	Total natural resources	32.4	31.6	19.3	21.3	22.9	17.1	16.6	11.7	2.3	−0.3
Yemen	Natural gas	0.0	0.0	0.2	0.7	1.9	1.9	2.3	1.8	0.3	1.7
Yemen	Oil	32.4	31.5	19.1	20.5	21.0	15.2	14.3	9.8	1.9	−0.3

(Continued)

Table 2.1. *(Continued)*

		(2007–2015)									
Country Name	Series Name	2007	2008	2009	2010	2011	2012	2013	2014	2015	SLOPE
OECD	Agriculture	1.6	1.6	1.5	1.6	1.7	1.6	1.7	1.6	—	0.0
OECD	Industry	26.1	25.7	24.1	24.6	24.7	24.5	24.2	24.2	—	−2.6
OECD	Manufacturing	15.9	15.4	14.4	15.0	15.0	14.9	14.9	15.0	—	−2.7
OECD	Services	72.3	72.7	74.3	73.8	73.6	73.9	74.1	74.2	—	2.5
OECD	Total natural resources	1.2	1.7	0.8	1.1	1.4	1.2	1.1	1.0	0.5	−4.8
OECD	Natural gas	0.3	0.4	0.1	0.0	0.1	0.1	0.1	0.1	0.0	0.0
OECD	Oil	0.4	0.6	0.3	0.4	0.5	0.5	0.5	0.4	0.1	0.0

Source: World Bank Development Indicators, 2017. For Israel, The Israel Central Bureau of Statistics.

total natural resource rents as a percent of GDP. The latter is subdivided into revenue from natural gas and oil.

The most common characteristics of the region in terms of endowment include natural resources, people and human capital. With the exception of Cyprus and Israel, the majority of MENA countries are dependent on natural resources and/or on the natural resource producing countries, through labor remittances and aid flows. The value-added composition as a percent of GDP listed in Table 2.1 point to a clear concentration of resources in industry and services with very little in manufacturing and agriculture. For Israel, Cyprus and Turkey the service sector is the predominant component of GDP along the lines of the OECD. A number of countries within MENA, e.g., Bahrain, Egypt, Morocco and Tunisia, have a sizeable agriculture sector. Overall, one can be confident that these aggregate data point to a status quo ante scenario for most of MENA. There are no recorded major structural changes in the composition of these economies. This proved to be the Achilles heel for those MENA countries involved in the Arab Spring.

The MENA economies, since their independence, have adopted a succession of industrial policies designed to reverse the market failure of private sector development. As can be seen from the aggregate data in Table 2.1, many decades of experience with industrial policy has resulted in limited success. Despite aggressive actions to drive industrial development, structural transformation and job creation, the results for most of the economies have been very low. There is some success within MENA, notably Israel, which suggest that MENA governments should rely more on market forces and less on government direction.

On the contrary, most MENA economies were guided by a development model with a strong interventionist-redistributive orientation (Richards and Waterbury, 2007). The key characteristics of this model consisted of reliance on state planning in determining economic priorities; the adoption of import-substitution industrialization policies; the implementation of a wave of inconsistent agrarian reform programs; sweeping nationalizations of private and foreign assets; programs for state provision of education, housing, health care and food subsidies; and the emergence of centralized, hierarchical and tightly controlled trade unions, professional associations and ruling-party governments with little or no democratic freedoms. Overall, these policies established "the State" as the instrument of social transformation, political mobilization and economic distribution. The market as is conventionally understood disappeared.

Focusing on the positive role of the State, appears particularly attractive to policymakers and analysts who observe the remarkable success of East Asian economies and the PRC, where the government role has been large and ongoing (Pelzman, 2016). One can make a convincing argument that intervention by the State when structural transformation is required but is threatened by a non-existent market or when the market institutions are dysfunctional. This has been and continues to be the long-standing pro-industrial policy argument made in the development literature. Despite the allure of this argument, it holds predominantly only for small closed economies. Once an economy is open to world market competition, this industrial policy argument loses its attractive appeal (Harrison and Rodriguez-Clare, 2010). An economy that is open to global forces, such as the PRC, benefits from learning externalities. The resulting knowledge spillovers yield large productivity benefits for all firms across industries (Pelzman, 2016; Hausmann and Rodrik, 2003). When market forces are disrupted because of xenophobia and artificial barriers to "globalization" as is common in many MENA countries, it should not be surprising to find the existence of information asymmetries related to the economic returns to investment; coordination difficulties among entrepreneurs in complementary industries; and the call for State intervention. Ironically the State, in most of these MENA economies, is the source of the absence of markets.

The extent to which these industrial policy programs are likely to succeed depends on whether or not the State wants to remove obstacles to market competitiveness. Unfortunately, a long history of State intervention within MENA has proven that the State places a higher priority on alternative uses of funds or pursue other goals that are potentially incompatible with growth; these include, but are not limited to, incentives to extend open-ended benefits to political supporters. In order to avoid State corruption within MENA, industrial policy aimed at attenuating the effects of market failure must be directed at industries and sectors, not at the level of firms. Research by Aghion *et al.* (2012) indicates that industrial policy can promote productivity growth when it favors competition — and not a direct transfer to political supporters. The example of the industrial policy in the People's Republic of China has done precisely this (Pelzman, 2016).

In contrast, interest groups and other State actors within Arab MENA molded state policy since the 1950s. Interest and pressure groups and, most broadly, proprietary classes sought to protect and promote their own interests through the state. In the context of Arab MENA, the impact of the

State on class, on gender equality, on the nature of education, on the nature of religious indoctrination and intolerance is especially striking — as the State redistributed property through nationalizations, land reforms, and privatizations. One of the new actors in Arab MENA associated with the structural transformation occurring in the 1960s, 1970s and 1980s was the "foreign entrepreneurial class." It was this new economic actor who could assure continued growth for the beneficiary State without having to liberalize and democratize the indigenous economy. That policy of growth via a surrogate has run out of steam.

As the UNDP (1992) noted, the pattern of governance in Arab MENA is characterized by a powerful State that exerts complete control over all other branches of the economy, being free from institutional checks and balances. What is considered "representative democracy" is not genuine and is often absent. Moreover, "obsolete norms of legitimacy prevail." In a 2016 UNDP report on Youth and their prospects, the report noted that despite all the assessments since the 1990s and the joint work by the UNDP and the OECD and Arab MENA for the past two decades, on better governance, governance within Arab MENA remains firmly the domain of an often hereditary elite.

The UNDP report continues to note that within MENA the Arab youth population (aged 15–29) numbers 105 million and growing fast, but unemployment, poverty and marginalization are all growing faster. The average MENA youth unemployment rate, at 30 percent, stands at more than twice the world's average of 14 percent. Almost half of young Arab women looking for jobs fail to find them (against a global average of 16 percent). These figures are very sobering when you consider that in 2014 Arabs were only 5 percent of the world's population, yet the Arab world accounted for 45 percent of the world's terrorism, 68 percent of its battle-related deaths, 47 percent of its internally displaced and 58 percent of its refugees. These were not Arab-Israeli wars but internal Arab wars that not only kills and maims, but destroys vital infrastructure accelerating the disintegration of Arab MENA.

The new generation of Arabs are by far the most well educated and the most highly urbanized in the history of the Arab region. Yet they are also the most disillusioned with the slow path of change within Arab MENA. With these strong similarities in terms of economic policies, limited markets, dominant State actors, division between the educated youth and the undeveloped production infrastructure for economic growth and development, it is not surprising, then, that many of the development challenges facing Arab MENA today are also similar. Europe and the USA continue to be more attractive prospects for Arab youth than Arab MENA.

As repeated volumes of the UN Arab Human Development Reports have so eloquently noted, the limited economic reforms in most of the Arab MENA economies, to date, have led to very minimal results (UNDP, 2002, 2003, 2004, 2005, 2009a, 2009b, 2016a and 2016b).

The economic structural changes required for sustainable growth have remained weak throughout the Arab MENA. Israel, in contrast, has managed to limit the disruptive effects of the State and consequently has benefited from the acceptance of a market paradigm.

2.2. Labor in MENA

In two recent World Bank studies focusing on private sector employment in Arab MENA (2015 and 2016a) the authors analyze recently disclosed census data and enterprise survey data for Egypt, Tunisia, Morocco, Jordan, and Lebanon. Their comparison country was Turkey. They concluded that for over the past 20 years per capita GDP growth in Arab MENA was not driven by labor productivity but by demographic changes. Furthermore, they conclude that the per capita GDP growth did not create sufficient formal private sector jobs. While these results are not new, the authors of these studies neglected the basic underlying business model within Arab MENA. Had the authors compared this sample of Arab MENA countries to Israel and or the OECD average they would have stumbled on the bitter truth — that the economic policies in Arab MENA did not and still do not encourage private sector employment.

There are many reasonable explanations for the appalling private sector job creation within Arab MENA. The authors of these World Bank studies focus on the lack of entry and exit in the private sector and the slow growth in private sector productivity. While these are factors for most normal market-based economies, they are not dispositive of the current situation in Arab MENA. Moreover, the World Bank authors do not point to the basic fact that within Arab MENA those who are job candidates attempt to minimize job market risk and therefore opt into government employment. Even more humorous, the authors attempt to make economic sense from data gathered for Gaza and the West Bank and ignore two basic facts. One, that within Gaza there is no private sector employment other than smuggling and bomb making. Currently over 50 percent of active labor participants within Gaza are unemployed. That outcome is driven by the choices made by the leaders in Gaza. Within the West Bank the only private sector employers are Israeli firms, which are conveniently missing in any these World Bank studies. Furthermore, the small number of private Arab-owned West Bank firms are too busy dealing with local corruption as a cost of doing business and therefore have limited resources for new employment.

The political instability within Arab MENA should be a signal for the current governments to increase private sector employment for the young and better-educated, more skilled labor force. The unfortunate reality is that Arab MENA is characterized by the world's highest youth unemployment rate and the lowest female labor force participation. The social contract of those in power is driven by the easy fix of a large, overpaid and under productive public sector that in most Arab MENA provides most formal jobs. The public sector in Arab MENA remains the primary employer, employing anywhere between 20 percent and 40 percent of all workers (World Bank, 2016b). The crowding out of the private sector is an old economic strategy well tested in Arab MENA. Government institutions in Arab MENA are overstaffed by government employees who are paid more than the private sector, and have access to lifelong security and large 'grey market' side payments.

Table 2.2 presents the latest 2015 IMF data on government remuneration as a percent of GDP for those MENA countries that have reported the data to the IMF. Data on the USA is presented as a hypothetical target where the private sector is the predominant economic actor. The central government official wages including social security is in the double digits, which is the highest rate worldwide (World Bank, 2016b). Despite this fact, the IMF data reported is a lower bound estimate because we do not have reliable extrabudgetary expenditures for public sector employees. Furthermore, we do not have estimates of 'in kind' payments to public sector employees, nor their income from "grey market" activities. There is no sign that the size of the public sector is going to be reduced in the foreseeable future. It should not be a surprise to find that the educated youth within Arab MENA will continue to wait for "comfortable" public sector positions rather than exposing themselves to the uncertainties of the market-driven demand and supply mechanisms within their distorted economies. The long history of economic thinking within Arab MENA was to both treat the public sector as employer of last resort and as a social protection mechanism to avoid a revolution. After the Arab Spring that old economic model has become unusable.

Table 2.2. Public Sector Remuneration for 2015 within MENA (% of GDP)

Country	2015
Bahrain	11.7
Cyprus	12.1
Egypt	8.6
Iraq	11.6
Israel	8.4
Jordan	13.2
Kuwait	17.0
Morocco	12.9
Turkey	8.5
USA	2.2

Source: IMF. Government Finance Statistics (GFS), 2017. The data presented is compensation of employees by the Central government including social security as a percent of GDP.

To add to the problem of private sector development within Arab MENA is the fact that the industrial structure is a uniquely protected oligarchic structure which leaves the private sector permanently small and undercapitalized (World Bank, 2015, 2016a, 2016b). It is no surprise that within Arab MENA there is a thriving underground economy which is unable to handle the flood of new and educated Arab youth. Within this environment, why would any foreign investors consider risking their funds in Arab MENA, other than in large oligarchic structures. Those World Bank authors who consider foreign participation as a viable solution to solving the job creation problem have overlooked the prohibitive cost of local corruption. Until the governments in Arab MENA deregulate their economies and eliminate local corruption, they will never be able to deal with the demographic time bomb awaiting them. The only viable example of the benefits of eliminating the oligarchic structure can be found in Israel. It is unfortunate that the authors of the World Bank studies (2015, 2016a, 2016b) could not locate Israel on their map of MENA.

To understand the nature of the demographic time bomb awaiting the leadership in Arab MENA we present in Table 2.3 a profile of the population and labor force for the entire MENA region. Table 2.3 presents the 2014 profile of the MENA labor participation rate by gender and population by age for 2015. The first characteristic of the Arab MENA labor market is the very low participation rate of the female population, except for Kuwait, Qatar and the UAE. Within Israel, female labor market participation is 57.7 percent, which is in line with the OECD average and the participation

Table 2.3. Profile of MENA Labor Force Participation, 2014 and Population, 2015

	Total Labor force	Labor participation rate			Population					
		Female (% of female population)	Male (% of male population)	Total (% of total population)		ages 0–14	ages 15–64	ages 65+	Female	Urban
	(thousands)	ages 15+			Total	(% of total)				
Algeria	12,355	15.4	72.5	44.2	39,667	28.5	65.5	5.9	49.7	70.7
Bahrain	750	39.1	86.7	69.9	1,377	21.5	76.1	2.4	38.0	88.8
Cyprus	614	56.2	71.3	63.9	1,165	16.6	70.6	12.8	49.0	66.9
Djibouti	307	36.5	68.0	52.3	888	32.7	63.1	4.2	49.8	77.3
Egypt	29,597	23.8	75.0	49.3	91,508	33.2	61.6	5.2	49.5	43.1
Iran	27,133	16.7	74.0	45.4	79,109	23.6	71.3	5.1	49.6	73.4
Iraq	8,802	15.0	69.8	42.4	36,423	41.0	56.0	3.1	49.4	69.5
Israel	3,738	57.7	68.6	63.0	8,380	27.8	60.9	11.2	50.4	92.1
Jordan	1,989	15.8	66.9	41.8	7,595	35.5	60.7	3.8	48.8	83.7
Kuwait	1,993	43.8	83.3	68.5	3,892	22.3	75.7	2.0	43.8	98.3
Lebanon	2,037	23.7	71.2	47.8	5,851	24.0	67.9	8.1	49.8	87.8
Libya	2,324	30.0	76.4	52.8	6,278	29.8	65.6	4.5	49.7	78.6
Morocco	12,498	26.7	75.9	50.7	34,378	27.2	66.6	6.2	50.6	60.2
Oman	2,216	29.3	83.2	66.3	4,491	20.5	76.9	2.6	33.7	77.6
Qatar	1,594	50.7	95.5	86.6	2,235	15.5	83.3	1.2	27.4	99.2
SA	12,135	20.4	78.4	55.2	31,540	28.6	68.6	2.9	43.5	83.1
Syria	5,172	13.6	72.6	43.6	18,502	37.1	58.8	4.1	49.4	57.7
Tunisia	4,023	25.2	71.0	47.7	11,108	23.4	69.1	7.6	50.6	66.8
Turkey	28,361	29.3	70.8	49.4	78,666	25.7	66.8	7.5	50.8	73.4
UAE	6,302	46.4	92.9	80.5	9,157	13.9	84.9	1.1	26.7	85.5
Yemen	7,628	25.6	72.5	49.1	26,832	40.3	56.9	2.8	49.5	34.6
OECD	621,429	50.9	68.9	59.6	1,282,975	18.1	65.6	16.2	50.8	80.3
USA	161,074	56.3	68.8	62.4	321,419	19.0	66.3	14.8	50.4	81.6

Source: World Bank Development Indicators, 2017.

rate of women in the USA. There is no valid economic reason to justify such sparse participation rates for Arab women in MENA. Among the lowest labor participation rates for women is found in the Hashemite Kingdom of Jordan, which has a free trade area agreement with the USA, assuring labor market equality and non-discrimination

The structure of employment in Arab MENA's formal private sector is in many ways very different from similar economies in Asia, Latin America and Africa. Within Arab MENA the role of the manufacturing sector and exporting firms play a comparatively larger role in providing employment than the service sector. The employment of women in a typical firm within Arab MENA is much lower than elsewhere in the world, and the same is true for women as top managers and firm owners. Given the relative anti-women bias in Arab MENA it is not surprising to find that the share of women's employment is higher in labor-intensive sectors (World Bank, 2015, 2016a, 2016b).

Research on gender bias within Arab MENA makes two reasonable conclusions. First, gender inequality and women's marginalization has been a barrier to human development in large parts of Arab MENA for the past 5 decades. Second, continued resistance to women's economic and political emancipation and their full participation in all aspects of national life threatens to hinder many countries' future progress, whether measured in terms of economic growth, human development, or democratization. Empirical research shows that women have been locked into a patriarchal family structure for decades, which has had profound negative economic and social costs for the majority of countries in Arab MENA (UNDP, 2005, 2016a, 2016b).

The untenable position of women in Arab MENA has been documented by many studies within the UN and the ILO (UNDP, 2005, 2009a, 2009b, 2016a, 2016b; ILO, 2016). The reports conclude that the shortcomings of current and past social and economic arrangements with respect to the status of women represent a major negative burden for Arab MENA. Women in this part of the world remain severely marginalized with no prospects of a gender equality solution. The political leaders within Arab MENA do not see the economic value of their women population. Clearly, this labor market discrimination is inconsistent with current development efforts of the smaller Arab MENA countries like Qatar and UAE, and with the standards for women in the third world, and the rest of the world.

A noteworthy testament to the failed development model in Arab MENA is in two outcome variables. The first is the position of women in MENA in terms of gender gap in the work force. The latest ILO data is reflected in Figure 2.1. The darker areas represent the greatest degree of gender bias in employment. For example, for Syria the gender gap is 58.5 percent, for Egypt it is 50.1 percent, for Iran it is 56.9 percent, for Saudi Arabia it is 58.5 percent, and for Israel it is 10.5 percent. Overall for Arab MENA the figures for gender bias in the workforce are very large when compared to Israel as well as the rest of the world. In fact, by world standards they are among the highest. The second outcome variable is the share of women in the unemployed pool. The latest ILO data is reflected in Figure 2.2. The difference between the share of women and men who are either employed or looking for work as a percentage of their respective population, compared to the rest of the world and to Israel is also substantial for Arab MENA. The gender gap in the unemployed pool for Egypt is 15.6 percent, for Saudi Arabia it is 17.2 percent, for Syria it is 21.1 percent, and for Israel it is 0.4 percent.

The largest component of the Arab MENA population is the youth. The age structure of the population is significantly younger than the global average, reflecting the large proportion of children ages 0–14 and the relatively small proportion of those age 65 and older.

The age structures vary widely, with the proportion of those under 15 years ranging from 13.9 percent in the UAE to 41.0 percent in Iraq. The Hashemite Kingdom of Jordan, which is not abiding by the terms of its FTA with the USA with respect to gender equality, has 35.5 percent of the population under 15 years old. This is clearly a time bomb for Hashemite Kingdom. With respect to the elderly, the percentage of the national populations age 65 and over is very low, pointing to the low life expectancy in Arab MENA. Within Israel, the percentage of those 65 plus is 11.2 percent.

To repeat the basic fact that two-thirds of the Arab MENA's population is below 30 years of age, half of which fall within the 15–29-year age bracket is to admit that it is unprecedented to find such a mass of young people at the prime of their working and productive abilities. This mass can either be considered an enormous potential for advancing Arab MENA economic and social development or, if not given an opportunity, the destruction of the MENA's Arab leadership. As the UNDP (2016a, b) points out, it is not clear that the Arab leaders within MENA will positively capture the benefits of this demographic gift.

The UNDP (2016a, b) reminds us that today's generation of young people within Arab MENA is "more educated, active and connected to the outside world, and hence have a greater awareness of their realities and

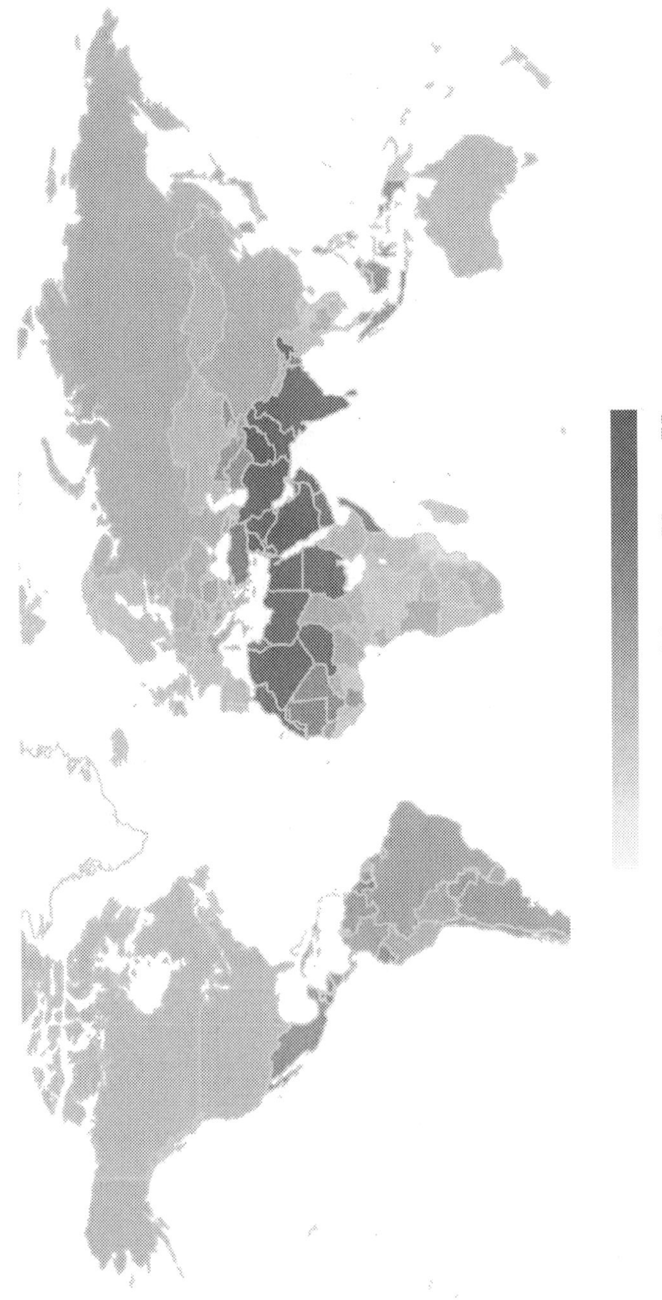

Figure 2.1. The Difference between the Share of Women and Men who are Either Employed or Looking for Work as a Percentage of their Respective Population

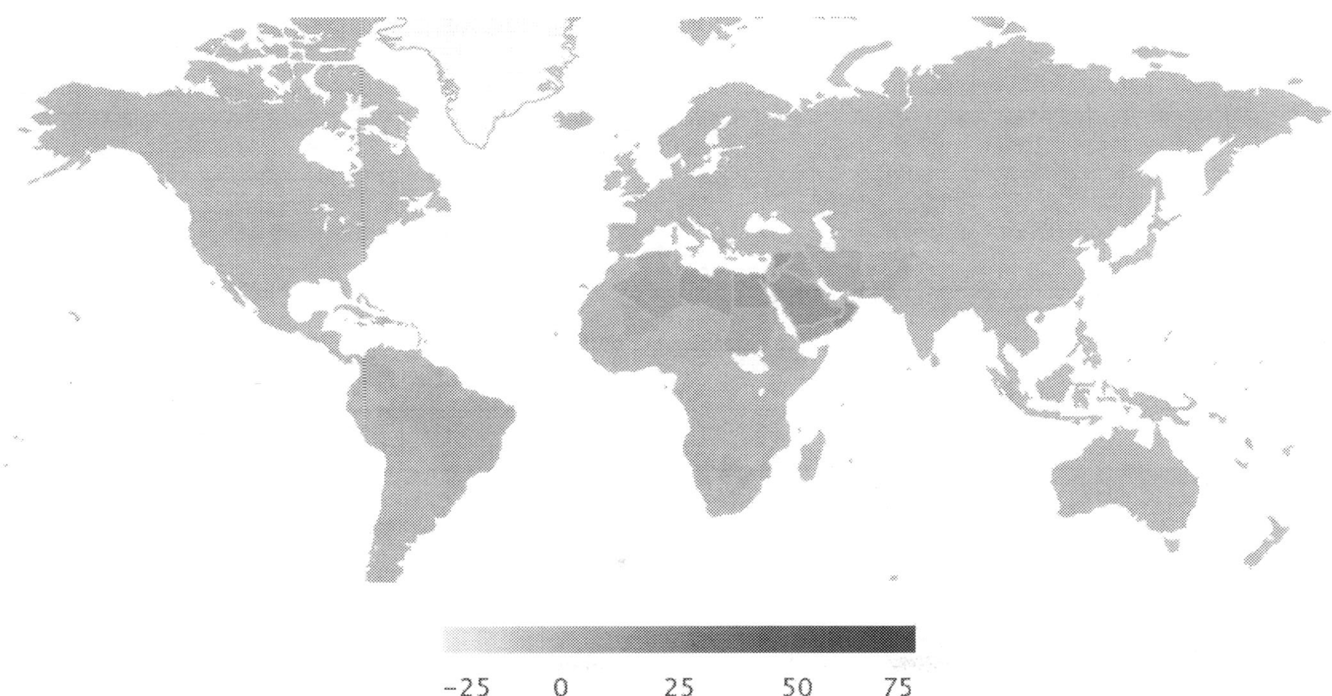

Figure 2.2. The Difference between the Share of Women and Men who Would Like to Work but are Unable to Find Jobs as a Share of their Respective Population

higher aspirations for a better future."... "These realities collide with the reality, that the current leaders in Arab MENA marginalizes them and blocks their pathways to express their opinions, actively participate or earn a living." Consequently, the mass of young Arabs will most likely become an overwhelming power for internal revolution.

2.3. Education and Human Capital in MENA

Acquisition of human capital is an important dimension of economic development. It is now generally accepted that knowledge is a core factor of production and a principal determinant of productivity and economic development. Human capital is an asset, and differences in educational attainment prevent poor people from becoming part of the high-productivity growth process. Democratizing education, particularly tertiary education, would benefit people from poorer backgrounds (UNDP, 2016b).

As the UNDP (2016b) has repeatedly advocated, investing in girls and women has multidimensional benefits. For development purposes, women need support to pursue higher education, particularly in science, technology, engineering and mathematics, where the future employment will be.

The case of Israel is an important proof of the synergy between knowledge acquisition and the productive power of human capital to a society's strength. This synergy is especially strong in high value- added productive activities, which are becoming increasingly based on both advanced technical knowledge and the need to constantly improve human capital capabilities given the short lifespan of existing innovations. The process of continuous innovation and upgrading is the bulwark of current and future international competitiveness.

In the 21st century, it should be obvious to Arab MENA that the knowledge gap, rather than the income gap or the oil gap, is likely to be the most critical determinant of the fortunes of countries across the world. Israel, a member of MENA, has already demonstrated that knowledge and human capital constitute the road to economic development, especially in a world of intensive globalization (UNDP, 2016b).

There are many indicators of the reality of MENA country investment in human capital. We start in Table 2.4 to examine one of the outcome variables of MENA country policies — namely the Human Development Indicator (HDI) index for education. This index measures the mean years of schooling and expected years of schooling and ranks it over the entire world. The UN data is crystal clear in listing Israel as the only country within

Table 2.4. International Human Development Indicators — Education index for MENA

(1980–2013)

HDI Rank	Country	1980	1985	1990	1995	2000	2005	2006	2007	2008	2009	2010	2011	2012	2013
93	Algeria	0.321	0.347	0.382	0.424	0.493	0.563	0.570	0.581	0.598	0.615	0.631	0.643	0.643	0.643
44	Bahrain	0.425	0.535	0.574	0.619	0.656	0.711	0.703	0.706	0.708	0.711	0.714	0.714	0.714	0.714
32	Cyprus	0.465	0.513	0.546	0.655	0.676	0.731	0.740	0.751	0.765	0.778	0.765	0.771	0.776	0.776
170	Djibouti	—	—	—	—	—	0.248	0.253	0.267	0.278	0.284	0.295	0.306	0.306	0.306
110	Egypt	0.279	0.349	0.386	0.434	0.486	0.525	0.534	0.544	0.553	0.562	0.573	0.573	0.573	0.573
75	Iran	0.309	0.333	0.382	0.477	0.526	0.554	0.570	0.587	0.606	0.617	0.625	0.639	0.683	0.683
120	Iraq	0.341	0.342	0.362	0.381	0.401	0.456	0.458	0.460	0.462	0.465	0.467	0.467	0.467	0.467
19	Israel	0.675	0.706	0.714	0.764	0.820	0.848	0.846	0.849	0.844	0.847	0.848	0.851	0.854	0.854
77	Jordan	0.433	0.466	0.495	0.644	0.671	0.707	0.706	0.707	0.714	0.708	0.703	0.700	0.700	0.700
46	Kuwait	0.454	0.514	0.471	0.524	0.637	0.609	0.610	0.612	0.619	0.626	0.633	0.639	0.646	0.646
65	Lebanon	—	—	—	—	—	0.633	0.622	0.625	0.625	0.628	0.628	0.633	0.631	0.631
55	Libya	0.421	0.459	0.516	0.571	0.625	0.660	0.667	0.675	0.683	0.690	0.698	0.698	0.698	0.698
129	Morocco	0.205	0.242	0.254	0.292	0.346	0.408	0.411	0.422	0.431	0.440	0.454	0.468	0.468	0.468
56	Oman	—	—	—	—	—	0.527	0.527	0.539	0.556	0.589	0.596	0.603	0.603	0.603
31	Qatar	0.479	0.513	0.508	0.562	0.612	0.673	0.686	0.699	0.703	0.689	0.680	0.671	0.686	0.686
34	SA	0.304	0.363	0.427	0.482	0.565	0.617	0.624	0.630	0.641	0.660	0.688	0.707	0.721	0.723
118	Syria	0.347	0.399	0.422	0.420	0.451	0.534	—	0.539	0.538	0.545	0.548	0.553	0.553	0.553
90	Tunisia	0.298	0.362	0.403	0.460	0.525	0.580	0.588	0.597	0.605	0.610	0.619	0.621	0.621	0.621
69	Turkey	0.304	0.363	0.398	0.427	0.493	0.531	0.545	0.557	0.563	0.582	0.625	0.648	0.652	0.652
40	UAE	0.358	0.416	0.471	0.543	0.604	0.649	0.654	0.659	0.664	0.669	0.673	0.673	0.673	0.673
154	Yemen	—	—	0.218	0.229	0.257	0.304	0.307	0.310	0.313	0.321	0.328	0.339	0.339	0.339

Source: UNDP, Human Development Report. 2016. Calculated using Mean Years of Schooling and Expected Years of Schooling. Data in the tables are those available to the Human Development Report Office as of 15 November, 2013, unless otherwise specified.

MENA with the highest world rank in terms of mean years of education. Qatar, Cyprus, Saudi Arabia, UAE and Kuwait follow behind them in the ranking. At the bottom of the ranking we have Egypt, Syria, Morocco, Yemen and Djibouti. The Hashemite Kingdom ranks along with Turkey in the bottom of the first 100 countries.

In Table 2.5 we present the HDI composite data for education achievements within MENA, ranked across the world. Those with the very high human development in education include, Israel, Cyprus, Qatar, Saudi Arabia, the UAE, Bahrain and Kuwait. The second group making up the bottom 100 countries is composed of Oman, Iran, Turkey, Lebanon, Algeria, Jordan and Tunisia. That is followed by countries ranked between 107 and 147 which include Egypt, Iraq, and Morocco. Those in the bottom group ranked from 148 to 188 include Syria, Yemen and Djibouti. The common factor explaining this ranking is the government spending on education. Those countries in the upper tier have expenditures on education resembling that of the OECD norm. The other countries are far behind.

In order to explore in more detail, the question of government commitment to fund public education in MENA we present in Table 2.6 total government expenditure as a percent of GDP, and expenditure per tertiary student, per student in secondary and primary school, as a percentage of GDP per capita. The comparison group is Israel and the OECD.

If we take the OECD average as a standard, we get expenditure numbers ranging from 20 to 30 percent. Israel, a non-Arab MENA member, has expenditure figures ranging from 20 to 23 percent. The majority of Arab MENA countries have expenditure figures in the single digit range, primarily focused on the primary level.

The 21st century may be best referred to as the age of knowledge intensity. In this century, poor knowledge acquisition is a serious short-fall. A telling indicator of the poor level of educational attainment in Arab MENA is the persistence of illiteracy rates that are higher, educational enrolment rates that are lower and expenditure on students that are lower, than those of dynamic less developed countries in East Asia and Latin America, let alone the more developed non-Arab MENA country, Israel.

While it may be true that the current cohort of young men and women in Arab MENA are more educated than their parents, it avoids a comparison with a world norm. Given the need for accelerated private sector job creation in Arab MENA, these low education expenditure figures will only make this goal harder to achieve.

Table 2.5. Education Achievements in MENA (2005–2015)

HDI rank	Country	Literacy rate: Adult	Literacy rate: Youth (% ages 15–24) Female	Literacy rate: Youth (% ages 15–24) Male	Population with at least some secondary education	Gross enrolment ratio: Pre-primary	Gross enrolment ratio: Primary	Gross enrolment ratio: Secondary	Gross enrolment ratio: Tertiary	Education quality: Primary school dropout rate	Education quality: Primary school teachers trained to teach	Education quality: Pupil-teacher ratio, primary school	Government expenditure on education
					(% ages 25 and older)	(% of preschool-age children)	(% of primary school-age population)	(% of secondary school-age population)	(% of tertiary school-age population)	(% of primary school cohort)	(%)	(number of pupils per teacher)	(% of GDP)
		2005–2015	2005–2015	2005–2015	2005–2015	2010–2015	2010–2015	2010–2015	2010–2015	2005–2015	2005–2015	2010–2015	2010–2014
	Very high human development												
19	Israel	—	—	—	88.8	110.7	104.2	101.9	66.2	0.8	—	12.5	5.9
33	Cyprus	99.1	99.9	99.8	79.0	77.1	99.2	99.4	53.1	9.2	—	13.4	6.6
33	Qatar	97.8	99.7	98.3	68.4	58.5	101.4	109.4	15.8	2.3	48.9	11.2	3.5
38	SA	94.7	99.3	99.4	66.5	16.3	108.7	108.3	61.1	1.3	100.0	10.8	—
42	UAE	93.8	99.1	99.6	67.7	92.0	106.7	—	22.0	8.0	100.0	18.9	—
47	Bahrain	95.7	99.7	99.8	57.9	55.2	—	—	36.8	2.2	82.8	11.7	2.6
51	Kuwait	96.2	99.5	99.6	57.4	81.0	102.7	93.6	27.0	4.3	79.5	8.8	—
	High human development												
52	Oman	94.8	99.1	99.1	58.8	54.4	110.3	101.9	28.6	1.3	—	—	5.0
69	Iran	86.8	98.2	98.5	67.7	42.4	109.2	88.4	66.0	3.8	100.0	25.9	3.0
71	Turkey	95.0	98.8	99.7	54.0	27.6	106.9	100.3	79.0	10.0	—	19.8	—
76	Lebanon	93.9	99.3	98.8	54.2	84.5	97.1	68.2	42.8	6.7	97.0	12.0	2.6
83	Algeria	80.2	95.5	95.6	34.9	79.2	118.7	99.9	34.6	6.6	94.7	23.7	—

(Continued)

Table 2.5. (Continued)

		Literacy rate				Gross enrolment ratio				Education quality			
		Adult	Youth (% ages 15–24)		Population with at least some secondary education	Pre-Primary	Primary	Secondary	Tertiary	Primary school dropout rate	Primary school teachers trained to teach	Pupil-teacher ratio, primary school	Government expenditure on education
HDI rank	Country		Female	Male	(% ages 25 and older)	(% of preschool-age children)	(% of primary school-age population)	(% of secondary school-age population)	(% of tertiary school-age population)	(% of primary school cohort)	(%)	(number of pupils per teacher)	(% of GDP)
		2005–2015	2005–2015	2005–2015	2005–2015	2010–2015	2010–2015	2010–2015	2010–2015	2005–2015	2005–2015	2010–2015	2010–2014
86	Jordan	96.7	99.4	99.0	81.3	32.2	88.7	84.3	47.6	2.1	—	—	—
97	Tunisia	81.8	97.8	98.3	43.9	42.8	113.1	87.6	34.6	6.0	100.0	16.5	6.2
	Medium human development												
111	Egypt	75.2	92.1	94.5	61.4	30.3	103.9	86.1	31.7	3.9	72.7	23.1	—
121	Iraq	79.7	80.6	82.4	45.6	—	—	—	—	—	—	—	—
123	Morocco	72.4	93.5	96.6	29.4	59.6	116.1	69.1	24.6	10.7	100.0	25.7	—
	Low human development												
149	Syria	86.4	95.6	97.1	38.9	5.9	80.1	50.5	33.0	83.9	—	—	—
168	Yemen	70.1	82.7	97.6	24.4	1.3	97.5	48.6	10.0	30.5	—	30.3	—
172	Djibouti	—	—	—	—	4.7	66.3	47.1	5.0	15.6	100.0	33.0	4.5

Human development groups												
Very high human	—	—	—	88.8	83.9	102.4	106.0	75.2	—	—	14.3	5.1
High human	95.3	99.3	99.2	70.6	74.2	105.1	95.0	42.5	—	—	17.8	—
Medium human	76.4	88.5	91.5	49.1	33.7	108.5	68.3	23.3	—	—	29.1	3.9
Low human	60.9	69.1	77.5	20.3	17.6	98.4	39.9	8.2	42.2	76.4	42.1	3.8
OECD	—	—	—	85.5	79.9	102.5	103.9	70.2	—	—	15.9	5.1

Definitions

Adult literacy rate: Percentage of the population ages 15 and older that can, with understanding, both read and write a short simple statement on everyday life.

Youth literacy rate: Percentage of the population ages 15–24 that can, with understanding, both read and write a short simple statement on everyday life.

Population with at least some secondary education: Percentage of the population ages 25 and older that has reached (but not necessarily completed) a secondary level of education.

Gross enrolment ratio: Total enrolment in a given level of education (pre-primary, primary, secondary or tertiary), regardless of age, expressed as a percentage of the official school-age population for the same level of education.

Primary school dropout rate: Percentage of students from a given cohort who have enrolled in primary school but who drop out before reaching the last grade of primary education. It is calculated as 100 minus the survival rate to the last grade of primary education and assumes that observed flow rates remain unchanged throughout the cohort life and that dropouts do not re-enter school.

Primary school teachers trained to teach: Percentage of primary school teachers who have received the minimum organized teacher training (pre-service or in-service) required for teaching at the primary level.

Pupil-teacher ratio, primary school: Average number of pupils per teacher in primary education in a given school year.

Government expenditure on education: Current, capital and transfers spending on education, expressed as a percentage of GDP.

Source: UNDP, Human Development Report. 2016b.

Table 2.6. Government Expenditure on Education and Per Student in Tertiary, Secondary and Primary Education in MENA

(2007–2014)

Country	Series Name	2007	2008	2009	2010	2011	2012	2013	2014
Algeria	Government expenditure per tertiary student as % of GDP per capita (%)	—	—	—	—	—	—	—	—
Algeria	Government expenditure per student, secondary (% of GDP per capita)	—	—	—	—	—	—	—	—
Algeria	Government expenditure per student, primary (% of GDP per capita)	—	—	—	—	—	—	—	—
Algeria	Government expenditure on education, total (% of GDP)	—	4.3	—	—	—	—	—	—
Bahrain	Government expenditure per tertiary student as % of GDP per capita (%)	—	—	—	—	—	—	—	—
Bahrain	Government expenditure per student, secondary (% of GDP per capita)	—	—	—	—	—	—	—	—
Bahrain	Government expenditure per student, primary (% of GDP per capita)	—	—	—	—	—	—	—	—
Bahrain	Government expenditure on education, total (% of GDP)	2.6	2.5	—	—	—	2.6	—	—
Cyprus	Government expenditure per tertiary student as % of GDP per capita (%)	51.1	52.1	49.1	35.1	36.0	—	—	—
Cyprus	Government expenditure per student, secondary (% of GDP per capita)	32.9	35.0	37.8	37.3	38.3	—	—	—
Cyprus	Government expenditure per student, primary (% of GDP per capita)	23.7	26.2	29.3	31.3	32.6	—	—	—
Cyprus	Government expenditure on education, total (% of GDP)	6.3	6.8	7.3	6.7	6.6	—	—	—

Djibouti	Government expenditure per tertiary student as % of GDP per capita (%)	—	—	—	190.9	—	—	—	—
Djibouti	Government expenditure per student, secondary (% of GDP per capita)	—	30.8	—	—	—	—	—	—
Djibouti	Government expenditure per student, primary (% of GDP per capita)	22.5	22.9	—	—	—	—	—	—
Djibouti	Government expenditure on education, total (% of GDP)	8.4	—	—	4.5	—	—	—	—
Egypt	Government expenditure per tertiary student as % of GDP per capita (%)	—	—	—	—	—	—	—	—
Egypt	Government expenditure per student, secondary (% of GDP per capita)	—	—	—	—	—	—	—	—
Egypt	Government expenditure per student, primary (% of GDP per capita)	—	—	—	—	—	—	—	—
Egypt	Government expenditure on education, total (% of GDP)	3.7	3.8	—	—	—	—	—	—
Iran	Government expenditure per tertiary student as % of GDP per capita (%)	24.2	17.7	19.0	16.0	18.0	15.2	12.6	13.8
Iran	Government expenditure per student, secondary (% of GDP per capita)	19.4	17.4	18.1	19.0	14.7	14.1	18.5	15.5
Iran	Government expenditure per student, primary (% of GDP per capita)	16.5	14.2	12.9	12.5	13.0	10.7	8.0	8.2
Iran	Government expenditure on education, total (% of GDP)	4.7	4.1	4.0	3.9	3.7	3.2	3.2	3.0
Iraq	Government expenditure per tertiary student as % of GDP per capita (%)	—	—	—	—	—	—	—	—
Iraq	Government expenditure per student, secondary (% of GDP per capita)	—	—	—	—	—	—	—	—
Iraq	Government expenditure per student, primary (% of GDP per capita)	—	—	—	—	—	—	—	—
Iraq	Government expenditure on education, total (% of GDP)	—	—	—	—	—	—	—	—

(Continued)

Table 2.6. (*Continued*)

	(2007–2014)								
Country	Series Name	2007	2008	2009	2010	2011	2012	2013	2014
Israel	Government expenditure per tertiary student as % of GDP per capita (%)	21.1	19.8	20.7	19.7	19.2	19.3	—	—
Israel	Government expenditure per student, secondary (% of GDP per capita)	15.9	17.0	15.9	15.3	15.3	16.0	16.2	—
Israel	Government expenditure per student, primary (% of GDP per capita)	19.7	19.8	19.9	21.5	22.4	22.9	22.1	—
Israel	Government expenditure on education, total (% of GDP)	5.5	5.5	5.5	5.5	5.6	—	5.9	—
Jordan	Government expenditure per tertiary student as % of GDP per capita (%)	—	—	—	—	—	—	—	—
Jordan	Government expenditure per student, secondary (% of GDP per capita)	16.1	14.8	—	—	15.1	—	—	—
Jordan	Government expenditure per student, primary (% of GDP per capita)	12.6	12.3	—	—	12.2	—	—	—
Jordan	Government expenditure on education, total (% of GDP)	—	—	—	—	—	—	—	—
Kuwait	Government expenditure per tertiary student as % of GDP per capita (%)	—	—	—	—	—	—	—	—
Kuwait	Government expenditure per student, secondary (% of GDP per capita)	—	14.2	—	—	22.2	—	—	—
Kuwait	Government expenditure per student, primary (% of GDP per capita)	—	10.4	—	—	17.8	—	—	—
Kuwait	Government expenditure on education, total (% of GDP)	—	—	—	—	—	—	—	—
Lebanon	Government expenditure per tertiary student as % of GDP per capita (%)	14.4	12.3	9.9	9.5	8.8	14.1	15.6	—
Lebanon	Government expenditure per student, secondary (% of GDP per capita)	—	—	—	—	—	3.7	5.1	—

Lebanon	Government expenditure per student, primary (% of GDP per capita)	—	—	—	—	—	—	—	—
Lebanon	Government expenditure on education, total (% of GDP)	2.6	2.0	1.8	1.6	1.6	2.2	2.6	—
Libya	Government expenditure per tertiary student as % of GDP per capita (%)	—	—	—	—	—	—	—	—
Libya	Government expenditure per student, secondary (% of GDP per capita)	—	—	—	—	—	—	—	—
Libya	Government expenditure per student, primary (% of GDP per capita)	—	—	—	—	—	—	—	—
Libya	Government expenditure on education, total (% of GDP)	—	—	—	—	—	—	—	—
Morocco	Government expenditure per tertiary student as % of GDP per capita (%)	—	—	81.6	—	—	—	—	—
Morocco	Government expenditure per student, secondary (% of GDP per capita)	37.2	32.7	30.5	34.0	33.6	36.1	—	—
Morocco	Government expenditure per student, primary (% of GDP per capita)	13.8	15.6	16.6	17.8	17.9	18.8	19.3	—
Morocco	Government expenditure on education, total (% of GDP)	—	5.3	5.3	—	—	—	—	—
Oman	Government expenditure per tertiary student as % of GDP per capita (%)	—	—	41.1	—	—	—	—	—
Oman	Government expenditure per student, secondary (% of GDP per capita)	—	—	14.4	—	17.4	—	21.5	—
Oman	Government expenditure per student, primary (% of GDP per capita)	—	—	12.6	—	15.4	—	—	—
Oman	Government expenditure on education, total (% of GDP)	—	—	4.2	—	—	—	5.0	—
Qatar	Government expenditure per tertiary student as % of GDP per capita (%)	—	—	—	—	—	—	—	—
Qatar	Government expenditure per student, secondary (% of GDP per capita)	—	—	10.5	—	—	—	—	—

(Continued)

Table 2.6. *(Continued)*

		(2007–2014)							
Country	Series Name	2007	2008	2009	2010	2011	2012	2013	2014
Qatar	Government expenditure per student, primary (% of GDP per capita)	—	—	9.9	—	—	—	—	—
Qatar	Government expenditure on education, total (% of GDP)	2.5	4.2	3.4	4.5	4.0	3.5	4.0	3.5
SA	Government expenditure per tertiary student as % of GDP per capita (%)	—	—	—	—	—	—	—	—
SA	Government expenditure per student, secondary (% of GDP per capita)	18.2	—	—	—	—	—	—	—
SA	Government expenditure per student, primary (% of GDP per capita)	18.3	—	—	—	—	—	—	—
SA	Government expenditure on education, total (% of GDP)	—	5.1	—	—	—	—	—	—
Syria	Government expenditure per tertiary student as % of GDP per capita (%)	42.7	44.2	47.9	—	—	—	—	—
Syria	Government expenditure per student, secondary (% of GDP per capita)	13.3	—	14.6	—	—	15.4	—	—
Syria	Government expenditure per student, primary (% of GDP per capita)	17.5	—	17.2	—	—	18.3	—	—
Syria	Government expenditure on education, total (% of GDP)	4.9	4.6	5.1	—	—	—	—	—
Tunisia	Government expenditure per tertiary student as % of GDP per capita (%)	47.2	45.4	49.9	50.2	—	52.9	56.7	53.7
Tunisia	Government expenditure per student, secondary (% of GDP per capita)	—	24.4	—	—	—	—	—	—
Tunisia	Government expenditure per student, primary (% of GDP per capita)	—	17.3	—	—	—	—	—	—
Tunisia	Government expenditure on education, total (% of GDP)	6.5	6.3	6.5	6.3	—	6.2	—	—

Turkey	Government expenditure per tertiary student as % of GDP per capita (%)	—	—	—	—	—	—	—	—
Turkey	Government expenditure per student, secondary (% of GDP per capita)	—	—	—	—	—	—	—	—
Turkey	Government expenditure per student, primary (% of GDP per capita)	—	—	—	—	—	—	—	—
Turkey	Government expenditure on education, total (% of GDP)	—	—	—	—	—	—	—	—
UAE	Government expenditure per tertiary student as % of GDP per capita (%)	—	—	—	—	—	—	—	—
UAE	Government expenditure per student, secondary (% of GDP per capita)	—	—	—	—	17.2	17.8	—	—
UAE	Government expenditure per student, primary (% of GDP per capita)	—	—	—	—	11.3	10.4	—	—
UAE	Government expenditure on education, total (% of GDP)	—	—	—	—	—	—	—	—
Yemen	Government expenditure per tertiary student as % of GDP per capita (%)	—	—	—	—	—	—	—	—
Yemen	Government expenditure per student, secondary (% of GDP per capita)	—	—	—	—	12.6	—	—	—
Yemen	Government expenditure per student, primary (% of GDP per capita)	—	—	—	—	19.4	—	—	—
Yemen	Government expenditure on education, total (% of GDP)	—	4.6	—	—	—	—	—	—
OECD	Government expenditure per tertiary student as % of GDP per capita (%)	24.6	24.3	28.2	26.7	27.8	23.8	—	—
OECD	Government expenditure per student, secondary (% of GDP per capita)	22.9	24.6	26.1	26.1	25.6	24.3	—	—
OECD	Government expenditure per student, primary (% of GDP per capita)	19.2	19.2	21.3	22.0	21.0	20.6	—	—
OECD	Government expenditure on education, total (% of GDP)	4.9	5.1	5.4	5.5	5.2	4.9	—	—

Source: World Bank Development Indicators, 2017.

One proxy for access to knowledge in this age of connectivity and globalization is the number of Internet users per 100 people. Table 2.7 presents the data for the period 2007–2015. Arab MENA has the lowest level of access to the Internet of all regions of the world, even lower than sub-Saharan Africa. While there have been improvements they still fall substantially behind Israel and the OECD. A second outcome variable listed in Table 2.7 is the expenditure on research and development relative to GDP. Arab MENA spends on average less than 1 percent of their GDP on research and development compared to Israel's 4.1 percent and the OECD average of 2.4 percent. These numbers are further corroborated by the sparse number of scientific and technical research articles published in accredited and ranked journals by Arab MENA scientists and researchers.

A discussion of the size of human capital investment in the MENA and the resulting returns and earnings inequality developed is presented in Chapter 4. A discussion of the demographic explosion within Arab MENA, especially among the educated and female, accompanied by a targeting of employment opportunities by citizenship (the state sector for local citizens, and the high-tech private sector delegated to non-citizens) and the use of low-wage workers for infrastructure development, is presented within Chapter 5. The resulting technology gap between Arab MENA and the OECD and Israel is explored in Chapter 7.

2.4. Health Expenditure in MENA

In addition to focusing on expenditure on human capital and its outcome on literacy, labor market participation and potential economic growth, one must address the current condition of health expenditure in MENA and the resulting impact on life expectancy.

From the existing literature on cross-country comparison of social welfare (Dasgupta and Weale, 1992; Murray *et al.*, 2006), it is a well-established fact that life expectancy at birth — defined as the average length of a lifespan in a population, given current age-specific mortality rates — is one of the most widely used indicators of social welfare. It is also one of three factors that make up the Human Development Index (HDI).

A number of factors are known to affect life expectancy. The first set of indicators are specific to the health system. That includes health spending per capita and physicians and hospital beds per capita. Falkingham (2004) and Kabir (2008) point out that there is a strong positive relationship between the amount spent on health and life expectancy. The magic cut

Table 2.7. MENA Country Expenditure on Research and Development and Internet Users

(2007–2015)

Country	Series Name	2007	2008	2009	2010	2011	2012	2013	2014	2015
Algeria	Internet users (per 100 people)	9.5	10.2	11.2	12.5	14.0	15.2	16.5	25.0	38.2
Algeria	R & D expenditure (% of GDP)	—	—	—	—	—	—	—	—	—
Bahrain	Internet users (per 100 people)	32.9	52.0	53.0	55.0	77.0	88.0	90.0	90.5	93.5
Bahrain	R & D expenditure (% of GDP)	—	—	—	—	—	—	—	0.1	—
Cyprus	Internet users (per 100 people)	40.8	42.3	49.8	53.0	56.9	60.7	65.5	69.3	71.7
Cyprus	R & D expenditure (% of GDP)	0.4	0.4	0.5	0.5	0.5	0.4	0.5	0.5	—
Djibouti	Internet users (per 100 people)	1.6	2.3	4.0	6.5	7.0	8.3	9.5	10.7	11.9
Djibouti	R & D expenditure (% of GDP)	—	—	—	—	—	—	—	—	—
Egypt	Internet users (per 100 people)	16.0	18.0	20.0	21.6	25.6	26.4	29.4	33.9	35.9
Egypt	R & D expenditure (% of GDP)	0.3	0.3	0.4	0.4	0.5	0.5	0.7	0.7	—
Iran	Internet users (per 100 people)	9.5	12.0	13.8	15.9	19.0	22.7	30.0	39.4	44.1
Iran	R & D expenditure (% of GDP)	—	0.7	0.3	0.3	—	0.3	—	—	—
Iraq	Internet users (per 100 people)	0.9	1.0	1.1	2.5	5.0	7.1	9.2	13.2	17.2
Iraq	R & D expenditure (% of GDP)	0.0	0.0	0.0	0.0	0.0	—	—	0.0	—
Israel	Internet users (per 100 people)	48.1	59.4	63.1	67.5	68.9	70.8	70.3	75.0	78.9
Israel	R & D expenditure (% of GDP)	4.4	4.3	4.1	3.9	4.0	4.1	4.1	4.1	—
Jordan	Internet users (per 100 people)	20.0	23.0	26.0	27.2	34.9	37.0	41.4	46.2	53.4
Jordan	R & D expenditure (% of GDP)	—	0.4	—	—	—	—	—	—	—

(*Continued*)

Table 2.7. *(Continued)*

		(2007–2015)								
Country	Series Name	2007	2008	2009	2010	2011	2012	2013	2014	2015
Kuwait	Internet users (per 100 people)	34.8	42.0	50.8	61.4	65.8	70.5	75.5	78.7	82.1
Kuwait	R & D expenditure (% of GDP)	0.1	0.1	0.1	0.1	0.1	0.1	0.3	—	—
Lebanon	Internet users (per 100 people)	18.7	22.5	30.1	43.7	52.0	61.2	70.5	73.0	74.0
Lebanon	R & D expenditure (% of GDP)	—	—	—	—	—	—	—	—	—
Libya	Internet users (per 100 people)	4.7	9.0	10.8	14.0	14.0	—	16.5	17.8	19.0
Libya	R & D expenditure (% of GDP)	—	—	—	—	—	—	—	—	—
Morocco	Internet users (per 100 people)	21.5	33.1	41.3	52.0	46.1	55.4	56.0	56.8	57.1
Morocco	R & D expenditure (% of GDP)	—	—	—	0.7	—	—	—	—	—
Oman	Internet users (per 100 people)	16.7	20.0	26.8	35.8	48.0	60.0	66.5	70.2	74.2
Oman	R & D expenditure (% of GDP)	—	—	—	—	0.1	0.2	0.2	—	—
Qatar	Internet users (per 100 people)	37.0	44.3	53.1	69.0	69.0	69.3	85.3	91.5	92.9
Qatar	R & D expenditure (% of GDP)	—	—	—	—	—	0.5	—	—	—
SA	Internet users (per 100 people)	30.0	36.0	38.0	41.0	47.5	54.0	60.5	64.7	69.6
SA	R & D expenditure (% of GDP)	0.0	0.0	0.1	—	—	—	—	—	—

Syria	Internet users (per 100 people)	11.5	14.0	17.3	20.7	22.5	24.3	26.2	28.1	30.0
Syria	R & D expenditure (% of GDP)	—	—	—	—	—	—	—	—	—
Tunisia	Internet users (per 100 people)	17.1	27.5	34.1	36.8	39.1	41.4	43.8	46.2	48.5
Tunisia	R & D expenditure (% of GDP)	0.7	0.6	0.7	0.7	0.7	0.7	0.7	0.6	—
Turkey	Internet users (per 100 people)	28.6	34.4	36.4	39.8	43.1	45.1	46.3	51.0	53.7
Turkey	R & D expenditure (% of GDP)	0.7	0.7	0.8	0.8	0.9	0.9	0.9	1.0	—
UAE	Internet users (per 100 people)	61.0	63.0	64.0	68.0	78.0	85.0	88.0	90.4	91.2
UAE	R & D expenditure (% of GDP)	—	—	—	—	0.5	—	—	0.7	—
Yemen	Internet users (per 100 people)	5.0	6.9	10.0	12.4	14.9	17.4	20.0	22.6	25.1
Yemen	R & D expenditure (% of GDP)	—	—	—	—	—	—	—	—	—
OECD	Internet users (per 100 people)	61.9	63.9	65.3	67.6	68.6	71.0	72.3	74.3	77.2
OECD	R & D expenditure (% of GDP)	2.2	2.3	2.4	2.4	2.4	2.4	2.4	—	—

Source: World Bank Development Indicators, 2017.

off point used by researchers is $2,500 per capita. Beyond that amount one reaches diminishing returns. In addition to health care expenditure, accessibility and quality of health services also affects a population's health and life expectancy. Not having access to basic services, especially preventive services, clearly has a significantly negative impact on health and life expectancy. In Table 2.8 we present the health expenditure figures for MENA. These include private, public and total health expenditure as a share of GDP and health expenditure per capita, PPP expressed in constant 2011 international dollars. The data is presented for 2007–2014 with a compound annual growth rate.

For most of the MENA countries, the total health expenditure as a percent of GDP is on the low side, despite the marginal improvement over the 2007–2014 period. The real health expenditure per capita for the majority of MENA countries is far below $2,500. The exceptions are Israel and Qatar who surpass the $2,500 figure, and Saudi Arabia and the UAE that are very close to $2,500. The next group of MENA countries cluster around $1,000, with the balance in the $200–$600 range. Overall the first indicator on health spending will predict a lower life expectancy at birth for the majority in MENA.

In Tables 2.9 and 2.10 we present the data on the second institutional factor concerning the health system, that is the question of accessibility of health services. Table 2.9 presents the latest data on the number of hospital beds per 10,000 population. Apart from Cyprus, Israel, Lebanon, Libya, Oman, Saudi Arabia, Tunisia and Turkey, there is a real issue of accessibility of hospital space in MENA. Table 2.10 goes further and presents the number of physicians per 1,000 people over the period 1990–2014. Here again we have an access problem in MENA. Apart from Cyprus, Israel, Jordan, Lebanon, Libya, Saudi Arabia, there are less than 2 physicians per 1,000 people for the majority of MENA. The data for the OECD and the USA while above 2 is less than the Israeli figure of 3.6 per 1,000 people.

We now turn to the outcome variable, life expectancy at birth in 2015. Table 2.11 presents data on life expectancy at birth for both males and females. It also presents data on healthy life expectancy at birth. According to the World Health Organization, life expectancy in Arab MENA is, on average, 5 plus years lower than the comparable figures for Europe, the USA and Israel.

The figures vary from a low of around 61.8 years for males in Djibouti to a level approaching 76.4 years for males in the UAE. By contrast, life expectancy in Israel stands at 80.6 for males and 84.3 for females. For the

Table 2.8. Health Expenditure — Total, Public and Private and Per Capita in MENA Percent of GDP and PPP Constant 2011 International $

(2007–2014)

Country	Series Name	2007	2008	2009	2010	2011	2012	2013	2014	Compound Annual Growth Rate
Algeria	Health expenditure, total (% of GDP)	3.8	4.2	5.4	5.1	5.3	6.1	7.1	7.2	0.095
Algeria	Health expenditure, public (% of GDP)	2.7	3.1	3.8	3.6	3.8	4.5	5.2	5.2	0.099
Algeria	Health expenditure, private (% of GDP)	1.1	1.1	1.5	1.5	1.5	1.6	1.9	2.0	0.084
Algeria	Health expenditure per capita, PPP (constant 2011 international $)	453.2	510.1	655.0	644.3	686.2	821.3	858.9	932.1	0.108
Bahrain	Health expenditure, total (% of GDP)	3.1	3.2	3.8	3.6	3.4	4.4	4.7	5.0	0.071
Bahrain	Health expenditure, public (% of GDP)	2.2	2.3	2.7	2.6	2.4	2.8	3.0	3.2	0.054
Bahrain	Health expenditure, private (% of GDP)	0.9	0.9	1.0	1.0	1.0	1.6	1.7	1.8	0.108
Bahrain	Health expenditure per capita, PPP (constant 2011 international $)	1,261.2	1,294.1	1,489.7	1,434.1	1,349.8	1,788.9	2,028.7	2,272.9	0.088

(Continued)

Table 2.8. *(Continued)*

		(2007–2014)								
Country	Series Name	2007	2008	2009	2010	2011	2012	2013	2014	Compound Annual Growth Rate
Cyprus	Health expenditure, total (% of GDP)	6.1	6.9	7.4	7.2	7.5	7.4	7.5	7.4	0.028
Cyprus	Health expenditure, public (% of GDP)	2.6	2.9	3.3	3.4	3.5	3.4	3.5	3.3	0.037
Cyprus	Health expenditure, private (% of GDP)	3.5	4.0	4.1	3.8	4.0	4.0	3.9	4.0	0.022
Cyprus	Health expenditure per capita, PPP (constant 2011 international $)	1,780.1	2,224.2	2,343.9	2,270.0	2,313.1	2,215.7	2,112.0	2,062.4	0.021
Djibouti	Health expenditure, total (% of GDP)	7.7	8.0	8.4	8.8	8.7	8.9	9.1	10.6	0.046
Djibouti	Health expenditure, public (% of GDP)	5.3	5.7	6.0	5.1	5.0	5.3	5.3	6.8	0.034
Djibouti	Health expenditure, private (% of GDP)	2.4	2.3	2.4	3.7	3.7	3.7	3.8	3.8	0.070
Djibouti	Health expenditure per capita, PPP (constant 2011 international $)	174.4	190.4	184.0	231.8	242.4	257.6	276.7	338.0	0.099
Egypt	Health expenditure, total (% of GDP)	5.0	4.8	5.0	4.8	5.0	5.3	5.5	5.6	0.019
Egypt	Health expenditure, public (% of GDP)	2.0	2.0	2.1	1.9	2.0	1.9	2.1	2.2	0.007

Egypt	Health expenditure, private (% of GDP)	2.9	2.8	3.0	2.9	3.0	3.4	3.4	3.5	0.026
Egypt	Health expenditure per capita, PPP (constant 2011 international $)	422.3	441.5	475.1	474.8	507.5	542.5	567.2	594.1	0.050
Iran	Health expenditure, total (% of GDP)	5.8	6.3	7.6	8.0	7.1	7.0	6.5	6.9	0.024
Iran	Health expenditure, public (% of GDP)	2.4	2.4	2.9	2.7	2.5	2.7	2.7	2.8	0.023
Iran	Health expenditure, private (% of GDP)	3.4	3.8	4.8	5.3	4.6	4.3	3.8	4.1	0.025
Iran	Health expenditure per capita, PPP (constant 2011 international $)	890.0	984.0	1,205.0	1,335.2	1,242.8	1,143.9	1,045.0	1,081.7	0.028
Iraq	Health expenditure, total (% of GDP)	3.7	3.9	4.6	3.8	3.3	5.3	5.9	5.5	0.060
Iraq	Health expenditure, public (% of GDP)	2.6	2.9	3.5	2.8	2.5	3.3	3.7	3.3	0.038
Iraq	Health expenditure, private (% of GDP)	1.1	1.0	1.2	1.0	0.8	2.0	2.2	2.2	0.100
Iraq	Health expenditure per capita, PPP (constant 2011 international $)	122.4	144.6	460.2	391.5	371.6	650.8	774.4	667.0	0.274
Israel	Health expenditure, total (% of GDP)	7.4	7.3	7.5	7.4	7.4	7.7	7.9	7.8	0.008
Israel	Health expenditure, public (% of GDP)	4.6	4.5	4.6	4.6	4.6	4.9	4.9	4.8	0.006
Israel	Health expenditure, private (% of GDP)	2.8	2.8	2.8	2.7	2.7	2.9	3.0	3.1	0.012

(*Continued*)

Table 2.8. ***(Continued)***

		(2007–2014)								
Country	Series Name	2007	2008	2009	2010	2011	2012	2013	2014	Compound Annual Growth Rate
Israel	Health expenditure per capita, PPP (constant 2011 international $)	2,004.4	1,990.5	2,041.1	2,116.1	2,231.8	2,446.1	2,571.9	2,599.1	0.038
Jordan	Health expenditure, total (% of GDP)	8.3	8.8	9.5	8.4	8.4	8.0	7.2	7.5	−0.016
Jordan	Health expenditure, public (% of GDP)	5.0	5.4	6.7	5.9	5.9	5.5	4.9	5.2	0.006
Jordan	Health expenditure, private (% of GDP)	3.4	3.3	2.8	2.5	2.5	2.5	2.4	2.3	−0.055
Jordan	Health expenditure per capita, PPP (constant 2011 international $)	802.7	884.5	980.3	861.1	865.8	834.7	763.1	797.6	−0.001
Kuwait	Health expenditure, total (% of GDP)	2.1	1.9	3.9	2.8	2.6	2.6	2.6	3.0	0.052
Kuwait	Health expenditure, public (% of GDP)	1.7	1.5	3.4	2.3	2.3	2.2	2.2	2.6	0.065
Kuwait	Health expenditure, private (% of GDP)	0.5	0.4	0.5	0.4	0.4	0.4	0.4	0.4	−0.008
Kuwait	Health expenditure per capita, PPP (constant 2011 international $)	1,919.6	1,704.5	3,004.5	1,992.5	1,996.6	2,017.9	1,968.3	2,319.6	0.027
Lebanon	Health expenditure, public (% of GDP)	3.7	3.1	3.1	2.7	2.7	3.2	3.1	3.0	−0.028

Lebanon	Health expenditure, total (% of GDP)	8.9	8.1	7.4	7.2	7.1	7.0	6.6	6.4	−0.046
Lebanon	Health expenditure, private (% of GDP)	5.2	4.9	4.3	4.5	4.4	3.8	3.6	3.3	−0.061
Lebanon	Health expenditure per capita, PPP (constant 2011 international $)	1,115.5	1,118.3	1,123.5	1,146.9	1,117.4	1,085.7	1,033.0	987.4	−0.017
Libya	Health expenditure, total (% of GDP)	2.6	2.0	3.2	3.1	4.8	4.3	4.3	5.0	0.095
Libya	Health expenditure, public (% of GDP)	1.7	1.4	2.2	2.1	3.0	3.0	3.0	3.7	0.111
Libya	Health expenditure, private (% of GDP)	0.9	0.7	1.0	0.9	1.8	1.3	1.3	1.3	0.059
Libya	Health expenditure per capita, PPP (constant 2011 international $)	605.9	555.5	955.5	942.5	617.8	1,148.5	911.4	806.2	0.042
Morocco	Health expenditure, total (% of GDP)	5.5	5.4	5.7	5.9	6.0	6.1	5.9	5.9	0.011
Morocco	Health expenditure, public (% of GDP)	1.9	1.9	2.0	2.1	2.1	2.2	2.0	2.0	0.008
Morocco	Health expenditure, private (% of GDP)	3.6	3.5	3.6	3.8	3.9	4.0	4.0	3.9	0.013
Morocco	Health expenditure per capita, PPP (constant 2011 international $)	301.7	317.7	346.9	278.0	401.8	425.1	428.8	446.6	0.058
Oman	Health expenditure, total (% of GDP)	2.4	2.0	2.8	2.7	2.5	2.5	2.8	3.6	0.056
Oman	Health expenditure, public (% of GDP)	2.0	1.6	2.3	2.3	2.0	2.1	2.4	3.2	0.071

(Continued)

Table 2.8. (*Continued*)

		(2007–2014)								
Country	Series Name	2007	2008	2009	2010	2011	2012	2013	2014	Compound Annual Growth Rate
Oman	Health expenditure, private (% of GDP)	0.5	0.4	0.5	0.5	0.5	0.4	0.4	0.4	−0.032
Oman	Health expenditure per capita, PPP (constant 2011 international $)	1,009.6	903.5	1,304.6	1,259.1	1,083.6	1,073.9	1,128.6	1,442.0	0.052
Qatar	Health expenditure, total (% of GDP)	2.3	1.9	2.6	2.1	1.9	2.2	2.1	2.2	−0.008
Qatar	Health expenditure, public (% of GDP)	1.9	1.6	2.1	1.6	1.5	1.8	1.9	1.9	−0.005
Qatar	Health expenditure, private (% of GDP)	0.4	0.3	0.6	0.5	0.4	0.3	0.3	0.3	−0.024
Qatar	Health expenditure per capita, PPP (constant 2011 international $)	2,684.9	2,212.2	3,053.2	2,583.0	2,582.4	2,855.5	2,916.9	3,071.2	0.019
SA	Health expenditure, total (% of GDP)	3.5	2.9	4.1	3.5	3.6	3.9	4.2	4.7	0.043
SA	Health expenditure, public (% of GDP)	2.5	1.9	2.8	2.3	2.5	2.8	3.1	3.5	0.048
SA	Health expenditure, private (% of GDP)	1.0	1.0	1.3	1.2	1.1	1.1	1.1	1.2	0.029
SA	Health expenditure per capita, PPP (constant 2011 international $)	1,353.6	1,201.2	1,712.1	1,514.3	1,692.8	1,920.4	2,159.4	2,466.0	0.089

Syria	Health expenditure, total (% of GDP)	3.7	3.4	3.5	3.3	3.2	3.3	3.3	3.3	−0.019
Syria	Health expenditure, public (% of GDP)	1.8	1.6	1.6	1.5	1.5	1.5	1.5	1.5	−0.024
Syria	Health expenditure, private (% of GDP)	1.9	1.8	1.9	1.8	1.7	1.7	1.7	1.7	−0.014
Syria	Health expenditure per capita, PPP (constant 2011 international $)	172.9	162.8	177.5	171.9	188.1	163.2	270.7	375.9	0.117
Tunisia	Health expenditure, total (% of GDP)	5.6	5.6	6.2	6.5	7.2	7.2	7.3	7.0	0.031
Tunisia	Health expenditure, public (% of GDP)	3.0	3.0	3.5	3.8	4.2	4.2	4.2	4.0	0.043
Tunisia	Health expenditure, private (% of GDP)	2.7	2.6	2.7	2.7	3.0	3.0	3.0	3.0	0.017
Tunisia	Health expenditure per capita, PPP (constant 2011 international $)	505.8	533.3	605.0	656.1	725.3	766.0	797.5	785.3	0.065
Turkey	Health expenditure, total (% of GDP)	6.0	6.1	6.1	5.6	5.3	5.2	5.4	5.4	−0.015
Turkey	Health expenditure, public (% of GDP)	4.1	4.4	4.9	4.4	4.2	4.1	4.2	4.2	0.003
Turkey	Health expenditure, private (% of GDP)	1.9	1.6	1.2	1.2	1.1	1.1	1.2	1.2	−0.064
Turkey	Health expenditure per capita, PPP (constant 2011 international $)	843.9	918.2	887.1	904.1	941.4	948.7	1,007.0	1,036.5	0.030
UAE	Health expenditure, total (% of GDP)	2.6	2.9	4.0	3.9	3.7	3.4	3.5	3.6	0.051

(Continued)

Table 2.8. *(Continued)*

Country	Series Name	2007	2008	2009	2010	2011	2012	2013	2014	Compound Annual Growth Rate
	(2007–2014)									
UAE	Health expenditure, public (% of GDP)	1.6	1.9	3.0	2.8	2.7	2.6	2.6	2.6	0.078
UAE	Health expenditure, private (% of GDP)	1.0	1.0	1.0	1.1	1.0	0.9	0.9	1.0	0.000
UAE	Health expenditure per capita, PPP (constant 2011 international $)	1,953.4	2,040.3	2,410.9	2,232.4	2,130.3	1,993.6	2,208.3	2,405.4	0.030
Yemen	Health expenditure, total (% of GDP)	4.9	5.1	5.3	5.2	5.0	5.7	5.8	5.6	0.020
Yemen	Health expenditure, public (% of GDP)	1.5	1.6	1.3	1.3	1.4	1.6	1.4	1.3	−0.020
Yemen	Health expenditure, private (% of GDP)	3.5	3.6	4.0	3.9	3.7	4.2	4.4	4.4	0.034
Yemen	Health expenditure per capita, PPP (constant 2011 international $)	196.9	211.3	224.0	221.7	182.3	210.6	211.0	202.2	0.004
OECD	Health expenditure, total (% of GDP)	11.0	11.3	12.2	12.1	12.1	12.2	12.2	12.4	0.016
OECD	Health expenditure, public (% of GDP)	6.7	7.0	7.7	7.6	7.6	7.6	7.6	7.7	0.020
OECD	Health expenditure, private (% of GDP)	4.3	4.3	4.6	4.5	4.5	4.6	4.6	4.7	0.010
OECD	Health expenditure per capita, PPP (constant 2011 international $)	3,721.3	3,912.3	4,073.6	4,190.0	4,335.0	4,451.6	4,541.5	4,697.9	0.034

Source: World Bank Development Indicators, 2017.

Table 2.9. Hospital Beds (Per 10,000 Population)

Reported for the Period (2004–2010)

Country	Hospital beds (per 10,000 population) (numeric)
Algeria	17
Bahrain	18
Cyprus	38
Djibouti	14
Egypt	17
Iran	17
Iraq	13
Israel	58
Jordan	18
Kuwait	20
Lebanon	35
Libya	37
Morocco	11
Oman	19
Qatar	14
Qatar	12
SA	22
Syria	15
Tunisia	21
Turkey	25
UAE	19
Yemen	7

Source: World Health Organization.

USA life expectancy for males is 76.9 years and for females it is 81.6 years. For Europe the numbers are 73.2 years for males and 80.2 for females. For the entire WHO globe the average for males is 69.1 years and 73.8 for women. What is the most disturbing is the implications contained in the new set of indicators that the WHO has published for healthy life expectancy at birth. Only Israel stands out with the highest number — 72.8 years. The USA figure is 69.1 years and Europe is 68 years. For Arab MENA the numbers are disturbingly low reflecting the fact that in 2015 health care institutions were not meeting the needs of its citizens.

2.5. Growth and Capital Formation in MENA

Economic growth is usually measured by gross domestic product (GDP) in a unit of common currency, usually dollars. When expressed in per capita

Table 2.10. Physicians (Per 1,000 People)

Country	1990	2000	2010	2014
Algeria	0.942		1.207	
Bahrain		1.017	0.934	0.939
Cyprus	1.564		2.174	2.496
Djibouti	0.162		0.229	0.229
Egypt	0.760	2.118	2.830	0.814
Iran			0.890	1.491
Iraq	0.603		0.639	0.854
Israel	3.207	3.766	3.414	3.619
Jordan		2.008	2.487	2.650
Kuwait	0.183		2.500	1.949
Lebanon			2.671	2.380
Libya	1.071		1.900	2.092
Morocco			0.620	0.618
Oman	0.795	1.455	1.991	1.541
Qatar	1.500		3.919	1.964
SA	1.433	0.699	2.350	2.568
Syria	0.835	1.370	1.505	1.546
Tunisia	0.537	0.767	1.222	1.648
Turkey	0.938	1.348	1.707	1.749
UAE			1.531	1.558
Yemen	0.007			0.311
OECD	1.994	2.534		2.812
USA	1.800	2.583	2.429	2.554

Source: World Health Organization's Global Health Workforce Statistics.

terms, the GDP is often employed as a crude indicator of average social welfare. We know that if negative externalities are not priced, it follows that measured GDP overestimates social welfare. This problem is likely to be particularly acute for those countries that sell oil. Most of this revenue is not income that can be sustained over time. One can think of GDP in the case of Saudi Arabia and the Gulf as "liquidation of capital" rather than "income."

Economic growth invariably involves unevenness across sectors, or structural transformation. Despite the wide variation in the patterns of economic growth, in virtually all countries, rising per capita income is accompanied by a decline in agriculture's share of output and employment and a corresponding increase in the share of industry and services. As an economy's income level rises, its production structure tends to move away from the predominance of agriculture, toward a larger manufacturing base, and eventually to a service-oriented economy. Structural transformation, so defined,

Table 2.11. Life Expectancy at Birth and Healthy Life Expectancy at Birth, 2015

	Total population (000s)	Life expectancy at birth (years)			Healthy life expectancy at birth (years)
		Male	Female	Both sexes	
Country	2015	2015			2015
Algeria	39,667	73.8	77.5	75.6	66.0
Bahrain	1,377	76.2	77.9	76.9	67.0
Cyprus	1,165	78.3	82.7	80.5	71.3
Djibouti	888	61.8	65.3	63.5	55.8
Egypt	91,508	68.8	73.2	70.9	62.2
Iran	79,109	74.5	76.6	75.5	66.6
Iraq	36,423	66.2	71.8	68.9	60.0
Israel	8,064	80.6	84.3	82.5	72.8
Jordan	7,595	72.5	75.9	74.1	65.0
Kuwait	3,892	73.7	76.0	74.7	65.8
Lebanon	5,851	73.5	76.5	74.9	65.7
Libya	6,278	70.1	75.6	72.7	63.8
Morocco	34,378	73.3	75.4	74.3	64.9
Oman	4,491	75.0	79.2	76.6	66.7
Qatar	2,235	77.4	80.0	78.2	67.7
SA	31,540	73.2	76.0	74.5	64.5
Syria	18,502	59.9	69.9	64.5	56.1
Tunisia	11,254	73.0	77.8	75.3	66.7
Turkey	78,666	72.6	78.9	75.8	66.2
UAE	9,157	76.4	78.6	77.1	67.9
Yemen	26,832	64.3	67.2	65.7	57.7
USA	321,774	76.9	81.6	79.3	69.1
Europe	910,053	73.2	80.2	76.8	68
Global	7,313,015	69.1	73.8	71.4	63.1

Source: World Health Statistics 2016: Annex B.

is one of the very few "universals" of modern economic history. Furthermore, as average income levels rise, an analogous shift can be expected to occur in investment patterns.

Since labor productivity and therefore incomes are much higher in industry than in agriculture, the transfer of population to industry raises national income.

Furthermore, the rate of technological change that raises income per person is typically faster in industry. Consequently, the accepted paradigm has been to see industry and accumulation of human capital and technological changes as the leading actors of economic development.

In Table 2.12 we present aggregate data on gross capital formation and gross fixed capital formation and the sources of this funding from local savings to foreign direct investment for the period 2007–2015. A detailed analysis of investment on human capital is provided in Chapter 4.

Since 2000, there has been an unmistakable shift in the pattern of gross capital formation at the worldwide level, with developing countries becoming increasingly important in the global investment picture. One of the mainstream explanations for this shift is attributed to the robust economic growth in the developing world relative to the developed world and by greater convergence in investment rates between the two. To what extent this growth has translated to the experience of MENA countries is relevant for our purposes.

Over this period, gross fixed-capital formation relative to GDP was, on par with the OECD average of approximately 20 percent. There were substantial outliers within MENA. For Algeria, gross fixed capital formation grew from 26.3 percent of GDP in 2007 to 36.7 percent in 2014, representing a compound annual growth of 4.9 percent. In contrast, for Bahrain gross fixed capital formation as a percent of GDP declined from 33.6 percent in 2007 to 15.5 percent in 2014, representing a negative compound annual growth rate of 10.5 percent. Likewise, in Cyprus there was a negative compound annual growth rate of 7.8 percent. Similarly, for Egypt there was a negative compound annual growth rate of 5.1 percent for gross fixed capital formation as a percent of GDP from 2007 to 2015. For Jordan, gross fixed capital formation declined from 27.5 percent of GDP in 2007 to 22.9 percent in 2015, representing a compound annual decline of 2.3 percent. The trend in gross capital formation, gross domestic saving, gross saving and gross national expenditure, all as a percent of GDP follow the same trend of gross fixed capital formation.

The contribution of these investments to growth depends not only on the size and rate of investment but also on the efficiency with which it is used. The correlation between the rate of economic growth and investment efficiency is quite strong and significant on a world scale. For Arab MENA, we have relatively low levels of both investment efficiency and growth.

It is a well-understood development paradigm that policymakers must institute a national innovation system that is capable of innovating from both internal and external sources. Both are key to the efficient management of technology transfer, absorption, adaptation and diffusion in knowledge economies. The basic concept behind such systems is that it takes multiple actors to innovate and produce knowledge. The process is

Table 2.12. Capital Formation and Financing in MENA

Country	Series Name	2007	2008	2009	2010	2011	2012	2013	2014	2015	Compound Annual Growth Rate
	Percent of GDP for 2007–2015 and Annual Growth Rate										
Algeria	Gross capital formation (% of GDP)	34.5	37.3	46.9	41.4	38.0	39.1	43.4	45.6	—	0.041
Algeria	Gross domestic savings (% of GDP)	56.7	56.6	46.3	48.5	48.2	47.5	46.2	44.2	—	−0.035
Algeria	Gross fixed capital formation (% of GDP)	26.3	29.2	38.2	36.3	31.7	30.8	34.2	36.7	—	0.049
Algeria	Gross national expenditure (% of GDP)	77.8	80.7	100.6	93.0	89.8	91.6	97.2	101.5	—	0.039
Algeria	Gross savings (% of GDP)	57.0	57.4	47.3	50.0	48.6	47.9	45.7	43.5	—	−0.038
Algeria	Foreign direct investment, net inflows (% of GDP)	1.2	1.5	2.0	1.4	1.3	0.7	0.8	0.7	−0.2	−0.079
Algeria	Foreign direct investment, net outflows (% of GDP)	0.1	0.2	0.2	0.1	0.3	0.0	−0.1	0.0	0.1	−0.077
Bahrain	Gross capital formation (% of GDP)	34.7	35.2	26.1	27.3	16.5	20.1	17.1	16.5	—	−0.101
Bahrain	Gross domestic savings (% of GDP)	56.3	54.4	45.1	45.9	48.0	46.6	44.8	43.9	—	−0.035
Bahrain	Gross fixed capital formation (% of GDP)	33.6	34.5	25.3	26.0	15.8	19.4	15.7	15.5	—	−0.105
Bahrain	Gross national expenditure (% of GDP)	78.4	80.7	81.0	81.4	68.5	73.5	72.3	72.6	—	−0.011

(Continued)

Table 2.12. *(Continued)*

Percent of GDP for 2007–2015 and Annual Growth Rate											
Country	Series Name	2007	2008	2009	2010	2011	2012	2013	2014	2015	Compound Annual Growth Rate
Bahrain	Gross savings (% of GDP)	48.1	43.9	28.6	30.3	27.8	27.4	25.0	19.9	—	−0.118
Bahrain	Foreign direct investment, net inflows (% of GDP)	8.1	7.0	1.1	0.6	2.7	2.9	3.0	2.9	−4.7	−0.138
Bahrain	Foreign direct investment, net outflows (% of GDP)	7.7	6.3	−7.8	1.3	3.1	3.0	3.2	−0.2	1.6	−0.178
Cyprus	Gross capital formation (% of GDP)	24.5	29.2	23.1	23.8	18.8	16.1	13.2	12.3	14.5	−0.064
Cyprus	Gross domestic savings (% of GDP)	19.7	16.4	17.8	16.5	15.8	14.6	15.0	14.4	14.8	−0.035
Cyprus	Gross fixed capital formation (% of GDP)	25.5	27.2	23.4	22.3	18.9	15.1	14.1	11.7	13.3	−0.078
Cyprus	Gross national expenditure (% of GDP)	104.8	112.8	105.3	107.3	102.9	101.5	98.2	97.9	99.7	−0.006
Cyprus	Gross savings (% of GDP)	18.1	14.1	15.4	12.5	14.7	10.1	8.2	8.0	11.6	−0.055
Cyprus	Foreign direct investment, net inflows (% of GDP)	9.5	8.4	10.9	53.2	−43.5	198.3	−25.0	−3.2	41.0	0.200
Cyprus	Foreign direct investment, net outflows (% of GDP)	5.2	16.6	2.9	66.8	−58.8	44.4	−27.0	−10.3	88.9	0.425
Djibouti	Gross capital formation (% of GDP)	37.5	—	—	—	—	—	—	—	—	—
Djibouti	Gross domestic savings (% of GDP)	17.4	—	—	—	—	—	—	—	—	—

Djibouti	Gross fixed capital formation (% of GDP)	37.5	—	—	—	—	—	—	—	—	—
Djibouti	Gross national expenditure (% of GDP)	120.1	—	—	—	—	—	—	—	—	—
Djibouti	Gross savings (% of GDP)	—	—	—	—	—	—	—	—	—	—
Djibouti	Foreign direct investment, net inflows (% of GDP)	23.0	22.8	9.2	3.2	6.4	8.1	19.7	9.6	7.2	−0.136
Djibouti	Foreign direct investment, net outflows (% of GDP)	—	—	—	—	—	—	—	—	—	—
Egypt	Gross capital formation (% of GDP)	20.9	22.4	19.2	19.5	17.1	16.2	14.3	13.8	14.4	−0.045
Egypt	Gross domestic savings (% of GDP)	16.3	16.8	12.6	14.3	13.0	8.2	7.9	5.3	5.9	−0.119
Egypt	Gross fixed capital formation (% of GDP)	20.9	22.3	18.9	19.2	16.7	14.9	13.1	12.6	13.7	−0.051
Egypt	Gross national expenditure (% of GDP)	104.6	105.6	106.6	105.2	104.1	108.0	106.4	108.5	108.4	0.005
Egypt	Gross savings (% of GDP)	23.6	23.6	16.8	18.0	16.9	13.0	13.8	12.0	9.6	−0.106
Egypt	Foreign direct investment, net inflows (% of GDP)	8.9	5.8	3.6	2.9	−0.2	1.0	1.5	1.6	2.1	−0.166
Egypt	Foreign direct investment, net outflows (% of GDP)	0.5	1.2	0.3	0.5	0.3	0.1	0.1	0.1	0.1	−0.243
Iran	Gross capital formation (% of GDP)	37.2	39.2	38.0	37.1	35.0	38.2	32.1	33.4	—	−0.015
Iran	Gross domestic savings (% of GDP)	45.1	44.1	39.7	42.2	44.2	39.8	39.8	38.7	—	−0.022
Iran	Gross fixed capital formation (% of GDP)	28.1	31.6	30.9	27.8	26.2	27.6	26.8	26.2	—	−0.010
Iran	Gross national expenditure (% of GDP)	92.1	95.1	98.4	94.9	90.9	98.4	92.3	94.7	—	0.004
Iran	Gross savings (% of GDP)	—	—	—	—	—	—	—	—	—	—

(Continued)

Table 2.12. *(Continued)*

Country	Series Name	2007	2008	2009	2010	2011	2012	2013	2014	2015	Compound Annual Growth Rate
	Percent of GDP for 2007–2015 and Annual Growth Rate										
Iran	Foreign direct investment, net inflows (% of GDP)	0.6	0.5	0.7	0.8	0.7	0.8	0.6	0.5	—	−0.027
Iran	Foreign direct investment, net outflows (% of GDP)	0.1	0.1	0.0	0.0	0.0	0.0	0.0	0.0	—	−0.207
Iraq	Gross capital formation (% of GDP)	9.3	15.2	11.3	15.9	15.5	13.4	29.5	30.7	19.7	0.098
Iraq	Gross domestic savings (% of GDP)	27.0	34.8	11.4	21.2	32.1	28.9	46.5	52.2	32.4	0.023
Iraq	Gross fixed capital formation (% of GDP)	6.8	14.8	10.3	16.2	13.0	22.0	26.9	26.2	25.8	0.182
Iraq	Gross national expenditure (% of GDP)	82.3	80.4	99.9	94.7	83.3	84.6	83.0	78.5	87.3	0.007
Iraq	Gross savings (% of GDP)	28.3	37.9	12.4	20.5	29.7	27.0	—	—	—	−0.009
Iraq	Foreign direct investment, net inflows (% of GDP)	1.1	1.4	1.4	1.0	1.1	1.6	2.2	2.1	1.9	0.073
Iraq	Foreign direct investment, net outflows (% of GDP)	0.0	0.0	0.1	0.1	0.2	0.2	0.1	0.1	0.1	0.325
Israel	Gross capital formation (% of GDP)	20.9	19.7	18.0	18.5	20.4	21.3	20.0	20.1	19.9	−0.006
Israel	Gross domestic savings (% of GDP)	20.2	19.3	20.9	20.7	21.0	21.5	22.2	22.0	23.0	0.016

Israel	Gross fixed capital formation (% of GDP)	19.8	19.6	18.4	18.9	20.5	20.8	20.3	19.9	19.1	−0.004
Israel	Gross national expenditure (% of GDP)	100.6	100.4	97.1	97.8	99.4	99.8	97.7	98.2	97.0	−0.005
Israel	Gross savings (% of GDP)	22.6	20.1	21.2	22.0	22.9	21.9	23.3	24.0	24.5	0.010
Israel	Foreign direct investment, net inflows (% of GDP)	4.9	5.0	2.1	2.4	3.3	3.3	4.2	2.2	3.8	−0.030
Israel	Foreign direct investment, net outflows (% of GDP)	4.8	3.3	0.8	3.9	3.5	1.3	1.9	1.2	3.3	−0.046
Jordan	Gross capital formation (% of GDP)	30.3	29.9	26.3	24.0	25.5	26.9	28.1	28.0	23.6	−0.031
Jordan	Gross domestic savings (% of GDP)	−7.3	0.2	3.6	3.2	−0.8	−1.1	−1.5	1.6	0.7	0.215
Jordan	Gross fixed capital formation (% of GDP)	27.5	27.9	25.2	23.0	24.5	26.0	27.2	27.2	22.9	−0.023
Jordan	Gross national expenditure (% of GDP)	137.5	129.7	122.7	120.8	126.2	128.0	129.6	126.4	122.9	−0.014
Jordan	Gross savings (% of GDP)	13.5	21.8	21.6	16.9	15.2	11.7	17.6	20.7	14.2	0.007
Jordan	Foreign direct investment, net inflows (% of GDP)	15.3	12.9	10.1	6.4	5.2	4.9	5.4	5.6	3.4	−0.172
Jordan	Foreign direct investment, net outflows (% of GDP)	0.3	0.1	0.3	0.1	0.1	0.0	0.0	0.2	0.0	−0.442
Kuwait	Gross capital formation (% of GDP)	20.5	17.6	18.0	17.7	13.5	12.8	14.4	16.3	25.0	0.025
Kuwait	Gross domestic savings (% of GDP)	55.6	58.5	48.1	54.0	60.9	61.3	58.5	53.3	34.1	−0.059
Kuwait	Gross fixed capital formation (% of GDP)	20.5	17.6	18.0	—	—	—	—	—	—	—

(*Continued*)

Table 2.12. (*Continued*)

		Percent of GDP for 2007–2015 and Annual Growth Rate									
Country	Series Name	2007	2008	2009	2010	2011	2012	2013	2014	2015	Compound Annual Growth Rate
Kuwait	Gross national expenditure (% of GDP)	64.9	59.2	69.9	63.7	52.7	51.5	55.9	63.0	90.9	0.043
Kuwait	Gross savings (% of GDP)	57.2	58.5	45.3	50.7	57.5	59.0	55.1	49.6	32.6	−0.068
Kuwait	Foreign direct investment, net inflows (% of GDP)	0.1	0.0	1.1	1.1	2.1	1.7	0.8	0.3	0.2	0.125
Kuwait	Foreign direct investment, net outflows (% of GDP)	8.5	6.2	8.1	5.1	7.0	3.9	9.6	8.1	4.8	−0.070
Lebanon	Gross capital formation (% of GDP)	24.1	27.7	26.3	24.8	26.7	29.4	30.4	31.2	27.6	0.017
Lebanon	Gross domestic savings (% of GDP)	−0.7	−2.5	1.8	−0.8	−1.2	8.8	16.1	19.3	19.6	−0.379
Lebanon	Gross fixed capital formation (% of GDP)	24.1	27.7	26.3	24.8	26.7	29.4	30.4	31.2	27.6	0.017
Lebanon	Gross national expenditure (% of GDP)	124.8	130.2	124.5	125.6	128.0	120.6	114.3	111.9	108.0	−0.018
Lebanon	Gross savings (% of GDP)	13.6	7.2	6.3	4.3	4.7	12.5	18.6	23.0	25.5	0.082
Lebanon	Foreign direct investment, net inflows (% of GDP)	13.7	15.0	13.7	11.3	8.7	7.3	6.1	6.4	5.0	−0.119
Lebanon	Foreign direct investment, net outflows (% of GDP)	3.5	3.4	3.2	1.3	1.9	2.3	4.4	2.7	1.3	−0.114
Libya	Gross capital formation (% of GDP)	26.1	29.8	—	—	—	—	—	—	—	—
Libya	Gross domestic savings (% of GDP)	69.3	73.4	—	—	—	—	—	—	—	—

Libya	Gross fixed capital formation (% of GDP)	25.7	29.8	—	—	—	—	—	—	—	—
Libya	Gross national expenditure (% of GDP)	56.8	56.5	—	—	—	—	—	—	—	—
Libya	Gross savings (% of GDP)	70.2	73.0	—	—	—	—	—	—	—	—
Libya	Foreign direct investment, net inflows (% of GDP)	6.9	4.7	2.2	2.4	—	—	—	—	—	—
Libya	Foreign direct investment, net outflows (% of GDP)	5.8	6.8	1.8	3.6	0.4	—	—	—	—	—
Morocco	Gross capital formation (% of GDP)	33.9	39.1	35.0	34.1	35.8	35.0	34.7	32.2	30.2	−0.014
Morocco	Gross domestic savings (% of GDP)	24.5	24.9	23.1	23.3	21.8	19.8	20.2	19.7	22.5	−0.011
Morocco	Gross fixed capital formation (% of GDP)	32.2	34.4	31.7	30.7	31.5	32.6	30.8	29.7	28.7	−0.014
Morocco	Gross national expenditure (% of GDP)	109.3	114.2	111.9	110.8	114.0	115.3	114.5	112.5	107.8	−0.002
Morocco	Gross savings (% of GDP)	33.9	34.2	29.8	29.7	28.1	25.3	26.8	26.4	28.2	−0.023
Morocco	Foreign direct investment, net inflows (% of GDP)	3.6	2.7	2.1	1.3	2.5	2.9	3.1	3.2	3.2	−0.012
Morocco	Foreign direct investment, net outflows (% of GDP)	0.8	0.3	0.5	0.6	0.2	0.4	0.4	0.4	0.7	−0.025
Oman	Gross capital formation (% of GDP)	34.3	36.5	28.2	25.4	23.8	24.7	29.8	24.8	35.9	0.006
Oman	Gross domestic savings (% of GDP)	50.8	57.8	44.2	49.9	53.7	51.3	52.1	47.6	39.5	−0.031
Oman	Gross fixed capital formation (% of GDP)	28.9	30.6	33.3	27.0	24.2	27.2	29.1	28.8	33.8	0.020

(Continued)

Table 2.12. (*Continued*)

Percent of GDP for 2007–2015 and Annual Growth Rate											
Country	Series Name	2007	2008	2009	2010	2011	2012	2013	2014	2015	Compound Annual Growth Rate
Oman	Gross national expenditure (% of GDP)	83.5	78.7	84.0	75.6	70.1	73.4	77.8	77.2	96.4	0.018
Oman	Gross savings (% of GDP)	39.7	44.8	27.2	34.0	37.0	34.9	36.4	29.5	20.4	−0.080
Oman	Foreign direct investment, net inflows (% of GDP)	7.9	4.8	3.1	2.1	2.4	1.8	2.0	1.9	−3.9	−0.166
Oman	Foreign direct investment, net outflows (% of GDP)	−0.1	1.0	0.2	2.6	1.8	1.2	1.2	1.7	0.4	−0.098
Qatar	Gross capital formation (% of GDP)	46.0	41.1	43.0	31.3	29.0	27.1	27.8	31.8	38.2	−0.023
Qatar	Gross domestic savings (% of GDP)	70.5	74.4	65.1	69.8	75.5	74.3	70.9	68.8	58.3	−0.023
Qatar	Gross fixed capital formation (% of GDP)	—	—	—	—	—	—	—	—	—	—
Qatar	Gross national expenditure (% of GDP)	75.6	66.7	77.9	61.4	53.5	52.8	56.9	63.0	79.9	0.007
Qatar	Gross savings (% of GDP)	—	—	—	—	60.1	60.3	58.3	55.7	46.6	−0.062
Qatar	Foreign direct investment, net inflows (% of GDP)	5.9	3.3	8.3	3.7	0.6	0.2	−0.4	0.5	0.7	−0.241
Qatar	Foreign direct investment, net outflows (% of GDP)	6.5	3.2	3.3	1.5	6.0	1.0	4.0	3.3	2.4	−0.115
SA	Gross capital formation (% of GDP)	26.5	27.3	31.7	30.7	26.8	26.3	26.2	28.5	34.6	0.034

SA	Gross domestic savings (% of GDP)	51.5	55.4	41.0	47.4	53.4	51.4	47.4	41.7	29.6	−0.067
SA	Gross fixed capital formation (% of GDP)	23.7	22.8	25.8	24.5	22.7	22.3	23.7	25.3	28.8	0.025
SA	Gross national expenditure (% of GDP)	75.0	71.9	90.7	83.4	73.4	74.9	78.8	86.8	105.0	0.043
SA	Gross savings (% of GDP)	48.9	52.8	36.6	43.4	50.5	48.8	44.4	38.7	25.7	−0.077
SA	Foreign direct investment, net inflows (% of GDP)	5.8	7.6	8.5	5.5	2.4	1.7	1.2	1.1	1.3	−0.175
SA	Foreign direct investment, net outflows (% of GDP)	0.0	0.7	0.5	0.7	0.5	0.6	0.7	0.7	0.9	0.030
Syria	Gross capital formation (% of GDP)	27.8	—	—	—	—	—	—	—	—	—
Syria	Gross domestic savings (% of GDP)	28.6	—	—	—	—	—	—	—	—	—
Syria	Gross fixed capital formation (% of GDP)	20.4	—	—	—	—	—	—	—	—	—
Syria	Gross national expenditure (% of GDP)	99.2	—	—	—	—	—	—	—	—	—
Syria	Gross savings (% of GDP)	28.9	—	—	—	—	—	—	—	—	—
Syria	Foreign direct investment, net inflows (% of GDP)	3.1	—	—	—	—	—	—	—	—	—
Syria	Foreign direct investment, net outflows (% of GDP)	0.0	—	—	—	—	—	—	—	—	—
Tunisia	Gross capital formation (% of GDP)	23.8	25.9	25.0	26.7	23.3	24.7	23.0	23.8	21.6	−0.012
Tunisia	Gross domestic savings (% of GDP)	21.9	22.9	22.3	21.9	16.1	15.5	13.7	12.8	10.7	−0.086

(Continued)

Table 2.12. *(Continued)*

Country	Series Name	2007	2008	2009	2010	2011	2012	2013	2014	2015	Compound Annual Growth Rate
Percent of GDP for 2007–2015 and Annual Growth Rate											
Tunisia	Gross fixed capital formation (% of GDP)	23.0	23.5	24.2	24.7	21.9	22.5	21.9	20.6	19.7	−0.019
Tunisia	Gross national expenditure (% of GDP)	101.9	103.0	102.7	104.8	107.2	109.2	109.3	111.0	111.0	0.011
Tunisia	Gross savings (% of GDP)	20.7	21.4	22.0	21.6	15.2	15.7	13.8	13.9	12.0	−0.066
Tunisia	Foreign direct investment, net inflows (% of GDP)	3.9	5.8	3.5	3.0	0.9	3.5	2.3	2.2	2.2	−0.067
Tunisia	Foreign direct investment, net outflows (% of GDP)	0.1	0.1	0.2	0.2	0.0	0.0	0.0	0.0	0.1	0.050
Turkey	Gross capital formation (% of GDP)	21.1	21.8	14.9	19.5	23.6	20.1	20.6	20.0	18.1	−0.019
Turkey	Gross domestic savings (% of GDP)	15.9	17.3	13.8	14.0	14.9	15.0	14.1	15.8	15.2	−0.005
Turkey	Gross fixed capital formation (% of GDP)	21.4	19.9	16.9	18.9	21.8	20.3	20.3	20.1	20.4	−0.006
Turkey	Gross national expenditure (% of GDP)	105.2	104.4	101.1	105.6	108.7	105.2	106.5	104.2	102.9	−0.003
Turkey	Gross savings (% of GDP)	15.3	16.6	13.0	13.3	14.2	14.3	13.2	14.9	14.1	−0.010
Turkey	Foreign direct investment, net inflows (% of GDP)	3.4	2.7	1.4	1.2	2.1	1.7	1.5	1.6	2.4	−0.045
Turkey	Foreign direct investment, net outflows (% of GDP)	0.3	0.3	0.3	0.2	0.3	0.5	0.4	0.9	0.7	0.102
UAE	Gross capital formation (% of GDP)	25.1	25.1	31.6	27.4	23.4	23.2	22.9	24.1	27.5	0.011

UAE	Gross domestic savings (% of GDP)	33.1	34.3	37.5	33.9	41.4	48.5	48.5	45.4	41.7	0.029
UAE	Gross fixed capital formation (% of GDP)	23.6	22.4	28.9	25.0	21.4	21.9	21.7	22.8	26.1	0.013
UAE	Gross national expenditure (% of GDP)	92.0	90.8	94.2	93.5	82.0	74.7	74.4	78.7	85.8	−0.009
UAE	Gross savings (% of GDP)	—	—	—	—	—	—	—	—	—	
UAE	Foreign direct investment, net inflows (% of GDP)	5.5	1.6	0.4	3.1	2.1	2.4	2.4	2.7	3.0	−0.074
UAE	Foreign direct investment, net outflows (% of GDP)	5.6	5.0	1.1	0.7	0.6	0.7	2.3	2.2	2.5	−0.097
Yemen	Gross capital formation (% of GDP)	17.2	15.4	13.5	11.7	5.5	8.7	8.1	7.8	1.7	−0.250
Yemen	Gross domestic savings (% of GDP)	9.9	9.8	2.1	7.3	3.1	−2.9	0.3	1.0	−10.5	−0.252
Yemen	Gross fixed capital formation (% of GDP)	17.2	15.4	13.5	11.7	5.5	8.7	8.1	7.8	1.7	−0.250
Yemen	Gross national expenditure (% of GDP)	107.3	105.6	111.4	104.4	102.4	111.6	107.8	106.9	112.2	0.006
Yemen	Gross savings (% of GDP)	10.2	10.8	3.5	8.3	2.5	8.1	4.8	8.9	−5.2	−0.017
Yemen	Foreign direct investment, net inflows (% of GDP)	4.2	5.8	0.5	0.6	−1.6	0.0	−0.3	−0.5	0.0	—
Yemen	Foreign direct investment, net outflows (% of GDP)	0.2	0.9	0.3	0.2	0.2	0.0	0.0	0.0	0.0	−0.232
OECD	Gross capital formation (% of GDP)	23.3	22.7	19.5	20.3	20.7	20.6	20.5	20.8	20.9	−0.013
OECD	Gross domestic savings (% of GDP)	22.4	21.4	19.4	19.8	19.9	20.1	20.4	20.7	21.3	−0.007

(*Continued*)

Table 2.12. *(Continued)*

		Percent of GDP for 2007–2015 and Annual Growth Rate									
Country	Series Name	2007	2008	2009	2010	2011	2012	2013	2014	2015	Compound Annual Growth Rate
OECD	Gross fixed capital formation (% of GDP)	22.7	22.3	20.4	19.9	20.2	20.4	20.3	20.5	20.6	−0.012
OECD	Gross national expenditure (% of GDP)	—	—	—	—	—	—	—	—	—	—
OECD	Gross savings (% of GDP)	22.2	20.8	19.0	19.8	20.1	20.6	20.8	21.3	21.8	−0.003
OECD	Foreign direct investment, net inflows (% of GDP)	5.3	3.6	1.8	2.2	2.8	2.4	2.3	1.7	2.6	−0.085
OECD	Foreign direct investment, net outflows (% of GDP)	6.5	4.8	2.3	2.9	3.6	2.8	2.9	2.0	2.8	−0.100

Source: World Bank Development Indicators, 2017.

not conducive to stand-alone research institutions or universities, but to a system of integrated players both domestic and foreign. Efficient and productive innovation systems are flexible global networks capable of using existing technologies and human capital to create new forms of technology that raise productivity.

With few exceptions, the experience of Arab MENA in technology transfer, management and adaptation has been less than stellar despite the fact that technology transfer has always been a top national priority. The polemics in Arab MENA have consistently stressed the need to restructure their economies toward industrial sectors and to non-basic export-based industries. However, the local socio-cultural-political realities in Arab MENA made it impossible to translate the polemics into reality (UNDP, 2002, 2003, 2004, 2005, 2009a, 2009b, 2016a and 2016b). The countries in Arab MENA, unlike Cyprus and Israel, focused on the acquisition of production facilities and on production technology under the umbrella of protectionism. Such a policy framework was undertaken by the erroneous belief that this transplantation of production capacity would miraculously constitute a technology transfer that would be a prelude to the indigenization of technology and innovation.

These simple acquisition policies did not recognize the importance of innovation. The externality that it created was a very unproductive domestic sector based on outdated technology which pressured local government officials to pass and enforce protection laws, which inevitably prolonged the life of the least efficient production units. These industrial dinosaurs eventually become a drain on national resources and a major impediment to socio-economic development.

Some Arab MENA countries created a host of legal and financial incentives to entice FDI in order to integrate local Arab production systems into a global network which would lead to an inward flow of knowledge and technology. Unfortunately, the same countries that wanted to open their economies to FDI also had to appease local domestic interest groups that continued their anti-Israel and anti-Jewish boycott and xenophobia. This religious intolerance came with a price — the inability to attract the best human capital in the global market. As El-Baradei notes (UNDP, 2009a, p. 205): "*The solution will not lie in reconstructing history. And it will not lie in redressing all past injustice. If we are to solve the central conflict of the Middle East, we must begin by looking forward, not backward, by being ready to reconcile and recognize mutual rights, and above all by finding in our hearts the ability to forgive.*"[1]

While the idea that liberalizing international trade and adopting market-based industrial policies would encourage the advanced world to invest in the growth of the region, strengthening its national infrastructure and creating an environment conducive to free flows of technology, it must be accompanied by a major reversal in local cultural and political intolerance toward the only advanced economy in MENA. The political conflict between Arab MENA (including Israel's so-called friends, Egypt and Jordan) with Israel has been far more devastating for Arab MENA than for Israel (UNDP, 2002, 2003, 2004, 2005, 2009a, 2009b, 2016a and 2016b).

The traditional industrialization policies of Arab countries did not lead to the transfer and adaptation of technology, nor did they encourage economic development. A revised Arab MENA program which will provide greater incentives in order to encourage FDI will not lead to expanded technology transfer either unless Arab MENA revises its internal domestic conditions for the creation of a knowledge-flow environment free from old anti-Israel and anti-Jewish boycotts and xenophobia. The basic and most important factor in the process of technology transfer and adaptation remains a global, free and open R&D sector, which drives the process of technological change with an effective participation in the world technological system unencumbered by "old" and "outdated" hatreds.

[1]Every UNDP Human Development Report since 2002 continues the basic lie that the term "Palestinian" refers to Arabs on both sides of the Jordan River. From the fifth century BC, following the historian Herodotus, Greeks called the eastern coast of the Mediterranean "the Philistine Syria" using the Greek language form of the name. In AD 135, after putting down the Bar Kochba revolt, the Emperor Hadrian wanted to blot out the name of the Roman "Provincia Judaea" and so renamed it "Provincia Syria Palaestina," the Latin version of the Greek name and the first use of the name as an administrative unit. The name "Provincia Syria Palaestina" was later shortened to "Palaestina," from which the modern, anglicized "Palestine" is derived. The name "Falastin" that Arabs today use for "Palestine" is not an Arabic name. It is the Arab pronunciation of the Roman "Palaestina." In the Qur'an, the term "Holy Land" is mentioned at least seven times, once when Moses proclaims to the Children of Israel: "*O my people! Enter the holy land which Allah hath assigned unto you, and turn not back ignominiously, for then will ye be overthrown, to your own ruin*" (Surah 5:21). "Palestine" was first officially applied to the country in modern times in 1920 when the peace negotiators at the San Remo Conference juridically established the country as the Jewish National Home. (An agreed text was confirmed by the Council of the League of Nations on July 24, 1922, and it came into operation in September 1923.) It appears that the term "Palestine" really applies to both the current Israel and what is now called Jordan, and "Palestinian" applies to both Jews and Arabs. See Krämer (2008).

Understanding that in the 21st century R&D is the weakest link in Arab MENA innovation systems is the first step in overcoming impediments to knowledge production.

It remains a fact that Arab MENA has so far been unsuccessful in attracting FDI. The data presented in Table 2.12 corroborate the low level of FDI in terms of net inflows and net outflows as a percent of GDP for most of Arab MENA. It would be unrealistic to expect to see any Arab MENA countries listed among the top ten recipients of FDI worldwide, given current global patterns favoring economies with an existing strong R&D sector accompanied by an open exchange of ideas and flow of human capital. It should be no surprise that given the socio-economic self- imposed constraints, not one Arab MENA country appears in the top ten among developing countries, nor in the top ten in terms of patents and innovations.

Whatever gains that Arab MENA experienced from inducing a limited flow of FDI was temporary and in the resource extraction sectors, because their economies were not effectively involved in the global economy. In much of Arab MENA, general market failure, lack of globalization, corrupt domestic markets, lack of rule of law and intolerant and xenophobic mind- sets undermined economic growth and structural transformation. As Posner (1980) noted, these characteristics are common to "primitive" societies, not to those that wish to compete in the 21st century.

Along these lines, Bosworth and Collins (2003) find that a very large portion of the cross-country variation in economic growth experiences over the past four decades can be related to differences in initial conditions and government institutions. The more open the local institutions, the greater the economy's growth. In contrast, the more intolerant and xenophobic the local government institutions, the lower is the economy's growth. This would be in line with the experience of Arab MENA in the latter case, and in non-Arab MENA in the former. Moreover, they find that the size of capital stock and not the size of investment flows is a far more important explanatory variable for economic growth. This is a further distinction between the Arab and non-Arab members of MENA.

2.6. Decomposition of MENA International Trade "Openness"

The degree of a country's openness, in the aggregate, can be detected by measuring its international trade exposure relative to GDP, the commodity composition of its trade portfolio and its direction. A summary view for

MENA is presented in Tables 2.13 to 2.16. A more detailed investigation of inter- and intra-MENA trade and its competitiveness is presented in Chapter 8.

The first indicator that we present in Table 2.13 is exports of goods and services as a share of GDP, which represents the value of all goods and other market services provided to the rest of the world. They include the value of merchandise, freight, insurance, transport, travel, royalties, license fees and other services, such as communication, construction, financial, information, business, personal and government services. They exclude compensation of employees and investment income (formerly called factor services) and transfer payments. The OECD average for this indicator is approximately 28.5 percent with a compound growth rate of 1.1 percent over the 2007–2015 period. Within MENA, apart from Cyprus, Turkey and the UAE, who experienced a positive growth rate in exports of goods in services, the balance of countries in MENA showed a compound growth decline ranging from −1.0 to −6.0 percent.

The second indicator that we present in Table 2.13 is imports of goods and services as a share of GDP, which represent the value of all goods and other market services received from the rest of the world. They include the value of merchandise, freight, insurance, transport, travel, royalties, license fees and other services, such as communication, construction, financial, information, business, personal and government services. They exclude compensation of employees and investment income (formerly called factor services) and transfer payments. The OECD average for this indicator is approximately 28.2 percent with a compound growth rate of 0.5 percent over the 2007–2015 period. Within MENA, except for Algeria, Kuwait, Oman, Saudi Arabia, Turkey and the UAE, who had experienced a positive growth rate in imports of goods in services, the balance of countries in MENA showed a compound growth decline ranging from −1.0 to −5.0 percent.

The third indicator that we present in Table 2.13 is the current account balance (CA) as a share of GDP. This figure calculated by the IMF as part of its balance of payments statistics represents the sum of net exports of goods and services, net primary income and net secondary income. These figures capture the importance of a country's trade position (surplus or deficit) relative to its GDP and its compound annual growth over a 9-year period. Some countries within MENA have a clear trend line rather than several shocks, either as deficit or surplus countries. For example, Algeria which had a substantial current account surplus in 2007 experienced

Table 2.13. MENA Country International Trade Exposure

Percent of GDP for 2007–2015 and Annual Growth Rate

Country		2007	2008	2009	2010	2011	2012	2013	2014	2015	Compound Annual Growth Rate
Algeria	Exports of goods and services (% of GDP)	47.1	48.0	35.4	38.4	38.8	36.9	33.2	30.5	—	−0.060
Algeria	Imports of goods and services (% of GDP)	24.9	28.7	36.0	31.4	28.6	28.5	30.4	32.0	—	0.037
Algeria	Current account balance (% of GDP)	22.5	19.9	0.3	7.6	8.8	5.8	0.6	−4.5	−16.3	−1.793
Algeria	External balance on goods and services (% of GDP)	22.2	19.3	−0.6	7.0	10.2	8.4	2.8	−1.5	—	−1.677
Algeria	Merchandise trade (% of GDP)	65.0	69.5	61.6	60.5	60.4	58.5	57.2	56.9	53.5	−0.024
Algeria	Trade (% of GDP)	71.9	76.7	71.3	69.9	67.4	65.3	63.6	62.5	—	−0.020
Algeria	Trade in services (% of GDP)	7.1	8.5	10.6	9.5	8.1	7.0	6.9	7.2	8.7	0.025
Bahrain	Exports of goods and services (% of GDP)	79.7	82.6	68.5	69.5	79.7	74.3	74.5	72.1	—	−0.014
Bahrain	Imports of goods and services (% of GDP)	58.1	63.3	49.5	50.9	48.2	47.9	46.8	44.7	—	−0.037
Bahrain	Current account balance (% of GDP)	13.4	8.8	2.4	3.0	11.3	7.2	7.9	3.4	—	−0.179
Bahrain	External balance on goods and services (% of GDP)	21.6	19.3	19.0	18.6	31.5	26.5	27.7	27.4	—	0.035
Bahrain	Merchandise trade (% of GDP)	115.6	125.6	95.8	105.9	112.5	106.0	108.4	103.1	67.1	−0.066
Bahrain	Trade (% of GDP)	137.8	145.9	118.0	120.5	128.0	122.2	121.2	116.9	—	−0.023
Bahrain	Trade in services (% of GDP)	24.8	23.1	24.3	23.9	17.6	14.8	14.9	14.8	—	−0.071

(*Continued*)

Table 2.13. *(Continued)*

Country		Percent of GDP for 2007–2015 and Annual Growth Rate									
		2007	2008	2009	2010	2011	2012	2013	2014	2015	Compound Annual Growth Rate
Cyprus	Exports of goods and services (% of GDP)	53.3	50.1	48.7	50.2	52.9	53.5	58.7	62.2	61.2	0.018
Cyprus	Imports of goods and services (% of GDP)	58.0	62.9	54.1	57.5	55.9	55.0	56.9	60.1	60.9	0.006
Cyprus	Current account balance (% of GDP)	−7.6	−15.2	−7.7	−11.4	−4.0	−6.1	−5.0	−4.3	−2.9	−0.112
Cyprus	External balance on goods and services (% of GDP)	−4.8	−12.8	−5.3	−7.3	−2.9	−1.5	1.8	2.1	0.3	−1.684
Cyprus	Merchandise trade (% of GDP)	41.6	44.1	35.0	39.0	38.3	36.1	34.6	36.8	37.8	−0.012
Cyprus	Trade (% of GDP)	111.3	112.9	102.8	107.7	108.8	108.5	115.6	122.3	122.1	0.012
Cyprus	Trade in services (% of GDP)	50.1	59.0	55.3	56.0	57.1	58.2	69.6	72.9	75.6	0.053
Djibouti	Exports of goods and services (% of GDP)	57.1	—	—	—	—	—	—	—	—	—
Djibouti	Imports of goods and services (% of GDP)	77.1	—	—	—	—	—	—	—	—	—
Djibouti	Current account balance (% of GDP)	−20.2	−22.6	−6.8	4.5	−13.9	−10.9	−21.2	−24.8	−31.7	0.058
Djibouti	External balance on goods and services (% of GDP)	−20.1	—	—	—	—	—	—	—	—	—
Djibouti	Merchandise trade (% of GDP)	62.7	64.3	50.3	40.7	48.7	50.4	57.7	58.7	59.2	−0.007
Djibouti	Trade (% of GDP)	134.2	—	—	—	—	—	—	—	—	—
Djibouti	Trade in services (% of GDP)	42.0	42.7	42.9	40.3	38.3	35.8	37.4	—	—	−0.019

Egypt	Exports of goods and services (% of GDP)	30.2	33.0	25.0	21.3	20.6	16.6	17.2	14.4	13.2	−0.098
Egypt	Imports of goods and services (% of GDP)	34.8	38.6	31.6	26.6	24.7	24.6	23.6	23.0	21.6	−0.058
Egypt	Current account balance (% of GDP)	0.3	−0.9	−1.8	−2.1	−2.3	−2.5	−1.2	−2.0	−5.1	−2.487
Egypt	External balance on goods and services (% of GDP)	−4.6	−5.6	−6.6	−5.2	−4.1	−8.0	−6.4	−8.5	−8.4	0.079
Egypt	Merchandise trade (% of GDP)	43.2	45.8	36.0	36.3	37.9	35.7	30.8	32.4	25.4	−0.064
Egypt	Trade (% of GDP)	65.1	71.7	56.6	47.9	45.3	41.2	40.7	37.4	34.9	−0.075
Egypt	Trade in services (% of GDP)	26.3	26.1	18.8	17.6	14.1	13.8	12.1	13.1	—	−0.095
Iran	Exports of goods and services (% of GDP)	29.7	27.4	23.5	25.4	25.7	22.4	27.5	24.2	—	−0.029
Iran	Imports of goods and services (% of GDP)	21.8	22.5	21.9	20.3	16.5	20.7	19.8	18.9	—	−0.020
Iran	Current account balance (% of GDP)	—	—	—	—	—	—	—	—	—	—
Iran	External balance on goods and services (% of GDP)	7.9	4.9	1.6	5.1	9.1	1.6	7.7	5.3	—	−0.056
Iran	Merchandise trade (% of GDP)	39.6	43.1	32.5	35.6	32.7	27.4	25.7	32.9	—	−0.026
Iran	Trade (% of GDP)	51.5	49.9	45.4	45.7	42.2	43.1	47.3	43.1	—	−0.025
Iran	Trade in services (% of GDP)	—	—	—	—	—	—	—	—	—	—
Iraq	Exports of goods and services (% of GDP)	45.9	50.3	39.4	39.4	44.4	44.5	37.7	42.4	34.8	−0.034
Iraq	Imports of goods and services (% of GDP)	28.2	30.7	39.3	34.1	27.8	29.1	20.7	20.9	22.1	−0.030
Iraq	Current account balance (% of GDP)	17.5	21.6	−1.0	4.7	14.1	13.6	—	—	—	−0.050
Iraq	External balance on goods and services (% of GDP)	17.7	19.6	0.1	5.3	16.7	15.4	17.0	21.5	12.7	−0.041

(Continued)

Table 2.13. *(Continued)*

Country	Percent of GDP for 2007–2015 and Annual Growth Rate	2007	2008	2009	2010	2011	2012	2013	2014	2015	Compound Annual Growth Rate
Iraq	Merchandise trade (% of GDP)	70.7	71.6	72.0	69.6	70.5	69.1	64.2	62.8	56.3	−0.028
Iraq	Trade (% of GDP)	74.1	81.1	78.7	73.5	72.2	73.6	58.4	63.3	56.9	−0.032
Iraq	Trade in services (% of GDP)	6.5	6.9	9.6	9.2	7.5	7.4	—	—	—	0.028
Israel	Exports of goods and services (% of GDP)	40.4	38.5	33.3	35.1	36.1	36.1	33.4	32.2	30.7	−0.034
Israel	Imports of goods and services (% of GDP)	41.1	38.8	30.4	32.9	35.5	35.9	31.1	30.4	27.7	−0.048
Israel	Current account balance (% of GDP)	3.1	1.5	3.8	3.4	2.6	0.6	3.3	3.8	4.6	0.050
Israel	External balance on goods and services (% of GDP)	−0.6	−0.4	2.9	2.2	0.6	0.2	2.3	1.8	3.0	0.007
Israel	Merchandise trade (% of GDP)	63.0	59.5	46.7	51.2	55.0	53.8	48.3	46.7	42.9	−0.047
Israel	Trade (% of GDP)	81.5	77.3	63.8	68.0	71.7	72.1	64.5	62.6	58.4	−0.041
Israel	Trade in services (% of GDP)	21.8	20.7	19.2	18.8	19.0	20.9	19.1	19.0	19.4	−0.014
Jordan	Exports of goods and services (% of GDP)	54.2	57.8	46.4	48.2	47.7	46.2	42.4	43.3	37.6	−0.045
Jordan	Imports of goods and services (% of GDP)	91.8	87.5	69.1	69.0	73.9	74.3	72.0	69.7	60.5	−0.051
Jordan	Current account balance (% of GDP)	−16.8	−9.3	−5.2	−7.1	−10.2	−15.2	−10.4	−7.3	−8.9	−0.077
Jordan	External balance on goods and services (% of GDP)	−37.5	−29.7	−22.7	−20.8	−26.2	−28.0	−29.6	−26.4	−22.9	−0.060

Jordan	Merchandise trade (% of GDP)	113.4	113.5	86.5	85.5	93.4	92.6	89.2	87.4	75.1	−0.050
Jordan	Trade (% of GDP)	146.0	145.3	115.5	117.3	121.5	120.5	114.3	113.1	98.1	−0.049
Jordan	Trade in services (% of GDP)	41.9	40.5	35.7	38.4	35.4	35.4	32.5	32.9	28.8	−0.046
Kuwait	Exports of goods and services (% of GDP)	63.4	66.8	59.5	66.7	73.2	74.7	70.9	68.5	54.4	−0.019
Kuwait	Imports of goods and services (% of GDP)	28.3	25.9	29.4	30.4	25.9	26.3	26.7	31.5	45.3	0.060
Kuwait	Current account balance (% of GDP)	36.1	40.9	27.4	32.0	42.9	45.5	39.9	33.2	7.5	−0.178
Kuwait	External balance on goods and services (% of GDP)	35.1	40.8	30.1	36.3	47.3	48.5	44.1	37.0	9.1	−0.155
Kuwait	Merchandise trade (% of GDP)	73.3	76.2	69.8	80.3	82.6	84.0	82.9	83.5	76.0	0.004
Kuwait	Trade (% of GDP)	91.7	92.7	88.9	97.0	99.1	101.0	97.6	100.0	99.6	0.010
Kuwait	Trade in services (% of GDP)	20.5	18.8	23.8	21.5	18.9	17.2	15.6	18.5	26.2	0.031
Lebanon	Exports of goods and services (% of GDP)	38.2	39.7	34.1	36.3	36.2	56.5	56.9	57.5	57.0	0.051
Lebanon	Imports of goods and services (% of GDP)	63.1	69.9	58.6	61.9	64.2	77.1	71.2	69.4	65.0	0.004
Lebanon	Current account balance (% of GDP)	−6.5	−14.2	−19.2	−19.9	−12.1	−22.1	−25.9	−25.5	−17.3	0.130
Lebanon	External balance on goods and services (% of GDP)	−24.8	−30.2	−24.5	−25.6	−28.0	−20.6	−14.3	−11.9	−8.0	−0.132
Lebanon	Merchandise trade (% of GDP)	64.4	73.6	59.1	61.8	65.9	63.8	61.3	56.2	47.6	−0.037
Lebanon	Trade (% of GDP)	101.3	109.5	92.7	98.1	100.4	133.5	128.0	126.9	121.9	0.023
Lebanon	Trade in services (% of GDP)	92.5	107.9	88.1	76.5	81.4	61.5	63.9	61.0	62.4	−0.048
Libya	Exports of goods and services (% of GDP)	72.7	72.5	59.2	65.6	54.8	—	—	—	—	−0.068
Libya	Imports of goods and services (% of GDP)	29.5	29.0	42.8	42.1	44.8	—	—	—	—	0.110
Libya	Current account balance (% of GDP)	42.2	41.0	14.9	22.5	9.2	—	—	—	—	−0.317

(Continued)

Table 2.13. (*Continued*)

Country	Percent of GDP for 2007–2015 and Annual Growth Rate	2007	2008	2009	2010	2011	2012	2013	2014	2015	Compound Annual Growth Rate
Libya	External balance on goods and services (% of GDP)	43.2	43.5	16.4	23.5	10.0	—	—	—	—	−0.306
Libya	Merchandise trade (% of GDP)	79.5	81.8	79.0	88.7	77.8	—	—	—	—	−0.006
Libya	Trade (% of GDP)	102.2	101.5	102.1	107.7	99.6	—	—	—	—	−0.006
Libya	Trade in services (% of GDP)	4.0	5.2	8.6	8.7	12.8	—	—	—	—	0.332
Morocco	Exports of goods and services (% of GDP)	34.6	35.7	28.0	32.2	34.7	34.9	32.8	34.3	34.3	−0.001
Morocco	Imports of goods and services (% of GDP)	43.9	49.9	39.9	43.0	48.7	50.2	47.2	46.8	42.1	−0.005
Morocco	Current account balance (% of GDP)	−0.2	−4.9	−5.4	−4.2	−7.9	−9.7	−7.3	−5.7	−2.1	0.390
Morocco	External balance on goods and services (% of GDP)	−9.3	−14.2	−11.9	−10.8	−14.0	−15.3	−14.5	−12.5	−7.8	−0.022
Morocco	Merchandise trade (% of GDP)	59.9	67.8	50.5	57.0	65.0	67.5	62.9	63.4	59.0	−0.002
Morocco	Trade (% of GDP)	78.5	85.7	67.9	75.2	83.4	85.1	80.0	81.2	76.4	−0.003
Morocco	Trade in services (% of GDP)	24.6	23.8	23.4	23.7	24.1	23.9	20.5	22.4	22.5	−0.012
Oman	Exports of goods and services (% of GDP)	56.5	58.5	50.6	57.1	72.9	71.5	75.2	69.5	56.1	−0.001
Oman	Imports of goods and services (% of GDP)	40.0	37.2	34.6	32.7	43.0	44.9	53.0	46.7	52.5	0.035
Oman	Current account balance (% of GDP)	5.9	8.2	−1.0	8.3	13.0	10.2	6.6	5.2	−15.5	−0.018

Oman	External balance on goods and services (% of GDP)	16.5	21.3	16.0	24.4	29.9	26.6	22.2	22.8	3.6	−0.174
Oman	Merchandise trade (% of GDP)	96.7	99.9	94.2	96.5	104.7	105.3	116.6	101.8	70.7	−0.039
Oman	Trade (% of GDP)	96.5	95.7	85.3	89.8	115.9	116.3	128.2	116.3	108.6	0.015
Oman	Trade in services (% of GDP)	16.1	12.6	14.7	13.9	14.8	14.9	16.2	16.5	—	0.003
Qatar	Exports of goods and services (% of GDP)	60.3	61.4	51.1	62.3	72.6	76.5	72.7	68.0	56.1	−0.009
Qatar	Imports of goods and services (% of GDP)	35.8	28.1	29.0	23.8	26.1	29.3	29.7	31.0	36.0	0.001
Qatar	Current account balance (% of GDP)	—	—	—	—	31.1	33.2	30.4	24.0	8.4	−0.280
Qatar	External balance on goods and services (% of GDP)	24.4	33.3	22.1	38.6	46.5	47.2	43.1	37.0	20.1	−0.024
Qatar	Merchandise trade (% of GDP)	82.1	82.6	74.6	78.5	86.0	89.5	86.4	78.2	69.4	−0.021
Qatar	Trade (% of GDP)	96.1	89.4	80.1	86.1	98.7	105.7	102.4	99.0	92.1	−0.005
Qatar	Trade in services (% of GDP)	—	—	—	—	14.5	18.1	19.5	22.5	27.8	0.178
SA	Exports of goods and services (% of GDP)	59.9	62.1	47.1	49.7	56.2	54.4	52.1	47.0	33.7	−0.069
SA	Imports of goods and services (% of GDP)	34.9	34.0	37.8	33.1	29.6	29.3	30.9	33.9	38.8	0.013
SA	Current account balance (% of GDP)	22.4	25.5	4.9	12.7	23.7	22.4	18.2	9.8	−8.3	−0.099
SA	External balance on goods and services (% of GDP)	25.0	28.1	9.3	16.6	26.6	25.1	21.2	13.2	−5.0	−0.077
SA	Merchandise trade (% of GDP)	77.8	82.5	67.1	68.0	74.1	74.1	73.1	68.5	57.9	−0.036
SA	Trade (% of GDP)	94.9	96.1	84.9	82.8	85.8	83.7	83.0	80.9	72.5	−0.033
SA	Trade in services (% of GDP)	19.1	16.3	19.7	16.6	13.4	11.5	11.9	15.0	16.2	−0.020
Syria	Exports of goods and services (% of GDP)	38.6	—	—	—	—	—	—	—	—	—
Syria	Imports of goods and services (% of GDP)	37.8	—	—	—	—	—	—	—	—	—

(Continued)

Table 2.13. *(Continued)*

Country	Percent of GDP for 2007–2015 and Annual Growth Rate	2007	2008	2009	2010	2011	2012	2013	2014	2015	Compound Annual Growth Rate
Syria	Current account balance (% of GDP)	1.1	—	—	—	—	—	—	—	—	—
Syria	External balance on goods and services (% of GDP)	0.8	—	—	—	—	—	—	—	—	—
Syria	Merchandise trade (% of GDP)	64.8	—	—	—	—	—	—	—	—	—
Syria	Trade (% of GDP)	76.5	—	—	—	—	—	—	—	—	—
Syria	Trade in services (% of GDP)	17.0	—	—	—	—	—	—	—	—	—
Tunisia	Exports of goods and services (% of GDP)	51.1	56.2	45.8	50.5	49.3	49.4	47.7	45.6	40.8	−0.028
Tunisia	Imports of goods and services (% of GDP)	53.0	59.2	48.5	55.3	56.6	58.6	57.1	56.6	51.8	−0.003
Tunisia	Current account balance (% of GDP)	−2.4	−3.8	−2.8	−4.8	−7.4	−8.3	−8.4	−9.1	−8.9	0.182
Tunisia	External balance on goods and services (% of GDP)	−1.9	−3.0	−2.7	−4.8	−7.2	−9.2	−9.3	−11.0	−11.0	0.245
Tunisia	Merchandise trade (% of GDP)	88.1	98.0	77.2	87.7	91.2	92.1	89.3	87.4	79.7	−0.012
Tunisia	Trade (% of GDP)	104.1	115.4	94.4	105.8	105.9	108.0	104.8	102.1	92.6	−0.015
Tunisia	Trade in services (% of GDP)	19.2	20.3	18.9	20.1	17.0	18.4	17.6	17.1	—	−0.015
Turkey	Exports of goods and services (% of GDP)	22.3	23.9	23.3	21.2	24.0	26.3	25.6	27.9	28.0	0.029
Turkey	Imports of goods and services (% of GDP)	27.5	28.3	24.4	26.8	32.6	31.5	32.2	32.1	30.8	0.015

Turkey	Current account balance (% of GDP)	−5.7	−5.4	−1.8	−6.1	−9.6	−6.1	−7.7	−5.5	−4.5	−0.030
Turkey	External balance on goods and services (% of GDP)	−5.2	−4.4	−1.1	−5.6	−8.7	−5.2	−6.5	−4.2	−2.9	−0.070
Turkey	Merchandise trade (% of GDP)	42.9	45.7	39.6	41.0	48.5	49.3	49.0	50.0	48.9	0.017
Turkey	Trade (% of GDP)	49.8	52.2	47.7	48.0	56.6	57.8	57.8	60.0	58.8	0.021
Turkey	Trade in services (% of GDP)	7.1	7.6	8.6	7.7	8.0	8.2	8.8	9.6	9.6	0.039
UAE	Exports of goods and services (% of GDP)	72.4	78.9	79.7	78.8	90.3	100.6	101.0	97.3	97.4	0.038
UAE	Imports of goods and services (% of GDP)	64.4	69.6	73.8	72.2	72.3	75.3	75.4	76.0	83.1	0.032
UAE	Current account balance (% of GDP)	—	—	—	—	—	—	—	—	—	—
UAE	External balance on goods and services (% of GDP)	8.0	9.2	5.8	6.5	18.0	25.3	25.6	21.3	14.2	0.075
UAE	Merchandise trade (% of GDP)	120.6	131.9	134.9	132.5	144.9	154.0	159.0	155.5	133.7	0.013
UAE	Trade (% of GDP)	136.8	148.5	153.5	151.0	162.6	176.0	176.4	173.4	180.5	0.035
UAE	Trade in services (% of GDP)	—	—	—	—	—	—	—	—	—	—
Yemen	Exports of goods and services (% of GDP)	35.9	37.8	28.3	30.0	30.3	24.9	22.4	21.5	10.2	−0.145
Yemen	Imports of goods and services (% of GDP)	43.2	43.4	39.7	34.4	32.7	36.5	30.2	28.4	22.5	−0.078
Yemen	Current account balance (% of GDP)	−7.0	−4.6	−10.1	−3.4	−1.6	−0.9	−3.8	−3.4	−8.0	0.018
Yemen	External balance on goods and services (% of GDP)	−7.3	−5.6	−11.4	−4.4	−2.4	−11.6	−7.8	−6.9	−12.2	0.066
Yemen	Merchandise trade (% of GDP)	68.4	67.4	61.5	56.2	64.0	60.9	53.5	48.0	36.8	−0.074
Yemen	Trade (% of GDP)	79.1	81.2	68.1	64.4	63.1	61.4	52.5	49.8	32.7	−0.104
Yemen	Trade in services (% of GDP)	12.0	13.2	13.4	12.2	10.5	11.1	9.9	9.8	—	−0.025

(Continued)

Table 2.13. *(Continued)*

Country	Percent of GDP for 2007–2015 and Annual Growth Rate										
		2007	2008	2009	2010	2011	2012	2013	2014	2015	Compound Annual Growth Rate
OECD	Exports of goods and services (% of GDP)	26.1	27.0	23.8	26.2	27.9	28.4	28.5	28.8	28.5	0.011
OECD	Imports of goods and services (% of GDP)	26.9	28.3	24.0	26.6	28.8	28.9	28.7	28.9	28.2	0.005
OECD	Current account balance (% of GDP)	—	—	—	—	—	—	—	—	—	—
OECD	External balance on goods and services (% of GDP)	−0.8	−1.2	−0.2	−0.5	−0.9	−0.5	−0.2	−0.1	0.4	−0.265
OECD	Merchandise trade (% of GDP)	43.7	46.2	37.9	42.6	46.5	46.0	46.1	45.7	43.0	−0.002
OECD	Trade (% of GDP)	53.1	55.3	47.9	52.8	56.7	57.3	57.3	57.6	56.7	0.008
OECD	Trade in services (% of GDP)	11.7	12.4	11.8	11.9	12.3	12.4	13.0	13.6	13.6	0.018

Source: World Bank Development Indicators, 2017.

a rapid deterioration in its trade account ending in 2015 with a deficit equivalent to −16.3 percent of its GDP. The same experience was evident in Bahrain where the CA surplus declined from 13.4 percent to 3.4 percent of GDP. Cyprus experienced an improvement in its CA deficit which declined from −7.6 percent to −2.9 percent of GDP. In contrast, the CA deficit in Djibouti increased from −20.2 percent to −31.7 percent of GDP. Likewise, the CA deficit expanded in Egypt from a positive 0.3 percent surplus to a deficit of 5.1 percent of GDP. Data for Iran, Iraq, Libya and Syria are somewhat misleading or unavailable given the internal conflicts in those countries. Israel, in stark contrast to its Arab MENA neighbors, experienced a growing CA surplus from 3.1 percent in 2007 to 4.6 percent of GDP in 2015. Jordan's CA deficit shrank from −16.8 percent to −8.9 percent of GDP during the same period. Surprisingly, the CA surplus in Kuwait was drastically reduced from 36.1 percent of GDP in 2007 to 7.5 percent of GDP in 2015 representing a negative compound growth rate of −17.8 percent. The deterioration of the CA balance in Lebanon was as devastating as that in Kuwait. The CA balance for Saudi Arabia reflects the role of world oil prices. Its CA surplus was drastically cut from a high of 25.5 percent of GDP in 2008 to a deficit of −8.3 percent of GDP in 2015.

The fourth indicator that we present in Table 2.13 is the external balance on goods and services (formerly resource balance), which is equal to exports of goods and services minus imports of goods and services (previously nonfactor services) as a share of GDP. The external deficit (ED) is considered as a CA deficit. It is a negative net flow of liquid assets to the citizens of a particular country. The external balance (EB) includes the trade gap, the net foreign factor revenue and the net foreign aid received. Usually the most important cause of an external deficit is a trade deficit. This is clearly the case in Algeria, Bahrain, Cyprus, Egypt, Israel, Jordan, Kuwait, Morocco, Qatar and Saudi Arabia.

The fifth indicator that we present in Table 2.13 is the merchandise trade as a share of GDP which is the sum of merchandise exports and imports divided by the value of GDP, all in current U.S. dollars. Merchandise trade data continue to constitute the core of trade relations between a country and the rest of the world. The OECD average for this indicator is approximately 43.0 percent with a compound growth rate of −0.002 percent over the 2007–2015 period. For Cyprus and Israel, merchandise trade is at the OECD average. For Egypt, the indicator declined to 25.4 percent in 2015. It has been declining by an annual compound growth rate of −6.4 percent over the 2007–2015 period. For Jordan the 2015 indicator was 75.1 percent, a decline from the 2007 figure of 113.4 percent. Similarly, for Oman the indicator declined from 96.7 percent to 70.7 percent from 2007 to 2015. The balance of Arab MENA countries had similar indicators.

The sixth indicator that we present in Table 2.13 is trade which is the sum of exports and imports of goods and services measured as a share of gross domestic product. The OECD average for this indicator is approximately 56.7 percent with a compound growth rate of 0.008 percent over the 2007–2015 period. Israel and Saudi Arabia are at the OECD average. The balance of the MENA countries are either at the low end like Egypt or high end like Tunisia.

The seventh indicator that we present in Table 2.13 is trade in services, which is the sum of service exports and imports divided by the value of GDP, all in current U.S. dollars. The OECD average for this indicator is approximately 13.6 percent with a compound growth rate of 1.8 percent over the 2007–2015 period. It is expected that trade in services will rise with economic development. This is the case for Israel where this indicator is 19.4 percent in 2015. For Egypt it was 13.1 percent and for Bahrain it was 14.8, both in 2015. The highest provider of service trade was Cyprus with 75.6 in 2015.

The 1990s saw a significant shift in MENA trade policy. Since 1993, Tunisia, Morocco, Israel and Jordan have signed bilateral Free Trade Agreements with the EU in the form of Euro-Med Partnership Agreements (EMAs). Algeria, Egypt, Lebanon and Syria are involved in similar negotiations. In addition to removing trade barriers on industrial goods, these agreements will ultimately grant preferential and reciprocal access for agricultural products and establish conditions for the gradual liberalization of trade in services and capital. At the intra-regional level, Arab MENA countries revived in 1997 the almost defunct 1981 Executive Program for Arab Free Trade for the creation of a Greater Arab Free Trade Area (GAFTA).[2]

This provides for an across-the-board reduction or elimination of tariffs, tariff-like charges and non-tariff barriers on industrial goods over a period of 10 years.

[2]To date, the member states of the Arab League that signed the Arab FTA Agreement include: Bahrain, Egypt, Iraq, Jordan, Kuwait, Lebanon, Libya, Morocco, Oman, Qatar, Saudi Arabia, Syria, Tunisia and the UAE. Algeria has expressed an intention to ratify the Agreement at a later stage. Djibouti, Mauritania, Sudan and Yemen are in the process of ratifying it.

As François (1997, pp. 35–36) has noted:

> "[The] recent movement to market-based policies has ... served to highlight the importance of political economy constraints in the economic reform process. As North (1990) has emphasized, not all stable policy regimes are characterized by good practice. In fact, through most of history, and across most of the world, regimes conducive to stagnation and decline have been remarkably tenacious and even robust. At this point, the fundamental problem of development economics is perhaps not so much the identification of good practices, but rather the identification of the institutional arrangements necessary for the sustainability of such practices. Not surprisingly, given the demonstrated difficulties inherent in pursuing good long-run policies both through painful short- and medium-run adjustments, and through sustained pressures of rent seeking (and rent preservation), a common theme to emerge in some of the recent development literature is the potentially positive role, at least in the economic arena, that can be played by a strong, stable central government in anchoring such policies."

The structure of MENA exports, compared with the OECD, is presented in Tables 2.14, 2.15 and 2.16. In terms of merchandise trade, the list of fuel exporters is well known — Algeria, Bahrain, Iraq, Kuwait, Oman, Qatar, Saudi Arabia and the UAE. For these countries, the concentration on fossil fuel exports has not changed over the 2007–2014 period. Data on Iran, Syria and Djibouti is unavailable. The major food exporters within MENA remain Cyprus, Morocco and Jordan... Those who are exporting manufactured goods include Cyprus, Egypt, Israel, Jordan, Lebanon, Morocco, Tunisia and Turkey. On the import side, all of MENA is importing manufactured goods and some food. The non-oil exporting countries are net importers.

Turning to Table 2.15 which summarizes the key components of service trade, it is not surprising to find that exports of computer, communication and other services are led by Israel, Algeria, Kuwait and Morocco. On the import side it is led by Algeria, Israel, Lebanon, Morocco, Oman, and Saudi Arabia. Cyprus and Lebanon not surprisingly, have a predominant position in financial service exports. Travel services both in terms of exports and imports are led by Bahrain, Cyprus, Egypt, Iraq, Israel, Jordan, Kuwait, Lebanon, Morocco, Oman, Qatar, Saudi Arabia, Tunisia, Turkey and Yemen.

Trade in services as a share of GDP has substantially changed over the 2007–2015 period. (see Table 2.13). The largest increase in this category occurred in Qatar whose trade in services expanded by a 17.8 compound annual growth rate. Likewise, trade in services as a share of GDP in Cyprus expanded by a 5.3 compound annual growth rate.

Table 2.14. Commodity Composition of MENA Merchandise Trade

Country	Percent of Merchandise Exports and Merchandise Imports for 2007–2015 and Annual Growth Rate	2007	2008	2009	2010	2011	2012	2013	2014	2015	Compound Annual Growth Rate
Algeria	Food exports (% of merchandise exports)	0.2	0.2	0.3	0.6	0.5	0.4	0.6	0.5	0.7	0.196
Algeria	Fuel exports (% of merchandise exports)	97.8	97.6	97.7	97.3	97.2	97.1	96.7	95.8	94.3	−0.004
Algeria	Manufactures exports (% of merchandise exports)	1.5	1.6	1.6	1.8	2.0	2.2	2.5	3.5	4.7	0.149
Algeria	Food imports (% of merchandise imports)	19.8	21.4	16.3	16.3	22.8	19.9	19.1	20.1	19.3	−0.003
Algeria	Fuel imports (% of merchandise imports)	1.1	1.4	1.1	2.1	2.3	9.7	7.8	4.9	4.6	0.193
Algeria	Manufactures imports (% of merchandise imports)	74.9	74.0	79.8	78.4	71.8	67.4	70.1	72.0	73.1	−0.003
Bahrain	Food exports (% of merchandise exports)	0.4	2.1	3.4	1.9	1.7	2.6	3.9	3.2	2.8	0.283
Bahrain	Fuel exports (% of merchandise exports)	80.8	69.1	68.6	74.3	71.8	64.1	59.0	58.5	50.4	−0.057
Bahrain	Manufactures exports (% of merchandise exports)	8.0	11.8	12.6	5.6	4.9	12.1	18.6	19.7	23.9	0.148
Bahrain	Food imports (% of merchandise imports)	5.2	6.3	8.0	7.6	8.3	10.9	9.3	9.5	11.8	0.109
Bahrain	Fuel imports (% of merchandise imports)	52.0	44.4	44.7	38.0	43.9	28.2	47.2	40.7	26.1	−0.082
Bahrain	Manufactures imports (% of merchandise imports)	40.9	45.1	43.7	41.5	38.1	53.1	38.7	42.1	56.2	0.041

Cyprus	Food exports (% of merchandise exports)	39.8	37.8	37.1	34.4	37.7	36.4	38.0	36.8	31.8	−0.028
Cyprus	Fuel exports (% of merchandise exports)	0.0	0.0	0.0	0.0	0.0	0.0	0.0	0.0	11.9	1.506
Cyprus	Manufactures exports (% of merchandise exports)	44.6	48.0	50.4	50.2	43.3	43.4	47.7	51.4	47.4	0.008
Cyprus	Food imports (% of merchandise imports)	12.9	13.4	15.5	14.8	15.7	17.5	20.0	19.6	20.2	0.057
Cyprus	Fuel imports (% of merchandise imports)	16.8	19.7	17.6	20.2	25.1	30.2	28.9	24.7	22.0	0.034
Cyprus	Manufactures imports (% of merchandise imports)	67.5	64.2	65.0	61.6	56.6	50.3	49.6	54.3	56.3	−0.022
Djibouti	Food exports (% of merchandise exports)	—	—	—	—	—	—	—	—	—	—
Djibouti	Fuel exports (% of merchandise exports)	—	—	6.5	—	—	—	—	—	—	—
Djibouti	Manufactures exports (% of merchandise exports)	—	—	90.7	—	—	—	—	—	—	—
Djibouti	Food imports (% of merchandise imports)	—	—	29.3	—	—	—	—	—	—	—
Djibouti	Fuel imports (% of merchandise imports)	—	—	6.5	—	—	—	—	—	—	—
Djibouti	Manufactures imports (% of merchandise imports)	—	—	62.4	—	—	—	—	—	—	—
Egypt	Food exports (% of merchandise exports)	7.9	10.7	17.4	17.2	15.0	14.3	16.4	17.1	20.4	0.126
Egypt	Fuel exports (% of merchandise exports)	52.5	44.4	28.9	29.8	30.9	31.5	26.9	23.9	18.4	−0.123
Egypt	Manufactures exports (% of merchandise exports)	18.8	36.5	43.8	43.4	45.1	45.5	48.7	51.5	52.9	0.138

(*Continued*)

Table 2.14. *(Continued)*

Percent of Merchandise Exports and Merchandise Imports for 2007–2015 and Annual Growth Rate											
Country		2007	2008	2009	2010	2011	2012	2013	2014	2015	Compound Annual Growth Rate
Egypt	Food imports (% of merchandise imports)	20.3	17.2	17.2	19.1	23.7	22.4	17.7	21.1	19.4	−0.006
Egypt	Fuel imports (% of merchandise imports)	14.8	11.1	9.9	13.4	14.9	18.7	14.2	14.0	15.7	0.008
Egypt	Manufactures imports (% of merchandise imports)	42.4	59.9	65.2	60.1	52.3	50.9	55.9	56.8	58.9	0.042
Iran	Food exports (% of merchandise exports)	—	—	—	6.2	3.7	—	—	—	—	—
Iran	Fuel exports (% of merchandise exports)	—	—	—	70.8	70.5	—	—	—	—	—
Iran	Manufactures exports (% of merchandise exports)	—	—	—	15.6	12.1	—	—	—	—	—
Iran	Food imports (% of merchandise imports)	—	—	—	15.4	14.1	—	—	—	—	—
Iran	Fuel imports (% of merchandise imports)	—	—	—	2.8	1.4	—	—	—	—	—
Iran	Manufactures imports (% of merchandise imports)	—	—	—	70.5	62.1	—	—	—	—	—
Iraq	Food exports (% of merchandise exports)	—	—	0.0	0.0	0.0	0.0	0.0	0.0	0.0	—
Iraq	Fuel exports (% of merchandise exports)	—	99.9	98.6	99.6	99.8	99.7	99.8	99.9	100.0	—
Iraq	Manufactures exports (% of merchandise exports)	—	—	0.2	0.0	0.2	0.2	0.2	0.1	0.0	—

Iraq	Food imports (% of merchandise imports)	—	1.8	—	—	—	—	—	7.2	—	—
Iraq	Fuel imports (% of merchandise imports)	—	65.7	—	—	—	—	—	23.0	—	—
Iraq	Manufactures imports (% of merchandise imports)	—	0.1	—	—	—	—	—	66.3	—	—
Israel	Food exports (% of merchandise exports)	2.6	2.7	3.4	3.0	2.9	3.1	3.2	3.0	2.7	0.007
Israel	Fuel exports (% of merchandise exports)	0.2	0.9	0.0	0.9	1.0	1.7	1.6	1.1	0.8	0.228
Israel	Manufactures exports (% of merchandise exports)	75.9	92.1	93.5	93.3	93.3	92.2	92.5	92.8	93.9	0.027
Israel	Food imports (% of merchandise imports)	5.9	6.6	7.6	7.3	7.2	7.1	7.5	7.7	8.4	0.046
Israel	Fuel imports (% of merchandise imports)	15.8	19.8	17.1	17.7	18.6	22.0	20.2	17.7	11.9	−0.035
Israel	Manufactures imports (% of merchandise imports)	74.1	69.5	71.9	71.4	70.8	67.7	69.1	71.4	76.1	0.003
Jordan	Food exports (% of merchandise exports)	15.4	13.7	16.6	16.6	17.1	18.5	20.3	20.4	20.9	0.039
Jordan	Fuel exports (% of merchandise exports)	0.8	0.2	0.6	1.1	0.2	0.3	0.2	0.2	0.1	−0.214
Jordan	Manufactures exports (% of merchandise exports)	76.3	75.4	73.3	73.6	70.4	69.6	71.9	70.9	69.6	−0.011
Jordan	Food imports (% of merchandise imports)	15.1	16.8	17.0	16.2	16.1	17.4	17.5	18.2	19.8	0.034
Jordan	Fuel imports (% of merchandise imports)	21.9	22.0	17.8	22.1	29.0	32.5	26.4	28.0	18.1	−0.024

(Continued)

Table 2.14. *(Continued)*

Percent of Merchandise Exports and Merchandise Imports for 2007–2015 and Annual Growth Rate											
Country		2007	2008	2009	2010	2011	2012	2013	2014	2015	Compound Annual Growth Rate
Jordan	Manufactures imports (% of merchandise imports)	57.6	55.7	59.6	56.3	49.5	45.4	51.1	49.0	57.1	−0.001
Kuwait	Food exports (% of merchandise exports)	0.2	0.2	0.3	0.3	0.3	—	0.4	0.4	0.9	0.231
Kuwait	Fuel exports (% of merchandise exports)	96.3	96.5	93.2	92.8	94.8	—	94.2	95.2	89.1	−0.010
Kuwait	Manufactures exports (% of merchandise exports)	3.3	3.2	6.2	6.6	4.6	—	5.1	4.1	9.2	0.138
Kuwait	Food imports (% of merchandise imports)	13.0	14.7	—	15.4	17.0	—	15.3	15.9	16.2	0.028
Kuwait	Fuel imports (% of merchandise imports)	0.6	0.6	—	0.8	0.7	—	0.7	0.7	0.6	0.015
Kuwait	Manufactures imports (% of merchandise imports)	83.1	81.2	—	80.9	79.1	—	81.0	80.1	79.8	−0.005
Lebanon	Food exports (% of merchandise exports)	14.7	14.0	16.4	14.9	18.4	19.9	21.4	26.2	—	0.074
Lebanon	Fuel exports (% of merchandise exports)	0.2	0.4	0.5	0.2	0.1	2.9	10.0	1.1	—	0.204
Lebanon	Manufactures exports (% of merchandise exports)	67.0	71.5	72.5	63.6	66.9	64.2	55.2	62.6	—	−0.008
Lebanon	Food imports (% of merchandise imports)	16.4	14.4	15.3	16.3	16.8	16.2	16.5	17.8	—	0.010

Lebanon	Fuel imports (% of merchandise imports)	22.7	26.1	20.5	21.4	24.2	29.6	24.6	24.0	—	0.007
Lebanon	Manufactures imports (% of merchandise imports)	57.1	55.4	61.1	59.0	55.4	51.2	56.0	55.0	—	−0.005
Libya	Food exports (% of merchandise exports)	0.0	0.0	0.0	0.0	—	—	—	—	—	—
Libya	Fuel exports (% of merchandise exports)	96.6	96.7	97.9	97.7	—	—	—	—	—	—
Libya	Manufactures exports (% of merchandise exports)	3.4	3.2	2.1	2.3	—	—	—	—	—	—
Libya	Food imports (% of merchandise imports)	16.1	16.4	11.7	12.1	—	—	—	—	—	—
Libya	Fuel imports (% of merchandise imports)	1.0	1.2	0.9	1.1	—	—	—	—	—	—
Libya	Manufactures imports (% of merchandise imports)	80.2	80.6	85.1	84.1	—	—	—	—	—	—
Morocco	Food exports (% of merchandise exports)	19.1	17.4	23.0	19.0	17.3	17.2	18.9	18.9	19.9	0.005
Morocco	Fuel exports (% of merchandise exports)	2.3	2.2	2.3	1.1	2.6	4.0	5.0	3.3	1.5	−0.052
Morocco	Manufactures exports (% of merchandise exports)	66.8	63.9	64.7	66.3	65.7	65.4	66.1	69.0	69.4	0.005
Morocco	Food imports (% of merchandise imports)	12.3	11.8	11.2	11.4	12.6	12.4	10.8	12.2	11.2	−0.012
Morocco	Fuel imports (% of merchandise imports)	20.1	22.4	20.6	23.1	25.3	27.7	27.0	24.1	18.2	−0.012
Morocco	Manufactures imports (% of merchandise imports)	61.4	57.5	62.9	58.8	55.3	53.7	57.0	58.0	64.1	0.005

(*Continued*)

Table 2.14. *(Continued)*

Percent of Merchandise Exports and Merchandise Imports for 2007–2015 and Annual Growth Rate											
Country		2007	2008	2009	2010	2011	2012	2013	2014	2015	Compound Annual Growth Rate
Oman	Food exports (% of merchandise exports)	2.1	2.5	3.1	2.5	2.2	2.1	2.4	2.3	4.5	0.103
Oman	Fuel exports (% of merchandise exports)	89.1	86.4	75.0	77.8	74.4	83.5	82.5	83.5	62.0	−0.044
Oman	Manufactures exports (% of merchandise exports)	7.5	7.3	10.3	10.5	12.7	10.8	10.1	10.5	15.5	0.096
Oman	Food imports (% of merchandise imports)	9.8	10.9	10.9	12.1	11.0	10.3	9.3	12.4	12.4	0.030
Oman	Fuel imports (% of merchandise imports)	3.5	2.7	5.5	7.1	10.3	7.7	21.5	5.8	11.2	0.156
Oman	Manufactures imports (% of merchandise imports)	81.0	79.9	77.2	74.6	70.9	51.3	61.8	74.4	56.2	−0.045
Qatar	Food exports (% of merchandise exports)	0.0	0.0	0.0	0.0	0.0	—	0.0	0.0	0.2	0.293
Qatar	Fuel exports (% of merchandise exports)	90.7	92.1	73.9	92.6	93.0	—	88.7	87.8	82.8	−0.011
Qatar	Manufactures exports (% of merchandise exports)	8.5	2.2	7.5	2.0	1.8	—	3.6	0.1	5.2	−0.061
Qatar	Food imports (% of merchandise imports)	4.7	6.0	—	8.2	—	—	9.1	9.4	9.7	0.094
Qatar	Fuel imports (% of merchandise imports)	0.5	0.7	—	0.9	—	—	1.0	1.1	1.2	0.109
Qatar	Manufactures imports (% of merchandise imports)	91.2	89.5	—	83.9	—	—	82.9	83.5	81.9	−0.013

SA	Food exports (% of merchandise exports)	0.8	0.7	1.4	1.2	0.9	0.9	0.9	1.0	1.8	0.100
SA	Fuel exports (% of merchandise exports)	90.1	91.4	87.9	87.5	88.6	88.5	87.4	84.9	78.4	−0.017
SA	Manufactures exports (% of merchandise exports)	8.7	7.6	10.4	11.1	10.3	10.5	11.3	13.2	18.4	0.098
SA	Food imports (% of merchandise imports)	13.3	14.6	15.1	16.1	15.5	14.2	14.9	14.6	14.1	0.007
SA	Fuel imports (% of merchandise imports)	0.2	0.3	0.2	0.3	0.3	0.5	1.4	1.6	0.8	0.155
SA	Manufactures imports (% of merchandise imports)	81.0	79.4	80.2	77.7	77.8	79.5	78.6	78.7	80.7	−0.001
Syria	Food exports (% of merchandise exports)	20.8	22.0	27.3	21.0	—	—	—	—	—	—
Syria	Fuel exports (% of merchandise exports)	41.1	38.6	37.8	49.9	—	—	—	—	—	—
Syria	Manufactures exports (% of merchandise exports)	34.8	33.0	31.0	24.7	—	—	—	—	—	—
Syria	Food imports (% of merchandise imports)	12.6	14.0	22.9	21.0	—	—	—	—	—	—
Syria	Fuel imports (% of merchandise imports)	32.6	31.4	12.8	19.7	—	—	—	—	—	—
Syria	Manufactures imports (% of merchandise imports)	47.6	46.6	57.1	54.1	—	—	—	—	—	—
Tunisia	Food exports (% of merchandise exports)	9.5	8.9	9.2	7.7	10.1	9.3	9.7	7.9	14.2	0.052
Tunisia	Fuel exports (% of merchandise exports)	16.2	17.3	13.6	14.2	14.6	16.8	15.2	13.2	7.2	−0.096
Tunisia	Manufactures exports (% of merchandise exports)	69.8	71.6	75.4	76.0	73.2	71.3	73.1	76.9	76.5	0.012

(*Continued*)

Table 2.14. *(Continued)*

Country	Percent of Merchandise Exports and Merchandise Imports for 2007–2015 and Annual Growth Rate	2007	2008	2009	2010	2011	2012	2013	2014	2015	Compound Annual Growth Rate
Tunisia	Food imports (% of merchandise imports)	9.8	10.2	8.6	9.3	11.3	9.1	10.6	9.7	11.2	0.016
Tunisia	Fuel imports (% of merchandise imports)	12.9	16.9	11.5	12.6	14.8	17.4	17.8	18.3	14.3	0.013
Tunisia	Manufactures imports (% of merchandise imports)	70.8	64.6	74.8	72.3	67.9	66.1	66.4	66.8	69.1	−0.003
Turkey	Food exports (% of merchandise exports)	8.4	8.3	10.8	10.6	10.6	10.8	11.2	11.4	12.1	0.046
Turkey	Fuel exports (% of merchandise exports)	4.8	5.8	4.0	3.9	4.7	5.3	4.3	3.8	3.1	−0.054
Turkey	Manufactures exports (% of merchandise exports)	81.7	81.0	80.2	79.2	78.3	77.7	78.1	78.5	78.8	−0.004
Turkey	Food imports (% of merchandise imports)	3.1	4.3	4.4	4.0	4.5	4.5	4.6	5.1	5.3	0.069
Turkey	Fuel imports (% of merchandise imports)	14.6	7.8	8.4	8.3	8.5	9.1	8.6	8.6	7.1	−0.086
Turkey	Manufactures imports (% of merchandise imports)	64.9	59.8	64.2	63.3	60.6	57.8	61.7	61.5	66.6	0.003
UAE	Food exports (% of merchandise exports)	0.9	0.8	—	—	—	1.7	1.8	1.8	—	0.094
UAE	Fuel exports (% of merchandise exports)	65.3	64.8	—	—	—	53.5	51.5	42.5	—	−0.052
UAE	Manufactures exports (% of merchandise exports)	3.1	4.0	—	—	—	6.2	6.0	7.5	—	0.115

UAE	Food imports (% of merchandise imports)	6.5	6.6	—	—	—	7.0	7.1	7.6	—	0.020
UAE	Fuel imports (% of merchandise imports)	0.9	1.0	—	—	—	3.8	3.2	3.3	—	0.178
UAE	Manufactures imports (% of merchandise imports)	69.8	73.2	—	—	—	79.5	73.1	74.8	—	0.009
Yemen	Food exports (% of merchandise exports)	5.3	5.3	5.7	6.6	7.3	6.3	6.2	23.7	81.0	0.206
Yemen	Fuel exports (% of merchandise exports)	91.2	92.4	92.2	91.2	89.1	89.5	75.9	70.3	0.2	−0.032
Yemen	Manufactures exports (% of merchandise exports)	3.0	2.1	1.7	1.8	3.2	4.0	10.7	5.3	16.8	0.071
Yemen	Food imports (% of merchandise imports)	25.0	24.8	27.8	30.8	31.5	32.5	28.7	40.4	46.9	0.062
Yemen	Fuel imports (% of merchandise imports)	21.5	28.9	20.9	21.0	29.8	27.3	1.5	2.2	10.1	−0.247
Yemen	Manufactures imports (% of merchandise imports)	52.3	45.0	49.7	46.7	37.5	36.0	36.8	55.5	41.1	0.007
OECD	Food exports (% of merchandise exports)	6.9	7.4	8.4	7.9	8.1	8.3	8.6	8.6	8.3	0.023
OECD	Fuel exports (% of merchandise exports)	6.8	8.8	7.3	8.0	9.4	9.6	9.7	9.2	7.0	0.003
OECD	Manufactures exports (% of merchandise exports)	75.6	73.6	72.8	72.5	71.7	71.4	71.5	72.2	74.2	−0.002
OECD	Food imports (% of merchandise imports)	6.7	6.9	8.1	7.4	7.6	7.7	8.0	8.1	8.0	0.023
OECD	Fuel imports (% of merchandise imports)	14.5	18.0	14.8	15.8	18.2	18.8	18.1	16.2	10.9	−0.035
OECD	Manufactures imports (% of merchandise imports)	69.1	65.5	67.8	67.6	65.8	65.3	66.6	68.4	73.9	0.008

Source: World Bank Development Indicators, 2017.

Table 2.15. Commodity Composition of MENA's Major Components of Service Trade

Percent of Commercial Service Exports or Imports for 2007–2015 and Annual Growth Rate											
Country		2007	2008	2009	2010	2011	2012	2013	2014	2015	Compound Annual Growth Rate
Algeria	Computer, communications and other services Exports	51.3	53.2	53.7	62.9	65.7	64.1	63.9	59.1	58.5	0.017
Algeria	Computer, communications and other services Imports	56.6	62.4	67.5	66.5	65.4	56.6	53.6	56.0	56.0	−0.002
Algeria	Insurance and financial services Exports	5.7	8.3	9.1	8.6	8.4	9.2	8.1	9.3	12.5	0.102
Algeria	Insurance and financial services Imports	3.9	3.7	2.2	2.4	1.9	2.2	2.5	2.4	2.6	−0.052
Algeria	Travel services Exports	7.8	9.5	9.0	6.4	5.9	6.1	6.7	7.4	9.1	0.018
Algeria	Travel services Imports	5.9	4.5	4.1	5.2	4.4	5.1	4.6	5.4	6.5	0.012
Bahrain	Computer, communications and other services Exports	27.4	27.4	28.9	27.5	35.7	31.5	31.3	30.3	—	0.013
Bahrain	Computer, communications and other services Imports	10.1	9.5	11.5	11.0	18.6	7.6	7.2	7.0	—	−0.045
Bahrain	Insurance and financial services Exports	22.3	23.4	22.2	21.4	10.7	12.1	12.2	12.2	—	−0.072
Bahrain	Insurance and financial services Imports	20.7	21.1	24.0	22.7	4.8	3.2	3.7	3.3	—	−0.205
Bahrain	Travel services Exports	30.0	29.8	29.2	32.2	31.4	34.1	35.3	35.9	—	0.023
Bahrain	Travel services Imports	28.1	24.8	23.4	26.5	40.4	49.2	45.7	44.4	—	0.059

Cyprus	Computer, communications and other services Exports	27.4	14.3	14.3	10.9	10.2	11.1	16.4	15.4	16.7	−0.060
Cyprus	Computer, communications and other services Imports	19.4	22.7	23.9	21.7	26.1	26.4	36.4	31.7	35.8	0.080
Cyprus	Insurance and financial services Exports	10.9	27.9	27.8	30.9	30.9	27.5	24.2	28.7	27.4	0.122
Cyprus	Insurance and financial services Imports	6.8	18.0	18.9	18.7	15.7	14.7	14.6	18.8	17.6	0.127
Cyprus	Travel services Exports	34.4	26.1	23.6	23.2	25.3	27.6	27.7	26.7	27.1	−0.029
Cyprus	Travel services Imports	40.6	28.8	27.8	24.1	23.8	24.4	20.2	20.5	19.1	−0.090
Djibouti	Computer, communications and other services Exports	15.1	11.2	11.0	10.7	10.8	11.9	12.0	12.6	13.5	−0.014
Djibouti	Computer, communications and other services Imports	12.5	10.8	11.9	14.1	11.2	10.8	8.9	8.1	6.8	−0.073
Djibouti	Insurance and financial services Exports	—	—	—	—	—	—	—	—	—	—
Djibouti	Insurance and financial services Imports	8.7	12.0	10.0	10.6	8.7	8.3	11.1	12.3	11.2	0.031
Djibouti	Travel services Exports	7.4	6.0	11.3	12.1	12.6	13.1	12.2	12.8	13.2	0.076
Djibouti	Travel services Imports	2.6	3.0	5.1	8.3	14.7	12.9	10.9	10.8	9.5	0.175
Egypt	Computer, communications and other services Exports	16.5	20.4	16.8	12.3	9.7	10.7	12.1	14.9	10.5	−0.054
Egypt	Computer, communications and other services Imports	24.9	27.2	24.1	20.7	22.4	24.1	21.3	22.5	26.3	0.007
Egypt	Insurance and financial services Exports	0.9	2.0	1.3	1.2	1.4	1.1	1.4	1.3	2.2	0.124
Egypt	Insurance and financial services Imports	10.4	10.1	11.3	11.5	11.5	10.5	10.6	10.5	10.3	−0.002
Egypt	Travel services Exports	47.3	44.5	50.5	53.0	45.8	46.6	33.8	35.6	33.5	−0.042
Egypt	Travel services Imports	18.7	17.8	19.9	17.2	16.8	16.8	20.4	18.7	20.6	0.013
Iran	Computer, communications and other services Exports	—	—	—	—	—	—	—	—	—	—
Iran	Computer, communications and other services Imports	—	—	—	—	—	—	—	—	—	—

(Continued)

Table 2.15. *(Continued)*

Country	Percent of GDP for 2007–2015 and Annual Growth Rate	2007	2008	2009	2010	2011	2012	2013	2014	2015	Compound Annual Growth Rate
Iran	Insurance and financial services Exports	—	—	—	—	—	—	—	—	—	—
Iran	Insurance and financial services Imports	—	—	—	—	—	—	—	—	—	—
Iran	Travel services Exports	—	—	—	—	—	—	—	—	—	—
Iran	Travel services Imports	—	—	—	—	—	—	—	—	—	—
Iraq	Computer, communications and other services Exports	5.3	2.0	3.9	6.0	5.8	12.8	20.5	28.9	27.6	0.228
Iraq	Computer, communications and other services Imports	13.9	4.6	1.2	3.1	5.9	4.1	5.1	6.6	4.3	−0.136
Iraq	Insurance and financial services Exports	2.3	0.3	0.2	0.9	2.1	1.1	0.8	0.8	1.0	−0.104
Iraq	Insurance and financial services Imports	24.5	28.3	29.6	28.8	27.9	27.3	25.0	22.0	20.3	−0.023
Iraq	Travel services Exports	61.5	67.7	81.2	75.5	71.5	61.5	68.0	62.1	66.1	0.009
Iraq	Travel services Imports	13.5	11.1	14.3	16.9	16.9	17.5	22.9	28.6	38.6	0.140
Israel	Computer, communications and other services Exports	61.5	60.2	65.7	62.8	66.5	68.5	70.9	72.2	73.8	0.023
Israel	Computer, communications and other services Imports	44.0	45.2	47.2	46.2	44.7	50.8	47.2	51.4	49.7	0.016
Israel	Insurance and financial services Exports	0.1	0.1	0.1	0.1	0.1	0.1	0.1	0.1	0.1	−0.024
Israel	Insurance and financial services Imports	2.2	2.4	2.2	2.2	3.3	2.8	2.9	2.2	2.1	−0.010
Israel	Travel services Exports	17.6	19.0	19.7	20.1	18.1	17.1	16.2	15.8	15.1	−0.019
Israel	Travel services Imports	21.1	18.8	19.1	20.1	19.2	17.2	19.0	18.4	20.7	−0.002
Jordan	Computer, communications and other services Exports	13.5	13.2	11.7	9.9	10.4	8.6	8.4	8.2	8.1	−0.062

Jordan	Computer, communications and other services Imports	11.5	8.7	10.3	7.1	7.3	6.9	6.7	5.1	6.3	−0.073
Jordan	Insurance and financial services Exports	0.0	0.0	0.0	0.0	0.0	0.0	0.0	1.2	1.6	—
Jordan	Insurance and financial services Imports	8.2	8.6	7.7	7.2	8.7	9.3	9.8	11.0	10.5	0.032
Jordan	Travel services Exports	67.2	67.6	69.4	68.7	65.2	67.4	68.2	66.3	68.7	0.003
Jordan	Travel services Imports	26.3	25.6	29.0	36.4	26.6	25.6	24.4	25.1	26.3	0.000
Kuwait	Computer, communications and other services Exports	58.3	53.4	63.2	42.2	37.9	41.8	60.3	54.4	49.9	−0.019
Kuwait	Computer, communications and other services Imports	1.3	8.7	12.3	18.4	11.1	13.4	21.8	21.7	16.5	0.378
Kuwait	Insurance and financial services Exports	1.3	3.9	3.5	4.2	5.2	3.6	11.4	9.8	10.8	0.302
Kuwait	Insurance and financial services Imports	1.6	2.5	4.5	8.6	8.4	8.2	3.6	3.0	4.1	0.123
Kuwait	Travel services Exports	2.5	2.3	3.3	3.4	3.4	5.2	5.3	6.5	9.1	0.179
Kuwait	Travel services Imports	63.2	51.2	48.0	44.9	45.9	46.2	48.6	50.4	56.1	−0.015
Lebanon	Computer, communications and other services Exports	51.6	62.1	55.5	32.8	52.3	35.0	39.6	33.3	31.1	−0.061
Lebanon	Computer, communications and other services Imports	48.4	56.6	55.9	40.6	47.5	34.7	38.8	33.9	31.2	−0.054
Lebanon	Insurance and financial services Exports	2.9	2.1	2.1	13.9	7.5	11.8	11.0	13.6	15.6	0.234
Lebanon	Insurance and financial services Imports	3.1	2.4	0.1	10.6	5.6	9.0	9.2	11.3	15.2	0.221
Lebanon	Travel services Exports	40.9	33.0	40.1	49.2	33.4	45.6	42.1	44.4	44.0	0.009
Lebanon	Travel services Imports	31.2	26.5	28.6	34.7	30.9	36.8	34.2	38.1	35.6	0.016
Libya	Computer, communications and other services Exports	8.4	5.3	2.6	2.9	25.4	6.6	7.0	—	—	−0.022
Libya	Computer, communications and other services Imports	4.6	15.9	1.7	4.1	1.2	0.6	0.7	—	—	−0.211
Libya	Insurance and financial services Exports	0.0	2.2	16.4	18.4	0.0	21.4	20.0	—	—	0.316

(Continued)

Table 2.15. *(Continued)*

Country	Percent of GDP for 2007–2015 and Annual Growth Rate	2007	2008	2009	2010	2011	2012	2013	2014	2015	Compound Annual Growth Rate
Libya	Insurance and financial services Imports	7.7	6.8	13.7	12.4	7.0	20.0	22.2	—	—	0.141
Libya	Travel services Exports	68.4	35.7	13.0	14.6	—	—	—	—	—	—
Libya	Travel services Imports	36.2	35.8	36.7	39.0	63.8	40.7	32.8	—	—	−0.012
Morocco	Computer, communications and other services Exports	32.3	32.9	37.8	36.8	33.9	35.6	32.9	32.9	35.0	0.010
Morocco	Computer, communications and other services Imports	29.2	30.3	30.2	27.6	26.4	25.5	29.2	33.2	33.6	0.018
Morocco	Insurance and financial services Exports	0.5	1.0	1.5	1.3	1.2	1.2	1.4	1.2	1.3	0.115
Morocco	Insurance and financial services Imports	2.5	3.0	4.7	4.3	3.7	4.2	4.3	2.2	3.0	0.024
Morocco	Travel services Exports	53.6	49.0	46.1	46.8	47.3	44.8	49.2	45.8	44.4	−0.023
Morocco	Travel services Imports	19.4	19.4	20.9	21.3	20.3	19.1	20.5	17.9	20.1	0.004
Oman	Computer, communications and other services Exports	38.0	29.8	21.3	26.2	16.8	16.3	17.7	17.4	18.5	−0.086
Oman	Computer, communications and other services Imports	40.4	32.2	33.9	31.1	34.9	34.5	31.7	34.2	34.1	−0.021
Oman	Insurance and financial services Exports	0.5	0.9	1.4	1.4	1.5	1.5	1.6	1.5	1.2	0.124
Oman	Insurance and financial services Imports	11.0	10.0	11.4	11.2	9.8	9.3	8.8	9.2	10.0	−0.013

Oman	Travel services Exports	38.5	43.6	42.5	43.3	42.9	40.8	43.8	44.0	44.2	0.018
Oman	Travel services Imports	14.8	14.6	16.5	15.7	15.1	14.6	14.6	16.6	17.2	0.019
Qatar	Computer, communications and other services Exports	—	—	—	—	2.0	8.0	4.7	7.0	7.8	0.182
Qatar	Computer, communications and other services Imports	—	—	—	—	17.9	25.2	26.4	22.8	21.3	0.022
Qatar	Insurance and financial services Exports	—	—	—	—	6.6	7.0	7.3	6.8	3.9	−0.063
Qatar	Insurance and financial services Imports	—	—	—	—	7.1	4.6	5.8	7.9	9.6	0.038
Qatar	Travel services Exports	—	—	—	—	21.0	32.3	33.6	35.9	35.7	0.069
Qatar	Travel services Imports	—	—	—	—	11.6	25.5	26.6	28.9	28.8	0.120
SA	Computer, communications and other services Exports	49.1	2.8	2.8	3.5	3.0	3.8	3.4	3.8	1.9	−0.332
SA	Computer, communications and other services Imports	28.2	31.2	26.6	28.3	34.1	23.3	22.3	24.5	23.9	−0.020
SA	Insurance and financial services Exports	0.0	6.3	13.1	12.0	3.1	4.5	5.4	3.2	4.0	−0.055
SA	Insurance and financial services Imports	7.6	6.7	5.7	5.3	6.5	6.8	6.4	5.2	5.3	−0.045
SA	Travel services Exports	37.0	64.7	63.6	64.8	76.1	70.3	67.7	68.9	73.4	0.090
SA	Travel services Imports	43.5	30.5	43.4	41.4	31.4	34.1	34.1	38.5	34.7	−0.028
Syria	Computer, communications and other services Exports	9.8	6.8	5.7	3.4	—	—	—	—	—	—
Syria	Computer, communications and other services Imports	10.6	7.5	6.6	5.7	—	—	—	—	—	—
Syria	Insurance and financial services Exports	2.9	3.5	2.9	1.1	—	—	—	—	—	—
Syria	Insurance and financial services Imports	9.3	7.9	5.1	3.9	—	—	—	—	—	—
Syria	Travel services Exports	81.0	76.0	82.0	87.9	—	—	—	—	—	—
Syria	Travel services Imports	22.1	25.8	33.6	43.9	—	—	—	—	—	—
Tunisia	Computer, communications and other services Exports	10.7	11.9	15.8	18.4	20.8	19.4	21.3	19.7	23.7	0.104

(Continued)

Table 2.15. (Continued)

Country	Percent of GDP for 2007–2015 and Annual Growth Rate	2007	2008	2009	2010	2011	2012	2013	2014	2015	Compound Annual Growth Rate
Tunisia	Computer, communications and other services Imports	17.5	16.7	19.7	20.4	16.7	16.8	16.8	15.3	15.4	−0.016
Tunisia	Insurance and financial services Exports	2.4	2.3	2.3	2.6	3.0	2.9	3.0	3.0	3.8	0.055
Tunisia	Insurance and financial services Imports	8.7	8.5	10.2	9.4	9.2	8.8	8.3	9.5	9.9	0.015
Tunisia	Travel services Exports	55.7	52.3	54.6	49.9	44.7	46.8	47.9	51.8	44.2	−0.029
Tunisia	Travel services Imports	17.0	14.7	15.3	17.9	20.2	19.8	21.5	21.9	25.1	0.050
Turkey	Computer, communications and other services Exports	8.8	9.1	8.2	7.7	8.1	8.0	7.1	7.6	7.1	−0.026
Turkey	Computer, communications and other services Imports	14.5	16.0	17.8	17.6	18.1	20.2	21.2	18.4	18.5	0.031
Turkey	Insurance and financial services Exports	3.5	4.4	3.2	3.4	3.3	3.3	3.8	3.9	3.7	0.008
Turkey	Insurance and financial services Imports	14.4	14.2	12.9	10.7	12.9	12.7	13.3	15.6	15.7	0.011
Turkey	Travel services Exports	65.6	63.8	65.0	62.8	61.5	59.2	59.1	57.9	57.8	−0.016
Turkey	Travel services Imports	24.4	22.4	28.6	28.1	24.9	21.1	20.9	22.0	25.8	0.007
UAE	Computer, communications and other services Exports	—	—	—	—	—	—	—	—	—	—
UAE	Computer, communications and other services Imports	—	—	—	—	—	—	—	—	—	—

UAE	Insurance and financial services Exports	—	—	—	—	—	—	—	—	—	—
UAE	Insurance and financial services Imports	—	—	—	—	—	—	—	—	—	—
UAE	Travel services Exports	—	—	—	—	—	—	—	—	—	—
UAE	Travel services Imports	—	—	—	—	—	—	—	—	—	—
Yemen	Computer, communications and other services Exports	18.6	11.2	12.9	8.0	11.7	23.2	24.5	14.8	28.9	0.056
Yemen	Computer, communications and other services Imports	30.0	34.5	34.3	31.6	31.1	24.7	24.8	29.7	20.7	−0.045
Yemen	Insurance and financial services Exports	—	—	—	—	—	—	—	—	—	—
Yemen	Insurance and financial services Imports	9.4	9.1	8.7	10.3	10.3	12.4	12.2	11.5	13.8	0.049
Yemen	Travel services Exports	73.5	84.5	82.9	78.9	70.2	60.0	60.6	68.1	38.1	−0.079
Yemen	Travel services Imports	10.1	8.0	10.6	8.7	8.6	3.2	3.9	2.8	5.8	−0.067
OECD	Computer, communications and other services Exports	42.8	43.2	45.3	44.7	45.5	46.4	46.4	47.1	47.3	0.013
OECD	Computer, communications and other services Imports	39.9	40.6	43.6	42.6	43.8	44.5	44.3	45.1	46.1	0.018
OECD	Insurance and financial services Exports	11.2	10.6	11.1	10.6	10.8	10.3	10.3	10.3	10.3	−0.011
OECD	Insurance and financial services Imports	9.7	9.9	10.6	10.1	9.6	9.1	9.4	9.2	8.8	−0.011
OECD	Travel services Exports	23.9	23.7	24.0	23.5	23.2	23.2	22.9	23.2	23.5	−0.002
OECD	Travel services Imports	25.8	24.7	24.6	24.1	23.6	23.4	22.9	22.9	22.8	−0.015

Source: World Bank Development Indicators, 2017.

Table 2.16. Commodity Composition of MENA High-Technology Exports and Tourism Trade

Percent of Manufactured Exports and Percent of Total Imports and Exports, respectively for 2007–2015 and Annual Growth Rate

Country		2007	2008	2009	2010	2011	2012	2013	2014	2015	Compound Annual Growth Rate
Algeria	High-technology exports (% of manufactured exports)	0.7	0.7	0.6	0.5	0.2	0.1	0.2	0.2	0.2	−0.177
Algeria	International tourism, expenditures (% of total imports)	1.5	1.2	1.2	1.4	1.0	1.0	0.8	1.0	1.2	−0.027
Algeria	International tourism, receipts (% of total exports)	0.5	0.6	0.8	0.5	0.4	0.4	0.5	0.5	0.9	0.076
Bahrain	High-technology exports (% of manufactured exports)	0.0	2.5	0.0	0.1	0.2	0.4	0.6	1.5	1.0	0.462
Bahrain	International tourism, expenditures (% of total imports)	5.3	4.3	5.3	5.2	6.5	6.0	5.7	5.8	—	0.011
Bahrain	International tourism, receipts (% of total exports)	10.7	9.1	11.9	12.1	7.7	7.6	7.7	7.9	—	−0.037
Cyprus	High-technology exports (% of manufactured exports)	29.4	30.4	30.9	36.9	27.3	13.0	7.2	6.2	6.2	−0.177
Cyprus	International tourism, expenditures (% of total imports)	13.2	11.2	12.4	11.0	11.3	12.3	11.9	12.6	12.1	−0.011
Cyprus	International tourism, receipts (% of total exports)	30.1	22.9	19.3	18.9	18.6	20.5	21.4	20.1	20.8	−0.045

Djibouti	High-technology exports (% of manufactured exports)	—	—	0.1	—	—	—	—	—	—	—
Djibouti	International tourism, expenditures (% of total imports)	2.4	2.2	3.0	4.2	5.0	4.1	3.4	2.1	1.7	−0.042
Djibouti	International tourism, receipts (% of total exports)	2.2	2.1	4.0	4.3	4.6	4.5	4.4	4.8	5.3	0.114
Egypt	High-technology exports (% of manufactured exports)	0.2	1.0	0.8	0.9	1.0	0.6	0.5	1.3	0.8	0.194
Egypt	International tourism, expenditures (% of total imports)	5.4	5.0	5.5	4.5	4.2	4.4	5.0	4.7	5.4	0.000
Egypt	International tourism, receipts (% of total exports)	23.3	22.1	26.4	27.9	19.8	22.3	15.1	16.9	18.4	−0.029
Iran	High-technology exports (% of manufactured exports)	—	—	—	4.5	4.1	—	—	—	—	—
Iran	International tourism, expenditures (% of total imports)	—	—	—	—	—	—	—	—	—	—
Iran	International tourism, receipts (% of total exports)	—	—	—	—	—	—	—	—	—	—
Iraq	High-technology exports (% of manufactured exports)	—	—	—	—	0.1	—	—	—	—	—
Iraq	International tourism, expenditures (% of total imports)	3.3	2.2	2.8	3.5	3.6	3.7	5.2	7.3	10.8	0.161
Iraq	International tourism, receipts (% of total exports)	1.4	1.3	3.4	3.2	1.9	1.7	2.4	2.8	8.2	0.250
Israel	High-technology exports (% of manufactured exports)	7.5	11.1	17.6	14.7	14.0	15.8	15.6	16.0	19.7	0.128

(Continued)

Table 2.16. *(Continued)*

Percent of Manufactured Exports and Percent of Total Imports and Exports, respectively for 2007–2015 and Annual Growth Rate

Country		2007	2008	2009	2010	2011	2012	2013	2014	2015	Compound Annual Growth Rate
Israel	International tourism, expenditures (% of total imports)	6.3	5.6	6.7	6.1	5.3	5.2	5.7	6.0	7.5	0.022
Israel	International tourism, receipts (% of total exports)	6.1	6.6	7.3	7.1	6.4	6.6	6.5	6.4	6.6	0.010
Jordan	High-technology exports (% of manufactured exports)	1.1	0.9	1.4	2.9	2.5	2.3	1.6	1.6	1.8	0.062
Jordan	International tourism, expenditures (% of total imports)	6.5	5.9	7.3	9.5	6.0	5.5	5.0	5.0	5.6	−0.018
Jordan	International tourism, receipts (% of total exports)	29.3	27.9	31.4	34.4	31.7	35.8	36.2	35.5	35.3	0.024
Kuwait	High-technology exports (% of manufactured exports)	0.5	0.3	0.5	3.0	2.7	—	1.4	0.1	2.7	0.243
Kuwait	International tourism, expenditures (% of total imports)	21.8	21.5	21.1	20.1	21.3	22.2	22.7	24.0	25.7	0.021
Kuwait	International tourism, receipts (% of total exports)	0.7	0.6	1.0	0.8	0.6	0.6	0.5	0.6	1.5	0.096
Lebanon	High-technology exports (% of manufactured exports)	2.2	2.4	4.5	12.8	2.4	2.0	2.2	2.1	—	−0.010
Lebanon	International tourism, expenditures (% of total imports)	18.3	14.8	16.7	16.1	13.8	14.4	14.4	16.1	17.1	−0.008
Lebanon	International tourism, receipts (% of total exports)	35.5	28.6	33.9	38.7	27.1	36.6	35.2	36.3	36.6	0.004

Libya	High-technology exports (% of manufactured exports)	—	—	—	—	—	—	—	—	—	—
Libya	International tourism, expenditures (% of total imports)	5.0	5.1	6.2	7.1	—	8.1	6.1	—	—	—
Libya	International tourism, receipts (% of total exports)	0.2	0.2	0.4	0.3	—	—	—	—	—	—
Morocco	High-technology exports (% of manufactured exports)	8.8	6.0	7.3	7.7	6.1	6.4	6.6	5.3	3.5	−0.108
Morocco	International tourism, expenditures (% of total imports)	4.5	4.4	4.9	5.1	4.9	4.5	4.2	4.5	5.2	0.018
Morocco	International tourism, receipts (% of total exports)	34.7	29.1	33.3	30.2	28.6	26.3	25.1	24.4	23.3	−0.048
Oman	High-technology exports (% of manufactured exports)	0.5	0.7	0.3	0.6	2.6	3.4	3.4	4.3	4.1	0.317
Oman	International tourism, expenditures (% of total imports)	4.9	4.5	6.0	5.1	5.1	4.8	4.4	5.5	5.9	0.024
Oman	International tourism, receipts (% of total exports)	3.4	2.8	3.7	2.8	3.1	3.1	3.2	3.5	5.7	0.066
Qatar	High-technology exports (% of manufactured exports)	0.1	0.0	0.0	0.0	0.0	—	0.0	0.0	3.4	—
Qatar	International tourism, expenditures (% of total imports)	—	—	—	—	17.8	19.6	19.9	20.1	19.6	0.012
Qatar	International tourism, receipts (% of total exports)	—	—	—	—	3.7	5.1	5.8	7.5	13.1	0.173
SA	High-technology exports (% of manufactured exports)	0.7	0.8	1.1	0.7	0.6	0.6	0.7	0.6	0.8	0.020

(Continued)

Table 2.16. *(Continued)*

Percent of Manufactured Exports and Percent of Total Imports and Exports, respectively for 2007–2015 and Annual Growth Rate											
Country		2007	2008	2009	2010	2011	2012	2013	2014	2015	Compound Annual Growth Rate
SA	International tourism, expenditures (% of total imports)	14.4	9.1	13.1	12.7	9.2	8.4	8.1	9.7	8.8	−0.060
SA	International tourism, receipts (% of total exports)	2.8	2.1	3.3	2.9	2.5	2.1	2.2	2.6	5.1	0.080
Syria	High-technology exports (% of manufactured exports)	1.3	1.8	1.6	1.3	—	—	—	—	—	—
Syria	International tourism, expenditures (% of total imports)	4.6	4.7	5.9	8.2	—	—	—	—	—	—
Syria	International tourism, receipts (% of total exports)	19.0	16.1	24.1	32.2	—	—	—	—	—	—
Tunisia	High-technology exports (% of manufactured exports)	5.4	4.5	4.1	4.9	5.6	4.7	4.9	5.5	6.3	0.020
Tunisia	International tourism, expenditures (% of total imports)	2.6	2.1	2.3	2.5	2.6	2.6	2.9	2.9	3.5	0.038
Tunisia	International tourism, receipts (% of total exports)	16.9	15.6	17.8	15.7	11.2	13.2	13.0	14.1	10.7	−0.055
Turkey	High-technology exports (% of manufactured exports)	1.9	1.6	1.7	1.9	1.8	1.8	1.9	1.9	2.2	0.017

Turkey	International tourism, expenditures (% of total imports)	2.4	2.1	3.3	3.0	2.1	1.8	2.0	2.1	2.6	0.008
Turkey	International tourism, receipts (% of total exports)	14.9	14.9	18.1	16.7	16.5	15.4	17.2	17.6	17.8	0.023
UAE	High-technology exports (% of manufactured exports)	1.1	3.2	—	—	—	3.7	3.2	8.5	—	—
UAE	International tourism, expenditures (% of total imports)	—	—	—	—	—	—	—	—	—	—
UAE	International tourism, receipts (% of total exports)	—	—	—	—	—	—	—	—	—	—
Yemen	High-technology exports (% of manufactured exports)	0.4	0.3	0.4	0.4	0.3	0.2	0.4	1.2	4.7	0.368
Yemen	International tourism, expenditures (% of total imports)	2.6	2.1	2.8	2.4	2.4	1.1	1.2	1.0	1.0	−0.111
Yemen	International tourism, receipts (% of total exports)	5.5	8.7	12.6	13.9	8.8	10.7	11.5	12.7	6.2	0.016
OECD	High-technology exports (% of manufactured exports)	17.0	16.4	17.2	17.0	16.3	16.6	16.8	16.8	17.7	0.005
OECD	International tourism, expenditures (% of total imports)	5.8	5.5	6.1	5.5	5.1	5.3	5.3	5.4	5.5	−0.006
OECD	International tourism, receipts (% of total exports)	6.0	5.9	6.5	6.0	5.7	5.9	6.1	6.3	6.6	0.012

Source: World Bank Development Indicators, 2017.

In contrast, trade in services as a share of GDP for Bahrain declined by a 7.1 compound annual growth rate. Trade in services as a share of GDP in Egypt declined by 9.5 compound annual growth rate. Trade in services as a share of GDP in Jordan declined by 4.6 compound annual growth rate. Likewise, trade in services as a share of GDP in Lebanon declined by 4.8 compound annual growth rate.

Shifting to high-technology exports as listed in Table 2.16, we again face the inevitable that within MENA, only Israel has a growing high-technology sector. Between 2007 and 2015, Israeli exports in high technology expended at a compound growth rate of 12.8 percent. In 2015, 20 percent of Israel's manufacturing exports were in high technology. Despite a few attempts in the oil-rich countries in MENA to alter this reality, they have not been successful.[3]

When we shift to tourism, Table 2.16 presents two indicators — *international tourism receipts* which are expenditures by international inbound visitors, including payments to national carriers for international transport. These receipts include any other prepayment made for goods or services received in the destination country. They also may include receipts from same-day visitors, except when these are important enough to justify separate classification. For some countries, they do not include receipts for passenger transport items. Their share in exports is calculated as a ratio to exports of goods and services, which comprise all transactions between residents of a country and the rest of the world involving a change of ownership from residents to non-residents of general merchandise, goods sent for processing and repairs, non-monetary gold, and services; and *international tourism expenditures* which are expenditures of international outbound visitors in other countries, including payments to foreign carriers for

[3]These trade outcomes are occurring despite the establishment of the King Abdullah University for Science and Technology, which offers Arab graduates, purportedly regardless of gender, grants to conduct scientific research with state-of-the-art facilities and resources. There is also the Mohammed Bin Rashid Al Maktoum Foundation, with the objective of developing the knowledge and human capabilities of the Arab region, as well as the Arab Open University financed by the Prince Talal Bin Abdul Aziz. One should not minimize these initiatives to promote the development of human capital among Arab MENA, but the question remains: are the rich Arabs just building Pyramids in the desert for their own aggrandizement, or if not, are these institutional expenditures simply too little and too late? None of these institutions have opened up their doors to the wider scientific community, in large part because those scientists belong to the group which is being constantly vilified in elementary school textbooks and whose hatred keeps the Arab elites in power. In the Arab MENA there is some truth to the statement that "ignorance is bliss" (UNDP, 2009a).

international transport. These expenditures may include those by residents traveling abroad as same-day visitors, except in cases where these are important enough to justify separate classification. For some countries, they do not include expenditures for passenger transport items. Their share in imports is calculated as a ratio to imports of goods and services, which comprise all transactions between residents of a country and the rest of the world involving a change of ownership from non-residents to residents of general merchandise, goods sent for processing and repairs, non-monetary gold and services. A limited number of MENA countries are tied to the tourism revenue stream. They include Cyprus, Egypt, Jordan, Morocco, Qatar and, to a lower degree, Turkey and Tunisia. Israel has been in the tourism business for decades and remains an outlier both in this sector as well as in high-technology exports.

2.7. Impediments to Business Activity within MENA

The overriding explanatory variable for the post-1980 devastating growth in the non-oil producing Arab MENA is the domestic regulatory environments which discouraged private investment and impeded the development of export-oriented industrial sectors, creating obstacles to the integration of the regional economy into global markets. The most recent World Bank (2018) report on doing business commends the MENA countries for attempting to limit regulations affecting their business sector. Despite these attempts, however, the score card for most of the MENA countries is not very impressive. There are a multitude of domestic factors, policies and institutions that negatively affect the quality of MENA's business environment or its competitiveness. For example, there are a variety of macro policies that affect economic stability and impose above normal risk on business activity. In addition, there are concerns raised about developments in the financial system, competition rules that affect firm behavior, the incidence of bribery and corruption and the quality of the labor force. All of these forces inhibit private sector activity within MENA.

The growth slowdown prompted countries, led by Morocco, Tunisia and Jordan (to a limited extent), to initiate domestic policies of reduced government expenditures and cross-sector subsidies, and reformed exchange rate regimes. It was not until the 1990s that these three governments initiated a gradual transition to structural adjustment focusing on privatization of state-owned enterprises (SOEs), trade liberalization and deregulation, and strengthening the institutional foundations for a market-based economy.

These reforms were in response to World Bank and IMF instructions rather than "grass root" pressure.

Given the lack of markets and local pressure, it is not surprising that implementation of these structural economic reforms was uneven, hesitant and incomplete (World Bank, 2009). The oil-exporting MENA countries faced no great pressure to reform their economies, as long as oil prices were high. Over the entire 2007–2015 time period, the compound growth rate of GDP per capita measured in constant 2010 US dollars, for Arab MENA was on average below one percent. (See Table 1.1) The only non-oil economy in MENA that experienced a positive compound growth rate in real GDP per capita was Israel, which had a 1.4 percent compound growth rate. Despite the size of Arab MENA with its huge natural resource endowment, non-military physical capital accumulation, productivity growth remained almost non-existent across the region in the late 20th and early 21st century. A number of scholars have noted that this performance within Arab MENA is tied to the "curse of natural resources" (Auty, 2001a, b; Sachs and Warner, 1997a, b).

This "Dutch disease" phenomenon which will be addressed in greater detail in Chapter 6 is arguably common in countries with natural-resource abundance. The lack of economic growth in these countries is attributed to the fact that the positive wealth shocks from the export of natural resources raise demand for non-tradable products, drawing skilled workers, physical capital investment and entrepreneurial ability from other sectors. Consequently, productive sectors (including the tradable sector) decline and economic growth suffers. Furthermore, it has been found that countries with large natural resource endowments also exhibit policy distortions and weak institutional structures that handicap progress, with reforms aimed at curtailing government expenditures and reorienting economic activity.

Within Arab MENA, the non-existence of market economies with strong institutional support was translated to perpetual non-reforms. The local governments interested in their survival were hard pressed to reduce cross-sector subsidies and inefficient distortions. Violent mass protests which took place in Egypt in 1977, Morocco in 1983, Tunisia in 1984, Algeria in 1988 and Jordan in 1989 were sufficient justification for the autocratic governments of Arab MENA to continuously postpone the reform pressure from the World Bank and the IMF. The uprising in the Arab Spring has not generated sufficient market reforms to eliminate prospects of future local instability and revolutions. (UNDP, 2016a and 2016b)

Table 2.17. Ease of Doing Business Index in MENA (2015–2016)

(1 = most business-friendly regulations)		
	2015	2016
Algeria	163	156
Bahrain	66	63
Cyprus	41	45
Djibouti	168	171
Egypt	126	122
Iran	117	120
Iraq	166	165
Israel	49	52
Jordan	119	118
Kuwait	98	102
Lebanon	122	126
Morocco	68	68
Oman	69	66
Qatar	74	83
SA	96	94
Syria	172	173
Tunisia	75	77
Turkey	63	69
UAE	34	26
Yemen	179	179

Source: World Bank, Doing Business project.

In addition to the lack of substantial reforms as reported by the United Nations (UNDP, 2002, 2003, 2004, 2005, 2009a, 2009b, 2016a, and 2016b), the World Bank survey work on *Doing Business*[4] provides a quantitative ranking of a multiple set of issues that apply to the private sector in MENA. By quantifying the degree to which these factors are discouraging private entrepreneurial activity, we may be able to shed some light on why there is such a disappointing economic performance in Arab MENA.

In Table 2.17 we present an overall index of "Ease of Doing Business in MENA. This index ranks economies from 1 to 190, with first place being the best. A high ranking (a low numerical rank) means that the regulatory environment is conducive to business operation. The index averages

[4] "*Doing Business* (2018) provides a quantitative measure of regulations for starting a business, dealing with construction permits, employing workers, registering property, getting credit, protecting investors, paying taxes, trading across borders, enforcing contracts and closing a business — as they apply to domestic small and medium-size enterprises" (*Doing Business*, 2018).

the country's percentile rankings on 10 topics covered in the World Bank's *Doing Business*. The ranking on each topic is the simple average of the percentile rankings on its component indicators. Despite the reforms undertaken in some MENA countries in 2008–2010, the overall index shows only marginal gains. For example, Bahrain increased from 66 to 63, while Cyprus declined from 41 to 45. The UAE is the single MENA country with the largest improvement from 34 to 26, between 2015 and 2016.

It is not startling to find that the majority of Arab MENA economies in 2016 rank above 100 relative to 190 countries: Jordan — 118; Egypt — 122; Lebanon — 126; Iran — 120; Syria — 173; Iraq — 165 and Yemen — 179.

In order to determine the complexity and bureaucracy of starting a business within MENA, we present in Table 2.18 six indexes over the period 2007 and 2016. The first index is the "business extent of disclosure index" (0 = less disclosure to 10 = more disclosure), which measures the extent to which investors are protected through disclosure of ownership and financial information. The index ranges from 0 to 10, with higher values indicating more disclosure. Within MENA Bahrain, Cyprus, Egypt, Israel, Lebanon, Morocco, Oman, Saudi Arabia, Turkey and the UAE have indexes between 7 and 10.

The second variable is the "cost of business start-up procedures' (% of GNI per capita) which measures the cost to register a business normalized as a percentage of gross national income (GNI) per capita. These figures range from a high of 167 percent in Djibouti to a low of 3.3 percent for Israel and 2.8 percent for Kuwait. What is surprising is the cost of registering a business in Turkey which in 2016 was 16.4 percent of GNI per capita. For the OECD, the average cost of registering a business was 3.9 percent of GNI per capita. Israel and a number of Gulf states fit the OECD average.

The third variable is "new business density" (new registrations per 1,000 people ages 15–64) which is measured as the number of new limited liability corporations (LLC) registered in the calendar year. The OECD average for 2014 was 5.4. For Arab MENA the average is closer to 1, and for Israel in 2014 it was 3.1 and for Cyprus it was 137. Overall, the numbers suggest a slow increase in LLCs within MENA. The fourth variable which supports the density figures is the number of "new businesses registered." (number). These new entities are all LLCs. It is unclear if the data on numbers of new firms is primarily affected by the cost of entry or the general macro downcycle. The World Bank (2017) in its report suggests the former.

The fifth variable is the number of "start-up procedures to register a business." These start up procedures are those required to start a business,

Table 2.18. Complexity and Bureaucracy of Starting a Business in MENA

	(2007–2016)										
Country		2007	2008	2009	2010	2011	2012	2013	2014	2015	2016
Algeria	Business extent of disclosure index (0 = less disclosure to 10 = more disclosure)	4	4	4	4	4	4	4	4	4	4
Algeria	Cost of business start-up procedures (% of GNI per capita)	13.2	10.8	12.1	12.9	12.1	12.1	12.4	11	10.9	11.1
Algeria	New business density (new registrations per 1,000 people ages 15–64)	0.3	0.5	0.4	0.4	0.5	0.5	—	0.6	—	—
Algeria	New businesses registered (number)	7,955	11,120	10,661	9,564	12,256	13,938	—	15,574	—	—
Algeria	Start-up procedures to register a business (number)	13	13	13	13	13	13	13	13	12	12
Algeria	Time required to start a business (days)	24	24	24	24	24	24	24	22	20	20
Bahrain	Business extent of disclosure index (0 = less disclosure to 10 = more disclosure)	8	8	8	8	8	8	8	8	8	8

(Continued)

Table 2.18. *(Continued)*

Country		2007	2008	2009	2010	2011	2012	2013	2014	2015	2016
		(2007–2016)									
Bahrain	Cost of business start-up procedures (% of GNI per capita)	0.7	0.6	0.5	0.6	0.9	0.8	1	0.8	0.8	1.2
Bahrain	New business density (new registrations per 1,000 people ages 15–64)	—	—	—	—	—	—	—	—	—	—
Bahrain	New businesses registered (number)	—	—	—	—	—	—	—	—	—	—
Bahrain	Start-up procedures to register a business (number)	7	7	7	7	7	7	7	7	7	7
Bahrain	Time required to start a business (days)	9.4	9.4	9.3	9.3	9.3	9.3	9.3	9.3	9.4	9.3
Cyprus	Business extent of disclosure index (0 = less disclosure to 10 = more disclosure)	—	4	4	4	8	8	8	8	8	8
Cyprus	Cost of business start-up procedures (% of GNI per capita)	—	14.1	11.7	12.6	13.1	12.4	12.6	13	12.5	12.2
Cyprus	New business density (new registrations per 1,000 people ages 15–64)	39.0	32.3	20.9	24.7	24.7	22.5	—	13.7	—	—

Cyprus	New businesses registered (number)	29,016	24,453	16,101	19,278	19,538	17,999	—	11, 169	—	—
Cyprus	Start-up procedures to register a business (number)	—	6	6	6	6	6	6	6	6	5
Cyprus	Time required to start a business (days)	—	8	8	8	8	8	8	8	8	6
Djibouti	Business extent of disclosure index (0 = less disclosure to 10 = more disclosure)	4	4	4	4	4	4	4	4	4	4
Djibouti	Cost of business start-up procedures (% of GNI per capita)	251.6	245.2	240.1	214.9	214.8	195.7	184.7	175.2	170.7	167.0
Djibouti	New business density (new registrations per 1,000 people ages 15–64)	—	—	—	—	—	—	—	—	—	—
Djibouti	New businesses registered (number)	—	—	—	—	—	—	—	—	—	—
Djibouti	Start-up procedures to register a business (number)	11	11	11	11	11	11	9	7	7	7
Djibouti	Time required to start a business (days)	44	37	37	37	37	37	17	14	14	14
Egypt	Business extent of disclosure index (0 = less disclosure to 10 = more disclosure)	4	5	5	5	5	5	5	8	8	8

(*Continued*)

Table 2.18. *(Continued)*

		(2007–2016)									
Country		2007	2008	2009	2010	2011	2012	2013	2014	2015	2016
Egypt	Cost of business start-up procedures (% of GNI per capita)	28.9	22.7	20.7	10.9	10.4	10.4	9.7	9.2	7.6	7.4
Egypt	New business density (new registrations per 1,000 people ages 15–64)	0.2	0.1	0.1	—	—	—	—	—	—	—
Egypt	New businesses registered (number)	7,941	6,291	6,308	—	—	—	—	—	—	—
Egypt	Start-up procedures to register a business (number)	8	7	7	7	7	7	7	7	7	4
Egypt	Time required to start a business (days)	10.5	8.5	8.5	8.5	8.5	8.5	8.5	8.5	8.5	6.5
Iran	Business extent of disclosure index (0 = less disclosure to 10 = more disclosure)	5	5	5	5	5	7	7	7	7	7
Iran	Cost of business start-up procedures (% of GNI per capita)	5.3	4.6	3.9	4.2	3.9	3.4	3.1	3.1	2.7	1.1
Iran	New business density (new registrations per 1,000 people ages 15–64)	—	—	—	—	—	—	—	—	—	—

Iran	New businesses registered (number)	—	—	—	—	—	—	—	—	—	—
Iran	Start-up procedures to register a business (number)	9	9	8	8	8	9	10	9	9	9
Iran	Time required to start a business (days)	30.5	30.5	11.5	13.5	13.5	18.5	18.5	15.5	15.5	15.5
Iraq	Business extent of disclosure index (0 = less disclosure to 10 = more disclosure)	4	4	4	4	4	4	4	4	4	4
Iraq	Cost of business start-up procedures (% of GNI per capita)	68.5	126.9	64.6	92.5	102.3	70.5	36.7	35.9	37.4	51.9
Iraq	New business density (new registrations per 1,000 people ages 15–64)	0.2	0.3	0.3	0.1	0.1	0.1	—	—	—	—
Iraq	New businesses registered (number)	3,600	5,134	4,534	2,500	1,943	2,309	—	—	—	—
Iraq	Start-up procedures to register a business (number)	11	11	11	11	11	10	10	10	9	9
Iraq	Time required to start a business (days)	30.5	30.5	30.5	30.5	30.5	27.5	27.5	27.5	34.5	34.5
Israel	Business extent of disclosure index (0 = less disclosure to 10 = more disclosure)	7	7	7	7	7	7	7	7	7	7
Israel	Cost of business start-up procedures (% of GNI per capita)	4.4	4.4	4.2	4.3	4.4	4	4.1	3.5	3.4	3.3
Israel	New business density (new registrations per 1,000 people ages 15–64)	3.5	3.3	3.3	3.6	3.4	3.0	—	3.1	—	—

(*Continued*)

Table 2.18. (*Continued*)

Country		(2007–2016)									
		2007	2008	2009	2010	2011	2012	2013	2014	2015	2016
Israel	New businesses registered (number)	15,871	14,836	15,211	16,898	16,383	14,504	—	15, 680	—	—
Israel	Start-up procedures to register a business (number)	5	5	5	5	5	5	5	5	5	4
Israel	Time required to start a business (days)	19	19	19	19	19	20	13	13	13	12
Jordan	Business extent of disclosure index (0 = less disclosure to 10 = more disclosure)	4	4	4	4	4	4	4	4	4	4
Jordan	Cost of business start-up procedures (% of GNI per capita)	23.8	35.9	30.6	27.6	23.6	23.4	22.3	21.4	20.7	22.4
Jordan	New business density (new registrations per 1,000 people ages 15–64)	0.6	0.7	0.8	0.8	0.8	1.0	—	1.0	—	—
Jordan	New businesses registered (number)	1,982	2,315	2,735	3,106	3,039	3,868	—	4, 093	—	—
Jordan	Start-up procedures to register a business (number)	8	8	7	7	7	7	7	7	7	7
Jordan	Time required to start a business (days)	13.5	13.5	12.5	12.5	12.5	12.5	12.5	12.5	12.5	12.5

Kuwait	Business extent of disclosure index (0 = less disclosure to 10 = more disclosure)	4	4	4	4	4	4	4	4	4	4
Kuwait	Cost of business start-up procedures (% of GNI per capita)	1.6	1.3	1	1.3	1.2	1.1	1.2	2	2.3	2.8
Kuwait	New business density (new registrations per 1,000 people ages 15–64)	—	—	—	—	—	—	—	—	—	—
Kuwait	New businesses registered (number)	—	—	—	—	—	—	—	—	—	—
Kuwait	Start-up procedures to register a business (number)	13	13	13	13	12	12	12	12	12	12
Kuwait	Time required to start a business (days)	35.4	35.4	35.4	35.4	32.4	32.4	32.4	31.4	31.4	61.4
Lebanon	Business extent of disclosure index (0 = less disclosure to 10 = more disclosure)	9	9	9	9	9	9	9	9	9	9
Lebanon	Cost of business start-up procedures (% of GNI per capita)	94.5	87.8	78.5	75.3	67.3	35.5	35.1	33.6	34.2	40.6
Lebanon	New business density (new registrations per 1,000 people ages 15–64)	—	—	—	—	—	—	—	—	—	—
Lebanon	New businesses registered (number)	—	—	—	—	—	—	—	—	—	—
Lebanon	Start-up procedures to register a business (number)	9	8	8	8	8	8	8	8	8	8
Lebanon	Time required to start a business (days)	53	18	15	15	15	15	15	15	15	15

(Continued)

Table 2.18. ***(Continued)***

		(2007–2016)									
Country		2007	2008	2009	2010	2011	2012	2013	2014	2015	2016
Morocco	Business extent of disclosure index (0 = less disclosure to 10 = more disclosure)	5	5	5	6	6	6	6	6	6	9
Morocco	Cost of business start-up procedures (% of GNI per capita)	13.6	12	10.8	10.3	10	9.6	9.5	9.2	9.1	7.9
Morocco	New business density (new registrations per 1,000 people ages 15–64)	1.2	1.3	1.3	—	—	—	—	1.5	—	—
Morocco	New businesses registered (number)	24,676	26,280	26,166	—	—	—	—	34, 658	—	—
Morocco	Start-up procedures to register a business (number)	6	6	6	6	6	6	5	5	4	4
Morocco	Time required to start a business (days)	12	12	12	12	12	12	11	11	10	9.5
Oman	Business extent of disclosure index (0 = less disclosure to 10 = more disclosure)	8	8	8	8	8	8	8	8	8	8
Oman	Cost of business start-up procedures (% of GNI per capita)	4.3	3.6	2.2	3.3	3.1	2.6	2.4	2.4	3.2	4

Oman	New business density (new registrations per 1,000 people ages 15–64)	2.0	2.3	1.7	—	—	—	1.0	—	—	—
Oman	New businesses registered (number)	3,350	3,929	3,165	—	—	—	2, 730	—	—	—
Oman	Start-up procedures to register a business (number)	11	8	6	6	6	6	6	6	6	4
Oman	Time required to start a business (days)	39.4	14.4	12.4	12.4	8.3	8.3	8.3	8.3	8.3	6.3
Qatar	Business extent of disclosure index (0 = less disclosure to 10 = more disclosure)	5	5	5	5	5	5	5	5	5	2
Qatar	Cost of business start-up procedures (% of GNI per capita)	5.7	5.7	4.7	7.2	6.1	4.9	5.1	5.2	5.1	6.2
Qatar	New business density (new registrations per 1,000 people ages 15–64)	2.2	1.9	1.4	1.5	2.1	1.7	—	1.7	—	—
Qatar	New businesses registered (number)	2,026	2,158	1,846	2,247	3,373	3,053	—	3, 288	—	—
Qatar	Start-up procedures to register a business (number)	7	7	7	9	8	8	8	8	8	8
Qatar	Time required to start a business (days)	7.2	7.2	7.2	9.7	8.7	8.7	8.7	8.7	8.7	8.7
SA	Business extent of disclosure index (0 = less disclosure to 10 = more disclosure)	7	8	8	8	8	8	8	8	8	8
SA	Cost of business start-up procedures (% of GNI per capita)	27.5	15.4	5.8	7.4	6.4	5.1	5	4	4.1	4.1
SA	New business density (new registrations per 1,000 people ages 15–64)	—	—	—	—	—	—	—	—	—	—

(Continued)

Table 2.18. ***(Continued)***

Country		2007	2008	2009	2010	2011	2012	2013	2014	2015	2016
		(2007–2016)									
SA	New businesses registered (number)	—	—	—	—	—	—	—	—	—	—
SA	Start-up procedures to register a business (number)	12	12	13	13	13	13	13	13	13	13
SA	Time required to start a business (days)	24.2	24.2	24.2	24.2	24.2	21.2	21.7	21.7	20.2	16.2
Syria	Business extent of disclosure index (0 = less disclosure to 10 = more disclosure)	6	6	6	7	7	7	7	7	7	7
Syria	Cost of business start-up procedures (% of GNI per capita)	55.7	18.2	27.8	38.1	17.1	15.6	12.5	14.4	8.5	8.9
Syria	New business density (new registrations per 1,000 people ages 15–64)	0.0	0.0	0.0	0.1	0.0	—	—	—	—	—
Syria	New businesses registered (number)	296	472	500	713	598	—	—	—	—	—
Syria	Start-up procedures to register a business (number)	13	8	7	7	7	7	7	7	7	7
Syria	Time required to start a business (days)	43.5	16.5	15.5	13.5	13.5	13.5	13.5	13.5	13.5	15.5

Tunisia	Business extent of disclosure index (0 = less disclosure to 10 = more disclosure)	0	0	4	4	4	4	4	4	4	4
Tunisia	Cost of business start-up procedures (% of GNI per capita)	8.3	7.9	5.7	5	4.2	4.1	4.7	4.2	3.9	4.7
Tunisia	New business density (new registrations per 1,000 people ages 15–64)	1.3	1.2	1.3	1.5	1.5	—	1.5	—	—	—
Tunisia	New businesses registered (number)	8,997	8,297	9,138	11,317	11,307	—	12, 691	—	—	—
Tunisia	Start-up procedures to register a business (number)	9	9	9	9	9	9	9	9	9	9
Tunisia	Time required to start a business (days)	11	11	11	11	11	11	11	11	11	11
Turkey	Business extent of disclosure index (0 = less disclosure to 10 = more disclosure)	8	9	9	9	9	9	9	9	9	9
Turkey	Cost of business start-up procedures (% of GNI per capita)	20.7	14.9	14.2	17.2	11.2	10.5	12.7	16.4	16.6	16.4
Turkey	New business density (new registrations per 1,000 people ages 15–64)	1.2	1.0	0.9	1.1	1.1	0.8	—	1.1	—	—
Turkey	New businesses registered (number)	54,101	47,983	42,237	50,414	53,383	38,823	—	57, 760	—	—
Turkey	Start-up procedures to register a business (number)	7	7	7	7	7	7	7	8	8	7
Turkey	Time required to start a business (days)	7	7	7	7	7	7	7	7.5	7.5	6.5
UAE	Business extent of disclosure index (0 = less disclosure to 10 = more disclosure)	4	4	4	4	4	4	6	10	10	10

(*Continued*)

Table 2.18. *(Continued)*

Country		2007	2008	2009	2010	2011	2012	2013	2014	2015	2016
		(2007–2016)									
UAE	Cost of business start-up procedures (% of GNI per capita)	13.9	11.6	11.1	12.6	13.4	11	11.4	11.3	11.2	13
UAE	New business density (new registrations per 1,000 people ages 15–64)	1.8	1.6	0.9	1.1	1.2	1.4	—	—	—	—
UAE	New businesses registered (number)	8,810	9,259	6,086	7,700	9,127	10,814	—	—	—	—
UAE	Start-up procedures to register a business (number)	9	9	8	8	7	6	6	6	6	4
UAE	Time required to start a business (days)	18.2	18.2	15.2	15.2	13.2	8.2	8.2	8.2	8.2	8.2
Yemen	Business extent of disclosure index (0 = less disclosure to 10 = more disclosure)	6	6	6	6	6	6	6	6	6	6
Yemen	Cost of business start-up procedures (% of GNI per capita)	178.8	93	83	82.1	83.8	71.9	66.1	66.3	68	82.2
Yemen	New business density (new registrations per 1,000 people ages 15–64)	—	—	—	—	—	—	—	—	—	—

Yemen	New businesses registered (number)	—	—	—	—	—	—	—	—	—	—
Yemen	Start-up procedures to register a business (number)	12	7	6	6	6	6	6	6	6	6
Yemen	Time required to start a business (days)	63.5	13.5	12.5	12.5	12.5	40.5	40.5	40.5	40.5	40.5
OECD	Business extent of disclosure index (0 = less disclosure to 10 = more disclosure)	6	6	6	6	6	6	6	6	6	6
OECD	Cost of business start-up procedures (% of GNI per capita)	7.3	6.3	5.8	6.0	5.2	5.1	4.6	4.4	4.0	3.9
OECD	New business density (new registrations per 1,000 people ages 15–64)	5.0	4.4	4.1	4.2	4.6	4.7	1.7	5.4	—	—
OECD	New businesses registered (number)	—	—	—	—	—	—	—	—	—	—
OECD	Start-up procedures to register a business (number)	7	6	6	6	6	6	5	5	5	5
OECD	Time required to start a business (days)	17.8	15.1	14.4	13.6	11.3	11.0	10.7	9.4	8.5	8.2

Source: World Bank, Doing Business project (http://www.doingbusiness.org/).

including interactions to obtain necessary permits and licenses and to complete all inscriptions, verifications and notifications to start operations. Data are for businesses with specific characteristics of ownership, size and type of production. For the OECD the 2016 average is 5 procedures. Cyprus and Israel fall in this average along with Morocco and the UAE. For balance the number of procedures is in double digits.

The sixth variable is the "time required to start a business, in terms of calendar days needed to complete the procedures to legally operate a business. If a procedure can be speeded up at additional cost, the fastest procedure, independent of cost, is chosen. The 2016 OECD average is 8.2 days. Within MENA, for 2016, the numbers of days vary by the degree of pro-business environment. For Cyprus it is 6.0 days, Egypt 6.5 days, Oman, 6.3 days and Turkey 6.5 days. The least business friendly was Kuwait with 61.4 days followed by Yemen with a requirement of 40.5 days, followed by Iraq with 34.5 days and followed by Algeria with 20 days. To shorten these days, it is possible to provide facilitation funds which are legal by international law but do substantially increase the cost of start-up activity within Arab MENA. What is surprising is that for Israel that is well known as the start-up nation, the number of days required to complete the procedures to legally operate a business in 2016 was 12, substantially larger than the OECD average of 8.2 days.

Doing Business (2018) measures aspects of regulation affecting 11 areas of the life of a business. Above, we discussed ease of doing business and the bureaucracy of starting a business in MENA. We now turn to dealing with construction permits within MENA. *Doing Business* (2018) records all procedures required for a business in the construction industry to build a warehouse along with the time and cost to complete each procedure. In addition, *Doing Business* (2018) measures the building quality control index, evaluating the quality of building regulations, the strength of quality control and safety mechanisms, liability and insurance regimes, and professional certification requirements. Information is collected through a questionnaire administered to experts in construction licensing, including architects, civil engineers, construction lawyers, construction firms, utility service providers and public officials who deal with building regulations, including approvals, permit issuance and inspections. The ranking of economies on the ease of dealing with construction permits is determined by sorting their distance to frontier scores for dealing with construction permits. These scores are the simple average of the distance to frontier scores for each of the component indicators. The distance to frontier score, presented in Column (1) of

Table 2.19. Dealing with Construction Permits in MENA, 2016

Economy	Dealing with Construction Permits DTF (1)	Dealing with Construction Permits rank (2)	Procedures (Number) (3)	Time (Days) (4)	Cost (% of Warehouse Value) (5)	Building Quality Control Index (0–15) (6)
Algeria	59	146	19	146	8	10
Bahrain	74	47	11	174	4	12
Cyprus	64	120	8	507	1	11
Djibouti	68	84	17	111	5	11
Egypt	71	66	19	172	2	14
Iran	78	25	15	99	2	13
Iraq	68	93	11	167	0	6
Israel	72	65	15	209	1	13
Jordan	66	110	15	62	12	11
Kuwait	62	129	23	236	1	13
Lebanon	60	142	19	249	6	13
Morocco	80	17	13	89	4	13
Oman	72	60	14	172	1	11
Qatar	79	19	16	58	2	12
SA	76	38	17	90	2	12
Tunisia	67	95	18	96	6	11
Turkey	67	96	18	103	4	10
UAE	86	2	14	51	2	15
OECD	75	46	13	155	2	11

Source: World Bank, Doing Business project (http://www.doingbusiness.org/).

Table 2.19, helps assess the absolute level of regulatory performance over time. It measures the distance of each economy to the "frontier," which represents the best performance observed on each of the indicators across all economies in the *Doing Business*. An economy's distance to frontier is reflected on a scale from 0 to 100, where 0 represents the lowest performance and 100 represents the frontier. For example, a score of 59 for Algeria in 2016 means that it was 41 percentage points away from the frontier constructed from the best performances across all economies and across time. Within MENA, the top score belongs to the UAE, which in 2016 was 14 points away from the best performers. The UAE made dealing with construction permits easier by implementing risk-based inspections and streamlining the final joint inspection with the process of obtaining a completion certificate. In terms of country ranking for MENA the UAE, post reforms, ranks at the top of the list.

The average number of procedures for MENA was well above the OECD norm of 13. Bahrain and Cyprus have the smallest number of procedures — 11 and 8, respectively, exceeding the OECD standard. Despite the decline in procedures, the time involved, in terms of days, was very substantial. For Bahrain it is 174 days and for Cyprus it is 507 days. For the OECD, the 13 procedures translated to 155 days. For Israel the 15 procedures translated to 209 days as compared to Jordan whose 15 procedures translated to 62 days. The UAE translated its 14 procedures to 51 days.

These procedures and time involved translate to financial cost. For the OECD this bureaucratic process costs 2 percent of the value of the project. For most of the MENA countries, with the exception of Cyprus, Israel, Kuwait and Oman, these costs were substantially higher. The most expensive country in the permitting business was Jordan with 12 percent of the project value.

The building quality control index, presented in the Column (6) in Table 2.19 is the sum of the scores on the quality of building regulations, quality control before construction, quality control during construction, quality control after construction, liability and insurance regimes and professional certifications indices. The index ranges from 0 to 15, with higher values indicating better quality control and safety mechanisms in the construction regulatory system. The OECD average is 12. Most of the MENA countries were in the OECD target standard. The only outlier was Iraq with a score of 6.

Economic activity depends on a system of transparent and legally binding transfers of land and other property. When property rights are poorly defined and/or poorly administered, this can prevent the transfer of assets to more productive uses or to be used as collateral for other investments. De Soto (2000) describes such land as "dead capital," assets whose use is limited or that cannot be used as collateral. *Doing Business* (2018) records the full sequence of procedures necessary for a business (the buyer) to purchase a property from another business (the seller) and to transfer the property title to the buyer's name so that the buyer can use the property for expanding its business, use the property as collateral in taking new loans or, if necessary, sell the property to another business. It also measures the time and cost to complete each of these procedures. *Doing Business* (2018) also measures the quality of the land administration system in each economy. The quality of land administration index has five dimensions: reliability of infrastructure, transparency of information, geographic coverage, land dispute resolution and equal access to property rights.

Column (1) of Table 2.20 ranks the MENA economies in terms of its distance to the optimal frontier score with respect to property registration and transfer. Column (2) presents the individual countries' ranking *vis-à-vis* the

Table 2.20. Registering Property in MENA, 2016

Economy	Registering Property DTF (1)	Registering Property Rank (2)	Procedures (Number) (3)	Time (Days) (4)	Cost (% of Property Value) (5)	Quality of the Land Administration Index (0–30) (6)
Algeria	44	163	10	55	7	7
Bahrain	81	25	2	31	2	18
Cyprus	63	92	7	9	10	23
Djibouti	43	168	6	39	13	5
Egypt	56	119	8	75	1	7
Iran	64	87	7	12	6	15
Iraq	60	101	5	51	6	11
Israel	53	130	6	81	8	14
Jordan	66	72	6	17	9	23
Kuwait	68	70	9	35	1	17
Lebanon	60	102	8	34	6	16
Morocco	64	86	6	22	6	16
Oman	74	54	2	16	5	13
Qatar	81	26	7	13	0	25
SA	81	24	2	2	0	10
Tunisia	63	93	4	39	6	11
Turkey	75	46	7	7	3	22
UAE	90	10	2	2	0	21
Yemen	65	82	6	19	2	7
OECD	77	44	5	22	4	23

Source: World Bank, Doing Business project (http://www.doingbusiness.org/).

190-country total. At the top of the list is the UAE with a score of 90, making it number 10 in the world ranking. Not far behind are Saudi Arabia, Bahrain and Qatar, which rank 24, 25 and 26. Column (3) presents the number of procedures that are legally or in practice required for registering property. If a procedure can be accelerated legally for an additional cost, the fastest procedure is chosen if that option is more beneficial to the economy's distance to frontier score and if is used by most of property owners. Although the buyer may use lawyers or other professionals where necessary in the registration process, it is assumed that the buyer does not employ an outside facilitator in the registration process unless legally or in practice required to do so. This includes the required steps to check encumbrances, obtain clearance certificates and prepare deed and transfer titles so that the property can be occupied, sold or used as collateral. Saudi Arabia, the UAE and Bahrain have the lowest barriers to the transfer of property within MENA.

Column (4) measures the median duration that property lawyers, notaries or registry officials indicate is necessary to complete a procedure. It is assumed that the minimum time required for each procedure is one day, except for procedures that can be fully completed online, for which the time required is recorded as half a day. Although procedures may take place simultaneously, they cannot start on the same day, again apart from procedures that can be fully completed online. It is assumed that the buyer does not waste time and commits to completing each remaining procedure without delay. If a procedure can be accelerated for an additional cost, the fastest legal procedure available and used by most of property owners is chosen. If procedures can be undertaken simultaneously, it is assumed that they are. It is assumed that the parties involved are aware of all requirements and their sequence from the beginning. Time spent on gathering information is not considered. If time estimates differ among sources, the median reported value is used by *Doing Business* (2018). Saudi Arabia and the UAE have the shortest number of days to record property. The average for the OECD is 22 days, which on the low end for most MENA economies.

Cost recorded as a percentage of the property value, assumed to be equivalent to 50 times income per capita is presented in the 5th Column. Only official costs required by law are recorded, including fees, transfer taxes, stamp duties and any other payment to the property registry, notaries, public agencies or lawyers. Other taxes, such as capital gains tax or value added tax, are excluded from the cost measure. Both costs borne by the buyer and the seller are included. If cost estimates differ among sources, the median reported value is used. The OECD average cost is 4 percent of the property value. UAE, Saudi Arabia, Qatar, Bahrain, Egypt and Kuwait have costs far below the OECD average. An interesting anomaly is the case of Israel where the total number of procedures is 6, but the number of days to execute the property registration is 81 days at a total cost of 8 percent of the value of the property. This is either a reflection of the complexity of the recording process, given all the various prior empires that controlled land in the area, or of a very inefficient bureaucracy.

The quality of land administration index, which is the 6th Column in Table 2.20, is composed of five other indices from *Doing Business* (2018): the reliability of infrastructure, transparency of information, geographic coverage, land dispute resolution and equal access to property rights. Data are collected for each economy's largest business city. The index ranges from 0 to 30, with higher values indicating better quality of the land administration system. The OECD average in 2017 is 23. Within MENA, Cyprus,

Qatar, Turkey and Jordan are on par with the OECD average. The balance of MENA economies are below that average. The lowest score of 7 is shared by Algeria, Egypt and Yemen.

Along with a clear and transparent property registration system, the ability of small and medium-size firms to access the credit market is highly reliant on the availability of objective credit information and on a registry of assets which could be used as collateral. Lenders must assess not only the viability of a project in search of funding but also the creditworthiness of potential future borrowers. When this is combined with a strong legal system assuring creditors' rights, it facilitates the flow of credit to viable projects. It is a well-established principle that in the absence of market failure, the economies that provide effective collateral laws and credit registries are objective and well-functioning banks are more likely to extend loans. By way of contrast, questionable enforcement rules dependent on political connections and inefficient regulations of contractual enforcement induce informal relationships based on family ties, previous transactions or criminal connections.

Doing Business (2018) measures the legal rights of borrowers and lenders with respect to secured transactions through one set of indicators and the reporting of credit information through another. The first set of indicators, presented in Table 2.21, measures whether certain features that facilitate lending exist within the applicable collateral and bankruptcy laws. The second set measures the coverage, scope and accessibility of credit information available through credit reporting service providers such as credit bureaus or credit registries. The ranking of economies on the ease of getting credit is determined by sorting their distance to frontier scores for getting credit. These scores are the distance to frontier score for the sum of the strength of legal rights index and the depth of credit information index.

The first two columns in Table 2.21 measure an economy's relative position in the provision of credit. The OECD score is 63 in the distance to frontier and 62 in the 190-country ranking. Within MENA, the bottom of the list is held by Iraq, Yemen, Djibouti and Algeria. At the top of the list is Israel, followed by Cyprus, Turkey and the UAE. The balance of the countries is ranked above 100.

The data on the legal rights of borrowers and lenders which are presented in the last 4 Columns of Table 2.21, are gathered by *Doing Business* (2018) through a questionnaire administered to financial lawyers and verified through analysis of laws and regulations as well as public sources of information on collateral and bankruptcy laws. Questionnaire responses are

Table 2.21. Ease of Getting Credit in MENA, 2016

Economy	Getting Credit DTF (1)	Getting Credit Rank (2)	Strength of Legal Rights Index (0–12) (3)	Depth of Credit Information Index (0–8) (4)	Credit Registry Coverage (% of Adults) (5)	Credit Bureau Coverage (% of Adults) (6)
Algeria	10	177	2	0	3	0
Bahrain	45	105	1	8	0	28
Cyprus	60	68	7	5	0	73
Djibouti	5	183	1	0	0	0
Egypt	50	90	2	8	8	25
Iran	50	90	2	8	55	56
Iraq	0	186	0	0	1	0
Israel	65	55	6	7	0	71
Jordan	25	159	0	5	2	15
Kuwait	35	133	1	6	15	31
Lebanon	40	122	2	6	23	0
Morocco	45	105	2	7	0	25
Oman	35	133	1	6	27	0
Qatar	35	133	1	6	28	0
SA	50	90	2	8	0	50
Tunisia	45	105	3	6	27	0
Turkey	55	77	4	7	80	0
UAE	50	90	2	8	9	55
Yemen	0	186	0	0	1	0
OECD	63	62	6	7	18	64

Source: World Bank, Doing Business project (http://www.doingbusiness.org/).

verified through several rounds of follow-up communication with respondents as well as by contacting third parties and consulting public sources. The questionnaire data are confirmed through teleconference calls or on-site visits in all economies. The strength of legal rights index measures the degree to which collateral and bankruptcy laws protect the rights of borrowers and lenders and thus facilitate lending. This index measures the strength of legal rights focuses on the regulations on non-possessory security interests in movable property. The fourth index focuses on the depth of credit information available to creditors. The depth of credit information index measures rules and practices affecting the coverage, scope and accessibility of credit information available through either a credit bureau or a credit registry. *Doing Business* (2018) assigns a score of 1 for each of the following eight features of the credit bureau or credit registry (or both): (a) Data on firms and individuals are distributed; (b) Both positive credit information (for example, original loan amounts, outstanding loan amounts and a pattern of on-time repayments) and negative information (for example, late payments and the number and amount of defaults) are distributed; (c) Data from retailers or utility companies are distributed in addition to data from financial institutions; (d) At least 2 years of historical data are distributed. Credit bureaus and registries that erase data on defaults as soon as they are repaid or distribute negative information more than 10 years after defaults are repaid receive a score of 0 for this component; (e) Data on loan amounts below 1 percent of income per capita are distributed; (f) By law, borrowers have the right to access their data in the largest credit bureau or registry in the economy. Credit bureaus and registries that charge more than 1 percent of income per capita for borrowers to inspect their data receive a score of 0 for this component; (g) Banks and other financial institutions have online access to the credit information (for example, through a web interface, a system-to-system connection or both); (h) Bureau or registry credit scores are offered as a value-added service to help banks and other financial institutions assess the creditworthiness of borrowers. The index ranges from 0 to 8, with higher values indicating the availability of more credit information, from either a credit bureau or a credit registry, to facilitate lending decisions.

It should not be surprising that Israel in 2016 ranks number 6 (identical to the OECD) in terms of the strength of the legal rights index. Likewise, data on the depth of credit information in Israel and in the OECD was ranked as 7 on a 0-8 index scale. Most of the MENA countries had an index in the same range. The negative outliers in 2016 included Algeria, Djibouti, Iraq and Yemen who had indexes at 0. The key information variable was access to either credit registry or credit bureau data on borrowers. Within the OECD, 64 percent of adults are covered by credit bureaus and 18 percent by credit registries. In the case of Israel, credit bureaus provide information on 71 percent of the adult population, well within the OECD norm. The overall MENA average was 5–12 percent, far below the OECD norm. The improvement in credit reporting by 2016 was made in the UAE, Saudi Arabia, and Iran. These countries had credit bureau coverage equal to, or above, 50 percent of adults.

Djankov *et al.* (2003, 2008) raise a whole series of issues concerning existing issues of corporate governance affecting investor confidence, particularly in developing economies where corporate ownership tends to be highly concentrated. The most common problems concern related-party transactions — those between company insiders and other companies they control. These include sales of goods or services to the company at inflated prices, or purchases from it at excessively low prices.

Investors typically look for transparency in such corporate dealings, accountability from company directors for improper corporate practices, and ability to take part in the major decisions of the company. If a country's laws do not provide these, investors may be reluctant to invest, except to become the controlling shareholder.

Doing Business (2018) measures the protection of minority investors from conflicts of interest and shareholders' rights in corporate governance. The data come from a questionnaire administered to corporate and securities lawyers and are based on securities regulations, company laws, civil procedure codes and court rules of evidence. The ranking of economies on the strength of minority investor protections is determined by sorting their distance to frontier (DTF) scores for protecting minority investors. These scores are the simple average of the distance to frontier scores for the extent of conflict of interest regulation index and the extent of shareholder governance index. Columns (1) and (2) in Table 2.22 present the DTF index and index ranked. The OECD average DTF index is 64, which translates to a departure from the frontier by 36 percent and ranking of the index of 47 out of 190. The overall average index rank for MENA is 96 and the DTF is 52. The countries within MENA with the best record for protecting minority investor rights in 2016 are the UAE and Saudi Arabia, both ranked at 10 and Israel ranked at 16. The worst performers for protecting minority investor rights in 2016 were Qatar ranked at 177, Algeria and Iran, both ranked at 170. In the case of Lebanon, which was historically considered a reasonably safe place to invest, the DTF score was 42 and the index was raked 138. These results go a long way in explaining why it is so risky to invest in certain parts of MENA.

Column (3) in Table 2.22 presents the extent of conflict of interest regulation index. This index measures the protection of shareholders against directors' misuse of corporate assets for personal gain by distinguishing three dimensions of regulation that address conflicts of interest: transparency of related-party transactions, shareholders' ability to sue and hold directors liable for self-dealing and access to evidence and allocation of legal expenses in shareholder litigation. In order to make the data comparable across economies, *Doing Business* (2018) has made several assumptions about the business and the transaction that are used. It has been assumed that the corporation is a publicly traded corporation listed on the economy's most important stock exchange. If no reputable exchange is available,

Table 2.22. Protecting Minority Investors in MENA, 2016

Economy	Protecting Minority Investors DTF (1)	Protecting Minority Investors Rank (2)	Extent of Conflict of Interest Regulation Index (0–10) (3)	Extent of Shareholder Governance Index (0–10) (4)
Algeria	33	170	3	3
Bahrain	50	108	5	5
Cyprus	63	43	6	6
Djibouti	52	96	6	5
Egypt	55	81	5	6
Iran	33	170	4	3
Iraq	47	124	5	5
Israel	73	16	8	6
Jordan	40	146	3	5
Kuwait	55	81	6	5
Lebanon	42	138	5	3
Morocco	58	62	6	6
Oman	47	124	5	4
Qatar	27	177	2	3
SA	75	10	7	8
Tunisia	48	119	5	4
Turkey	72	20	7	8
UAE	75	10	8	7
Yemen	43	132	4	4
OECD	64	47	6	6

Source: World Bank, Doing Business project (http://www.doingbusiness.org/).

it is assumed that the corporation is a large private company with multiple shareholders. The corporate governance structure assumed is one where the corporation has a board of directors and a chief executive officer who may legally act on the firm's behalf. Furthermore, it is assumed that the corporation has a supervisory board on which 60 percent of the shareholder-elected members have been appointed by the controlling shareholder who is also a member of the board of directors. The index ranges from 0 to 10, with higher values indicating stronger conflict of interest regulation.

The OECD score is 6 for this index. The average conflict of interest regulation index for MENA is 5. On the low end of the spectrum, we have Qatar with an index of 2 and Algeria and Jordan with a score of 3 for both. On the high end of the distribution, we have Israel and the UAE with an index score of 8, followed by Saudi Arabia with a score of 7. Column (4) reports the index of the extent of shareholder governance. This index is the average of the extent of shareholder rights index, the extent of ownership and control index and the extent of corporate transparency index. The index ranges from 0 to 10, with higher values indicating stronger rights of shareholders in corporate governance. For the OECD the score is 6 for this index. The average extent of shareholder governance index for MENA is 5. On the low end of the spectrum we have Algeria, Iran, Lebanon and Qatar with an index of 3. On the high end of the distribution we have Turkey, Saudi Arabia, the UAE and Israel and with an index score above the OECD norm of 6.

As noted in Djankov *et al.* (2003, 2008), economies that rank high on the strength of investor protection index protect minority investors from self-dealing through more disclosure, clear duties for directors and easy access to corporate information.

The need for tax revenue to fund public sector services is not new. Equally true is the business sector acceptance of the benefits that the public sector provides in terms of infrastructure, education, courts, public record keeping, and regulations. The issue across both developed and developing countries is the manner by which taxes are levied and upon whom. As always, the primary concern is tax equity and the impact of an inefficient tax on firm and consumer behavior. From the point of view of the tax authorities, the key concern is how to ensure public compliance as opposed to a move to the informal sector (World Economic Forum, 2007, 2008).

In Table 2.23 we present the *Doing Business* (2018) data on taxes and mandatory contributions that a medium-size company must pay or withhold in a given year, as well as measures the administrative burden in paying taxes and contributions. The most recent round of data collection by *Doing Business* covers taxes paid for the calendar year 2016. This data has been expanded relative to prior years to better understand the overall tax environment in an economy. It now includes data on post-filing processes, VAT refunds and tax audits. The data shows what drives the differences in the overall tax compliance cost across economies.

Doing Business (2018) records the taxes and mandatory contributions that a medium-size company must pay in a given year as well as the administrative burden of paying taxes and contributions and complying with post filing procedures. Taxes and contributions measured include the profit or corporate income tax, social contributions and labor taxes paid by the employer, property taxes, property transfer taxes, dividend tax, capital gains tax, financial transactions tax, waste collection taxes, vehicle and road taxes and any other small taxes or fees.

Table 2.23. Paying Taxes in MENA, 2016

Economy	Paying Taxes DTF (1)	Paying Taxes Rank (2)	Payments (Number Per Year) (3)	Time (Hours Per Year) (4)	Total Tax and Contribution Rate (% of Profit) (5)	Postfiling Index (0–100) (6)
Algeria	54	157	27	265	66	50
Bahrain	94	5	14	29	14	—
Cyprus	81	44	28	127	23	76
Djibouti	69	108	35	76	38	50
Egypt	51	167	29	392	45	27
Iran	57	150	20	344	45	27
Iraq	64	129	15	312	31	21
Israel	70	99	33	235	27	61
Jordan	71	97	25	129	28	35
Kuwait	92	6	12	98	13	—
Lebanon	68	113	20	181	30	27
Morocco	86	25	6	155	50	99
Oman	91	11	15	68	24	85
Qatar	99	1	4	41	11	—
SA	75	76	3	47	16	0
Tunisia	60	140	9	145	64	23
Turkey	72	88	11	216	41	50
UAE	99	1	4	12	16	—
Yemen	74	80	44	248	27	96
OECD	83	40	11	161	40	83

Source: World Bank, Doing Business project (http://www.doingbusiness.org/).

The ranking of economies on the ease of paying taxes is determined by sorting their distance to frontier scores for paying taxes. These scores are the simple average of the distance to frontier scores for each of the component indicators, with a threshold and a nonlinear transformation applied to one of the component indicators, the total tax and contribution rate. The threshold is defined as the total tax and contribution rate at the 15th percentile of the overall distribution of the total tax rate indicator for all years included in the analysis up to and including *Doing Business* (2018). The threshold is set at 26.1 percent.

The threshold is not based on any economic theory of an "optimal tax rate" that minimizes distortions or maximizes efficiency in an economy's overall tax system. Instead, it is mainly empirical in nature, set at the lower end of the distribution of tax rates levied on medium-size enterprises in the manufacturing sector as observed through the paying taxes indicators. *Doing Business* (2018) measures all taxes and contributions that are government mandated and that apply to the standardized business and have an impact in its financial statements. In doing so, *Doing Business* (2018) goes beyond the traditional definition of a tax. As defined for the purposes of government national accounts, taxes include only compulsory, unrequited payments to general government. *Doing Business* (2018) departs from this definition because it measures imposed charges that affect business accounts, not government accounts. One main difference relates to labor contributions. The *Doing Business* (2018) measurement includes government-mandated contributions paid by the employer to a requited private pension fund or workers' insurance fund.

For MENA, Column (1) presents paying taxes relative to the frontier and Column (2) ranks the countries. Under this rubric, Qatar, UAE rank number 1 with an index of 99 percent relative to DTF. Following this lead, we have Bahrain and Kuwait with a rank of 5 and 6, with a corresponding DTF score of 94 and 92, respectively. Oman comes in with rank of 11 and DTF rank of 91. The average for the OECD is a rank of 40 with a DTF score of 83. At the bottom of the ranking scale are Egypt, Algeria and Iran with a rank of 167, 157, 150 and a DTF score of 51, 54 and 57, respectively.

The tax payments indicator contained in Column (3) reflects the total number of taxes and contributions paid, the method of payment, the frequency of payment, the frequency of filing and the number of agencies involved for the standardized case study company during the second year of operation. It includes taxes withheld by the company, such as sales tax, VAT and employee-borne labor taxes. These taxes are traditionally collected by the company from the consumer or employee on behalf of the tax agencies. Although they do not affect the income statements of the company, they add to the administrative burden of complying with the tax system and so are included in the tax payments measure.

For MENA the number of payments varies substantially from a low 3 for Saudi Arabia to 4 for Yemen. The OECD standard is 11. On the low end in addition to Saudi Arabia, the UAE and Qatar have 4 payments, and Morocco has 6 payments. Overall, the tax burden of complying with a burdensome tax system is found within MENA if the number of tax payments goes beyond 12.

Column (4) presents the additional burden of the tax system, e.g. the "time" indicator which measures the time taken to prepare, file and pay three major types of taxes and contributions: the corporate income tax, value added or sales tax, and labor taxes, including payroll taxes and social contributions. Preparation time includes the time to collect all information necessary to compute the tax payable and to calculate the amount payable.

If separate accounting books must be kept for tax purposes — or separate calculations made — the time associated with these processes is included. Filing time includes the time to complete all necessary tax return forms and file the relevant returns at the tax authority. Payment time considers the hours needed to make the payment online or in person. Where taxes and contributions are paid in person, the time includes delays while waiting.

For MENA the highest time cost is borne by businesses operating in Egypt with 392 hours per year, Iran with 344 hours per year, Iraq with 312 hours per year, Yemen with 248 hours per year, Israel with 235 hours per year, and Turkey with 216 hours per year. The OECD standard is 161 hours per year. On the low end we have the UAE with 12 hours per year, Qatar with 41 hours per year, and Saudi Arabia with 47 hours per year. Overall, the tax burden of complying with a burdensome tax system in terms of time devoted to complying with the local tax laws is very large and not business friendly.

Column (5) presents the total tax and contribution rate which measures the amount of taxes and mandatory contributions borne by the business in the second year of operation, expressed as a share of commercial profit. The total amount of taxes and contributions borne is the sum of all the different taxes and contributions payable after accounting for allowable deductions and exemptions. The taxes withheld or collected by the company and remitted to the tax authorities but not borne by the company are excluded. The taxes included can be divided into five categories: profit or corporate income tax, social contributions and labor taxes paid by the employer, property taxes, turnover taxes and other taxes, such as municipal fees and vehicle taxes.

The total tax and contribution rate is designed to provide a comprehensive measure of the cost of all the taxes a business bears. It differs from the statutory tax rate, which merely provides the factor to be applied to the tax base. In computing the total tax and contribution rate, *Doing Business* (2018) uses the actual tax or contribution payable, divided by commercial profit.

Commercial profit is essentially net profit before all taxes and contributions borne. It differs from the conventional profit before tax, reported in financial statements. In computing profit before tax, many of the taxes borne by a firm are deductible. In computing commercial profit, these taxes are not deductible. Commercial profit therefore presents a clear picture of the actual profit of a business before any of the taxes it bears during the fiscal year.

Commercial profit is computed as sales minus cost of goods sold, minus gross salaries, minus administrative expenses, minus other expenses, minus provisions, plus capital gains minus interest expense, plus interest income and minus commercial depreciation. To compute the commercial depreciation, a straight-line depreciation method is applied, with the following rates: 0 percent for the land, 5 percent for the building, 10 percent for the machinery, 33 percent for the computers, 20 percent for the office equipment, 20 percent for the truck and 10 percent for business development expenses. Commercial profit amounts to 59.4 times income per capita.

For the OECD the total tax and contribution rate in 2016 was 40 percent. Most of the MENA countries were below that rate. On the low end we have Qatar with a 11 percent, Kuwait with 13 percent, Bahrain with 14 percent, Saudi Arabia with 16 percent, and the UAE with 16 percent. In the mid range we have Cyprus with 23 percent, Oman with 24 percent, Israel and Yemen with 27 percent and Jordan with 28 percent.

Column (6) presents the post filing index. It is based on four components — time to comply with VAT refund, time to obtain VAT refund, time to comply with corporate income tax audit and time to complete a corporate income tax audit. If both VAT and corporate income tax apply, the post filing index is the simple average of the distance to frontier scores for each of the four components. If only VAT or corporate income tax applies, the post filing index is the simple average of the scores for only the two components pertaining to the applicable tax. If neither VAT nor corporate income tax applies, the post filing index is not included in the ranking of the ease of paying taxes.

For the OECD the post filing index is 83. For Morocco it is 99 percent. For Yemen the index is 96. For Oman it is 85. For Cyprus the index is 76. For Israel the index is 61. For the balance of MENA it is below the OECD standard.

It is a well-understood fact in international economics that eliminating impediments at the border facilitates trade, increases domestic efficiency and leads to an expansion in the export sector. The cost of red tape and burdensome procedural requirements to export and import serve as taxes on the firms. Many economies, while promising to lower tariff barriers at their borders, resort to cumbersome trade procedures, long delays and high storage and other transaction costs at their ports as a subtle alternative tax.

In Table 2.24 we present the *Doing Business* (2018) data on the time and cost associated with the logistical process of exporting and importing goods. *Doing Business* (2018) measures the time and cost (excluding tariffs)

Table 2.24. Cost of Trading Across Borders in MENA, 2016

Economy	Trading Across Borders DTF (1)	Trading Across Borders Rank (2)	Time to Export: Border Compliance (Hours) (3)	Cost to Export: Border Compliance (USD) (4)	Time to Export: Documentary Compliance (Hours) (5)	Cost to Export: Documentary Compliance (USD) (6)	Time to Import: Border Compliance (Hours) (7)	Cost to Import: Border Compliance (USD) (8)	Time to Import: Documentary Compliance (Hours) (9)	Cost to Import: Documentary Compliance (USD) (10)
Algeria	24	181	118	593	149	374	327	466	249	400
Bahrain	76	78	71	47	24	100	54	397	84	130
Cyprus	88	45	18	300	2	50	15	335	2	50
Djibouti	52	159	109	944	72	95	78	1209	50	100
Egypt	42	170	48	258	88	100	240	554	265	1000
Iran	46	166	101	565	120	125	141	660	192	197
Iraq	25	179	85	1118	504	1800	131	644	176	500
Israel	83	60	36	150	13	73	64	307	44	70
Jordan	86	53	38	131	6	16	79	181	55	30
Kuwait	54	154	96	602	72	191	89	491	96	332
Lebanon	60	140	96	410	48	100	180	695	72	135
Morocco	81	65	19	156	26	107	106	228	26	116
Oman	79	72	52	261	7	107	70	394	7	124
Qatar	72	90	25	382	10	150	48	558	72	290
SA	50	161	69	363	81	105	228	779	122	390
Syria	30	176	84	1113	48	725	141	828	149	742
Tunisia	71	96	50	469	3	200	80	596	27	144
Turkey	80	71	16	376	5	87	41	655	11	142
UAE	72	91	27	462	6	178	54	678	12	283
OECD	94	25	13	150	2	35	9	112	4	26

Source: World Bank, Doing Business project (http://www.doingbusiness.org/).

associated with three sets of procedures — documentary compliance, border compliance and domestic transport — within the overall process of exporting or importing a shipment of goods. The ranking of economies in Column (1) on the ease of trading across borders is determined by sorting their distance to frontier (DTF) scores for trading across borders. These scores are the simple average of the distance to frontier scores for the time and cost for documentary compliance and border compliance to export and import. The country-specific ranking out of 190 countries is presented in Column (2). For the OECD the DTF ranking in 2016 is 94 with a country ranking of 25. The average MENA DTF score was 62 and the average rank was 116 out of 190. The highest DTF ranking within MENA was experienced in Cyprus, Israel, Jordan, Morocco and Turkey. The highest rank within MENA for Column (2) was experienced in Cyprus, Jordan, Israel and Morocco. The worst performance was in Algeria, Syria, Iraq, Saudi Arabia, Egypt, Iran, Kuwait, and Lebanon.

Column (3) presents data on the time, measured in hours, for export processing at the border. For the OECD the time allocated to this activity is 13 hours. For MENA, on average, it is 61 hours. Countries below this average include Cyprus, Turkey, Morocco, Qatar, Israel, Jordan, Oman and the UAE. The balance within MENA consume much more time. In Algeria it takes 118 hours to process exports at the border. In Column (4) these times are translated into costs in US dollars. Insurance cost and informal payments for which no receipt is issued are excluded from the costs recorded. For the OECD the cost at the border for exports is \$150. The average for MENA is \$458. The MENA countries who experience the OECD level of border costs include Israel with \$150 and Jordan with \$131. The costs for the balance of countries within MENA are substantially higher, with Iraq and Syria topping the list at \$1,118 and \$1,113, respectively.

Documentary compliance captures the time and cost associated with compliance with the documentary requirements of all government agencies of the origin economy, the destination economy and any transit economies. The time and cost for documentary compliance include the time and cost for obtaining documents (such as time spent to get the document issued and stamped); preparing documents (such as time spent gathering information to complete the customs declaration or certificate of origin); processing documents (such as time spent waiting for the relevant authority to issue a phytosanitary certificate); presenting documents (such as time spent showing a port terminal receipt to port authorities); and submitting documents (such as time spent submitting a customs declaration to the customs agency in person or electronically).

Documentary compliance for exports in terms hours is presented in Column (5) and in US dollars in Column (6). The OECD cost in terms of hours is 2 with a financial cost of $35. For the MENA the average costs in hours is 68 which translates to an average financial cost of $246. On the low end of time consumption, we have Cyprus, Tunisia, Turkey, the UAE, Jordan, Oman, and Israel. Iraq tops the list of the largest time cost of 504 hours to export at a cost of $1,800.

Columns (7) and (8) present data on border compliance in terms of time and dollar cost. These refers to compliance with the economy's customs regulations and with regulations relating to other inspections that are mandatory in order for the shipment to cross the economy's border, as well as the time and cost for handling that takes place at its port or border. The time and cost for this segment include time and cost for customs clearance and inspection procedures conducted by other agencies. For example, the time and cost for conducting a phytosanitary inspection would be included here.

The computation of border compliance time and cost depends on where the border compliance procedures take place, who requires and conducts the procedures and what is the probability that inspections will be conducted. If all customs clearance and other inspections take place at the port or border at the same time, the time estimate for border compliance takes this simultaneity into account. The average for the OECD is 9 hours for border compliance translated to US dollars to be $116. For the MENA countries the average is 114 hours at a cost of $561. Those counties at the low end of the cost structure include Cyprus, Turkey, the UAE, Bahrain and Israel. The great majority of countries within MENA are above the MENA average of 114 hours and $561. The highest border compliance cost is borne in Egypt with 240 hours.

Documentary compliance for imports in terms hours is presented in Column (9) and in US dollars in Column (10). The OECD cost in terms of hours is 4 with a financial cost of $26. For the MENA the average costs in hours is 90 which translates to an average financial cost of $272. On the low end of time consumption, we have Cyprus, Oman, Tunisia, Turkey, the UAE, Jordan and Israel. Egypt tops the list of the largest time cost of 265 hours to import at a cost of $1,000.

Overall, the cost of trading across borders in MENA in 2016 is substantially higher than the OECD standard and the Gulf states, Cyprus and Israel.

Djankov *et al.* (2003) reinforce an old paradigm where it is taken for granted that in developed countries, a system of courts is responsible for enforcing contracts between debtors and creditors, and between suppliers and customers, as opposed to many third world countries where the courts increase transaction costs because they are slow, inefficient and oftentimes corrupt. If you hypothesize that the performance of courts is determined by how the law regulates their operations, or via procedural formalism, then developing country courts are found to be at the lower end of the performance scale. Furthermore, they find significant inefficiencies in terms of the expected duration of dispute resolution, which is often extraordinarily high. This suggests that courts in developing countries are not an attractive venue for resolving disputes. As one major Egyptian entrepreneur confirmed in an interview with the author, "he paid his legal staff a high salary in order to keep his firm out of the Egyptian courts," primarily because of the high transaction costs involved and the level of uncertainty with respect to outcome, regardless of the merits of the case.

Doing Business (2018) measures the time and cost for resolving a commercial dispute through a local first-instance court and the quality of judicial processes index, evaluating whether each economy has adopted a series of good practices that promote quality and efficiency in the court system. The data are collected through study of the codes of civil procedure and other court regulations as well as questionnaires completed by local litigation lawyers and judges. The ranking of economies on the ease of enforcing contracts is determined by sorting their distance to frontier scores for enforcing contracts. These scores are the simple average of the distance to frontier scores for each of the component indicators.

Column (1) and (2) of Table 2.25 present the ranking of enforcing contracts in terms of DTF and rank order. The average OECD DTF score is 67, which translates to shortfall of 33 percent from the optimal legal enforcement. This translates to a country ranking of 47. For the MENA the average, DTF score is 55 and the average country rank is 104. Most of the MENA countries around have a DTF score around the mean. Djibouti is an outlier at 35 on one side of the distribution, and UAE with a DTF score of 74 on the other side of the distribution.

Time in terms of days for contract enforcement is presented in Column (3). Time counted from the moment that one of the parties decides to file the lawsuit in court. This includes both the days when actions take place and the waiting periods in between. The average duration of the following three different stages of dispute resolution is recorded: (i) filing and

Table 2.25. Enforcing Contracts in MENA, 2016

Economy	Enforcing Contracts DTF (1)	Enforcing Contracts Rank (2)	Time (Days) (3)	Cost (% of Claim Value) (4)	Quality of Judicial Processes Index (0–18) (5)
Algeria	55	103	630	20	6
Bahrain	55	111	635	15	4
Cyprus	49	138	1100	16	8
Djibouti	35	175	1025	34	3
Egypt	43	160	1010	26	6
Iran	59	80	505	17	5
Iraq	48	144	520	28	2
Israel	58	92	975	25	13
Jordan	54	118	642	31	7
Kuwait	60	73	566	19	7
Lebanon	50	134	721	31	6
Morocco	62	57	510	27	9
Oman	60	67	598	15	7
Qatar	53	123	570	22	4
SA	59	83	575	28	8
Syria	43	161	872	29	4
Tunisia	59	76	565	22	7
Turkey	69	30	580	25	13
UAE	74	12	445	21	13
Yemen	49	140	645	30	4
OECD	67	47	578	22	11

Source: World Bank, Doing Business project (http://www.doingbusiness.org/).

service; (ii) trial and judgment; and (iii) enforcement. Time is recorded in practice, regardless of time limits set by law if such time limits are not respected in the majority of cases.

The OECD average is 578 days. The average for MENA is 684 days. The outliers in MENA with the longest time are in Cyprus with 1,100 days, Djibouti with 1,025 days, Egypt with 1,010 days and Israel with 975 days.

The cost of contract enforcement, measured as a percent of the value of the claim, is presented in Column (4). The OECD average cost is 22 percent of the value of the claim. For the MENA the average cost is 24 percent of the value of the claim, which is not very different from the OECD average. The costliest counties to litigate are in Djibouti, Jordan and Lebanon.

The quality of judicial processes index presented in Column (5) measures whether each economy has adopted a series of good practices in its court system in four areas: court structure and proceedings, case management, court automation and alternative dispute resolution. The index ranges from 0 to 18. The OECD average is 11. The MENA average is 7. Within MENA the best judicial process is in Israel, Turkey and the UAE. The worst judicial process is found in Iraq and Djibouti.

Doing Business (2018) studies the time, cost and outcome of insolvency proceedings involving domestic entities as well as the strength of the legal framework applicable to judicial liquidation and reorganization proceedings. The data for the resolving insolvency indicators are derived from questionnaire responses by local insolvency practitioners and verified through a study of laws and regulations as well as public information on insolvency systems. The ranking of economies on the ease of resolving insolvency is determined by sorting their distance to frontier scores for resolving insolvency. These scores are the simple average of the distance to frontier (DTF) scores for the recovery rate and the strength of insolvency framework index.

Column (1) and (2) in Table 2.26 present the DTF scores and the country ranking. For the OECD DTF score is 76 and the country ranking is 24. For MENA the average, DTF score is 38 with a county average of 112. On the positive side of the distribution we have Cyprus with a 78 DTF score and 21 country ranking. This is followed by Israel with a DTF score of 73 and a country ranking of 29. The balance of MENA countries is at the other side of the distribution (Iran, Iraq and Syria and Saudi Arabia).

The recovery rate presented in Columns (3), (4) and (5) is calculated based on the time, cost and outcome of insolvency proceedings in each economy. To make the data on the time, cost and outcome of insolvency proceedings comparable across economies, several assumptions about the business and the case are used. First, *Doing Business* (2018) assumes that the insolvent business is experiencing liquidity problems. Furthermore, the affected company's loss in 2016 reduced its net worth to a negative figure. There is no cash to pay the bank interest or principal in full. The business will therefore default on its loan. Management believes that losses will be incurred in the immediate future.

For the best-case scenario, *Doing Business* (2018) assumes that the amount outstanding under the loan agreement is exactly equal to the market value of the business and represents 74 percent of the company's total debt. The other 26 percent of its debt is held by unsecured creditors (suppliers, employees, tax authorities). Furthermore, it is assumed that the insolvent company has too many creditors to negotiate an informal out-of-court workout. The following options are available: a judicial procedure aimed at

Table 2.26. Resolving Insolvency in MENA, 2016

Economy	Resolving Insolvency DTF (1)	Resolving Insolvency Rank (2)	Recovery Rate (Cents on the Dollar) (3)	Time (Years) (4)	Cost (% of Estate) (5)	Outcome (0 as Piecemeal Sale and 1 as Going Concern) (6)	Strength of Insolvency Framework Index (0–16) (7)
Algeria	49	71	51	1	7	0	7
Bahrain	44	90	42	3	10	0	7
Cyprus	78	21	73	2	15	1	13
Djibouti	48	73	38	2	11	0	9
Egypt	39	115	26	3	22	0	8
Iran	24	160	15	5	15	0	5
Iraq	0	168	—	—	—	—	—
Israel	73	29	63	2	23	1	13
Jordan	31	146	28	3	20	0	5
Kuwait	39	110	33	4	10	0	7
Lebanon	29	147	31	3	15	0	4
Morocco	34	134	28	4	18	0	6
Oman	42	98	38	4	4	0	7
Qatar	38	116	31	3	22	0	7
SA	0	168	—	—	—	—	—
Syria	21	163	11	4	16	0	5
Tunisia	55	63	52	1	7	0	9
Turkey	33	139	15	5	15	0	8
UAE	50	69	29	3	20	0	11
Yemen	26	156	20	3	15	0	5
OECD	76	24	71	2	9	—	12

Source: World Bank, Doing Business project (http://www.doingbusiness.org/).

the rehabilitation or reorganization of the company to permit its continued operation; a judicial procedure aimed at the liquidation or winding-up of the company; or a judicial debt enforcement procedure (foreclosure or receivership) against the company.

The recovery rate for the OECD is 71 cents to a dollar. For MENA the average recovery rate is 31 cents to a dollar. The highest recovery rates can be found in Cyprus with 73 cents to the dollar and Israel with 63 cents to the dollar. For the majority of MENA countries, the recovery rate is as low as 15 cents per dollar in Turkey and Iran, or slightly above. The length of the insolvency procedure for the OECD is 2 years (Column 4). For the MENA the average is 3 years. For Tunisia, Algeria and Israel the insolvency procedure is below the OECD average. For the balance of MENA countries, it is 3 or 4 years.

Column (5) presents the cost of the proceedings which is recorded as a percentage of the value of the debtor's estate. The cost is calculated by

Doing Business (2018) on the basis of questionnaire responses and includes court fees and government levies; fees of insolvency administrators, auctioneers, assessors and lawyers; and all other fees and costs. For the OECD the average cost is 9 percent of the debtor's estate. The average for MENA is 15 percent of the debtor's estate. On the high end of the distribution we have Israel with 23 percent, Egypt and Qatar with 22 percent, Jordan and the UAE with 20 percent. Oman has the lowest rate at 4 percent of the debtor's estate.

Recovery by creditors (Column 6) depends on whether the business emerges from the proceedings as a going concern or the company's assets are sold piecemeal. If the business continues operating, 100 percent of the hotel value is preserved. If the assets are sold piecemeal, the maximum amount that can be recovered is 70 percent of the value of the business. Within MENA all but Cyprus and Israel the company's assets are sold piecemeal. For cases in Cyprus and Israel the insolvent business emerges from the proceedings as a going concern.

The strength of insolvency framework index (Column 7) is based on four other indices: commencement of proceedings index, management of debtor's assets index, reorganization proceedings index and creditor participation index. The strength of insolvency framework index is the sum of the scores of the other indices. The aggregate index ranges from 0 to 16, with higher values indicating insolvency legislation that is better designed for rehabilitating viable firms and liquidating non-viable ones. For the OECD we have average score of 12. For MENA the average score is 7, with Cyprus and Israel having scores of 13, above the OECD average. Below the OECD average we have the UAE with a score of 11. The balance of MENA countries do not have insolvency legislation that is better designed for rehabilitating viable firms and liquidating non-viable ones. Overall, the majority of MENA countries have instituted sufficient reforms in their bankruptcy procedures.

The data presented in this chapter point to a series of measures which, by themselves, may go a long way in explaining the poor performance of Arab MENA. We now turn to the Islamic institutional factors that some analysts argue are so antithetical to markets that they are primarily responsible for the lackluster performance of Arab MENA.

Chapter 3

Islamic Economics: The Role of Interest-Free Finance in MENA's Development

Is it possible that institutional Islamic restrictions were a major contributing factor for the fact that the Arab MENA region, in contrast to non-Arab MENA, became less developed, did not invest in human capital of its younger generation, did not honor gender equality, did not honor religious freedom, and did not honor market institutions or the elimination of State terror? These are just a few of the list of factors outlined in the post-Williamson's "Washington Consensus" that are being discussed in the development literature and especially in the UN *Arab Human Development Reports* (UNDP, 2002, 2003, 2004, 2005, 2009a).

Kuran (2004, p. 74) argues that the Arab MENA has preserved a series of *institutional bottlenecks* — rooted in the Islamic religious tradition — that continue to negatively affect its current development. Specifically he points to three institutional constraints: (1) the Islamic law of inheritance, which inhibited capital accumulation; (2) the strict individualism of Islamic law and its lack of a concept of corporation or public sector; and (3) the *waqf*, Islam's distinct form of trust, which locked vast resources into organizations likely to become dysfunctional over time. Kuran (1997, p. 302) goes further and argues that Islamic economics is a 20th-century construct that emerged in late-colonial India as an instrument of identity: "Initially, the economics of Islamic economics was merely incidental to its Islamic character." In fact, "it is hardly obvious why the doctrine exists, to say nothing of why it has generated Islamic norms, banks, and redistribution systems." "Islamic economics is at present in a muddled state and lacks direction." (Hasan, 2016, p. 411). As we shall see below, some of the economic ideas and practices that are now characterized as inherently "Islamic" are copied from Jewish traditions, and others, "while not new, acquired religious significance only recently."

Once the doctrine had been developed, a number of stakeholders within MENA adopted it because it represented a convenient vehicle for advancing their political and economic aims. (Kuran, 1995). During the oil boom of the 1970s, Saudi Arabia became one of the lead advocates of Islamic economics. It is therefore not surprising that in 1975, the first Islamic commercial banks were started along with the Islamic Development Bank. The latter established a process of transferring petrodollars to predominantly Muslim developing countries through interest-free instruments. Several countries, notably Pakistan, have gone so far as to outlaw every form of interest, thus forcing all banks, including foreign subsidiaries, to adopt ostensibly Islamic methods of deposit and loan management. Pakistan, Saudi Arabia, Malaysia and a few other Muslim majority countries have instituted official redistribution systems to collect an ancient religious tax and disburse the proceeds to causes endorsed by religious councils. Separating out Islam as a religion from economic rationality became impossible and a new sub-economy was created (Kuran, 1995, p. 155).

Because Islamic economics was developed to negate a Western economic system based on markets, it is best characterized as a political movement to serve religious, cultural and political ends. Consequently, it did not have to abide by reasonable scientific standards of coherence, quantifiable precision, or realism. Unlike Marxist criticism of Capitalism, Islamic economics, as a political movement, needed only to differentiate itself from the Western intellectual traditions that it was aiming to displace. Accordingly, contributions to Islamic economics typically begin by focusing on Islam and an Islamic religious moral standard as a religious filter and not on rational economics as the distinguishing characteristics of an Islamic economy.

During this period, new institutes of Islamic economics came into being, and departments of Islamic economics were started in various parts of the Islamic world. With the flow of petrodollars came journals of Islamic economics as well as well-funded international conferences of Islamic economics. With academic respectability and funding, academic researchers steeped in Islamic economics went looking for new problems to address, and various applications of Islamic economic principles. The primary starting point and one considered to be the most fundamental of these characteristics has been the prohibition of interest. This Marxist idea was retooled with a religious Islamic moral filter, without attribution to Marx. Two other

Islamic religious norms turned into economic practices is the *zakat*, which is an ancient Islamic redistribution system, and the requirement that all economic decisions must pass through an Islamic religious hierarchy (Kuran, 1997, p. 329).

In order to get a better understanding of the implications of some of the core concepts peddled as "Islamic Economics" on the MENA region, 60 plus years after its creation, we must first reconstruct the basic mainstream macro-inter-temporal model with savings and investment and identify the important economic role of interest, one of the elements that Islamic Economics intends to eliminate worldwide.

For any economy, investment represents a trade-off between present and future consumption. In this inter-temporal setting, the primary characteristic of investment is that it consists of the goods that are produced currently for future use in the production of goods and services. Within this framework, the real interest rate is a key determinant of investment as it represents investment's opportunity cost. A higher real interest rate implies that the opportunity cost of investment is larger, at the margin, and therefore investment will decline. In addition to interest rates, a firm's investment decision depends on credit market risk, as perceived by lenders. If banks and other financial institutions perceive lending to be more risky, then firms may find it more difficult to borrow and to finance investment projects.

We start the model by considering the *representative consumer* who makes a work–leisure decision in each of the current and future periods, and makes a consumption–savings decision in the current period. The representative consumer works and consumes in both periods.

The representative consumer has h units of time in each period and divides this time between work and leisure in each period. Let w denote the real wage in the current period, w_{t+n} the real wage in the future period, and r the real interest rate. The consumer pays lump-sum taxes to the government of T in the current period and T_{t+n} in the future period. The representative consumer has to, subject to the inter-temporal budget constraints, choose current consumption C, future consumption C_{t+n}, leisure time in the current l and future periods l_{t+n}, and savings in the current period s, in order to maximize his or her utility.[8]

The consumer's current period budget constraint is:

$$C + s = w(h - l) + \pi - T, \tag{3.1}$$

[8] We assume that the representative consumer is a price-taker with respect to w, r and T across periods.

where π is dividend income.

The consumer's future budget constraint is:

$$C_{t+n} = w_{t+n}(h - l_{t+n}) + \pi_{t+n} - T_{t+n} + (1+r)S. \tag{3.2}$$

The lifetime budget constraint for our representative consumer will be:

$$C + \frac{C_{t+n}}{1+r} = w(h-l) + \pi - T + \frac{w_{t+n}(h - l_{t+n}) + \pi_{t+n} - T_{t+n}}{1+r}. \tag{3.3}$$

The representative consumer makes the work–leisure choice each period based on equilibrium between his or her marginal rate of substation and the real wage. In terms of the choice between current and future consumption, the optimization decision must rest with $(1+r)$, that is, the relative price of current consumption in terms of future consumption. It is what we have come to refer to as one plus the real interest rate.

Now let us introduce the representative firm, which produces goods using inputs of labor and capital in both the current and future periods. In effect, the firm can invest in the current period by accumulating capital so as to expand the capacity to produce future output. In the current period, the representative firm produces output according to the production function:

$$Y = zF(K, L), \tag{3.4}$$

where Y is current output, z is total factor productivity, F is the production function, K is current capital, and L is current labor input.

Future period output is produced according to the following production function:

$$Y_{t+n} = z_{t+n}F(K_{t+n}, L_{t+n}), \tag{3.5}$$

where $(t+n)$ refers to the future periods.

The obvious issue for our discussion is what is the basic inter-temporal economic concern for the representative firm when it makes its investment decision? The essence of the investment decision is that something must be foregone in the current period to gain something in the future. That is, the firm uses some of the current output it produces to invest in capital, which becomes productive in the future. Letting I denote the quantity of current investment, the future capital stock is given by:

$$K_{t+n} = (1-\delta)K + I, \tag{3.6}$$

where δ is the depreciation rate.

The goal of the firm is to maximize the present value of profits over the current and future periods. This will allow it to determine the firm's demand for current labor, as well as the firm's quantity of investment.

For the representative firm, current and future profits, respectively, are given by:

$$\pi = Y - wL - l, \tag{3.7}$$

$$\pi_{t+n} = Y_{t+n} - w_{t+n}L_{t+n} + (1-\delta)K_{t+n}. \tag{3.8}$$

We assume that profits (π) earned by the firm in the current and future periods are paid out to the shareholders of the firm as dividend income in each period.

The beauty of this assumption in mainstream economics is that it implies that the firm maximizes the present value of the consumer's dividend income, which serves to maximize the lifetime wealth of the consumer. Letting V denote the present value of profits for the firm, the firm then maximizes:

$$V = \pi + \frac{\pi_{t+n}}{(1+r)}. \tag{3.9}$$

In Equation (3.9), all the benefits from investment come in terms of future profits and there are two components to the marginal benefit. First, an additional unit of current investment adds one unit to the future capital stock. This implies that the firm will produce more output in the future, and the additional output produced is equal to the firm's future marginal product of capital, (MPK_{t+n}). Second, each unit of current investment implies that there will be an additional $(1-\delta)$ units of capital remaining at the end of the future period which can be liquidated. Formally we have:

$$\text{marginal benefits } (I) = \frac{MPK_{t+n} + 1 - \delta}{1+r}. \tag{3.10}$$

Or in equilibrium:

$$MPK_{t+n} - \delta = r. \tag{3.11}$$

The optimal investment rule as stated in Equation (3.11) basically states that an efficient firm will invest until the net marginal product of capital is equal to the real interest rate. The real interest rate is the rate of return on the alternative asset in this economy. How can economic agents make efficient inter-temporal consumption and investment decisions without the help of an interest rate?

3.1. Basic Principles of Islamic Law Applicable to a Loan Agreement: Prohibition of Interest (*Riba*) and Risk/Uncertainty (*Gharar*)

Posner (1980) reminds the reader that throughout history, no country has been able to successfully eliminate interest rates despite countless attempts by various groups, both religious and secular, who are hostile to the concept of opportunity cost. There is a rich and voluminous set of legal treaties on Islamic Law (Sharī'a)[9] and a raging debate on Islamic finance and its assertion that Islamic Law forbids all forms of interest (Bonner, 2005; Iqbal, 2005; Kuran, 2005 and 2007; Pamuk, 2000; Qureshi, 1990; Roy, 1994). In fact, one analyst (El-Gamal, 2003) notes that excluding interest in Islamic finance is a misleading notion in light of the actual practices of Islamic financial providers over the past three decades to formally base rates of return or costs of capital on a benchmark interest rate such as LIBOR.

In its strict interpretation, classical Islamic law[10] requires every loan, regardless of size or purpose, to be free of interest. The principal justification for this ban is that it is stated in the Qur'an.[11] What the Qur'an explicitly prohibits is *riba*, an ancient Arabian practice whereby the debt of a borrower doubled if he failed to make restitution on time.[12] Was the ban on interest a new phenomenon created by the Qur'an or did it represent the ongoing trend of the period? According to Kuran (2005, pp. 595–596), the logic for a general prohibition against interest was developed well before Islam.[13] Citing Homer and Sylla (1996, p. 3), Kuran (2005) points out

[9]The reference material on Islamic Law is enormous. The starting point for most is Coulson (1964), Schacht (1964) and Zwaini and Peters (1994).

[10]Schools of Islamic jurisprudence have developed separately and the content of Shari'a can vary considerably from one school to another.

[11]The Qur'an itself provides no detailed rationale for the prohibition of interest (Ahmad, 1995).

[12]*Riba* commonly resulted in confiscation of the borrower's assets and may include enslavement (Qur'an 2:274–280, 3:130, 4:160–161, quoted in Kuran, 2005, p. 595). Currently, *Riba* generally means an excess or increase in return from a transaction (http://www.nubank.com/islamic/primer.pdf). The Qur'an strictly prohibits such excesses and a transaction involving *riba* is void under Shari'a Law (Islamic religious law).

[13]Badr (1978, p. 188) reminds the reader that "*the Qur'an is far from being a legal code. In fact it contains very few legal provisions. Out of a total of 6237 verses, only 190 verses or 3% of the total can be said to contain legal provisions. Most of these deal with family law and inheritance. In its Mu'amlat branch, which is all that other legal systems deal with, Islamic law is indeed a man-made law and has no pretense to being*

that legal codes of the Middle East included stipulations to limit borrowers' exposure to risk. In fact, the code of Hammurabi (mid-18th century BCE) capped the interest rate on grain loans at 33 percent per annum and that on silver loans at 20 percent. Furthermore, it restricted slavery for debt to 3 years. The laws of Solon (around 600 BCE) reduced or annulled most pre-existing debts, and prohibited slavery for overdue obligations. The Roman Twelve Tables (around 450 BCE) capped interest at 8.3 percent per annum and imposed four-fold damages on creditors who demanded more.

Before the birth of Islam, the Torah prohibited lending at interest among Jews (Deuteronomy 23:20).[14] It also banned collecting interest from the poor (Exodus 22:24–26)[15] and from non-Jewish residents (Leviticus 25:35–37).[16] It is instructive to read how Islamic scholars minimize and distort the relationship between Islamic and Jewish law (Mallat, 2003, 2004). Mr. Gamal Moursi Badr, who was a prominent Member of the Egyptian National Bar Association and former Algerian Justice of the Supreme Court, as well as member of the United Nations Secretariat in New York, in a 1978 article published in the *American Journal of Comparative Law*, stated:

> "It is often maintained that Jewish law has influenced the early development of Islamic jurisprudence. As in the case of Roman law, no solid evidence is adduced in support of this position other than priority in time and some apparent

a religious law except that it may be said to lay more emphasis on moral considerations than is usually the case with other legal systems."

[14] "*You may not cause your brother to pay interest — interest on money, interest on food or interest on any other item for which interest may be taken.*" The Gutnick Edition of the Chumash (2009, pp. 1278–1281).

[15] "*When you lend money (prioritize first) My people (i.e. Jews), the poor person, and (the inhabitant of your city) who is with you. (If you know he cannot yet repay your loan), do not behave towards him as a lender (claiming your money forcibly). Do not place interest payments upon him. If (he fails to pay the loan on time and) you take your friend's (daytime) garment as security, you must return it to him (for the entire day) until the sun sets. (You must also return his night garments by night) for it is his only covering; it is his garment for his skin. With what shall he sleep? If he cries out to Me, I will listen because I am compassionate.*" The Gutnick Edition of the Chumash (2009, pp. 492–495).

[16] "*If your fellow among you becomes needy and his hand is wavering, you should support him (before he becomes completely destitute) so that he can live with you — even if he is a convert or a resident (non-Jewish) alien, (provided he is not an idol-worshiper.) You should not take interest from him, (for taking) interest (is a double sin. While this may be difficult for you) you should fear your God, and (help) your fellow to live with you. You should not lend him your money with interest, nor should you lend your food with interest.*" The Gutnick Edition of the Chumash (2009, pp. 820–821).

parallels even less numerous than those which purport to link Islamic law to Roman law. The Jewish legal system which offers interesting comparisons with Islamic law . . . does not qualify as a major world legal system by our criteria."

The Qur'an refers to *riba* in different contexts among which most relevant to modern financial transactions is the loan context. Shari'a considers any loan made in order to profit as involving *riba* and absolutely prohibits it. As one scholar puts it, "[i]n Islam, one does not lend to make money, and one does not borrow to finance business. Loans are a charitable contract."[17]

In recent years there has been considerable debate over the scope of this prohibition. Only in Iran, Pakistan and Sudan, conventional financial markets do not exist and the entire banking system operates under the Islamic system. A substantial minority of Muslim scholars argue that the prohibition on *riba* does not necessarily outlaw all forms of interest on loans (El-Gamal, 2003). Some have stated that an interest rate below the inflation rate (which only guarantees the return of the purchasing power of the money lent) or interest on loans for production, as opposed to consumption, can be excluded from the definition of *riba*.

In Iran, two important exceptions have been recognized to the prohibition of *riba*. First, banks are allowed to charge a penalty for a late payment (although this is not called *riba*, but rather is deemed an incentive to comply with a repayment schedule). A late fee in most Western bank terms is not interest either. Second, charging interest in a transaction with foreign entities is permissible. The majority view today, however, holds that any type of interest on a loan is *riba* and thus prohibited (Sabahi, 2004).

Another rule in Shari'a which is indirectly related to banking and financial activities, but which does not directly affect the structure of a credit facility, is the prohibition of *gharar*, which means an "unacceptable" level of risk or uncertainty. "Acceptable" is a term of art based on fact-specific issues in each transaction and must be determined on a case-by-case basis. In effect it becomes discretionary.[18]

El-Gamal (2003) points out that the sale of an object which is not yet in existence is unenforceable (*adam* or non-existence, e.g., an unborn calf) and the sale of an object which is not under the control of the seller is also unenforceable (e.g., fish in the sea). Under this prohibition, derivatives (including forward contracts, futures and options) are generally invalid. Moreover, when the consideration furnished by either party to the contract

[17]Under US law, tax rules are designed to induce charitable transactions.
[18]A transaction involving a prohibited level of *gharar* is void under Islamic jurisprudence.

is indeterminable, the contract will not be enforceable (*jahala* or ignorance, e.g., payment of a fixed price for a diver's catch the next day).

This prohibition can be extended to traditional forms of insurance and thus made impermissible. Sabahi (2004) points out that there would be an unacceptable level of uncertainty in an insurance contract because the total amount of the premiums that the policyholder pays is not predetermined.

The prohibitions on *riba* and *gharar* have enormous repercussions for financial transactions. Under the Islamic model, banks cannot charge interest on loans or pay interest on deposits, two traditional operations of Western banks. In fact, under the Islamic model, there can be no banks in the traditional sense of the word. Therefore, Islamic banks have to operate under a different model that conforms to Islamic principles. This model is based mainly on contractual modes of financing.

3.2. Contractual Modes of Financing under Islamic Law

As a result of the above institutional problems, banks and their customers have to use other methods to finance a business operation in accordance with Islamic principles. The main method which banks and businesses use for this purpose is structuring the credit facility through contracts permissible under Shari'a.

3.2.1. *Partnerships (Musharaka and Mudharaba)*

The main types of contracts used to structure a financing transaction are partnerships (*musharaka* and *mudharaba*), leases (*ijara* and *ijara va iqtina*), mark-up sales or cost-plus financing (*murabaha*), and commissioned manufacturing (*istisna'*). *Musharaka* and *mudharaba* are partnerships, or "profit and loss" sharing ventures, and are used as a common financing method in the Islamic financial markets. *Musharaka*, an equity-based partnership, involves two parties both of whom contribute capital and share the profits and losses of the operations in proportion to their respective contributions. In this sense, *musharaka* is very similar to the partnership concept in the US legal system. Banks use this type of contract in long-term investment projects. Both parties have the right to participate in the management of the partnership, but they can also delegate that right (El-Gamal, 2000; Sabahi, 2004).

One type of *musharaka* is *musharaka mutinaqiza* (diminishing partnership), in which the financing agency and the customer are both owners of the real estate. The periodic payments made by the customer are divided into a rental payment and a buyout payment. The contract terminates when the ownership of the property is completely transferred to the customer (El-Gamal, 2000; Sabahi, 2004).

Another type of Islamic partnership that banks commonly use is *mudharaba* (participation or trust financing). Under this type of partnership agreement, one party provides the capital and the other provides the labor (management) and expertise. Banks use this type of arrangement to provide venture capital for entrepreneurial projects. The bank bears any losses from the project and the entrepreneur's loss is limited to his "time and efforts." Both parties share in the profits, which must be divided according to a percentage agreement (as opposed to a lump-sum agreement) (El-Gamal, 2000; Sabahi, 2004).

Islamic banks also use *mudharaba* on the deposit-taking side of their operations. In this case, the depositor is the provider of the capital and the bank provides the labor and expertise in the joint investment. This system, where banks use *mudharaba* on both sides, is called two-tier *mudharaba* (El-Gamal, 2000; Sabahi, 2004).

Clearly, in these transactions, the depositor bears the risk of loss. In some banks, however, demand deposits are held as *amanat*, in which the bank is only a safekeeper. Then the bank is responsible for the total amount of the deposit and cannot use the funds to provide credit to the borrowers (El-Gamal, 2000; Sabahi, 2004).

3.2.2. *Lease (Ijara and "Ijara va iqtina")*

Lease (*ijara*) financing methods are among the most popular vehicles for providing credit to businesses which operate under Islamic principles. In a typical lease financing situation, the bank buys the asset that its customer needs and then leases the asset to the customer. These leases are different from traditional financing transactions in that the bank must own the leased item. If the bank provides the manufacturer with a loan in the amount of the present value of lease payments, and the manufacturer leases the object to the customer, the customer will still, in fact, indirectly pay interest to the bank.[19]

However, some Islamic supervisory boards have stated that in such transactions, the lessee cannot be required to pay the cost of insurance (because the asset belongs to the bank); even if the bank incorporates that

[19]See Taqi Usmani, M. (1998) for a partial list of conditions for lease financing to be valid.

cost into the amount of the rent, the bank is responsible for paying the premiums. In lease financing transactions, the customer typically has an option to buy the asset upon expiration of the lease. These transactions, called *ijara va iqtina*, have been used extensively in cross-border transactions for a wide range of assets including ships, aircraft, telecommunications equipment and power station turbines (Norton Rose, 2008).

3.2.3. *Mark-Up Sale (Murabaha)*

In *murabaha*, the bank buys the item that its customer needs and sells the item to the customer at a marked-up price (hence the alternative name for these transactions, mark-up sale). The customer usually pays the sale price on a deferred basis or in installments. Islamic financial institutions use this type of transaction mostly to provide trade financing for their customers. In these transactions, as in lease financing transactions, the bank takes title to the item (when it buys it from a third party) and therefore assumes the risk, which entitles it to profit from the transaction (Norton Rose, 2008).

3.2.4. *Commissioned Manufacturing (Istisna')*

Another round-about for financial institutions who need a contract form to finance the manufacturing or construction of an item such as buildings, equipment, aircraft, etc., is called *Istisna'*. This is a type of contract whereby, either by pre-payment or by installment payments, the financial institution that takes title to the item will be able to then either sell or lease it to the customer (El-Gamal, 2000).

This part of the transaction is similar to *murabaha* (cost-plus sale) or *ijara* (lease). The core of the transaction is the financing of the manufacturing or construction of the item that the customer needs. Under the principle of prohibition of *gharar* (risk/uncertainty), *istisna'* is technically prohibited because payment for something which is not yet in existence entails too much risk (Norton Rose, 2008).

Islamic scholars, however, have allowed this type of contract by analogy (*qiyas*) to another type of Islamic contract called *bai' salam*, which is similar to a forward contract. Under *bai' salam*, the buyer pays for an item in full and arranges to take delivery at a future date. *Bai' salam* is only available for products whose quality and quantity is fully specified at the time of the contract, e.g., agricultural or manufactured products (Norton Rose, 2008; McMillen, 2001; Ebrahim and Rahman, 2005).

This type of contract is permitted by Islamic principles in order to facilitate commercial transactions. Islamic scholars by analogy have concluded that prepayment to finance the manufacturing or construction of an item is also permissible. *Istisna'* has been used in present-day transactions in order to provide advance funding for major industrial projects or for expensive equipment like turbines for power plants, ships and aircraft (Norton Rose, 2008; Ambinder, de Silva and Dewar, 2001).

3.2.5. *Empirical Evidence: Is Islamic Banking Interest-Free?*

The first Islamic financial institution was a mutual savings bank formed in the Egyptian town of Mit Ghamar in 1963. Over the past four decades, however, Islamic banking has grown rapidly in terms of size and the number of players. Islamic banking can now be found in more than 50 countries worldwide.[20] In Iran, Pakistan and Sudan, only Islamic banking is allowed. In other countries, such as Bangladesh, Egypt, Indonesia, Jordan and Malaysia, Islamic banking co-exists with conventional banking. In August 2004, the Islamic Bank of Britain became the first bank licensed by a non-Muslim country to engage in Islamic banking. The HSBC, University Bank in Ann Arbor and Devon Bank in Chicago offer Islamic banking products in the United States. Islamic banking services in 2013 and 2014 sum up to a global industry amounting to around $2 trillion in assets, of which 80 percent is accounted for by Islamic banks (including Islamic windows of conventional banks), 15 percent *Sukuk* (Islamic bonds), 24 percent Islamic mutual funds and 1 percent *Takaful* (Islamic insurance) (*The Economist*, 2014). According to the Islamic Financial Services Board (2013), Iran is the biggest Islamic banking market (accounting for around 40 percent of global Islamic banking assets) followed by Saudi Arabia (14 percent), Malaysia (10 percent) and the United Arab Emirates (UAE) and Kuwait (both with 9 percent shares). Only Iran and Sudan have solely Islamic banks. For the other Muslim countries, Islamic banks compete head-on with conventional

[20]One can find Islamic banking in the following countries: Albania, Algeria, Australia, Bahamas, Bahrain, Bangladesh, British Virgin Islands, Brunei, Canada, Cayman Islands, North Cyprus, Djibouti, Egypt, France, Gambia, Germany, Guinea, India, Indonesia, Iran, Iraq, Italy, Ivory Coast, Jordan, Kazakhstan, Kuwait, Lebanon, Luxembourg, Malaysia, Mauritania, Morocco, Netherlands, Niger, Nigeria, Oman, Pakistan, Palestine, Philippines, Qatar, Russia, Saudi Arabia, Senegal, Singapore, South Africa, Sri Lanka, Sudan, Switzerland, Tunisia, Turkey, Trinidad & Tobago, United Arab Emirates, United Kingdom, United States and Yemen.

banks. In Saudi Arabia around 35 percent of banking sector assets are Islamic law compliant. In the UAE (22 percent), Qatar (20 percent) and Malaysia (20 percent). For the world market, Islamic banking and financial assets are trivial, comprising under 1 percent of total global financial assets (Credit Suisse, 2016).

The growth of Islamic banking raises a series of important questions. Have Islamic banks established a whole system of contracts to get around issues of interest and unreasonable risk, thereby establishing a new comparative advantage of the Islamic banking paradigm? Could it represent just an upward shift in the worldwide Islamic resurgence with lots of petrodollars? The literature has called this feature of Islamic banking, the profit-and-loss sharing (PLS) paradigm (Aggarwal and Yousef, 2000). A number of empirical studies have attempted to determine if in fact these practices are actually implemented.

In one such study, Chong and Liu (2009) found that Islamic banking is not very different from conventional banking. Their work on Malaysia[21] shows that only a negligible portion of Islamic bank financing is strictly PLS-based and that Islamic deposits are not interest-free, but are closely pegged to conventional deposits.[22] Their findings suggest that the rapid growth in Islamic banking was largely driven by the Islamic resurgence worldwide rather than by the advantages of the PLS paradigm. Furthermore, they propose that Islamic banks should be subject to regulations similar to those of their Western counterparts.

The Chong and Liu (2009) results rely on the monthly series of Islamic investment rates and conventional deposit rates from April 1995 to April 2004. The sample size was 109 for each time series. They examined the rates provided by two types of financial institutions: banks and finance companies. For each type of institution, they compared Islamic investment rates and conventional deposit rates on savings deposits as well as time deposits of various maturities, ranging from 1 month to 12 months.

Islamic investment rates were, on average, significantly lower than the conventional deposit rates. This finding was true for both the banks and the finance companies. Furthermore, the volatility and the minimum–maximum range of Islamic investment rates were significantly lower than those of conventional deposit rates, except for the investment rates on Islamic banks'

[21]Their study focused on Malaysia, where a full-fledged Islamic banking system has developed alongside a conventional banking system. This provided them a unique setting to compare Islamic banking practices with those of conventional banking.

[22]See El-Gamal (2003) for a similar conclusion.

savings deposits. These results arise because the returns on Islamic deposits were administratively linked to the deposit rates offered by conventional banks.

Overall, the Chong and Liu (2009) results suggest that in the case of Malaysia, "the Islamic deposits, in practice, are not very different from conventional deposits. In particular, we found that the Islamic investment rates for both the banks and the finance companies are closely pegged to the conventional deposit rates. In theory, *mudarabah* deposits are structured based on a 'profit-sharing' basis, whereas the *al-wadiah* savings deposits are structured based on the 'savings with guarantee' concept. In practice, however, we found that both the *mudarabah* deposits and the *al-wadiah* savings deposits are not 'interest-free,' and their investment rates are closely linked to conventional deposit rates."

What would explain these results? In a country like Malaysia where both banking institutions exist, the actual implementation of the PLS paradigm is constrained by competition from conventional banking practices. Religion notwithstanding, consumers and firms can choose to bank with an Islamic bank and/or a conventional bank. Consequently, Islamic banking practices cannot deviate substantially from those of conventional banking because of market competition.

Recently, a comprehensive study done by Beck *et al.* (2013) found that there are very few significant differences between Islamic and conventional banks. Their study investigates Islamic bank performance issues using a sample of banks from 141 countries over 1995 and 2007. Econometrically comparing, risk, efficiency and business model features, they find that Islamic bankers developed products that resemble conventional banking products, replacing interest rate payments and discounting with fees and contingent payment structures.

Beck *et al.* confirm the findings of Chong and Liu (2009), where it was concluded that in Malaysia only a small portion of Islamic bank financing is based on profit–loss sharing and that Islamic deposits are not interest-free, but closely pegged to conventional deposits. These results were also confirmed by Khan (2010) for a sample of large Islamic banks across several countries.

The interest-free focus of the discussion on Islamic banking is not warranted by the empirical results. Unlike interest-free loans, leasing-like products are the most popular among Islamic banks, as they are directly linked to real-sector transactions. The residual equity-style risk that Islamic banks and their depositors are taking has implications for the agency relationships on both sides of the balance sheet. Overall, the empirical research on Islamic banking does not support the political argument that Islamic banking is ethically superior to conventional Western banking. There are no differences between those banks that are constrained by Islam and conventional Western banks that are not constrained by any religion.

Chapter 4

Investment in Human Capital

Persistent differences in the standards of living across Arab MENA and between Arab and non-Arab MENA have historically been attributable to resource differences. If the large disparity in income per capita across MENA is, however, partly due to barriers to the adoption of technology and allocative inefficiencies, then we need to consider an alternative explanation. In order to explain these differences, this chapter concentrates on the contribution of the accumulation of skills and education to economic growth. This framework is based on the endogenous growth models developed by Lucas (1988) and Romer (1986 and 1990).

4.1. A Simplified Endogenous Growth Model

Taking the endogenous growth model as the germane paradigm, Hsieh and Klenow (2009) estimated that, if capital and labor were allocated as efficiently across firms in China and India as in the United States, then total factor productivity would be 30–50 percent higher in China, and 40–60 percent higher in India. The improvement in factor productivity could be achieved by the elimination of government corruption, inefficiencies in the financial sector, and inefficient taxes and subsidies. This line of research becomes critical to explaining differences in standards of living within MENA.

From our earlier discussion of the Washington Consensus (Chapter 1), we know that if MENA governments discontinue protecting local monopoly power, then firms would have to develop and implement new technologies to remain competitive, so that productivity will be higher. Along these lines, MENA governments can promote the free flow of goods and factors of production. Greater competition between countries promotes innovation and the adoption of the best technologies. In cases where there is no market failure, MENA governments should privatize production. The existence of State-Owned Enterprises (SOEs) often leads to protection of employment at the expense of efficiency, and this tends to lower total factor productivity. Total factor productivity growth involves research and development by firms, education, and training on the job, and all of these activities are responsive to the enabling economic environment found in a given economy. As the Washington Consensus continues to stress, MENA governments can improve their country's economic performance by promoting the enforcing laws, so as to mitigate political corruption.

We begin with our simplified endogenous growth model by considering the case of a representative consumer who allocates his or her time between supplying labor to produce output and/or accumulating human capital.[23]

It is generally assumed that a higher level of human capital translates into potentially faster economic growth. The accumulation of human capital is best viewed as investment, just like investment in plant and equipment. Both inter-temporal activities are associated with current costs and future benefits. The major difference between the two is the assumption that diminishing marginal returns to the accumulation of physical capital is not present when we consider the accumulation of human capital. As Romer (1990) argues, a key feature of knowledge is non-rivalry, that is, there appears to be no limit to how productive individuals can become given increases in knowledge and skills. A particular person's acquisition of knowledge does not reduce the ability of someone else to acquire the same knowledge. This is not the case when we consider physical capital accumulation, where the acquisition of plant and equipment by a firm i depletes resources that could be used by firms j to n to acquire plant and equipment. As Romer (1990) stresses, the lack of diminishing returns to human capital investment along with non-rivalry leads to unbounded growth.

We begin a discussion of the endogenous growth model by first considering the decision of our representative consumer between work and accumulating human capital.[24] The consumer's budget constraint is as follows:

$$C = w\gamma H^S, \tag{4.1}$$

[23]Human capital can be viewed as the accumulated stock of skills and education that a worker has at a specific point in time.

[24]We ignore the leisure question.

where:

$C =$ consumption or total labor earnings
$w =$ current real wage
$\gamma =$ fraction of time devoted to work in a given period
$H^S =$ initial units of human capital in period 1.

Without savings, the representative consumer can only trade-off current for future consumption by accumulating human capital. The technology for accumulating human capital is given by:

$$H^S_{t+n} = \alpha(1-\gamma)H^S, \tag{4.2}$$

where $(1-\gamma)H^S$ represents the number of current efficiency units of labor devoted to human capital accumulation. We assume that $\alpha > 0$, reflecting the efficiency of human capital accumulation technology. Implicit in Equation (4.2) is the assumption that the ease and speed of future accumulation of human capital is closely tied to prior stocks of education and skills.

Following the same set of assumptions about human capital, we start our discussion of the representative firm which produces output using only efficiency units of labor. The resulting production function which has constant returns to scale will be:

$$Y = z\gamma H^D, \tag{4.3}$$

where:

$Y =$ current output
$z =$ marginal product of efficiency units of labor assumed to be > 0
$\gamma H^D =$ the current input of efficiency units of labor into production. That is, it is the demand for efficient units of labor by the representative firm.

The representative firm hires the quantity of efficiency units of labor, γH^D, that maximizes current prices, where profits are:

$$\pi = Y - w\gamma H^D.$$

Substituting for Y from Equation (4.3), we have:

$$\pi = z\gamma H^D - w\gamma H^D = (z-w)\gamma H^D. \tag{4.4}$$

	$z-w$	γH^D	π
Case 1	<0	>0	<0
Case 2	>0	>0	$(z-w)\gamma H^D$
Equilibrium	$w=z$	>0	0

The three cases noted above are as follows. In case 1, if $(z - w) < 0$, then profits are negative. If the firm hires a positive quantity of efficiency units of labor, the firm maximizes profits by setting $\gamma H^D = 0$. In case 2, if $(z - w) > 0$, then profits are $z - w$ for each efficiency unit hired, so that the firm wants to hire an infinite quantity of workers to maximize profits. In case 3, if $z = w$, then the firm's profits are zero for any quantity of workers hired.

The equilibrium real wage per efficiency unit of labor is always $w = z$, which implies that the real wage per hour of work is $wH^D = zH^D$. That is, the real wage changes in proportion to the quantity of human capital of the representative consumer.

Market clearing occurs when:

$$\gamma H^S = \gamma H^D.$$

That is, the supply of efficiency units of labor is equal to the demand. Therefore, $H^S = H^D = H$. Substituting Equations (4.1) and (4.2) for w and H^S, we have:

$$C = z\gamma H \tag{4.5}$$

and

$$H_{t+n} = \alpha(1 - \gamma)H. \tag{4.6}$$

If $\alpha(1 - \gamma) > 1$, then we have $H_{t+n} > H$. That is, future human capital is always greater than current human capital, and therefore, human capital grows over time without bounds. The growth rate of human capital based on Equation (4.6) is:

$$\frac{H_{t+n}}{H} - 1 = \alpha(1 - \gamma) - 1, \tag{4.7}$$

which is a constant. The crucial element in this model is that the growth rate of human capital increases if α increases or if γ decreases.

The endogenous growth model predicts that countries with more efficient education systems should experience higher rates of growth in human capital.

As long as $C_{t+n} = z\gamma H_{t+n}$, we can determine the rate of growth of consumption to be:

$$\frac{C_{t+n}}{C} - 1 = \frac{z\gamma H_{t+n}}{z\gamma H} - 1 = \frac{H_{t+n}}{H} - 1 = \alpha(1 - \gamma) - 1. \tag{4.8}$$

The conclusion that one develops from the endogenous growth model is that the growth rate of consumption is identical to the growth rate of human capital. That is, $C = Y$ from the classic income–expenditure identity.

Given the results of a simplified endogenous model as noted above, what would be the most appropriate options for State intervention? Can the State increase the quantity of public funds spent on public education and be able to generate an increase in total factor productivity? Will subsidies to research and development have any positive and meaningful impact on growth of total factor productivity? More generally, does the State have any positive role in the promotion of economic growth?

The endogenous growth model suggests that there is a role for State intervention. The common growth rate of human capital, consumption and output depends on two parameters: α and γ. Consequently, the question becomes, can the State influence these two parameters? By making a country's educational system more efficient, the State can affect the efficiency of the human capital accumulation technology (α). Exactly what policies the various MENA countries have pursued to increase α will be the focus of the next section of this chapter. Moreover, the State could change its fiscal policies with respect to taxes or subsidies as applied to education in order to change γ. If the State decided to subsidize education, then resources would shift to the sector which would make human capital accumulation more desirable relative to current production, and so γ would decrease, and the growth rate of output and consumption would increase. However, a decrease in γ which increases the growth rate of consumption, $\alpha(1-\gamma)-1$, will also lead to a reduction in C. That is, $C = z\gamma H$, and in the first period, if γ decreases, then C must also fall because the initial human capital (H) is given. Clearly the representative consumer must consider the trade-off of initial reduction of consumption, in order to increase future consumption. The problem for the State would be to forecast the specific country's switch to a higher consumption path.

4.2. Human Capital Acquisition in MENA

It is well-understood within Arab MENA that the acquisition of human capital involves not only the formal acquisition of education but also the removal of cultural and systemic barriers to learning. As the authors of the countless *UN Arab Human Development Report* (UNDP, 2002, 2003,

2004, 2005, 2009a, 2009b, 2016a, 2016b) have so forcefully acknowledged, the effective use of knowledge in societal activities will not only increasingly expand the frontiers of human potential but will also enlarge the scope of human freedoms. It is this latter externality which generates official platitudes in favor of educational reforms but at the same time creates institutional barriers to its acquisition. Knowledge has the potential to force the public to demand good governance and the promotion of equity and freedom, justice and human dignity. Why would the Arab MENA succumb to these externalities? In the non-Arab MENA there is no similar issue — human capital acquisition is its defining characteristic.

As we noted in Section 4.1, human capital has become an essential factor of production, and a basic determinant of productivity. There is a strong connection between the acquisition of human capital and the productive capacity of a society. This connection figures prominently in high value-added production activities, which are increasingly based on human capital intensity, and which lead to the rapid obsolescence of knowledge, technology and skills. Such activities are the backbone of competitive economies like Israel and other world-class economies, but not Arab MENA (UNDP, 2003, p. 37). In most Arab MENA countries, the knowledge system faces a dual crisis. On the one hand, the system itself suffers from the backwardness of the local society; and on the other hand, the same backward society, in order to preserve its power structure, imposes restrictions on the acquisition of human capital by all its citizens and consequently on the development of Arab MENA.

As the endogenous growth model has demonstrated, the global stock of human capital is renewable and grows ceaselessly. As a recent UNDP Human Development report (2016b, p12) stated, "Human capital is an asset, and differences in educational attainment prevent poor people from becoming part of the high-productivity growth process. Democratizing education, particularly tertiary education, would benefit people from poorer backgrounds." Yet its human, cultural and economic potential will not blossom in any country where the social climate does not actively encourage knowledge acquisition dissemination, production and use: "Local conditions within Arab MENA influence whether education, learning R&D and literary and artistic expression flourish or fail and therefore whether productivity and human development prosper or not" (UNDP, 2003 p. 38).

According to the *UN Arab Human Development Report* (UNDP, 2016a p. 47), the four most significant aspects of the local Arab MENA societal constraints affecting their development of a knowledge system are:

(a) "links with societal activities, especially production;
(b) the role of the state;
(c) the regional context; and
(d) the international environment."

The political leadership within Arab MENA that does not support knowledge acquisition and use through education, technical research and development traps itself on the lowest rungs of learning. Moreover, those Arab MENA leaders that do not value knowledge highly do not provide adequate funding and support for the process of human capital acquisition for its effective activity. The outcome is lower productivity, lower economic development, limited freedom and greater reliance on fear as a political instrument of control (UNDP, 2002, 2003, 2004, 2005, 2009a, 2009b, 2016a, and 2016b).

The reality of Arab MENA, as the various *UN Arab Human Development Reports* have stressed, is that there are certain "structural impediments" that prevent the production of human capital in Arab countries. The cultural conflict over the Islamization of human capital is the most difficult impediment in Arab MENA. This conflict is tied to xenophobia, religious intolerance, gender bias, intellectual reluctance to discuss their own political and economic history, and their present-day position in the global economy. As the authors of the *UN Arab Human Development Report* have stressed, "no essential characteristic or aspect of Arab society should be excluded from a scientific perspective."

The supply of institutions and their funding is a real constraint in Arab MENA, especially when autocratic and absolute regimes restrict freedom of expression and the circulation of knowledge, ideas and information that are critical to their authority. Nevertheless, there is a growing demand for human capital within Arab MENA which is not fully extinguished by the authoritarian regimes of Arab MENA. As the authors of the *UN Arab Human Development Report* have repeatedly pointed out, "Arab mentality is a project, not a fixed construct.. [I]t is ... in the process of formation" (UNDP, 2003, p. 45).

4.2.1. *The Demand Side*

Let us begin by asserting that the households in both Arab and non-Arab MENA demand certain kinds of institutional infrastructure to help them accumulate human capital. These families demand knowledge as a way to invest in the human capital of their members, and to make social and economic decisions within the family. The state, civil societies, and the business sectors, likewise, demand human capital in order to perform their respective functions. In the 21st century, the major drivers of dissemination and demand are the institutional components of the knowledge system. The most well-known of these are the components of the global economy we call access to the Internet.

The Internet has become the primary international vehicle for conveying ideas. It has helped destabilize regimes that have used access to information as a source of control. The Internet is now the largest depository of reference information for all areas of human capital. The globalized Internet infrastructure is not restricted to a single country. The abundant information made available on the Internet can either propel an economy's development or scare it. The dependent factor is the stock of human capital that is utilizing it. As we noted in Section 4.1, the larger the initial stock of human capital, the greater is the potential for growth.

In Table 4.1 we present data on the availability of Information and Communication Technologies (ICT) for the MENA region over the period 2007 and 2016. A compound annual growth rate is calculated to present a trend for each of the countries. The only country within MENA not reporting data on ICT is Iraq. The first and second sets of observations is for fixed broadband subscriptions in total and per 100 people. This data refers to fixed subscriptions to high-speed access to the public Internet (a TCP/IP connection), at downstream speeds equal to, or greater than, 256 kbit/s. This includes cable modem, DSL, fiber-to-the-home/building, other fixed (wired) broadband subscriptions, satellite broadband and terrestrial fixed wireless broadband. This total is measured irrespective of the method of payment. It excludes subscriptions that have access to data communications (including the Internet) via mobile-cellular networks. It should include fixed WiMAX and any other fixed wireless technologies. It includes both residential subscriptions and subscriptions for organizations.

The OECD average for fixed broadband subscriptions per 100 people in 2016 was 30. For the Arab world the fixed broadband subscriptions per 100 people in 2016 was 5. This figure represents a compound annual growth rate of 21 percent from 2007 where the number for fixed broadband subscriptions per 100 people was 1. With the exception of Cyprus, Israel, Iran and Lebanon who are at the OECD average, the balance of MENA countries,

Table 4.1. Availability of Information and Communication Technologies (ICT)

(2007–2016)

Country Name	Indicator Name	2007	2008	2009	2010	2011	2012	2013	2014	2015	2016	Compound Annual Growth Rate
Algeria	Fixed broadband subscriptions	287,039	485,000	818,000	900,000	980,752	1,154,748	1,280,000	1,599,692	2,269,348	2,858,906	0.291
Algeria	Fixed broadband subscriptions (per 100 people)	1	1	2	2	3	3	3	4	6	7	0.268
Algeria	Fixed telephone subscriptions (per 100 people)	9	9	7	8	8	9	8	8	8	8	−0.007
Algeria	Mobile cellular subscriptions	27,562,721	27,031,472	32,729,824	32,780,165	35,615,926	37,527,703	39,517,045	43,298,174	43,227,643	48,348,505	0.064
Algeria	Mobile cellular subscriptions (per 100 people)	79	76	90	88	94	98	101	108	106	117	0.045
Algeria	Secure Internet servers	8	18	19	31	34	49	60	77	101	146	0.381
Algeria	Secure Internet servers (per 1 million people)	0	1	1	1	1	1	2	2	3	4	0.355
Algeria	Individuals using the Internet (% of population)	9.5	10.2	11.2	12.5	14.9	18.2	22.5	29.5	38.2	42.9	0.183

(Continued)

Table 4.1. (*Continued*)

		(2007–2016)										
Country Name	Indicator Name	2007	2008	2009	2010	2011	2012	2013	2014	2015	2016	Compound Annual Growth Rate
Bahrain	Fixed broadband subscriptions	68,253	93,618	139,513	154,912	291,521	295,387	300,056	287,572	253,041	232,210	0.146
Bahrain	Fixed broadband subscriptions (per 100 people)	7	8	12	12	23	22	23	21	19	17	0.109
Bahrain	Fixed telephone subscriptions (per 100 people)	20	20	20	18	21	23	22	21	21	21	0.006
Bahrain	Mobile cellular subscriptions	1,115,979	1,440,782	1,401,974	1,567,000	1,693,650	2,123,903	2,210,190	2,328,994	2,519,055	2,994,865	0.116
Bahrain	Mobile cellular subscriptions (per 100 people)	108	129	118	125	131	161	166	173	185	217	0.080
Bahrain	Secure Internet servers	42	60	75	123	156	179	189	241	258	279	0.234
Bahrain	Secure Internet servers (per 1 million people)	41	54	63	99	122	138	144	180	188	196	0.191
Bahrain	Individuals using the Internet (% of population)	32.9	52.0	53.0	55.0	77.0	88.0	90.0	90.5	93.5	98.0	0.129

Cyprus	Fixed broadband subscriptions	97,613	147,276	176,024	194,455	212,149	220,580	229,195	243,611	260,640	278,483	0.124
Cyprus	Fixed broadband subscriptions (per 100 people)	9	19	22	23	25	26	27	29	31	33	0.153
Cyprus	Fixed telephone subscriptions (per 100 people)	38	53	51	50	48	43	41	38	38	38	−0.001
Cyprus	Mobile cellular subscriptions	988,312	1,016,739	977,521	1,034,071	1,090,944	1,110,935	1,099,621	1,110,802	1,111,123	1,133,780	0.015
Cyprus	Mobile cellular subscriptions (per 100 people)	93	129	121	125	128	129	128	130	132	134	0.042
Cyprus	Secure Internet servers	312	370	481	925	1252	888	709	700	789	890	0.124
Cyprus	Secure Internet servers (per 1 million people)	293	342	438	831	1113	782	620	607	680	761	0.112
Cyprus	Individuals using the Internet (% of population)	40.8	42.3	49.8	53.0	56.9	60.7	65.5	69.3	71.7	75.9	0.071
Djibouti	Fixed broadband subscriptions	1,092	2,451	5,285	8,058	11,302	14,907	17,705	20,102	24,165	27,000	0.428
Djibouti	Fixed broadband subscriptions (per 100 people)	0	0	1	1	1	2	2	2	3	3	0.407
Djibouti	Fixed telephone subscriptions (per 100 people)	2	2	2	2	2	2	2	2	3	3	0.050
Djibouti	Mobile cellular subscriptions	69,539	112,848	128,776	165,613	193,049	212,468	244,123	287,049	314,350	345,246	0.195
Djibouti	Mobile cellular subscriptions (per 100 people)	9	14	16	20	23	25	28	32	35	38	0.177
Djibouti	Secure Internet servers	1	1	4	5	5	4	4	9	8	7	0.241

(Continued)

Table 4.1. *(Continued)*

Country Name	Indicator Name	2007	2008	2009	2010	2011	2012	2013	2014	2015	2016	Compound Annual Growth Rate
		(2007–2016)										
Djibouti	Secure Internet servers (per 1 million people)	1	1	5	6	6	5	4	10	9	7	0.221
Djibouti	Individuals using the Internet (% of population)	1.6	2.3	4.0	6.5	7.0	8.3	9.5	10.7	11.9	13.1	0.262
Egypt	Fixed broadband subscriptions	477,432	769,744	1,077,489	1,451,628	1,845,249	2,288,773	2,676,263	3,067,878	3,826,410	4,469,164	0.282
Egypt	Fixed broadband subscriptions (per 100 people)	1	1	1	2	2	3	3	4	5	5	0.261
Egypt	Fixed telephone subscriptions (per 100 people)	15	16	13	12	11	11	8	8	7	7	−0.080
Egypt	Mobile cellular subscriptions	30,093,673	41,286,662	55,352,233	70,661,005	83,425,145	96,798,801	99,704,976	95,316,034	94,016,152	97,791,441	0.140
Egypt	Mobile cellular subscriptions (per 100 people)	41	55	72	91	105	120	122	114	111	114	0.121
Egypt	Secure Internet servers	64	81	119	186	248	299	285	429	498	498	0.256
Egypt	Secure Internet servers (per 1 million people)	1	1	1	2	3	3	3	5	5	5	0.231

Egypt	Individuals using the Internet (% of population)	16.0	18.0	20.0	21.6	25.6	26.4	29.4	33.9	37.8	39.2	0.105
Iran	Fixed broadband subscriptions	200,000	300,000	400,000	987,549	2,119,708	3,803,692	5,161,156	7,425,807	8,633,861	9,318,943	0.532
Iran	Fixed broadband subscriptions (per 100 people)	0	0	1	1	3	5	7	9	11	12	0.513
Iran	Fixed telephone subscriptions (per 100 people)	33	34	35	35	37	38	38	37	38	38	0.016
Iran	Mobile cellular subscriptions	29,770,000	43,000,000	52,555,000	54,051,764	56,043,006	58,157,539	65,246,219	68,891,151	74,218,815	80,520,249	0.117
Iran	Mobile cellular subscriptions (per 100 people)	41	59	71	73	74	76	84	88	93	100	0.103
Iran	Secure Internet servers	22	20	24	55	76	103	98	167	437	1139	0.550
Iran	Secure Internet servers (per 1 million people)	0	0	0	1	1	1	1	2	6	14	0.532
Iran	Individuals using the Internet (% of population)	9.5	12.0	13.8	15.9	19.0	22.7	30.0	39.4	45.3	53.2	0.211
Israel	Fixed broadband subscriptions	1,528,500	1,684,000	1,723,000	1,762,000	1,879,029	1,937,000	2,003,000	2,131,000	2,173,000	2,258,000	0.044
Israel	Fixed broadband subscriptions (per 100 people)	22	24	24	24	25	25	26	27	27	28	0.027
Israel	Fixed telephone subscriptions (per 100 people)	44	45	46	46	46	47	44	44	43	42	−0.007

(*Continued*)

Table 4.1. (*Continued*)

(2007–2016)

Country Name	Indicator Name	2007	2008	2009	2010	2011	2012	2013	2014	2015	2016	Compound Annual Growth Rate
Israel	Mobile cellular subscriptions	8,902,000	8,982,000	9,022,000	9,111,000	9,200,000	9,225,000	9,500,000	9,500,000	10,570,000	10,570,000	0.019
Israel	Mobile cellular subscriptions (per 100 people)	128	126	124	123	122	121	123	121	133	132	0.003
Israel	Secure Internet servers	1.637	1.993	2.165	3,024	3,651	3.135	2.179	2,089	2,420	2.506	0.048
Israel	Secure Internet servers (per 1 million people)	228	273	289	397	470	396	270	254	289	293	0.028
Israel	Individuals using the Internet (% of population)	48.1	59.4	63.1	67.5	68.9	70.8	70.3	75.0	77.4	79.8	0.058
Jordan	Fixed broadband subscriptions	88.818	145.838	237.996	293.276	296.612	300,294	328.382	351.783	320.205	456.610	0.200
Jordan	Fixed broadband subscriptions (per 100 people)	2	2	4	5	4	4	5	5	4	6	0.157
Jordan	Fixed telephone subscriptions (per 100 people)	10	9	8	8	7	6	5	5	5	5	−0.083
Jordan	Mobile cellular subscriptions	4,771,641	5,313,564	6,014,366	6,620,000	7,482,561	8,984,252	10,313,976	11,092,404	13,797,968	15,352,000	0.139
Jordan	Mobile cellular subscriptions (per 100 people)	84	90	97	103	111	128	142	148	179	196	0.098
Jordan	Secure Internet servers	34	52	72	120	156	185	174	201	210	227	0.235

Jordan	Secure Internet servers (per 1 million people)	5	8	11	17	21	23	21	23	23	24	0.178
Jordan	Individuals using the Internet (% of population)	20.0	23.0	26.0	27.2	34.9	37.0	41.4	46.2	60.1	62.3	0.135
Kuwait	Fixed broadband subscriptions	35,000	40,000	45,000	46,000	47,000	47,000	47,000	48,000	55,000	101,390	0.125
Kuwait	Fixed broadband subscriptions (per 100 people)	1	1	2	2	2	1	1	1	2	3	0.081
Kuwait	Fixed telephone subscriptions (per 100 people)	21	19	19	17	16	16	15	14	13	11	−0.070
Kuwait	Mobile cellular subscriptions	1,426,395	1,499,912	2,618,413	3,979,145	4,934,160	5,100,000	6,410,000	7,600,000	5,846,335	5,392,806	0.159
Kuwait	Mobile cellular subscriptions (per 100 people)	56	56	92	133	158	157	190	218	163	147	0.113
Kuwait	Secure Internet servers	135	177	238	380	505	582	623	746	869	954	0.243
Kuwait	Secure Internet servers (per 1 million people)	54	67	84	127	158	171	173	197	221	235	0.178
Kuwait	Individuals using the Internet (% of population)	34.8	42.0	50.8	61.4	65.8	70.5	75.5	78.7	77.5	78.4	0.094
Lebanon	Fixed broadband subscriptions	50,000	100,000	197,000	331,089	402,329	476,185	480,000	1,132,139	1,283,258	1,300,000	0.436
Lebanon	Fixed broadband subscriptions (per 100 people)	1	2	5	8	9	10	10	23	25	26	0.404
Lebanon	Fixed telephone subscriptions (per 100 people)	17	18	19	19	19	19	18	19	20	21	0.025

(Continued)

Table 4.1. (*Continued*)

		(2007–2016)										
Country Name	Indicator Name	2007	2008	2009	2010	2011	2012	2013	2014	2015	2016	Compound Annual Growth Rate
Lebanon	Mobile cellular subscriptions	1,260,000	1,427,000	2,390,317	2,863,664	3,456,650	3,755,169	3,884,757	4,387,275	4,657,651	4,890,534	0.163
Lebanon	Mobile cellular subscriptions (per 100 people)	30	34	56	66	77	81	81	88	92	96	0.137
Lebanon	Secure Internet servers	45	54	65	121	175	215	192	248	282	297	0.233
Lebanon	Secure Internet servers (per 1 million people)	11	13	16	28	38	44	36	44	48	49	0.182
Lebanon	Individuals using the Internet (% of population)	18.7	22.5	30.1	43.7	52.0	61.2	70.5	73.0	74.0	76.1	0.169
Morocco	Fixed broadband subscriptions	477,360	493,228	479,503	504,499	595,207	689,541	843,940	993,451	1,147,533	1,255,428	0.113
Morocco	Fixed broadband subscriptions (per 100 people)	2	2	2	2	2	2	3	3	3	4	0.099
Morocco	Fixed telephone subscriptions (per 100 people)	8	10	11	12	11	10	9	7	7	6	−0.028

Morocco	Mobile cellular subscriptions	20,029,300	22,815,694	25,310,761	31,982,279	36,553,943	39,016,336	42,423,794	44,114,534	43,079,696	41,513,933	0.084
Morocco	Mobile cellular subscriptions (per 100 people)	65	74	81	101	114	120	129	132	127	121	0.071
Morocco	Secure Internet servers	33	44	62	95	139	116	120	167	212	252	0.253
Morocco	Secure Internet servers (per 1 million people)	1	1	2	3	4	3	4	5	6	7	0.237
Morocco	Individuals using the Internet (% of population)	21.5	33.1	41.3	52.0	46.1	55.4	56.0	56.8	57.1	58.3	0.117
Oman	Fixed broadband subscriptions	20,177	32,447	41,131	58,556	78,217	113,324	154,290	177,063	233,234	266,983	0.332
Oman	Fixed broadband subscriptions (per 100 people)	1	1	2	2	3	3	4	5	6	6	0.258
Oman	Fixed telephone subscriptions (per 100 people)	11	12	11	10	9	9	10	10	10	10	−0.017
Oman	Mobile cellular subscriptions	2,500,000	3,219,349	3,970,563	4,606,133	4,809,248	5,277,591	5,617,426	6,194,169	6,646,655	6,866,260	0.119
Oman	Mobile cellular subscriptions (per 100 people)	97	124	149	164	159	159	155	158	160	159	0.056
Oman	Secure Internet servers	15	32	—	77	152	186	228	336	394	426	0.450
Oman	Secure Internet servers (per 1 million people)	6	12	—	25	47	54	61	85	94	96	0.371

(Continued)

Table 4.1. (*Continued*)

		(2007–2016)										
Country Name	Indicator Name	2007	2008	2009	2010	2011	2012	2013	2014	2015	2016	Compound Annual Growth Rate
Oman	Individuals using the Internet (% of population)	16.7	20.0	26.8	35.8	48.0	60.0	66.5	70.2	66.1	69.8	0.172
Qatar	Fixed broadband subscriptions	87,673	106,177	144,760	145,787	164,601	185,127	215,487	224,633	237,774	260,002	0.128
Qatar	Fixed broadband subscriptions (per 100 people)	8	8	9	8	9	9	10	10	10	11	0.039
Qatar	Fixed telephone subscriptions (per 100 people)	21	20	18	15	16	19	19	18	18	19	−0.007
Qatar	Mobile cellular subscriptions	1,264,206	1,429,486	1,948,770	2,186,447	2,302,225	2,601,210	3,310,353	3,305,822	3,740,469	3,552,579	0.122
Qatar	Mobile cellular subscriptions (per 100 people)	110	105	125	125	120	127	153	146	159	147	0.033
Qatar	Secure Internet servers	41	65	90	150	236	289	351	503	663	691	0.369
Qatar	Secure Internet servers (per 1 million people)	34	47	57	84	121	137	156	212	267	269	0.256

Qatar	Individuals using the Internet (% of population)	37.0	44.3	53.1	69.0	69.0	69.3	85.3	91.5	92.9	94.3	0.110
SA	Fixed broadband subscriptions	623,116	1,048,098	1,437,718	1,711,598	1,951,457	2,540,151	2,919,701	3,032,237	3,564,976	3,287,663	0.203
SA	Fixed broadband subscriptions (per 100 people)	2	4	5	6	7	9	10	10	12	11	0.182
SA	Fixed telephone subscriptions (per 100 people)	15	16	16	15	17	17	17	12	13	12	−0.028
SA	Mobile cellular subscriptions	28,400,000	36,000,000	44,864,355	51,564,375	54,000,000	53,000,000	53,104,000	52,735,000	52,796,066	47,932,521	0.060
SA	Mobile cellular subscriptions (per 100 people)	110	137	167	189	195	187	184	180	177	158	0.041
SA	Secure Internet servers	160	204	279	480	605	864	987	1,417	1,695	1,860	0.313
SA	Secure Internet servers (per 1 million people)	6	8	10	18	21	30	33	46	54	58	0.278
SA	Individuals using the Internet (% of population)	30.0	36.0	38.0	41.0	47.5	54.0	60.5	64.7	69.6	73.8	0.105
Syria	Fixed broadband subscriptions	6,957	11,055	34,657	69,817	121,300	242,154	346,146	501,194	700,000	913,684	0.719
Syria	Fixed broadband subscriptions (per 100 people)	0	0	0	0	1	1	2	2	3	4	0.691

(*Continued*)

Table 4.1. (*Continued*)

		(2007–2016)										
Country Name	Indicator Name	2007	2008	2009	2010	2011	2012	2013	2014	2015	2016	Compound Annual Growth Rate
Syria	Fixed telephone subscriptions (per 100 people)	18	18	18	19	20	19	20	17	16	15	−0.016
Syria	Mobile cellular subscriptions	6,234,682	7,056,158	10,021,861	11,696,000	12,917,000	12,980,000	12,291,150	14,039,749	14,312,271	12,350,927	0.079
Syria	Mobile cellular subscriptions (per 100 people)	32	35	48	54	59	59	56	64	64	54	0.061
Syria	Secure Internet servers	2	3	7	2	5	8	10	11	17	11	0.209
Syria	Secure Internet servers (per 1 million people)	0	0	0	0	0	0	1	1	1	1	0.217
Syria	Individuals using the Internet (% of population)	11.5	14.0	17.3	20.7	22.5	24.3	26.2	28.1	30.0	31.9	0.120
Tunisia	Fixed broadband subscriptions	95,916	227,328	372,887	482,204	559,358	527,308	519,984	498,730	573,977	641,113	0.235

Tunisia	Fixed broadband subscriptions (per 100 people)	1	2	4	5	5	5	5	4	5	6	0.221
Tunisia	Fixed telephone subscriptions (per 100 people)	12	12	12	12	11	10	9	9	8	9	−0.040
Tunisia	Mobile cellular subscriptions	7,842,619	8,602,164	9,797,026	11,114,206	12,387,656	12,843,889	12,712,365	14,283,633	14,595,875	14,282,078	0.069
Tunisia	Mobile cellular subscriptions (per 100 people)	76	83	93	105	115	118	116	128	130	126	0.057
Tunisia	Secure Internet servers	91	110	130	149	206	141	185	197	147	153	0.059
Tunisia	Secure Internet servers (per 1 million people)	9	11	12	14	19	13	17	18	13	13	0.047
Tunisia	Individuals using the Internet (% of population)	17.1	27.5	34.1	36.8	39.1	41.4	43.8	46.2	48.5	50.9	0.129
Turkey	Fixed broadband subscriptions	4,753,757	5,756,965	6,450,287	7,098,163	7.591.367	7,868,968	8,893,391	8,866,361	9,504.594	10,499.692	0.092
Turkey	Fixed broadband subscriptions (per 100 people)	7	8	9	10	10	11	12	12	12	14	0.079
Turkey	Fixed telephone subscriptions (per 100 people)	26	25	23	22	21	19	18	17	15	14	−0.065
Turkey	Mobile cellular subscriptions	61,975,807	65,824,110	62,779,554	61,769,635	65,321,745	67,680,547	69,661,108	71,888,416	73,639,261	75,061,699	0.022

(*Continued*)

Table 4.1. (*Continued*)

Country Name	Indicator Name	(2007–2016) 2007	2008	2009	2010	2011	2012	2013	2014	2015	2016	Compound Annual Growth Rate
Turkey	Mobile cellular subscriptions (per 100 people)	89	94	88	86	89	91	93	95	96	97	0.009
Turkey	Secure Internet servers	2,818	4,230	4,947	7,202	10,494	8,640	3,779	4,354	5,278	6,367	0.095
Turkey	Secure Internet servers (per 1 million people)	40	60	69	100	143	116	50	57	67	80	0.079
Turkey	Individuals using the Internet (% of population)	28.6	34.4	36.4	39.8	43.1	45.1	46.3	51.0	53.7	58.3	0.082
UAE	Fixed broadband subscriptions	379,800	557,577	690,424	786,818	866,968	954,988	1,041,934	1,091,763	1,234,447	1,297,585	0.146
UAE	Fixed broadband subscriptions (per 100 people)	7	8	9	9	10	10	11	12	13	13	0.082
UAE	Fixed telephone subscriptions (per 100 people)	24	23	20	18	20	21	22	22	24	23	−0.002
UAE	Mobile cellular subscriptions	7,731,508	9,357,735	10,671,878	10,926,019	11,727,401	13,775,252	16,063,547	16,819,024	17,942,560	19,905,093	0.111

UAE	Mobile cellular subscriptions (per 100 people)	133	138	138	129	131	150	172	178	187	204	0.048
UAE	Secure Internet servers	417	564	758	1,145	1,423	1,691	1,815	2,675	3,248	3,623	0.272
UAE	Secure Internet servers (per 1 million people)	69	82	99	138	164	190	202	295	355	391	0.213
UAE	Individuals using the Internet (% of population)	61.0	63.0	64.0	68.0	78.0	85.0	88.0	90.4	90.5	90.6	0.045
Yemen	Fixed broadband subscriptions	11,000	26,000	54,000	84,000	109,000	167,300	256,800	340,000	395,000	430,400	0.503
Yemen	Fixed broadband subscriptions (per 100 people)	0	0	0	0	0	1	1	1	2	2	0.468
Yemen	Fixed telephone subscriptions (per 100 people)	5	4	4	5	5	5	5	5	5	5	−0.004
Yemen	Mobile cellular subscriptions	4,349,000	6,445,000	8,313,000	11,085,000	11,668,000	13,900,000	16,844,700	17,100,000	17,359,000	17,536,000	0.168
Yemen	Mobile cellular subscriptions (per 100 people)	21	30	37	49	50	58	69	68	68	67	0.141
Yemen	Secure Internet servers	2	4	5	7	10	11	16	19	17	17	0.268
Yemen	Secure Internet servers (per 1 million people)	0	0	0	0	0	0	1	1	1	1	0.235

(*Continued*)

Table 4.1. *(Continued)*

		(2007–2016)										
Country Name	Indicator Name	2007	2008	2009	2010	2011	2012	2013	2014	2015	2016	Compound Annual Growth Rate
Yemen	Individuals using the Internet (% of population)	5.0	6.9	10.0	12.4	14.9	17.4	20.0	22.6	24.1	24.6	0.193
Arab World	Fixed broadband subscriptions	2,811,961	4,235,468	5,845,325	7,123,797	8,570,787	10,323,586	11,799,992	13,764,423	16,575,189	18,419,019	0.232
Arab World	Fixed broadband subscriptions (per 100 people)	1	1	2	2	3	3	4	4	5	5	0.217
Arab World	Fixed telephone subscriptions (per 100 people)	10	10	10	10	10	10	9	8	8	8	−0.030
Arab World	Mobile cellular subscriptions	174,488,139	214,062,549	265,270,824	312,247,800	351,957,968	381,641,858	407,704,505	415,029,432	419,532,602	419,028,364	0.102

Arab World	Mobile cellular subscriptions (per 100 people)	53	63	76	88	99	105	110	110	109	107	0.082
Arab World	Secure Internet servers	1,103	1,489	1,951	3,109	4,100	4,865	5,299	7,354	8,731	9,592	0.272
Arab World	Secure Internet servers (per 1 million people)	4	4	6	9	11	13	14	19	22	24	0.231
Arab World	Individuals using the Internet (% of population)	14.2	18.6	21.5	24.5	26.6	30.3	33.0	36.5	39.9	42.0	0.128
OECD	Fixed broadband subscriptions	238,168,990	268,647,254	288,558,103	306,017,375	322,102,317	334,799,023	347,182,044	357,403,815	373,091,645	386,446,916	0.055
OECD	Fixed broadband subscriptions (per 100 people)	20	22	23	25	26	27	27	28	29	30	0.047
OECD	Fixed telephone subscriptions (per 100 people)	44	44	45	44	43	42	40	39	38	38	−0.017

(*Continued*)

Table 4.1. (*Continued*)

Country Name	Indicator Name	2007	2008	2009	2010	2011	2012	2013	2014	2015	2016	Compound Annual Growth Rate
		(2007–2016)										
OECD	Mobile cellular subscriptions	1,146,822,765	1,205,103,884	1,236,161,941	1,261,091,698	1,312,536,754	1,352,985,422	1,384,002,555	1,435,902,332	1,472,810,933	1,520,536,105	0.032
OECD	Mobile cellular subscriptions (per 100 people)	94	98	100	101	105	107	109	113	115	118	0.025
OECD	Secure Internet servers	601,270	705,599	724,979	1,011,239	1,207,059	1,198,856	1,059,349	1,262,894	1,394,006	1,414,662	0.100
OECD	Secure Internet servers (per 1 million people)	495	576	619	814	967	954	838	992	1,088	1,097	0.093
OECD	Individuals using the Internet (% of population)	61.9	63.9	65.3	67.6	68.5	70.9	72.3	73.9	76.5	78.6	0.027

Source: World Bank Development Indicators, 2017; International Telecommunication Union, World Telecommunication/ICT Development Report and database; Netcraft (http://www.netcraft.com/) and World Bank population estimates.

regardless of their oil wealth, are far behind what would be acceptable for internet access in a modern digital world.

The third set of observations is for fixed telephone subscriptions per 100 people. This refers to the sum of active number of analogue fixed-telephone lines, voice-over-IP (VoIP) subscriptions, fixed wireless local loop (WLL) subscriptions, ISDN voice-channel equivalents and fixed public payphones. The OECD average for 2016 was 30 subscriptions, down from 44 subscriptions in 2007, reflecting the change in technology to wireless. For the Arab world the 2016 number of subscriptions per 100 people was 38. For the MENA countries, with the exception of Cyprus, Israel, Iran and Lebanon who are at the OECD average, the balance of MENA countries, are far behind what would be acceptable for communication needs.

The fourth and fifth set of observations is for mobile cellular telephone subscriptions, in total and per 100 people. These subscriptions are to a public mobile telephone service that provide access to the PSTN using cellular technology. The indicator includes (and is split into) the number of postpaid subscriptions and the number of active prepaid accounts (i.e., that have been used during the last three months). The indicator applies to all mobile cellular subscriptions that offer voice communications. It excludes subscriptions via data cards or USB modems, subscriptions to public mobile data services, private trunked mobile radio, telepoint, radio paging and telemetry services. The OECD average for 2016 was 118 subscriptions per 100 people, up from 94 subscriptions in 2007, reflecting the change in technology to wireless. For the Arab world, the 2016 number of subscriptions per 100 people was 107 up from 53 in 2007. For the MENA countries, except for the poorest countries, the OECD standard for mobile cellular telephone subscriptions per 100 was met, if not substantially overpassed.

The sixth and seventh set of observations is for total secure servers and per 1 million people. These are servers using encryption technology in Internet transactions. For the OECD the number of secure Internet servers per million people in 2016 was 1,097. For the Arab world the number of secure Internet servers per million people in 2016 was exceptionally low, at 24 per million. For MENA the lowest number of secure Internet servers per million people in 2016 was in Syria and Yemen both with 1, Algeria with 4, Egypt with 5, Djibouti and Morocco both with 7, Tunisia with 13, Iran with 14, Jordan with 24 and Lebanon with 49. At the upper end of the distribution, the highest number of secure Internet servers per million people in 2016 was in Cyprus with 761, UAE with 391, Israel with 293, Qatar with 269, Kuwait with 235 and Bahrain with 196.

Eight observations are for the number of individuals have used the Internet (from any location) in the last 3 months, measured as percent of the population. The measure considers that the Internet can be used via a computer, mobile phone, personal digital assistant, games machine, digital TV etc. For the OECD the percent of the population using the Internet in 2016 was 78.6. For the Arab world the percent of the population using the Internet in 2016 was 42.0. At the upper end of the distribution within MENA, the largest percent of the population using the Internet in 2016 was in Bahrain with 98 percent, Qatar with 94.3 percent, UAE with 90.6 percent, Israel with 79.8 percent, Cyprus with 75.9 percent, Kuwait with 78.4 percent, Lebanon with 76.1 percent and Saudi Arabia with 73.8 percent.

Despite the changes in availability of the Internet within MENA over the 2007–2016 period there is still a long path to travel for more than 50 percent of the MENA countries to get to the OECD average standard.

To assess the ranking of the MENA countries in the general ICT area we present in Table 4.2 a number indices ranking each MENA country relative to the world (in Panel A) and in terms of each country's score ranging from 0 to 100 (in Panel B). All indices present both the rank and the country score. The first index presented is the overall ICT world ranking and country score. The average rank for MENA was 64 and the average country score was 56. There was a major divide between those countries with a 'world-class' ICT infrastructure and those who fell behind. On the positive side, the UAE, Israel and Bahrain ranked 23, 24 and 25, respectively in the world. Their ICT scores were 78. The remaining MENA countries were closer to the MENA average.

The second index is the ICT access index. This index is a composite index that weights five ICT indicators (20 percent each): (1) Fixed telephone subscriptions per 100 inhabitants; (2) Mobile cellular telephone subscriptions per 100 inhabitants; (3) International Internet bandwidth (bit/s) per Internet user; (4) Percentage of households with a computer; and (5) Percentage of households with Internet access. It is the first sub-index in International Telecommunication Union's (ITU) ICT Development Index (IDI). For the MENA region, as a whole, their average ICT access index rank was 57, with a score of 65. The best performers in terms of ICT access within MENA included Israel with a rank of 18, the UAE with a rank of 23 and Bahrain with a rank of 29. The other members of the MENA community did not rank well as providers of ICT access. These figures were matched in terms of the ICT access scores, where Israel's score was 83, followed by the UAE with a score of 81 and Bahrain with a score of 79.

Table 4.2. Ranking Information and Communication Technologies (ICTs) Infrastructure in MENA, 2016

	Panel A: RANK					Panel B: SCORE (0–100)				
	Information and communication technologies (ICTs)	ICT access	ICT use	Government's online service	Online e-participation	Information and communication technologies (ICTs)	ICT access	ICT use	Government's online service	Online e-participation
Algeria	113	82	89	125	122	25	50	29	7	12
Bahrain	25	29	20	22	32	78	79	75	83	75
Cyprus	65	51	50	78	82	58	70	55	54	53
Egypt	91	78	84	90	97	43	53	31	47	41
Iran	98	68	91	104	113	36	63	27	33	20
Israel	24	18	38	18	17	78	83	60	86	83
Jordan	87	70	83	91	95	46	61	32	46	46
Kuwait	45	39	36	53	54	66	74	62	65	64
Lebanon	70	62	48	81	89	55	66	55	52	49
Morocco	53	71	79	36	17	63	61	34	74	83
Oman	57	41	53	67	74	61	74	54	59	56
Qatar	39	29	31	49	54	69	79	63	67	64
Saudi Arabia	38	42	31	49	39	69	73	63	67	71
Tunisia	64	79	70	40	43	58	53	40	72	70
Turkey	67	69	67	64	59	57	62	42	60	63
UAE	23	23	25	13	32	78	81	68	89	75
Yemen	121	116	111	119	121	17	27	11	15	14
MENA Average	64	57	59	65	67	56	65	47	57	55

Sources: ICT access and ICT use -International Telecommunication Union, Measuring the Information Society 2016, ICT Development Index 2016. http://www.itu.int/en/ITU-D/Statistics/Pages/publications/mis2016.aspx;

Government's online service and Online e-participation — United Nations Public Administration Network, e-Government Survey 2016. https://publicadministration.un.org/egovkb/en-us/Reports/UN-E-Government-Survey-2016.

Unfortunately, most MENA countries did not fulfil their citizen's desire for ICT access.

The third index is the ICT use index. This index is a composite index that weighs three ICT indicators (33 percent each): (1) Percentage of individuals using the Internet; (2) Fixed (wired)-broadband Internet subscriptions per 100 inhabitants; (3) Active Mobile-broadband subscriptions per 100 inhabitants. It is the second sub-index in ITU's ICT Development Index (IDI). For the MENA the average ICT use index rank was 59 and the ICT use score was 47, both on the low end of the spectrum. The individual ranking of the MENA countries in terms of ICT use has Bahrain, the UAE, Saudi Arabia, Qatar, Kuwait and Israel, at the lead, ranking 20, 25, 31, 31, 36 and 38. In terms of ICT use scores the top ranks include Bahrain, the UAE, Kuwait, Saudi Arabia, Qatar and Israel, with scores of 75, 68, 62, 63, 63 and 60.

The fourth index is the Government's online service index. This index is compiled by the United Nations as part of their ongoing survey work on e-Government. The UN assesses each country's national website in the native language, including the national portal, e-services portal, and e-participation portal, as well as the websites of the related ministries of education, labor, social services, health, finance and environment as applicable. The average MENA rank for these services was 65 and the average score was 57. As usual, the subgroup with the best services include the UAE with a score of 13, Israel with a score of 18 and Bahrain with a score of 22. Their respective scores were 89 for the UAE, 86 for Israel and 83 for Bahrain. The balance of the MENA countries were far closer to the average rank and score.

The fifth and final index is the Online e-Participation Index. This index is derived as a supplementary index to the UN e-Government Survey. It extends the dimension of the Survey by focusing on the use of online services to facilitate provision of information by governments to citizens ('e-information sharing'), interaction with stakeholders ('e-consultation') and engagement in decision-making processes. A country's Online e-Participation Index reflects its e-participation mechanisms that are deployed by the government as compared to all other countries. The purpose of this measure is to provide information on how different countries are using online tools to promote interaction between citizen and government, as well as among citizens, for the benefit of the public. Because the Online e-Participation Index is a qualitative assessment based on the availability and relevance of participatory services available on government websites, the comparative ranking of countries should serve as an indicator of the broad trends in promoting citizen engagement. This index is designed to capture the e-participation performance of counties relative to one another at a particular point in time. The index ranges from 0 to 1, with 1 showing greater e-participation.[25] For MENA the average rank for Online e-Participation Index was 67 and the average score was 55. The most efficient providers of government services online included Israel with a rank of 17, the UAE and Bahrain both with a rank of 32. Their scores were 83 for Israel, and 75 for both the UAE and Bahrain.

The importance of unrestricted access to ICT and government-citizen services provided by efficient ICT providers cannot be understated. Within MENA there are only a few countries that have responded to this consumer demand. Those few countries include Israel, the UAE, Kuwait, Saudi Arabia, Qatar and Bahrain. Consequently, these countries will be able to take advantage of the downstream positive implications of investing in ICT. The immediate positive impact is the integration of these few MENA countries into the global innovation infrastructure. The majority of MENA countries will be left further behind in the development path, in part because of their inability to invest in the ICT infrastructure of the 21st century.

4.2.2. *The Supply Side*

There are many factors that are considered to be the building blocks of a knowledge economy. The development literature has historically focused on indicators such as increased education levels, the growing globalization of an economy in terms of trade in goods and services, and the internationalization of innovation, and the advancements in the utilization of the Internet for consumer activity and government services combined with an expansion of investment in ICT.

The World Bank Institute as part of its endeavor to measure the knowledge economy created the Knowledge Assessment Methodology (KAM) which focuses on a number of accepted indicators. That primary indicators used as building blocks in the KAM project include a country's transition from an industrial economy to a service-based economy, the education of increasing numbers of professional and technical workers and

[25]The precise meaning of the UN indices varies from one edition of the Survey to the next as understanding of the potential of e-government changes and the underlying technology evolves. Read about the methodology at http://unpan3.un.org/egovkb/en-us/About/Methodology.

their integration into the economy, the transition to an information society organized around knowledge and information, enhanced scientific research and development, alongside the integration of science and technology with the economy, and the focus on advancing the focus on intellectual technology. Consequently, the KAM project views the pillars of knowledge in the knowledge economy the development of ICT and progress in investing in human capital.

The KAM Knowledge Index (KI) measures a country's ability to generate, adopt and diffuse knowledge. This is an indication of overall potential of knowledge development in a given country. The Knowledge Economy Index (KEI) takes into account whether the environment is conducive for knowledge to be used effectively for economic development. It is an aggregate index that represents the overall level of development of a country or region toward the Knowledge Economy. The KEI is calculated based on the average of the normalized performance scores of a country or region on all four pillars related to the knowledge economy — economic incentive and institutional regime, education and human resources, the innovation system, and ICT (World Bank, KAM).

Table 4.3 presents the KEI, the KI, and the Economy Incentive Index, the Innovation Index, the Education index, the ICT index and the country's rank as a knowledge economy. Taking the first two major education indicators used by the World Bank to assess a country's preparedness to compete in the knowledge economy, it is very revealing that in the 21st century, few Arab MENA countries belong to the upper half of the world's countries on these indices. Only Israel and Cyprus has KEI and KI indices over 7 in 1995, 2000 and 2012. The overall knowledge ranking was 16 for Israel in 1995 dropping to 25 in 2012, 32 for Cyprus in 1995 dropping to 35 in 2012, and 36 for Bahrain in 1995 dropping to 43 in 2012. None of the other MENA countries had attained indices and ranks close to these three countries.

In order to better understand the barriers that citizens in MENA face in the struggle to become a knowledge economy, we look at the World Bank's indices for Economic Incentive Regime, Innovation, Education, and ICT as the building blocks for the facilitation of a world-class human capital delivery system. These indices cover physical resources, finance and administration, curricula and teaching methods, evaluation and monitoring, motivation and rewards, and information and "public accountability."

In terms of the Economic Incentive Regime Index, Israel is the only country within MENA that had an index above 8 for 1995, 2000 and 2012. Cyprus had an index above 8 in 1995 dropping to 7.71 in 2012. For Iran

Table 4.3. Various Knowledge Economy Indices, Weighted by Population for MENA

(1995, 2000, 2012)

[Each index (0 = lowest & 10 = highest) and Rank (1 = the Best)]

Country	Indicator	1995	2000	2012
Algeria	Knowledge Economy Index	3.5	2.85	3.79
Algeria	Knowledge Index	4.05	3.44	4.28
Algeria	Economic Incentive Regime Index	1.85	1.09	2.33
Algeria	Innovation Index	3.41	3.25	3.54
Algeria	Education Index	3.88	3.96	5.27
Algeria	ICT Index	4.87	3.11	4.04
Algeria	Knowledge Economy Rank	108	110	96
Bahrain	Knowledge Economy Index	6.97	6.85	6.9
Bahrain	Knowledge Index	6.98	6.66	6.98
Bahrain	Economic Incentive Regime Index	6.95	7.45	6.69
Bahrain	Innovation Index	6.93	6.37	4.61
Bahrain	Education Index	6.49	6.34	6.78
Bahrain	ICT Index	7.52	7.26	9.54
Bahrain	Knowledge Economy Rank	36	41	43
Cyprus	Knowledge Economy Index	7.68	7.53	7.56
Cyprus	Knowledge Index	7.43	7.46	7.5
Cyprus	Economic Incentive Regime Index	8.43	7.73	7.71
Cyprus	Innovation Index	7.47	7.4	7.71
Cyprus	Education Index	6.75	6.95	7.23
Cyprus	ICT Index	8.05	8.04	7.57
Cyprus	Knowledge Economy Rank	32	32	35
Djibouti	Knowledge Economy Index	3.01	1.59	1.34
Djibouti	Knowledge Index	2.7	1.43	1.17
Djibouti	Economic Incentive Regime Index	3.94	2.07	1.85
Djibouti	Innovation Index	2.66	1.34	1.44
Djibouti	Education Index	0.35	0.35	0.73
Djibouti	ICT Index	5.11	2.6	1.33
Djibouti	Knowledge Economy Rank	115	136	139
Egypt	Knowledge Economy Index	4.68	4.29	3.78
Egypt	Knowledge Index	4.86	4.49	3.54
Egypt	Economic Incentive Regime Index	4.14	3.68	4.5
Egypt	Innovation Index	5.08	5.03	4.11
Egypt	Education Index	4.64	4.66	3.37
Egypt	ICT Index	4.87	3.77	3.12
Egypt	Knowledge Economy Rank	87	88	97

(Continued)

Table 4.3. (*Continued*)

Country	Indicator	1995	2000	2012
Iran	Knowledge Economy Index	3.59	3.6	3.91
Iran	Knowledge Index	4.58	4.05	4.97
Iran	Economic Incentive Regime Index	0.63	2.25	0.73
Iran	Innovation Index	2.86	2.62	5.02
Iran	Education Index	4.47	4.42	4.61
Iran	ICT Index	6.41	5.1	5.28
Iran	Knowledge Economy Rank	105	95	94
Israel	Knowledge Economy Index	8.79	8.8	8.14
Israel	Knowledge Index	8.73	8.79	8.07
Israel	Economic Incentive Regime Index	8.96	8.85	8.33
Israel	Innovation Index	9.18	9.53	9.39
Israel	Education Index	8.5	8.28	7.47
Israel	ICT Index	8.51	8.55	7.36
Israel	Knowledge Economy Rank	16	18	25
Jordan	Knowledge Economy Index	5.55	5.58	4.95
Jordan	Knowledge Index	5.51	5.68	4.71
Jordan	Economic Incentive Regime Index	5.67	5.28	5.65
Jordan	Innovation Index	6.17	6.2	4.05
Jordan	Education Index	4.48	5.62	5.55
Jordan	ICT Index	5.89	5.22	4.54
Jordan	Knowledge Economy Rank	61	57	75
Kuwait	Knowledge Economy Index	5.71	6.16	5.33
Kuwait	Knowledge Index	5.82	5.88	5.15
Kuwait	Economic Incentive Regime Index	5.36	7	5.86
Kuwait	Innovation Index	5.5	5.38	5.22
Kuwait	Education Index	4.51	5.17	3.7
Kuwait	ICT Index	7.46	7.09	6.53
Kuwait	Knowledge Economy Rank	57	46	64
Lebanon	Knowledge Economy Index	5.38	4.95	4.56
Lebanon	Knowledge Index	5.75	5.58	4.65
Lebanon	Economic Incentive Regime Index	4.29	3.04	4.28
Lebanon	Innovation Index	4.26	4.47	4.86
Lebanon	Education Index	6.65	5.77	5.51
Lebanon	ICT Index	6.32	6.49	3.58
Lebanon	Knowledge Economy Rank	63	68	81
Morocco	Knowledge Economy Index	4.17	3.74	3.61
Morocco	Knowledge Index	4.03	3.33	3.25
Morocco	Economic Incentive Regime Index	4.6	4.99	4.66

(*Continued*)

Table 4.3. (*Continued*)

Country	Indicator	1995	2000	2012
Morocco	Innovation Index	4.79	4.04	3.67
Morocco	Education Index	2.44	2.02	2.07
Morocco	ICT Index	4.87	3.93	4.02
Morocco	Knowledge Economy Rank	96	92	102
Oman	Knowledge Economy Index	5.34	5.28	6.14
Oman	Knowledge Index	5.01	4.53	5.87
Oman	Economic Incentive Regime Index	6.33	7.51	6.96
Oman	Innovation Index	5.48	4.25	5.88
Oman	Education Index	3.65	4.22	5.23
Oman	ICT Index	5.89	5.12	6.49
Oman	Knowledge Economy Rank	65	65	47
Qatar	Knowledge Economy Index	5.86	6.01	5.84
Qatar	Knowledge Index	5.93	5.81	5.5
Qatar	Economic Incentive Regime Index	5.64	6.64	6.87
Qatar	Innovation Index	4.79	5.51	6.42
Qatar	Education Index	5.52	4.85	3.41
Qatar	ICT Index	7.49	7.05	6.65
Qatar	Knowledge Eonomy Rank	54	49	54
SA	Knowledge Economy Index	5.02	4.6	5.96
SA	Knowledge Index	5.21	4.67	6.05
SA	Economic Incentive Regime Index	4.45	4.4	5.68
SA	Innovation Index	5	4.24	4.14
SA	Education Index	4.11	4.28	5.65
SA	ICT Index	6.51	5.49	8.37
SA	Knowledge Economy Rank	78	76	50
Syria	Knowledge Economy Index	3.49	2.85	2.77
Syria	Knowledge Index	3.97	3.23	3.01
Syria	Economic Incentive Regime Index	2.05	1.72	2.04
Syria	Innovation Index	3.07	3.53	3.07
Syria	Education Index	3.11	2.57	2.4
Syria	ICT Index	5.73	3.58	3.55
Syria	Knowledge Economy Rank	109	111	112
Tunisia	Knowledge Economy Index	4.54	4.15	4.56
Tunisia	Knowledge Index	4.51	4.24	4.8
Tunisia	Economic Incentive Regime Index	4.65	3.89	3.81
Tunisia	Innovation Index	4.29	4.24	4.97
Tunisia	Education Index	3.57	3.92	4.55
Tunisia	ICT Index	5.66	4.54	4.89
Tunisia	Knowledge Economy Rank	89	89	80

(*Continued*)

Table 4.3. (*Continued*)

Country	Indicator	1995	2000	2012
Turkey	Knowledge Economy Index	5.46	5.42	5.16
Turkey	Knowledge Index	5.2	5.18	4.81
Turkey	Economic Incentive Regime Index	6.23	6.13	6.19
Turkey	Innovation Index	5.04	5.23	5.83
Turkey	Education Index	4	4.05	4.11
Turkey	ICT Index	6.55	6.26	4.5
Turkey	Knowledge Economy Rank	62	62	69
UAE	Knowledge Economy Index	6.39	6.05	6.94
UAE	Knowledge Index	6.22	5.56	7.09
UAE	Economic Incentive Regime Index	6.9	7.51	6.5
UAE	Innovation Index	6.59	4.32	6.6
UAE	Education Index	4.46	4.44	5.8
UAE	ICT Index	7.62	7.92	8.88
UAE	Knowledge Economy Rank	46	48	42
Yemen	Knowledge Economy Index	2.44	1.98	1.92
Yemen	Knowledge Index	2.64	1.95	1.58
Yemen	Economic Incentive Regime Index	1.85	2.07	2.91
Yemen	Innovation Index	2.03	1.58	1.96
Yemen	Education Index	1.38	1.96	1.62
Yemen	ICT Index	4.5	2.3	1.17
Yemen	Knowledge Economy Rank	132	128	122

Source: http://knoema.com/WBKEI2013/knowledge-economy-index-world-bank-2012.

the Economic Incentive Regime index was below 1 for all years. Some of the other MENA countries were able over the 1995 to 2012 period to reach an index above 5.

With respect to the Innovation index, only Israel had an index above 9 in all periods. The only MENA countries that may be able to compete with Israel on Innovation include Cyprus and the UAE. The balance of MENA countries have problems achieving the Israeli standard for innovation.

With respect to the Education index, Israel's 8.5 index in 1995 dropped to 7.47 in 2012. In Bahrain the Education index increased from 6.49 in 1995 to 6.78 in 2012. In Cyprus the Education index increased from 6.75 in 1995 to 7.23 in 2012. In Kuwait the Education index decreased from 4.51 in 1995 to 3.7 in 2012. In Oman the Education index increased from 3.65 in 1995 to 5.23 in 2012. In Qatar the Education index decreased from 5.52 in 1995 to 3.41 in 2012. In Saudi Arabia the Education index increased from 4.11 in 1995 to 5.65 in 2012.

With respect to the ICT index, the leading country within MENA in 2012 was Bahrain with an index of 9.54, followed by the UAE with an index of 8.88, followed by Saudi Arabia with an index of 8.37, followed by Cyprus with an index of 7.57, followed by Israel with an index of 7.36, followed by Qatar with an index of 6.65, followed by Kuwait with an index of 6.53.

Overall, the data in Table 4.3 suggest that a small minority of countries within MENA have human capital acquisition systems that feature a good mix of education, innovation, economic incentives, and public accountability. The great majority of MENA countries have a long path to travel in order to catch up with the lead group within MENA.

What indeed has prevented most of Arab MENA from emerging into the knowledge society of the 21st century? The UNDP *Knowledge Report* (2009, p. 99) asks the same question a bit more keenly: "How can they (Arab MENA) even see the light at the end of this tunnel when more than 60 million of their people, two-thirds of them women, are illiterate, and when some nine million school-age children are out of school, most of these in the very countries that have failed to solve the illiteracy problem? How can these countries possibly build a knowledge economy if the rate of upper secondary school enrolment is less than 55 percent for both males and females at a time when this rate exceeds 80 percent in industrialized developed nations and the countries of Central Asia?" (World Bank, Development Indicators, 2017).

To participate in the knowledge economy, the young within MENA must possess a range of skills in Mathematics and Science that are recognized by the international community. In Table 4.4 we present the distribution of MENA eighth graders achievements in Mathematics and Science tested by the Trends in International Mathematics and Science Study (TIMSS) for 2007, 2011 and 2015. This data provides reliable information on the mathematics and science achievement of US and international students compared to an international norm.

The first and second sets of test results is for eighth-grade students reaching the "advanced international benchmark" of mathematics achievement and science achievements. The data represents the share of eighth-grade students scoring at least 625 on the mathematics and science assessments. For the mathematics assessments at this benchmark, students can reason with information, draw conclusions, make generalizations and solve linear equations. Students can solve a variety of fraction, proportion and percent problems and justify their conclusions. Students can express generalizations algebraically and model situations. They can solve

Table 4.4. International Benchmark of Mathematics and Science Achievement in MENA

(2007, 2011 and 2015)

Country	Indicator Name	2007	2011	2015
Algeria	TIMSS: Eighth-grade students reaching the advanced international benchmark of mathematics achievement (%)	0	—	—
Algeria	TIMSS: Eighth-grade students reaching the advanced international benchmark of science achievement (%)	0	—	—
Algeria	TIMSS: Eighth-grade students reaching the high international benchmark of mathematics achievement (%)	0	—	—
Algeria	TIMSS: Eighth-grade students reaching the high international benchmark of science achievement (%)	1	—	—
Algeria	TIMSS: Eighth-grade students reaching the intermediate international benchmark of mathematics achievement (%)	7	—	—
Algeria	TIMSS: Eighth-grade students reaching the intermediate international benchmark of science achievement (%)	14	—	—
Algeria	TIMSS: Eighth-grade students reaching the low international benchmark of mathematics achievement (%)	41	—	—
Algeria	TIMSS: Eighth-grade students reaching the low international benchmark of science achievement (%)	55	—	—
Bahrain	TIMSS: Eighth-grade students reaching the advanced international benchmark of mathematics achievement (%)	0	1	2
Bahrain	TIMSS: Eighth-grade students reaching the advanced international benchmark of science achievement (%)	2	3	6
Bahrain	TIMSS: Eighth-grade students reaching the high international benchmark of mathematics achievement (%)	3	8	12
Bahrain	TIMSS: Eighth-grade students reaching the high international benchmark of science achievement (%)	17	17	22
Bahrain	TIMSS: Eighth-grade students reaching the intermediate international benchmark of mathematics achievement (%)	19	26	39
Bahrain	TIMSS: Eighth-grade students reaching the intermediate international benchmark of science achievement (%)	49	44	49

(*Continued*)

Table 4.4. (*Continued*)

Country	Indicator Name	2007	2011	2015
Bahrain	TIMSS: Eighth-grade students reaching the low international benchmark of mathematics achievement (%)	49	53	75
Bahrain	TIMSS: Eighth-grade students reaching the low international benchmark of science achievement (%)	78	70	73
Cyprus	TIMSS: Eighth-grade students reaching the advanced international benchmark of mathematics achievement (%)	2	—	—
Cyprus	TIMSS: Eighth-grade students reaching the advanced international benchmark of science achievement (%)	1	—	—
Cyprus	TIMSS: Eighth-grade students reaching the high international benchmark of mathematics achievement (%)	17	—	—
Cyprus	TIMSS: Eighth-grade students reaching the high international benchmark of science achievement (%)	12	—	—
Cyprus	TIMSS: Eighth-grade students reaching the intermediate international benchmark of mathematics achievement (%)	48	—	—
Cyprus	TIMSS: Eighth-grade students reaching the intermediate international benchmark of science achievement (%)	42	—	—
Cyprus	TIMSS: Eighth-grade students reaching the low international benchmark of mathematics achievement (%)	78	—	—
Cyprus	TIMSS: Eighth-grade students reaching the low international benchmark of science achievement (%)	74	—	—
Egypt	TIMSS: Eighth-grade students reaching the advanced international benchmark of mathematics achievement (%)	1	—	0
Egypt	TIMSS: Eighth-grade students reaching the advanced international benchmark of science achievement (%)	1	—	0
Egypt	TIMSS: Eighth-grade students reaching the high international benchmark of mathematics achievement (%)	5	—	5
Egypt	TIMSS: Eighth-grade students reaching the high international benchmark of science achievement (%)	7	—	5

(*Continued*)

Table 4.4. (*Continued*)

Country	Indicator Name	2007	2011	2015
Egypt	TIMSS: Eighth-grade students reaching the intermediate international benchmark of mathematics achievement (%)	21	—	21
Egypt	TIMSS: Eighth-grade students reaching the intermediate international benchmark of science achievement (%)	27	—	20
Egypt	TIMSS: Eighth-grade students reaching the low international benchmark of mathematics achievement (%)	47	—	47
Egypt	TIMSS: Eighth-grade students reaching the low international benchmark of science achievement (%)	55	—	42
Iran	TIMSS: Eighth-grade students reaching the advanced international benchmark of mathematics achievement (%)	1	2	2
Iran	TIMSS: Eighth-grade students reaching the advanced international benchmark of science achievement (%)	2	5	3
Iran	TIMSS: Eighth-grade students reaching the high international benchmark of mathematics achievement (%)	5	8	12
Iran	TIMSS: Eighth-grade students reaching the high international benchmark of science achievement (%)	14	21	15
Iran	TIMSS: Eighth-grade students reaching the intermediate international benchmark of mathematics achievement (%)	20	26	34
Iran	TIMSS: Eighth-grade students reaching the intermediate international benchmark of science achievement (%)	41	50	42
Iran	TIMSS: Eighth-grade students reaching the low international benchmark of mathematics achievement (%)	51	55	63
Iran	TIMSS: Eighth-grade students reaching the low international benchmark of science achievement (%)	76	79	73
Israel	TIMSS: Eighth-grade students reaching the advanced international benchmark of mathematics achievement (%)	4	12	13
Israel	TIMSS: Eighth-grade students reaching the advanced international benchmark of science achievement (%)	5	11	12

(*Continued*)

Table 4.4. (*Continued*)

Country	Indicator Name	2007	2011	2015
Israel	TIMSS: Eighth-grade students reaching the high international benchmark of mathematics achievement (%)	19	40	38
Israel	TIMSS: Eighth-grade students reaching the high international benchmark of science achievement (%)	21	39	37
Israel	TIMSS: Eighth-grade students reaching the intermediate international benchmark of mathematics achievement (%)	48	68	65
Israel	TIMSS: Eighth-grade students reaching the intermediate international benchmark of science achievement (%)	51	69	64
Israel	TIMSS: Eighth-grade students reaching the low international benchmark of mathematics achievement (%)	75	87	84
Israel	TIMSS: Eighth-grade students reaching the low international benchmark of science achievement (%)	75	88	84
Jordan	TIMSS: Eighth-grade students reaching the advanced international *benchmark* of mathematics achievement (%)	1	0	0
Jordan	TIMSS: Eighth-grade students reaching the advanced international benchmark of science achievement (%)	5	2	1
Jordan	TIMSS: Eighth-grade students reaching the high international benchmark of mathematics achievement (%)	11	6	3
Jordan	TIMSS: Eighth-grade students reaching the high international benchmark of science achievement (%)	26	15	9
Jordan	TIMSS: Eighth-grade students reaching the intermediate international benchmark of mathematics achievement (%)	35	26	18
Jordan	TIMSS: Eighth-grade students reaching the intermediate international benchmark of science achievement (%)	56	45	34
Jordan	TIMSS: Eighth-grade students reaching the low international benchmark of mathematics achievement (%)	61	55	45
Jordan	TIMSS: Eighth-grade students reaching the low international benchmark of science achievement (%)	79	72	63

(*Continued*)

Table 4.4. (*Continued*)

Country	Indicator Name	2007	2011	2015
Kuwait	TIMSS: Eighth-grade students reaching the advanced international benchmark of mathematics achievement (%)	0	—	0
Kuwait	TIMSS: Eighth-grade students reaching the advanced international benchmark of science achievement (%)	0	—	1
Kuwait	TIMSS: Eighth-grade students reaching the high international benchmark of mathematics achievement (%)	0	—	1
Kuwait	TIMSS: Eighth-grade students reaching the high international benchmark of science achievement (%)	6	—	6
Kuwait	TIMSS: Eighth-grade students reaching the intermediate international benchmark of mathematics achievement (%)	6	—	11
Kuwait	TIMSS: Eighth-grade students reaching the intermediate international benchmark of science achievement (%)	28	—	23
Kuwait	TIMSS: Eighth-grade students reaching the low international benchmark of mathematics achievement (%)	29	—	37
Kuwait	TIMSS: Eighth-grade students reaching the low international benchmark of science achievement (%)	60	—	49
Lebanon	TIMSS: Eighth-grade students reaching the advanced international benchmark of mathematics achievement (%)	1	1	0
Lebanon	TIMSS: Eighth-grade students reaching the advanced international benchmark of science achievement (%)	1	1	1
Lebanon	TIMSS: Eighth-grade students reaching the high international benchmark of mathematics achievement (%)	10	9	8
Lebanon	TIMSS: Eighth-grade students reaching the high international benchmark of science achievement (%)	8	7	7
Lebanon	TIMSS: Eighth-grade students reaching the intermediate international benchmark of mathematics achievement (%)	36	38	35
Lebanon	TIMSS: Eighth-grade students reaching the intermediate international benchmark of science achievement (%)	28	25	24

(*Continued*)

Table 4.4. (*Continued*)

Country	Indicator Name	2007	2011	2015
Lebanon	TIMSS: Eighth-grade students reaching the low international benchmark of mathematics achievement (%)	74	73	71
Lebanon	TIMSS: Eighth-grade students reaching the low international benchmark of science achievement (%)	55	54	50
Morocco	TIMSS: Eighth-grade students reaching the advanced international benchmark of mathematics achievement (%)	0	0	0
Morocco	TIMSS: Eighth-grade students reaching the advanced international benchmark of science achievement (%)	0	0	0
Morocco	TIMSS: Eighth-grade students reaching the high international benchmark of mathematics achievement (%)	1	2	2
Morocco	TIMSS: Eighth-grade students reaching the high international benchmark of science achievement (%)	3	2	3
Morocco	TIMSS: Eighth-grade students reaching the intermediate international benchmark of mathematics achievement (%)	13	12	14
Morocco	TIMSS: Eighth-grade students reaching the intermediate international benchmark of science achievement (%)	18	13	17
Morocco	TIMSS: Eighth-grade students reaching the low international benchmark of mathematics achievement (%)	41	36	41
Morocco	TIMSS: Eighth-grade students reaching the low international benchmark of science achievement (%)	51	39	47
Oman	TIMSS: Eighth-grade students reaching the advanced international benchmark of mathematics achievement (%)	0	0	1
Oman	TIMSS: Eighth-grade students reaching the advanced international benchmark of science achievement (%)	1	2	3
Oman	TIMSS: Eighth-grade students reaching the high international benchmark of mathematics achievement (%)	2	4	6
Oman	TIMSS: Eighth-grade students reaching the high international benchmark of science achievement (%)	8	11	17

(*Continued*)

Table 4.4. (*Continued*)

Country	Indicator Name	2007	2011	2015
Oman	TIMSS: Eighth-grade students reaching the intermediate international benchmark of mathematics achievement (%)	14	16	23
Oman	TIMSS: Eighth-grade students reaching the intermediate international benchmark of science achievement (%)	32	34	45
Oman	TIMSS: Eighth-grade students reaching the low international benchmark of mathematics achievement (%)	41	39	52
Oman	TIMSS: Eighth-grade students reaching the low international benchmark of science achievement (%)	61	59	72
Qatar	TIMSS: Eighth-grade students reaching the advanced international benchmark of mathematics achievement (%)	0	2	3
Qatar	TIMSS: Eighth-grade students reaching the advanced international benchmark of science achievement (%)	0	3	6
Qatar	TIMSS: Eighth-grade students reaching the high international benchmark of mathematics achievement (%)	0	10	14
Qatar	TIMSS: Eighth-grade students reaching the high international benchmark of science achievement (%)	2	14	21
Qatar	TIMSS: Eighth-grade students reaching the intermediate international benchmark of mathematics achievement (%)	4	29	36
Qatar	TIMSS: Eighth-grade students reaching the intermediate international benchmark of science achievement (%)	11	34	46
Qatar	TIMSS: Eighth-grade students reaching the low international benchmark of mathematics achievement (%)	16	54	63
Qatar	TIMSS: Eighth-grade students reaching the low international benchmark of science achievement (%)	29	58	70
SA	TIMSS: Eighth-grade students reaching the advanced international benchmark of mathematics achievement (%)	0	1	0
SA	TIMSS: Eighth-grade students reaching the advanced international benchmark of science achievement (%)	0	1	1

(*Continued*)

Table 4.4. (*Continued*)

Country	Indicator Name	2007	2011	2015
SA	TIMSS: Eighth-grade students reaching the high international benchmark of mathematics achievement (%)	0	5	2
SA	TIMSS: Eighth-grade students reaching the high international benchmark of science achievement (%)	2	8	6
SA	TIMSS: Eighth-grade students reaching the intermediate international benchmark of mathematics achievement (%)	3	20	11
SA	TIMSS: Eighth-grade students reaching the intermediate international benchmark of science achievement (%)	18	33	22
SA	TIMSS: Eighth-grade students reaching the low international benchmark of mathematics achievement (%)	18	47	34
SA	TIMSS: Eighth-grade students reaching the low international benchmark of science achievement (%)	52	68	49
Syria	TIMSS: Eighth-grade students reaching the advanced international benchmark of mathematics achievement (%)	0	0	—
Syria	TIMSS: Eighth-grade students reaching the advanced international benchmark of science achievement (%)	1	0	—
Syria	TIMSS: Eighth-grade students reaching the high international benchmark of mathematics achievement (%)	3	3	—
Syria	TIMSS: Eighth-grade students reaching the high international benchmark of science achievement (%)	9	6	—
Syria	TIMSS: Eighth-grade students reaching the intermediate international benchmark of mathematics achievement (%)	17	17	—
Syria	TIMSS: Eighth-grade students reaching the intermediate international benchmark of science achievement (%)	39	29	—
Syria	TIMSS: Eighth-grade students reaching the low international benchmark of mathematics achievement (%)	47	43	—
Syria	TIMSS: Eighth-grade students reaching the low international benchmark of science achievement (%)	76	63	—

(*Continued*)

Table 4.4. (*Continued*)

Country	Indicator Name	2007	2011	2015
Tunisia	TIMSS: Eighth-grade students reaching the advanced international benchmark of mathematics achievement (%)	0	0	—
Tunisia	TIMSS: Eighth-grade students reaching the advanced international benchmark of science achievement (%)	0	0	—
Tunisia	TIMSS: Eighth-grade students reaching the high international benchmark of mathematics achievement (%)	3	5	—
Tunisia	TIMSS: Eighth-grade students reaching the high international benchmark of science achievement (%)	4	5	—
Tunisia	TIMSS: Eighth-grade students reaching the intermediate international benchmark of mathematics achievement (%)	21	25	—
Tunisia	TIMSS: Eighth-grade students reaching the intermediate international benchmark of science achievement (%)	31	30	—
Tunisia	TIMSS: Eighth-grade students reaching the low international benchmark of mathematics achievement (%)	61	61	—
Tunisia	TIMSS: Eighth-grade students reaching the low international benchmark of science achievement (%)	77	72	—
Turkey	TIMSS: Eighth-grade students reaching the advanced international benchmark of mathematics achievement (%)	5	7	6
Turkey	TIMSS: Eighth-grade students reaching the advanced international benchmark of science achievement (%)	3	8	8
Turkey	TIMSS: Eighth-grade students reaching the high international benchmark of mathematics achievement (%)	15	20	20
Turkey	TIMSS: Eighth-grade students reaching the high international benchmark of science achievement (%)	16	26	29
Turkey	TIMSS: Eighth-grade students reaching the intermediate international benchmark of mathematics achievement (%)	33	40	42
Turkey	TIMSS: Eighth-grade students reaching the intermediate international benchmark of science achievement (%)	40	54	59

(*Continued*)

Table 4.4. (*Continued*)

Country	Indicator Name	2007	2011	2015
Turkey	TIMSS: Eighth-grade students reaching the low international benchmark of mathematics achievement (%)	59	67	70
Turkey	TIMSS: Eighth-grade students reaching the low international benchmark of science achievement (%)	71	79	83
UAE	TIMSS: Eighth-grade students reaching the advanced international benchmark of mathematics achievement (%)	—	2	5
UAE	TIMSS: Eighth-grade students reaching the advanced international benchmark of science achievement (%)	—	4	7
UAE	TIMSS: Eighth-grade students reaching the high international benchmark of mathematics achievement (%)	—	14	20
UAE	TIMSS: Eighth-grade students reaching the high international benchmark of science achievement (%)	—	19	26
UAE	TIMSS: Eighth-grade students reaching the intermediate international benchmark of mathematics achievement (%)	—	42	46
UAE	TIMSS: Eighth-grade students reaching the intermediate international benchmark of science achievement (%)	—	47	53
UAE	TIMSS: Eighth-grade students reaching the low international benchmark of mathematics achievement (%)	—	73	73
UAE	TIMSS: Eighth-grade students reaching the low international benchmark of science achievement (%)	—	75	76

Source: http://timss.bc.edu/

a variety of problems involving equations, formulas and functions. Students can reason with geometric figures to solve problems. Students can reason with data from several sources or unfamiliar representations to solve multi-step problems.

For the science assessments at this benchmark, students can communicate an understanding of complex and abstract concepts in biology, chemistry, physics and earth science. Students demonstrate some conceptual knowledge about cells and the characteristics, classification, and life processes of organisms. They communicate an understanding of the complexity of ecosystems and adaptations of organisms, and apply an understanding of life cycles and heredity. Students also communicate an understanding of the structure of matter and physical and chemical properties and changes and apply knowledge of forces, pressure, motion, sound and light. They reason about electrical circuits and properties of magnets. Students apply knowledge and communicate understanding of the solar system and Earth's processes, structures and physical features. They understand basic features of scientific investigation. They also combine information from several sources to solve problems and draw conclusions, and they provide written explanations to communicate scientific knowledge.

Apart from Israel which in 2015 had 13 and 12 percent of their eighth graders achieve the "advanced international benchmark" in mathematics and science, respectively, very few of the other countries within MENA have had one percent of their eighth graders assessed in this "advanced international benchmark."

The third and fourth set of test results is for eighth-grade students reaching the "high international benchmark" of mathematics achievement and science achievements. The data represents the share of eighth-grade students scoring at least 550 on the mathematics and science assessments. For the mathematics assessment at this benchmark, students can apply their understanding and knowledge in a variety of relatively complex situations. Students can use information from several sources to solve problems involving different types of numbers and operations. Students can relate fractions, decimals and percents to each other. Students at this level show basic procedural knowledge related to algebraic expressions. They can use properties of lines, angles, triangles, rectangles and rectangular prisms to solve problems. They can analyze data in a variety of graphs.

For the science assessments at this benchmark, students can demonstrate understanding of concepts related to science cycles, systems, and principles. They demonstrate understanding of aspects of human biology and of the characteristics, classification, and life processes of organisms. Students communicate understanding of processes and relationships in ecosystems. They show an understanding of the classification and compositions of matter and chemical and physical properties and changes. They apply knowledge to situations related to light and sound and demonstrate basic knowledge of heat and temperature, forces and motion, and electrical circuits and magnets. Students demonstrate an understanding of the solar system and of Earth's processes, physical features and resources. They demonstrate some scientific inquiry skills. They also combine and interpret information from various types of diagrams, contour maps, graphs and tables; select relevant information, analyze and draw conclusions; and provide short explanations conveying scientific knowledge.

Apart from Israel which in 2015 had 38 percent and 37 percent of their eighth graders achieve the "high international benchmark" in mathematics and science, respectively, very few countries within MENA have even achieved double digit assessments of their eighth graders in the "high international benchmark."

The fifth and sixth test results are for eighth grade students reaching the "intermediate international benchmark" of mathematics achievement and science achievements. The data represents the share of eighth-grade students scoring at least 475 on the mathematics and science assessments. For the mathematics assessment at this benchmark, students can apply basic mathematical knowledge in a variety of situations. Students can solve problems involving decimals, fractions, proportions and percentages. They understand simple algebraic relationships. Students can relate a two-dimensional drawing to a three-dimensional object. They can read, interpret and construct graphs and tables. They recognize basic notions of likelihood.

For the science assessments at this benchmark, students can recognize and apply their understanding of basic scientific knowledge in various contexts. Students apply knowledge and communicate an understanding of human health, life cycles, adaptation, and heredity and analyze information about ecosystems. They have some knowledge of chemistry in everyday life and elementary knowledge of properties of solutions and the concept of concentration. They are acquainted with some aspects of force, motion and energy. They demonstrate an understanding of Earth's processes and physical features, including the water cycle and atmosphere. Students interpret information from tables, graphs and pictorial diagrams and draw conclusions. They apply knowledge to practical situations and communicate their understanding through brief descriptive responses.

Apart from Israel which in 2015 had 65 and 64 percent of their eighth graders achieve the "intermediate international benchmark" in mathematics and science, respectively, very few of the other countries within MENA have had 30 to 40 percent of their eighth graders assessed in this "intermediate international benchmark."

The seventh and eight test results are for eighth-grade students reaching the "low international benchmark" of mathematics achievement and science achievements. The data represents the share of eighth-grade students scoring at least 400 on the mathematics and science assessments. For the mathematics assessment at this benchmark, students have some knowledge of whole numbers and decimals, operations and basic graphs.

For the science assessments at this benchmark, students can recognize some basic facts from the life and physical sciences. They have some knowledge of biology, and demonstrate some familiarity with physical phenomena. Students interpret simple pictorial diagrams, complete simple tables and apply basic knowledge to practical situations.

Israel in 2015 had 84 percent of their eighth graders achieve the "low international benchmark" in both mathematics and science. Bahrain in 2015 had 75 and 73 percent of their eighth graders achieve the "low international benchmark" in mathematics and science, respectively. Lebanon in 2015 had 71 and 50 percent of their eighth graders achieve the "low international benchmark" in mathematics and science, respectively. Oman in 2015 had 52 percent and 72 percent of their eighth graders achieve the "low international benchmark" in mathematics and science, respectively. Turkey in 2015 had 70 and 83 percent of their eighth graders achieve the "low international benchmark" in mathematics and science, respectively. The UAE in 2015 had 73 percent and 76 percent of their eighth graders achieve the "low international benchmark" in mathematics and science, respectively. The other countries within MENA had over 50 percent of their eighth graders unable to pass the "low international benchmark" in mathematics and science.

In a recent report entitled *The Road Not Traveled — Education Reform in the Middle East and North Africa* (World Bank, 2008), the authors[26] observe that, over the previous 50 years, the Arab MENA countries have drawn up extensive plans for reforming their educational systems at all levels and for all their types of education.[27] Despite all best intentions, over the 1990 to 2016 period, it appears that most of Arab MENA have fallen short of realizing the goals of *Education for All* (UNESCO, 2009) and from meeting global standards with regard to mathematics and science. Consequently, this poor performance places Arab MENA well behind Israel, its major non-Arab MENA competitor, as well as behind the industrialized developed nations and also behind many newly industrialized countries in Asia and Latin America. These other countries have made enormous strides

[26]The World Bank chose, in this report, to exclude Israel from the list of MENA countries. The comparison between Arab MENA and Israel must have been embarrassing for the management of the Bank.

[27]They estimated an average of 2.5 such plans per country during this period with an average of 25 measures per plan.

in the quality of their educational services and have obtained results equal or close to those of the advanced industrialized nations.[28]

Barring major revolutionary events, it is clear that Arab MENA, in general, does not have the critical mass needed to sustain the impetus of efforts aimed at elevating their educational systems to the standards achieved by Israel and other developed nations. Consequently, based on the endogenous growth model described at the beginning of this chapter, Arab MENA will not achieve the growth rate needed to fully employ its younger generation. That in turn will create pressures to overturn the existing autocratic regimes. The parties responsible for this set of events include the central leadership, the religious leadership and the educational system that all foster an environment of xenophobia and religious intolerance.

One does not have to go far in a review of Arab MENA human capital statistics to note that the formal education of a huge percentage of youth — currently over 40 percent in Arab MENA — does not extend beyond the level of basic education, hampering these countries' ability to engage in the 21st century knowledge economy, which requires theoretical and technical knowledge that can be acquired only in higher education. How can a xenophobic and religiously intolerant society that teaches hate to their young expect the same individuals to survive in a 21st century world that depends on "specialized sciences, modern technologies, and the information and communications revolution, as well as upon openness to the latest advances in knowledge, sustained and constructive interaction between countries and societies, and intensive networking between individuals and institutions"? (UNDP, 2009, p. 139).

[28]The World Bank report cites differences between Arab MENA on the basis of a compound index that combines measurements of enrolment at all educational levels, gender parity, primary education efficiency, and the quality of education as evidenced by adult literacy rates and results in international standardized tests.

Chapter 5

Labor Market in MENA

Most Arab countries in MENA have been growing slowly for a long time and see themselves increasingly poor relative to the rest of the world, to both advanced countries and peer countries like Israel and Cyprus within MENA. There are a whole set of reasons for this lackluster performance which have been explored in earlier chapters. Human capital occupies a central role in modern thinking about growth. The labor market is the place where human capital is created and deployed. If we are to understand growth and development within MENA, we need to understand the creation and deployment of human capital. The endogenous growth model which was discussed in Chapter 4 is the appropriate venue for a discussion of the labor market. This chapter accepts the argument that the study of the links between labor markets and growth should concentrate on a study of labor market influences on the quantity, quality and productivity of human capital. This requires an investigation of the institutions that influence the acquisition and employment of human capital and their effectiveness in enhancing growth (Aghion and Howitt, 1998; Agénor *et al.*, 2004; Benhabib and Spiegel, 1994; Pecorino, 1992).

The structure of the labor market will determine how much human capital is put into growth-enhancing activities and how much into other activities, such as the public sector. It will also determine what types of human capital will be required in different environments (Topel, 1999). In light of this research on growth and the labor market, we begin with an examination of the labor market institutions in the MENA countries that are likely to influence growth outcomes. However, there is virtually no literature explaining which labor market institutions are likely to be good for growth and which are bad [Aghion and Howitt, 1998; Topel, 1999 are perfect examples]. What we do have in discussions of MENA are recent studies analyzing the functioning of the labor market, and political and institutional constraints that lead to gender bias and youth unemployment; but there is very little discussion on the connections between labor market institutions and growth (World Bank, 2004a). In this chapter we examine the sectoral composition of employment and the institutional structure that governs wage determination and employment within MENA.

Human capital is created by formal education and formal training as well as by informal learning mechanisms. Each time someone develops the ability to do something new, he or she increases his or her human capital. Of course, measuring human capital in its full dimension is considered by many to be an impossible task. Consequently, the literature adopts the standard approach suggested by Hall and Jones (1999) that confines itself to measuring the years of schooling in the working population and using the outcome as a proxy for all human capital in the country. That is, one can construct the human capital index h as a function of the average years of schooling given by:

$$h = e^{\phi(s)}, \tag{5.1}$$

where the function $\phi(\cdot)$ is such that $\phi(0) = 0$ and $\phi^1(s)$ is the Mincerian return to education.[1]

5.1. Human Capital and Economic Growth

Using the Hall and Jones (1999) approach to MENA's labor market, we begin by looking at a series of data measuring years of schooling as a proxy for the stock of human capital. The literature is in agreement that an abundance of well-educated people and well-educated females is correlated with a high level of labor productivity. Furthermore, it goes without saying that with greater numbers of skilled workers there is a greater ability to absorb advanced technology from developed countries. (Lucas, 1988 and Mankiw *et al.*, 1992) Using the data from Barro and Lee (2013), we construct a trend of educational attainment for MENA's population aged 15 and above, covering the period 1950–2010 in Tables 5.1 and 5.2. The specific information that is relevant to address the human capital component include (1) the

[1]Using the returns suggested in Psacharopoulos (1994), the returns for MENA, in the public sector, can be assumed to be 15.5 percent for primary school, 11.2 percent for secondary school and 10.6 percent for higher education. In private education the returns are 17.4 percent for primary school, 15.9 percent for secondary school and 21.7 percent for higher education.

Table 5.1. Trends of Educational Attainment of Total MENA Population Aged 15 and Over

Country	Highest Level Attained	Unit	1950	1955	1960	1965	1970	1975	1980	1985	1990	1995	2000	2005	2010	Compound Annual Growth Rate
Algeria	Population (1000s)	thousands	5,241	5,699	6,073	6,374	7,100	8,392	10,188	12,172	14,404	17,068	20,070	23,113	25,853	0.027
Algeria	No Schooling Attained	%	80.7	81.1	82.6	80.9	73.6	64.5	55.8	45.8	38.9	32.9	28.2	29.6	21.1	−0.022
Algeria	Total Primary Schooling	%	17.6	17.0	14.3	14.4	19.2	25.2	29.5	33.1	35.2	38.0	43.2	43.9	43.9	0.016
Algeria	Total Primary Schooling Completed	%	3.8	3.5	3.1	4.0	5.2	4.3	4.6	13.0	14.7	19.3	24.0	27.2	25.9	0.033
Algeria	Total Secondary Schooling	%	1.6	1.7	3.7	6.3	10.2	13.8	17.6	23.6	27.1	28.3	24.4	21.6	23.9	0.047
Algeria	Total Secondary Schooling Completed	%	0.5	0.5	1.1	1.8	3.3	5.1	7.6	11.3	14.4	16.4	15.4	14.0	17.1	0.063
Algeria	Total Tertiary Schooling	%	0.3	0.3	0.3	0.4	0.3	0.7	1.5	2.5	3.7	4.7	6.3	6.9	11.8	0.064
Algeria	Total Tertiary Schooling Completed	%	0.2	0.1	0.2	0.2	0.2	0.4	0.8	1.3	2.0	2.5	3.4	3.8	6.7	0.065
Algeria	Average Years of Schooling Attained	Years	0.9	0.8	0.9	1.1	1.6	2.1	2.8	4.0	4.7	5.4	5.7	5.5	6.7	0.036
Algeria	Average Years of Primary Schooling Attained	Years	0.7	0.7	0.7	0.8	1.2	1.5	1.9	2.7	3.1	3.5	3.7	3.7	4.2	0.030
Algeria	Average Years of Secondary Schooling Attained	Years	0.1	0.1	0.2	0.3	0.4	0.6	0.9	1.3	1.6	1.8	1.7	1.6	2.1	0.055
Algeria	Average Years of Tertiary Schooling Attained	Years	0.0	0.0	0.0	0.0	0.0	0.0	0.1	0.1	0.1	0.1	0.2	0.2	0.4	0.063

(Continued)

Table 5.1. (*Continued*)

Country	Highest Level Attained	Unit	1950	1955	1960	1965	1970	1975	1980	1985	1990	1995	2000	2005	2010	Compound Annual Growth Rate
Bahrain	Population (1000s)	thousands	66	77	89	94	116	158	227	282	337	406	482	531	600	0.038
Bahrain	No Schooling Attained	%	86.9	86.0	83.5	77.8	61.7	50.8	41.9	38.0	32.2	28.1	25.3	27.8	28.9	−0.018
Bahrain	Total Primary Schooling	%	7.8	8.3	8.8	11.3	14.8	18.4	20.1	17.4	14.2	12.8	11.7	13.0	13.3	0.009
Bahrain	Total Primary Schooling Completed	%	5.4	5.7	6.0	7.9	6.4	8.2	8.9	7.7	6.4	5.8	5.4	6.0	6.3	0.002
Bahrain	Total Secondary Schooling	%	3.5	3.9	5.7	8.5	19.9	25.1	29.4	32.9	40.7	47.1	52.4	49.4	49.5	0.046
Bahrain	Total Secondary Schooling Completed	%	2.2	2.0	3.1	4.8	11.2	13.9	17.5	20.4	25.5	29.6	32.5	31.6	32.1	0.047
Bahrain	Total Tertiary Schooling	%	1.8	1.9	2.1	2.4	3.7	5.8	8.6	11.7	12.9	12.0	10.6	9.8	8.3	0.026
Bahrain	Total Tertiary Schooling Completed	%	1.5	1.4	1.5	1.8	2.1	2.5	3.4	6.3	8.5	9.2	9.1	8.8	7.8	0.029
Bahrain	Average Years of Schooling Attained	Years	1.0	1.1	1.3	1.8	3.1	4.0	4.9	5.7	6.5	7.1	7.5	7.2	7.1	0.034
Bahrain	Average Years of Primary Schooling Attained	Years	0.7	0.8	0.9	1.2	2.1	2.7	3.2	3.4	3.8	4.1	4.3	4.1	4.1	0.030
Bahrain	Average Years of Secondary Schooling Attained	Years	0.2	0.2	0.3	0.4	0.9	1.2	1.5	1.9	2.3	2.6	2.8	2.7	2.7	0.043
Bahrain	Average Years of Tertiary Schooling Attained	Years	0.1	0.1	0.1	0.1	0.1	0.2	0.2	0.4	0.4	0.4	0.4	0.4	0.3	0.029

Cyprus	Population (1000s)	thousands	324	349	363	382	423	450	462	485	505	548	609	669	725	0.014
Cyprus	No Schooling Attained	%	36.5	29.9	22.0	17.8	17.0	13.4	11.2	6.9	4.5	7.2	8.6	11.6	0.7	−0.064
Cyprus	Total Primary Schooling	%	54.3	56.1	57.1	56.2	53.7	50.4	44.1	40.6	36.6	27.1	20.6	23.8	20.7	−0.016
Cyprus	Total Primary Schooling Completed	%	29.4	32.8	36.6	33.9	32.5	33.7	31.0	30.0	27.8	21.0	17.0	17.5	15.5	−0.011
Cyprus	Total Secondary Schooling	%	7.7	12.6	19.7	24.2	26.3	31.3	36.4	40.1	42.7	45.2	48.5	44.4	49.8	0.032
Cyprus	Total Secondary Schooling Completed	%	4.2	7.6	12.2	12.8	15.7	19.2	23.1	26.6	28.7	30.7	33.3	30.6	35.1	0.037
Cyprus	Total Tertiary Schooling	%	1.5	1.4	1.2	1.8	3.0	5.0	8.3	12.4	16.3	20.5	22.4	20.3	28.8	0.051
Cyprus	Total Tertiary Schooling Completed	%	1.0	1.0	0.9	1.3	2.0	3.4	5.8	8.7	11.6	14.6	15.9	14.5	20.8	0.052
Cyprus	Average Years of Schooling Attained	Years	3.6	4.3	5.1	5.5	5.9	6.7	7.5	8.4	9.1	9.6	9.9	9.3	11.1	0.019
Cyprus	Average Years of Primary Schooling Attained	Years	3.1	3.5	4.1	4.3	4.3	4.7	4.9	5.3	5.5	5.4	5.4	5.1	5.8	0.011
Cyprus	Average Years of Secondary Schooling Attained	Years	0.5	0.7	1.0	1.2	1.4	1.8	2.3	2.8	3.1	3.5	3.8	3.5	4.3	0.039
Cyprus	Average Years of Tertiary Schooling Attained	Years	0.1	0.1	0.0	0.1	0.1	0.2	0.3	0.4	0.6	0.7	0.8	0.7	1.0	0.052

(Continued)

Table 5.1. (*Continued*)

Country	Highest Level Attained	Unit	1950	1955	1960	1965	1970	1975	1980	1985	1990	1995	2000	2005	2010	Compound Annual Growth Rate
Egypt	Population (1000s)	thousands	13,169	14,597	16,019	17,819	20,684	23,221	25,715	28,890	32,818	37,492	43,151	49,195	54,733	0.024
Egypt	No Schooling Attained	%	93.0	91.0	89.0	85.9	82.2	78.0	67.8	55.8	50.7	45.2	39.0	34.8	31.1	−0.018
Egypt	Total Primary Schooling	%	3.9	5.3	6.6	8.4	10.6	11.5	14.2	16.7	15.2	13.8	12.7	9.8	9.0	0.014
Egypt	Total Primary Schooling Completed	%	1.4	1.9	2.4	3.2	4.4	5.2	6.8	8.5	8.2	7.8	7.5	6.0	5.7	0.025
Egypt	Total Secondary Schooling	%	2.0	2.4	2.7	3.6	4.6	8.0	14.4	23.7	30.7	37.0	40.7	45.9	48.1	0.055
Egypt	Total Secondary Schooling Completed	%	0.7	0.9	1.0	1.4	1.8	3.2	6.2	10.6	14.5	18.1	20.4	24.0	26.4	0.063
Egypt	Total Tertiary Schooling	%	1.1	1.4	1.8	2.2	2.6	2.5	3.6	3.7	3.4	4.0	7.6	9.5	11.8	0.042
Egypt	Total Tertiary Schooling Completed	%	0.6	0.8	1.0	1.2	1.4	1.3	1.9	2.0	1.9	2.2	4.2	5.3	6.7	0.042
Egypt	Average Years of Schooling Attained	Years	0.5	0.7	0.8	1.0	1.3	1.7	2.7	3.8	4.4	5.1	6.0	6.7	7.2	0.045
Egypt	Average Years of Primary Schooling Attained	Years	0.3	0.4	0.5	0.7	0.9	1.1	1.7	2.4	2.8	3.1	3.5	3.7	3.8	0.042

Egypt	Average Years of Secondary Schooling Attained	Years	0.2	0.2	0.2	0.3	0.4	0.5	0.8	1.3	1.6	1.9	2.3	2.7	2.9	0.052
Egypt	Average Years of Tertiary Schooling Attained	Years	0.0	0.0	0.1	0.1	0.1	0.1	0.1	0.1	0.1	0.1	0.2	0.3	0.4	0.044
Iran	Population (1000s)	thousands	10,302	11,099	12,195	13,830	15,969	18,508	21,750	26,802	31,347	35,831	42,998	49,563	55,585	0.029
Iran	No Schooling Attained	%	92.0	90.6	87.1	80.7	74.6	68.5	58.2	47.8	39.1	29.3	21.3	17.5	14.2	−0.031
Iran	Total Primary Schooling	%	5.5	5.9	8.2	11.2	12.7	13.7	18.3	22.8	25.9	27.3	24.7	20.1	17.3	0.020
Iran	Total Primary Schooling Completed	%	3.6	4.0	5.2	6.6	7.5	8.1	10.6	13.1	14.8	15.5	14.0	11.3	9.8	0.017
Iran	Total Secondary Schooling	%	2.3	3.1	4.1	7.3	11.4	15.7	20.9	25.7	29.3	34.8	43.1	49.2	49.1	0.053
Iran	Total Secondary Schooling Completed	%	1.0	1.3	2.0	3.4	6.4	9.6	14.0	18.3	21.2	26.4	27.6	30.7	30.5	0.060
Iran	Total Tertiary Schooling	%	0.3	0.3	0.6	0.8	1.4	2.1	2.7	3.6	5.6	8.6	10.9	13.2	19.4	0.076
Iran	Total Tertiary Schooling Completed	%	0.2	0.2	0.4	0.6	0.9	1.5	1.9	2.6	4.1	6.4	8.0	9.7	14.7	0.077

(Continued)

Table 5.1. (*Continued*)

Country	Highest Level Attained	Unit	1950	1955	1960	1965	1970	1975	1980	1985	1990	1995	2000	2005	2010	Compound Annual Growth Rate
Iran	Average Years of Schooling Attained	Years	0.5	0.7	0.9	1.4	2.0	2.7	3.6	4.4	5.2	6.4	7.3	8.1	8.9	0.049
Iran	Average Years of Primary Schooling Attained	Years	0.4	0.5	0.7	1.0	1.4	1.7	2.3	2.8	3.1	3.6	4.0	4.2	4.3	0.040
Iran	Average Years of Secondary Schooling Attained	Years	0.1	0.2	0.2	0.4	0.6	0.9	1.2	1.5	1.9	2.5	3.0	3.5	3.9	0.062
Iran	Average Years of Tertiary Schooling Attained	Years	0.0	0.0	0.0	0.0	0.1	0.1	0.1	0.1	0.2	0.3	0.4	0.5	0.7	0.074
Iraq	Population (1000s)	thousands	3,177	3,517	3,954	4,441	5,318	6,238	7,456	8,826	10,254	12,209	14,374	16,997	19,846	0.032
Iraq	No Schooling Attained	%	97.4	95.9	93.4	88.8	80.5	74.0	66.3	55.4	45.1	37.7	30.9	29.3	24.7	−0.023
Iraq	Total Primary Schooling	%	0.8	1.6	3.2	5.6	10.6	13.6	15.0	18.9	24.6	30.4	31.1	29.9	27.1	0.062
Iraq	Total Primary Schooling Completed	%	0.3	0.6	1.2	2.2	4.5	6.1	7.3	9.8	13.6	17.6	18.7	18.8	17.6	0.073
Iraq	Total Secondary Schooling	%	1.2	1.9	2.6	4.1	6.8	9.1	14.4	20.0	23.1	24.0	28.1	28.4	32.1	0.057
Iraq	Total Secondary Schooling Completed	%	0.5	0.7	1.0	1.6	2.6	3.6	6.1	8.8	10.8	11.7	14.2	14.8	17.4	0.064

Iraq	Total Tertiary Schooling	%	0.6	0.6	0.9	1.5	2.2	3.3	4.3	5.7	7.3	7.8	9.9	12.5	16.2	0.057
Iraq	Total Tertiary Schooling Completed	%	0.3	0.3	0.5	0.8	1.1	1.7	2.2	3.0	3.8	4.2	5.3	6.8	8.8	0.057
Iraq	Average Years of Schooling Attained	Years	0.2	0.3	0.5	0.9	1.4	2.0	2.7	3.7	4.6	5.1	5.9	6.3	7.2	0.059
Iraq	Average Years of Primary Schooling Attained	Years	0.1	0.2	0.3	0.6	1.0	1.3	1.8	2.4	3.0	3.4	3.8	3.9	4.2	0.059
Iraq	Average Years of Secondary Schooling Attained	Years	0.1	0.1	0.1	0.2	0.4	0.5	0.8	1.2	1.4	1.5	1.8	2.0	2.4	0.060
Iraq	Average Years of Tertiary Schooling Attained	Years	0.0	0.0	0.0	0.1	0.1	0.1	0.1	0.2	0.2	0.2	0.3	0.4	0.5	0.056
Israel	Population (1000s)	thousands	860	1,146	1,352	1,676	1,937	2,254	2,515	2,768	3,100	3,803	4,364	4,858	5,328	0.031
Israel	No Schooling Attained	%	19.0	18.2	16.5	14.8	12.8	10.0	7.4	6.5	4.7	4.0	3.8	3.0	2.5	−0.034
Israel	Total Primary Schooling	%	44.2	43.7	42.7	40.1	35.8	30.8	26.4	26.8	26.9	26.8	25.3	25.1	10.5	−0.024
Israel	Total Primary Schooling Completed	%	40.5	38.0	36.1	34.2	30.2	26.5	22.6	23.3	23.9	23.7	22.6	22.3	8.6	−0.026
Israel	Total Secondary Schooling	%	28.2	29.4	31.4	33.5	38.9	41.5	46.4	43.5	42.6	39.7	38.2	39.0	51.9	0.010

(Continued)

Table 5.1. (Continued)

Country	Highest Level Attained	Unit	1950	1955	1960	1965	1970	1975	1980	1985	1990	1995	2000	2005	2010	Compound Annual Growth Rate
Israel	Total Secondary Schooling Completed	%	18.8	19.7	21.2	22.2	25.9	28.2	32.1	30.3	30.3	28.8	28.4	29.6	39.1	0.012
Israel	Total Tertiary Schooling	%	8.5	8.8	9.4	11.6	12.6	17.7	19.8	23.2	25.8	29.5	32.7	32.9	35.0	0.024
Israel	Total Tertiary Schooling Completed	%	4.8	4.9	5.3	6.3	6.8	9.6	11.0	12.8	14.2	16.3	18.3	18.8	20.3	0.025
Israel	Average Years of Schooling Attained	Years	7.3	7.4	7.7	8.1	8.7	9.6	10.3	10.5	10.8	11.1	11.3	11.5	12.3	0.009
Israel	Average Years of Primary Schooling Attained	Years	4.8	4.7	4.8	4.9	5.1	5.3	5.4	5.5	5.6	5.9	6.1	6.4	6.4	0.005
Israel	Average Years of Secondary Schooling Attained	Years	2.3	2.4	2.6	2.8	3.2	3.7	4.2	4.3	4.4	4.2	4.2	4.1	4.8	0.013
Israel	Average Years of Tertiary Schooling Attained	Years	0.3	0.3	0.3	0.4	0.4	0.6	0.6	0.7	0.8	0.9	1.0	1.0	1.1	0.024
Jordan	Population (1000s)	thousands	256	363	499	611	879	1,022	1,127	1,433	1,730	2,528	3,019	3,582	4,127	0.048
Jordan	No Schooling Attained	%	81.5	76.1	68.0	60.5	55.9	51.2	47.9	40.9	31.8	24.0	18.7	13.2	7.0	−0.041
Jordan	Total Primary Schooling	%	10.6	13.1	16.9	20.2	21.7	22.4	19.9	17.5	17.9	17.8	15.5	13.7	13.0	0.003

Jordan	Total Primary Schooling Completed	%	5.8	7.4	10.1	10.9	12.0	12.6	14.8	13.7	12.5	13.0	11.6	10.4	9.6	0.008
Jordan	Total Secondary Schooling	%	7.3	10.1	14.3	17.7	19.5	21.2	26.4	32.3	41.5	48.2	54.8	59.8	67.0	0.038
Jordan	Total Secondary Schooling Completed	%	2.9	4.5	6.3	7.5	8.4	9.0	8.9	15.2	22.0	28.5	32.0	31.2	27.1	0.039
Jordan	Total Tertiary Schooling	%	0.6	0.7	0.8	1.7	3.0	5.2	5.8	9.3	8.9	10.0	11.0	13.3	13.0	0.054
Jordan	Total Tertiary Schooling Completed	%	0.4	0.4	0.7	1.1	1.8	2.7	2.9	3.8	3.5	3.6	3.7	4.0	3.8	0.039
Jordan	Average Years of Schooling Attained	Years	1.3	1.8	2.4	3.0	3.5	4.0	4.6	5.7	6.6	7.6	8.4	9.1	9.6	0.034
Jordan	Average Years of Primary Schooling Attained	Years	1.0	1.3	1.7	2.1	2.4	2.6	3.0	3.4	3.9	4.4	4.8	5.1	5.5	0.030
Jordan	Average Years of Secondary Schooling Attained	Years	0.3	0.5	0.7	0.9	1.0	1.2	1.4	2.0	2.4	2.9	3.3	3.6	3.8	0.042
Jordan	Average Years of Tertiary Schooling Attained	Years	0.0	0.0	0.0	0.1	0.1	0.2	0.2	0.3	0.3	0.3	0.3	0.3	0.3	0.049
Kuwait	Population (1000s)	thousands	98	125	180	289	421	561	823	1,081	1,356	1,199	1,647	2,034	2,316	0.055
Kuwait	No Schooling Attained	%	66.5	61.1	54.8	48.6	44.8	58.6	50.7	44.8	40.8	39.6	23.2	6.7	6.1	−0.040
Kuwait	Total Primary Schooling	%	25.9	29.0	30.9	33.5	32.7	12.2	10.2	8.7	8.5	7.3	268	46.4	43.8	0.009
Kuwait	Total Primary Schooling Completed	%	4.6	5.4	7.3	9.1	9.0	4.7	3.9	2.8	2.4	1.6	5.2	9.2	9.6	0.013
Kuwait	Total Secondary Schooling	%	5.3	7.0	10.7	13.9	19.0	24.3	31.7	35.6	39.8	42.4	40.9	39.8	43.0	0.036
Kuwait	Total Secondary Schooling Completed	%	2.6	3.5	5.6	7.3	9.9	12.2	16.4	20.3	21.9	22.6	20.1	17.5	18.7	0.034

(Continued)

Table 5.1. *(Continued)*

Country	Highest Level Attained	Unit	1950	1955	1960	1965	1970	1975	1980	1985	1990	1995	2000	2005	2010	Compound Annual Growth Rate
Kuwait	Total Tertiary Schooling	%	2.3	3.0	3.6	4.0	3.5	4.9	7.6	10.9	10.9	10.8	9.1	7.0	7.1	0.019
Kuwait	Total Tertiary Schooling Completed	%	1.3	1.6	2.0	2.1	1.8	2.5	4.0	6.1	6.1	6.3	5.4	4.2	4.3	0.021
Kuwait	Average Years of Schooling Attained	Years	1.5	1.8	2.4	2.9	3.3	3.5	4.6	5.5	5.9	6.1	6.1	6.1	6.3	0.025
Kuwait	Average Years of Primary Schooling Attained	Years	0.9	1.1	1.3	1.6	1.7	1.5	1.9	2.1	2.2	2.3	2.6	3.0	3.1	0.021
Kuwait	Average Years of Secondary Schooling Attained	Years	0.5	0.7	0.9	1.2	1.4	1.9	2.5	3.1	3.3	3.5	3.2	2.9	3.0	0.031
Kuwait	Average Years of Tertiary Schooling Attained	Years	0.1	0.1	0.1	0.1	0.1	0.2	0.2	0.3	0.3	0.3	0.3	0.2	0.2	0.020
Morocco	Population (1000s)	thousands	4,981	5,612	6,416	7,209	8,028	9,140	11,140	12,907	14,893	17,063	19,465	21,690	23,834	0.027
Morocco	No Schooling Attained	%	96.4	95.1	93.7	91.3	87.1	81.8	77.0	71.1	64.8	59.4	54.9	49.5	43.8	−0.013
Morocco	Total Primary Schooling	%	1.4	1.8	2.5	2.9	5.4	8.8	11.2	14.0	17.2	19.2	21.0	23.2	24.8	0.049
Morocco	Total Primary Schooling Completed	%	0.6	0.7	1.0	1.2	2.4	4.1	5.8	8.2	11.5	14.5	16.9	19.6	21.7	0.064
Morocco	Total Secondary Schooling	%	2.0	2.8	3.4	5.3	6.5	7.7	9.0	10.7	12.6	14.7	16.8	19.0	22.1	0.042

Morocco	Total Secondary Schooling Completed	%	0.7	1.0	1.3	1.9	2.4	3.0	3.8	4.8	5.9	7.2	8.5	10.0	12.1	0.049
Morocco	Total Tertiary Schooling	%	0.2	0.2	0.5	0.6	0.9	1.7	2.8	4.2	5.5	6.8	7.4	8.3	9.4	0.064
Morocco	Total Tertiary Schooling Completed	%	0.0	0.0	0.1	0.1	0.2	0.6	0.7	2.2	3.0	3.7	4.1	4.7	5.4	0.099
Morocco	Average Years of Schooling Attained	Years	0.3	0.4	0.5	0.7	1.0	1.4	1.8	2.3	2.9	3.4	3.8	4.3	5.0	0.050
Morocco	Average Years of Primary Schooling Attained	Years	0.2	0.2	0.3	0.4	0.6	0.8	1.0	1.3	1.6	1.9	2.2	2.4	2.8	0.050
Morocco	Average Years of Secondary Schooling Attained	Years	0.1	0.2	0.2	0.3	0.4	0.5	0.7	0.9	1.1	1.3	1.4	1.6	1.9	0.048
Morocco	Average Years of Tertiary Schooling Attained	Years	0.0	0.0	0.0	0.0	0.0	0.1	0.1	0.1	0.2	0.2	0.2	0.3	0.3	0.059
Qatar	Population (1000s)	thousands	14	20	27	45	70	115	156	261	338	385	449	636	694	0.068
Qatar	No Schooling Attained	%	82.6	78.0	74.2	67.8	63.1	57.6	52.8	48.3	45.1	40.0	36.8	33.3	3.6	−0.052
Qatar	Total Primary Schooling	%	4.8	5.8	6.7	8.2	9.0	10.7	11.8	12.8	13.1	13.7	13.2	10.2	42.1	0.038
Qatar	Total Primary Schooling Completed	%	0.8	1.2	2.6	3.4	4.1	5.1	5.2	5.6	5.9	6.2	6.0	4.4	18.5	0.054
Qatar	Total Secondary Schooling	%	9.5	11.5	13.1	16.1	18.0	21.3	24.1	27.6	29.4	32.8	34.7	39.1	37.8	0.024
Qatar	Total Secondary Schooling Completed	%	4.5	5.2	6.0	7.5	8.9	10.4	12.0	14.0	15.4	17.4	18.6	22.9	23.6	0.028
Qatar	Total Tertiary Schooling	%	3.1	4.6	6.0	7.9	9.9	10.4	11.3	11.3	12.5	13.5	15.4	17.4	16.4	0.029
Qatar	Total Tertiary Schooling Completed	%	1.8	2.6	3.4	4.4	5.6	5.9	6.5	7.2	7.8	8.4	9.8	10.6	10.1	0.030

(*Continued*)

Table 5.1. *(Continued)*

Country	Highest Level Attained	Unit	1950	1955	1960	1965	1970	1975	1980	1985	1990	1995	2000	2005	2010	Compound Annual Growth Rate
Qatar	Average Years of Schooling Attained	Years	1.6	2.1	2.5	3.2	3.8	4.3	4.8	5.2	5.6	6.1	6.6	7.3	8.4	0.028
Qatar	Average Years of Primary Schooling Attained	Years	0.9	1.2	1.4	1.8	2.1	2.4	2.6	2.9	3.1	3.4	3.6	3.8	5.1	0.029
Qatar	Average Years of Secondary Schooling Attained	Years	0.6	0.8	0.9	1.2	1.4	1.6	1.8	1.9	2.1	2.3	2.5	2.9	2.8	0.026
Qatar	Average Years of Tertiary Schooling Attained	Years	0.1	0.1	0.2	0.3	0.3	0.3	0.4	0.4	0.4	0.4	0.5	0.6	0.5	0.029
SA	Population (1000s)	thousands	1,856	2,061	2,309	2,683	3,188	4,041	5,348	7,421	9,557	10,959	12,982	15,413	18,076	0.039
SA	No Schooling Attained	%	64.0	62.2	60.5	55.4	54.2	50.1	45.7	36.0	29.1	26.5	21.2	17.1	12.7	−0.027
SA	Total Primary Schooling	%	25.8	26.5	26.8	30.2	29.7	29.6	29.5	33.0	34.9	32.0	30.4	27.3	23.1	−0.002
SA	Total Primary Schooling Completed	%	10.8	12.0	12.7	14.4	14.1	14.8	15.0	17.4	18.7	17.4	17.2	16.1	15.0	0.005
SA	Total Secondary Schooling	%	6.9	7.6	8.4	9.8	11.2	14.2	17.6	22.3	26.0	30.4	36.0	43.9	52.3	0.035
SA	Total Secondary Schooling Completed	%	2.9	3.5	4.1	4.8	5.5	6.9	8.6	10.9	12.8	15.0	18.1	22.4	29.1	0.040
SA	Total Tertiary Schooling	%	3.3	37	4.2	4.5	4.9	6.1	73	8.8	10.0	11.1	12.4	11.7	12.0	0.022

SA	Total Tertiary Schooling Completed	%	1.8	2.0	2.3	2.4	2.6	3.1	37	4.7	5.5	6.2	6.9	6.5	6.7	0.022
SA	Average Years of Schooling Attained	Years	2.3	2.5	2.7	3.1	3.2	3.7	4.3	5.2	5.8	6.3	7.1	7.7	8.5	0.022
SA	Average Years of Primary Schooling Attained	Years	1.7	1.8	2.0	2.2	2.3	2.6	2.8	3.4	3.8	4.0	4.3	4.6	5.0	0.018
SA	Average Years of Secondary Schooling Attained	Years	0.5	0.6	0.6	0.7	0.8	1.0	1.2	1.5	1.8	2.0	2.4	2.7	3.2	0.032
SA	Average Years of Tertiary Schooling Attained	Years	0.1	0.1	0.1	0.1	0.2	0.2	0.2	0.3	0.3	0.3	0.4	0.4	0.4	0.022
Syria	Population (1000s)	thousands	2,046	2,255	2,507	2,837	3,323	3,879	4,565	5,486	6,664	8,174	10,042	12,023	13,910	0.033
Syria	No Schooling Attained	%	74.4	72.4	69.4	65.4	58.4	50.0	41.4	31.7	24.4	18.3	16.0	15.3	16.2	−0.026
Syria	Total Primary Schooling	%	24.0	25.1	26.7	28.2	31.5	35.5	39.2	43.7	50.1	58.6	62.5	53.2	43.5	0.010
Syria	Total Primary Schooling Completed	%	2.8	3.5	6.1	6.1	7.0	7.9	8.2	9.0	11.0	13.1	16.2	32.6	32.5	0.042
Syria	Total Secondary Schooling	%	1.3	2.1	3.5	5.3	9.1	12.7	16.1	20.6	20.9	18.7	17.9	27.2	35.7	0.058
Syria	Total Secondary Schooling Completed	%	0.3	0.4	0.8	1.3	2.4	3.6	3.8	4.3	5.1	4.8	4.1	8.8	18.1	0.070

(Continued)

Table 5.1. *(Continued)*

Country	Highest Level Attained	Unit	1950	1955	1960	1965	1970	1975	1980	1985	1990	1995	2000	2005	2010	Compound Annual Growth Rate
Syria	Total Tertiary Schooling	%	0.4	0.4	0.4	1.0	0.9	1.8	3.2	4.0	4.6	4.4	3.6	4.4	4.6	0.043
Syria	Total Tertiary Schooling Completed	%	0.2	0.2	0.2	0.5	0.5	0.9	1.6	2.1	2.4	2.3	1.9	2.3	2.6	0.043
Syria	Average Years of Schooling Attained	Years	0.9	1.0	1.2	1.5	2.0	2.7	3.4	4.1	4.5	4.6	4.6	5.9	6.7	0.036
Syria	Average Years of Primary Schooling Attained	Years	0.8	0.8	1.0	1.2	1.5	2.0	2.4	2.9	3.2	3.4	3.6	4.4	4.6	0.031
Syria	Average Years of Secondary Schooling Attained	Years	0.1	0.1	0.2	0.3	0.5	0.7	0.9	1.1	1.1	1.0	0.9	1.4	1.9	0.053
Syria	Average Years of Tertiary Schooling Attained	Years	0.0	0.0	0.0	0.0	0.0	0.1	0.1	0.1	0.1	0.1	0.1	0.1	0.1	0.046
Tunisia	Population (1000s)	thousands	2,160	2,283	2,391	2,485	2,758	3,184	3,745	4,397	5,098	5,879	6,674	7,483	8,180	0.023
Tunisia	No Schooling Attained	%	90.5	88.5	86.5	81.4	74.8	64.8	53.8	51.6	44.8	37.8	31.0	25.3	20.9	−0.025
Tunisia	Total Primary Schooling	%	5.9	7.3	8.6	11.4	15.2	21.8	29.2	26.9	29.1	31.0	31.8	30.5	29.4	0.027
Tunisia	Total Primary Schooling Completed	%	2.0	2.6	3.1	4.4	6.3	9.8	14.1	13.8	15.7	17.5	18.6	18.6	18.3	0.038

Tunisia	Total Secondary Schooling	%	3.1	3.7	4.3	6.3	9.0	12.3	15.2	18.9	22.4	26.7	30.5	34.1	37.1	0.043
Tunisia	Total Secondary Schooling Completed	%	1.4	1.7	2.0	2.9	4.2	5.9	7.3	9.0	10.6	12.5	14.0	15.3	16.4	0.043
Tunisia	Total Tertiary Schooling	%	0.5	0.5	0.6	0.9	1.0	1.1	1.9	2.6	3.8	4.5	6.7	10.1	12.7	0.058
Tunisia	Total Tertiary Schooling Completed	%	0.3	0.3	0.3	0.5	0.5	0.5	0.9	1.4	2.1	2.5	3.8	5.7	7.4	0.058
Tunisia	Average Years of Schooling Attained	Years	0.7	0.8	0.9	1.3	1.8	2.5	3.3	3.7	4.4	5.1	5.9	6.8	7.5	0.042
Tunisia	Average Years of Primary Schooling Attained	Years	0.5	0.6	0.7	0.9	1.3	1.8	2.3	2.5	2.9	3.3	3.8	4.1	4.4	0.039
Tunisia	Average Years of Secondary Schooling Attained	Years	0.2	0.2	0.3	0.4	0.5	0.7	0.9	1.1	1.4	1.6	1.9	2.3	27	0.047
Tunisia	Average Years of Tertiary Schooling Attained	Years	0.0	0.0	0.0	0.0	0.0	0.0	0.1	0.1	0.1	0.1	0.2	0.3	0.4	0.065
UAE	Population (1000s)	thousands	40	46	51	89	147	382	725	993	1,311	1,754	2,450	3,507	3,998	0.081
UAE	No Schooling Attained	%	90.9	87.3	83.6	78.0	74.2	69.9	61.8	52.9	41.9	29.7	18.1	10.0	9.7	−0.037
UAE	Total Primary Schooling	%	3.5	4.5	5.7	6.7	6.8	7.1	8.3	9.1	10.7	12.1	18.4	24.6	22.6	0.032
UAE	Total Primary Schooling Completed	%	0.6	1.0	1.3	2.0	2.2	2.6	3.3	3.8	4.7	5.5	8.6	11.5	11.3	0.050
UAE	Total Secondary Schooling	%	3.7	5.6	7.5	11.1	14.2	18.2	24.1	29.9	36.4	43.5	47.1	50.0	53.3	0.046

(Continued)

Table 5.1. *(Continued)*

Country	Highest Level Attained	Unit	1950	1955	1960	1965	1970	1975	1980	1985	1990	1995	2000	2005	2010	Compound Annual Growth Rate
UAE	Total Secondary Schooling Completed	%	1.8	3.0	4.5	7.1	9.3	12.0	16.1	19.7	23.5	27.7	30.0	32.2	35.7	0.052
UAE	Total Tertiary Schooling	%	1.9	2.6	3.3	4.1	4.8	4.7	5.9	8.1	11.0	14.8	16.3	15.4	14.4	0.035
UAE	Total Tertiary Schooling Completed	%	1.0	1.4	1.8	2.2	2.6	2.5	3.2	4.8	6.4	8.7	9.7	9.0	8.5	0.037
UAE	Average Years of Schooling Attained	Years	0.8	1.1	1.5	2.1	2.5	3.0	3.9	4.9	6.1	7.5	8.4	8.9	9.1	0.042
UAE	Average Years of Primary Schooling Attained	Years	0.5	0.7	0.9	1.2	1.4	1.7	2.1	2.7	3.3	4.0	4.6	5.0	5.1	0.042
UAE	Average Years of Secondary Schooling Attained	Years	0.3	0.4	0.6	0.8	1.0	1.2	1.6	2.0	2.5	3.0	3.3	3.4	3.5	0.044
UAE	Average Years of Tertiary Schooling Attained	Years	0.1	0.1	0.1	0.1	0.2	0.1	0.2	0.3	0.4	0.5	0.5	0.5	0.5	0.035
Yemen	Population (1000s)	thousands	2,489	2,630	2,812	3,055	3,256	3,490	4,105	4,875	5,829	7,637	9,281	11,251	13,540	0,029
Yemen	No Schooling Attained	%	99.6	99.5	99.2	99.0	98.7	98.8	95.8	91.1	84.0	78.2	70.8	65.0	57.5	−0.009
Yemen	Total Primary Schooling	%	0.3	0.5	0.7	1.0	1.2	0.5	3.5	5.6	8.6	11.5	13.7	13.5	16.0	0.068
Yemen	Total Primary Schooling Completed	%	0.1	0.2	0.3	0.4	0.5	0.2	1.7	3.0	4.8	6.7	8.4	8.6	10.6	0.076

Yemen	Total Secondary Schooling	%	0.0	0.0	0.0	0.0	0.0	0.5	0.5	2.9	6.6	8.9	13.6	19.3	23.7	0.114
Yemen	Total Secondary Schooling Completed	%	0.0	0.0	0.0	0.0	0.0	0.2	0.2	1.2	2.9	3.9	6.0	8.6	10.7	0.125
Yemen	Total Tertiary Schooling	%	0.0	0.0	0.0	0.0	0.0	0.1	0.1	0.4	0.8	1.4	1.8	2.3	2.9	0.075
Yemen	Total Tertiary Schooling Completed	%	0.0	0.0	0.0	0.0	0.0	0.1	0.1	0.2	0.4	0.7	0.9	1.2	1.5	0.076
Yemen	Average Years of Schooling Attained	Years	0.0	0.0	0.0	0.1	0.1	0.1	0.2	0.6	1.2	1.7	2.3	3.0	3.7	0.092
Yemen	Average Years of Primary Schooling Attained	Years	0.0	0.0	0.0	0.1	0.1	0.1	0.2	0.5	0.8	1.2	1.6	2.0	2.4	0.084
Yemen	Average Years of Secondary Schooling Attained	Years	0.0	0.0	0.0	0.0	0.0	0.0	0.0	0.2	0.3	0.5	0.7	1.0	1.2	0.036
Yemen	Average Years of Tertiary Schooling Attained	Years	0.0	0.0	0.0	0.0	0.0	0.0	0.0	0.0	0.0	0.0	0.1	0.1	0.1	0.038

Source: Barro and Lee (2013).

Table 5.2. Trends of Educational Attainment of the MENA's Female Population Aged 15 and Over

Country	Highest Level Attained	Unit	1950	1955	1960	1965	1970	1975	1980	1985	1990	1995	2000	2005	2010	Compound Annual Growth Rate
Algeria	Population (1000s)	thousands	2,531	2,795	3,048	3,216	3,766	4,375	5,142	6,125	7,222	8,534	10,018	11,514	12,870	0.028
Algeria	No Schooling Attained	%	83.8	84.4	87.6	89.7	87.4	79.8	72.1	62.5	54.6	45.8	38.6	38.0	28.2	−0.018
Algeria	Total Primary Schooling	%	14.7	13.9	10.4	8.0	8.8	14.3	18.4	22.5	25.8	30.3	35.7	36.9	36.7	0.016
Algeria	Total Primary Schooling Completed	%	3.2	3.0	2.3	2.1	2.3	2.9	3.6	8.2	10.3	14.2	18.3	22.0	20.4	0.032
Algeria	Total Secondary Schooling	%	1.4	1.6	1.9	2.1	3.6	5.7	8.9	13.6	17.4	20.6	20.3	18.8	22.5	0.049
Algeria	Total Secondary Schooling Completed	%	0.4	0.3	0.6	0.9	1.7	3.0	5.1	8.4	11.3	14.0	14.1	13.6	16.8	0.067
Algeria	Total Tertiary Schooling	%	0.2	0.1	0.1	0.1	0.1	0.3	0.7	1.5	2.2	3.3	5.5	6.3	12.5	0.078
Algeria	Total Tertiary Schooling Completed	%	0.1	0.1	0.1	0.1	0.1	0.1	0.3	0.8	1.2	1.8	3.0	3.5	7.1	0.081
Algeria	Average Years of Schooling Attained	Years	0.7	0.7	0.6	0.6	0.8	1.2	1.8	2.8	3.5	4.3	4.9	5.0	6.4	0.038
Algeria	Average Years of Primary Schooling Attained	Years	0.6	0.6	0.5	0.4	0.6	0.9	1.2	1.8	2.3	2.8	3.2	3.3	3.8	0.031
Algeria	Average Years of Secondary Schooling Attained	Years	0.1	0.1	0.1	0.1	0.2	0.3	0.6	0.9	1.2	1.5	1.6	1.5	2.1	0.060

Algeria	Average Years of Tertiary Schooling Attained	Years	0.0	0.0	0.0	0.0	0.0	0.0	0.0	0.0	0.1	0.1	0.2	0.2	0.4	0.064
Bahrain	Population (1000s)	thousands	30	34	39	49	52	66	85	106	129	160	192	214	249	0.037
Bahrain	No Schooling Attained	%	94.4	93.2	90.0	81.6	71.3	58.5	49.6	44.1	36.0	31.4	27.4	30.0	30.9	−0.019
Bahrain	Total Primary Schooling	%	2.5	3.3	4.6	9.6	10.8	14.4	13.7	11.8	10.6	10.1	9.7	9.5	8.2	0.020
Bahrain	Total Primary Schooling Completed	%	1.6	1.7	2.6	6.3	4.6	6.1	5.7	4.9	4.4	4.2	4.1	4.0	3.5	0.013
Bahrain	Total Secondary Schooling	%	2.3	2.7	4.3	6.8	15.3	22.3	29.0	32.0	40.0	46.0	52.0	50.2	51.9	0.054
Bahrain	Total Secondary Schooling Completed	%	1.2	1.3	2.1	3.5	7.8	11.7	16.4	19.8	25.5	30.0	34.4	34.1	34.7	0.058
Bahrain	Total Tertiary Schooling	%	0.8	0.9	1.2	2.1	2.6	4.8	7.7	12.1	13.4	12.5	10.9	10.3	9.1	0.042
Bahrain	Total Tertiary Schooling Completed	%	0.6	0.6	0.8	1.6	1.2	1.8	3.0	6.0	8.4	9.2	9.0	8.7	8.2	0.044
Bahrain	Average Years of Schooling Attained	Years	0.5	0.5	0.8	1.4	2.3	3.4	4.5	5.4	6.4	7.0	7.5	7.3	7.3	0.048
Bahrain	Average Years of Primary Schooling Attained	Years	0.3	0.4	0.5	1.0	1.5	2.2	2.8	3.2	3.7	3.9	4.2	4.0	4.0	0.044

(Continued)

Table 5.2. *(Continued)*

Country	Highest Level Attained	Unit	1950	1955	1960	1965	1970	1975	1980	1985	1990	1995	2000	2005	2010	Compound Annual Growth Rate
Bahrain	Average Years of Secondary Schooling Attained	Years	0.1	0.1	0.2	0.4	0.7	1.0	1.5	1.8	2.3	2.6	2.9	2.8	2.9	0.055
Bahrain	Average Years of Tertiary Schooling Attained	Years	0.0	0.0	0.0	0.1	0.1	0.1	0.2	0.4	0.4	0.4	0.4	0.4	0.4	0.043
Cyprus	Population (1000s)	thousands	167	181	186	200	214	231	233	245	255	278	313	348	376	0.014
Cyprus	No Schooling Attained	%	52.1	42.7	32.5	26.7	24.8	19.3	15.7	10.3	7.0	10.2	11.8	18.1	1.2	−0.062
Cyprus	Total Primary Schooling	%	42.1	47.8	52.8	53.7	51.8	49.8	44.5	42.2	38.8	28.8	20.7	23.9	22.9	−0.010
Cyprus	Total Primary Schooling Completed	%	18.4	22.8	29.4	28.5	25.4	26.8	26.3	27.1	26.2	20.1	15.6	16.2	16.0	−0.002
Cyprus	Total Secondary Schooling	%	4.9	8.8	14.2	18.7	21.5	27.3	33.0	36.9	39.2	41.5	45.2	39.4	46.4	0.039
Cyprus	Total Secondary Schooling Completed	%	2.5	5.1	8.4	9.7	12.5	16.3	20.5	23.8	25.6	27.6	30.7	27.1	32.3	0.044
Cyprus	Total Tertiary Schooling	%	1.0	0.7	0.5	0.9	1.9	3.6	6.8	10.5	15.0	19.6	22.3	18.6	29.6	0.060
Cyprus	Total Tertiary Schooling Completed	%	0.6	0.4	0.4	0.6	1.2	2.2	4.5	7.0	10.1	13.2	15.0	12.6	20.2	0.062
Cyprus	Average Years of Schooling Attained	Years	2.5	3.2	4.1	4.6	4.9	5.8	6.8	7.7	8.5	9.0	9.5	8.4	10.9	0.025

Cyprus	Average Years of Primary Schooling Attained	Years	2.2	2.7	3.4	3.6	3.7	4.2	4.5	4.9	5.2	5.1	5.1	4.7	5.7	0.017
Cyprus	Average Years of Secondary Schooling Attained	Years	0.3	0.5	0.7	0.9	1.1	1.5	2.0	2.5	2.8	3.3	3.6	3.1	4.1	0.047
Cyprus	Average Years of Tertiary Schooling Attained	Years	0.0	0.0	0.0	0.0	0.1	0.1	0.2	0.4	0.5	0.7	0.8	0.6	1.0	0.061
Egypt	Population (1000s)	thousands	6,684	7,375	8,050	8,944	10,359	11,653	12,950	14,498	16,453	18,808	21,670	24,746	27,585	0.024
Egypt	No Schooling Attained	%	97.6	96.2	94.8	92.4	89.4	86.0	79.0	69.5	64.0	56.7	49.0	43.4	38.3	−0.016
Egypt	Total Primary Schooling	%	1.5	2.6	3.6	5.1	7.1	7.8	9.6	11.6	10.2	10.5	10.6	8.3	8.2	0.029
Egypt	Total Primary Schooling Completed	%	0.5	0.9	1.3	1.9	2.9	3.4	4.5	5.8	5.4	5.9	6.2	5.1	5.8	0.042
Egypt	Total Secondary Schooling	%	0.7	1.0	1.2	1.8	2.4	5.1	9.9	17.3	24.0	30.0	36.0	41.8	44.0	0.072
Egypt	Total Secondary Schooling Completed	%	0.3	0.4	0.5	0.7	0.9	2.0	4.1	7.6	11.3	14.7	18.1	22.0	24.4	0.080
Egypt	Total Tertiary Schooling	%	0.2	0.3	0.4	0.7	1.0	1.1	1.6	1.6	1.8	2.8	4.4	6.5	9.6	0.072
Egypt	Total Tertiary Schooling Completed	%	0.1	0.1	0.2	0.3	0.5	0.6	0.8	0.9	1.0	1.6	2.4	3.6	5.4	0.074

(Continued)

Table 5.2. (*Continued*)

Country	Highest Level Attained	Unit	1950	1955	1960	1965	1970	1975	1980	1985	1990	1995	2000	2005	2010	Compound Annual Growth Rate
Egypt	Average Years of Schooling Attained	Years	0.2	0.3	0.3	0.5	0.7	1.0	1.7	2.6	3.2	4.1	5.0	5.7	6.4	0.064
Egypt	Average Years of Primary Schooling Attained	Years	0.1	0.2	0.2	0.4	0.5	0.7	1.1	1.7	2.0	2.5	2.9	3.2	3.5	0.059
Egypt	Average Years of Secondary Schooling Attained	Years	0.0	0.1	0.1	0.1	0.2	0.3	0.5	0.8	1.2	1.5	1.9	2.3	2.6	0.074
Egypt	Average Years of Tertiary Schooling Attained	Years	0.0	0.0	0.0	0.0	0.0	0.0	0.1	0.1	0.1	0.1	0.1	0.2	0.3	0.059
Iran	Population (1000s)	thousands	5,052	5.463	6,014	6,834	7,872	9,109	10,686	13,055	15,290	17,657	21,264	24,543	27,562	0.029
Iran	No Schooling Attained	%	96.2	95.3	92.9	88.5	83.5	77.1	68.3	57.8	48.2	37.0	26.9	23.2	17.2	−0.029
Iran	Total Primary Schooling	%	2.5	3.0	4.2	6.6	8.9	11.0	15.0	20.4	24.8	27.0	24.9	20.7	17.1	0.033
Iran	Total Primary Schooling Completed	%	1.8	2.2	2.7	4.0	5.6	7.0	9.9	13.9	17.5	19.7	18.9	16.3	14.0	0.036
Iran	Total Secondary Schooling	%	1.2	1.6	2.7	4.5	6.9	10.7	15.1	19.6	23.3	29.8	38.9	44.3	47.3	0.064
Iran	Total Secondary Schooling Completed	%	0.5	0.6	1.2	2.1	3.8	6.3	9.7	13.4	16.5	22.4	25.4	28.4	31.3	0.073
Iran	Total Tertiary Schooling	%	0.1	0.0	0.2	0.3	0.6	1.2	1.6	2.2	3.5	6.1	9.4	11.8	18.4	0.102

Iran	Total Tertiary Schooling Completed	%	0.0	0.0	0.1	0.2	0.5	0.9	1.1	1.6	2.6	4.6	6.8	8.4	12.7	0.102
Iran	Average Years of Schooling Attained	Years	0.3	0.3	0.5	0.8	1.3	1.9	2.7	3.5	4.3	5.5	6.8	7.5	8.7	0.061
Iran	Average Years of Primary Schooling Attained	Years	0.2	0.3	0.4	0.6	0.9	1.3	1.8	2.3	2.7	3.3	3.8	4.0	4.3	0.052
Iran	Average Years of Secondary Schooling Attained	Years	0.1	0.1	0.1	0.2	0.4	0.6	0.8	1.1	1.4	2.0	2.7	3.1	3.8	0.076
Iran	Average Years of Tertiary Schooling Attained	Years	0.0	00	0.0	0.0	0.0	0.0	0.1	0.1	0.1	0.2	0.3	0.4	0.6	0.072
Iraq	Population (1000s)	thousands	1,594	1,766	1,986	2,231	2,665	3,113	3,712	4,390	5,094	6,055	7,127	8,424	9,838	0.031
Iraq	No Schooling Attained	%	99.0	98.3	97.2	94.8	89.7	85.5	80.2	70.5	56.9	48.5	41.5	39.0	33.9	−0.018
Iraq	Total Primary Schooling	%	0.4	0.8	1.4	2.6	5.7	7.8	9.0	13.7	23.4	30.1	31.7	30.1	25.5	0.074
Iraq	Total Primary Schooling Completed	%	0.1	0.3	0.5	1.0	2.4	3.4	4.3	7.0	12.9	17.4	19.0	19.0	18.8	0.089
Iraq	Total Secondary Schooling	%	0.5	0.8	1.1	1.8	3.5	4.8	8.1	11.9	14.5	15.6	19.8	21.8	28.4	0.071
Iraq	Total Secondary Schooling Completed	%	0.2	0.3	0.4	0.7	1.3	1.8	3.4	5.2	6.8	7.7	10.0	11.5	15.6	0.079

(Continued)

Table 5.2. *(Continued)*

Country	Highest Level Attained	Unit	1950	1955	1960	1965	1970	1975	1980	1985	1990	1995	2000	2005	2010	Compound Annual Growth Rate
Iraq	Total Tertiary Schooling	%	0.2	0.2	0.3	0.7	1.0	2.0	2.7	3.9	5.2	5.8	7.0	9.0	12.2	0.076
Iraq	Total Tertiary Schooling Completed	%	0.1	0.1	0.2	0.4	0.5	0.9	1.3	2.0	2.7	3.1	3.8	4.9	6.7	0.078
Iraq	Average Years of Schooling Attained	Years	0.1	0.1	0.2	0.4	0.7	1.1	1.6	2.4	3.3	3.9	4.6	5.1	6.2	0.074
Iraq	Average Years of Primary Schooling Attained	Years	0.1	0.1	0.1	0.3	0.5	0.7	1.1	1.6	2.3	2.7	3.1	3.3	3.8	0.076
Iraq	Average Years of Secondary Schooling Attained	Years	0.0	0.0	0.1	0.1	0.2	0.3	0.5	0.7	0.9	1.0	1.3	1.5	2.0	0.074
Iraq	Average Years of Tertiary Schooling Attained	Years	0.0	0.0	0.0	0.0	0.0	0.1	0.1	0.1	0.2	0.2	0.2	0.3	0.4	0.064
Israel	Population (1000s)	thousands	416	570	669	836	972	1,140	1,275	1,406	1,580	1,958	2,241	2,490	2,722	0.032
Israel	No Schooling Attained	%	25.9	25.0	23.0	20.3	17.0	13.6	10.8	9.3	6.4	5.3	4.8	4.2	3.6	−0.033
Israel	Total Primary Schooling	%	42.3	40.9	40.4	38.2	34.7	30.3	26.1	25.6	25.5	25.2	23.5	23.1	10.6	−0.023
Israel	Total Primary Schooling Completed	%	39.5	34.7	33.4	32.3	28.8	25.7	22.0	22.0	22.3	22.0	20.6	20.1	8.5	−0.026

Israel	Total Secondary Schooling	%	25.9	27.7	29.2	31.8	36.9	39.9	44.5	42.7	42.5	39.5	37.5	37.8	48.0	0.011
Israel	Total Secondary Schooling Completed	%	17.9	19.3	20.4	21.7	25.4	27.9	31.8	30.7	31.3	30.0	29.0	29.8	37.1	0.012
Israel	Total Tertiary Schooling	%	5.9	6.3	7.4	9.7	11.3	16.2	18.7	22.3	25.7	30.0	34.1	34.9	37.8	0.032
Israel	Total Tertiary Schooling Completed	%	2.6	2.9	3.4	4.4	5.1	7.6	8.9	11.0	13.4	15.8	18.4	19.3	21.3	0.036
Israel	Average Years of Schooling Attained	Years	6.5	6.6	6.9	7.5	8.2	9.1	9.8	10.2	10.7	11.1	11.4	11.5	12.3	0.011
Israel	Average Years of Primary Schooling Attained	Years	4.4	4.3	4.4	4.6	4.8	5.1	5.2	5.3	5.5	5.8	6.1	6.3	6.3	0.006
Israel	Average Years of Secondary Schooling Attained	Years	2.0	2.1	2.3	2.6	3.0	3.6	4.0	4.2	4.4	4.3	4.3	4.2	4.9	0.015
Israel	Average Years of Tertiary Schooling Attained	Years	0.2	0.2	0.2	0.3	0.3	0.5	0.6	0.7	0.8	0.9	1.1	1.1	1.2	0.033
Jordan	Population (1000s)	thousands	125	179	243	296	423	496	545	686	820	1,187	1,429	1,705	1,974	0.048
Jordan	No Schooling Attained	%	91.7	89.1	83.6	77.2	71.0	64.7	59.0	49.5	39.2	28.8	23.0	17.0	10.5	−0.036
Jordan	Total Primary Schooling	%	4.0	5.6	9.0	13.2	16.7	19.1	16.5	15.1	18.8	23.1	18.6	15.3	12.3	0.019

(Continued)

Table 5.2. *(Continued)*

Country	Highest Level Attained	Unit	1950	1955	1960	1965	1970	1975	1980	1985	1990	1995	2000	2005	2010	Compound Annual Growth Rate
Jordan	Total Primary Schooling Completed	%	2.6	3.6	5.7	7.3	8.9	10.0	10.6	9.8	12.4	15.9	13.2	11.0	8.8	0.021
Jordan	Total Secondary Schooling	%	4.2	5.1	7.1	9.1	11.0	13.5	21.0	29.3	35.7	40.7	50.2	57.2	65.7	0.048
Jordan	Total Secondary Schooling Completed	%	1.3	1.9	2.6	3.4	4.2	5.2	6.7	13.4	18.9	24.4	30.0	31.3	29.6	0.054
Jordan	Total Tertiary Schooling	%	0.2	0.2	0.3	0.6	1.3	2.7	3.5	6.2	6.3	7.4	8.3	10.8	11.5	0.074
Jordan	Total Tertiary Schooling Completed	%	0.1	0.1	0.2	0.3	0.6	1.0	3.5	1.7	1.7	1.8	1.9	2.1	2.2	0.052
Jordan	Average Years of Schooling Attained	Years	0.6	0.8	1.2	1.6	2.1	2.6	3.5	4.7	5.6	6.6	7.6	8.5	9.3	0.046
Jordan	Average Years of Primary Schooling Attained	Years	0.5	0.6	0.9	1.2	1.5	1.8	2.3	2.9	3.5	4.1	4.5	4.9	5.3	0.042
Jordan	Average Years of Secondary Schooling Attained	Years	0.2	0.2	0.3	0.4	0.5	0.7	1.0	1.7	2.0	2.4	2.9	3.4	3.7	0.054
Jordan	Average Years of Tertiary Schooling Attained	Years	0.0	0.0	0.0	0.0	0.0	0.1	0.1	0.2	0.2	0.2	0.2	0.3	0.3	0.057

Kuwait	Population (1000s)	thousands	35	45	57	96	167	236	313	430	539	432	591	756	886	0.056
Kuwait	No Schooling Attained	%	86.2	81.5	74.6	66.3	58.5	62.7	51.8	42.8	40.5	41.0	24.9	9.2	8.2	−0.039
Kuwait	Total Primary Schooling	%	10.4	13.4	15.9	19.8	21.6	10.5	9.3	8.2	7.5	6.2	23.6	39.3	37.5	0.022
Kuwait	Total Primary Schooling Completed	%	2.2	3.1	4.7	6.5	7.2	4.1	3.5	2.4	1.9	1.4	4.7	9.5	10.4	0.027
Kuwait	Total Secondary Schooling	%	2.8	4.3	8.0	11.9	17.9	23.7	33.2	39.3	42.0	42.8	41.3	42.1	44.8	0.048
Kuwait	Total Secondary Schooling Completed	%	1.4	2.2	4.3	6.5	9.7	12.1	17.5	22.8	23.6	23.4	21.3	20.2	21.6	0.047
Kuwait	Total Tertiary Schooling	%	0.5	0.8	1.4	2.0	2.0	3.1	5.7	9.7	10.0	9.9	10.3	9.4	9.5	0.050
Kuwait	Total Tertiary Schooling Completed	%	0.3	0.4	0.7	1.0	1.0	1.5	2.8	5.2	5.4	5.6	5.9	5.4	5.6	0.054
Kuwait	Average Years of Schooling Attained	Years	0.6	0.9	1.4	2.0	2.7	3.1	4.5	5.7	6.0	6.0	6.3	6.6	6.9	0.042
Kuwait	Average Years of Primary Schooling Attained	Years	0.4	0.5	0.8	1.1	1.4	1.4	1.8	2.2	2.3	2.3	2.6	3.0	3.1	0.036
Kuwait	Average Years of Secondary Schooling Attained	Years	0.2	0.3	0.6	0.9	1.3	1.7	2.5	3.3	3.4	3.4	3.3	3.2	3.4	0.048

(Continued)

Table 5.2. (*Continued*)

Country	Highest Level Attained	Unit	1950	1955	1960	1965	1970	1975	1980	1985	1990	1995	2000	2005	2010	Compound Annual Growth Rate
Kuwait	Average Years of Tertiary Schooling Attained	Years	0.0	0.0	0.0	0.1	0.1	0.1	0.2	0.3	0.3	0.3	0.3	0.3	0.3	0.047
Morocco	Population (1000s)	thousands	2,499	2,819	3,226	3,658	4,095	4,643	5,651	6,548	7,561	8,664	9,883	11,023	12,111	0.027
Morocco	No Schooling Attained	%	97.5	96.9	95.7	94.6	92.3	89.0	85.1	80.3	75.0	70.4	66.1	60.7	54.4	−0.010
Morocco	Total Primary Schooling	%	0.7	0.9	1.7	1.7	3.3	5.1	7.0	9.1	11.4	13.0	14.6	16.3	17.8	0.056
Morocco	Total Primary Schooling Completed	%	0.4	0.4	0.7	0.8	1.6	2.6	4.0	5.9	8.4	10.4	12.2	14.2	15.9	0.067
Morocco	Total Secondary Schooling	%	1.5	1.8	2.4	3.5	3.8	4.9	6.5	8.4	10.3	12.3	14.4	17.2	21.0	0.046
Morocco	Total Secondary Schooling Completed	%	0.5	0.6	0.9	1.1	1.4	1.9	2.7	3.7	4.9	6.0	7.3	9.1	11.7	0.055
Morocco	Total Tertiary Schooling	%	0.4	0.3	0.2	0.3	0.5	1.0	1.5	2.3	3.3	4.3	4.9	5.8	6.8	0.051
Morocco	Total Tertiary Schooling Completed	%	0.0	0.0	0.0	0.1	0.1	0.3	0.3	1.2	1.8	2.4	2.7	3.3	3.9	0.093
Morocco	Average Years of Schooling Attained	Years	0.2	0.3	0.3	0.4	0.6	0.8	1.2	1.6	2.1	2.5	2.9	3.5	4.1	0.051
Morocco	Average Years of Primary Schooling Attained	Years	0.1	0.1	0.2	0.3	0.3	0.5	0.7	0.9	1.2	1.4	1.6	1.9	2.3	0.051

Morocco	Average Years of Secondary Schooling Attained	Years	0.1	0.1	0.1	0.2	0.2	0.3	0.5	0.6	0.8	1.0	1.1	1.4	1.6	0.048
Morocco	Average Years of Tertiary Schooling Attained	Years	0.0	0.0	0.0	0.0	0.0	0.0	0.0	0.1	0.1	0.1	0.2	0.2	0.2	0.053
Qatar	Population (1000s)	thousands	6	8	11	14	18	29	48	69	90	111	139	180	208	0.062
Qatar	No Schooling Attained	%	87.5	81.7	80.0	77.2	70.2	62.1	53.2	46.0	41.8	36.9	33.1	30.4	4.4	−0.049
Qatar	Total Primary Schooling	%	3.7	5.5	5.2	5.4	6.9	9.0	10.2	11.0	11.1	11.1	10.2	7.0	29.2	0.036
Qatar	Total Primary Schooling Completed	%	1.0	1.5	2.5	2.5	3.5	4.8	5.8	5.8	5.1	5.0	4.6	2.5	10.1	0.041
Qatar	Total Secondary Schooling	%	7.6	11.1	11.8	13.0	16.8	21.1	25.3	30.6	32.0	35.1	36.8	40.1	40.5	0.029
Qatar	Total Secondary Schooling Completed	%	3.0	4.5	5.3	6.3	8.4	10.2	13.1	16.5	18.4	20.6	21.1	25.7	26.8	0.038
Qatar	Total Tertiary Schooling	%	1.3	1.7	3.0	4.4	6.2	7.8	11.3	12.4	15.2	17.0	19.9	22.5	25.9	0.053
Qatar	Total Tertiary Schooling Completed	%	0.7	0.9	1.5	2.3	3.2	4.0	6.1	7.6	8.8	10.2	12.2	13.1	15.2	0.054
Qatar	Average Years of Schooling Attained	Years	1.1	1.6	1.9	2.3	3.0	3.8	4.9	5.6	6.2	6.8	7.4	8.1	9.6	0.037

(*Continued*)

Table 5.2. *(Continued)*

Country	Highest Level Attained	Unit	1950	1955	1960	1965	1970	1975	1980	1985	1990	1995	2000	2005	2010	Compound Annual Growth Rate
Qatar	Average Years of Primary Schooling Attained	Years	0.7	1.0	1.1	1.3	1.7	2.2	2.7	3.1	3.3	3.6	3.8	4.0	5.2	0.035
Qatar	Average Years of Secondary Schooling Attained	Years	0.4	0.6	0.7	0.8	1.1	1.4	1.8	2.2	2.4	2.7	2.9	3.3	3.6	0.038
Qatar	Average Years of Tertiary Schooling Attained	Years	0.0	0.1	0.1	0.1	0.2	0.2	0.4	0.4	0.5	0.5	0.6	0.7	0.8	0.053
SA	Population (1000s)	thousands	914	1,019	1,142	1,311	1,534	1,871	2,312	3,055	3,893	4,431	5,634	6,825	8,156	0.038
SA	No Schooling Attained	%	79.6	78.4	77.4	72.1	71.5	67.5	64.0	55.1	42.3	39.0	31.0	23.7	18.0	−0.025
SA	Total Primary Schooling	%	16.9	17.7	18.2	22.8	22.8	23.4	23.5	25.0	31.6	27.7	26.5	23.7	19.8	0.003
SA	Total Primary Schooling Completed	%	5.2	5.9	6.3	7.9	7.9	9.3	9.7	11.8	15.5	13.9	14.0	13.9	12.5	0.015
SA	Total Secondary Schooling	%	2.7	2.9	3.2	3.9	4.4	6.9	9.5	14.8	19.3	24.8	31.0	41.1	49.7	0.051
SA	Total Secondary Schooling Completed	%	1.1	1.3	1.5	1.8	2.1	3.3	4.6	7.3	9.6	12.4	16.4	22.0	29.3	0.058
SA	Total Tertiary Schooling	%	0.8	1.0	1.2	1.2	1.3	2.2	3.0	5.1	6.8	8.6	11.6	11.5	12.6	0.048
SA	Total Tertiary Schooling Completed	%	0.4	0.5	0.6	0.6	0.6	1.1	1.5	2.6	3.6	4.6	6.3	6.3	6.9	0.049

SA	Average Years of Schooling Attained	Years	1.1	1.2	1.2	1.5	1.6	2.0	2.4	3.4	4.5	5.1	6.2	7.2	8.2	0.035
SA	Average Years of Primary Schooling Attained	Years	0.9	0.9	1.0	1.2	1.3	1.5	1.8	2.3	3.0	3.3	3.8	4.3	4.7	0.029
SA	Average Years of Secondary Schooling Attained	Years	0.2	0.2	0.2	0.2	0.3	0.4	0.6	1.0	1.3	1.6	2.1	2.6	3.1	0.052
SA	Average Years of Tertiary Schooling Attained	Years	0.0	0.0	0.0	0.0	0.0	0.1	0.1	0.2	0.2	0.3	0.4	0.4	0.4	0.052
Syria	Population (1000s)	thousands	986	1,101	1,234	1,400	1,647	1,938	2,302	2,769	3,364	4,112	5,041	6,025	6,951	0.034
Syria	No Schooling Attained	%	90.8	89.5	87.2	84.3	79.0	71.2	61.4	50.0	39.6	29.8	23.5	23.4	23.4	−0.023
Syria	Total Primary Schooling	%	8.5	9.3	11.0	12.9	16.1	20.8	25.4	30.9	39.7	50.1	53.9	47.1	39.7	0.026
Syria	Total Primary Schooling Completed	%	1.4	1.7	2.9	2.7	2.8	3.2	4.1	4.9	7.1	9.5	13.3	27.5	28.9	0.053
Syria	Total Secondary Schooling	%	0.6	1.1	1.7	2.5	4.6	7.1	11.2	16.6	17.5	17.3	20.7	26.5	33.4	0.072
Syria	Total Secondary Schooling Completed	%	0.2	0.3	0.5	0.7	1.4	2.3	2.9	3.6	4.5	4.5	3.7	8.9	17.4	0.080
Syria	Total Tertiary Schooling	%	0.1	0.1	0.1	0.3	0.3	0.9	1.9	2.6	3.2	2.9	2.0	3.1	3.5	0.068

(Continued)

Table 5.2. *(Continued)*

Country	Highest Level Attained	Unit	1950	1955	1960	1965	1970	1975	1980	1985	1990	1995	2000	2005	2010	Compound Annual Growth Rate
Syria	Total Tertiary Schooling Completed	%	0.0	0.0	0.0	0.2	0.1	0.4	0.9	1.3	1.7	1.5	1.0	1.7	1.9	0.073
Syria	Average Years of Schooling Attained	Years	0.3	0.4	0.5	0.7	1.0	1.5	2.2	3.0	3.5	3.8	4.2	5.3	6.1	0.052
Syria	Average Years of Primary Schooling Attained	Years	0.3	0.3	0.4	0.5	0.8	1.1	1.5	2.1	2.5	2.9	3.3	3.9	4.2	0.047
Syria	Average Years of Secondary Schooling Attained	Years	0.0	0.1	0.1	0.1	0.2	0.4	0.6	0.8	0.9	0.9	0.9	1.3	1.8	0.071
Syria	Average Years of Tertiary Schooling Attained	Years	0.0	0.0	0.0	0.0	0.0	0.0	0.1	0.1	0.1	0.1	0.1	0.1	0.1	0.041
Tunisia	Population (1000s)	thousands	1,090	1,164	1,194	1,230	1,426	1,583	1,864	2,187	2,543	2,931	3,332	3,740	4,092	0.023
Tunisia	No Schooling Attained	%	95.5	94.6	93.5	89.6	84.4	75.5	67.5	64.4	56.6	48.3	41.3	34.8	28.9	−0.020
Tunisia	Total Primary Schooling	%	2.6	3.4	4.3	6.8	10.4	16.8	22.0	21.5	24.8	27.7	28.0	27.0	26.5	0.040
Tunisia	Total Primary Schooling Completed	%	0.9	1.1	1.5	2.5	4.2	7.3	10.4	10.9	13.3	15.5	16.3	16.4	18.6	0.053
Tunisia	Total Secondary Schooling	%	1.7	1.8	2.0	3.3	4.8	7.3	9.8	12.8	16.4	21.0	25.7	29.5	32.6	0.051

Tunisia	Total Secondary Schooling Completed	%	0.6	0.6	0.7	1.2	1.9	3.1	4.3	5.8	7.7	10.0	12.4	14.4	16.2	0.057
Tunisia	Total Tertiary Schooling	%	0.1	0.2	0.2	0.4	0.4	0.5	0.8	1.4	2.2	2.9	5.0	8.7	12.0	0.080
Tunisia	Total Tertiary Schooling Completed	%	0.1	0.1	0.1	0.2	0.2	0.2	0.4	0.7	1.2	1.6	2.8	4.9	7.0	0.081
Tunisia	Average Years of Schooling Attained	Years	0.3	0.4	0.4	0.7	1.0	1.6	2.2	2.6	3.3	4.1	4.9	5.9	6.9	0.055
Tunisia	Average Years of Primary Schooling Attained	Years	0.2	0.3	0.3	0.5	0.8	1.2	1.6	1.8	2.3	2.7	3.2	3.6	4.0	0.051
Tunisia	Average Years of Secondary Schooling Attained	Years	0.1	0.1	0.1	0.2	0.3	0.4	0.5	0.7	1.0	1.2	1.6	2.1	2.5	0.060
Tunisia	Average Years of Tertiary Schooling Attained	Years	0.0	0.0	0.0	0.0	0.0	0.0	0.0	0.0	0.1	0.1	0.2	0.3	0.4	0.064
UAE	Population (1000s)	thousands	19	22	24	34	47	91	175	294	372	498	667	945	1,152	0.072
UAE	No Schooling Attained	%	96.2	93.7	90.9	85.5	80.7	74.0	61.9	51.0	39.7	26.4	16.0	8.5	8.4	−0.041
UAE	Total Primary Schooling	%	1.3	2.1	2.5	3.5	4.1	5.5	7.4	8.2	10.1	11.3	15.5	16.9	15.6	0.043
UAE	Total Primary Schooling Completed	%	0.2	0.5	0.6	0.9	1.1	1.8	2.7	3.3	4.3	5.0	7.1	7.5	7.3	0.060

(Continued)

Table 5.2. *(Continued)*

Country	Highest Level Attained	Unit	1950	1955	1960	1965	1970	1975	1980	1985	1990	1995	2000	2005	2010	Compound Annual Growth Rate
UAE	Total Secondary Schooling	%	2.0	3.3	5.3	8.9	12.2	17.2	25.1	32.3	38.7	46.2	49.4	54.7	57.0	0.058
UAE	Total Secondary Schooling Completed	%	1.0	1.8	3.2	5.6	7.9	11.6	17.4	22.8	27.4	32.7	35.3	39.5	42.5	0.066
UAE	Total Tertiary Schooling	%	0.4	0.8	1.3	2.2	3.0	3.4	5.5	8.5	11.5	16.0	19.1	19.9	19.0	0.066
UAE	Total Tertiary Schooling Completed	%	0.2	0.4	0.6	1.1	1.5	1.7	2.8	4.6	6.3	8.9	10.7	11.0	10.7	0.068
UAE	Average Years of Schooling Attained	Years	0.3	0.6	0.9	1.4	1.9	2.6	3.9	5.2	6.5	8.1	9.1	9.9	10.0	0.060
UAE	Average Years of Primary Schooling Attained	Years	0.2	0.3	0.5	0.8	1.1	1.5	2.1	2.8	3.4	4.2	4.8	5.2	5.3	0.058
UAE	Average Years of Secondary Schooling Attained	Years	0.1	0.2	0.3	0.6	0.8	1.1	1.6	2.2	2.7	3.3	3.7	4.0	4.1	0.062
UAE	Average Years of Tertiary Schooling Attained	Years	0.0	0.0	0.0	0.1	0.1	0.1	0.2	0.3	0.4	0.5	0.6	0.6	0.6	0.072
Yemen	Population (1000s)	thousands	1,239	1,311	1,405	1,531	1,654	1,799	2,097	2,469	2,933	3,789	4,595	5,577	6,718	0.029
Yemen	No Schooling Attained	%	99.6	99.6	99.6	99.5	99.4	99.7	98.6	97.2	94.1	90.7	86.2	81.1	72.5	−0.005
Yemen	Total Primary Schooling	%	0.3	0.3	0.3	0.4	0.5	0.2	1.2	2.1	3.6	5.1	6.4	5.1	7.1	0.054

Yemen	Total Primary Schooling Completed	%	0.1	0.1	0.1	0.2	0.2	0.1	0.6	1.1	2.0	3.0	3.9	3.3	5.4	0.065
Yemen	Total Secondary Schooling	%	0.0	0.0	0.0	0.0	0.0	0.0	0.2	0.6	1.9	3.6	6.1	11.8	17.6	0.109
Yemen	Total Secondary Schooling Completed	%	0.0	0.0	0.0	0.0	0.0	0.0	0.1	0.3	0.9	1.8	3.1	6.1	9.6	0.123
Yemen	Total Tertiary Schooling	%	0.0	0.0	0.0	0.0	0.0	0.0	0.1	0.1	0.5	0.6	1.3	2.1	2.8	0.074
Yemen	Total Tertiary Schooling Completed	%	0.0	0.0	0.0	0.0	0.0	0.0	0.0	0.1	0.2	0.3	0.7	1.1	1.5	0.075
Yemen	Average Years of Schooling Attained	Years	0.0	0.0	0.0	0.0	0.0	0.0	0.1	0.2	0.4	0.7	1.2	1.8	2.7	0.086
Yemen	Average Years of Primary Schooling Attained	Years	0.0	0.0	0.0	0.0	0.0	0.0	0.1	0.1	0.3	0.5	0.8	1.1	1.6	0.077
Yemen	Average Years of Secondary Schooling Attained	Years	0.0	0.0	0.0	0.0	0.0	0.0	0.0	0.0	0.1	0.2	0.4	0.7	1.0	0.081
Yemen	Average Years of Tertiary Schooling Attained	Years	0.0	0.0	0.0	0.0	0.0	0.0	0.0	0.0	0.0	0.0	0.0	0.1	0.1	0.036

Source: Barro and Lee (2013).

percentage of primary schooling attained in the relevant population; (2) the percentage of those completing primary schooling in the relevant population; (3) the percentage of secondary schooling attained in the relevant population; (4) the percentage of those completing secondary schooling in the relevant population; (5) the percentage of tertiary schooling attained in the relevant population; (6) the percentage of those completing tertiary schooling in the relevant population. The relevant population for Table 5.1 is the total population aged 15 and above. The relevant population for Table 5.2 is the total female population aged 15 and above. The data from Barro and Lee (2013) follows the classification scheme fond in UNESCO's 'International Standard Classification of Education (ISCED)' and, thereby, facilitates comparisons of education statistics and indicators across countries on the basis of uniform and internationally agreed definitions. Under this classification, primary schooling is typically designed to provide students with fundamental skills in reading, writing and mathematics and to establish a solid foundation for learning. Secondary education starts by building on primary education, typically with a more subject-oriented curriculum. It is followed by preparing for tertiary education and/or providing skills relevant to employment usually with an increased range of subject options and streams. Tertiary schooling is typically practical-based, occupationally specific and prepares students for labor market entry. These programs may also provide a pathway to other tertiary programs. These other pathways are designed to provide intermediate academic and/or professional knowledge, skills and competencies leading to a first tertiary degree or equivalent qualification.

Despite efforts within MENA to provide education to its citizens over the 1950–2010-time period, the proportion of the population within Arab MENA countries with no schooling in 2010 is still very high. Qatar is the only country within Arab MENA that has substantially seen a drop in the percent of the total population aged 15 and above with no schooling from 82.6 percent in 1950 to 3.6 in 2010 and a drop in the female population aged 15 and above that did not receive any education from 87.5 in 1950 to 4.4 in 2010. In Algeria, 21.1 percent of the total population aged 15 and above and 28.2 percent of the female population aged 15 and above did not receive any education. For Bahrain the number in 2010 is 28.9 percent for total population and 30.9 percent for women; for Egypt it was 31.1 percent for total and 38.3 percent for women; for Iran it was 14.2 percent for total and 17.2 percent for women; for Iraq it was 24.7 percent for total and 33.9 percent for women; for Jordan it was 7.0 percent for total and

10.5 percent for women; for Kuwait it was 6.1 percent for total and 8.2 percent for women; for Syria it was 16.2 percent for total and 23.4 percent for women; for Tunisia it was 20.9 percent for total and 28.9 percent for women; and for the UAE it was 9.7 for total and 8.4 for women; for Yemen it was over 57.5 percent for total and over 72.5 percent for women. For the non-Arab MENA members, these figures are substantially lower — for Cyprus it was 0.7 percent for the total population aged 15 and above and 1.2 percent for women, and for Israel it was 2.5 percent for total and 3.6 percent for women, reflecting the large number of Bedouins who do not attend school.

In addition to the large number of people without any education, the data in Tables 5.1 and 5.2 also highlight the limited formal education that citizens in Arab MENA complete. At every level of education in Arab MENA, a small share of the relevant population complete primary schooling, secondary schooling, and far less, tertiary education. The average percentage that completed tertiary education in Arab MENA in 2010 was 6.8 percent for both the total population aged 15 and female population aged 15 and above. In Israel it was 20.3 percent for total and 21.3 percent for women, and in Cyprus it was 20.8 percent for total and 20.2 percent for women.

Despite educational reforms in Arab MENA, as evidenced by the increase in the years of formal education attained at all levels, the degree of effective reforms is limited. In the case of Egypt, despite the well-funded reforms, the country operates two parallel education systems: the secular system and the Al-Azhar (Islamic) system. Universal primary education throughout the country is compulsory until Grade 8. Despite the increased enrollment, however, overall adult illiteracy remains high — 43 percent — and the rate for women is even higher at 54 percent. This gender gap is especially high at the secondary and tertiary level. Quality remains an issue at all educational levels in Egypt.

Economists, when measuring a country's human capital, focus on measuring the number of years the average member of the workforce had attended school or college. This information has been easily obtained at the international level as seen in Table 5.1 and 5.2. Using time spent in school as a measure of human capital, "they were able to show that individuals who spent more years in school or college would be more prosperous in their economic career later in life. Furthermore, they showed that countries where a higher percentage of the population was in school or college for a longer period of time enjoyed a higher level of economic growth."

However, that time spent in school does not reflect the level of learning in these institutions. Ideally, measures of a person's human capital, or a nation's total human capital, would be observed by test scores. Days and years spent in formal education is a necessary but not sufficient condition for an indicator of human capital. (Hanushek, Peterson and Woessmann, 2013).

For MENA we have observed in Chapter 4 that despite the increase in enrolment in formal education the test results demonstrate a very inferior performance by international standards. Furthermore, the fact that in 2010 the total population 15 and above for Arab MENA that did not attend formal schooling remained at 21.2 percent and for the female population aged 15 and above that did not attending formal education was even higher at 26.9 percent corroborates the recent results presented by UNESCO (2017) that there are today "millions of children and youth not going to school." Despite efforts by individual countries to reverse this situation, they remain ineffective.

In a USAID (2004) report, the social evaluation of the Egyptian reform effort was less than enthusiastic. In particular, in the case of Egypt:

> "the quality of primary education is declining. The teacher-focused learning and authoritarian teaching styles that prevail in most Egyptian classrooms promote passive learning. Thus, even though more than 90 percent of primary school-aged children enroll in schools, the poor teaching-learning environment means that learning achievements are not optimized. The quality problems are even more pronounced at the secondary level, where an increasing number of students are entering. It is clear that Egypt will need a more sophisticated education system that produces students with critical thinking skills and the ability to enter the competitive job market. Thus far, the increased investment in the education sector has not translated into an improved quality of secondary education. Its inadequacy is reflected in the shortcomings of the curriculum and examination system and in deficient pedagogical skills. Another factor contributing to poor quality is that teachers must organize their lessons according to national directives on lesson planning instead of the learning needs of their students. In addition, strategies that incorporate good science and technology programs at the higher education level are not yet in place." [USAID, 2004, p. 11 quoting World Bank, Secondary Education Enhancement Project, Project Appraisal (March 22, 1999). http://www-wds.worldbank.org/].

Jamison *et al.* (2006), report their empirical results to support the existence of a link between educational quality and economic outcomes such as income per capita. Their results indicate that performance on international mathematics tests appear to be measuring an element of human capital that is important to growth in income per capita and that is not captured by quantity (years) of schooling on its own. Their work points out that a one standard deviation increase in test scores is associated with an increase in annual growth in income per capita of 0.5–0.9 percent.

They further report that "we find the strongest support for the idea that quality impacts economic output through changes in the rate of technical progress" (Jamison *et al.*, 2006, p. 20). Furthermore, their results support the hypothesis that "openness of the economy" is a major determinant in affecting cognitive skills and the rate of technical progress. Consequently, education quality improves productivity most significantly in an economic environment that is open to outside trade and influence. Their results indicate that "higher test scores are associated with higher rates of technical progress only in countries where openness is greater than a certain minimal level" (Jamison *et al.*, 2006, p. 20).[2]

Given these results and the educational attainment figures for Arab MENA through 2010, it is not surprising that the Arab MENA is a long way from "closing the educational gap with the more advanced developing economies." Moreover, given the empirical evidence supporting positive results on educational quality coming from an economic environment that is open to outside "influence", the continued policy of xenophobia, religious intolerance, gender bias and aversion to critical thinking will guarantee that Arab MENA will never close the educational gap between itself and the rest of the developing and developed world.

5.2. Measuring Aggregate Productivity

Standard economic analysis estimates aggregate productivity, or TFP, by looking at the annual output Y (measured by the gross domestic product, GDP) that is produced on the basis of the accumulated factors of production, or capital, which are available as inputs. For any given stock of capital, the higher the output, the more productive the economy. Capital is composed of physical capital K and human capital H. Physical capital takes the form of means of production, such as machines and buildings. Human capital is the productive capacity of the labor force, which in turn corresponds to the headcount of the labor force or raw labor, L, multiplied by its average level of skill or education h, so that $H = hL$. TFP measures the effectiveness with which accumulated factors of production, or capital, are used to produce output. Consequently, output growth over

[2]For comparable results, see Schultz (1993), Easterly (2001), Hanushek and Woessmann (2010), and Pritchett (2006).

time results from accumulation of factors of production and productivity growth. Customarily the literature begins with a Cobb–Douglas production function given by:

$$Y = AK^{\alpha}H^{1-\alpha} = AK^{\alpha}(hL)^{1-\alpha}, \tag{5.2}$$

where A is the output elasticity to (physical) capital. The production function parameter α is set equal to 1/3, a standard value in the literature (Klenow and Rodríguez-Clare, 2005). This assumption has been questioned by many. In particular, Gollin (2002) shows that once informal labor and household entrepreneurship are taken into account, there is no systematic difference across countries associated with level of development (GDP per capita), nor any time trend.

One approach would be to construct the relevant series for output, physical capital and human capital (Y, K, H) based on available statistics. Using these series, one can compute the measure of TFP by:

$$A = \frac{Y}{K^{\alpha}(hL)^{1-\alpha}}, \tag{5.3}$$

which is a full measure of the efficiency with which the economy is able to transform its accumulated factors of production into output. However, given that part of MENA is natural resource rich while the other is natural resource poor, it may bias this measure of TFP in favor of the oil-rich. If the results show lower total factor productivity, then we may be facing the popular "natural resource curse hypothesis." This will be addressed in Chapter 6.

A slight alternative to the above measure would be defined with respect to the size of the labor force L rather than the total human capital H. Consequently, education would not be considered a factor of production. Higher average education h would be reflected in higher productivity:

$$A_1 = Ah^{1-\alpha} = \frac{Y}{K^{\alpha}L^{1-\alpha}}. \tag{5.4}$$

A second alternative measure would be to eliminate K as a factor of production. Consequently, an economy whose labor has more capital would exhibit higher productivity:

$$A_2 = A\left(\frac{K}{L}\right)^{\alpha} h^{1-\alpha} = \frac{Y}{L}. \tag{5.5}$$

Both alternative TFP measures provide difficulties. An increase in the labor productivity measure cannot differentiate between better quality of the labor input, due to increased education, from the mere accumulation of physical capital or something else totally unrelated to factor inputs. TFP measures which are based on L cannot measure the effect of education. Being able to distinguish between these different sources of growth is relevant for policy.

TFP measures the efficiency with which available factors of production are transformed into final output. This measure of productivity includes a technological component and tends to increase as the technological frontier expands and new technology or ideas become available and are adopted, but these may be affected by the efficiency of local markets and the institutional constraints imposed by the leadership. Consequently, an economy populated by technologically advanced firms may produce inefficient aggregate results and therefore translate into low aggregate productivity. When market failure exists, it may distort the efficiency with which factors are allocated across sectors, and across firms within sectors, thus depressing efficiency when measured at the aggregate level.

The production function framework noted in Equations (5.2)–(5.5) can be directly applied to account for output per worker Y/L in terms of TFP and per-worker factor intensities $k = K/L$ and $h = H/L$. It is useful to relate this production function framework to a welfare framework, such as the traditional measure of GDP per capita ($y = Y/N$), where N is the size of the population. Differences in income per capita, or in its growth, can be attributed to TFP and per-worker factor intensities:

$$y = \frac{Y}{N} = A\left(\frac{K}{L}\right)^{\alpha} h^{1-\alpha}\frac{L}{N} = Ak^{\alpha}h^{1-\alpha}. \tag{5.6}$$

Keller and Nabli (2007) utilize Equation (5.6) to compare the components behind income per capita between country i and a benchmark economy, denoted by (*), or level gaps:

$$\bar{y} = \frac{y_i}{y^*} = \frac{A_i}{A^*}\left(\frac{k_i}{k^*}\right)^{\alpha}\left(\frac{h_i}{h^*}\right)^{1-\alpha} = \bar{A}\bar{k}^{\alpha}\bar{h}^{1-\alpha}. \tag{5.7}$$

A logarithmic transformation of Equation (5.7) can then be used to account for the contribution of the TFP gap and that of factor intensities to the overall income per capita gap at a point in time:

$$\log(\bar{y}) = \log(\bar{A}) + \alpha\log(\bar{k}) + (1-\alpha)\log(\bar{h}). \tag{5.8}$$

The time difference over a period of n years (say from $t-n$ to t) yields a decomposition of how the level gaps opened during the period, to be interpreted as a decomposition of the accumulated growth gap in the period, found in Equation (5.9) below:

$$\Delta_n \log \bar{y}_t = \log\left(\frac{\bar{y}_t}{\bar{y}_{t-n}}\right)$$
$$= \log\left(\frac{\bar{A}_t}{\bar{A}_{t-n}}\right) + \alpha \log\left(\frac{\bar{k}_t}{\bar{k}_{t-n}}\right) + (1-\alpha)\log\left(\frac{\bar{h}_t}{\bar{h}_{t-n}}\right). \quad (5.9)$$

Keller and Nabli (2007) calculated TFP growth over 10-year periods from 1960–2000. To determine the coefficients on capital and human capital-augmented labor, α and $(1-\alpha)$, the average annual rate of GDP per capita growth over the decade was regressed on average growth of physical capital per worker and human-capital per worker with a least squares trend over the entire period of availability (1960–2000).

Table 5.3 presents Keller and Nabli's calculated TFP using three distinct calculations of factor shares — $\alpha k = 0.3$; $\alpha k = 0.4$; $\alpha k = 0.5$ — to check the sensitivity of the region's growth performance to the assumptions made on the output elasticities.

The TFP growth calculated by Keller and Nabli (2007) is the simple residual between output growth and the growth of factor inputs (capital and labor). From their estimates we observe that Arab MENA exhibited a pattern of high TFP growth in the 1960s, declining dramatically over the 1970s and continuing to decline throughout the 1980s and 1990s. Israel, a non-Arab MENA member,[3] by way of contrast, had a very high rate of TFP in the entire period between the 1960s to the 1980s, declining in the 1990s below the world average, but still in the positive range.

Keller and Nabli argue that the high TFP in Arab MENA in the 1960s reflected "a two-decade period of massive public investment in infrastructure, health, and education, which in this early period of development was able to translate into high growth" (Keller and Nabli, 2007, p. 177). Their conclusion would imply that all of the investments undertaken during the 1960s were exceptionally productive. The reality is very different. Most of Arab MENA devoted their energy in the 1960s to funding investment in

[3]The World Bank study *Breaking the Barriers to Higher Economic Growth: Better Governance and Deeper Reforms in the Middle East and North Africa* (2007), which includes the chapter by Keller and Nabli (pp. 169–201), has for some unexplained reason placed Israel within the OECD rather than MENA. This reflects either a new World Bank consensus designed to move Israel, on paper at least, out of the Middle East, or the power of oil funds in determining unilateral World Bank behavior. This kind of behavior speaks volumes about Arab intolerance and lack of self-worth.

Table 5.3. TFP Estimates Under Various Assumptions of Elasticity of Output with Respect to Physical Capital

Country	1960s TFP $\alpha =$			1970s TFP $\alpha =$			1980s TFP $\alpha =$			1990s TFP $\alpha =$		
	(0.3)	(0.4)	(0.5)	(0.3)	(0.4)	(0.5)	(0.3)	(0.4)	(0.5)	(0.3)	(0.4)	(0.5)
Algeria	2.16	2.08	2	0.28	−0.14	−0.55	−2.45	−2.4	−2.36	−2.38	−1.99	−1.6
Bahrain	...	...	...	...	...	...	−5.28	−5.24	−5.2	0.23	0.36	0.49
Egypt	1.81	1.52	1.23	1.98	1.51	1.04	0.01	−0.31	−0.63	0.58	0.73	0.88
Iran	3.29	2.34	1.39	4.72	5.52	−6.33	−1.26	−1.1	−0.93	0.02	0.16	0.31
Israel	3.3	3.06	2.81	0.72	0.49	0.25	1.05	0.98	0.92	0.46	0.21	−0.05
Jordan	−2.97	−3.49	−4.02	3.18	2.38	1.58	−4.45	−4.43	−4.41	−0.81	−0.55	−0.29
Kuwait	−0.16	0.72	1.61	−6.95	−6.33	−5.72	−5.12	−4.61	−4.1	−2.1	−1.79	−1.49
Morocco	1.98	1.84	1.71	0.04	−0.32	−0.68	0.29	0.21	0.13	−1.14	−1.15	−1.15
Saudi Arabia	4.85	4.53	4.2	0.82	−0.83	−2.48	−6.41	−5.88	−5.35	0.47	0.88	1.28
Syria	2.11	2.04	1.98	2.12	1.17	0.22	−3.92	−4.42	−4.92	0.68	0.89	1.1
Tunisia	1.64	1.24	0.83	1.61	1.43	1.25	−0.45	−0.54	−0.64	0.51	0.55	0.59
Comparison Group												
Africa	−0.01	−0.49	−0.97	−0.07	−0.31	−0.55	−0.62	−0.7	−0.77	−0.07	−0.11	−0.15
E. Asia	1.07	1.04	1.01	1.61	1.18	0.76	3.58	3.08	2.59	4.11	3.32	2.54
ECA	3.42	3.07	2.72	0.58	0.08	−0.42	0.95	0.89	0.83	−0.57	−0.55	−0.54
LAC	1.46	1.2	0.94	1.23	0.91	0.59	−2.37	−2.29	−2.22	0.02	0.03	0.04
MENA	2.36	1.96	1.55	−0.35	−0.96	−1.56	−1.39	−1.44	−1.48	−0.22	−0.03	0.15
OECD	2.18	1.67	1.15	−0.17	−0.39	−0.62	0.92	0.71	0.5	0.45	0.28	0.11
S. Asia	0.62	0.27	−0.09	−0.57	−0.66	−0.76	1.79	1.56	1.33	1.39	1.11	0.83
World	1.28	1.01	0.74	0.52	0.22	−0.07	1.62	1.34	1.07	1.88	1.51	1.13
World (excluding China)	1.37	0.97	0.56	0.01	−0.26	−0.53	0.58	0.39	0.19	0.55	0.37	0.18

Source: Sub-sample of countries reported in Annex Table 1 of Keller and Nabli (2007, pp. 193–201).

protected state industries, especially state-owned industries. Furthermore, the industrial development programs in Arab MENA in the 1960s were based on a concerted effort to protect local markets and subsidize factor inputs. That is, these calculated TFP numbers reflected "distortionary" investment and trade programs, not market conditions. The futility of these industrial policies became evident in the post-1970s when the TFP numbers declined across the entire Arab MENA. Only Israel saw actual improvements in total factor productivity between the 1970s and 1990s.

In the 1990s, the MENA region experienced a small recovery of GDP and TFP growth, despite a continued decline in investment projects, especially in the public sector. This recovery, however, was not sufficient to allow Arab MENA to close the gap neither with Israel, the more advanced developing countries, nor with Asia. The growth of TFPs in Arab MENA compared poorly even with the rest of Africa.

Because human capital accumulation was higher in Arab MENA than in the rest of Africa, its performance net of human capital was even worse than Keller and Nabli (2007) report. This suggests a far lower contribution of human capital to growth in Arab MENA when compared to the rest of the world.

5.3. Labor Market Structure

Labor markets in developing countries differ in important ways from those in industrial countries. Key structural differences are the importance of the agricultural sector in economic activity, the importance of self-employment, and the persistence of irregular work activities. These labor market characteristics add a seasonal pattern to employment and unemployment data.

Rosenzweig (1988) points out that development economics typically differentiates between three sectors in the developing-country labor markets. The rural sector is often characterized by a large share of self-employed persons and unpaid family workers. The informal urban sector is characterized by self-employed individuals with limited skill levels or small privately owned enterprises with limited access to credit markets and producing mainly services and other non-tradables. Tansel (2000, pp. 15–16) finds that in Turkey, male workers in the formal sector earn on average 35 percent more than their counterparts in the informal sector; for women, the differential is about 80 percent. Similar figures are suggested by Tunali (2003). The third segment of the labor market is the formal urban sector, consisting of medium and large enterprises producing both tradable and non-tradable goods, and using workers with a wide range of skills.

Thus far we know that in a large number of Arab MENA countries, agriculture still employs a large share of the labor force in rural areas, whereas the urban sector, despite a sharp expansion in some MENA countries, continues to provide limited employment opportunities. Consequently, the public sector (including both parastatal enterprises and regular government services) is often the dominant employer of educated labor within Arab MENA. The distribution of public sector employment across the various levels of government and public enterprises varies substantially across countries within MENA. In part, this is related to alternative wages and the availability of employment in the private sector. Employment in the public sector tends to increase not only in response to growing demand for public services but also partly in response to adverse conditions in private labor markets — sometimes giving governments the role of "employer of last resort." Historically, that was the case for Arab MENA.

In much of Arab MENA, public sector employment provided a variety of benefits that helped attract workers. That is, relative job security and sometimes less-than-complete enforcement of performance standards, non-wage entitlements, enhanced social status, and opportunities for moonlighting and rent-seeking (Gelb, Knight and Sabot, 1991). However, Rodrik (2000) points out that a high level of government employment may be the result of risk-averse behavior designed to minimize the effects of external risk faced by the domestic economy. There is indeed some evidence suggesting that countries that are greatly exposed to external risk also have higher levels of public employment. The combination of attractive public sector jobs and government hiring policies may be an important source of delayed unemployment, particularly among the skilled. Therefore, public sector employment will be inefficient and unproductive, and the cost in terms of foregone income may be high.

Consequently, in the next section we shift our attention to the second argument presented in the literature, which is based on the premise that the low performance in Arab MENA may also be due to a misallocation of labor resources away from growth-enhancing activities. That is, we begin an examination of the labor market's static efficiency.

5.3.1. *Static Efficiency*

Static efficiency investigates the allocation of labor across sectors of the economy. The data presented in Table 5.4 covers all persons of working age who, during the 2008–2016 period, were in the following categories: (a) paid employment (whether at work or with a job but not at work); or

Table 5.4. Employment by Sex and Economic Activity, Thousands, (ISIC-Rev.4)

			Total	A. Agriculture; forestry and fishing	B. Mining and quarrying	C. Manufacturing	D. Electricity; gas, steam and air conditioning supply	E. Water supply; sewerage, waste management and remediation activities	F. Construction	G. Wholesale and retail trade; repair of motor vehicles and motorcycles	H. Transportation and storage
Algeria		Total									
	2011		9,599	1,034	192	1,175			1,595	1,232	627
		Male									
	2011		8,038	987	179	840			1,571	1,174	594
		Female									
	2011		1561	46	12	336			24	58	33
Bahrain		Total									
	2015		770	8	2	92	1	1	172	119	19
		Male									
	2015		608	8	2	84	1	1	165	104	16
		Female									
	2015		161	0	0	8	0	0	6	15	3
Cyprus		Total									
	2008		383	16	0	37	3	2	46	69	15
	2009		383	15	1	35	3	1	44	72	16
	2010		395	15	1	33	2	2	44	75	16
	2011		398	15	1	31	1	4	46	74	15
	2012		385	11	1	29	2	6	40	72	15
	2013		365	11	1	27	2	5	30	68	15
	2014		363	16	0	30	2	3	25	64	14
	2015		358	14	1	28	2	2	25	67	14
	2016		363	13	1	26	2	3	30	65	16

(Continued)

Table 5.4. *(Continued)*

			Total	I. Accommodation and food service activities	J. Information and communication	K. Financial and insurance activities	L. Real estate activities	M. Professional, scientific and technical activities	N. Administrative and support service activities	O. Public administration and defence; compulsory social security	P. Education
Algeria		Total									
	2011		9,599	323						3,421	
		Male									
	2011		8,038	256						2,437	
		Female									
	2011		1561	67						984	
Bahrain		Total									
	2015		770	38	8	20	8	15	21	95	28
		Male									
	2015		608	31	6	14	7	11	19	78	12
		Female									
	2015		161	7	2	6	1	4	2	17	15
Cyprus		Total									
	2008		383	26	9	20	3	20	10	31	27
	2009		383	28	8	19	2	20	12	29	26
	2010		395	29	8	20	2	22	10	29	29
	2011		398	28	10	20	2	23	9	28	32
	2012		385	30	10	23	2	25	8	25	29
	2013		365	29	9	22	1	25	9	26	29
	2014		363	28	9	21	1	26	9	27	33
	2015		358	29	9	17	2	26	10	29	29
	2016		363	33	10	19	3	25	10	30	28

(Continued)

Table 5.4. (*Continued*)

			Total	Q. Human health and social work activities	R. Arts, entertainment and recreation	S. Other service activities	T. Activities of households as employers; undifferentiated goods- and services-producing activities of households for own use	U. Activities of extraterritorial organizations and bodies	X. Not elsewhere classified
Algeria		Total							
	2011		9,599						
		Male							
	2011		8,038						
		Female							
	2011		1561						
Bahrain		Total							
	2015		770	4	1	14	2	92	11
		Male							
	2015		608	2	1	10	2	26	9
		Female							
	2015		161	2	0	4	0	66	2
Cyprus		Total							
	2008		383	16	4	11	17	3	
	2009		383	16	5	11	18	2	
	2010		395	17	7	11	22	2	
	2011		398	16	8	11	23	2	
	2012		385	16	6	11	24	1	
	2013		365	16	5	10	22	1	
	2014		363	18	5	10	20	1	
	2015		358	18	6	10	18	1	
	2016		363	20	6	11	12	1	

(*Continued*)

Table 5.4. *(Continued)*

	Total	A. Agriculture; forestry and fishing	B. Mining and quarrying	C. Manufacturing	D. Electricity; gas, steam and air conditioning supply	E. Water supply; sewerage, waste management and remediation activities	F. Construction	G. Wholesale and retail trade; repair of motor vehicles and motorcycles	H. Transportation and storage
Male									
2008	212	12	0	25	2	2	42	38	10
2009	205	10	1	23	2	1	40	40	11
2010	209	10	1	21	1	2	39	41	11
2011	209	11	1	20	1	3	42	40	10
2012	202	8	1	19	1	4	37	37	10
2013	190	8	0	19	1	4	27	37	11
2014	185	12	0	20	2	2	23	34	10
2015	184	11	0	20	1	2	23	34	10
2016	188	10	1	18	2	3	27	33	11
Female									
2008	171	5	0	12	0	0	4	31	5
2009	178	5	0	12	1	0	4	32	5
2010	186	5	0	12	0	0	5	34	5
2011	189	5	0	11	0	1	4	35	4
2012	184	3	0	10	1	1	4	35	5
2013	175	3	0	9	0	1	3	30	5
2014	178	4	0	10	1	0	2	29	5
2015	175	4	0	8	0	0	2	32	4
2016	175	3	0	8	0	0	3	32	4

(Continued)

Table 5.4. *(Continued)*

		Total	I. Accommodation and food service activities	J. Information and communication	K. Financial and insurance activities	L. Real estate activities	M. Professional, scientific and technical activities	N. Administrative and support service activities	O. Public administration and defence; compulsory social security	P. Education
	Male									
2008		212	12	6	8	2	8	4	19	7
2009		205	14	5	8	1	8	4	17	7
2010		209	14	5	8	1	9	4	18	8
2011		209	13	6	8	1	9	4	16	8
2012		202	15	6	12	1	12	3	15	7
2013		190	14	5	12	1	12	4	16	7
2014		185	13	5	10	1	10	4	16	9
2015		184	15	6	8	1	11	4	17	7
2016		188	16	6	7	1	11	4	16	7
	Female									
2008		171	13	3	11	1	12	6	12	20
2009		178	15	3	11	1	12	7	12	19
2010		186	15	3	12	1	13	6	11	21
2011		189	14	4	12	1	14	5	11	24
2012		184	15	4	11	1	13	5	10	22
2013		175	15	4	11	1	13	5	11	22
2014		178	15	4	10	1	15	5	11	23
2015		175	15	3	10	1	15	6	12	22
2016		175	17	4	12	1	14	6	13	21

(Continued)

Table 5.4. (*Continued*)

	Total	Q. Human health and social work activities	R. Arts, entertainment and recreation	S. Other service activities	T. Activities of households as employers; undifferentiated goods- and services-producing activities of households for own use	U. Activities of extraterritorial organizations and bodies	X. Not elsewhere classified
Male							
2008	212	5	3	4	0	2	
2009	205	5	4	4	0	2	
2010	209	5	4	4	1	1	
2011	209	4	5	5	1	1	
2012	202	4	4	4	1	1	
2013	190	4	3	4	1	1	
2014	185	5	3	4	1	1	
2015	184	6	4	4	1	1	
2016	188	5	4	4	0	1	
Female							
2008	171	10	1	7	17	1	
2009	178	11	2	7	18	1	
2010	186	12	3	6	21	1	
2011	189	12	3	7	23	0	
2012	184	12	2	6	23	0	
2013	175	12	2	7	22	0	
2014	178	13	2	6	20	0	
2015	175	13	2	6	18	1	
2016	175	14	3	7	12	0	

(*Continued*)

Table 5.4. (*Continued*)

			Total	A. Agriculture; forestry and fishing	B. Mining and quarrying	C. Manufacturing	D. Electricity; gas, steam and air conditioning supply	E. Water supply; sewerage, waste management and remediation activities	F. Construction	G. Wholesale and retail trade; repair of motor vehicles and motorcycles	H. Transportation and storage
Egypt		Total									
	2009		22,975	6,876	32	2,658	205	116	2,441	2,464	1,498
	2010		23,829	6,728	47	2,882	266	150	2,694	2,694	1,471
	2011		23,346	6,810	49	2,292	260	172	2,716	2,572	1,602
	2012		23,564	6,379	40	2,616	252	158	2,791	2,583	1,644
	2013		23,975	6,703	41	2,571	226	214	2,728	2,689	1,699
	2014		24,299	6,694	48	2,707	222	211	2,742	2,713	1,756
	2015		24,779	6,397	39	2,781	204	187	3,005	2,935	1,903
	2016		25,371	6,478	41	2,900	202	307	3,009	3,004	1,887
		Male									
	2009		18,397	4,769	32	2,466	188	106	2,426	2,185	1,459
	2010										
	2011		18,719	4,806	49	2,104	243	161	2,698	2,297	1,567
	2012		18,903	4,626	40	2,416	230	142	2,773	2,261	1,608
	2013		19,083	4,606	41	2,367	214	195	2,716	2,358	1,662
	2014		19,264	4,518	48	2,503	207	194	2,726	2,367	1,728
	2015		19,694	4,354	37	2,544	191	171	2,985	2,493	1,871
	2016		20,009	4,427	40	2,611	190	291	2,993	2,497	1,856

(*Continued*)

Table 5.4. *(Continued)*

			Total	I. Accommodation and food service activities	J. Information and communication	K. Financial and insurance activities	L. Real estate activities	M. Professional, scientific and technical activities	N. Administrative and support service activities	O. Public administration and defence; compulsory social security	P. Education
Egypt		Total									
	2009		22,975	451	208	203	14	381	150	1,899	2,083
	2010		23,829	529	211	193	8	231	147	1,855	2,080
	2011		23,346	465	198	201	11	415	164	1,862	2,123
	2012		23,564	519	200	195	17	378	148	1,886	2,235
	2013		23,975	525	189	167	26	372	147	1,886	2,300
	2014		24,299	549	190	158	32	414	145	1,913	2,293
	2015		24,779	648	206	160	38	408	186	1,791	2,216
	2016		25,371	668	188	181	36	377	201	1,729	2,283
		Male									
	2009		18,397	434	169	153	13	322	129	1,458	1,167
	2010										
	2011		18,719	447	158	152	10	351	146	1,433	1,100
	2012		18,903	504	162	138	15	320	134	1,412	1,124
	2013		19,083	507	156	125	25	317	132	1,431	1,208
	2014		19,264	520	150	120	29	358	129	1,460	1,168
	2015		19,694	623	168	121	35	339	164	1,379	1,146
	2016		20,009	620	153	144	34	319	181	1,332	1,185

(Continued)

Table 5.4. (*Continued*)

			Total	Q. Human health and social work activities	R. Arts, entertainment and recreation	S. Other service activities	T. Activities of households as employers; undifferentiated goods- and services-producing activities of households for own use	U. Activities of extraterritorial organizations and bodies	X. Not elsewhere classified
Egypt		Total							
	2009		22,975	560	101	527	78	6	24
	2010		23,829	593	82	365	115	3	488
	2011		23,346	625	115	516	119	2	54
	2012		23,564	666	120	549	184	3	2
	2013		23,975	646	113	597	133	2	
	2014		24,299	667	121	602	119	4	1
	2015		24,779	747	115	590	220	3	
	2016		25,371	780	117	608	330	4	41
		Male							
	2009		18,397	254	84	505	53	4	20
	2010								
	2011		18,719	262	98	497	90	1	49
	2012		18,903	283	97	529	85	2	2
	2013		19,083	267	88	576	89	2	
	2014		19,264	277	100	576	86	3	1
	2015		19,694	294	95	558	124	3	
	2016		20,009	327	93	573	117	2	23

(*Continued*)

Table 5.4. (Continued)

			Total	A. Agriculture; forestry and fishing	B. Mining and quarrying	C. Manufacturing	D. Electricity; gas, steam and air conditioning supply	E. Water supply; sewerage, waste management and remediation activities	F. Construction	G. Wholesale and retail trade; repair of motor vehicles and motorcycles	H. Transportation and storage
		Female									
	2009		4,578	2,107		192	17	10	14	279	38
	2010										
	2011		4,627	2,004		188	17	11	18	275	35
	2012		4,662	1,752		200	22	16	18	322	35
	2013		4,892	2,097		204	12	19	12	330	37
	2014		5,035	2,176	1	204	15	17	16	347	28
	2015		5,085	2,043	2	237	12	16	20	443	31
	2016		5,362	2,051		289	12	16	16	507	31
Iran		Total									
	2014		21,304	3,812	159	3,587	141	102	3,202	3,117	2,044
	2015		21,972	3,961	157	3,697	153	94	3,047	3,280	2,178
	2016		22,588	4,061	156	3,817	158	100	2,969	3,520	2,179
		Male									
	2014		18,205	3,135	152	2,879	136	93	3,177	2,904	2,018
	2015		18,511	3,171	152	2,921	144	87	3,019	3,024	2,148
	2016		18,707	3,208	149	2,900	148	94	2,932	3,211	2,144
		Female									
	2014		3,099	677	7	708	5	9	25	213	26
	2015		3,461	790	4	776	9	7	28	255	30
	2016		3,881	853	7	917	10	6	36	309	35

(Continued)

Table 5.4. (Continued)

			Total	I. Accommodation and food service activities	J. Information and communication	K. Financial and insurance activities	L. Real estate activities	M. Professional, scientific and technical activities	N. Administrative and support service activities	O. Public administration and defence; compulsory social security	P. Education
		Female									
	2009		4,578	16	39	51		58	21	441	917
	2010										
	2011		4,627	17	40	49	1	65	19	429	1,024
	2012		4,662	16	39	57	1	58	14	475	1,111
	2013		4,892	18	33	42		55	15	455	1,092
	2014		5,035	29	40	38	3	56	16	453	1,125
	2015		5,085	24	38	38	3	70	23	412	1,070
	2016		5,362	48	35	37	2	58	20	397	1,098
Iran		Total									
	2014		21,304	250	194	338	133	223	258	1,341	1,284
	2015		21,972	289	213	338	136	254	258	1,430	1,284
	2016		22,588	309	235	319	133	281	280	1,418	1,323
		Male									
	2014		18,205	225	158	284	133	165	211	1,227	628
	2015		18,511	258	178	275	135	172	211	1,285	611
	2016		18,707	265	180	263	132	186	214	1,267	612
		Female									
	2014		3,099	25	36	54	1	58	47	114	655
	2015		3,461	31	36	63	1	82	47	145	673
	2016		3,881	43	54	56	1	96	66	151	711

(Continued)

Table 5.4. *(Continued)*

			Total	Q. Human health and social work activities	R. Arts, entertainment and recreation	S. Other service activities	T. Activities of households as employers; undifferentiated goods- and services-producing activities of households for own use	U. Activities of extraterritorial organizations and bodies	X. Not elsewhere classified
		Female							
	2009		4,578	306	17	23	26	1	4
	2010								
	2011		4,627	363	17	19	28		6
	2012		4,662	383	23	20	99		
	2013		4,892	379	25	21	44		
	2014		5,035	390	21	26	34	1	0
	2015		5,085	453	21	33	96		
	2016		5,362	453	24	35	214	2	18
Iran		Total							
	2014		21,304	555	95	441	24	0	3
	2015		21,972	615	93	455	37	1	3
	2016		22,588	645	122	510	48	1	4
		Male							
	2014		18,205	268	62	332	13	0	3
	2015		18,511	287	68	341	21	0	3
	2016		18,707	304	88	378	26	1	3
		Female							
	2014		3,099	287	33	109	11	0	0
	2015		3,461	328	25	114	16	1	0
	2016		3,881	341	35	132	22	0	1

(Continued)

Table 5.4. *(Continued)*

		Total	A. Agriculture; forestry and fishing	B. Mining and quarrying	C. Manufacturing	D. Electricity; gas, steam and air conditioning supply	E. Water supply; sewerage, waste management and remediation activities	F. Construction	G. Wholesale and retail trade; repair of motor vehicles and motorcycles	H. Transportation and storage
Israel	Total									
2013		3,450	43	3	408	15	16	165	403	147
2014		3,556	40	3	417	16	14	172	406	147
2015		3,644	37	3	419	16	15	181	420	151
	Male									
2013		1,835	32	3	291	12	13	153	229	119
2014		1,880	30	3	299	13	12	159	231	119
2015		1,928	27	3	302	13	13	166	236	121
	Female									
2013		1,614	11		118	3	3	12	174	28
2014		1,675	10		118	3	2	13	176	28
2015		1,715	10		117	3	2	15	184	30
Qatar	Total									
2011		1,270	17	82	101	5	1	498	142	33
2012		1,341	18	83	103	8	1	499	169	38
2013		1,539	21	95	119	9	3	568	194	45
2015		1,947	24	101	135	20	13	785	253	66
2016		2,049	25	100	144	17	9	847	254	59
	Male									
2011		1,117	17	79	100	5	1	495	137	29
2012		1,173	18	80	102	7	1	496	164	33
2013		1,346	21	92	118	8	3	565	187	39
2015		1,690	24	95	133	19	12	780	227	56
2016		1,780	25	94	142	16	9	841	227	49

(Continued)

Table 5.4. (Continued)

			Total	I. Accommodation and food service activities	J. Information and communication	K. Financial and insurance activities	L. Real estate activities	M. Professional, scientific and technical activities	N. Administrative and support service activities	O. Public administration and defence; compulsory social security	P. Education
Israel		Total									
	2013		3,450	150	166	119	28	237	148	363	413
	2014		3,556	153	174	125	29	253	147	367	434
	2015		3,644	154	180	124	28	258	153	371	455
		Male									
	2013		1,835	88	105	49	17	122	91	219	104
	2014		1,880	91	108	53	17	130	88	221	107
	2015		1,928	95	111	53	16	134	92	227	114
		Female									
	2013		1,614	62	61	70	11	115	57	144	309
	2014		1,675	61	66	72	12	123	59	146	327
	2015		1,715	60	70	71	12	124	61	144	342
Qatar		Total									
	2011		1,270	30	10	11	9	24	40	76	27
	2012		1,341	32	11	11	9	26	41	81	30
	2013		1,539	39	13	12	10	29	48	95	39
	2015		1,947	51	13	15	12	29	56	99	49
	2016		2,049	73	16	16	12	29	85	87	46
		Male									
	2011		1,117	28	8	8	9	23	38	62	11
	2012		1,173	29	9	8	9	24	39	68	12
	2013		1,346	35	9	9	10	27	44	80	13
	2015		1,690	38	10	9	11	27	52	83	16
	2016		1,780	55	13	10	11	25	79	71	13

(Continued)

Table 5.4. *(Continued)*

			Total	Q. Human health and social work activities	R. Arts, entertainment and recreation	S. Other service activities	T. Activities of households as employers; undifferentiated goods- and services-producing activities of households for own use	U. Activities of extraterritorial organizations and bodies	X. Not elsewhere classified
Israel		Total							
	2013		3,450	354	61	89	64	2	54
	2014		3,556	377	67	87	67	3	59
	2015		3,644	393	67	85	66	3	65
		Male							
	2013		1,835	76	33	36	6	1	35
	2014		1,880	80	38	35	8	2	38
	2015		1,928	87	36	33	8	2	41
		Female							
	2013		1,614	278	28	54	58		19
	2014		1,675	297	29	53	59	1	21
	2015		1,715	305	31	52	58	1	24
Qatar		Total							
	2011		1,270	21	5	4	132	2	
	2012		1,341	23	8	5	140	2	
	2013		1,539	28	9	7	152	2	3
	2015		1,947	30	14	14	161	4	
	2016		2,049	30	6	16	173	5	
		Male							
	2011		1,117	11	4	4	48	1	
	2012		1,173	12	7	4	50	1	
	2013		1,346	13	8	6	56	1	1
	2015		1,690	14	13	11	57	3	
	2016		1,780	14	5	11	66	3	

(Continued)

Table 5.4. (Continued)

			Total	A. Agriculture; forestry and fishing	B. Mining and quarrying	C. Manufacturing	D. Electricity; gas, steam and air conditioning supply	E. Water supply; sewerage, waste management and remediation activities	F. Construction	G. Wholesale and retail trade; repair of motor vehicles and motorcycles	H. Transportation and storage
		Female									
	2011		153	0	2	1	0	0	3	5	4
	2012		167	0	3	1	0	0	3	6	5
	2013		193	0	3	1	1	0	3	7	6
	2015		257	0	7	2	1	1	5	26	11
	2016		269	0	7	2	1	1	6	28	10
SA		Total									
	2013		10,729	477	118	760	82	73	1,518	1,678	381
	2014		11,068	582	153	796	107	77	1,417	1,607	392
	2015		11,485	700	138	945	88	84	1,357	1,590	386
	2016		11,686	581	142	906	89	67	1,659	1,329	363
		Male									
	2013		9,332	474	116	746	81	72	1,510	1,649	377
	2014		9,617	578	153	779	107	76	1,410	1,575	389
	2015		9,895	692	137	926	87	83	1,353	1,564	385
	2016		10,039	579	137	885	89	66	1,651	1,297	359
		Female									
	2013		1,397	3	2	14	1	1	8	29	4
	2014		1,450	4	0	17	0	1	6	31	3
	2015		1,589	9	1	19	0	1	4	26	0
	2016		1,648	2	4	21	0	1	8	32	3

(Continued)

Table 5.4. (Continued)

		Total	I. Accommodation and food service activities	J. Information and communication	K. Financial and insurance activities	L. Real estate activities	M. Professional, scientific and technical activities	N. Administrative and support service activities	O. Public administration and defence; compulsory social security	P. Education
	Female									
	2011	153	3	2	3	0	1	3	14	16
	2012	167	3	3	3	0	2	2	14	18
	2013	193	4	3	4	1	2	4	15	26
	2015	257	13	3	6	1	2	4	17	34
	2016	269	17	2	6	1	3	6	15	33
SA	Total									
	2013	10,729	259	104	119	98	109	200	1,820	1,265
	2014	11,068	377	129	142	127	158	183	1,780	1,308
	2015	11,485	333	111	137	110	175	253	1,791	1,389
	2016	11,686	295	128	157	116	191	209	1,825	1,311
	Male									
	2013	9,332	254	101	109	97	106	195	1,773	715
	2014	9,617	371	125	136	126	155	176	1,743	705
	2015	9,895	325	106	125	109	169	246	1,741	792
	2016	10,039	288	125	140	115	184	202	1,779	732
	Female									
	2013	1,397	5	3	10	1	3	5	46	550
	2014	1,450	6	4	6	1	4	7	37	603
	2015	1,589	8	5	12	1	6	8	50	597
	2016	1,648	7	3	16	1	8	7	45	579

(Continued)

Table 5.4. (*Continued*)

			Total	Q. Human health and social work activities	R. Arts, entertain-ment and recreation	S. Other service activities	T. Activities of households as employers; undifferentiated goods- and services-producing activities of households for own use	U. Activities of extraterri-torial organiza-tions and bodies	X. Not elsewhere classified
		Female							
	2011		153	10	1	0	84	0	
	2012		167	12	1	1	90	0	
	2013		193	15	1	1	96	0	1
	2015		257	16	1	3	105	1	
	2016		269	16	1	5	107	2	
SA		Total							
	2013		10,729	480	16	230	930	12	
	2014		11,068	610	18	243	853	8	0
	2015		11,485	554	16	230	1,083	13	0
	2016		11,686	591	14	246	1,459	9	
		Male							
	2013		9,332	346	14	205	381	11	
	2014		9,617	436	16	222	330	8	0
	2015		9,895	387	16	199	441	12	0
	2016		10,039	404	11	226	758	9	
		Female							
	2013		1,397	134	2	25	550	1	
	2014		1,450	174	1	21	523	0	0
	2015		1,589	167	1	32	642	1	0
	2016		1,648	188	2	19	701	0	

(Continued)

Table 5.4. *(Continued)*

			Total	A. Agricul-ture; forestry and fishing	B. Mining and quarry-ing	C. Manu-factur-ing	D. Electricity; gas, steam and air condition-ing supply	E. Water supply; sewerage, waste management and remediation activities	F. Con-struction	G. Wholesale and retail trade; repair of motor vehicles and motorcycles	H. Trans-porta-tion and storage
Tunisia		Total									
	2008		3,155	558	37	603	399	363	181		125
	2009		3,199	579	35	565	413	379	189		130
	2010		3,277	576	34	598	440	387	194		125
	2011		3,140	510	32	578	442	388	175		106
	2012		3,232	550	37	598	432	386	194		111
		Male									
	2008		2,337	410	33	339	393	300	162		109
	2009		2,391	425	32	327	407	319	169		114
	2010		2,458	415	30	346	435	324	172		110
	2011		2,394	399	29	338	437	324	160		96
	2012		2,435	427	34	341	428	319	172		99
		Female									
	2008		819	147	3	263	5	63	19		16
	2009		807	154	4	238	6	61	20		16
	2010		820	161	4	252	6	62	22		15
	2011		746	111	3	240	5	65	15		10
	2012		797	124	3	256	5	67	21		13
Turkey		Total									
	2009		21,271	4,881	98	3,867	64	48	1,305	3,381	986
	2010		22,593	5,355	114	4,213	73	92	1,432	3,326	1,010
	2011		24,099	5,822	124	4,366	81	131	1,674	3,476	1,045

(Continued)

Table 5.4. *(Continued)*

			Total	I. Accommodation and food service activities	J. Information and communication	K. Financial and insurance activities	L. Real estate activities	M. Professional, scientific and technical activities	N. Administrative and support service activities	O. Public administration and defence; compulsory social security	P. Education
Tunisia		Total									
	2008		3,155		26	119		140		577	
	2009		3,199		27	128		140		585	
	2010		3,277		27	132		143		591	
	2011		3,140		26	134		139		588	
	2012		3,232		31	141		129		612	
		Male									
	2008		2,337		18	99		78		381	
	2009		2,391		18	105		72		385	
	2010		2,458		18	105		82		395	
	2011		2,394		19	107		77		391	
	2012		2,435		21	113		69		406	
		Female									
	2008		819		8	20		62		196	
	2009		807		9	23		68		200	
	2010		820		9	27		60		196	
	2011		746		7	27		62		197	
	2012		797		11	28		60		205	
Turkey		Total									
	2009		21,271	1,051	157	273	63	398	598	1,206	967
	2010		22,593	1,084	204	273	60	429	767	1,291	1,019
	2011		24,099	1,140	211	280	154	428	778	1,338	1,107

(Continued)

Table 5.4. *(Continued)*

			Total	Q. Human health and social work activities	R. Arts, entertain-ment and recreation	S. Other service activities	T. Activities of households as employers; undifferentiated goods- and services-producing activities of households for own use	U. Activities of extraterri-torial organiza-tions and bodies	X. Not elsewhere classified
Tunisia		Total							
	2008		3,155						28
	2009		3,199						29
	2010		3,277						30
	2011		3,140						23
	2012		3,232						10
		Male							
	2008		2,337						14
	2009		2,391						19
	2010		2,458						24
	2011		2,394						17
	2012		2,435						8
		Female							
	2008		819						14
	2009		807						10
	2010		820						6
	2011		746						6
	2012		797						3
Turkey		Total							
	2009		21,271	591	130	612	589	5	
	2010		22,593	590	102	582	572	4	
	2011		24,099	693	100	595	553	5	

(Continued)

Table 5.4. *(Continued)*

	Total	A. Agriculture; forestry and fishing	B. Mining and quarrying	C. Manufacturing	D. Electricity; gas, steam and air conditioning supply	E. Water supply; sewerage, waste management and remediation activities	F. Construction	G. Wholesale and retail trade; repair of motor vehicles and motorcycles	H. Transportation and storage
2012	24,819	5,846	113	4,419	97	121	1,709	3,501	1,094
2013	25,520	5,850	105	4,632	96	122	1,780	3,518	1,151
2014	25,931	5,468	133	4,935	92	154	1,911	3,586	1,119
2015	26,619	5,432	119	4,966	103	153	1,907	3,693	1,110
2016	27,216	5,307	125	4,918	106	151	1,987	3,757	1,186
Male									
2009	15,402	2,656	96	3,022	60	44	1,265	2,779	924
2010	16,168	2,828	110	3,263	68	86	1,376	2,697	950
2011	17,131	3,076	122	3,379	76	122	1,620	2,787	979
2012	17,511	3,125	111	3,408	90	111	1,652	2,750	1,029
2013	17,878	3,122	102	3,546	88	110	1,718	2,733	1,074
2014	18,241	2,937	130	3,725	85	138	1,831	2,795	1,039
2015	18,578	2,929	116	3,762	95	137	1,836	2,831	1,025
2016	18,898	2,921	120	3,711	95	135	1,903	2,864	1,075
Female									
2009	5,868	2,225	3	845	5	4	40	602	62
2010	6,424	2,527	4	950	5	6	56	629	59
2011	6,969	2,746	2	987	5	9	54	689	66
2012	7,308	2,722	2	1,012	7	10	57	751	65
2013	7,641	2,728	3	1,086	8	12	61	785	78

(Continued)

Table 5.4. (Continued)

	Total	I. Accommodation and food service activities	J. Information and communication	K. Financial and insurance activities	L. Real estate activities	M. Professional, scientific and technical activities	N. Administrative and support service activities	O. Public administration and defence; compulsory social security	P. Education
2012	24,819	1,206	238	265	184	507	924	1,459	1,225
2013	25,520	1,308	254	288	186	553	1,019	1,463	1,248
2014	25,931	1,351	228	301	205	684	1,155	1,385	1,321
2015	26,619	1,446	253	296	213	752	1,295	1,458	1,420
2016	27,216	1,471	248	301	243	846	1,397	1,455	1,607
Male									
2009	15,402	890	115	156	53	272	469	1,031	516
2010	16,168	917	153	158	47	293	592	1,099	541
2011	17,131	935	159	157	126	284	587	1,136	593
2012	17,511	965	176	143	151	329	629	1,238	633
2013	17,878	1,024	186	159	153	348	684	1,228	625
2014	18,241	1,073	172	162	174	434	768	1,166	674
2015	18,578	1,129	189	159	175	452	859	1,215	707
2016	18,898	1,128	186	169	199	507	929	1,204	758
Female									
2009	5,868	161	42	117	10	125	129	175	451
2010	6,424	168	51	115	13	136	175	191	477
2011	6,969	204	52	123	28	144	191	202	513
2012	7,308	242	62	121	33	178	295	221	592
2013	7,641	284	68	129	33	205	335	235	623

(Continued)

Table 5.4. *(Continued)*

	Total	Q. Human health and social work activities	R. Arts, entertainment and recreation	S. Other service activities	T. Activities of households as employers; undifferentiated goods- and services-producing activities of households for own use	U. Activities of extraterritorial organizations and bodies	X. Not elsewhere classified
2012	24,819	808	108	588	403	5	
2013	25,520	858	121	636	326	6	
2014	25,931	974	131	638	160	2	
2015	26,619	1,056	150	649	145	4	
2016	27,216	1,123	141	682	157	6	
Male							
2009	15,402	264	110	497	184	2	
2010	16,168	259	84	473	173	2	
2011	17,131	279	84	480	146	2	
2012	17,511	299	83	477	110	3	
2013	17,878	299	95	505	74	3	
2014	18,241	318	102	503	12	2	
2015	18,578	329	117	502	10	2	
2016	18,898	328	107	541	16	4	
Female							
2009	5,868	327	20	114	405	3	
2010	6,424	331	18	109	399	2	
2011	6,969	413	16	115	407	2	
2012	7,308	509	25	111	293	3	
2013	7,641	559	26	131	251	2	

(Continued)

Table 5.4. *(Continued)*

			Total	A. Agriculture; forestry and fishing	B. Mining and quarrying	C. Manufacturing	D. Electricity; gas, steam and air conditioning supply	E. Water supply; sewerage, waste management and remediation activities	F. Construction	G. Wholesale and retail trade; repair of motor vehicles and motorcycles	H. Transportation and storage
	2014		7,690	2,531	3	1,209	7	16	80	790	80
	2015		8,041	2,503	3	1,204	8	16	71	863	85
	2016		8,317	2,386	4	1,208	12	16	84	893	112
UAE		Total									
	2016		7,450	10	172	460	28	25	1,464	651	355
		Male									
	2016		6,188	10	163	437	24	23	1,440	563	330
		Female									
	2016		1,262	0	9	23	4	1	24	88	25

(Continued)

Table 5.4. *(Continued)*

			Total	I. Accommodation and food service activities	J. Information and communication	K. Financial and insurance activities	L. Real estate activities	M. Professional, scientific and technical activities	N. Administrative and support service activities	O. Public administration and defence; compulsory social security	P. Education
	2014		7,690	277	56	139	31	250	386	219	647
	2015		8,041	316	64	137	37	301	436	243	713
	2016		8,317	343	63	132	43	340	468	251	849
UAE		Total									
	2016		7,450	356	102	138	158	168	518	236	138
		Male									
	2016		6,188	322	90	99	141	133	479	199	58
		Female									
	2016		1,262	34	12	39	16	35	40	37	80

(Continued)

Table 5.4. *(Continued)*

			Total	Q. Human health and social work activities	R. Arts, entertainment and recreation	S. Other service activities	T. Activities of households as employers; undifferentiated goods- and services-producing activities of households for own use	U. Activities of extraterritorial organizations and bodies	X. Not elsewhere classified
	2014		7,690	655	29	136	148	0	
	2015		8,041	727	32	147	135	2	
	2016		8,317	795	34	141	141	3	
UAE		Total							
	2016		7,450	98	38	50	900	4	1,380
		Male							
	2016		6,188	56	35	33	307	3	1,242
		Female							
	2016		1,262	41	4	17	593	1	138

Source: ILO.

(b) self-employment (whether at work or with an enterprise but not at work). Data are disaggregated by ISIC (Rev. 4) in terms of economic activity, which refers to the main activity of the establishment in which a person worked during the reference period and does not depend on the specific duties or functions of the person's job, but on the characteristics of the economic unit in which this person works. The concern is whether the allocation of skilled labor is the one most likely to maximize the country's growth potential. The data point to a number of specific characterizes in MENA. First, the role of women in the labor pool is very limited except for Cyprus and Israel. In the Arab MENA labor market there is a clear gender bias against women. Second, manufacturing occupies a smaller fraction of the labor force than in other industrializing countries. Third, within Arab MENA the biggest employer is the State public sector.

For Algeria the data for 2011 show a concentration of employment, for both men and women, in public administration and defense; and compulsory social security. For Egypt, the primary sectors for employment over the 2009–2016 period was in (a) agriculture; forestry and fishing; (b) manufacturing; (c) construction; (d) wholesale and retail trade; repair of motor vehicles and motorcycle; (e) transportation and storage; (f) public administration and defense; compulsory social security; and (g) education. Women in Egypt were predominantly assigned to the education sector. There was no significant change in this distribution of employment over the entire 2009–2016 period.

In Qatar the main employment sectors for men are (a) construction and (b) wholesale and retail trade; repair of motor vehicles and motorcycles. For the minority of women that can work in Qatar the primary sector is activities of households as employers; undifferentiated goods- and services-producing activities of households for own use. In Saudi Arabia the main employment sectors for men are (a) construction and (b) wholesale and retail trade; repair of motor vehicles and motorcycles; (c) public administration and defense; compulsory social security; and (d) education. For the minority of women that can work in Saudi Arabia the primary sectors where they are employed include (a) activities of households as employers; undifferentiated goods- and services-producing activities of households for own use and (b) education. There was no significant change in this distribution of employment over the entire 2013–2016 period.

In Tunisia the sector distribution of male employees over the period 2008 to 2012 is concentrated in (a) agriculture; forestry and fishing; (b) manufacturing; (c) electricity; gas, steam and air conditioning supply;

(d) water supply; sewerage, waste management and remediation activities; and (e) public administration and defense; compulsory social security. For the minority of women that can work in Tunisia the primary sectors where they are employed include (a) manufacturing; (b) public administration and defense; compulsory social security; and (c) agriculture; forestry and fishing. There was no significant change in this distribution of employment over the entire 2008–2012 period.

In Turkey, which has been considered a more modern Arab MENA country, the sector distribution of male employees over the period 2009–2016 paints a different picture. Over this period its male employees are concentrated in (a) agriculture; forestry and fishing; (b) wholesale and retail trade; repair of motor vehicles and motorcycles; (c) manufacturing; (d) construction; and (e) public administration and defense; compulsory social security. For the minority of women that can work in Turkey the primary sector where they are employed is manufacturing. The data for the UAE for 2016 point to a single primary sector of employment for males — construction. For the minority of women that can work in the UAE they are primarily employed in activities of households as employers; undifferentiated goods- and services-producing activities of households for own use.

For non-Arab MENA, the distribution is very different. In the case of Cyprus, the concentration of its male employees are in (a) wholesale and retail trade; repair of motor vehicles and motorcycles; (b) construction; (c) accommodation and food service activities; (d) financial and insurance activities; and (e) transportation and storage. For women in Cyprus the employment concentration is in (a) wholesale and retail trade; repair of motor vehicles and motorcycles; (b) human health and social work activities; (c) professional, scientific and technical activities; (d) education; (e) public administration and defense; compulsory social security; and (f) activities of households as employers; undifferentiated goods- and services-producing activities of households for own use.

For Israel, the concentration of employment in the 2013–2015 period for men was in (a) manufacturing; (b) public administration and defense; compulsory social security; (c) wholesale and retail trade; repair of motor vehicles and motorcycles; (d) construction; and (e) professional, scientific and technical activities. For women in Israel the employment concentration is in (a) education; (b) human health and social work activities; (c) wholesale and retail trade; repair of motor vehicles and motorcycles; (d) professional, scientific and technical activities; and (e) manufacturing.

Economic studies show that low productivity is exacerbated in the public sector of countries in Arab MENA by encouraging overstaffing (World Bank, 2004a). The World Bank finds that the share of underutilized workers in the public sector ranged from 17 percent (Algeria) to 21 percent (Egypt) and to over 40 percent in the oil-exporting countries in the late 1990s. Nothing has changed in the past 15 years. (World Bank, 2015). Berthelemy *et al.* (1999) find that the share of the public sector has, despite its substantial size, increased to 35 percent in Egypt and 40 percent in Jordan, and that the resulting estimated average loss of GDP growth is approximately 5–10 percent.[4] This translates to the assertion that if one assumes that public sector employees are not utilizing their human capital in a productive manner, then the larger the public sector in a given country, the smaller the economy's GDP growth.

In Table 5.5 we dig deeper into the skill characteristics of MENA's employed labor force. We use the ISIC rev. 4 to disaggregate sector employment and then match it to the ILO ISCO08 skill level designations. The four skill level designations are — Skills 1–4. Skill Level 1 covers occupations that typically involve the performance of simple and routine physical or manual tasks. They may require the use of hand-held tools, such as shovels, or of simple electrical equipment, such as vacuum cleaners. They involve tasks such as cleaning; digging; lifting and carrying materials by hand; sorting, storing or assembling goods by hand (sometimes in the context of mechanized operations); operating non-motorized vehicles; and picking fruit and vegetables. Many occupations at Skill Level 1 may require physical strength and/or endurance. For some jobs basic skills in literacy and numeracy may be required. For competent performance in some occupations at Skill Level 1, completion of primary education or the first stage of basic education may be required (ILO, 2012, pp. 12–13)

Skill Level 2 occupations typically involve the performance of tasks such as operating machinery and electronic equipment; driving vehicles; maintenance and repair of electrical and mechanical equipment; and manipulation, ordering and storage of information. For almost all occupations at Skill Level 2 the ability to read information such as safety instructions, to make written records of work completed, and to accurately perform simple arithmetic calculations is essential. Many occupations at this skill level require a high level of manual dexterity. The knowledge and skills required

[4]Their estimates are based on the strong assumption that public sector employees do not contribute at all to growth of the economy.

Table 5.5. Employment by Skill Level ISIC Rev 4 in Thousands and Percent.

	Year	Total	(Thousands) Skill Level 1 (Low)	Skill Level 2 (Medium)	Skill Levels 3 and 4 (High)	(Percent) Skill Level 1 (Low)	Skill Level 2 (Medium)	Skill Levels 3 and 4 (High)
				Algeria				
A. Agriculture; forestry and fishing	2014	899	232	650	15	25.8	72.3	1.7
B. Mining and quarrying	2014	131	15	78	39	11.5	59.5	29.8
C. Manufacturing	2014	1,159	111	931	116	9.6	80.3	10.0
D. Electricity; gas, steam and air conditioning supply	2014	1,826	619	1,087	120	33.9	59.5	6.6
E. Water supply; sewerage, waste management and remediation activities	2014	1,516	101	1,340	75	6.7	88.4	4.9
F. Construction	2014	646	37	553	55	5.7	85.6	8.5
G. Wholesale and retail trade; repair of motor vehicles and motorcycles	2014	450	46	259	144	10.2	57.6	32.0
H. Transportation and storage	2014	3,612	358	1,963	1,178	9.9	54.3	32.6
TOTAL	2014	10,239	1,519	6,863	1,742	14.8	67.0	17.0
				Cyprus				
A. Agriculture; forestry and fishing								
	2008	16	3	11	0	18.8	68.8	0.0
	2009	15	3	11	0	20.0	73.3	0.0
	2010	14	4	10	0	28.6	71.4	0.0
	2011	15	3	10	0	20.0	66.7	0.0
	2012	11	3	7	0	27.3	63.6	0.0
	2013	11	3	7	0	27.3	63.6	0.0
	2014	16	5	9	0	31.3	56.3	0.0
	2015	14	5	8	0	35.7	57.1	0.0
	2016	13	4	8	0	30.8	61.5	0.0
C. Manufacturing								
	2008	37	6	25	5	16.2	67.6	13.5
	2009	34	5	23	5	14.7	67.6	14.7
	2010	32	5	22	5	15.6	68.8	15.6
	2011	31	5	19	5	16.1	61.3	16.1
	2012	28	4	18	5	14.3	64.3	17.9
	2013	27	3	18	5	11.1	66.7	18.5
	2014	29	3	20	5	10.3	69.0	17.2
	2015	27	3	19	5	11.1	70.4	18.5
	2016	26	2	17	5	7.7	65.4	19.2

(Continued)

Table 5.5. (*Continued*)

	Year	Total	(Thousands) Skill Level 1 (Low)	Skill Level 2 (Medium)	Skill Levels 3 and 4 (High)	(Percent) Skill Level 1 (Low)	Skill Level 2 (Medium)	Skill Levels 3 and 4 (High)
D. Electricity; gas, steam and air conditioning supply								
	2008	2	0	1	1	0.0	50.0	50.0
	2009	3	0	1	1	0.0	33.3	33.3
	2010	1	0	0	0	0.0	0.0	0.0
	2011	1	0	0	0	0.0	0.0	0.0
	2012	2	0	0	0	0.0	0.0	0.0
	2013	1	0	0	0	0.0	0.0	0.0
	2014	2	0	1	0	0.0	50.0	0.0
	2015	1	0	0	0	0.0	0.0	0.0
	2016	1	0	0	0	0.0	0.0	0.0
E. Water supply; sewerage, waste management and remediation activities								
	2008	1	0	0	0	0.0	0.0	0.0
	2009	1	0	0	0	0.0	0.0	0.0
	2010	2	1	0	0	50.0	0.0	0.0
	2011	3	1	1	0	33.3	33.3	0.0
	2012	5	2	1	1	40.0	20.0	20.0
	2013	4	2	1	0	50.0	25.0	0.0
	2014	2	1	0	0	50.0	0.0	0.0
	2015	2	1	0	0	50.0	0.0	0.0
	2016	3	1	1	0	33.3	33.3	0.0
F. Construction								
	2008	46	6	33	6	13.0	71.7	13.0
	2009	43	6	30	5	14.0	69.8	11.6
	2010	43	7	29	6	16.3	67.4	14.0
	2011	45	7	29	8	15.6	64.4	17.8
	2012	40	5	25	9	12.5	62.5	22.5
	2013	29	4	18	7	13.8	62.1	24.1
	2014	25	3	15	5	12.0	60.0	20.0
	2015	25	2	16	5	8.0	64.0	20.0
	2016	30	4	19	6	13.3	63.3	20.0
G. Wholesale and retail trade; repair of motor vehicles and motorcycles								
	2008	68	4	50	13	5.9	73.5	19.1
	2009	72	4	50	17	5.6	69.4	23.6
	2010	75	5	52	16	6.7	69.3	21.3
	2011	74	5	51	17	6.8	68.9	23.0
	2012	72	5	52	14	6.9	72.2	19.4
	2013	67	5	50	12	7.5	74.6	17.9
	2014	63	4	46	13	6.3	73.0	20.6
	2015	66	4	47	14	6.1	71.2	21.2
	2016	65	4	48	12	6.2	73.8	18.5
H. Transportation and storage								
	2008	14	0	9	3	0.0	64.3	21.4
	2009	16	1	10	3	6.3	62.5	18.8
	2010	16	1	9	4	6.3	56.3	25.0
	2011	14	1	8	4	7.1	57.1	28.6
	2012	14	1	8	4	7.1	57.1	28.6
	2013	15	0	8	5	0.0	53.3	33.3

(*Continued*)

Table 5.5. (*Continued*)

Year	Total	(Thousands) Skill Level 1 (Low)	Skill Level 2 (Medium)	Skill Levels 3 and 4 (High)	(Percent) Skill Level 1 (Low)	Skill Level 2 (Medium)	Skill Levels 3 and 4 (High)
2014	14	1	8	5	7.1	57.1	35.7
2015	14	1	9	3	7.1	64.3	21.4
2016	15	1	9	4	6.7	60.0	26.7
I. Accommodation and food service activities							
2008	25	4	17	3	16.0	68.0	12.0
2009	28	6	18	3	21.4	64.3	10.7
2010	28	6	18	3	21.4	64.3	10.7
2011	27	6	17	3	22.2	63.0	11.1
2012	29	7	19	2	24.1	65.5	6.9
2013	29	7	18	3	24.1	62.1	10.3
2014	28	7	18	2	25.0	64.3	7.1
2015	29	7	19	2	24.1	65.5	6.9
2016	32	9	20	3	28.1	62.5	9.4
J. Information and communication							
2008	9	0	2	6	0.0	22.2	66.7
2009	8	0	2	5	0.0	25.0	62.5
2010	8	0	2	5	0.0	25.0	62.5
2011	10	0	2	7	0.0	20.0	70.0
2012	10	0	2	7	0.0	20.0	70.0
2013	8	0	3	5	0.0	37.5	62.5
2014	9	0	3	6	0.0	33.3	66.7
2015	9	0	2	6	0.0	22.2	66.7
2016	9	0	2	7	0.0	22.2	77.8
K. Financial and insurance activities							
2008	19	0	8	10	0.0	42.1	52.6
2009	19	0	7	10	0.0	36.8	52.6
2010	20	0	8	11	0.0	40.0	55.0
2011	20	0	7	11	0.0	35.0	55.0
2012	23	0	6	15	0.0	26.1	65.2
2013	22	0	6	15	0.0	27.3	68.2
2014	20	0	5	14	0.0	25.0	70.0
2015	17	0	4	12	0.0	23.5	70.6
2016	19	0	5	12	0.0	26.3	63.2
L. Real estate activities							
2008	2	0	0	2	0.0	0.0	100.0
2009	2	0	0	1	0.0	0.0	50.0
2010	2	0	0	1	0.0	0.0	50.0
2011	1	0	0	1	0.0	0.0	100.0
2012	2	0	0	1	0.0	0.0	50.0
2013	1	0	0	1	0.0	0.0	100.0
2014	1	0	0	1	0.0	0.0	100.0
2015	1	0	0	0	0.0	0.0	0.0
2016	2	0	0	1	0.0	0.0	50.0
M. Professional, scientific and technical activities							
2008	19	0	4	14	0.0	21.1	73.7
2009	19	0	4	15	0.0	21.1	78.9
2010	22	0	3	17	0.0	13.6	77.3
2011	23	0	3	18	0.0	13.0	78.3

(*Continued*)

Table 5.5. (*Continued*)

	Year	Total	(Thousands) Skill Level 1 (Low)	Skill Level 2 (Medium)	Skill Levels 3 and 4 (High)	(Percent) Skill Level 1 (Low)	Skill Level 2 (Medium)	Skill Levels 3 and 4 (High)
	2012	24	0	4	20	0.0	16.7	83.3
	2013	24	0	3	20	0.0	12.5	83.3
	2014	25	1	3	20	4.0	12.0	80.0
	2015	25	0	4	20	0.0	16.0	80.0
	2016	24	0	4	19	0.0	16.7	79.2
N. Administrative and support service activities								
	2008	9	3	3	2	33.3	33.3	22.2
	2009	11	4	4	1	36.4	36.4	9.1
	2010	9	4	3	1	44.4	33.3	11.1
	2011	8	4	3	1	50.0	37.5	12.5
	2012	7	3	3	1	42.9	42.9	14.3
	2013	9	4	4	1	44.4	44.4	11.1
	2014	9	3	4	1	33.3	44.4	11.1
	2015	10	3	4	1	30.0	40.0	10.0
	2016	9	4	4	0	44.4	44.4	0.0
O. Public administration and defence; compulsory social security								
	2008	30	2	11	11	6.7	36.7	36.7
	2009	28	2	11	10	7.1	39.3	35.7
	2010	29	2	12	11	6.9	41.4	37.9
	2011	27	2	10	11	7.4	37.0	40.7
	2012	24	1	9	9	4.2	37.5	37.5
	2013	26	1	10	9	3.8	38.5	34.6
	2014	26	2	10	9	7.7	38.5	34.6
	2015	28	3	13	8	10.7	46.4	28.6
	2016	29	3	12	10	10.3	41.4	34.5
P. Education								
	2008	27	1	2	23	3.7	7.4	85.2
	2009	25	1	2	20	4.0	8.0	80.0
	2010	28	2	3	23	7.1	10.7	82.1
	2011	31	2	3	25	6.5	9.7	80.6
	2012	28	1	3	23	3.6	10.7	82.1
	2013	29	1	4	23	3.4	13.8	79.3
	2014	32	1	4	26	3.1	12.5	81.3
	2015	28	0	2	25	0.0	7.1	89.3
	2016	27	0	3	23	0.0	11.1	85.2
Q. Human health and social work activities								
	2008	15	1	3	10	6.7	20.0	66.7
	2009	16	1	4	10	6.3	25.0	62.5
	2010	17	1	4	10	5.9	23.5	58.8
	2011	15	2	3	10	13.3	20.0	66.7
	2012	16	1	4	10	6.3	25.0	62.5
	2013	16	1	4	10	6.3	25.0	62.5
	2014	17	1	4	11	5.9	23.5	64.7
	2015	18	1	3	12	5.6	16.7	66.7
	2016	19	2	3	13	10.5	15.8	68.4

(*Continued*)

Table 5.5. (*Continued*)

	Year	Total	(Thousands) Skill Level 1 (Low)	Skill Level 2 (Medium)	Skill Levels 3 and 4 (High)	(Percent) Skill Level 1 (Low)	Skill Level 2 (Medium)	Skill Levels 3 and 4 (High)
R. Arts, entertainment and recreation								
	2008	4	0	1	2	0.0	25.0	50.0
	2009	5	0	1	2	0.0	20.0	40.0
	2010	7	1	2	3	14.3	28.6	42.9
	2011	7	0	2	4	0.0	28.6	57.1
	2012	6	0	2	3	0.0	33.3	50.0
	2013	4	0	2	2	0.0	50.0	50.0
	2014	4	0	1	2	0.0	25.0	50.0
	2015	5	0	2	2	0.0	40.0	40.0
	2016	6	0	3	2	0.0	50.0	33.3
S. Other service activities								
	2008	10	0	8	2	0.0	80.0	20.0
	2009	10	0	8	1	0.0	80.0	10.0
	2010	10	0	7	1	0.0	70.0	10.0
	2011	11	0	8	1	0.0	72.7	9.1
	2012	10	0	7	2	0.0	70.0	20.0
	2013	10	0	7	2	0.0	70.0	20.0
	2014	10	0	7	1	0.0	70.0	10.0
	2015	10	0	8	1	0.0	80.0	10.0
	2016	11	0	8	2	0.0	72.7	18.2
T. Activities of households as employers; undifferentiated goods- and services-producing activities of households for own use								
	2008	16	16	0	0	100.0	0.0	0.0
	2009	17	17	0	0	100.0	0.0	0.0
	2010	22	21	0	0	95.5	0.0	0.0
	2011	23	22	0	0	95.7	0.0	0.0
	2012	23	23	0	0	100.0	0.0	0.0
	2013	22	22	0	0	100.0	0.0	0.0
	2014	20	20	0	0	100.0	0.0	0.0
	2015	18	17	0	0	94.4	0.0	0.0
	2016	12	12	0	0	100.0	0.0	0.0
TOTAL								
	2008	382	57	200	120	14.9	52.4	31.4
	2009	382	61	197	119	16.0	51.6	31.2
	2010	395	70	194	126	17.7	49.1	31.9
	2011	398	70	189	134	17.6	47.5	33.7
	2012	385	65	181	134	16.9	47.0	34.8
	2013	365	60	172	128	16.4	47.1	35.1
	2014	362	59	168	129	16.3	46.4	35.6
	2015	358	57	170	126	15.9	47.5	35.2
	2016	363	53	178	126	14.6	49.0	34.7

(*Continued*)

Table 5.5. ***(Continued)***

	Year	Total	(Thousands) Skill Level 1 (Low)	Skill Level 2 (Medium)	Skill Levels 3 and 4 (High)	(Percent) Skill Level 1 (Low)	Skill Level 2 (Medium)	Skill Levels 3 and 4 (High)
				Egypt				
A. Agriculture; forestry and fishing								
	2009	6,875	150	6,658	66	2.2	96.8	1.0
	2011	6,810	98	6,636	75	1.4	97.4	1.1
	2012	6,378	87	5,278	1,012	1.4	82.8	15.9
	2013	6,703	118	4,474	2,110	1.8	66.7	31.5
	2015	6,396	579	3,927	1,889	9.1	61.4	29.5
	2016	6,477	77	4,432	1,967	1.2	68.4	30.4
B. Mining and quarrying								
	2009	32	5	19	6	15.6	59.4	18.8
	2011	49	5	35	8	10.2	71.4	16.3
	2012	40	4	22	13	10.0	55.0	32.5
	2013	41	5	23	12	12.2	56.1	29.3
	2015	38	3	20	14	7.9	52.6	36.8
	2016	40	4	24	12	10.0	60.0	30.0
C. Manufacturing								
	2009	2,657	95	2,059	502	3.6	77.5	18.9
	2011	2,292	87	1,707	496	3.8	74.5	21.6
	2012	2,616	114	1,864	637	4.4	71.3	24.4
	2013	2,570	121	1,842	606	4.7	71.7	23.6
	2015	2,780	121	1,985	674	4.4	71.4	24.2
	2016	2,900	134	2,101	664	4.6	72.4	22.9
D. Electricity; gas, steam and air conditioning supply								
	2009	204	20	77	106	9.8	37.7	52.0
	2011	260	22	91	146	8.5	35.0	56.2
	2012	251	20	87	143	8.0	34.7	57.0
	2013	226	20	87	118	8.8	38.5	52.2
	2015	203	24	78	100	11.8	38.4	49.3
	2016	202	20	82	99	9.9	40.6	49.0
E. Water supply; sewerage, waste management and remediation activities								
	2009	116	26	47	42	22.4	40.5	36.2
	2011	172	40	62	68	23.3	36.0	39.5
	2012	157	44	52	60	28.0	33.1	38.2
	2013	214	76	72	65	35.5	33.6	30.4
	2015	186	55	67	63	29.6	36.0	33.9
	2016	306	53	201	51	17.3	65.7	16.7
F. Construction								
	2009	2,440	33	2,215	190	1.4	90.8	7.8
	2011	2,715	43	2,486	186	1.6	91.6	6.9
	2012	2,791	76	2,453	260	2.7	87.9	9.3
	2013	2,728	87	2,449	190	3.2	89.8	7.0
	2015	3,004	107	2,719	178	3.6	90.5	5.9
	2016	3,009	132	2,705	171	4.4	89.9	5.7
G. Wholesale and retail trade; repair of motor vehicles and motorcycles								
	2009	2,464	514	1,194	755	20.9	48.5	30.6
	2011	2,571	528	1,240	802	20.5	48.2	31.2
	2012	2,583	486	1,130	965	18.8	43.7	37.4

(*Continued*)

Table 5.5. (*Continued*)

		(Thousands)			(Percent)		
Year	Total	Skill Level 1 (Low)	Skill Level 2 (Medium)	Skill Levels 3 and 4 (High)	Skill Level 1 (Low)	Skill Level 2 (Medium)	Skill Levels 3 and 4 (High)
2013	2,688	521	1,413	752	19.4	52.6	28.0
2015	2,935	539	1,713	682	18.4	58.4	23.2
2016	3,003	531	1,857	614	17.7	61.8	20.4
H. Transportation and storage							
2009	1,497	126	1,225	144	8.4	81.8	9.6
2011	1,602	144	1,322	135	9.0	82.5	8.4
2012	1,643	140	1,337	165	8.5	81.4	10.0
2013	1,699	130	1,427	141	7.7	84.0	8.3
2015	1,902	138	1,627	136	7.3	85.5	7.2
2016	1,887	106	1,658	122	5.6	87.9	6.5
I. Accommodation and food service activities							
2009	450	47	341	60	10.4	75.8	13.3
2011	464	42	355	66	9.1	76.5	14.2
2012	519	54	368	96	10.4	70.9	18.5
2013	525	52	375	97	9.9	71.4	18.5
2015	647	77	466	103	11.9	72.0	15.9
2016	667	90	488	88	13.5	73.2	13.2
J. Information and communication							
2009	208	12	68	126	5.8	32.7	60.6
2011	197	14	65	118	7.1	33.0	59.9
2012	200	15	63	121	7.5	31.5	60.5
2013	188	16	64	107	8.5	34.0	56.9
2015	206	16	75	114	7.8	36.4	55.3
2016	188	19	56	111	10.1	29.8	59.0
K. Financial and insurance activities							
2009	203	21	44	137	10.3	21.7	67.5
2011	201	19	40	140	9.5	19.9	69.7
2012	195	22	34	138	11.3	17.4	70.8
2013	167	17	39	110	10.2	23.4	65.9
2015	159	23	35	100	14.5	22.0	62.9
2016	181	19	76	85	10.5	42.0	47.0
L. Real estate activities							
2009	13	0	1	11	0.0	7.7	84.6
2011	11	0	1	9	0.0	9.1	81.8
2012	16	0	3	12	0.0	18.8	75.0
2013	25	0	3	21	0.0	12.0	84.0
2015	37	0	7	29	0.0	18.9	78.4
2016	36	0	5	29	0.0	13.9	80.6
M. Professional, scientific and technical activities							
2009	380	9	27	344	2.4	7.1	90.5
2011	415	9	30	375	2.2	7.2	90.4
2012	377	9	32	336	2.4	8.5	89.1
2013	371	9	42	319	2.4	11.3	86.0
2015	408	12	46	349	2.9	11.3	85.5
2016	376	11	44	320	2.9	11.7	85.1
N. Administrative and support service activities							
2009	149	42	67	39	28.2	45.0	26.2
2011	164	48	71	43	29.3	43.3	26.2

(*Continued*)

Table 5.5. ***(Continued)***

	Year	Total	(Thousands) Skill Level 1 (Low)	Skill Level 2 (Medium)	Skill Levels 3 and 4 (High)	(Percent) Skill Level 1 (Low)	Skill Level 2 (Medium)	Skill Levels 3 and 4 (High)
	2012	148	51	55	41	34.5	37.2	27.7
	2013	147	49	53	43	33.3	36.1	29.3
	2015	186	60	81	44	32.3	43.5	23.7
	2016	200	59	100	40	29.5	50.0	20.0
O. Public administration and defence; compulsory social security								
	2009	1,898	183	563	1,139	9.6	29.7	60.0
	2011	1,862	181	534	1,137	9.7	28.7	61.1
	2012	1,886	164	558	1,157	8.7	29.6	61.3
	2013	1,886	162	545	1,175	8.6	28.9	62.3
	2015	1,790	167	517	1,105	9.3	28.9	61.7
	2016	1,728	171	584	973	9.9	33.8	56.3
P. Education								
	2009	2,083	164	79	1,837	7.9	3.8	88.2
	2011	2,123	137	57	1,925	6.5	2.7	90.7
	2012	2,234	139	62	2,032	6.2	2.8	91.0
	2013	2,299	176	69	2,052	7.7	3.0	89.3
	2015	2,216	178	64	1,973	8.0	2.9	89.0
	2016	2,282	166	65	2,050	7.3	2.8	89.8
Q. Human health and social work activities								
	2009	560	41	84	433	7.3	15.0	77.3
	2011	625	33	75	514	5.3	12.0	82.2
	2012	665	33	84	546	5.0	12.6	82.1
	2013	646	62	86	497	9.6	13.3	76.9
	2015	746	72	109	564	9.7	14.6	75.6
	2016	779	88	125	565	11.3	16.0	72.5
R. Arts, entertainment and recreation								
	2009	100	14	18	67	14.0	18.0	67.0
	2011	114	12	20	82	10.5	17.5	71.9
	2012	120	15	24	80	12.5	20.0	66.7
	2013	113	17	28	67	15.0	24.8	59.3
	2015	115	16	22	77	13.9	19.1	67.0
	2016	116	18	22	75	15.5	19.0	64.7
S. Other service activities								
	2009	527	173	218	135	32.8	41.4	25.6
	2011	516	167	207	141	32.4	40.1	27.3
	2012	548	182	185	180	33.2	33.8	32.8
	2013	596	189	215	191	31.7	36.1	32.0
	2015	590	173	221	195	29.3	37.5	33.1
	2016	607	185	231	190	30.5	38.1	31.3
T. Activities of households as employers; undifferentiated goods- and services-producing activities of households for own use								
	2009	78	61	15	1	78.2	19.2	1.3
	2011	118	100	15	3	84.7	12.7	2.5
	2012	183	84	93	5	45.9	50.8	2.7
	2013	133	111	15	5	83.5	11.3	3.8
	2015	219	179	31	9	81.7	14.2	4.1
	2016	330	131	109	88	39.7	33.0	26.7

(Continued)

Table 5.5. (*Continued*)

	Year	Total	(Thousands) Skill Level 1 (Low)	Skill Level 2 (Medium)	Skill Levels 3 and 4 (High)	(Percent) Skill Level 1 (Low)	Skill Level 2 (Medium)	Skill Levels 3 and 4 (High)
TOTAL								
	2009	22,975	1,747	15,038	6,163	7.6	65.5	26.8
	2011	23,345	1,741	15,067	6,494	7.5	64.5	27.8
	2012	23,564	1,749	13,794	8,011	7.4	58.5	34.0
	2013	23,975	1,951	13,330	8,690	8.1	55.6	36.2
	2015	24,778	2,549	13,821	8,407	10.3	55.8	33.9
	2016	25,371	2,026	14,976	8,328	8.0	59.0	32.8
Israel								
A. Agriculture; forestry and fishing								
	2013	42	6	28	6	14.3	66.7	14.3
	2014	39	5	26	6	12.8	66.7	15.4
	2015	37	5	24	5	13.5	64.9	13.5
	2016	37	4	24	6	10.8	64.9	16.2
C. Manufacturing								
	2013	408	27	207	161	6.6	50.7	39.5
	2014	417	30	209	167	7.2	50.1	40.0
	2015	418	27	206	174	6.5	49.3	41.6
	2016	422	26	202	182	6.2	47.9	43.1
D. Electricity; gas, steam and air conditioning supply								
	2013	15		6	5		40.0	33.3
	2014	16		7	8		43.8	50.0
	2015	15		6	7		40.0	46.7
	2016	16		6	8		37.5	50.0
E. Water supply; sewerage, waste management and remediation activities								
	2013	16	3	6	5	18.8	37.5	31.3
	2014	14	3	5	4	21.4	35.7	28.6
	2015	15	3	5	5	20.0	33.3	33.3
	2016	17	4	5	6	23.5	29.4	35.3
F. Construction								
	2013	165	14	121	27	8.5	73.3	16.4
	2014	172	17	126	27	9.9	73.3	15.7
	2015	180	20	131	28	11.1	72.8	15.6
	2016	186	16	135	32	8.6	72.6	17.2
G. Wholesale and retail trade; repair of motor vehicles and motorcycles								
	2013	402	26	245	127	6.5	60.9	31.6
	2014	406	28	244	131	6.9	60.1	32.3
	2015	420	26	251	138	6.2	59.8	32.9
	2016	429	29	254	143	6.8	59.2	33.3
H. Transportation and storage								
	2013	146	5	115	24	3.4	78.8	16.4
	2014	147	6	114	26	4.1	77.6	17.7
	2015	151	6	114	29	4.0	75.5	19.2
	2016	154	6	116	29	3.9	75.3	18.8
I. Accommodation and food service activities								
	2013	150	19	102	27	12.7	68.0	18.0
	2014	152	19	102	29	12.5	67.1	19.1
	2015	154	21	102	27	13.6	66.2	17.5
	2016	164	23	106	31	14.0	64.6	18.9

(*Continued*)

Table 5.5. (*Continued*)

	Year	Total	(Thousands) Skill Level 1 (Low)	Skill Level 2 (Medium)	Skill Levels 3 and 4 (High)	(Percent) Skill Level 1 (Low)	Skill Level 2 (Medium)	Skill Levels 3 and 4 (High)
J. Information and communication								
	2013	165		30	132	0.0	18.2	80.0
	2014	173	1	28	142	0.6	16.2	82.1
	2015	180	1	24	152	0.6	13.3	84.4
	2016	185	1	22	160	0.5	11.9	86.5
K. Financial and insurance activities								
	2013	118		36	80		30.5	67.8
	2014	124		37	85		29.8	68.5
	2015	123		35	85		28.5	69.1
	2016	124		34	87		27.4	70.2
L. Real estate activities								
	2013	28		4	22		14.3	78.6
	2014	29	1	4	23	0.0	13.8	79.3
	2015	27		4	22		14.8	81.5
	2016	32		4	26		12.5	81.3
M. Professional, scientific and technical activities								
	2013	236		24	208	0.0	10.2	88.1
	2014	252	1	23	225	0.4	9.1	89.3
	2015	257	1	18	234	0.4	7.0	91.1
	2016	269	1	15	249	0.4	5.6	92.6
N. Administrative and support service activities								
	2013	148	29	91	26	19.6	61.5	17.6
	2014	146	31	86	27	21.2	58.9	18.5
	2015	152	34	89	28	22.4	58.6	18.4
	2016	160	34	98	26	21.3	61.3	16.3
O. Public administration and defence; compulsory social security								
	2013	362	24	60	130	6.6	16.6	35.9
	2014	366	27	56	135	7.4	15.3	36.9
	2015	371	25	55	137	6.7	14.8	36.9
	2016	375	26	56	138	6.9	14.9	36.8
P. Education								
	2013	413	4	93	312	1.0	22.5	75.5
	2014	434	3	95	333	0.7	21.9	76.7
	2015	455	4	100	348	0.9	22.0	76.5
	2016	456	4	100	349	0.9	21.9	76.5
Q. Human health and social work activities								
	2013	353	10	131	210	2.8	37.1	59.5
	2014	377	9	139	226	2.4	36.9	59.9
	2015	392	9	145	235	2.3	37.0	59.9
	2016	398	9	146	241	2.3	36.7	60.6
R. Arts, entertainment and recreation								
	2013	61	2	13	43	3.3	21.3	70.5
	2014	66	4	13	47	6.1	19.7	71.2
	2015	66	3	14	47	4.5	21.2	71.2
	2016	71	3	14	52	4.2	19.7	73.2
S. Other service activities								
	2013	89	3	49	35	3.4	55.1	39.3
	2014	87	4	49	33	4.6	56.3	37.9

(*Continued*)

Table 5.5. (*Continued*)

	Year	Total	(Thousands) Skill Level 1 (Low)	Skill Level 2 (Medium)	Skill Levels 3 and 4 (High)	(Percent) Skill Level 1 (Low)	Skill Level 2 (Medium)	Skill Levels 3 and 4 (High)
	2015	84	3	46	33	3.6	54.8	39.3
	2016	89	3	48	36	3.4	53.9	40.4
T. Activities of households as employers; undifferentiated goods- and services-producing activities of households for own use								
	2013	64	16	46		25.0	71.9	
	2014	66	16	49		24.2	74.2	
	2015	66	17	48		25.8	72.7	
	2016	67	17	49		25.4	73.1	
TOTAL	2013	3,449	201	1,439	1,603	5.8	41.7	46.5
	2014	3,555	218	1,435	1,695	6.1	40.4	47.7
	2015	3,643	219	1,446	1,760	6.0	39.7	48.3
	2016	3,736	218	1,464	1,823	5.8	39.2	48.8
				Qatar				
A. Agriculture; forestry and fishing								
	2010	17	1	15	0	5.9	88.2	0.0
	2013	21	10	10	0	47.6	47.6	0.0
	2015	24	2	20	0	8.3	83.3	0.0
	2016	24	1	22	0	4.2	91.7	0.0
B. Mining and quarrying								
	2010	85	8	57	19	9.4	67.1	22.4
	2013	95	18	50	25	18.9	52.6	26.3
	2015	101	12	57	31	11.9	56.4	30.7
	2016	100	12	61	26	12.0	61.0	26.0
C. Manufacturing								
	2010	100	15	73	11	15.0	73.0	11.0
	2013	119	17	74	27	14.3	62.2	22.7
	2015	135	14	98	22	10.4	72.6	16.3
	2016	144	12	102	28	8.3	70.8	19.4
D. Electricity; gas, steam and air conditioning supply								
	2010	4	0	1	2	0.0	25.0	50.0
	2013	8	0	4	3	0.0	50.0	37.5
	2015	19	1	10	8	5.3	52.6	42.1
	2016	17	1	10	5	5.9	58.8	29.4
E. Water supply; sewerage, waste management and remediation activities								
	2010	0	0	0	0	0	0	0
	2013	2	0	1	1	0.0	50.0	50.0
	2015	13	0	5	7	0.0	38.5	53.8
	2016	9	2	5	1	22.2	55.6	11.1
F. Construction								
	2010	506	118	349	38	23.3	69.0	7.5
	2013	568	112	400	55	19.7	70.4	9.7
	2015	784	107	611	65	13.6	77.9	8.3
	2016	847	152	603	90	17.9	71.2	10.6
G. Wholesale and retail trade; repair of motor vehicles and motorcycles								
	2010	142	15	102	24	10.6	71.8	16.9
	2013	194	34	131	28	17.5	67.5	14.4
	2015	252	46	176	30	18.3	69.8	11.9
	2016	254	28	183	42	11.0	72.0	16.5

(*Continued*)

Table 5.5. (*Continued*)

	Year	Total	(Thousands) Skill Level 1 (Low)	Skill Level 2 (Medium)	Skill Levels 3 and 4 (High)	(Percent) Skill Level 1 (Low)	Skill Level 2 (Medium)	Skill Levels 3 and 4 (High)
H. Transportation and storage								
	2010	34	5	23	5	14.7	67.6	14.7
	2013	44	3	31	9	6.8	70.5	20.5
	2015	66	9	42	13	13.6	63.6	19.7
	2016	59	5	43	10	8.5	72.9	16.9
I. Accommodation and food service activities								
	2010	29	6	19	2	20.7	65.5	6.9
	2013	38	6	27	4	15.8	71.1	10.5
	2015	51	14	32	4	27.5	62.7	7.8
	2016	72	17	49	5	23.6	68.1	6.9
J. Information and communication								
	2010	9	0	2	6	0.0	22.2	66.7
	2013	12	1	4	6	8.3	33.3	50.0
	2015	13	0	3	9	0.0	23.1	69.2
	2016	15	1	2	11	6.7	13.3	73.3
K. Financial and insurance activities								
	2010	10	0	3	6	0.0	30.0	60.0
	2013	12	0	3	7	0.0	25.0	58.3
	2015	15	3	3	8	20.0	20.0	53.3
	2016	15	2	3	9	13.3	20.0	60.0
L. Real estate activities								
	2010	8	2	4	2	25.0	50.0	25.0
	2013	10	1	4	3	10.0	40.0	30.0
	2015	12	4	5	2	33.3	41.7	16.7
	2016	12	1	5	5	8.3	41.7	41.7
M. Professional, scientific and technical activities								
	2010	20	2	8	9	10.0	40.0	45.0
	2013	28	3	19	5	10.7	67.9	17.9
	2015	28	5	16	6	17.9	57.1	21.4
	2016	28	8	9	10	28.6	32.1	35.7
N. Administrative and support service activities								
	2010	39	14	21	3	35.9	53.8	7.7
	2013	47	18	20	8	38.3	42.6	17.0
	2015	55	30	21	3	54.5	38.2	5.5
	2016	84	36	37	11	42.9	44.0	13.1
O. Public administration and defence; compulsory social security								
	2010	72	12	30	28	16.7	41.7	38.9
	2013	94	12	40	42	12.8	42.6	44.7
	2015	99	12	49	37	12.1	49.5	37.4
	2016	87	8	46	32	9.2	52.9	36.8
P. Education								
	2010	26	1	2	22	3.8	7.7	84.6
	2013	39	2	11	25	5.1	28.2	64.1
	2015	49	3	12	33	6.1	24.5	67.3
	2016	46	2	10	34	4.3	21.7	73.9
Q. Human health and social work activities								
	2010	19	1	3	14	5.3	15.8	73.7
	2013	27	1	7	18	3.7	25.9	66.7

(*Continued*)

Table 5.5. ***(Continued)***

	Year	Total	(Thousands) Skill Level 1 (Low)	Skill Level 2 (Medium)	Skill Levels 3 and 4 (High)	(Percent) Skill Level 1 (Low)	Skill Level 2 (Medium)	Skill Levels 3 and 4 (High)
	2015	30	3	8	17	10.0	26.7	56.7
	2016	29	0	5	23	0.0	17.2	79.3
R. Arts, entertainment and recreation								
	2010	5	0	1	2	0.0	20.0	40.0
	2013	9	0	5	3	0.0	55.6	33.3
	2015	14	2	8	3	14.3	57.1	21.4
	2016	6	0	1	3	0.0	16.7	50.0
S. Other service activities								
	2010	5	1	3	1	20.0	60.0	20.0
	2013	6	2	3	1	33.3	50.0	16.7
	2015	14	5	6	2	35.7	42.9	14.3
	2016	16	2	7	5	12.5	43.8	31.3
T. Activities of households as employers; undifferentiated goods- and services-producing activities of households for own use								
	2010	132	90	41	0	68.2	31.1	0.0
	2013	151	94	57	0	62.3	37.7	0.0
	2015	161	87	72	0	54.0	44.7	0.0
	2016	173	90	81	1	52.0	46.8	0.6
TOTAL								
	2010	1,271	298	770	203	23.4	60.6	16.0
	2013	1,539	344	911	280	22.4	59.2	18.2
	2015	1,946	368	1,265	312	18.9	65.0	16.0
	2016	2,052	389	1,295	367	19.0	63.1	17.9
				Saudi Arabia				
A. Agriculture; forestry and fishing	2014	582		557	24	0.0	95.7	4.1
B. Mining and quarrying	2014	152		86	66	0.0	56.6	43.4
C. Manufacturing	2014	795		569	226	0.0	71.6	28.4
D. Electricity; gas, steam and air conditioning supply	2014	106		47	59	0.0	44.3	55.7
E. Water supply; sewerage, waste management and remediation activities	2014	77		57	19	0.0	74.0	24.7
F. Construction	2014	1,416		1,098	318	0.0	77.5	22.5
G. Wholesale and retail trade; repair of motor vehicles and motorcycles	2014	1,606		1,379	227	0.0	85.9	14.1
H. Transportation and storage	2014	392		325	66	0.0	82.9	16.8

(Continued)

Table 5.5. (*Continued*)

			(Thousands)			(Percent)		
	Year	Total	Skill Level 1 (Low)	Skill Level 2 (Medium)	Skill Levels 3 and 4 (High)	Skill Level 1 (Low)	Skill Level 2 (Medium)	Skill Levels 3 and 4 (High)
I. Accommodation and food service activities	2014	377		332	44	0.0	88.1	11.7
J. Information and communication	2014	128		43	85	0.0	33.6	66.4
K. Financial and insurance activities	2014	142		79	62	0.0	55.6	43.7
L. Real estate activities	2014	126		109	17	0.0	86.5	13.5
N. Administrative and support service activities	2014	183		148	34	0.0	80.9	18.6
O. Public administration and defence; compulsory social security	2014	1,780		1,624	155	0.0	91.2	8.7
P. Education	2014	1,307		232	1,074	0.0	17.8	82.2
Q. Human health and social work activities	2014	610		158	451	0.0	25.9	73.9
R. Arts, entertainment and recreation	2014	17		9	8	0.0	52.9	47.1
S. Other service activities	2014	243		194	49	0.0	79.8	20.2
T. Activities of households as employers; undifferentiated goods- and services-producing activities of households for own use	2014	853		849	3	0.0	99.5	0.4
TOTAL	2014	11,067		7,959	3,108	0.0	71.9	28.1
				Turkey				
A. Agriculture; forestry and fishing								
	2009	4,881	923	3,950	7	18.9	80.9	0.1
	2010	5,355	966	4,378	10	18.0	81.8	0.2
	2011	5,822	1,155	4,651	14	19.8	79.9	0.2
	2012	5,846	1,134	4,698	13	19.4	80.4	0.2
	2013	5,850	1,170	4,667	12	20.0	79.8	0.2
	2014	5,467	1,145	4,312	9	20.9	78.9	0.2
	2015	5,431	1,230	4,188	13	22.6	77.1	0.2
	2016	5,307	1,236	4,054	17	23.3	76.4	0.3

(*Continued*)

Table 5.5. (*Continued*)

	Year	Total	(Thousands) Skill Level 1 (Low)	Skill Level 2 (Medium)	Skill Levels 3 and 4 (High)	(Percent) Skill Level 1 (Low)	Skill Level 2 (Medium)	Skill Levels 3 and 4 (High)
B. Mining and quarrying								
	2009	98	26	57	14	26.5	58.2	14.3
	2010	114	26	66	20	22.8	57.9	17.5
	2011	124	36	67	19	29.0	54.0	15.3
	2012	113	31	65	16	27.4	57.5	14.2
	2013	105	22	67	15	21.0	63.8	14.3
	2014	132	36	79	16	27.3	59.8	12.1
	2015	118	30	70	18	25.4	59.3	15.3
	2016	124	30	76	18	24.2	61.3	14.5
C. Manufacturing								
	2009	3,866	557	2,726	582	14.4	70.5	15.1
	2010	4,213	497	3,067	647	11.8	72.8	15.4
	2011	4,366	544	3,181	640	12.5	72.9	14.7
	2012	4,419	540	3,230	648	12.2	73.1	14.7
	2013	4,631	584	3,397	649	12.6	73.4	14.0
	2014	4,934	757	3,483	693	15.3	70.6	14.0
	2015	4,965	756	3,486	722	15.2	70.2	14.5
	2016	4,918	757	3,477	683	15.4	70.7	13.9
D. Electricity; gas, steam and air conditioning supply								
	2009	64	6	32	25	9.4	50.0	39.1
	2010	72	6	39	26	8.3	54.2	36.1
	2011	81	6	36	37	7.4	44.4	45.7
	2012	96	9	47	39	9.4	49.0	40.6
	2013	95	8	49	37	8.4	51.6	38.9
	2014	91	8	49	33	8.8	53.8	36.3
	2015	102	10	52	39	9.8	51.0	38.2
	2016	106	8	51	47	7.5	48.1	44.3
E. Water supply; sewerage, waste management and remediation activities								
	2009	47	25	15	7	53.2	31.9	14.9
	2010	91	59	23	8	64.8	25.3	8.8
	2011	130	85	32	13	65.4	24.6	10.0
	2012	121	75	30	14	62.0	24.8	11.6
	2013	122	72	34	15	59.0	27.9	12.3
	2014	153	94	46	12	61.4	30.1	7.8
	2015	152	92	45	14	60.5	29.6	9.2
	2016	151	100	34	16	66.2	22.5	10.6
F. Construction								
	2009	1,304	315	843	146	24.2	64.6	11.2
	2010	1,431	323	942	165	22.6	65.8	11.5
	2011	1,674	395	1,090	188	23.6	65.1	11.2
	2012	1,709	397	1,111	200	23.2	65.0	11.7
	2013	1,779	368	1,218	192	20.7	68.5	10.8
	2014	1,910	385	1,309	215	20.2	68.5	11.3
	2015	1,906	370	1,323	213	19.4	69.4	11.2
	2016	1,986	377	1,364	245	19.0	68.7	12.3

(*Continued*)

Table 5.5. (*Continued*)

Year	Total	(Thousands) Skill level 1 (low)	Skill level 2 (medium)	Skill levels 3 and 4 (high)	(Percent) Skill level 1 (low)	Skill level 2 (medium)	Skill levels 3 and 4 (high)
G. Wholesale and retail trade; repair of motor vehicles and motorcycles							
2009	3,381	385	1,916	1,079	11.4	56.7	31.9
2010	3,326	352	1,910	1,063	10.6	57.4	32.0
2011	3,475	271	2,438	766	7.8	70.2	22.0
2012	3,501	257	2,528	715	7.3	72.2	20.4
2013	3,518	246	2,755	516	7.0	78.3	14.7
2014	3,585	256	2,790	537	7.1	77.8	15.0
2015	3,693	263	2,865	563	7.1	77.6	15.2
2016	3,756	244	2,944	568	6.5	78.4	15.1
H. Transportation and storage							
2009	986	97	779	108	9.8	79.0	11.0
2010	1,009	109	795	104	10.8	78.8	10.3
2011	1,044	102	825	116	9.8	79.0	11.1
2012	1,093	110	873	109	10.1	79.9	10.0
2013	1,151	109	931	111	9.5	80.9	9.6
2014	1,118	110	908	99	9.8	81.2	8.9
2015	1,109	101	909	98	9.1	82.0	8.8
2016	1,186	93	984	107	7.8	83.0	9.0
I. Accommodation and food service activities							
2009	1,050	165	635	249	15.7	60.5	23.7
2010	1,084	173	665	245	16.0	61.3	22.6
2011	1,139	179	715	244	15.7	62.8	21.4
2012	1,206	208	746	251	17.2	61.9	20.8
2013	1,307	263	798	245	20.1	61.1	18.7
2014	1,350	294	811	244	21.8	60.1	18.1
2015	1,445	303	899	242	21.0	62.2	16.7
2016	1,470	316	911	242	21.5	62.0	16.5
J. Information and communication							
2009	157	6	65	85	3.8	41.4	54.1
2010	204	6	83	113	2.9	40.7	55.4
2011	210	5	86	118	2.4	41.0	56.2
2012	237	7	84	146	3.0	35.4	61.6
2013	254	12	83	158	4.7	32.7	62.2
2014	228	9	70	147	3.9	30.7	64.5
2015	253	9	80	163	3.6	31.6	64.4
2016	248	12	74	161	4.8	29.8	64.9
K. Financial and insurance activities							
2009	273	10	147	115	3.7	53.8	42.1
2010	273	9	153	110	3.3	56.0	40.3
2011	280	8	152	118	2.9	54.3	42.1
2012	264	8	142	114	3.0	53.8	43.2
2013	287	9	159	119	3.1	55.4	41.5
2014	300	9	168	123	3.0	56.0	41.0
2015	296	8	177	109	2.7	59.8	36.8
2016	300	5	178	116	1.7	59.3	38.7

(*Continued*)

Table 5.5. (*Continued*)

			(Thousands)			(Percent)		
	Year	Total	Skill level 1 (low)	Skill level 2 (medium)	Skill levels 3 and 4 (high)	Skill level 1 (low)	Skill level 2 (medium)	Skill levels 3 and 4 (high)
L. Real estate activities								
	2009	62	5	8	48	8.1	12.9	77.4
	2010	60	1	10	48	1.7	16.7	80.0
	2011	153	4	88	60	2.6	57.5	39.2
	2012	183	5	117	60	2.7	63.9	32.8
	2013	185	4	116	64	2.2	62.7	34.6
	2014	205	5	114	84	2.4	55.6	41.0
	2015	212	11	115	85	5.2	54.2	40.1
	2016	242	11	136	94	4.5	56.2	38.8
M. Professional, scientific and technical activities								
	2009	397	7	152	237	1.8	38.3	59.7
	2010	428	10	167	250	2.3	39.0	58.4
	2011	427	10	158	258	2.3	37.0	60.4
	2012	506	13	166	327	2.6	32.8	64.6
	2013	553	15	186	351	2.7	33.6	63.5
	2014	684	16	229	438	2.3	33.5	64.0
	2015	752	19	222	510	2.5	29.5	67.8
	2016	846	27	253	565	3.2	29.9	66.8
N. Administrative and support service activities								
	2009	598	271	272	54	45.3	45.5	9.0
	2010	767	357	336	72	46.5	43.8	9.4
	2011	777	277	418	81	35.6	53.8	10.4
	2012	923	371	467	84	40.2	50.6	9.1
	2013	1,018	382	545	90	37.5	53.5	8.8
	2014	1,154	407	649	97	35.3	56.2	8.4
	2015	1,295	457	722	114	35.3	55.8	8.8
	2016	1,397	494	778	124	35.4	55.7	8.9
O. Public administration and defence; compulsory social security								
	2009	1,206	105	571	528	8.7	47.3	43.8
	2010	1,290	103	666	521	8.0	51.6	40.4
	2011	1,337	80	729	527	6.0	54.5	39.4
	2012	1,458	91	765	602	6.2	52.5	41.3
	2013	1,463	82	762	619	5.6	52.1	42.3
	2014	1,385	79	711	594	5.7	51.3	42.9
	2015	1,457	88	735	633	6.0	50.4	43.4
	2016	1,454	88	721	645	6.1	49.6	44.4
P. Education								
	2009	967	56	84	825	5.8	8.7	85.3
	2010	1,018	66	94	857	6.5	9.2	84.2
	2011	1,106	63	132	910	5.7	11.9	82.3
	2012	1,224	87	128	1,008	7.1	10.5	82.4
	2013	1,247	91	130	1,025	7.3	10.4	82.2
	2014	1,320	81	161	1,077	6.1	12.2	81.6
	2015	1,419	100	161	1,157	7.0	11.3	81.5
	2016	1,607	128	195	1,283	8.0	12.1	79.8

(*Continued*)

Table 5.5. (*Continued*)

	Year	Total	(Thousands) Skill level 1 (low)	Skill level 2 (medium)	Skill levels 3 and 4 (high)	(Percent) Skill level 1 (low)	Skill level 2 (medium)	Skill levels 3 and 4 (high)
Q. Human health and social work activities								
	2009	590	40	166	384	6.8	28.1	65.1
	2010	590	28	181	380	4.7	30.7	64.4
	2011	692	31	233	427	4.5	33.7	61.7
	2012	807	36	296	475	4.5	36.7	58.9
	2013	858	40	341	476	4.7	39.7	55.5
	2014	973	28	441	504	2.9	45.3	51.8
	2015	1,055	29	484	541	2.7	45.9	51.3
	2016	1,123	32	510	580	2.8	45.4	51.6
R. Arts, entertainment and recreation								
	2009	130	11	49	69	8.5	37.7	53.1
	2010	101	11	35	54	10.9	34.7	53.5
	2011	100	11	33	54	11.0	33.0	54.0
	2012	107	11	40	56	10.3	37.4	52.3
	2013	121	12	47	61	9.9	38.8	50.4
	2014	130	12	54	64	9.2	41.5	49.2
	2015	149	14	53	81	9.4	35.6	54.4
	2016	141	16	46	77	11.3	32.6	54.6
S. Other service activities								
	2009	611	104	400	106	17.0	65.5	17.3
	2010	582	82	373	126	14.1	64.1	21.6
	2011	595	73	384	136	12.3	64.5	22.9
	2012	587	74	384	127	12.6	65.4	21.6
	2013	636	83	427	125	13.1	67.1	19.7
	2014	638	112	407	118	17.6	63.8	18.5
	2015	649	110	414	123	16.9	63.8	19.0
	2016	682	130	432	119	19.1	63.3	17.4
T. Activities of households as employers; undifferentiated goods- and services-producing activities of households for own use								
	2009	589	170	415	3	28.9	70.5	0.5
	2010	572	170	400	0	29.7	69.9	0.0
	2011	552	134	416	1	24.3	75.4	0.2
	2012	403	68	333	0	16.9	82.6	0.0
	2013	325	57	267	1	17.5	82.2	0.3
	2014	160	54	104	1	33.8	65.0	0.6
	2015	145	47	94	3	32.4	64.8	2.1
	2016	156	46	106	4	29.5	67.9	2.6
TOTAL								
	2009	21,270	3,294	13,293	4,682	15.5	62.5	22.0
	2010	22,592	3,366	14,395	4,831	14.9	63.7	21.4
	2011	24,099	3,481	15,877	4,740	14.4	65.9	19.7
	2012	24,819	3,542	16,261	5,015	14.3	65.5	20.2
	2013	25,519	3,638	16,990	4,890	14.3	66.6	19.2
	2014	25,930	3,907	16,906	5,116	15.1	65.2	19.7
	2015	26,618	4,059	17,105	5,453	15.2	64.3	20.5
	2016	27,215	4,158	17,335	5,721	15.3	63.7	21.0

Source: ILO

for competent performance in occupations at Skill Level 2 are generally obtained through completion of the first stage of secondary education. Some occupations require the completion of the second stage of secondary education, which may include a significant component of specialized vocational education and on-the-job training. Some occupations require completion of vocation-specific education undertaken after completion of secondary education. Occupations classified at Skill Level 2 include butchers, bus drivers, secretaries, accounts clerks, sewing machinists, dressmakers, shop sales assistants, police officers, hairdressers, building electricians and motor vehicle mechanics.

Occupations at Skill Level 3 typically involve the performance of complex technical and practical tasks that require an extensive body of factual, technical and procedural knowledge in a specialized field. These occupations require tasks which assume that workers can ensure compliance with health, safety and related regulations; prepare detailed estimates of quantities and costs of materials and labor required for specific projects; coordinate, supervise, control and schedule the activities of other workers; and perform technical functions in support of professionals. Occupations at this skill level generally require a high level of literacy and numeracy and well-developed interpersonal communication skills. These skills may include the ability to understand complex written material, prepare factual reports and communicate verbally in difficult circumstances. The knowledge and skills required for competent performance in occupations at Skill Level 3 are usually obtained as the result of study at a higher educational institution for a period of 1–3 years following completion of secondary education. Occupations classified at Skill Level 3 include shop managers. medical laboratory technicians, legal secretaries, commercial sales representatives, diagnostic medical radiographers, computer support technicians and broadcasting and recording technicians.

Occupations at Skill Level 4 typically involve the performance of tasks that require complex problem-solving, decision-making and creativity based on an extensive body of theoretical and factual knowledge in a specialized field. The tasks performed typically include analysis and research to extend the body of human knowledge in a particular field, diagnosis and treatment of disease, imparting knowledge to others, and design of structures or machinery and of processes for construction and production. The knowledge and skills required for competent performance in occupations at Skill Level 4 are usually obtained as the result of study at a higher educational institution for a period of 3–6 years leading to the award of a first degree or higher qualification. Occupations classified at Skill Level 4 include sales and marketing managers, civil engineers, secondary school teachers, medical practitioners, musicians, operating theatre nurses and computer systems analysts.

The data in Table 5.5 verifies that most of Arab MENA's labor force is not trained in skills for the 21st century. For Algeria, in 2014, 67 percent of the employees are in Skill Level 2. For Cyprus, 49 percent of the employees, in 2016 are in Skill Level 2 and 34.7 percent are in Skill Level 3 and 4, combined. Over the 2008–2016 period there was no structural change in the accumulation of skills. For Egypt, 59 percent of the employed were in Skill Level 2 and 32.8 percent were in Skill Level 3 and 4 combined. Over the 2009–2016 period, the Skill level of those employed in occupations requiring Skill Level 3 and 4 combined, increased from 26.8 percent to 32.8 percent.

For Israel, the skill level distribution of its employed labor force in Skill Level 3 and 4 combined increased from 46.5 percent in 2013 to 48.8 percent in 2016. Those in Skill level 2 decreased from 41.7 percent in 2013 to 39.2 percent in 2016. Overall, the Skill Level characteristic of Israel's working population is the highest within MENA.

When we compare these results to those of Qatar which has the financial ability to improve its labor skill levels via a well-funded education program, we are totally disappointed at their lack of foresight. Between 2010 and 2016, the predominant Skill Level of Qatar's labor force is parked in Skill Level 2. In 2010, 60.6 percent of their labor force was at Skill Level 2. In 2016, 63.1 percent of its employed labor force was at Skill Level 2. This performance will not be sufficient for the 21st century. Saudi Arabia, which is another very wealthy Arab MENA country has performed as poorly, if not worse that Qatar, in their education program. The data for 2014 (the only data they reported) has 71.9 of the working labor force with a Skill Level of 2.

Turkey which boasts that it is a NIC and not an LDC, cannot support that characteristic given the Skill Level of its working population. The data that Turkey reported for the period 2009–2016 places the majority of its employed work force (63.7 percent) in Skill Level 2. For Skill Level 3 and 4 combined, Turkey's employed labor force is 21.0 percent in 2016, down from 22.0 in 2009. Turkey's labor force Skill Level characteristic makes it very appropriate as a source of unskilled labor for Europe and not as a source of 21st century skill requirements for a Newly Industrialized Country.

Having sorted out the supply side for those in the labor market, we shift the focus to the demand for labor by looking at the disclosed unemployment data. In Table 5.6 we present the unemployment distribution

Table 5.6. Unemployment Distribution by Aggregate Education Levels (By Sex and Age) (Percent)

	Total								Male			
	15–24				25+				15–24			
Year	<basic	Basic	Intermediate	Advanced	<basic	Basic	Intermediate	Advanced	<basic	Basic	Intermediate	Advanced
						Egypt						
2008	2.7	3.2	68.1	26.0	3.5	2.5	49.7	44.4	4.2	5.1	67.1	23.6
2009	2.4	4.9	61.9	30.9	8.8	2.6	45.2	43.4	3.8	4.2	61.0	31.0
2011	6.6	7.2	55.1	31.2	14.2	7.9	44.7	33.2	9.8	10.5	54.0	25.7
2012	6.3	10.8	53.7	29.2	6.3	6.3	49.7	37.8	9.5	15.4	52.3	22.9
2013	12.9	10.4	50.0	26.8	13.5	6.6	43.9	36.0	15.4	14.1	50.4	20.1
2014	14.6	12.5	49.0	23.8	18.8	8.2	42.1	30.9	15.7	18.1	48.7	17.5
2015	11.0	12.7	50.6	25.7	6.1	5.6	49.5	38.8	13.8	17.1	50.3	18.7
2016	10.1	14.3	48.3	27.1	7.3	3.7	52.3	36.7	9.8	20.1	50.2	19.6
						Israel						
2009		20.5	71.4	7.2		17.7	40.3	38.0		25.3	70.4	
2010		24.0	65.7	9.7		17.5	41.7	36.1		24.5	63.7	
2011		17.2	65.4	12.8		15.3	41.6	39.9		21.8	61.6	
2012		30.1	62.3	7.1	0.6	16.1	44.5	36.4		41.8	54.8	
2013		27.5	65.6	6.5		14.6	43.3	39.6		35.1	61.4	3.2
						Morocco						
2011	3.4	63.8	31.3		8.4	40.1	49.2		3.6	71.7	23.4	
2012	2.9	63.8	32.3		8.6	41.6	47.4		2.7	72.3	23.8	
						Qatar						
2009	3.8	18.2	53.5	24.5	6.0	30.1	41.0	22.9	8.4	26.5	29.3	35.7
2011	2.7	16.3	46.2	34.8	4.2	22.7	30.9	42.3	8.5	37.4	11.0	43.0
2012	0.0	23.8	52.0	24.2	0.0	27.5	19.8	52.7	0.0	36.8	47.1	16.1
2013	0.0	19.4	47.8	32.8	0.0	16.2	38.4	45.4	0.0	27.3	33.5	39.3

(Continued)

Table 5.6. (*Continued*)

	Male				Female							
	25+				15–24				25+			
Year	<basic	Basic	Intermediate	Advanced	<basic	Basic	Intermediate	Advanced	<basic	Basic	Intermediate	Advanced
						Egypt						
2008	5.8	3.8	42.0	48.4	1.2	1.3	69.1	28.5	1.2	1.1	57.4	40.3
2009	4.8	3.0	40.1	52.1	1.1	5.5	62.6	30.8	11.0	2.4	48.1	38.4
2011	23.1	11.8	40.2	24.9	2.1	2.6	56.5	38.8	2.7	2.9	50.6	43.9
2012	11.9	9.5	45.7	32.9	0.9	3.1	56.2	39.8	0.8	3.2	53.5	42.5
2013	23.1	10.8	36.1	30.0	8.4	3.7	49.3	38.7	4.1	2.5	51.5	41.9
2014	23.6	14.0	36.4	26.1	12.8	2.5	49.5	35.2	14.1	2.5	47.7	35.7
2015	11.6	10.0	41.7	36.8	6.5	5.5	51.0	36.9	1.3	1.8	56.3	40.7
2016	10.3	5.7	46.5	37.4	10.5	5.3	45.4	38.6	4.7	1.9	57.4	36.0
						Israel						
2009		20.7	40.1	33.0		11.7	72.5	11.4		7.2	41.9	45.2
2010		24.2	41.7	30.1		13.4	67.7	15.0		6.6	43.2	44.7
2011		15.4	43.0	33.1		12.8	68.9	16.6			41.6	49.6
2012		21.3	45.1	30.0		16.8	69.7	11.6		6.2	42.7	43.3
2013		20.0	43.7	33.2		17.6	70.1	10.1		4.2	42.2	46.2
						Morocco						
2011	7.6	47.6	42.2		2.9	40.4	54.9		9.9	25.4	62.7	
2012	8.3	49.4	40.1		3.5	39.6	56.3		9.3	24.4	64.0	
						Qatar						
2009	14.6	44.5	14.9	26.0	1.0	13.2	68.1	17.8	0.0	20.0	59.2	20.8
2011	6.8	37.0	17.2	39.0	0.9	9.8	57.1	32.2	3.2	17.0	36.3	43.6
2012	0.0	37.0	38.8	24.2	0.0	18.0	54.2	27.8	0.0	25.1	15.1	59.8
2013	0.0	36.1	57.1	6.8	0.0	15.8	54.6	29.7	0.0	10.7	26.1	63.2

(*Continued*)

Table 5.6. *(Continued)*

	Total								Male			
	15–24				25+				15–24			
Year	<basic	Basic	Intermediate	Advanced	<basic	Basic	Intermediate	Advanced	<basic	Basic	Intermediate	Advanced
						Saudi Arabia						
2009	0.8	14	48.8	36.4	1.6	19	29.8	49.6	1.2	22	62.6	14.2
2011	0	11.3	63.4	25.3	0.1	14.4	40.3	45.2	0	14.8	75.9	9.4
2012	0.1	7.1	55.2	37.6	0.2	10.5	31.4	58	0.3	11.9	74.7	13.2
2014	0	6.5	52.2	41.3	0.1	8.7	34.6	56.7	0	10.3	70.2	19.5
						Turkey						
2006	6.4	42.3	38.6	12.7	6.6	59.5	22	11.9	7.8	49.1	34.3	8.9
2007	7.8	39.9	37.8	14.5	6.7	58.2	22.5	12.5	9.1	47.4	33.8	9.8
2008	8.5	39.7	36.2	15.6	7.3	59.5	20.2	13	10.1	48.4	32.4	9
2009	9.1	41.6	35.3	14	6.8	59.3	21.1	12.8	10.2	49.6	31.7	8.5
2010	8.9	41.9	32.3	17	6.5	58.5	21.7	13.4	10.7	50.7	28.3	10.3
2011	8.2	39.6	31.9	20.3	7.2	55.4	20.7	16.7	10.1	49	28.3	12.6
2012	7.4	40.2	29.7	22.7	6.7	53.1	21.4	18.8	9.7	49.7	26.4	14.3
2013	5.8	42.3	29.5	22.4	7.2	52.4	21.2	19.2	7.2	52.6	26.1	14.1
2014	6.5	43.8	27.2	22.5	7.3	51.1	21.3	20.3	7.2	54.5	23.7	14.6
2015	5.3	43.4	27	24.3	6.3	51.7	20.5	21.5	6.5	55.4	24.3	13.8
2016	5	39.2	29.4	26.4	5.9	49.1	21.2	23.9	6.5	50.3	26.2	17

(Continued)

Table 5.6. (*Continued*)

	Male				Female							
	25+				15–24				25+			
	<basic	Basic	Intermediate	Advanced	<basic	Basic	Intermediate	Advanced	<basic	Basic	Intermediate	Advanced
					Saudi Arabia							
2009	2.9	36.1	41.8	19.2	0.2	0.6	26	73.3	0.2	1.6	17.7	80.5
2011	0.2	30.4	55.3	14.2	0	5.5	42.5	52	0.1	3.9	30.6	65.4
2012	0.5	26.9	56	16.6	0	1.7	33.1	65.1	0	2.6	19.4	78.1
2014	0.2	22.2	54.3	23.3	0	2.1	31.8	66.1	0	2.3	25.2	72.5
					Turkey							
2006	7	64.4	19.6	9	3.9	29.8	46.5	19.8	5	42.5	30.5	21.9
2007	7.6	64.1	19.6	8.8	5.2	25.1	45.8	23.9	3.8	38.5	32.5	25.2
2008	7.6	64.8	17.8	9.8	5.4	23.1	43.3	28.2	6.2	42.5	28	23.3
2009	7.1	65	18.5	9.4	6.7	25.8	42.5	25	5.9	42	29.1	23
2010	6.9	64.1	19.4	9.6	5.7	26.7	39.1	28.6	5.3	43.9	27.5	23.4
2011	7.6	61.9	18.1	12.4	5.2	25.1	37.4	32.3	6.3	40.8	26.7	26.3
2012	7.6	59.6	19.2	13.6	3.8	25.3	34.9	36.1	4.8	39.6	25.9	29.7
2013	8.1	59	18.6	14.4	3.8	27.1	34.6	34.5	5.7	40.3	25.9	28
2014	8.1	57.6	19.7	14.6	5.4	26.5	32.9	35.2	5.9	39.2	24.3	30.7
2015	6.5	59	19	15.6	3.6	27	30.8	38.6	6.1	39.1	23.1	31.8
2016	5.8	55.3	20.6	18.3	3.1	24.5	33.6	38.8	6	39	22.1	32.9

Source: ILO.

by aggregate education levels and age and gender. The aggregate levels of education used by the ILO include 4 levels. The first, called less than Basic refers to no schooling. Basic education refers to primary education and depending on the country may also include and age lower secondary or second stage of basic education. The third aggregate classification is called Intermediate education which includes upper secondary education and post-secondary non-tertiary education. The fourth aggregate classification is called Advanced education which refers to short-cycle tertiary education which does not lead directly to an advanced research qualification. At best it may lead to a Bachelor's or equivalent level.

The data in Table 5.6 point to a shortage of jobs for those in the intermediate and advanced education attainment levels. For women and older women especially, the situation is even worse. For Egypt unemployed women over 25 years old, represented 36 percent of the total unemployed in 2016 if they had advanced education and 57.4 percent with intermediate education. The distribution of unemployment for those without education above basic is very low. That speaks volume about the lack of respectable jobs for the 21st century. (World Bank, 2016a, 2016b and 2017)

For Israel the over-representation of women over 25 years old with intermediate and advanced education in 2013 among those unemployed was equally large. Morocco had a similar outcome in terms of unemployment for women with intermediate education. Morocco did not report unemployment levels for women with advanced education. The data for Qatar, Saudi Arabia and Turkey had similar problems for both women and men. There was insufficient employment for those with more education.

The World Bank in a number of reports (2007, 2008, 2009, 2015, 2016a, 2016b, and 2017) has repeatedly concluded that the situation for labor in Arab MENA has worsened in the past 3 decades. The burden of unemployment in Arab MENA is disproportionally born by women and the educated of both genders. The primary cause for this outcome is the lack of a private sector. To avoid unemployment, the educated have to enter the public sector, where they are clearly overqualified.

Chapter 6

Oil Money and the 'Dutch Disease'

Traditional concepts of comparative advantage stress endowments of labor, land, capital and natural resources. Following the framework in Leamer (1984) and assuming Leontief technology, we begin with the system of equations that relate factor supplies to factor demands as follows:

$$K = \alpha_{K1}Y_1 + \alpha_{K2}Y_2, \tag{6.1}$$

$$L = \alpha_{L1}Y_1 + \alpha_{L2}Y_2. \tag{6.2}$$

K and L are the amounts of two factors of production (capital and labor) available in a given country. These amounts are country-specific and are assumed to be internationally immobile. The Y's denote the quantity produced in the given country of two commodities (labeled 1 and 2). The α's are the traditional factor intensities determined by the available production technologies in each sector, and they represent the units of each factor required to produce a unit of output. Equations (6.1) and (6.2) represent a system that can be solved for outputs Y as a function of the inputs K and L and the factor intensities.

In matrix notation, this setup can be generalized to a model with multiple products and multiple factors of production as long as the latter do not exceed the number of products, or as long as the model is just identified or under-identified. Then:

$$\mathbf{Y} = \mathbf{A}^{-1}\mathbf{V}, \tag{6.3}$$

where $\mathbf{Y}$ is the vector of product outputs and $\mathbf{V}$ is the vector of endowments. The $\mathbf{A}$ is the vector of factor intensities, which is invertible as long as the production technologies are different across sectors so that the ratios of factor intensities across sectors are not identical.

Continuing with the presentation in Leamer (1984), the production of the world economy as a whole can also be written in the same format:

$$\mathbf{Y}_W = \mathbf{A}^{-1}\mathbf{V}_W. \tag{6.4}$$

Assuming that countries consume commodities in the same proportions, the country consumption levels can be expressed as:

$$C = s\mathbf{Y}_W, \tag{6.5}$$

where $\mathbf{Y}_W$ is the world's output vector and s is the proportion consumed by each country.

The vector of net exports is simply the product of the inverse of the vector of factor intensities across product clusters and the difference between each country's vector of endowments and the world's vector of endowments. Net exports are the difference between domestic production and consumption:

$$NX = Y - C = \mathbf{A}^{-1}(\mathbf{V} - s\mathbf{V}_W). \tag{6.6}$$

Empirical models of neoclassical trade theory use net exports as the dependent variable, and excess factor endowments as the explanatory variables. The signs of the estimated coefficients on the endowment variables, or the values inside the inverted $\mathbf{A}$ matrix, reflect the factor intensities of production. The inverted vector $\mathbf{A}$ contains factor intensities across product clusters, not relative factor abundances across countries. However, each country's consumption share (relative to the world) is a weighted average of its factor shares (also relative to the world's endowments), so that s is

$$\frac{K}{K_W} > s > \frac{L}{L_W}, \quad \text{or} \quad \frac{K}{K_W} < s < \frac{L}{L_W}. \tag{6.7}$$

That is, a capital-abundant country will have:

$$\frac{K}{K_W} > s > \frac{L}{L_W},$$

while a labor-abundant country will have:

$$\frac{K}{K_W} < s < \frac{L}{L_W}.$$

The "new" trade theories, however, stress that factor "endowments" are not the only factors that explain trade. Other "endowments" such as geography (distance to large markets), technical knowledge, human capital, public infrastructure, quality of institutions, and more generally, the ability of firms to provide the right products to the right markets at the right time, may be just as important.

The theory of international trade has been transformed in recent decades, with the focus of study shifting away from the stylized world of perfect markets, identical technologies across countries, and immobility of factors and inputs of production across borders. Recent literature instead has tended to emphasize the following:

- The role of input trade (Jones, 2000; Findlay and Jones, 2001);
- Frictions in international trade and investment flows due to geography, institutions, transport, and information costs (Venables, 2001; Bond, 2001);
- The transmission of knowledge across borders (Grossman and Helpman, 1991);
- Technological differences across borders (Trefler, 1995; Hakura, 2001); and
- Monopolistic competition in differentiated products with increasing returns to scale (Krugman, 1979; Ruffin, 1999).

While trade theory has evolved to consider the importance of "endowments" in determining comparative advantage, another strand of research that can be traced back to Adam Smith (1776, p. 562) raises the concern that dependence on natural resource rather than on human capital will misdirect a country's comparative advantage and become a "curse." During the past decade, the popular notion referred to as the resource curse hypothesis has re-emerged.

In Tables 6.1 and 6.2 we present basic data for the MENA oil-producing countries. In Table 6.1 we present data on the crude oil production and oil rents as a percent of GDP for the oil-rich MENA countries. Crude oil production is defined as the quantities of oil extracted from the ground after the removal of inert matter or impurities. It includes crude oil, natural gas liquids (NGLs) and additives. This indicator is measured in thousand tonne of oil equivalent (toe). Refinery production refers to the output of secondary oil products from an oil refinery. Oil rents are the difference between the value of crude oil production at world prices and total costs of production. Combined, the data presented for the period 2000–2016 for production and for oil rents up to 2015 paint a credible picture of these countries' dependence on oil revenue, or depletable natural resource savings. In Table 6.2 we present data on the proven reserves for the oil rich MENA countries. At the end of 2016 the proven reserves of these oil rich MENA

Table 6.1. Basic Data on MENA Oil Producing Countries (2000–2016)

	Oil Production in Millions of Toe (tonne of oil equivalent)							Oil Rents (% of GDP)						
Year	Bahrain	Kuwait	Oman	Qatar	SA	UAE	Yemen	Bahrain	Kuwait	Oman	Qatar	SA	UAE	Yemen
2000	9.5	102.5	51.2	31.5	410.1	109.4	21.5	3.0	44.9	41.8	30.4	39.3	18.0	38.7
2001	9.3	100.3	51.1	32.6	396.3	104.6	21.6	2.5	38.3	33.7	25.6	31.2	13.3	30.5
2002	9.4	89.9	48.0	34.1	359.2	97.8	21.6	2.5	32.3	31.5	25.0	29.6	12.2	28.9
2003	9.6	108.6	43.8	33.1	425.9	110.0	21.2	2.9	37.1	31.9	23.8	35.7	15.1	30.8
2004	9.6	118.2	41.8	37.7	451.8	115.0	19.9	2.9	43.8	35.8	27.1	41.3	18.0	33.0
2005	9.5	132.5	41.4	38.1	473.7	116.3	19.7	3.6	54.2	42.4	29.2	51.1	21.1	40.7
2006	9.3	136.2	39.5	40.6	466.3	125.6	18.0	3.7	53.2	40.5	27.3	51.0	23.3	39.1
2007	9.4	132.6	38.0	39.5	446.4	123.7	15.7	3.5	49.3	37.1	21.8	47.8	21.2	32.4
2008	9.3	138.2	37.9	42.1	467.1	126.2	14.0	3.8	54.2	37.1	21.8	54.9	24.2	31.5
2009	9.3	116.5	40.5	36.5	414.5	113.7	13.7	2.4	36.8	28.9	12.9	34.5	15.8	19.1
2010	9.2	119.1	43.1	36.5	413.5	117.8	13.0	3.0	48.0	35.3	14.0	41.6	20.2	20.5
2011	9.7	136.9	44.1	36.5	471.5	130.0	9.7	4.5	60.2	45.5	15.3	49.0	24.8	21.0
2012	8.8	153.7	46.0	36.7	495.8	134.9	7.6	4.8	59.8	41.9	13.7	46.3	24.8	15.2
2013	10.0	150.5	47.1	36.1	488.0	141.8	8.5	4.5	56.1	39.9	12.2	42.9	24.0	14.3
2014	10.3	147.6	47.2	35.3	491.9	141.6	7.1	4.5	53.4	35.3	10.4	38.9	21.4	9.8
2015	10.2	147.2	49.0	32.7	516.2	151.5	1.5	2.6	38.5	20.5	5.9	22.5	11.2	1.9
2016	10.0	154.3	50.1	32.6	531.0	156.4	0.6	NA	NA	NA	NA	NA	NA	NA

Source: Oil Rents from World Bank Data Bank; Oil Production from OECD.

Table 6.2. Oil — Total Proven Reserves for MENA

	At End 1996	At End 2006	At End 2015	At End 2016			
	Thousand Million Barrels	Thousand Million Barrels	Thousand Million Barrels	Thousand Million Barrels	Thousand Million Tonnes	Share of World Total	R/P Ratio
Kuwait	96.5	101.5	101.5	101.5	14	5.9%	88.0
Oman	5.3	5.6	5.3	5.4	0.7	0.3%	14.6
Qatar	3.7	27.4	25.2	25.2	2.6	1.5%	36.3
SA	261.4	264.3	266.6	266.5	36.6	15.6%	59.0
UAE	97.8	97.8	97.8	97.8	13	5.7%	65.6
Yemen	2	2.8	3	3	0.4	0.2%	N/A

Source: BP Statistical Review of World Energy, 2017. London. R/P Ratio is the proven reserves to production ratio.

countries represent 29 percent of the world's proven reserves. The size of the revenue surpluses generated by these oil dollars develop sizeable rents as well as resource misallocation as is demonstrated in the following theoretical section. Both of these sources account for the natural resource "curse", noted in the literature.

6.1. The Basic Model of a Resource Curse

Corden and Neary (1982) and Corden (1984) develop a core model which establishes the implications of having production biased in favor of a dominant resource sector. Assume three sectors: the natural resource sector (R), the non-resource domestic sector (D) and the non-tradeable sector (N). The first two sectors face world market prices. Output in each sector is produced by a factor specific to that sector, α_{ij}, and by labor which is mobile between all three sectors, so as to equalize its wage:

$$\alpha_{lR}X_R + \alpha_{lD}X_D + \alpha_{lN}X_N = L. \tag{6.8}$$

Add a full-employment condition for each of the three sector-specific stocks of "capital":

$$\alpha_{Kj}X_j = K_j, \; (j = R, D, N). \tag{6.9}$$

Using Jones (1965) and totally differentiating output, keeping in mind that the endowments of all factors are fixed, yields:

$$\lambda_{lR}(\hat{\alpha}_{lR} - \hat{\alpha}_{kR}) + \lambda_{lD}(\hat{\alpha}_{lD} - \hat{\alpha}_{kD}) + \lambda_{lN}(\hat{\alpha}_{lN} - \hat{\alpha}_{kN}) = 0, \tag{6.10}$$

where λ_{ij} is the proportion of factor i used in sector j. The elasticity of substitution between labor and capital is:

$$\hat{\alpha}_{Lj} - \hat{\alpha}_{Kj} = \sigma_j(\hat{w} - \hat{r}_j), \quad (j = R, D, N) \tag{6.11}$$

where w is the wage, equal in all sectors, and the three rents are r_R, r_D, r_N. All factor prices are flexible and all factors are internationally immobile.

The equilibrium prices are:

$$\hat{p}_R = \theta_{LR}\hat{w} + \theta_{KR}\hat{r}_R - \pi, \tag{6.12}$$

$$0 = \theta_{LD}\hat{w} + \theta_{KD}\hat{r}_D, \tag{6.13}$$

$$\hat{p}_N = \theta_{LN}\hat{w} + \theta_{KN}\hat{r}_N, \tag{6.14}$$

where θ_{ij} is the share of factor i in the value of output in sector j, and $\hat{p}_D = 0$. Substituting (6.11)–(6.14) into (6.10), holding p_R constant, the impact on w is equal to:

$$\hat{w} = \xi_R\pi + \xi_N\hat{p}_N, \tag{6.15}$$

where ξ_j is the proportional contribution of sector j to Δ, the wage elasticity of the aggregate demand for labor:

$$\xi_j \equiv \frac{I}{\Delta}\lambda_{Lj}\frac{\sigma_j}{\theta_{Kj}}, \quad (j = R, D, N) \quad . \tag{6.16}$$

where

$$\Delta \equiv \lambda_{LR}\frac{\sigma_R}{\theta_{KR}} + \lambda_{LD}\frac{\sigma_D}{\theta_{KD}} + \lambda_{LN}\frac{\sigma_N}{\theta_{KN}}.$$

A boom in R will initially raise aggregate incomes of the factors initially employed there. This boom, according to Corden and Neary (1982) and Corden (1984), can be thought of as happening in a number of ways. An exogenous change in technology improving the output in sector R and confined to the country concerned is one possibility. A second possibility is the windfall gain from a discovery of new resources in sector R. A third possibility is created by an exogenous increase in price of sector R output, relative to the price of imports, which is only for export with no sales at home.

As Corden and Neary (1982) and Corden (1984) point out, if a portion of the extra income generated by R is spent, directly or by the government after R's profits are taxed, and provided the income elasticity of demand for N is positive, the price of N relative to the prices of tradeables must rise.

This in turn will draw resources out of R and D into N, as well as shifting demand away from N toward R and D.

As factors move out of sector R, the marginal product of labor, at a constant wage in terms of tradeables, the demand for labor in R rises and this induces a movement of labor out of D and out of N. First, the movement of labor out of D into R lowers output in D. This can be called direct de-industrialization because it does not involve the market for N and thus does not require an appreciation of the real exchange rate. Second, there is a movement of labor out of N into R at a constant real exchange rate.

The two effects combined, leading to a movement of labor from D to N, bring about what can be called indirect de-industrialization, which supplements the direct de-industrialization that resulted from the movement of labor from D to R. The output of N could finally be higher or lower than initially. The spending effect tends to make it higher and the resource movement effect tends to make it lower.

Corden (1984, footnote 5, pp. 361–362) points out that the spending effect on its own is unambiguous, since (to isolate it) it is assumed that no labor is employed in R (or any labor is specific): hence, before P_N rises, the income of only one factor changes, all extra spending thus coming out of r_R. But the resource movement effect, before P_N changes, raises w, and lowers r_D and r_N.

Spending on N out of r_R and w will rise, and out of r_R and r_N will fall. Only in the special case where the marginal propensities to spend on N are the same and positive for all factors will the spending effect be independent of the resource movement effect, and must always be positive.

In the general case, with marginal propensities differing, the spending effect will depend on the resource movement effect via income distribution. When the marginal propensities to spend on N of initial losers are sufficiently higher than of gainers, the spending effect could actually be negative.

Corden (1984) demonstrates that both effects lower the real rents of the specific factor in D, this being the essential problem of the Dutch Disease, at least as seen from the point of view of this factor. In addition, both effects raise the wage w defined in terms of D, because both increase the demand for labor. But p_N rises, so — bearing in mind that wage-earners also consume N — there is a question whether the "true" real wage w^* (the real wage defined in terms of a consumption basket of tradeables and N) rises or falls. The answer is unambiguous in the case of the resource movement effect: since output of N falls as a result of that effect, the real wage in terms of N (i.e., $\frac{w}{p_N}$) must rise, and since w also rises, w^* must then rise. On the other hand, the spending effect causes N to rise, and hence $\frac{w}{p_N}$ to fall, so that, with w having risen, w^* could have risen or fallen.

Corden and Neary (1982) formally show that the market for the non-tradeables, their supply in the core model depends only on the real wage in this sector:

$$\hat{X}_N = \phi_N(\hat{p}_N - \hat{w}), \tag{6.17}$$

where ϕ_S, the price elasticity of supply, equals $\frac{\sigma_S \theta_{LN}}{\theta_{KN}}$.

The demand and supply for non-tradeables in equilibrium would be:

$$(\phi_N + \varepsilon_N)\hat{p}_N = \phi_N \hat{w} + \eta\phi_R \pi. \tag{6.18}$$

The effects of a shift in resources in R on p_N and w are:

$$A\hat{p}_N = (\eta\phi_R + \phi_N \xi_R)\pi > 0, \tag{6.19}$$

$$A\hat{w} = [\eta\xi_N \theta_R + (\phi_N + \varepsilon_N)\xi_R]\pi > 0, \tag{6.20}$$

where

$$A \equiv \phi_N(I - \xi_N) + \varepsilon_N > 0. \tag{6.21}$$

The expression $(\phi_N + \varepsilon_N)$ is the compensated elasticity of excess supply of non-tradeables at a given wage rate, while A is the same elasticity when the change in w induced by a change in p_N is taken into account.

6.2. The Empirical Evidence on the Resource Curse

The 1990s saw a potpourri of empirical studies that have offered numerical evidence using cross-country growth regressions that "endowments" of natural resources appeared to curse countries with slower growth (Auty, 1993, 2000, 2001a, 2001b, 2006; Davis, 1995; Gylfason, 2001; Gylfason *et al.*, 1999; Neumayer, 2004; Mehlum *et al.*, 2006). They all contend that the resource-rich developing countries across the world have grown more slowly than other developing countries since the 1960s.

Sachs and Warner (1995a, 1995b, 1997a, 1997b, 1999 and 2001) placed the resource curse on the front page in the economic development literature. Their basic idea was that economic growth in economy (i) between time $t = 0$ and $t = T$ should be a negative function of the initial income Y_0^i and a vector of other structural characteristics of the economy Z^i. SXP is the resource measure equal to the ratio of primary exports to GDP. Their reduced-form growth regression equation is as follows:

$$1/T \log\left(\frac{Y_T^i}{Y_0^i}\right) = \delta_0 + \delta_1 \log(Y^i) + \delta_2 SXP + \delta_3 Z^i + \varepsilon^i. \qquad (6.22)$$

Sachs and Warner found that a one standard deviation increase in their resource measure was associated with a reduction in the annual per capita growth rate of approximately 1 percent. Similar results were found using alternative specifications. Humphreys *et al.* (2007) added further credence to the empirical research on the natural resource curse.

Consequently, the conventional wisdom postulates that natural resources are a drag on development.

The research results suggest that an abundance of resources is associated with: (a) slow growth, (b) an enhanced risk of civil war, and (c) autocratic political regimes. In addition to the cross-country studies, country-specific research supports the conclusion that resources may be a hindrance to development. Ross (2001a and 2001b) analyzed the implications of a resource boom on both local institutions and democracy. His findings are as expected; resource booms lead to corruption both in the management of those resources and in democratic institutions that are created. Ross (2001a) along with Jensen and Wantchekon (2004) provide empirical evidence that links oil wealth to autocratic regimes. It is no surprise that oil wealth provides an authoritarian government with sufficient power to hinder or prevent the transition to democracy. That is, it creates a rent-seeking society that creates "pyramids in the desert" (Robinson and Torvik, 2005), patronage (Robinson *et al.*, 2006), military repression (Azam, 2001) and, within MENA, the underrepresentation of women in public service as well as the limited progress toward gender equality (Ross, 2008b). A large flow of "petrodollars" may also weaken an honest government's ability to manage the economy, resulting in poor economic performance (Karl, 1997).

As was pointed out in the core model developed by Corden and Neary (1982) and Corden (1984), the resource-intensive sector, by attracting the flow of labor and specific capital, will create a disincentive to investment in human capital in the non-resource related sector. If the natural resource sector requires low skill levels, then incentives to invest in human capital are reduced further — both for individual workers and for the government. Consequently, there would be a negative impact on long-term growth, given that the endogenous growth models, discussed above, depend on the positive externalities associated with investment in human capital. A number of empirical studies point to a negative correlation between resources and various proxies of educational attainment in resource-rich countries such as the oil-rich Gulf States within Arab MENA. Moreover, the studies suggest that not only will there be a reduced investment in education; openness to trade will deteriorate as corruption increases (Gylfason *et al.*, 1999; Gylfason, 2001; and Papyrakis and Gerlagh, 2004). The various *UNDP Arab Human Development Reports* have suggested that one way of correcting for the "resource curse" would be to target all of these channels by which misallocation of resources occurs.

The shift in the empirical research on the Dutch disease in the late 1990s and early 21st century focused on poor institutions leading to non- optimal social outcomes. This literature can be divided into two broad areas — one focusing on rent-seeking models such as that of Mehlum *et al.* (2006) and the other focusing on patronage models such as that of Robinson *et al.* (2006). In Mehlum *et al.* (2006), entrepreneurs choose between rent-seeking and productive activity. The relative profitability of productive activities depends on the rule of law and bureaucratic efficiency within an economy. High institutional quality leads to equilibrium where all entrepreneurs are producers. In contrast, low institutional quality leads to equilibrium where a portion of entrepreneurs are rent-seekers. An abundance of natural resources lowers national income only in the rent-seeking paradigm. When private institutions are poor, the natural resources become a curse.

The outcome variables for the private sector in MENA are presented in Table 6.3. The variables that we highlight are: (1) the ranking of intellectual property protection with respect to the world and the value of the index from 1 to 7, where 7 is the best; (2) the ranking of soundness of banks with respect to the world and the value of the index from 1 to 7, where 7 is the best; (3) the ranking of the intensity of local competition with respect to the world and the value of the index from 1 to 7, where 7 is the best; (4) the cost of enforcing contracts as a percent of the claim; and (5) the perception of regulatory quality which reflects the private sector's perceptions of the ability of the government to formulate and implement sound policies and regulations that permit and promote private sector development. This index ranges in value from -2.5 (weak) to 2.5 (strong).

The data clearly demonstrates that in the oil-rich countries within MENA, intellectual property protection is less than the average, as is the intensity of private sector competition. Likewise, the regulatory quality is below that of the non-natural resource abundant countries. In the case of oil-abundant MENA countries, where institutions are dysfunctional, the rent-seekers are able to grab a large share of national income for their own

Table 6.3. Outcome Variables for the Private Sector in MENA (2007–2017)

			Weighted Averages									
	Indicator		2007–2008	2008–2009	2009–2010	2010–2011	2011–2012	2012–2013	2013–2014	2014–2015	2015–2016	2016–2017
Country	Indicator (1–7) Best											
Algeria	Intellectual property protection	Rank	95	120	110	—	135	142	145	114	105	108
Algeria	Intellectual property protection	Value	3.0	2.5	2.6	—	2.2	1.8	2.2	2.9	3.3	3.4
Algeria	Soundness of banks	Rank	129	134	127	121	138	143	140	133	128	123
Algeria	Soundness of banks	Value	4.1	3.9	3.7	4.2	3.6	2.9	3.3	3.4	3.4	3.6
Algeria	Intensity of local competition	Rank	95	113	109	93	131	144	141	136	138	136
Algeria	Intensity of local competition	Value	4.4	4.2	4.2	4.5	3.9	3.1	3.6	3.8	3.7	3.8
Algeria	Enforcing Contracts Cost % of claim	Value	21.9	21.9	21.9	21.9	21.9	21.9	21.9	19.9	19.9	19.9
Algeria	Regulatory Quality	Estimate	−0.6	−0.6	−0.8	−1.1	−1.2	−1.2	−1.3	−1.2	−1.3	−1.2
Bahrain	Intellectual property protection	Rank	33	27	25	—	20	28	32	31	31	30
Bahrain	Intellectual property protection	Value	4.7	4.9	5.1	—	5.3	5.1	4.8	4.7	4.8	5.0
Bahrain	Soundness of banks	Rank	23	22	18	19	18	28	44	28	29	47
Bahrain	Soundness of banks	Value	6.5	6.4	6.1	5.9	6.1	5.9	5.6	5.8	5.8	5.4
Bahrain	Intensity of local competition	Rank	56	46	51	40	25	33	40	46	47	61
Bahrain	Intensity of local competition	Value	5.1	5.3	5.2	5.2	5.5	5.4	5.3	5.4	5.3	5.2
Bahrain	Enforcing Contracts Cost % of claim	Value	14.7	14.7	14.7	14.7	14.7	14.7	14.7	14.7	14.7	14.7
Bahrain	Regulatory Quality	Estimate	0.7	0.8	0.7	0.7	0.7	0.7	0.7	0.6	0.7	0.8
Cyprus	Intellectual property protection	Rank	39	35	29	—	38	44	40	39	43	59
Cyprus	Intellectual property protection	Value	4.4	4.7	4.7	—	4.4	4.2	4.4	4.3	4.4	4.3
Cyprus	Soundness of banks	Rank	47	37	22	31	48	83	141	143	139	133
Cyprus	Soundness of banks	Value	5.9	6.1	6.0	5.7	5.6	4.9	3.3	2.4	2.7	2.9
Cyprus	Intensity of local competition	Rank	36	26	16	18	30	43	47	37	46	43

(*Continued*)

Table 6.3. *(Continued)*

	Indicator		Weighted Averages									
			2007–2008	2008–2009	2009–2010	2010–2011	2011–2012	2012–2013	2013–2014	2014–2015	2015–2016	2016–2017
Cyprus	Intensity of local competition	Value	5.4	5.6	5.7	5.6	5.4	5.1	5.2	5.4	5.3	5.3
Cyprus	Enforcing Contracts Cost % of claim	Value	16.4	16.4	16.4	16.4	16.4	16.4	16.4	16.4	16.4	16.4
Cyprus	Regulatory Quality	Estimate	1.3	1.3	1.4	1.4	1.4	1.2	1.1	0.9	1.1	1.1
Egypt	Intellectual property protection	Rank	64	60	58	—	80	83	94	110	108	124
Egypt	Intellectual property protection	Value	3.5	3.6	3.7	—	3.3	3.3	3.2	2.9	3.2	3.2
Egypt	Soundness of banks	Rank	106	111	86	61	102	123	125	110	70	70
Egypt	Soundness of banks	Value	4.7	4.7	5.0	5.3	4.6	4.3	4.0	4.2	4.8	4.8
Egypt	Intensity of local competition	Rank	73	92	83	91	114	121	131	133	128	127
Egypt	Intensity of local competition	Value	4.7	4.6	4.7	4.6	4.1	4.0	4.1	4.0	4.2	4.2
Egypt	Enforcing Contracts Cost % of claim	Value	26.2	26.2	26.2	26.2	26.2	26.2	26.2	26.2	26.2	26.2
Egypt	Regulatory Quality	Estimate	−0.4	−0.3	−0.2	−0.2	−0.2	−0.3	−0.5	−0.6	−0.7	−0.8
Iran	Intellectual property protection	Rank	—	—	—	—	111	112	122	127	130	126
Iran	Intellectual property protection	Value	—	—	—	—	2.7	2.9	2.8	2.7	2.9	3.2
Iran	Soundness of banks	Rank	—	—	—	113	113	104	121	125	121	122
Iran	Soundness of banks	Value	—	—	—	4.4	4.5	4.6	4.1	3.8	3.8	3.7
Iran	Intensity of local competition	Rank	—	—	—	112	106	106	121	119	121	126
Iran	Intensity of local competition	Value	—	—	—	4.2	4.2	4.3	4.3	4.4	4.3	4.2
Iran	Enforcing Contracts Cost % of claim	Value	—	—	—	17	17	17	17	17	17	17
Iran	Regulatory Quality	Estimate	—	—	—	−1.7	−1.7	−1.5	−1.4	−1.5	−1.5	−1.3
Israel	Intellectual property protection	Rank	26	39	44	—	35	33	34	33	29	22
Israel	Intellectual property protection	Value	5.1	4.5	4.0	—	4.6	4.8	4.6	4.6	5.0	5.7
Israel	Soundness of banks	Rank	27	34	19	13	14	17	22	18	19	18
Israel	Soundness of banks	Value	6.3	6.2	6.1	6.3	6.3	6.1	5.9	6.0	6.0	5.9

Israel	Intensity of local competition	Rank	21	32	29	22	27	66	95	126	116	65
Israel	Intensity of local competition	Value	5.6	5.5	5.5	5.6	5.4	4.9	4.7	4.2	4.4	5.2
Israel	Enforcing Contracts Cost % of claim	Value	25.3	25.3	25.3	25.3	25.3	25.3	25.3	25.3	25.3	25.3
Israel	Regulatory Quality	Estimate	1.0	1.1	1.2	1.1	1.2	1.3	1.2	1.2	1.2	1.3
Jordan	Intellectual property protection	Rank	40	36	30	—	40	39	36	34	35	31
Jordan	Intellectual property protection	Value	4.4	4.6	4.7	—	4.2	4.5	4.6	4.6	4.6	4.9
Jordan	Soundness of banks	Rank	57	58	37	51	55	61	59	57	62	48
Jordan	Soundness of banks	Value	5.7	5.8	5.7	5.4	5.5	5.4	5.2	5.2	5.0	5.4
Jordan	Intensity of local competition	Rank	33	24	30	46	34	31	44	57	57	38
Jordan	Intensity of local competition	Value	5.4	5.6	5.4	5.2	5.4	5.4	5.3	5.2	5.2	5.4
Jordan	Enforcing Contracts Cost % of claim	Value	31.2	31.2	31.2	31.2	31.2	31.2	31.2	31.2	31.2	31.2
Jordan	Regulatory Quality	Estimate	0.3	0.3	0.3	0.3	0.2	0.3	0.2	0.1	0.1	0.0
Kuwait	Intellectual property protection	Rank	61	62	47	—	51	46	62	83	84	89
Kuwait	Intellectual property protection	Value	3.6	3.6	4.0	—	3.9	4.0	3.8	3.5	3.7	3.8
Kuwait	Soundness of banks	Rank	30	29	48	64	58	55	45	50	37	30
Kuwait	Soundness of banks	Value	6.3	6.2	5.6	5.3	5.4	5.4	5.6	5.4	5.6	5.8
Kuwait	Intensity of local competition	Rank	60	54	45	60	80	81	110	114	69	59
Kuwait	Intensity of local competition	Value	5.0	5.1	5.3	5.0	4.7	4.7	4.5	4.5	5.0	5.2
Kuwait	Enforcing Contracts Cost % of claim	Value	14.3	14.3	14.3	14.3	14.3	14.3	14.3	18.6	18.6	18.6
Kuwait	Regulatory Quality	Estimate	0.3	0.3	0.2	0.2	0.2	0.1	0.0	−0.1	−0.1	−0.2
Lebanon	Intellectual property protection	Rank	—	—	—	—	112	124	136	139	122	123
Lebanon	Intellectual property protection	Value	—	—	—	—	2.7	2.6	2.4	2.2	3.1	3.2
Lebanon	Soundness of banks	Rank	—	—	—	4	9	12	29	27	23	34
Lebanon	Soundness of banks	Value	—	—	—	6.5	6.4	6.2	5.8	5.8	5.9	5.6

(*Continued*)

Table 6.3. *(Continued)*

	Indicator		Weighted Averages									
			2007–2008	2008–2009	2009–2010	2010–2011	2011–2012	2012–2013	2013–2014	2014–2015	2015–2016	2016–2017
Lebanon	Intensity of local competition	Rank	—	—	—	21	28	35	25	30	34	33
Lebanon	Intensity of local competition	Value	—	—	—	5.6	5.4	5.4	5.5	5.5	5.4	5.4
Lebanon	Enforcing Contracts Cost % of claim	Value	—	—	—	30.8	30.8	30.8	30.8	30.8	30.8	30.8
Lebanon	Regulatory Quality	Estimate	−0.2	−0.3	−0.2	0.0	0.1	0.0	−0.1	−0.1	−0.2	−0.3
Morocco	Intellectual property protection	Rank	54	78	86	—	71	82	90	64	61	55
Morocco	Intellectual property protection	Value	3.8	3.3	3.1	—	3.5	3.4	3.3	3.7	4.0	4.3
Morocco	Soundness of banks	Rank	79	89	78	69	65	53	41	42	54	61
Morocco	Soundness of banks	Value	5.3	5.2	5.2	5.2	5.3	5.5	5.7	5.6	5.2	5.1
Morocco	Intensity of local competition	Rank	84	89	89	69	53	57	60	48	73	70
Morocco	Intensity of local competition	Value	4.6	4.6	4.6	4.9	5.1	5.0	5.1	5.3	5.0	5.1
Morocco	Enforcing Contracts Cost % of claim	Value	25.2	25.2	25.2	25.2	25.2	25.2	25.2	25.2	25.2	25.2
Morocco	Regulatory Quality	Estimate	−0.2	−0.2	−0.2	0.0	−0.1	−0.1	−0.1	−0.1	−0.1	−0.2
Oman	Intellectual property protection	Rank	32	30	26	—	21	25	24	29	40	36
Oman	Intellectual property protection	Value	4.8	4.9	5.0	—	5.3	5.2	5.2	4.9	4.4	4.8
Oman	Soundness of banks	Rank	115	84	35	28	22	21	18	22	38	50
Oman	Soundness of banks	Value	4.6	5.4	5.7	5.7	6.0	6.0	6.0	5.9	5.6	5.3
Oman	Intensity of local competition	Rank	97	84	59	53	54	47	54	73	95	112
Oman	Intensity of local competition	Value	4.4	4.7	5.0	5.1	5.1	5.1	5.2	5.0	4.7	4.6
Oman	Enforcing Contracts Cost % of claim	Value	13.5	13.5	13.5	13.5	13.5	13.5	13.5	13.5	13.5	13.5
Oman	Regulatory Quality	Estimate	0.6	0.6	0.7	0.5	0.5	0.3	0.5	0.5	0.7	0.6
Qatar	Intellectual property protection	Rank	27	25	36	—	15	8	4	5	11	20
Qatar	Intellectual property protection	Value	5.0	5.1	4.5	—	5.5	5.8	6.0	6.0	5.9	5.8
Qatar	Soundness of banks	Rank	44	30	17	46	80	34	13	9	10	20
Qatar	Soundness of banks	Value	5.9	6.2	6.2	5.5	5.0	5.8	6.3	6.3	6.3	5.9

Qatar	Intensity of local competition	Rank	59	53	14	3	5	12	16	18	25	17
Qatar	Intensity of local competition	Value	5.0	5.1	5.7	6.1	5.9	5.7	5.8	5.7	5.5	5.7
Qatar	Enforcing Contracts Cost % of claim	Value	21.6	21.6	21.6	21.6	21.6	21.6	21.6	21.6	21.6	21.6
Qatar	Regulatory Quality	Estimate	0.3	0.4	0.7	0.7	0.6	0.5	0.8	0.8	0.6	0.7
SA	Intellectual property protection	Rank	53	38	31	—	25	27	27	28	30	34
SA	Intellectual property protection	Value	3.9	4.5	4.6	—	5.1	5.1	5.0	4.9	5.0	4.9
SA	Soundness of banks	Rank	62	63	33	20	20	16	15	17	18	27
SA	Soundness of banks	Value	5.6	5.7	5.8	5.9	6.0	6.1	6.1	6.0	6.0	5.8
SA	Intensity of local competition	Rank	51	50	37	24	17	14	18	40	40	37
SA	Intensity of local competition	Value	5.1	5.2	5.3	5.6	5.6	5.7	5.7	5.4	5.4	5.4
SA	Enforcing Contracts Cost % of claim	Value	27.5	27.5	27.5	27.5	27.5	27.5	27.5	27.5	27.5	27.5
SA	Regulatory Quality	Estimate	−0.1	0.0	0.1	0.2	0.2	0.0	0.1	0.1	0.0	0.0
Syria	Intellectual property protection	Rank	79	54	59	—	72	—	—	—	—	—
Syria	Intellectual property protection	Value	3.3	3.8	3.7	—	3.5	—	—	—	—	—
Syria	Soundness of banks	Rank	105	103	68	63	59	—	—	—	—	—
Syria	Soundness of banks	Value	4.7	5.0	5.2	5.3	5.4	—	—	—	—	—
Syria	Intensity of local competition	Rank	49	62	67	70	44	—	—	—	—	—
Syria	Intensity of local competition	Value	5.1	5.1	4.9	4.9	5.2	—	—	—	—	—
Syria	Enforcing Contracts Cost % of claim	Value	29.3	29.3	29.3	29.3	29.3	—	—	—	—	—
Syria	Regulatory Quality	Estimate	−1.4	−1.3	−1.1	−1.0	−0.9	−0.9	−1.5	−1.6	−1.7	−1.6
Tunisia	Intellectual property protection	Rank	35	40	43	—	56	—	97	102	90	79
Tunisia	Intellectual property protection	Value	4.6	4.4	4.0	—	3.8	—	3.2	3.1	3.5	3.9
Tunisia	Soundness of banks	Rank	76	85	76	59	84	—	131	128	131	127
Tunisia	Soundness of banks	Value	5.3	5.3	5.2	5.3	5.0	—	3.9	3.5	3.2	3.4
Tunisia	Intensity of local competition	Rank	41	34	40	34	42	—	80	92	90	84
Tunisia	Intensity of local competition	Value	5.3	5.4	5.3	5.4	5.2	—	4.9	4.8	4.7	4.9
Tunisia	Enforcing Contracts Cost % of claim	Value	21.8	21.8	21.8	21.8	21.8	21.8	21.8	21.8	21.8	21.8
Tunisia	Regulatory Quality	Estimate	0.1	0.1	0.1	0.0	0.0	-0.2	-0.2	-0.3	-0.4	-0.4

(Continued)

Table 6.3. (*Continued*)

	Indicator		Weighted Averages									
			2007–2008	2008–2009	2009–2010	2010–2011	2011–2012	2012–2013	2013–2014	2014–2015	2015–2016	2016–2017
Turkey	Intellectual property protection	Rank	69	93	105	—	108	86	74	72	82	95
Turkey	Intellectual property protection	Value	3.4	3.0	2.7	—	2.7	3.3	3.6	3.7	3.7	3.7
Turkey	Soundness of banks	Rank	92	114	89	36	33	22	20	38	51	55
Turkey	Soundness of banks	Value	5.0	4.7	5.0	5.6	5.8	6.0	6.0	5.7	5.3	5.2
Turkey	Intensity of local competition	Rank	31	42	32	15	13	16	15	11	10	12
Turkey	Intensity of local competition	Value	5.5	5.3	5.4	5.7	5.7	5.7	5.8	5.9	5.9	5.9
Turkey	Enforcing Contracts Cost % of claim	Value	27.3	27.3	27.3	27.3	27.3	27.3	27.3	27.9	27.9	24.9
Turkey	Regulatory Quality	Estimate	0.3	0.3	0.3	0.3	0.3	0.4	0.4	0.4	0.4	0.3
UAE	Intellectual property protection	Rank	31	24	15	—	27	23	20	18	22	24
UAE	Intellectual property protection	Value	4.8	5.2	5.6	—	5.0	5.2	5.3	5.5	5.5	5.7
UAE	Soundness of banks	Rank	38	31	36	50	54	48	38	23	21	17
UAE	Soundness of banks	Value	6.1	6.2	5.7	5.4	5.5	5.6	5.7	5.9	5.9	5.9
UAE	Intensity of local competition	Rank	35	28	9	13	19	15	17	9	8	9
UAE	Intensity of local competition	Value	5.4	5.6	5.8	5.7	5.6	5.7	5.7	6.0	6.0	5.9
UAE	Enforcing Contracts Cost % of claim	Value	19.5	19.5	19.5	19.5	19.5	19.5	19.5	19.5	19.5	20.1
UAE	Regulatory Quality	Estimate	0.6	0.6	0.6	0.5	0.3	0.5	0.7	0.8	1.0	1.1
Yemen	Intellectual property protection	Rank	—	—	—	—	141	139	138	137	—	137
Yemen	Intellectual property protection	Value	—	—	—	—	1.7	2.0	2.4	2.3	—	2.3
Yemen	Soundness of banks	Rank	—	—	—	—	137	138	142	137	—	132
Yemen	Soundness of banks	Value	—	—	—	—	3.7	3.4	3.1	3.0	—	3.1
Yemen	Intensity of local competition	Rank	—	—	—	—	77	80	118	125	—	125
Yemen	Intensity of local competition	Value	—	—	—	—	4.7	4.7	4.4	4.3	—	4.3
Yemen	Enforcing Contracts Cost % of claim	Value	—	—	—	—	26.5	26.5	26.5	30.0	30.0	30.0
Yemen	Regulatory Quality	Estimate	−0.8	−0.7	−0.7	−0.6	−0.6	−0.8	−0.7	−0.7	−0.8	−1.1

Source: World Bank, TC Data 360.

private benefit. Mehlum *et al.* (2006) predict that resource booms tend to reduce total income in rent-seeking economies and raise income in producer-friendly economies. The latter effect follows because of the extra income which the resource-rich country will receive. The former effect follows from the reallocation of talent from the manufacturing to the rent-seeking sector after a boom.

In reality, resource rents accrue to resource owners, who, in the oil-rich MENA, are the members of the government who in turn can allocate them to their preferred beneficiaries. It has been argued that such rents are easily appropriable by elites, leading to bribes and distortions in public policies (Karl, 1997; Tornell and Lane, 1999; Torvik, 2002). As noted in the core model above, rent-seeking may also affect economic production in the domestic economy through crowding out of talent, and it may shift entrepreneurial activity from the domestic and non-tradeable sectors to the resource sector. Atkinson and Hamilton (2003) captured the adverse effects of rent-seeking on an economy by using the concept that extracting a resource is equivalent to de-saving of national wealth. Their empirical analysis found that resource-rich countries like those in the oil-rich MENA use their resource money for government consumption rather than investment, and consequently become part of the resource curse.

Robinson *et al.* (2006) focused on the political foundations of the curse and highlighted perverse incentives for incumbent policymakers. Wealth generated by natural resources raises the value of staying in power for the elite. In the case of the oil-rich MENA, the autocracies that control the oil wealth are unaccountable to any constituency. Consequently, these same autocratic leaders have an incentive to create unproductive public sector employment via nepotism.

Robinson *et al.* (2006) point out that these elites are motivated by a desire to prolong their reign by appointing friends to positions of power, thereby redistributing income and consequently creating resource curse-type outcomes. The degree to which this outcome is possible depends on the institutional setting within which policymakers operate.

In Table 6.4 we present 5 global perception indices of the public sector and the Rule of Law in MENA for the period 1996 to 2016. These indices are developed by Kaufmann *et al.* (2010) for the World Bank as part of the Worldwide Governance Indicators (WGI) project. The first indicator — Rule of Law — "reflects perceptions of the extent to which agents have confidence in and abide by the rules of society, and the quality of contract enforcement, property rights, the police, and the courts, as well as

Table 6.4. Global Perceptions of the Public Sector and the Rule of Law in MENA

Country	Indicator		1996	1998	2000	2002	2003	2004	2005	2006	2007	2008	2009	2010	2011	2012	2013	2014	2015	2016
Algeria	Rule of Law	Rank	12.56	12.50	11.88	33.17	31.68	33.49	28.23	27.75	24.88	25.48	23.22	26.54	24.41	26.76	30.99	24.04	18.75	19.23
Algeria	Rule of Law	Estimate	−1.22	−1.16	−1.21	−0.63	−0.59	−0.62	−0.75	−0.71	−0.77	−0.74	−0.79	−0.78	−0.81	−0.77	−0.69	−0.77	−0.87	−0.85
Algeria	Government Effectiveness	Rank	13.11	19.69	14.87	31.12	31.12	34.48	39.22	38.05	32.52	31.07	35.41	38.76	36.02	35.07	35.07	35.10	35.58	35.10
Algeria	Government Effectiveness	Estimate	−1.09	−0.83	−0.96	−0.60	−0.61	−0.57	−0.47	−0.47	−0.57	−0.63	−0.58	−0.48	−0.56	−0.53	−0.53	−0.48	−0.50	−0.54
Algeria	Voice and Accountability	Rank	14.50	12.44	14.43	18.91	18.91	23.56	25.48	22.60	20.19	20.67	17.54	18.48	20.19	22.54	23.94	25.12	24.63	23.65
Algeria	Voice and Accountability	Estimate	−1.17	−1.24	−1.11	−1.04	−1.08	−0.80	−0.72	−0.92	−0.98	−0.98	−1.04	−1.02	−1.00	−0.91	−0.89	−0.82	−0.84	−0.88
Algeria	Regulatory Quality	Rank	20.11	22.80	23.08	29.59	32.14	30.05	42.65	29.41	27.18	21.36	12.92	9.57	9.95	9.00	11.85	8.17	10.58	10.10
Algeria	Regulatory Quality	Estimate	−0.91	−0.74	−0.71	−0.58	−0.52	−0.54	−0.38	−0.57	−0.62	−0.79	−1.07	−1.17	−1.19	−1.28	−1.17	−1.28	−1.17	−1.17
Algeria	Control of Corruption	Rank	33.33	22.16	18.78	23.23	28.79	27.80	40.00	36.59	34.47	33.01	33.49	36.67	35.07	37.44	39.34	32.21	28.85	27.40
Algeria	Control of Corruption	Estimate	−0.57	−0.88	−0.94	−0.88	−0.69	−0.68	−0.48	−0.52	−0.56	−0.59	−0.58	−0.52	−0.54	−0.50	−0.47	−0.60	−0.66	−0.69
Bahrain	Rule of Law	Rank	50.75	65.00	61.88	68.32	71.29	71.29	67.46	61.72	66.51	65.87	64.45	63.51	62.44	61.50	61.97	68.27	67.31	66.35
Bahrain	Rule of Law	Estimate	−0.01	0.38	0.30	0.57	0.62	0.71	0.61	0.38	0.53	0.53	0.52	0.44	0.35	0.26	0.33	0.41	0.43	0.46
Bahrain	Government Effectiveness	Rank	77.05	74.09	72.82	70.92	68.88	70.94	65.69	66.83	66.99	66.50	67.94	67.94	68.72	69.67	70.14	72.60	73.08	65.87

(Continued)

Table 6.4. *(Continued)*

Country	Indicator		1996	1998	2000	2002	2003	2004	2005	2006	2007	2008	2009	2010	2011	2012	2013	2014	2015	2016
Bahrain	Government Effectiveness	Estimate	0.78	0.60	0.59	0.55	0.48	0.55	0.40	0.40	0.41	0.39	0.48	0.46	0.52	0.55	0.59	0.57	0.56	0.32
Bahrain	Voice and Accountability	Rank	25.50	16.42	17.41	31.34	30.35	31.25	25.00	23.56	25.00	23.08	26.54	19.91	13.15	11.27	12.21	11.33	11.82	8.37
Bahrain	Voice and Accountability	Estimate	−0.72	−1.07	−1.06	−0.57	−0.59	−0.56	−0.74	−0.90	−0.86	−0.87	−0.79	−0.97	−1.22	−1.32	−1.32	−1.31	−1.31	−1.45
Bahrain	Regulatory Quality	Rank	74.46	75.65	78.46	77.04	70.41	72.91	70.10	71.08	73.30	73.30	73.68	74.64	75.83	73.93	71.56	74.04	76.44	72.12
Bahrain	Regulatory Quality	Estimate	0.79	0.81	0.79	0.91	0.65	0.71	0.66	0.68	0.77	0.71	0.69	0.71	0.72	0.69	0.61	0.71	0.82	0.61
Bahrain	Control of Corruption	Rank	63.98	63.92	68.02	79.29	70.71	70.24	66.34	61.46	60.68	62.14	63.64	63.33	63.98	67.77	68.72	63.94	61.06	56.25
Bahrain	Control of Corruption	Estimate	0.33	0.27	0.38	0.82	0.40	0.45	0.39	0.19	0.18	0.19	0.19	0.18	0.22	0.37	0.43	0.28	0.14	−0.06
Cyprus	Rule of Law	Rank	78.39	81.00	83.66	81.68	80.20	79.43	79.90	87.08	85.65	87.50	86.73	87.20	83.10	84.04	82.16	82.69	81.73	75.48
Cyprus	Rule of Law	Estimate	0.86	0.98	1.04	1.02	0.97	0.92	0.89	1.11	1.12	1.22	1.21	1.22	1.07	1.10	1.04	1.08	1.04	0.73
Cyprus	Government Effectiveness	Rank	85.25	87.05	85.13	87.24	84.69	83.25	84.31	86.34	88.35	89.81	88.04	90.91	92.42	88.15	88.15	83.65	81.25	78.37
Cyprus	Government Effectiveness	Estimate	1.17	1.25	1.13	1.35	1.18	1.13	1.16	1.27	1.43	1.53	1.42	1.53	1.56	1.39	1.37	1.14	1.05	0.98
Cyprus	Voice and Accountability	Rank	78.50	76.62	80.60	84.08	78.61	79.81	79.81	82.21	83.65	84.62	82.46	79.15	80.75	79.34	77.46	78.33	80.79	82.76

(Continued)

Table 6.4. *(Continued)*

Country	Indicator		1996	1998	2000	2002	2003	2004	2005	2006	2007	2008	2009	2010	2011	2012	2013	2014	2015	2016
Cyprus	Voice and Accountability	Estimate	1.04	0.98	1.06	1.12	0.99	0.95	0.96	1.05	1.07	1.08	1.07	1.02	1.05	1.02	0.98	1.02	1.03	1.08
Cyprus	Regulatory Quality	Rank	86.96	86.53	84.10	85.20	85.71	86.21	84.80	87.75	87.86	88.35	88.52	90.43	86.26	83.89	78.20	82.69	80.77	82.69
Cyprus	Regulatory Quality	Estimate	1.26	1.21	1.14	1.24	1.21	1.23	1.22	1.28	1.33	1.37	1.36	1.42	1.24	1.13	0.92	1.10	1.06	1.05
Cyprus	Control of Corruption	Rank	87.63	83.51	84.77	84.34	85.35	80.00	79.51	83.41	83.50	84.95	78.47	80.00	77.73	85.31	84.83	82.21	80.77	77.88
Cyprus	Control of Corruption	Estimate	1.33	1.10	1.12	1.16	1.23	0.89	0.91	1.09	1.08	1.20	0.91	0.97	0.87	1.25	1.25	1.08	1.01	0.82
Djibouti	Rule of Law	Rank	18.59	23.00	23.76	19.31	21.29	22.01	19.14	22.49	25.36	32.21	30.33	28.44	24.88	24.88	26.29	19.23	17.79	17.31
Djibouti	Rule of Law	Estimate	−0.97	−0.85	−0.89	−0.92	−0.87	−0.85	−0.96	−0.88	−0.76	−0.64	−0.68	−0.73	−0.81	−0.79	−0.77	−0.87	−0.92	−0.97
Djibouti	Government Effectiveness	Rank	20.22	13.47	11.79	23.47	28.57	33.99	24.51	20.49	19.90	19.42	20.57	15.79	17.54	14.69	17.06	16.35	16.83	16.83
Djibouti	Government Effectiveness	Estimate	−0.89	−1.03	−1.03	−0.80	−0.66	−0.59	−0.80	−0.88	−0.86	−0.87	−0.89	−0.97	−0.95	−1.06	−0.96	−0.97	−0.95	−0.97
Djibouti	Voice and Accountability	Rank	21.50	18.41	22.89	23.88	28.36	25.00	15.87	17.31	13.94	13.94	13.74	13.27	8.92	7.98	7.51	8.37	9.36	12.81
Djibouti	Voice and Accountability	Estimate	−0.88	−0.99	−0.88	−0.83	−0.67	−0.78	−1.11	−1.12	−1.20	−1.20	−1.21	−1.27	−1.41	−1.43	−1.47	−1.43	−1.41	−1.32
Djibouti	Regulatory Quality	Rank	16.30	14.51	22.56	32.65	22.45	25.62	23.04	22.55	23.30	27.18	28.71	27.75	32.70	36.49	32.23	31.73	27.88	25.48
Djibouti	Regulatory Quality	Estimate	−1.00	−1.02	−0.71	−0.53	−0.72	−0.65	−0.78	−0.75	−0.70	−0.66	−0.61	−0.63	−0.54	−0.43	−0.52	−0.53	−0.70	−0.70

(Continued)

Table 6.4. (Continued)

Country	Indicator		1996	1998	2000	2002	2003	2004	2005	2006	2007	2008	2009	2010	2011	2012	2013	2014	2015	2016
Djibouti	Control of Corruption	Rank	29.03	27.32	18.27	28.28	22.22	33.17	27.32	30.24	35.44	44.66	43.06	41.90	41.23	38.86	35.55	32.69	29.33	30.29
Djibouti	Control of Corruption	Estimate	−0.72	−0.78	−0.95	−0.74	−0.82	−0.58	−0.71	−0.66	−0.54	−0.33	−0.37	−0.40	−0.41	−0.46	−0.54	−0.60	−0.66	−0.65
Egypt	Rule of Law	Rank	51.76	50.00	50.99	54.46	53.96	52.63	52.63	47.37	48.33	51.44	52.61	49.76	41.78	40.38	33.33	29.33	31.25	35.58
Egypt	Rule of Law	Estimate	0.00	−0.04	−0.01	0.01	0.02	0.02	−0.02	−0.26	−0.23	−0.13	−0.11	−0.18	−0.45	−0.47	−0.63	−0.66	−0.59	−0.41
Egypt	Government Effectiveness	Rank	36.07	48.70	48.21	41.33	44.90	47.29	40.69	36.10	43.20	43.20	47.37	42.11	35.07	23.22	20.85	20.19	22.12	27.88
Egypt	Government Effectiveness	Estimate	−0.47	−0.23	−0.22	−0.41	−0.34	−0.27	−0.42	−0.51	−0.39	−0.37	−0.28	−0.37	−0.57	−0.81	−0.88	−0.82	−0.75	−0.66
Egypt	Voice and Accountability	Rank	22.00	21.39	22.39	16.42	18.41	21.63	21.15	14.42	14.90	13.46	14.22	13.74	14.08	25.82	16.90	14.78	14.78	14.29
Egypt	Voice and Accountability	Estimate	−0.84	−0.91	−0.89	−1.10	−1.08	−0.95	−0.96	−1.20	−1.17	−1.21	−1.16	−1.19	−1.14	−0.77	−1.05	−1.18	−1.18	−1.23
Egypt	Regulatory Qualtiy	Rank	53.26	37.31	36.92	35.71	27.55	33.00	38.73	36.76	43.20	49.51	46.89	46.89	41.23	33.65	29.38	26.44	22.12	17.79
Egypt	Regulatory Qualtiy	Estimate	−0.05	−0.33	−0.34	−0.48	−0.60	−0.51	−0.42	−0.44	−0.29	−0.18	−0.20	−0.17	−0.34	−0.48	−0.64	−0.76	−0.84	−0.92
Egypt	Control of Corruption	Rank	38.71	38.66	34.01	42.42	35.35	29.27	31.22	25.37	24.27	23.79	36.36	30.95	25.59	33.18	31.75	30.77	30.29	32.21
Egypt	Control of Corruption	Estimate	−0.47	−0.46	−0.55	−0.41	−0.55	−0.65	−0.62	−0.75	−0.76	−0.78	−0.52	−0.63	−0.70	−0.60	−0.63	−0.62	−0.64	−0.63

(Continued)

Table 6.4. *(Continued)*

Country	Indicator		1996	1998	2000	2002	2003	2004	2005	2006	2007	2008	2009	2010	2011	2012	2013	2014	2015	2016
Iran	Rule of Law	Rank	19.60	28.50	34.65	26.73	30.20	31.58	23.44	19.14	15.79	20.67	17.54	15.64	17.37	19.72	16.43	12.50	17.31	25.96
Iran	Rule of Law	Estimate	−0.94	−0.67	−0.51	−0.78	−0.64	−0.66	−0.83	−0.95	−0.97	−0.91	−0.97	−1.02	−0.97	−0.92	−1.00	−1.06	−0.92	−0.71
Iran	Government Effectiveness	Rank	32.79	35.75	36.92	34.18	38.27	40.39	33.33	35.12	30.10	30.58	36.84	39.23	41.23	35.55	28.91	37.98	46.63	45.67
Iran	Government Effectiveness	Estimate	−0.60	−0.48	−0.49	−0.54	−0.47	−0.44	−0.62	−0.53	−0.61	−0.64	−0.55	−0.48	−0.43	−0.53	−0.68	−0.43	−0.21	−0.20
Iran	Voice and Accountability	Rank	19.50	23.38	21.39	17.41	11.44	12.98	10.58	8.17	7.69	7.21	6.64	6.64	7.04	5.63	5.16	5.91	7.88	11.33
Iran	Voice and Accountability	Estimate	−0.95	−0.86	−0.93	−1.08	−1.25	−1.23	−1.28	−1.50	−1.55	−1.57	−1.58	−1.61	−1.58	−1.60	−1.61	−1.58	−1.51	−1.39
Iran	Regulatory Quality	Rank	7.07	6.22	6.67	8.16	11.73	9.36	11.76	5.88	3.40	2.91	2.87	2.87	5.69	7.11	5.69	4.81	6.73	9.13
Iran	Regulatory Quality	Estimate	−1.42	−1.64	−1.65	−1.29	−1.18	−1.26	−1.20	−1.46	−1.62	−1.63	−1.72	−1.71	−1.52	−1.43	−1.49	−1.46	−1.31	−1.23
Iran	Control of Corruption	Rank	37.63	39.69	39.59	50.00	47.47	42.44	39.51	38.05	34.95	24.27	20.57	17.62	20.38	23.22	27.96	31.25	31.73	25.96
Iran	Control of Corruption	Estimate	−0.48	−0.45	−0.40	−0.19	−0.27	−0.39	−0.48	−0.48	−0.55	−0.78	−0.84	−0.95	−0.87	−0.79	−0.69	−0.62	−0.60	−0.72
Israel	Rule of Law	Rank	88.44	83.00	82.67	83.66	79.70	76.56	75.60	77.99	74.64	75.48	74.41	79.62	80.28	78.87	80.75	83.65	85.10	81.25
Israel	Rule of Law	Estimate	1.28	1.03	1.02	1.10	0.94	0.86	0.82	0.90	0.83	0.85	0.84	0.92	1.01	0.93	0.98	1.11	1.16	1.02
Israel	Government Effectiveness	Rank	75.96	83.94	84.10	83.67	85.20	87.19	82.84	85.37	84.95	87.38	86.12	88.04	87.20	87.20	85.78	87.02	87.50	88.94

(Continued)

Table 6.4. *(Continued)*

Country	Indicator		1996	1998	2000	2002	2003	2004	2005	2006	2007	2008	2009	2010	2011	2012	2013	2014	2015	2016
Israel	Government Effectiveness	Estimate	0.77	1.09	1.11	1.08	1.20	1.26	1.04	1.25	1.24	1.33	1.28	1.39	1.34	1.28	1.25	1.21	1.39	1.35
Israel	Voice and Accountability	Rank	69.00	66.17	68.66	66.17	67.16	69.71	68.27	71.15	69.71	69.23	65.40	66.82	67.61	67.61	67.14	70.94	71.92	71.92
Israel	Voice and Accountability	Estimate	0.70	0.62	0.69	0.59	0.64	0.66	0.65	0.77	0.74	0.72	0.57	0.58	0.65	0.64	0.65	0.73	0.74	0.77
Israel	Regulatory Quality	Rank	83.15	85.49	83.59	78.57	76.53	76.35	73.04	78.92	83.98	85.44	83.25	84.69	87.20	85.78	85.78	86.54	86.06	87.50
Israel	Regulatory Quality	Estimate	1.08	1.10	1.13	0.96	0.94	0.83	0.86	1.00	1.10	1.17	1.10	1.22	1.32	1.18	1.17	1.22	1.27	1.31
Israel	Control of Corruption	Rank	88.17	84.54	84.26	85.35	83.33	81.95	79.02	80.49	77.18	78.64	74.64	74.29	76.30	77.73	78.67	78.85	79.33	81.73
Israel	Control of Corruption	Estimate	1.35	1.19	1.05	1.23	1.12	0.93	0.83	1.01	0.85	0.90	0.81	0.76	0.80	0.91	0.91	0.87	0.94	1.06
Jordan	Rule of Law	Rank	60.80	64.50	63.86	57.43	63.86	59.81	60.77	61.24	61.24	62.50	61.61	61.14	61.50	62.91	62.91	68.75	67.79	62.02
Jordan	Rule of Law	Estimate	0.28	0.35	0.37	0.11	0.36	0.32	0.33	0.33	0.39	0.41	0.25	0.19	0.24	0.37	0.39	0.46	0.44	0.31
Jordan	Government Effectiveness	Rank	56.83	59.07	55.90	61.22	64.29	60.10	56.86	60.98	61.65	62.14	62.20	58.85	58.77	55.92	53.55	59.13	59.13	58.65
Jordan	Government Effectiveness	Estimate	−0.03	0.05	−0.02	0.11	0.21	0.06	0.03	0.20	0.23	0.23	0.24	0.10	0.09	−0.01	−0.05	0.12	0.12	0.14
Jordan	Voice and Accountability	Rank	42.00	36.32	41.79	25.37	29.85	31.73	32.21	27.88	28.85	26.92	27.01	27.01	26.29	26.76	24.88	26.60	25.62	25.12

(Continued)

Table 6.4. *(Continued)*

Country	Indicator		1996	1998	2000	2002	2003	2004	2005	2006	2007	2008	2009	2010	2011	2012	2013	2014	2015	2016
Jordan	Voice and Accountability	Estimate	−0.24	−0.42	−0.28	−0.80	−0.63	−0.55	−0.51	−0.72	−0.68	−0.74	−0.78	−0.80	−0.80	−0.73	−0.81	−0.75	−0.77	−0.76
Jordan	Regulatory Quality	Rank	55.43	66.32	63.08	57.65	59.18	64.53	56.37	61.27	61.17	61.65	59.33	57.42	59.72	56.87	56.87	54.81	54.81	54.33
Jordan	Regulatory Quality	Estimate	0.02	0.42	0.26	0.04	0.21	0.29	0.10	0.33	0.31	0.32	0.27	0.23	0.30	0.19	0.14	0.08	0.08	0.05
Jordan	Control of Corruption	Rank	55.38	59.79	59.39	56.06	65.66	61.95	62.93	64.39	64.08	66.50	62.20	59.52	61.14	60.66	60.19	59.62	64.42	64.42
Jordan	Control of Corruption	Estimate	−0.04	0.10	0.08	−0.05	0.31	0.26	0.26	0.26	0.26	0.36	0.16	0.04	0.10	0.07	0.07	0.14	0.26	0.27
Kuwait	Rule of Law	Rank	67.34	70.50	67.82	69.31	68.32	66.03	65.07	65.07	68.90	68.27	66.82	66.82	66.20	62.44	62.44	59.62	57.21	56.73
Kuwait	Rule of Law	Estimate	0.60	0.64	0.57	0.61	0.57	0.52	0.54	0.54	0.60	0.59	0.59	0.59	0.55	0.37	0.37	0.02	0.00	0.03
Kuwait	Government Effectiveness	Rank	59.02	55.96	53.85	61.73	62.76	61.58	60.29	63.41	56.31	55.83	60.77	60.77	55.92	51.66	52.61	47.12	52.88	46.63
Kuwait	Government Effectiveness	Estimate	0.12	−0.06	−0.08	0.11	0.12	0.10	0.17	0.29	0.10	−0.01	0.20	0.17	0.02	−0.07	−0.07	−0.15	−0.03	−0.18
Kuwait	Voice and Accountability	Rank	41.50	41.29	39.80	39.80	38.31	39.90	33.65	30.77	32.21	30.29	31.75	30.33	30.05	27.70	28.17	28.57	28.08	28.08
Kuwait	Voice and Accountability	Estimate	−0.24	−0.30	−0.30	−0.36	−0.40	−0.30	−0.48	−0.58	−0.55	−0.54	−0.48	−0.52	−0.56	−0.64	−0.66	−0.66	−0.66	−0.69
Kuwait	Regulatory Quality	Rank	64.13	51.81	52.82	64.80	66.84	68.47	63.73	59.80	58.74	56.80	56.46	55.50	54.98	52.61	50.71	49.04	48.56	52.88
Kuwait	Regulatory Quality	Estimate	0.31	−0.04	−0.03	0.36	0.41	0.57	0.47	0.30	0.26	0.17	0.15	0.16	0.08	−0.04	−0.07	−0.15	−0.17	−0.07
Kuwait	Control of Corruption	Rank	70.43	74.23	73.60	82.83	77.27	76.10	69.27	69.76	69.42	68.93	67.46	65.24	59.72	52.13	52.61	50.96	51.44	50.00

(Continued)

Table 6.4. *(Continued)*

Country	Indicator		1996	1998	2000	2002	2003	2004	2005	2006	2007	2008	2009	2010	2011	2012	2013	2014	2015	2016
Kuwait	Control of Corruption	Estimate	0.48	0.59	0.59	1.01	0.80	0.79	0.51	0.43	0.37	0.42	0.31	0.30	0.09	−0.19	−0.19	−0.24	−0.23	−0.20
Lebanon	Rule of Law	Rank	42.21	41.50	46.04	44.55	42.08	44.02	43.54	30.62	28.71	28.85	28.91	29.38	29.58	27.23	25.82	24.52	21.15	18.75
Lebanon	Rule of Law	Estimate	−0.28	−0.31	−0.17	−0.31	−0.39	−0.26	−0.33	−0.64	−0.70	−0.67	−0.68	−0.71	−0.69	−0.75	−0.78	−0.77	−0.83	−0.86
Lebanon	Government Effectiveness	Rank	51.37	57.51	48.72	46.94	50.00	47.78	48.53	45.85	44.66	41.26	39.71	44.98	45.97	44.08	42.65	40.87	37.02	35.58
Lebanon	Government Effectiveness	Estimate	−0.13	−0.01	−0.19	−0.29	−0.21	−0.26	−0.19	−0.26	−0.33	−0.42	−0.47	−0.28	−0.27	−0.35	−0.40	−0.38	−0.47	−0.53
Lebanon	Voice and Accountability	Rank	39.00	37.31	39.30	28.86	33.33	36.54	40.38	33.65	33.65	34.13	35.55	36.02	34.74	35.21	35.21	33.50	31.03	31.53
Lebanon	Voice and Accountability	Estimate	−0.33	−0.40	−0.31	−0.66	−0.49	−0.41	−0.28	−0.39	−0.47	−0.42	−0.36	−0.33	−0.39	−0.39	−0.40	−0.42	−0.46	−0.52
Lebanon	Regulatory Quality	Rank	34.78	46.63	35.38	41.84	51.53	50.74	49.51	47.55	46.60	46.60	52.15	53.59	51.66	47.87	49.29	45.67	43.75	40.87
Lebanon	Regulatory Quality	Estimate	−0.41	−0.16	−0.37	−0.36	−0.11	−0.09	−0.16	−0.21	−0.26	−0.25	−0.05	0.05	−0.06	−0.12	−0.08	−0.25	−0.29	−0.34
Lebanon	Control of Corruption	Rank	31.18	40.72	34.52	38.38	30.30	28.29	37.56	18.54	19.42	20.87	21.53	20.00	19.43	19.43	19.43	13.94	19.23	13.94
Lebanon	Control of Corruption	Estimate	−0.66	−0.45	−0.54	−0.48	−0.67	−0.66	−0.53	−0.94	−0.89	−0.82	−0.83	−0.88	−0.90	−0.87	−0.92	−1.04	−0.88	−0.97
Morocco	Rule of Law	Rank	59.30	60.50	54.95	52.97	50.50	51.20	45.93	46.41	46.41	46.63	48.34	50.24	48.83	48.83	46.95	54.33	54.81	49.04
Morocco	Rule of Law	Estimate	0.22	0.23	0.13	−0.02	−0.08	−0.03	−0.16	−0.29	−0.30	−0.30	−0.21	−0.17	−0.23	−0.21	−0.25	−0.07	−0.09	−0.14

(Continued)

Table 6.4. *(Continued)*

Country	Indicator		1996	1998	2000	2002	2003	2004	2005	2006	2007	2008	2009	2010	2011	2012	2013	2014	2015	2016
Morocco	Government Effectiveness	Rank	55.19	58.03	54.36	51.02	53.06	53.20	46.57	51.22	50.97	48.54	50.72	50.24	48.82	52.61	54.03	50.48	50.96	50.96
Morocco	Government Effectiveness	Estimate	−0.10	0.00	−0.07	−0.15	−0.14	−0.13	−0.28	−0.16	−0.17	−0.18	−0.14	−0.10	−0.15	−0.06	−0.04	−0.07	−0.06	−0.10
Morocco	Voice and Accountability	Rank	36.50	42.79	34.33	34.83	26.87	33.65	26.44	28.85	27.88	25.96	27.96	28.91	27.70	29.11	27.23	27.59	28.57	29.06
Morocco	Voice and Accountability	Estimate	−0.42	−0.24	−0.45	−0.47	−0.75	−0.51	−0.69	−0.71	−0.71	−0.76	−0.75	−0.70	−0.71	−0.61	−0.70	−0.69	−0.63	−0.65
Morocco	Regulatory Quality	Rank	51.63	52.85	52.31	49.49	45.41	46.80	40.20	49.51	49.03	49.03	51.67	50.72	50.24	50.24	48.34	49.52	49.04	45.19
Morocco	Regulatory Quality	Estimate	−0.10	−0.02	−0.03	−0.14	−0.27	−0.25	−0.41	−0.18	−0.22	−0.19	−0.06	−0.08	−0.12	−0.08	−0.12	−0.13	−0.17	−0.23
Morocco	Control of Corruption	Rank	53.23	60.82	54.31	50.51	47.98	52.68	47.32	39.51	44.66	41.75	45.45	52.86	42.18	39.81	44.08	50.00	52.40	52.88
Morocco	Control of Corruption	Estimate	−0.11	0.11	−0.11	−0.19	−0.26	−0.14	−0.31	−0.41	−0.34	−0.38	−0.33	−0.20	−0.40	−0.44	−0.37	−0.27	−0.22	−0.15
Oman	Rule of Law	Rank	65.33	67.50	67.33	66.34	65.84	66.51	59.81	60.29	61.72	69.23	65.88	65.88	63.85	66.20	65.73	69.71	65.87	65.38
Oman	Rule of Law	Estimate	0.55	0.45	0.56	0.47	0.49	0.52	0.31	0.29	0.41	0.59	0.56	0.54	0.47	0.52	0.49	0.49	0.38	0.43
Oman	Government Effectiveness	Rank	65.57	70.47	65.13	66.84	70.92	69.95	63.24	64.39	64.56	66.99	66.03	66.03	62.56	61.61	61.14	63.94	55.77	61.54
Oman	Government Effectiveness	Estimate	0.44	0.45	0.32	0.39	0.50	0.48	0.33	0.31	0.34	0.42	0.38	0.38	0.25	0.26	0.21	0.27	0.08	0.19

(Continued)

Table 6.4. (Continued)

Country	Indicator		1996	1998	2000	2002	2003	2004	2005	2006	2007	2008	2009	2010	2011	2012	2013	2014	2015	2016
Oman	Voice and Accountability	Rank	26.00	22.39	26.87	26.37	25.37	28.85	22.12	16.83	17.79	17.79	16.11	18.01	18.78	16.90	17.37	19.21	20.69	20.20
Oman	Voice and Accountability	Estimate	−0.71	−0.89	−0.76	−0.79	−0.82	−0.66	−0.92	−1.16	−1.06	−1.07	−1.07	−1.04	−1.06	−1.02	−1.04	−1.09	−1.06	−1.11
Oman	Regulatory Quality	Rank	58.70	52.33	57.44	71.43	71.94	70.44	65.69	68.63	69.42	72.33	66.99	64.59	61.14	67.30	67.77	73.56	71.63	72.60
Oman	Regulatory Quality	Estimate	0.09	−0.03	0.08	0.72	0.71	0.66	0.55	0.60	0.61	0.70	0.53	0.44	0.32	0.47	0.48	0.69	0.57	0.61
Oman	Control of Corruption	Rank	67.74	77.32	78.17	81.82	75.25	75.12	66.83	67.32	68.45	72.33	67.94	66.19	62.09	63.03	63.03	65.38	64.90	66.35
Oman	Control of Corruption	Estimate	0.41	0.76	0.80	0.93	0.59	0.67	0.39	0.35	0.35	0.52	0.33	0.32	0.14	0.18	0.16	0.31	0.27	0.37
Qatar	Rule of Law	Rank	49.25	57.50	66.34	67.33	65.35	61.24	66.51	67.94	66.03	70.67	78.67	74.88	72.30	79.81	80.28	77.88	75.96	79.33
Qatar	Rule of Law	Estimate	−0.04	0.19	0.51	0.55	0.45	0.35	0.59	0.63	0.53	0.68	0.91	0.85	0.76	0.96	0.96	0.86	0.77	0.86
Qatar	Government Effectiveness	Rank	70.49	70.98	70.26	69.39	70.92	70.44	66.18	70.24	67.48	72.82	78.47	76.56	74.41	77.73	81.04	76.44	77.40	74.52
Qatar	Government Effectiveness	Estimate	0.56	0.46	0.45	0.50	0.50	0.53	0.40	0.58	0.44	0.60	0.97	0.85	0.75	0.94	1.06	0.94	0.96	0.75
Qatar	Voice and Accountability	Rank	26.50	26.87	29.35	27.36	27.86	35.58	32.69	15.00	19.71	18.75	19.43	18.96	17.37	21.13	20.19	16.75	16.75	15.76
Qatar	Voice and Accountability	Estimate	−0.71	−0.78	−0.65	−0.70	−0.69	−0.43	−0.51	−0.87	−1.04	−1.02	−1.00	−1.01	−1.08	−0.92	−0.98	−1.13	−1.14	−1.20
Qatar	Regulatory Quality	Rank	61.96	56.48	54.36	63.27	60.20	60.10	60.29	60.29	64.08	71.36	73.21	71.29	68.72	75.36	73.93	71.15	73.08	74.04

(Continued)

Table 6.4. (*Continued*)

Country	Indicator		1996	1998	2000	2002	2003	2004	2005	2006	2007	2008	2009	2010	2011	2012	2013	2014	2015	2016
Qatar	Regulatory Quality	Estimate	0.17	0.07	0.00	0.30	0.23	0.17	0.26	0.31	0.40	0.65	0.68	0.60	0.50	0.80	0.75	0.57	0.68	0.70
Qatar	Control of Corruption	Rank	54.84	69.59	72.59	76.77	73.74	72.20	73.66	79.51	74.27	79.13	91.39	89.05	80.09	81.52	81.99	80.29	78.37	79.81
Qatar	Control of Corruption	Estimate	−0.05	0.50	0.53	0.68	0.54	0.52	0.71	0.93	0.68	0.94	1.57	1.41	1.01	1.06	1.11	0.99	0.89	0.92
SA	Rule of Law	Rank	56.28	54.50	47.52	53.47	58.42	53.11	53.11	54.55	55.02	56.25	56.40	60.19	56.81	59.61	58.69	62.50	60.10	67.79
SA	Rule of Law	Estimate	0.11	0.07	−0.15	0.00	0.13	0.02	−0.01	0.02	0.08	0.07	0.05	0.16	0.05	0.15	0.16	0.13	0.12	0.47
SA	Government Effectiveness	Rank	49.18	50.26	47.69	45.92	46.43	45.81	42.65	49.76	51.46	52.91	51.20	55.50	45.50	58.29	58.29	62.02	60.58	63.46
SA	Government Effectiveness	Estimate	−0.18	−0.20	−0.22	−0.30	−0.30	−0.36	−0.37	−0.17	−0.12	−0.09	−0.10	−0.01	−0.30	0.03	0.07	0.21	0.20	0.24
SA	Voice and Accountability	Rank	9.00	5.47	5.97	3.98	5.47	10.10	6.25	3.85	5.77	4.33	3.32	3.79	2.35	2.82	2.82	2.96	3.45	3.94
SA	Voice and Accountability	Estimate	−1.50	−1.62	−1.60	−1.70	−1.64	−1.32	−1.54	−1.78	−1.71	−1.73	−1.82	−1.79	−1.91	−1.87	−1.88	−1.88	−1.84	−1.78
SA	Regulatory Quality	Rank	41.30	39.90	49.74	53.06	57.65	56.16	56.86	53.43	53.88	55.34	56.94	55.98	53.55	55.92	54.98	53.85	54.33	55.77
SA	Regulatory Quality	Estimate	−0.31	−0.27	−0.10	−0.05	0.11	0.05	0.11	−0.04	0.02	0.12	0.16	0.16	0.03	0.10	0.08	0.00	0.03	0.08
SA	Control of Corruption	Rank	51.08	47.94	50.76	62.63	55.05	48.78	54.63	51.71	53.40	58.74	58.85	59.05	48.82	57.82	59.24	59.13	58.65	62.98
SA	Control of Corruption	Estimate	−0.16	−0.25	−0.19	0.20	−0.15	−0.29	−0.10	−0.19	−0.17	−0.01	−0.02	0.04	−0.31	−0.04	−0.02	0.09	0.05	0.23

(*Continued*)

Table 6.4. (Continued)

Country	Indicator		1996	1998	2000	2002	2003	2004	2005	2006	2007	2008	2009	2010	2011	2012	2013	2014	2015	2016
Syria	Rule of Law	Rank	33.17	34.00	35.15	35.64	39.11	38.76	33.97	20.10	23.44	26.92	34.60	33.65	25.82	13.62	4.69	5.77	4.81	0.96
Syria	Rule of Law	Estimate	−0.55	−0.52	−0.49	−0.55	−0.47	−0.47	−0.59	−0.94	−0.80	−0.69	−0.57	−0.59	−0.78	−1.13	−1.41	−1.36	−1.42	−2.01
Syria	Government Effectiveness	Rank	21.86	11.92	15.90	18.88	11.22	11.33	11.76	19.02	22.33	29.61	34.45	32.06	38.39	12.32	6.64	7.21	5.29	1.92
Syria	Government Effectiveness	Estimate	−0.80	−1.06	−0.96	−0.88	−1.09	−1.04	−1.14	−0.92	−0.81	−0.66	−0.60	−0.61	−0.50	−1.15	−1.40	−1.40	−1.59	−1.82
Syria	Voice and Accountability	Rank	11.00	6.97	5.47	5.47	5.97	7.21	7.21	4.81	4.33	4.81	5.69	4.74	3.76	3.29	3.29	3.45	2.96	1.48
Syria	Voice and Accountability	Estimate	−1.40	−1.56	−1.63	−1.62	−1.62	−1.51	−1.51	−1.76	−1.78	−1.72	−1.69	−1.70	−1.81	−1.84	−1.83	−1.88	−1.92	−1.96
Syria	Regulatory Quality	Rank	14.67	9.33	9.74	16.33	16.33	13.79	17.65	8.33	8.25	13.11	18.18	19.62	19.91	4.27	4.27	3.85	4.33	3.85
Syria	Regulatory Quality	Estimate	−1.07	−1.25	−1.26	−1.01	−1.02	−1.10	−0.98	−1.36	−1.31	−1.14	−0.96	−0.90	−0.95	−1.53	−1.55	−1.69	−1.64	−1.67
Syria	Control of Corruption	Rank	19.89	20.10	14.21	43.43	24.75	22.93	20.98	14.63	12.14	10.68	11.96	12.86	13.74	9.95	8.53	2.40	1.92	2.40
Syria	Control of Corruption	Estimate	−0.88	−0.91	−1.03	−0.39	−0.80	−0.82	−0.85	−1.06	−1.10	−1.15	−1.13	−1.13	−1.09	−1.21	−1.26	−1.55	−1.55	−1.57
Tunisia	Rule of Law	Rank	41.21	43.50	43.56	49.50	48.02	55.50	53.59	56.46	55.50	55.29	59.24	57.35	50.70	51.17	49.30	52.88	55.29	55.77
Tunisia	Rule of Law	Estimate	−0.30	−0.24	−0.22	−0.12	−0.14	0.05	−0.01	0.11	0.09	0.07	0.13	0.06	−0.13	−0.13	−0.19	−0.11	−0.06	0.02
Tunisia	Government Effectiveness	Rank	62.84	72.54	71.28	72.45	71.43	68.47	64.71	72.20	67.96	66.02	65.55	63.16	55.45	54.98	52.13	48.08	49.04	45.19

(*Continued*)

Table 6.4. *(Continued)*

Country	Indicator		1996	1998	2000	2002	2003	2004	2005	2006	2007	2008	2009	2010	2011	2012	2013	2014	2015	2016
Tunisia	Government Effectiveness	Estimate	0.38	0.53	0.50	0.58	0.51	0.44	0.38	0.64	0.47	0.31	0.38	0.22	0.02	−0.03	−0.07	−0.12	−0.10	−0.21
Tunisia	Voice and Accountability	Rank	31.00	24.38	23.38	20.90	21.89	22.60	21.63	9.62	9.13	10.58	9.95	9.00	35.68	43.66	45.07	55.17	55.67	56.65
Tunisia	Voice and Accountability	Estimate	−0.60	−0.82	−0.81	−0.96	−0.92	−0.87	−0.95	−1.30	−1.38	−1.35	−1.36	−1.42	−0.37	−0.17	−0.08	0.19	0.24	0.33
Tunisia	Regulatory Quality	Rank	60.87	53.37	53.85	50.00	55.10	50.25	52.45	55.88	54.37	54.85	53.11	52.63	46.92	46.45	40.76	39.42	37.98	33.17
Tunisia	Regulatory Quality	Estimate	0.14	−0.02	−0.02	−0.12	0.03	−0.09	−0.08	0.11	0.03	0.06	0.00	−0.03	−0.19	−0.19	−0.33	−0.38	−0.41	−0.47
Tunisia	Control of Corruption	Rank	35.48	48.97	48.22	68.69	61.62	57.07	49.76	52.20	49.51	47.57	51.67	48.57	56.40	56.87	56.87	55.77	55.77	53.85
Tunisia	Control of Corruption	Estimate	−0.53	−0.24	−0.23	0.37	0.16	0.08	−0.26	−0.19	−0.25	−0.30	−0.22	−0.26	−0.06	−0.06	−0.07	−0.04	−0.07	−0.12
Turkey	Rule of Law	Rank	47.24	48.00	50.50	52.48	59.41	58.37	58.37	55.50	54.07	56.73	57.82	58.77	57.75	57.28	55.87	57.21	53.37	48.56
Turkey	Rule of Law	Estimate	−0.14	−0.06	−0.01	−0.03	0.15	0.13	0.16	0.05	0.02	0.08	0.10	0.11	0.07	0.04	0.07	0.01	−0.11	−0.16
Turkey	Government Effectiveness	Rank	55.74	46.11	56.92	60.71	60.71	57.64	58.82	59.02	64.08	63.59	63.16	64.11	65.40	65.40	64.45	67.79	62.02	54.81
Turkey	Government Effectiveness	Estimate	−0.08	−0.26	0.01	0.08	0.05	0.01	0.15	0.12	0.31	0.27	0.28	0.29	0.35	0.41	0.38	0.37	0.22	0.05
Turkey	Voice and Accountability	Rank	45.50	31.84	40.30	42.29	45.77	49.52	50.96	45.67	46.15	46.15	45.50	44.55	44.13	41.78	40.85	36.45	34.98	29.56

(Continued)

Table 6.4. (Continued)

Country	Indicator		1996	1998	2000	2002	2003	2004	2005	2006	2007	2008	2009	2010	2011	2012	2013	2014	2015	2016
Turkey	Voice and Accountability	Estimate	−0.13	−0.62	−0.29	−0.22	−0.03	0.01	0.00	−0.06	−0.05	−0.04	−0.06	−0.08	−0.14	−0.21	−0.25	−0.34	−0.37	−0.63
Turkey	Regulatory Quality	Rank	59.24	68.39	64.62	58.67	56.12	56.65	60.78	59.31	62.14	59.22	59.81	59.81	62.09	64.93	64.93	66.35	62.50	61.06
Turkey	Regulatory Quality	Estimate	0.10	0.50	0.35	0.10	0.04	0.06	0.28	0.29	0.32	0.26	0.28	0.30	0.37	0.42	0.43	0.40	0.27	0.20
Turkey	Control of Corruption	Rank	51.61	45.36	49.75	34.85	52.02	51.71	56.10	58.05	59.71	60.68	60.29	58.57	58.29	62.56	61.14	52.88	53.37	50.48
Turkey	Control of Corruption	Estimate	−0.15	−0.30	−0.20	−0.52	−0.18	−0.18	−0.03	0.03	0.11	0.11	0.09	0.03	0.04	0.16	0.09	−0.15	−0.15	−0.20
UAE	Rule of Law	Rank	68.84	73.50	72.77	73.27	67.82	64.11	61.24	60.77	59.33	62.98	63.03	62.56	65.26	67.14	69.01	75.00	73.08	79.81
UAE	Rule of Law	Estimate	0.69	0.75	0.68	0.73	0.57	0.44	0.40	0.32	0.29	0.42	0.40	0.32	0.50	0.54	0.62	0.65	0.64	0.89
UAE	Government Effectiveness	Rank	77.05	78.24	79.49	78.06	72.45	75.37	72.55	79.51	79.13	78.16	79.43	77.51	81.99	83.41	83.41	89.42	91.35	90.87
UAE	Government Effectiveness	Estimate	0.78	0.79	0.79	0.85	0.58	0.70	0.71	0.94	0.92	0.88	0.99	0.90	1.06	1.15	1.18	1.44	1.51	1.41
UAE	Voice and Accountability	Rank	37.00	33.83	31.34	30.35	22.89	26.44	25.96	20.67	23.08	22.12	25.59	23.22	23.47	18.31	19.25	20.20	19.21	19.21
UAE	Voice and Accountability	Estimate	−0.41	−0.52	−0.52	−0.63	−0.91	−0.69	−0.71	−1.00	−0.91	−0.91	−0.84	−0.90	−0.90	−1.00	−1.02	−1.06	−1.11	−1.12
UAE	Regulatory Quality	Rank	71.74	72.54	75.38	83.16	70.92	74.88	69.61	70.10	68.93	67.48	65.55	60.77	65.88	73.46	74.88	80.29	82.69	80.29
UAE	Regulatory Quality	Estimate	0.69	0.62	0.73	1.12	0.67	0.80	0.65	0.63	0.61	0.57	0.44	0.32	0.45	0.68	0.78	0.99	1.11	0.97

(Continued)

Table 6.4. *(Continued)*

Country	Indicator		1996	1998	2000	2002	2003	2004	2005	2006	2007	2008	2009	2010	2011	2012	2013	2014	2015	2016
UAE	Control of Corruption	Rank	57.53	57.22	61.42	83.84	78.28	83.90	81.46	79.02	81.07	83.01	78.95	78.57	81.99	83.89	87.20	83.17	82.69	88.46
UAE	Control of Corruption	Estimate	−0.01	0.05	0.12	1.15	0.86	1.06	1.00	0.89	1.01	1.08	0.91	0.90	1.08	1.16	1.28	1.20	1.07	1.28
Yemen	Rule of Law	Rank	9.05	7.50	3.47	3.96	10.89	11.00	9.09	14.35	17.22	16.83	14.69	13.27	7.98	8.92	11.27	7.69	7.21	4.81
Yemen	Rule of Law	Estimate	−1.38	−1.32	−1.46	−1.53	−1.21	−1.22	−1.26	−1.04	−0.97	−0.98	−1.09	−1.09	−1.29	−1.27	−1.18	−1.20	−1.27	−1.60
Yemen	Government Effectiveness	Rank	31.69	23.32	21.54	21.94	23.47	16.26	19.61	20.00	18.45	17.96	12.92	14.35	11.85	8.53	11.37	6.73	3.37	2.40
Yemen	Government Effectiveness	Estimate	−0.62	−0.74	−0.78	−0.81	−0.73	−0.91	−0.91	−0.90	−0.87	−0.88	−1.07	−1.02	−1.15	−1.27	−1.22	−1.41	−1.63	−1.82
Yemen	Voice and Accountability	Rank	27.50	26.37	24.38	14.93	23.88	20.19	17.31	16.35	16.35	12.98	12.80	11.37	9.39	9.39	11.74	11.82	7.39	5.91
Yemen	Voice and Accountability	Estimate	−0.68	−0.78	−0.80	−1.16	−0.89	−0.97	−1.05	−1.19	−1.11	−1.22	−1.27	−1.33	−1.39	−1.35	−1.33	−1.30	−1.52	−1.65
Yemen	Regulatory Quality	Rank	32.07	31.09	23.59	20.92	23.98	19.70	21.57	21.57	25.24	23.79	27.27	28.23	22.27	27.49	25.12	18.75	12.02	5.29
Yemen	Regulatory Quality	Estimate	−0.44	−0.44	−0.66	−0.80	−0.71	−0.85	−0.83	−0.77	−0.67	−0.72	−0.65	−0.62	−0.84	−0.69	−0.73	−0.89	−1.13	−1.48
Yemen	Control of Corruption	Rank	27.42	15.98	13.71	17.17	15.66	13.66	18.54	23.41	21.84	22.33	14.35	9.05	6.64	8.53	9.00	1.92	3.37	0.96
Yemen	Control of Corruption	Estimate	−0.74	−0.98	−1.05	−0.98	−0.94	−1.08	−0.89	−0.79	−0.79	−0.79	−1.07	−1.19	−1.23	−1.25	−1.25	−1.56	−1.47	−1.67

Source: The World Bank, The Worldwide Governance Indicators (WGI). See Daniel Kaufmann, Aart Kraay and Massimo Mastruzzi (2010). "The Worldwide Governance Indicators : A Summary of Methodology, Data and Analytical Issues". World Bank Policy Research Working Paper No. 5430

the likelihood of crime and violence" (Kaufmann *et al.*, 2010). There are two ways to present their indices. First, we present the rank among all countries expressed as a percent ranging from 0 (lowest) to 100 (highest). We normalize it to a grading scheme from A to F for easy interpretation. Second, the estimates range from approximately −2.5 (weak) to 2.5 (strong) and are highly correlated to the grading scheme. The Rule of Law indicator reports that Algeria, Djibouti, Egypt, Iran, Kuwait, Lebanon, Morocco, Syria, Tunisia, Turkey and Yemen earn an 'F' grade for the perception of Rule of Law. Bahrain, Jordan, Oman and Saudi Arabia earn a 'D' grade for the perception of Rule of Law. The only country within MENA that has highest grade for Rule of Law was Israel with a grade ranging from 'B' to 'B+'.

The second indicator is Governance Effectiveness which "reflects perceptions of the quality of public services, the quality of the civil service and the degree of its independence from political pressures, the quality of policy formulation and implementation, and the credibility of the government's commitment to such policies" (Kaufmann *et al.*, 2010). Algeria, Djibouti, Egypt, Iran, Jordan, Kuwait, Lebanon, Morocco, Syria, Tunisia, Turkey and Yemen earn an 'F' grade for the perception of Governance Effectiveness. Within MENA there were two countries who received a grade of 'A' for perception of Governance Effectiveness. They are Israel and the UAE.

The third indicator was Voice and Accountability which "reflects perceptions of the extent to which a country's citizens are able to participate in selecting their government, as well as freedom of expression, freedom of association, and a free media" (Kaufmann *et al.*, 2010). The Voice and Accountability indicator reports that none of the Arab MENA countries had a passing grade throughout the 1996–2016 period. Algeria, Bahrain, Djibouti, Egypt, Iran, Jordan, Kuwait, Lebanon, Morocco, Oman, Qatar, Saudi Arabia, Syria, Tunisia, Turkey, UAE and Yemen earn an 'F' grade for the perception of Voice and Accountability. Only Cyprus and Israel, the non-Arab MENA countries, passed with flying colors.

The fourth indicator was Regulatory Quality which "reflects perceptions of the ability of the government to formulate and implement sound policies and regulations that permit and promote private sector development" (Kaufmann *et al.*, 2010). This indicator captures the "Rule by Law" dimension of authoritarian systems. The Regulatory Quality indicator reports that for most Arab MENA countries they did not have a passing grade throughout the 1996–2016 period. Algeria, Djibouti, Egypt, Iran, Jordan, Kuwait, Lebanon, Morocco, Saudi Arabia, Syria, Tunisia, Turkey and Yemen earn an 'F' grade for the perception of Regulatory Quality. Bahrain, Oman and Qatar received a grade of 'C'; Cyprus and the UAE received a grade of 'B−'; and Israel received a grade of 'B+' for the perception of Regulatory Quality.

The fifth indicator was Control of Corruption which "reflects perceptions of the extent to which public power is exercised for private gain, including both petty and grand forms of corruption, as well as "capture" of the state by elites and private interests" (Kaufmann *et al.*, 2010). Algeria, Bahrain, Djibouti, Egypt, Iran, Kuwait, Lebanon, Morocco, Syria, Tunisia, Turkey and Yemen earn an 'F' grade for the perception of Control of Corruption. Bahrain and Cyprus receive a grade of 'C' and Israel receives a grade of 'B'. The balance of Arab MENA receive a grade of 'D' for Control of Corruption.

Bernheim and Whinston (1986) and Grossman and Helpman (1994) link resource abundance to a bilateral exchange between domestic interest groups, represented by the domestic and non-tradeable sectors and themselves, where bribes purchase political support. By paying bribes, these firms gain greater benefits from the autocrats' policies. Bulte and Damania (2008), in general equilibrium (GE) framework, model an exchange between the resource sector that purchases "favorable policies" from an autocratic government in the form of subsidized expenditure in infrastructure. In their GE framework, a favorable boom in the resource sector tilts the balance in favor of the resource sector, yielding a reorientation of support to this sector. The reduction in support for the non-resource sector induces an outmigration of entrepreneurs from that sector. Consequently, despite the windfall gain associated with the boom in the resource sector, aggregate income in the economy falls. This outcome is consistent with the realities in the oil-rich MENA economies. When institutions are properly functioning, with no rent-seeking, rents tend to be shared more equally, and the returns to rent-seeking are low or eliminated.

The Arab Human Development Reports (2002–2009) have gone to great lengths to point out that the oil-rich *paternalistic autocracies*, such as Saudi Arabia, Kuwait and some of the smaller states of the UAE in the Persian Gulf, have established their authority and legitimacy during the process of oil boom modernization, by increasing the living standards of their small tribal constituencies. These *paternalistic autocracies* can minimize the risk of overthrow as long as the oil wealth endures and is used to fund these artificial living standards. However, utilizing state spending in order to sustain political support generates a number of negative externalities.

These externalities include the ever increasing expenditure commitments — including subsidies; high levels of public employment in low-capacity, overstaffed bureaucracies; and protected, inefficient enterprises — that are hard to cut back and that constrain investment. Such entitlements will eventually push these states toward fiscal crisis (UNDP, 2002).

Mahdavy (1970), Luciani (1987), Vandewalle (1998) and many others have noted that oil-rich Arab MENA governments' access to rents, in the form of oil revenue, may have freed them from the need for taxation of their peoples, and that this in turn freed them from the need for democracy. The need for tax revenue is believed to require democracy under the theory "no taxation without representation." Huntington (1991) generalized this principle beyond Middle Eastern oil producers to states with natural resources in other parts of the developing world.

While the development programs implemented by the Gulf states over the past three and a half decades have had some success in establishing the possibility of increased competitiveness, they may be too little and too late. Their welfare-oriented strategies have created severe, unintended structural anomalies in the form of persistent dependence on oil for export earnings and fiscal revenues, overgrown public sectors whose omnipresence in the economy stifles the private sector, distorted work incentives, and extreme dependence on governments to provide jobs for Gulf nationals while at the same time depending on "unskilled guest workers" to build "pyramids in the desert" and on "skilled guest workers" to build an entrepreneurial class. As alternatives to oil are developed in the 21st century,[36] the Gulf States will face mounting fiscal pressures, an inability to expand public services, and an inability to maintain the public sector as the leading source to absorb the rapidly increasing number of new entrants to the labor market because of population growth.

As the UNDP *Human Development Reports* have continuously stressed, these trends create an urgent need to accelerate non-oil private sector growth to generate new job opportunities for Gulf nationals. However, to

[36]As an example of this trend, consider the joint venture by Carlos Ghosn (the CEO of Renault and Nissan) with Shai Agassi and his start-up "Better Place" designed to create in Israel the test case for an "oil-free economy" by introducing an electric car with a completed "smart grid" for battery replacement. Denmark, Australia, the San Francisco Bay Area, Hawaii and Ontario have all announced that they will join the Better Place plan. "If it succeeds, the global impact of Better Place on economics, politics, and the environment might well transcend that of the most important technology companies in the world. And the idea will have spread from Israel throughout the world" (Senor and Singer, 2009, p. 11).

realize this objective, Gulf governments will have to abandon development strategies pursued over the past quarter century and overcome severe political hurdles like xenophobia and religious intolerance which stand in the way of sustainable economic development strategies.

The negative impact of the natural resource sector on the economy can be mitigated by choosing a set of policies centered on a revised tax system and anti-corruption institutions. The tax system, by directly increasing taxes on the natural resource sector, could be instrumental in avoiding the Dutch disease and in assisting the development of the non-resource sector. The tax revenue generated by an increased resource tax should then be used to lower overall tax levels in the economy and, in particular, to cut non-wage labor costs. This should lead to lower total labor costs in sectors with low productivity. Taxing more of the resource "rent" away should also decrease wages in the resource sector and hence diminish the pressure on wages in other sectors. While orienting the tax system toward the resource sector can help reduce the rents associated with natural resources and thus alleviate the Dutch disease, it will make the economy dependent on an alternative source of revenue.

The economic literature cited above suggests a number of reasons why resource orientation may complicate economic development. Among those, the incentives for rent-seeking and its negative effects on economic development and corruption are predominant. Part of the solution is simply to tax away a fair share of the resource rent. While this is theoretically simple, in practice it is anything but simple. The main obstacle to achieving this result is that it requires a fairly efficient and non-corrupt administration — otherwise, resource rents are simply divided between resource companies and their bureaucratic counterparts, with only a minor share making it into state revenue. Therefore, the necessary and sufficient condition to eliminate the negative effects of the resource "curse" is an effective and relatively corruption-free state apparatus.

Cross-country research cited above shows that both the efficiency of the rule of law and the development of civil society are strongly and negatively correlated with corruption levels. The evidence also demonstrates that a lack of press freedom increases corruption. An independent justice, a free press, and a generally strong civil society are necessary and sufficient conditions to keeping down corruption, and thus to promote long-term economic development.

Chapter 7

Science, Technology and Innovation in MENA

Investment in science, technology and innovation has benefited from both increased globalization and economic growth. We are now entering the digital revolution where the availability inexpensive digital communications, processing and cloud computing has minimized the distances between connected population of active users of digital technologies around the globe. (Pelzman, 2018; WEF, 2016) Given the ease of real-time communication the distribution of research and development (R&D) is no longer confined predominantly to the OECD. In the past two decades, R&D activity has grown in China, Russia, India and in the MENA region (OECD, 2008a,b,c,d,e). An increasing share of R&D is funded through private business, public institutions or international organizations. The importance of foreign affiliates in business R&D is growing, as is the increased importance of scientific collaboration. The output of R&D in the form of patents and scientific publishing is increasing in those countries that have adopted knowledge economy-friendly policies that encourage and support internationalization.

The current paradigm on the internationalization process as developed by Silverberg *et al.* (1988) stresses that historically it was presumed that the more developed economies have sufficient human and physical capital to focus on innovation at the technology frontier, while less developed countries, by contrast, have opportunities to acquire these new technologies and to disseminate the relevant portions in their domestic economies. However, in the long-run, the ability of the developing countries to imitate these new technologies becomes the prime driver for economic development. It is this ability to make use of the integrated world of knowledge creation which will assure that developing countries have the ability to initiate new activities and to increase domestic productivity.

The process of innovation and diffusion is, however, highly dependent on a country's *a priori* institutional environment in terms of governance, education and infrastructure. In order to fully utilize the global human capital environment, one must develop a well-functioning innovation system. The first key component in the institutional construct is to achieve a better integration of the science and technology infrastructure with production needs, by increasing private sector participation in technology development, and by developing stronger linkages between industry, universities and research institutions. Innovation systems normally focus on building: (a) an environment conducive to business development; (b) a framework for the generation of new ideas; and (c) enterprise-level support to establish new knowledge economy-based companies, to carry out research and development activities, and to generate and sustain revenues.

The existence of an innovation system which is knowledge economy-friendly is particularly problematic in Arab MENA. A key priority addressed by the UNDP (2009a, 2009b, 2016a and 2016b) focusing on Arab MENA is the creation of an innovation-friendly institutional environment which requires reforms in education, trade, investment, finance and governance; the development of an incentive-driven research and development infrastructure; and a positive attitude toward collaboration with the rest of the world's scientific community, in spite of centuries of religious intolerance and gender bias.

Chen and Dahlman (2006) formalize this problem for the World Bank by disseminating what they refer to as the "four pillars" of the knowledge economy which become the core of the economic development process. The growth of a global knowledge-based economy creates great opportunities and poses interesting challenges for all countries, but particularly for those within Arab MENA who are struggling to promote sustainable development in an environment burdened by xenophobia, religious intolerance, gender bias, and by non-representative political, administrative and economic institutions.

The pre-requisites of the knowledge economy, as Chen and Dahlman (2006) postulate, are based on the elimination of these old cultural biases of Arab MENA and on adopting "knowledge" as the key engine of economic growth, regardless of the ethnicity, religion and gender of the innovators. It is an economy where "knowledge" is either acquired and transferred from the market and imitated, or created domestically within indigenous integrated research facilities and disseminated and used effectively to enhance economic development.

According to this research, the knowledge economy requires the establishment of the following four pillars (Chen and Dahlman, 2006, p. 4):

- An economic incentive and institutional regime that provides good economic policies and institutions that permit efficient mobilization and allocation of resources and stimulate creativity and incentives for the efficient creation, dissemination, and use of existing knowledge.
- Educated and skilled workers who can continuously upgrade and adapt their skills to efficiently create and use knowledge.
- An effective innovation system of firms, research centers, universities, consultants and other organizations that can keep up with the knowledge revolution and tap into the growing stock of global knowledge and assimilate and adapt it to local needs.
- A modern and adequate information infrastructure that can facilitate the effective communication, dissemination, and processing of information and knowledge.

These four pillars are used by the World Bank to gather and publish indexes for all of these pillars across both developed and developing countries. Using these indexes we quantify, in the next section, the relative knowledge- friendly developments in MENA over the 1995–2016 period.

What is the economic justification for this knowledge economy framework? Are investments in the four knowledge economy pillars a necessary and sufficient condition for sustained creation, adoption, adaptation and use of "knowledge" in domestic economic production? Moreover, will this lead to increased probability of economic success, and hence economic development, in the globalized world economy? In Section 7.1 we review the economic literature addressing the innovation process, present the case for the internalization of R&D activity, and present the latest statistics on the degree to which research and development is a shared innovation process. The latest data for 2000–2013 on the number of patents generated and the number of research publications presents a disturbing picture concerning the lack of Arab MENA's participation in the global economy. The causes for such a dismal outcome are addressed in Section 7.2 where we focus on the innovation system that is required to maximize the effectiveness of knowledge for economic development, and present the current statistical evidence on MENA's adoption of these prerequisites. The poor performance of the majority of MENA countries in this area is linked to the knowledge-unfriendly institutional environment and the aversion to globalization in terms of the free and unhindered flow of knowledge. Despite attempts by the oil-rich MENA countries to alter these domestic policies, their attempts may be too little, too late in a 21st century world where innovation is moving faster than their attempts to build sequestered science and research institutions in the desert.

7.1. The Output of Science, Technology and Innovation in MENA

The economics profession has been somewhat slow to acknowledge the role of innovation in the economic growth process. The standard models that have been used to discuss innovation start with a Cobb–Douglass production function where output is a function of capital and labor, and technological change enhanced the productivity of capital and labor. Equation (7.1) is a restatement of Equation (5.2) first presented in Chapter 5:

$$Y = AK^{\alpha}H^{1-\alpha} = AK^{\alpha}(hL)^{1-\alpha}, \tag{7.1}$$

where capital is composed of physical capital K and human capital H. Human capital is the productive capacity of the labor force, which in turn corresponds to the headcount of the labor force or raw labor, L, multiplied by its average level of skill or education h, so that $H = hL$. Technology is inserted as a separate factor (A), which augments the productivity of capital and labor.

With the advent of the endogenous growth models (Romer, 1990), technology was modeled as a result of R&D and human capital (H), as in Equation (7.2):

$$A = g(RD, H). \tag{7.2}$$

The endogenous growth model discussed in Chapter 4 includes a review of a large literature focusing on the determinants of total factor productivity (TFP), including inputs into the creation of knowledge (such as R&D and education), as well as access to foreign knowledge, human capital, physical infrastructure, the financial system, trade, the institutional regime (such as property rights, the rule of law, competitive pressure), and geography (climate, disease, distance from markets).

In a review of this literature, Isaksson (2007) concludes that capital accumulation is a very important determinant of growth, not only because

Table 7.1. Breakdown of Sources of Growth in a Number of MENA Economies (1970–2000)

	Average Annual Growth in Capital–Labor Ratio	Average Annual Growth in GDP per Worker	Average Annual Growth of TFP	Level of GDP/ Worker Relative to US	Level of TFP Relative to US	Projected Average Annual TFP Growth, 2001–2010
Algeria	1.02	0.59	1.01	0.34	0.48	−0.17
Egypt	3.72	2.39	1.01	0.16	0.42	−0.13
Iran	2.80	1.08	1.00	0.34	0.50	1.76
Israel	2.31	1.70	1.01	0.67	0.70	0.90
Jordan	3.95	1.34	0.99	0.28	0.50	−0.51
Morocco	2.87	1.16	1.00	0.18	0.35	−2.20
Syria	2.75	2.55	1.01	0.22	0.43	0.21
Turkey	4.69	2.03	1.00	0.22	0.43	0.29

Source: Calculated from UNIDO, World Productivity Database.

of capital deepening but also because more current technology embodies more productive processes. Furthermore, he finds that openness to foreign knowledge is a necessary and sufficient condition for the acquisition and absorption of important R&D. The necessity for developing countries to undertake some R&D is required if they are to absorb foreign knowledge. Simply importing "knowledge" from abroad will not create the positive externality to enable the absorption of foreign knowledge. Finally, the review finds that competition, the rule of law, and the enforcement of contracts are all positively related to greater TFP growth.

Using the UNIDO World Productivity Database constructed by Hulten and Isaksson (2007), the conventional analysis of the type in Equation (7.1) is presented in Table 7.1 for a subset of MENA countries within the current database. The results show that capital deepening explains more than 200 percent of the growth rate of output per worker in the majority of cases, with the exception of Algeria and Egypt. Differences in levels, however, are explained mostly by differences in TFP. As the data in Table 7.1 demonstrates, the level of TFP in Arab MENA is only 50 percent (or less) of that in the United States, while in the case of Israel it is at least 70 percent. Overall, the analysis as it currently stands points to innovation, as proxied by TFP, as the major contributor to the differences in development levels across countries.

The Growth Commission Report (2008), in supporting the four pillars of the knowledge economy as constructed by Chen and Dahlman (2006), lists five main macroeconomics elements explaining differentials in economic growth between economies. They are:

- Participation in the global economy;
- Maintaining macroeconomic stability;
- Maintaining high rates of savings and investment;
- Markets are allocating resources; and
- Credible, committed and capable governments.

To facilitate these changes requires a "credible, committed and capable government" which will promote technical change via:

- the direct pursuit of scientific and technological activities, as in the case of universities and other publicly funded research institutions;
- the financial support of innovation carried out in the business sector;
- the supply of the necessary productive infrastructures, including education and training, standards and norms, and a legal system of intellectual property rights, to allow individuals and firms to innovate.

The OECD (2008a, 2008b, 2008c, 2008d, 2008e) has reinforced the conclusion developed by the World Bank that the internationalization of R&D, while not a new phenomenon, is occurring at a much faster pace today. The primary motivation is led by a desire for outward investment in R&D. Multinational enterprises (MNEs) are seeking not only to exploit knowledge generated at home and in other countries, but also to source technology internationally and to utilize centers of increasingly multidisciplinary knowledge worldwide. Consequently, the distinction between imitation and innovation is not entirely clear (OECD, 2008a, 2008b, 2008c, 2008d, 2008e, and OECD, 2006a).

The literature on the internationalization of research activity makes the following observation: "The increasing similarity of technologies across sectors and the cross-fertilization of technology between sectors, coupled with the increasing costs and risks associated with innovation, has often led firms to consider international R&D alliances as a first-best option" (OECD, 2006a, p. 126). This process of R&D co-operation and strategic alliances enables leading international technological enterprises to stream-line the communication process between scattered research centers, universities, and technology labs. The formation of such "virtual research parks" enables companies to pool resources and risk, exploit research synergies and reduce research duplication. The ability to communicate in real time has enabled these research firms to carry out joint R&D projects with the best possible partners, either other firms, universities or science partners. According to Hagedoorn and Duysters (2002), the search for best partners is carried out on a global scale, resulting in a monumental increase, since the early 1980s, in the number of co-operation agreements or alliances between partners residing in Europe, North America, Israel, and more recently South-East Asia and the PRC. The actors in this global market of R&D investments and collaboration represent the world's most developed economies, paralleling the worldwide distribution of R&D resources and capabilities.

The internationalization of R&D activity is best demonstrated by looking at the resulting patents created by these ventures.

The data presented in Table 7.2 for the period 2000–2013 demonstrates the increasing importance of foreign affiliates in patenting. The OECD data reported in Table 7.2 confirms the growing world share of patents involving international co-invention. The prominent examples are India, the PRC and Taipei who in 2000 did not have a major share of world patent activity but after a number of years of entering the global R&D market managed to acquire over 1,000 patents per annum. Within MENA, Israel is the only successful country that has participated in the global R&D market for the entire period 2000–2013. Its share of the world supply of patents exceeds one percent comparable to Austria, Australia, Denmark, Finland and Korea. None of the Arab MENA countries appears to be active in the global R&D market, as demonstrated by the OECD patent data, during the 2000–2013 period.

The information contained in patent data which covers a long period and a large sample of firms and sectors is uniquely appropriate for the study of internationalization. The main disadvantage of patent statistics is that they fail to capture the full set of innovative activity because not all innovations are patented and not all patents lead to innovations (OECD, 2008a).

In addition to the ever growing internationalization of the production of patented innovations, the ownership structure of patents by foreign residents has also been substantial in small, open economies with the proper knowledge infrastructure. On average, the world has seen a 50 percent increase in the number of EPO patents where the share of foreign ownership of inventions made abroad is higher in the 2000–2013 period as compared to 1990.

The data in Table 7.3 lists those countries who in the 2000–2013 period had more than 1,000 patents where their local knowledge environment and infrastructure resulted in a large foreign ownership of domestic inventions.

Table 7.2. Patents with Foreign Co-Inventors (2000–2013)

(Number and Percent)

	2000			2001			2002		
Country	Total Patents	Foreign Co-Inventors (%)	Share of World Patents (%)	Total Patents	Foreign Co-Inventors (%)	Share of World Patents (%)	Total Patents	Foreign Co-Inventors (%)	Share of World Patents (%)
Australia	1,160	19.1	1.0	1,116	21.0	1.0	1,190	20.8	1.0
Austria	1,391	26.0	1.2	1,457	28.9	1.3	1,562	29.5	1.3
Belgium	1,655	35.6	1.4	1,541	36.3	1.3	1,667	34.7	1.4
Canada	2,073	32.0	1.8	2,182	33.5	1.9	2,226	31.7	1.9
Denmark	1,079	17.0	0.9	1,063	23.2	0.9	1,089	22.7	0.9
Finland	1,547	13.8	1.3	1,531	15.6	1.3	1,398	16.0	1.2
France	8,042	16.2	6.9	8,075	16.8	7.0	8,260	17.6	7.0
Germany	23,566	12.3	20.2	23,370	12.2	20.3	23,424	13.4	19.7
India	230	33.5	0.2	344	33.7	0.3	543	29.3	0.5
Israel	1,163	16.5	1.0	1,056	16.3	0.9	1,022	14.4	0.9
Italy	4,261	11.1	3.6	4,253	10.6	3.7	4,491	9.8	3.8
Japan	22,583	2.8	19.3	20,946	2.9	18.2	21,665	3.4	18.2
Korea	1,316	5.9	1.1	1,679	4.7	1.5	2,457	6.1	2.1
Netherlands	3,812	15.9	3.3	4,274	14.3	3.7	4,002	18.6	3.4
PRC	281	44.5	0.2	383	42.6	0.3	566	35.0	0.5
Spain	932	22.1	0.8	1,024	22.3	0.9	1,084	21.4	0.9
Sweden	2,525	16.5	2.2	2,405	19.1	2.1	2,285	16.5	1.9
Switzerland	3,308	31.7	2.8	3,417	31.6	3.0	3,326	34.2	2.8
Taipei	316	19.3	0.3	422	15.9	0.4	582	16.0	0.5
UK	6,953	22.3	6.0	6,605	24.5	5.7	6,564	24.0	5.5
USA	34,256	12.2	29.3	33,932	12.8	29.5	35,613	12.4	30.0
EU-28	54,050	8.1	46.3	53,858	8.3	46.8	53,982	8.6	45.5
World	116,762	7.0	100.0	115,115	7.3	100.0	118,736	7.4	100.0

(Continued)

Table 7.2. *(Continued)*

(Number and Percent)

Country	2003			2004			2005		
	Total Patents	Foreign Co-Inventors (%)	Share of World Patents (%)	Total Patents	Foreign Co-Inventors (%)	Share of World Patents (%)	Total Patents	Foreign Co-Inventors (%)	Share of World Patents (%)
Australia	1,230	21.0	1.0	1,328	21.9	1.0	1,318	20.9	1.0
Austria	1,618	25.0	1.3	1,715	26.8	1.3	1,778	25.2	1.3
Belgium	1,777	38.4	1.4	1,964	37.6	1.5	1,990	39.6	1.5
Canada	2,380	31.8	1.9	2,735	27.4	2.1	2,946	27.1	2.2
Denmark	1,245	19.6	1.0	1,269	23.5	1.0	1,338	19.4	1.0
Finland	1,394	13.8	1.1	1,517	14.2	1.1	1,465	16.9	1.1
France	8,881	17.9	7.1	9,309	18.3	7.0	9,456	19.6	6.9
Germany	23,833	13.4	19.2	24,920	14.0	18.9	25,982	14.6	19.0
India	658	34.7	0.5	671	36.2	0.5	736	33.0	0.5
Israel	1,182	16.1	1.0	1,364	18.9	1.0	1,592	17.5	1.2
Italy	4,691	10.3	3.8	4,900	10.6	3.7	5,230	10.5	3.8
Japan	22,720	3.0	18.3	23,813	3.1	18.0	22,698	3.5	16.6
Korea	3,456	4.9	2.8	4,608	4.3	3.5	5,345	4.8	3.9
Netherlands	3,971	20.2	3.2	4,109	19.2	3.1	3,992	19.6	2.9
PRC	835	34.4	0.7	1,019	29.9	0.8	1,784	26.7	1.3
Spain	1,129	24.0	0.9	1,403	22.1	1.1	1,559	20.3	1.1
Sweden	2,276	17.3	1.8	2,490	18.1	1.9	2,740	19.1	2.0
Switzerland	3,479	34.5	2.8	3,884	36.3	2.9	4,108	37.6	3.0
Taipei	632	11.9	0.5	720	13.8	0.5	871	12.2	0.6
UK	6,603	23.4	5.3	6,683	27.0	5.1	6,753	26.8	4.9
USA	36,706	12.9	29.5	38,669	13.2	29.3	40,381	13.2	29.5
EU-28	55,586	8.4	44.7	58,404	9.3	44.2	60,391	9.7	44.2
World	124,338	7.5	100.0	132,053	7.8	100.0	136,759	8.0	100.0

(Continued)

Table 7.2. (*Continued*)

(Number and Percent)

Country	2006 Total Patents	2006 Foreign Co-Inventors (%)	2006 Share of World Patents (%)	2007 Total Patents	2007 Foreign Co-Inventors (%)	2007 Share of World Patents (%)	2008 Total Patents	2008 Foreign Co-Inventors (%)	2008 Share of World Patents (%)
Australia	1,209	24.4	0.9	1,108	24.3	0.8	1,079	23.9	0.8
Austria	2,061	26.6	1.5	2,035	27.8	1.5	1,895	26.1	1.5
Belgium	2,026	38.7	1.5	2,016	36.7	1.5	1,958	37.5	1.5
Canada	2,978	31.6	2.2	2,877	33.0	2.2	2,667	32.1	2.1
Denmark	1,282	19.7	0.9	1,506	19.9	1.1	1,475	20.5	1.2
Finland	1,501	18.1	1.1	1,455	20.8	1.1	1,464	23.4	1.1
France	9,574	19.7	7.0	9,760	19.6	7.3	9,756	18.3	7.6
Germany	26,107	14.4	19.2	26,538	15.0	19.9	25,136	14.4	19.6
India	725	34.6	0.5	823	40.0	0.6	880	34.3	0.7
Israel	1,461	15.7	1.1	1,390	14.7	1.0	1,368	15.6	1.1
Italy	5,417	11.4	4.0	5,254	11.1	3.9	5,044	10.0	3.9
Japan	22,330	2.8	16.4	21,933	3.2	16.4	19,832	2.8	15.5
Korea	5,371	3.9	4.0	4,840	4.3	3.6	4,153	4.3	3.2
Netherlands	4,321	19.4	3.2	3,958	19.4	3.0	3,966	19.2	3.1
PRC	2,007	25.8	1.5	2,553	22.5	1.9	2,908	21.5	2.3
Spain	1,571	23.0	1.2	1,621	23.0	1.2	1,644	21.7	1.3
Sweden	2,969	19.8	2.2	3,249	21.8	2.4	3,135	20.3	2.4
Switzerland	4,208	37.1	3.1	4,292	39.4	3.2	4,043	36.4	3.2
Taipei	986	11.4	0.7	1,222	8.3	0.9	1,255	10.9	1.0
UK	6,924	25.1	5.1	6,851	26.2	5.1	6,443	25.0	5.0
USA	38,081	13.8	28.0	35,471	14.4	26.6	33,841	13.8	26.4
EU-28	61,842	9.4	45.5	62,287	9.4	46.7	60,188	8.6	47.0
World	135,848	8.1	100.0	133,511	8.4	100.0	128,079	8.2	100.0

(*Continued*)

Table 7.2. (*Continued*)

(Number and Percent)

Country	2009 Total Patents	2009 Foreign Co-Inventors (%)	2009 Share of World Patents (%)	2010 Total Patents	2010 Foreign Co-Inventors (%)	2010 Share of World Patents (%)	2011 Total Patents	2011 Foreign Co-Inventors (%)	2011 Share of World Patents (%)
Australia	1,083	25.3	0.8	995	27.4	0.7	1,040	27.1	0.8
Austria	2,014	26.8	1.5	2,084	27.2	1.6	2,139	27.5	1.6
Belgium	1,880	39.4	1.4	1,941	39.3	1.5	1,999	40.2	1.5
Canada	2,791	31.9	2.1	2,882	33.2	2.2	2,751	33.7	2.0
Denmark	1,344	20.2	1.0	1,476	22.2	1.1	1,672	21.3	1.2
Finland	1,454	17.5	1.1	1,566	19.4	1.2	1,505	18.8	1.1
France	9,693	17.7	7.4	9,513	19.0	7.1	9,983	18.9	7.3
Germany	25,437	14.8	19.5	25,404	14.3	19.0	24,919	14.6	18.2
India	1,052	35.7	0.8	1,283	40.5	1.0	1,460	41.4	1.1
Israel	1,295	16.9	1.0	1,272	16.0	1.0	1,237	17.1	0.9
Italy	4,755	11.4	3.7	4,832	11.4	3.6	4,780	12.6	3.5
Japan	20,302	3.0	15.6	22,367	2.8	16.8	22,280	2.8	16.3
Korea	5,033	3.9	3.9	5,598	4.7	4.2	5,572	4.5	4.1
Netherlands	3,908	19.0	3.0	3,434	19.2	2.6	3,844	17.5	2.8
PRC	4,196	18.1	3.2	4,510	17.7	3.4	5,039	18.9	3.7
Spain	1,735	18.9	1.3	1,707	19.2	1.3	1,661	19.3	1.2
Sweden	2,983	20.2	2.3	3,186	20.8	2.4	3,229	21.9	2.4
Switzerland	3,987	36.3	3.1	4,203	36.1	3.1	4,128	35.9	3.0
Taipei	1,379	7.5	1.1	1,519	10.6	1.1	1,517	13.8	1.1
UK	6,457	26.3	5.0	6,375	26.8	4.8	6,487	27.2	4.7
USA	33,176	14.1	25.5	33,450	15.1	25.1	35,668	15.0	26.1
EU-28	59,889	8.8	46.0	59,824	9.2	44.8	60,729	9.4	44.4
World	130,189	8.1	100.0	133,510	8.3	100.0	136,712	8.5	100.0

(*Continued*)

Table 7.2. *(Continued)*

(Number and Percent)

Country	2012 Total Patents	2012 Foreign Co-Inventors (%)	2012 Share of World Patents (%)	2013 Total Patents	2013 Foreign Co-Inventors (%)	2013 Share of World Patents (%)
Australia	1,017	24.5	0.7	976	24.3	0.7
Austria	2,197	27.3	1.6	2,248	26.9	1.6
Belgium	1,959	38.9	1.4	1,937	32.9	1.4
Canada	2,807	33.6	2.0	2,763	33.1	1.9
Denmark	1,513	22.0	1.1	1,532	20.0	1.1
Finland	1,827	18.2	1.3	1,696	17.8	1.2
France	9,886	17.9	7.1	10,160	17.5	7.2
Germany	23,912	15.0	17.2	23,464	14.9	16.6
India	1,478	41.1	1.1	1,459	43.2	1.0
Israel	1,405	18.4	1.0	1,452	20.7	1.0
Italy	4,685	11.9	3.4	4,658	12.3	3.3
Japan	21,554	2.8	15.5	20,081	2.8	14.2
Korea	6,045	4.1	4.4	6,677	3.4	4.7
Netherlands	3,807	18.2	2.7	3,840	18.8	2.7
PRC	6,492	16.6	4.7	6,886	16.4	4.9
Spain	1,730	20.1	1.2	1,742	18.9	1.2
Sweden	3,570	23.7	2.6	3,042	21.2	2.1
Switzerland	4,109	38.1	3.0	4,134	37.5	2.9
Taipei	1,422	13.6	1.0	1,280	13.8	0.9
UK	6,358	25.4	4.6	6,770	24.3	4.8
USA	37,320	15.0	26.9	40,707	13.7	28.7
EU-28	60,219	9.7	43.4	60,140	9.4	42.4
World	138,839	8.5	100.0	141,719	8.2	100.0

Note: Patent counts are based on the priority date, the inventor's country of residence, using simple counts. (1) Share of patent applications to the European Patent Office (EPO) with at least one foreign co-inventor in total patents invented domestically; (2) The EU is treated as one country; intra-EU co-operation is excluded: (3) Patents of OECD residents that involve international co-operation: (4) All EPO patents that involve international co-operation. Only Patents that exceed 1,000 during the 2000–2013 are listed.
Source: OECD Patent Database, 2017.

Table 7.3. Foreign Ownership of Domestic Inventions

Leading Countries (2000–2013)
(Number and Percent)

Country	2000		2001		2002		2003		2004		2005		2006	
	Total Patents	Patents Owned by Foreign Residents (%)	Total Patents	Patents Owned by Foreign Residents (%)	Total Patents	Patents Owned by Foreign Residents (%)	Total Patents	Patents Owned by Foreign Residents (%)	Total Patents	Patents Owned by Foreign Residents (%)	Total Patents	Patents Owned by Foreign Residents (%)	Total Patents	Patents Owned by Foreign Residents (%)
India	230	41.3	344	39.8	543	30.8	658	44.7	671	46.1	736	45.9	725	48.6
UK	6,953	39.8	6,605	39.9	6,564	42.3	6,603	42.7	6,683	44.8	6,753	42.7	6,924	41.2
Canada	2,073	36.9	2,182	40.1	2,226	40.5	2,380	44.8	2,735	41.3	2,946	38.3	2,978	42.6
Belgium	1,655	49.7	1,541	45.0	1,667	44.8	1,777	48.3	1,964	45.3	1,990	45.9	2,026	44.9
Israel	1,163	33.4	1,056	32.7	1,022	29.0	1,182	31.0	1,364	33.3	1,592	28.8	1,461	30.5
Australia	1,160	29.1	1,116	28.7	1,190	29.5	1,230	30.9	1,328	31.8	1,318	29.7	1,209	31.9
Spain	932	35.2	1,024	34.5	1,084	31.7	1,129	35.0	1,403	28.7	1,559	29.2	1,571	30.2
Austria	1,391	37.2	1,457	40.5	1,562	43.9	1,618	38.6	1,715	40.6	1,778	41.2	2,061	40.6
PRC	281	58.7	383	51.7	566	50.4	835	54.1	1,019	46.4	1,784	40.2	2,007	37.7
Sweden	2,525	19.5	2,405	22.7	2,285	22.4	2,276	22.3	2,490	23.5	2,740	23.1	2,969	25.4
Switzerland	3,308	24.4	3,417	25.6	3,326	26.5	3,479	26.2	3,884	26.3	4,108	27.4	4,208	25.3
Denmark	1,079	24.0	1,063	26.5	1,089	24.3	1,245	24.3	1,269	25.1	1,338	26.0	1,282	25.6
Italy	4,261	20.2	4,253	19.4	4,491	17.4	4,691	19.5	4,900	19.6	5,230	19.6	5,417	22.1
Netherlands	3,812	21.8	4,274	23.1	4,002	22.6	3,971	24.7	4,109	24.3	3,992	27.4	4,321	28.7
France	8,042	24.0	8,075	25.3	8,260	27.1	8,881	26.9	9,309	26.0	9,456	26.4	9,574	25.3
Germany	23,566	14.7	23,370	15.0	23,424	16.1	23,833	17.3	24,920	17.5	25,982	18.1	26,107	17.0
Finland	1,547	14.1	1,531	12.9	1,398	11.7	1,394	12.1	1,517	12.9	1,465	15.4	1,501	16.8
Taipei	316	27.2	422	19.2	582	24.4	632	18.8	720	16.5	871	18.5	986	20.4
USA	34,256	13.4	33,932	14.2	35,613	15.3	36,706	15.3	38,669	15.1	40,381	15.3	38,081	16.1
European U-28	54,050	12.7	53,858	12.6	53,982	12.6	55,586	12.9	58,404	13.3	60,391	13.6	61,842	13.3
Korea	1,316	5.9	1,679	4.6	2,457	6.0	3,456	4.8	4,608	4.2	5,345	3.8	5,371	3.3
Japan	22,583	4.5	20,946	4.5	21,665	4.9	22,720	4.8	23,813	4.6	22,698	4.7	22,330	4.2
World	116,762	16.7	115,115	17.3	118,736	18.0	124,338	18.5	132,053	18.4	136,759	18.8	135,848	18.9

(Continued)

Table 7.3. *(Continued)*

Leading Countries (2000–2013)
(Number and Percent)

Country	2007		2008		2009		2010		2011		2012		2013	
	Total Patents	Patents Owned by Foreign Residents (%)	Total Patents	Patents Owned by Foreign Residents (%)	Total Patents	Patents Owned by Foreign Residents (%)	Total Patents	Patents Owned by Foreign Residents (%)	Total Patents	Patents Owned by Foreign Residents (%)	Total Patents	Patents Owned by Foreign Residents (%)	Total Patents	Patents Owned by Foreign Residents (%)
India	823	59.7	880	57.2	1, 052	58.7	1, 283	63.1	1, 460	63.5	1, 478	69.5	1, 459	66.0
UK	6,851	40.9	6,443	41.8	6,457	43.2	6,375	45.8	6,487	45.6	6,358	44.1	6,770	43.3
Canada	2,877	41.8	2,667	40.8	2,791	36.7	2,882	33.8	2,751	36.6	2,807	39.8	2,763	42.1
Belgium	2,016	46.1	1,958	46.6	1,880	49.5	1,941	46.9	1,999	46.8	1,959	46.8	1,937	42.0
Israel	1,390	25.9	1,368	29.2	1,295	28.3	1,272	27.6	1,237	35.2	1,405	29.1	1,452	31.8
Australia	1,108	31.1	1,079	34.0	1,083	32.5	995	31.2	1,040	33.4	1,017	34.8	976	31.3
Spain	1,621	31.2	1,644	30.5	1,735	28.4	1,707	27.9	1,661	31.2	1,730	32.1	1,742	28.3
Austria	2,035	41.1	1,895	33.4	2,014	28.3	2,084	29.7	2,139	30.4	2,197	30.6	2,248	27.8
PRC	2,553	33.4	2,908	37.3	4,196	29.8	4,510	28.5	5,039	32.3	6,492	28.5	6,886	27.5
Sweden	3,249	24.1	3,135	22.8	2,983	24.4	3,186	23.4	3,229	21.9	3,570	22.5	3,042	25.7
Switzerland	4,292	30.0	4,043	28.5	3,987	26.3	4,203	24.1	4,128	24.4	4,109	24.4	4,134	25.5
Denmark	1,506	23.5	1,475	24.3	1,344	23.8	1,476	30.6	1,672	29.5	1,513	29.2	1,532	25.3
Italy	5,254	22.2	5,044	21.4	4,755	22.7	4,832	21.8	4,780	23.7	4,685	25.4	4,658	23.9
Netherlands	3,958	28.1	3,966	28.5	3,908	28.3	3,434	29.5	3,844	26.3	3,807	25.7	3,840	23.3
France	9,760	24.9	9,756	23.5	9,693	23.2	9,513	24.1	9,983	24.8	9,886	22.6	10,160	23.1
Germany	26,538	18.4	25,136	17.7	25,437	17.7	25,404	17.4	24,919	17.5	23,912	17.6	23,464	17.6
Finland	1,455	17.9	1,464	20.9	1,454	16.9	1,566	17.0	1,505	14.6	1,827	15.4	1,696	16.3
Taipei	1,222	15.3	1,255	12.6	1,379	11.9	1,519	11.5	1,517	16.9	1,422	15.1	1,280	15.7
USA	35,471	16.5	33,841	15.6	33,176	16.1	33,450	16.5	35,668	15.6	37,320	15.3	40,707	13.8
European U-28	62,287	13.4	60,188	12.3	59,889	12.2	59,824	12.3	60,729	12.8	60,219	12.5	60,140	13.0
Korea	4,840	4.8	4,153	5.0	5,033	4.3	5,598	5.2	5,572	6.4	6,046	4.5	6,677	3.3
Japan	21,933	4.6	19,832	4.1	20,302	4.2	22,367	3.5	22,280	3.7	21,554	3.5	20,081	3.3
World	133,511	19.3	128,079	19.1	130,189	18.8	133,510	18.6	136,712	19.1	138,839	18.8	141,719	18.4

Source: Share of patent applications to the European Patent Office (EPO) owned by foreign residents in total patents invented domestically. OECD, Patent Database, 2017. Ordered by 2013 share data only for patents that exceed 1,000 during the 2000–2013.

The leading economies are India, the UK, Canada, Belgium and Israel. Israel is the only member of MENA that has more than 1,000 patents annually and where 31.8 percent of its patents filed at the EPO in 2013 are foreign-owned. The remaining 68.2 percent are domestically owned. This balance reflects Israel's ability to sell its technology abroad and to provide both the infrastructure and the human capital to attract foreign partners to innovate their technologies within Israel. None of the Arab MENA countries appears on this list reflecting their inability to participate in the global R&D market, as demonstrated by the OECD patent data, during the 2000–2013 period.

The increase in research within countries and globally can also be observed in the growth of the number of research publications from around 162.1 articles per million population in 2000 to 306.2 articles per million population in 2013 for the entire world. Despite the fact that total world scientific publications are dominated by the OECD, the intensity of output (measured as scientific articles per million population) has increased in the majority of countries that have adopted pro-knowledge economy policies over the past decade.

Table 7.4 presents the number of science and engineering (S&E) articles per million population across all fields for the MENA countries. It is not surprising to find that within MENA, Israel and Cyprus lead the list of S&E articles published in internationally recognized and refereed journals. In 2013, Israeli scientists published 1402 scholarly articles and Cypriot scientists published 776 scholarly articles. These results are a tribute to the successful implementation of these countries' pro "knowledge economy" policies during the past five decades.

These results are in stark contrast to the figures reported by the UNDP (2009b p. 197), which claimed that within Arab MENA, "Egypt, Saudi Arabia, Tunisia, and Morocco lead the Arab countries in scientific publishing." The data on S&E publications based on internationally recognized sources, reported in Table 7.4, differ substantially from the UNDP claim for the entire period 2000–2013. Based on the NSF data reported in Table 7.4, we have Iran, Turkey and Tunisia among Arab-MENA in the top rank in 2013 as well as in earlier years. Egyptian scientists had only published 34 S&E articles in 2000 and 102 S&E articles per million population in 2013. This is a far cry from the "lead" position as asserted by the UNDP (2009b, p. 197). The bottom of this list is composed of Iraq, Syria and Yemen. Why the misrepresentation? The answer is found when one investigates the sources used by the UNDP in making this fallacious claim. The

Table 7.4. Number of Science & Engineering Articles in All Fields (Per Million Population)

(2000–2013)

Country	2000	2001	2002	2003	2004	2005	2006	2007	2008	2009	2010	2011	2012	2013
Algeria	11.3	12.4	14.6	18.1	25.0	27.9	38.7	42.2	52.5	63.1	62.5	71.2	84.5	95.3
Bahrain	110.1	113.5	73.7	152.7	157.5	176.1	185.0	170.6	144.5	159.5	162.5	141.0	120.9	159.4
Cyprus	141.8	120.1	153.6	142.2	215.3	258.5	300.1	343.1	401.8	524.0	557.7	584.0	649.2	776.8
Egypt	34.4	38.2	38.3	41.2	45.3	45.3	50.1	56.2	60.5	74.4	79.6	89.7	101.7	102.4
Iran	22.0	26.4	37.0	50.3	69.6	98.3	139.5	183.1	236.8	286.3	344.4	436.8	441.1	425.7
Iraq	3.6	3.7	4.1	4.6	3.4	5.2	8.8	8.5	11.0	13.7	19.7	25.0	28.8	27.9
Israel	1,358.2	1,327.0	1,376.9	1,385.5	1,468.4	1,474.9	1,539.9	1,541.1	1,530.7	1,479.2	1,408.3	1,418.7	1,456.0	1,402.1
Jordan	101.4	98.3	109.9	117.8	134.1	138.3	160.0	183.9	202.3	206.2	210.3	201.3	189.5	178.8
Kuwait	225.1	233.8	218.6	223.7	244.0	268.0	277.2	284.2	282.3	277.7	247.1	250.3	241.7	234.5
Lebanon	110.2	110.7	97.4	116.7	124.8	137.7	153.3	160.7	176.0	182.0	179.6	197.0	205.8	199.1
Morocco	29.0	31.9	31.3	30.2	31.2	30.0	32.0	33.6	38.5	46.9	52.0	62.3	71.4	75.0
Oman	77.2	100.5	98.2	118.4	120.0	125.2	126.3	140.9	134.8	147.0	155.4	186.4	169.8	177.2
Qatar	75.3	118.5	137.8	146.4	181.3	194.0	181.7	204.6	200.9	204.0	223.8	234.4	292.1	342.2
SA	70.9	69.3	69.3	73.6	72.7	72.1	76.3	79.3	86.1	108.6	136.9	184.3	214.1	255.0
Syria	5.6	4.9	4.7	5.7	7.4	7.8	6.2	7.9	9.9	7.7	11.1	13.5	15.4	15.7
Tunisia	60.8	72.8	91.9	98.1	132.8	165.3	188.1	225.3	264.1	303.6	325.4	350.5	354.5	381.9
Turkey	104.4	128.9	162.5	192.0	230.8	258.5	281.7	307.4	309.7	348.8	361.9	372.6	379.9	401.2
UAE	93.1	109.2	100.0	129.4	127.3	147.0	148.6	121.7	127.4	129.8	141.9	161.1	178.5	186.4
Yemen	1.2	2.1	1.4	1.5	1.9	2.2	2.5	2.1	2.6	3.5	4.5	4.9	4.8	5.0
World	162.1	163.1	167.6	175.9	195.8	220.5	232.2	243.2	253.9	266.3	277.2	293.5	301.6	306.2

Source: National Science Foundation, National Center for Science and Engineering Statistics; Science and Engineering Indicators 2016.

UNDP (2009b p. 197) relied on data taken from "studies of the Standing Committee on Scientific and Technical Cooperation (COMSTECH)." Who is COMSTECH? Is it an internationally recognized source? COMSTECH is in fact "a Ministerial Standing Committee on Scientific and Technological Cooperation established by the Third Summit of the Organization of Islamic Conference (OIC) held at Makkah, Saudi Arabia in January 1981." COMSTECH is a pro-active State actor "entrusted with the follow-up actions on science and technology-related decisions of the Summit" and not an independent internationally recognized nor impartial data source. Consequently, the claims made by the UNDP (2009b, p 199) can be ignored.

The next set of tables presents the distribution of scientific articles by key sub-branches. The empirical evidence unanimously supports the conclusion that in all the sub-branches of internationally recognized published research, the major non-OECD primary contributors to scientific research within MENA is Israel.

In agricultural sciences (Table 7.5), the leading country in the number of published S&E research over the 2000–2013 period was Israel with 16.7 articles per million population in 2013. Tunisia and Turkey ranked 2nd and 3rd with 14.9 and 14.2 articles per million population in 2013. In Table 7.6, we present the number of S&E research articles in Astronomy Sciences for the 2000–2013 period. The only country with a substantial record of publications in Astronomy Sciences is Israel with 11 publications per million population in 2013. The balance of MENA countries in this area were hard placed to reach 1 article per million population. Table 7.7 presents the numbers of S&E articles per million population in biological sciences for the 2000–2013 period. The overwhelming leading country in published research in this area is Israel with 231.4 articles per million population in 2013. The world average was 48.5 articles per million population in 2013. Israel's record of performance in this area of research has been the lead within MENA for the entire period 2000–2013. In the post 2007 period there was an uptick in research in Iran, Cyprus, Saudi Arabia, Turkey and Tunisia. Despite the changes in their performance they are still far behind the Israeli standard. Table 7.8 presents the numbers of S&E articles per million population in chemistry. The only large-scale publications in this area in the entire 2000–2013 period were from scientists in Israel. Israeli-published research in chemistry was consistently over 70 articles per year. Publications from Cyprus ranked 2nd place over the entire period. Scientists in Arab MENA were substantially less prolific.

Table 7.5. Number of Science & Engineering Articles in Agricultural Sciences (Per Million Population)

	(2000–2013)													
Country	2000	2001	2002	2003	2004	2005	2006	2007	2008	2009	2010	2011	2012	2013
Algeria	0.2	0.2	0.1	0.2	0.2	0.3	0.7	0.7	1.0	1.2	1.3	1.4	1.3	1.9
Bahrain	1.5	4.3	1.8	1.7	2.4	3.4	3.4	2.2	6.5	2.4	5.6	2.3	1.2	4.0
Cyprus	4.5	0.5	3.1	1.8	2.6	1.7	3.8	3.2	2.4	8.6	7.8	6.7	9.7	7.6
Egypt	1.1	1.2	1.1	0.9	0.7	0.8	1.4	2.2	2.1	2.0	2.1	2.8	2.5	3.0
Iran	0.5	0.5	0.8	0.9	1.7	2.5	6.6	12.3	12.5	12.4	15.0	18.1	16.9	13.6
Iraq	0.0	0.1	0.2	0.0	0.1	0.1	0.2	0.3	0.6	0.7	0.8	1.3	0.8	0.8
Israel	21.8	17.9	18.0	18.1	19.5	18.3	14.7	19.5	16.4	18.2	14.2	17.4	16.7	16.7
Jordan	4.7	5.8	6.6	7.2	8.0	5.5	9.6	12.5	12.5	10.0	7.6	7.9	8.5	7.0
Kuwait	5.0	2.8	2.1	3.0	3.6	2.6	3.5	3.9	4.0	4.3	2.7	2.9	2.9	3.6
Lebanon	4.1	4.0	1.5	2.7	1.7	2.8	2.9	1.7	1.9	2.7	4.0	3.2	2.1	1.3
Morocco	0.7	0.7	1.0	0.7	0.7	0.8	0.8	0.8	1.1	0.7	0.5	0.7	0.6	0.7
Oman	4.3	5.1	5.0	5.5	6.9	7.0	6.3	9.4	4.1	5.1	4.5	4.9	5.7	6.7
Qatar	5.1	0.8	6.2	4.4	1.3	1.2	0.3	0.4	1.2	1.3	0.6	1.7	0.6	1.2
SA	1.8	1.3	1.4	0.9	1.3	1.0	2.5	2.1	2.0	2.4	3.4	3.6	4.5	5.3
Syria	1.3	0.9	0.4	0.8	0.8	1.1	0.9	0.9	1.1	0.9	1.2	1.3	1.5	1.3
Tunisia	1.5	1.5	1.3	1.7	1.8	2.9	3.9	9.8	8.3	12.4	14.1	14.9	14.3	14.9
Turkey	3.4	3.5	4.8	6.0	8.6	8.5	12.4	12.0	12.6	18.4	18.3	17.4	14.6	14.2
UAE	1.3	1.4	0.8	2.1	2.3	2.1	4.6	1.6	1.5	2.1	1.4	1.4	1.7	2.0
Yemen	0.0	0.1	0.1	0.0	0.0	0.0	0.1	0.0	0.1	0.0	0.0	0.1	0.1	0.1
World	3.2	2.9	3.2	3.3	3.5	3.8	4.4	5.1	5.4	5.7	5.9	6.3	6.2	6.6

Source: National Science Foundation, National Center for Science and Engineering Statistics; Science and Engineering Indicators 2016.

Table 7.6. Number of Science & Engineering Articles in Astronomy Sciences (Per Million Population)

	(2000–2013)													
Country	2000	2001	2002	2003	2004	2005	2006	2007	2008	2009	2010	2011	2012	2013
Algeria	0.1	0.0	0.0	0.0	0.1	0.2	0.2	0.2	0.1	0.2	0.2	0.2	0.4	0.3
Bahrain	0.0	0.0	0.0	0.0	0.0	0.0	1.0	1.9	0.0	0.6	0.8	0.0	0.0	0.0
Cyprus	0.0	0.0	0.5	1.1	0.1	0.6	2.1	0.1	0.2	1.0	0.2	0.7	1.0	2.4
Egypt	0.1	0.1	0.1	0.2	0.1	0.1	0.2	0.2	0.2	0.2	0.6	0.5	0.6	0.7
Iran	0.1	0.1	0.2	0.2	0.2	0.2	0.4	0.3	0.4	0.4	0.5	0.9	1.3	1.2
Iraq	0.0	0.0	0.0	0.0	0.0	0.0	0.0	0.0	0.0	0.0	0.0	0.0	0.0	0.1
Israel	8.8	9.3	11.2	10.2	12.4	10.9	13.0	10.3	11.5	10.5	10.6	11.7	15.2	11.0
Jordan	0.5	0.1	0.0	0.1	0.2	0.2	0.0	0.2	0.1	0.2	0.0	0.1	0.2	0.1
Kuwait	0.0	0.0	0.0	0.0	0.0	0.0	0.1	0.5	0.4	0.1	0.0	0.1	0.0	0.0
Lebanon	0.6	0.1	0.4	0.0	0.1	0.0	0.4	0.3	0.0	0.5	0.1	0.3	0.4	0.1
Morocco	0.2	0.1	0.1	0.1	0.1	0.2	0.2	0.1	0.1	0.1	0.1	0.0	0.1	0.0
Oman	0.0	0.0	0.0	0.0	0.1	0.4	0.4	0.2	0.4	0.2	0.1	0.3	0.3	0.0
Qatar	0.0	0.0	0.0	0.3	0.0	0.0	0.0	0.0	0.1	0.0	0.2	0.7	0.3	1.7
SA	0.0	0.1	0.2	0.4	0.1	0.1	0.0	0.1	0.0	0.0	0.1	0.3	0.5	0.5
Syria	0.0	0.0	0.0	0.0	0.0	0.0	0.0	0.0	0.0	0.0	0.0	0.0	0.0	0.1
Tunisia	0.0	0.0	0.0	0.0	0.3	0.2	0.3	0.3	0.1	0.4	0.1	0.5	0.4	0.5
Turkey	0.2	0.3	0.3	0.4	0.5	0.7	1.0	0.6	0.7	0.6	0.6	0.7	0.9	0.9
UAE	0.3	0.3	0.4	0.1	0.1	0.1	0.5	0.3	0.1	0.2	0.1	0.3	0.1	0.0
Yemen	0.0	0.0	0.0	0.0	0.0	0.1	0.0	0.0	0.0	0.0	0.0	0.0	0.0	0.0
World	1.5	1.6	1.7	1.8	1.9	2.2	2.4	2.1	1.9	1.8	1.8	2.1	2.1	1.9

Source: National Science Foundation, National Center for Science and Engineering Statistics; Science and Engineering Indicators 2016.

Table 7.7. Number of Science & Engineering Articles in Biological Sciences (Per Million Population)

	(2000–2013)													
Country	2000	2001	2002	2003	2004	2005	2006	2007	2008	2009	2010	2011	2012	2013
Algeria	0.5	0.4	0.8	1.1	1.1	1.1	3.3	3.5	4.4	4.6	5.2	5.4	5.6	7.0
Bahrain	13.5	10.5	5.8	19.0	14.5	19.3	16.8	14.9	10.1	9.3	10.5	8.1	8.0	10.2
Cyprus	18.8	12.6	22.7	9.1	13.8	17.8	17.1	27.0	26.8	32.9	34.6	33.5	49.2	65.5
Egypt	4.2	4.7	4.6	5.1	4.6	4.3	5.3	5.8	7.4	10.9	11.2	18.0	20.2	20.5
Iran	2.7	3.0	4.5	5.5	7.3	9.2	15.6	21.2	27.0	32.6	38.8	74.0	65.3	65.8
Iraq	0.1	0.2	0.3	0.7	0.3	0.3	0.7	0.8	0.7	1.7	2.4	4.6	3.2	3.9
Israel	271.6	259.2	257.7	259.9	258.9	250.9	247.5	251.4	244.9	239.8	234.4	240.4	245.1	231.4
Jordan	13.8	13.9	13.9	17.4	16.1	15.8	21.3	24.7	20.2	31.6	29.0	28.8	24.5	21.5
Kuwait	39.5	40.8	34.5	42.6	39.1	43.3	39.9	38.3	36.0	33.1	30.1	33.4	30.4	26.2
Lebanon	9.8	16.2	13.4	18.4	17.9	14.8	14.6	17.3	19.0	18.3	19.6	21.4	22.5	21.5
Morocco	2.1	2.9	3.2	3.2	3.1	2.9	2.8	4.0	3.8	3.9	4.2	4.9	6.8	7.1
Oman	8.9	6.3	7.9	11.0	7.1	11.7	11.6	13.9	11.2	10.7	17.9	14.6	17.0	20.6
Qatar	2.2	6.5	5.7	14.1	17.9	9.6	9.4	12.9	13.6	13.2	17.6	17.2	21.7	25.2
SA	7.6	8.3	7.9	8.5	6.9	7.0	7.9	7.5	8.8	11.3	18.2	29.7	32.1	44.1
Syria	0.8	1.0	1.4	1.5	1.6	1.4	1.4	1.8	2.4	1.7	2.2	3.2	3.4	5.2
Tunisia	5.4	8.1	13.4	11.0	12.6	19.5	27.5	39.0	44.4	46.7	50.6	62.3	55.3	54.2
Turkey	11.9	15.8	20.0	23.3	26.0	28.6	31.1	32.0	31.6	36.7	40.4	44.6	39.7	40.9
UAE	17.4	17.3	11.3	13.8	14.5	17.4	15.1	12.0	13.4	10.7	12.9	12.6	11.7	13.8
Yemen	0.2	0.3	0.2	0.3	0.3	0.2	0.4	0.3	0.2	0.4	0.7	0.7	0.6	0.7
World	30.8	31.2	31.1	31.6	33.5	34.9	35.7	37.1	38.7	39.8	41.2	44.7	46.9	48.5

Source: National Science Foundation, National Center for Science and Engineering Statistics; Science and Engineering Indicators 2016.

Table 7.8. Number of Science & Engineering Articles in Chemistry (Per Million Population)

	(2000–2013)													
Country	2000	2001	2002	2003	2004	2005	2006	2007	2008	2009	2010	2011	2012	2013
Algeria	1.7	1.3	2.0	2.2	2.8	2.9	4.8	4.8	5.2	6.2	6.4	6.3	6.8	7.1
Bahrain	4.5	0.4	4.2	6.4	2.8	1.0	4.2	1.9	2.5	1.7	1.9	3.0	1.9	3.4
Cyprus	6.9	10.9	23.6	7.5	17.8	17.3	24.2	27.7	20.8	39.4	34.5	38.8	35.2	49.2
Egypt	7.7	7.7	8.6	8.8	8.8	8.8	9.7	10.6	10.7	10.2	10.4	10.6	11.3	11.6
Iran	6.1	7.8	9.3	12.1	14.5	18.8	22.7	28.5	31.4	34.9	40.0	48.2	53.3	54.6
Iraq	0.2	0.5	0.4	0.3	0.3	0.6	0.5	0.9	0.8	0.9	1.3	1.8	2.5	3.0
Israel	77.9	80.0	85.3	79.9	80.7	81.3	84.1	76.0	83.7	73.2	78.0	80.1	69.5	72.9
Jordan	5.9	7.7	9.3	8.8	9.8	9.0	12.4	14.8	14.7	12.2	11.1	10.4	10.6	10.3
Kuwait	13.5	15.8	15.4	8.6	14.9	20.6	23.8	20.2	19.4	13.0	13.8	12.5	11.9	9.3
Lebanon	3.1	2.4	2.4	1.8	2.1	3.0	3.7	3.2	5.7	4.9	4.3	7.5	5.4	7.5
Morocco	4.8	4.6	4.2	3.6	3.6	3.2	3.1	3.7	3.6	4.9	7.1	8.8	6.9	6.9
Oman	2.4	2.9	4.5	4.8	4.3	3.3	7.7	2.7	6.6	5.1	7.0	5.2	8.6	6.3
Qatar	8.1	5.0	4.6	6.8	21.9	13.1	7.5	6.1	13.0	6.3	13.9	16.4	14.9	15.0
SA	5.0	4.6	6.0	5.3	5.9	6.0	5.9	6.5	6.7	7.4	12.9	19.3	27.7	28.1
Syria	0.6	0.4	0.5	0.9	0.9	0.6	0.7	0.4	0.5	0.5	1.5	1.4	1.6	1.3
Tunisia	7.4	6.1	7.4	9.7	12.1	11.4	13.9	15.5	15.5	17.1	18.1	20.0	20.1	22.9
Turkey	9.1	11.0	12.5	13.7	17.7	17.8	20.7	23.9	22.7	24.5	24.6	23.8	23.6	26.2
UAE	3.7	6.0	3.5	3.7	3.4	4.6	5.2	5.4	3.3	3.7	5.5	7.7	6.5	8.1
Yemen	0.0	0.4	0.0	0.2	0.5	0.2	0.2	0.3	0.3	0.3	0.3	0.4	0.4	0.1
World	14.7	14.6	15.2	15.2	17.2	18.7	19.8	19.5	20.7	20.7	21.7	23.5	23.4	24.3

Source: National Science Foundation, National Center for Science and Engineering Statistics; Science and Engineering Indicators 2016.

In Table 7.9 we present the numbers of S&E articles per million population in computer sciences for the 2000–2013 period. The leading number of S&E scientific research publications in this area were from Israel and Cyprus. Scientists in Arab MENA were significantly less prolific in this line of research. Table 7.10 presents the numbers of S&E articles per million population in engineering. The leading published research consistently originated from Israel and Cyprus. Since 2007 there was an uptick in research in this area from Qatar, Tunisia and Iran.

Table 7.11 presents the number of S&E articles per million population in geosciences. Scientists from Israel remain the most prolific during the entire 2000–2013 period. Post 2007, scientists in Cyprus, Kuwait, Tunisia and Iran began to publish in this research area. The balance of Arab MENA has not participated in this research area significantly. Table 7.12 presents the numbers of S&E articles per million population in mathematics. Scientists from Israel have consistently ranked number one in terms of publications in mathematics during the entire 2000–2013 period. They have consistently published over 50 scientific articles per year per million population. The world average during this period ranges from 4 to 7.6 articles per year. Other MENA countries coming on board in mathematics include Cyprus, Saudi Arabia and Tunisia. Table 7.13 presents the numbers of S&E articles per million population in medical sciences. Scientists from Israel have outperformed all of the other MENA countries with the number of research articles ranging from 350 to 430 per year for the entire period. Scientists in Turkey place second place with a publication record ranging from 50 to 162 per year during the same period. The world average ranged from 44 to 65 articles per year.

Table 7.14 presents the numbers of S&E articles per million population in other life sciences. Scientists from Israel have maintained the lead position within MENA in terms of the number of articles in other life sciences during the entire 2000–2013 period. As of 2010, Cyprus has increased its scientific publications and now ranks second place within MENA. The world average during this period ranges from 4 to 7.6 articles per year. The balance of MENA countries have yet to reach one article per year per million population.

Table 7.15 presents the numbers of S&E articles per million population in physics. Scientists from Israel have maintained the lead position within MENA in terms of the number of articles in physics during the entire 2000–2013 period. Israel's publications ranged from 166 to 185 articles per year per million population. The world average ranged from 20 to 28 articles per

Table 7.9. Number of Science & Engineering Articles in Computer Sciences (Per Million Population)

(2000–2013)

Country	2000	2001	2002	2003	2004	2005	2006	2007	2008	2009	2010	2011	2012	2013
Algeria	0.3	0.5	1.2	1.3	1.7	3.3	5.8	6.0	6.2	9.8	9.9	12.4	14.7	14.3
Bahrain	0.0	4.7	1.4	5.1	3.1	7.6	7.3	12.1	13.6	15.9	24.3	17.1	17.7	16.0
Cyprus	13.4	18.2	16.3	25.8	43.8	61.6	79.4	71.5	84.5	106.2	100.8	108.8	162.1	144.0
Egypt	0.9	0.8	0.7	1.0	1.1	2.2	2.6	3.4	3.9	5.7	6.7	6.0	6.3	5.9
Iran	0.6	0.7	1.1	2.0	4.0	6.8	8.1	13.4	22.0	30.3	37.9	40.7	24.3	24.8
Iraq	0.1	0.2	0.0	0.6	0.0	0.0	0.6	0.3	0.5	1.0	1.7	2.7	2.0	1.6
Israel	58.0	67.7	65.1	92.2	117.6	127.8	147.5	144.9	151.7	144.6	142.2	137.7	168.8	140.9
Jordan	3.1	2.9	2.8	6.7	7.1	10.3	13.3	16.2	27.0	25.3	37.0	29.2	25.8	24.3
Kuwait	11.8	9.5	10.0	8.9	10.6	19.7	20.3	21.4	19.0	35.4	29.4	29.0	22.6	21.5
Lebanon	4.5	2.2	3.1	5.9	8.5	12.2	15.3	16.3	13.6	20.6	21.7	25.0	26.3	18.8
Morocco	0.9	0.5	0.4	0.6	0.5	0.9	1.3	1.1	2.5	4.9	5.6	8.6	11.5	11.7
Oman	2.7	1.7	3.9	6.5	6.8	6.3	9.1	10.0	11.2	18.7	14.7	16.5	16.2	13.3
Qatar	1.7	2.9	1.5	6.1	7.2	5.0	7.1	9.6	21.7	15.3	21.3	25.8	41.1	57.4
SA	1.8	1.5	1.6	2.1	2.3	2.5	3.6	4.3	7.0	10.1	14.7	17.4	17.7	22.9
Syria	0.0	0.0	0.0	0.0	0.1	0.2	0.4	0.4	0.3	0.7	0.4	0.4	0.3	0.5
Tunisia	3.3	1.6	9.8	3.4	5.6	13.3	17.1	20.3	27.7	37.4	42.8	40.9	55.4	59.0
Turkey	1.8	1.5	1.6	3.9	5.4	7.0	9.6	11.0	12.1	17.0	23.0	24.6	15.7	16.0
UAE	3.7	2.0	5.4	10.3	13.1	17.6	23.7	18.7	22.5	23.0	24.6	29.3	27.1	29.6
Yemen	0.0	0.0	0.0	0.0	0.0	0.1	0.1	0.0	0.0	0.3	0.4	0.6	0.2	0.4
World	4.9	5.1	5.5	8.2	12.1	15.9	17.1	19.2	21.2	24.5	27.1	26.0	25.9	24.7

Source: National Science Foundation, National Center for Science and Engineering Statistics; Science and Engineering Indicators 2016.

Table 7.10. Number of Science & Engineering Articles in Engineering (Per Million Population)

(2000–2013)

Country	2000	2001	2002	2003	2004	2005	2006	2007	2008	2009	2010	2011	2012	2013
Algeria	4.3	4.2	3.8	6.2	10.5	9.7	12.3	13.5	17.3	20.1	19.8	26.5	31.7	39.2
Bahrain	28.9	39.7	12.8	44.2	32.4	31.9	27.9	40.0	26.6	39.1	34.3	30.9	25.2	26.1
Cyprus	30.3	23.0	11.3	19.9	43.2	50.9	55.8	70.7	79.3	91.3	135.0	126.1	128.9	150.8
Egypt	8.0	11.0	10.1	9.4	14.1	11.8	12.5	13.5	14.0	16.1	16.8	16.7	19.5	21.4
Iran	4.6	5.8	7.6	12.1	18.2	24.3	34.0	42.4	60.0	71.1	93.4	108.9	122.7	106.9
Iraq	1.1	0.9	0.8	0.7	0.8	0.9	2.0	1.5	2.4	2.4	4.8	5.9	8.8	7.0
Israel	107.1	101.6	96.3	104.2	138.1	134.0	146.3	137.3	142.8	147.0	131.8	126.3	120.4	121.0
Jordan	23.2	22.8	22.5	25.3	31.3	30.4	28.8	40.6	41.0	39.8	39.8	42.8	36.7	38.6
Kuwait	51.3	57.0	41.6	59.1	55.5	57.5	54.1	70.0	58.4	61.5	56.5	64.4	68.0	63.4
Lebanon	15.9	10.5	11.9	14.7	22.2	20.8	24.4	24.6	31.4	33.4	31.8	44.7	48.8	50.0
Morocco	2.7	3.6	3.1	3.3	4.7	4.0	3.9	5.3	4.9	5.5	5.9	7.1	11.7	12.7
Oman	14.2	23.1	22.7	26.0	27.6	32.9	28.4	41.4	32.7	33.6	36.0	45.3	44.0	40.4
Qatar	12.7	26.1	23.7	19.5	37.3	42.1	31.6	40.6	49.7	48.7	67.3	58.3	94.9	116.5
SA	15.7	15.3	13.2	16.2	15.3	16.0	16.4	18.9	17.0	25.0	26.3	38.6	44.8	55.9
Syria	0.6	0.6	0.6	0.4	1.7	1.1	0.7	1.3	2.7	1.0	1.7	2.0	3.1	1.7
Tunisia	9.5	9.1	12.2	13.5	32.0	30.2	30.4	37.1	53.6	59.6	64.7	75.8	75.0	101.5
Turkey	12.8	14.4	18.8	21.4	32.8	34.5	40.9	47.0	48.5	52.9	52.8	53.2	62.2	67.8
UAE	15.5	27.9	22.6	37.9	38.5	42.6	42.3	35.9	28.6	40.0	46.6	55.8	71.1	73.8
Yemen	0.1	0.2	0.2	0.1	0.1	0.1	0.2	0.3	0.1	0.2	0.4	0.4	0.6	0.7
World	20.8	21.6	21.8	24.2	29.7	36.1	38.1	41.4	43.7	46.1	49.6	55.7	59.4	60.5

Source: National Science Foundation, National Center for Science and Engineering Statistics; Science and Engineering Indicators 2016.

Table 7.11. Number of Science & Engineering Articles in Geosciences (Per Million Population)

	(2000–2013)													
Country	2000	2001	2002	2003	2004	2005	2006	2007	2008	2009	2010	2011	2012	2013
Algeria	0.5	0.9	0.7	1.2	1.3	2.0	1.5	1.4	2.3	3.7	3.3	2.8	4.2	5.3
Bahrain	3.0	6.2	7.5	5.4	4.3	8.8	5.0	4.2	2.3	8.2	7.2	4.5	4.6	6.4
Cyprus	3.3	5.5	3.1	6.5	7.1	7.6	7.0	13.7	21.1	30.3	34.8	30.3	26.8	37.9
Egypt	2.1	2.1	2.1	2.4	2.1	2.2	2.6	3.0	3.2	5.5	5.2	5.0	8.1	5.0
Iran	0.8	0.7	1.1	1.8	2.5	3.8	5.9	7.5	10.2	15.1	17.6	20.1	20.9	22.2
Iraq	0.2	0.1	0.1	0.1	0.0	0.2	0.5	0.4	0.7	0.9	1.2	1.4	1.5	2.8
Israel	47.8	45.5	41.3	41.0	45.4	42.1	50.7	45.4	49.3	46.5	44.3	44.7	38.5	39.2
Jordan	8.0	8.9	7.8	8.4	8.7	11.6	11.4	17.9	18.0	20.4	13.3	11.3	12.8	14.8
Kuwait	17.4	18.0	12.8	14.2	16.1	13.8	16.7	23.6	19.5	26.6	17.7	21.3	25.6	27.2
Lebanon	5.1	6.5	5.7	5.9	6.9	7.5	8.1	9.7	6.7	7.6	5.7	5.9	7.1	7.4
Morocco	2.6	3.0	2.4	2.0	2.4	2.6	2.5	2.1	3.0	2.8	2.6	2.2	2.6	2.6
Oman	7.4	6.9	7.8	6.9	9.6	11.0	11.1	14.9	15.3	20.3	19.8	17.9	12.6	15.8
Qatar	11.8	5.5	11.2	11.5	2.8	7.1	2.9	7.8	7.3	35.8	10.5	10.8	11.4	10.8
SA	2.7	2.2	2.0	1.8	2.7	2.6	3.0	2.8	3.8	6.3	7.0	8.8	10.6	14.4
Syria	0.5	0.4	0.5	0.5	0.4	0.6	0.4	0.6	0.5	0.3	0.7	0.9	0.9	0.7
Tunisia	3.7	3.4	3.4	4.5	4.1	7.8	7.3	10.0	13.7	20.9	18.3	18.7	18.7	24.5
Turkey	4.9	6.9	7.7	9.4	11.6	12.2	13.9	16.7	18.5	19.7	19.5	20.4	18.7	19.7
UAE	10.8	5.4	6.8	8.2	6.2	9.0	6.3	8.2	15.2	8.9	9.5	7.9	12.3	10.3
Yemen	0.1	0.2	0.1	0.1	0.0	0.2	0.1	0.1	0.2	0.5	0.6	0.5	0.5	0.7
World	8.5	8.6	8.9	9.3	10.5	11.9	12.4	12.9	13.5	14.7	14.7	16.1	15.4	16.3

Source: National Science Foundation, National Center for Science and Engineering Statistics; Science and Engineering Indicators 2016.

Table 7.12. Number of Science & Engineering Articles in Mathematics (Per Million Population)

	(2000–2013)													
Country	2000	2001	2002	2003	2004	2005	2006	2007	2008	2009	2010	2011	2012	2013
Algeria	0.7	0.9	1.3	1.3	1.2	2.1	2.6	2.7	3.4	4.0	5.2	5.2	5.5	6.2
Bahrain	3.5	1.9	2.7	6.8	3.9	5.4	3.1	1.9	5.4	2.5	5.2	2.1	3.8	6.1
Cyprus	14.0	13.7	7.5	11.2	18.7	18.3	14.9	26.8	23.9	28.7	31.7	21.8	23.9	25.8
Egypt	0.9	1.0	1.5	2.3	2.5	2.0	1.7	1.6	2.2	2.5	2.0	2.4	2.8	2.7
Iran	1.1	1.2	1.4	1.8	3.0	4.7	6.2	7.5	7.4	9.6	10.4	15.4	17.2	16.5
Iraq	0.0	0.1	0.0	0.0	0.0	0.1	0.2	0.1	0.5	0.2	0.7	0.6	0.9	0.9
Israel	53.9	58.3	57.4	55.2	55.2	53.8	60.6	58.1	66.6	59.6	56.5	58.5	58.4	58.7
Jordan	1.7	3.1	5.1	5.3	7.4	8.9	9.2	8.8	12.1	8.8	10.5	10.8	17.2	10.8
Kuwait	14.7	10.9	10.4	7.8	5.8	7.6	10.2	6.7	10.0	6.8	9.2	8.1	6.4	10.4
Lebanon	2.6	3.2	2.4	3.2	3.2	2.5	3.6	3.1	3.0	3.8	4.4	4.4	7.1	5.4
Morocco	2.9	3.4	3.1	3.3	3.1	3.8	3.4	2.8	3.8	4.3	4.3	5.2	5.2	5.7
Oman	4.7	3.4	7.6	7.5	8.6	6.8	7.4	6.0	6.4	8.3	12.9	7.4	7.7	6.0
Qatar	0.0	1.1	3.9	2.5	7.9	5.8	4.5	9.5	7.6	5.6	4.9	7.9	5.4	4.9
SA	2.6	2.9	2.8	3.9	3.6	4.6	4.4	4.6	5.9	6.1	8.2	10.3	15.0	17.4
Syria	0.1	0.1	0.1	0.1	0.0	0.1	0.1	0.1	0.3	0.0	0.2	0.2	0.1	0.2
Tunisia	5.6	6.3	6.8	6.9	6.6	9.3	8.8	11.1	11.8	14.6	17.9	17.4	17.9	17.3
Turkey	2.4	2.2	2.8	3.6	5.3	5.3	6.7	6.6	7.5	9.3	10.2	12.5	11.7	15.8
UAE	2.7	3.2	7.0	8.2	10.0	8.8	6.3	4.7	4.0	3.8	3.6	4.6	5.4	3.7
Yemen	0.0	0.1	0.1	0.1	0.0	0.1	0.1	0.0	0.2	0.2	0.2	0.5	0.2	0.3
World	4.1	3.9	4.1	4.2	4.4	4.8	5.2	5.5	5.9	6.4	6.4	6.8	7.2	7.6

Source: National Science Foundation, National Center for Science and Engineering Statistics; Science and Engineering Indicators 2016.

Table 7.13. Number of Science & Engineering Articles in Medical Sciences (Per Million Population)

	(2000–2013)													
Country	2000	2001	2002	2003	2004	2005	2006	2007	2008	2009	2010	2011	2012	2013
Algeria	0.3	0.6	0.7	0.7	1.0	0.8	1.0	0.8	1.4	2.3	1.9	2.1	3.0	2.7
Bahrain	48.1	35.1	29.4	52.9	73.7	83.0	89.2	68.3	56.3	66.6	48.0	51.8	44.8	72.9
Cyprus	24.3	13.2	20.9	17.1	23.9	28.7	27.0	27.8	39.3	79.7	52.1	60.0	76.1	94.2
Egypt	5.4	5.1	5.1	6.1	6.4	7.7	8.5	9.4	10.8	14.1	17.8	21.2	23.7	24.6
Iran	2.8	3.7	6.6	9.0	11.3	19.3	27.5	34.4	44.8	54.7	62.5	77.7	83.0	81.8
Iraq	1.7	1.3	2.0	1.7	1.6	2.3	3.4	2.9	3.8	4.4	5.6	4.9	6.4	5.0
Israel	431.7	417.1	439.7	417.3	433.0	433.0	433.1	433.8	398.6	390.2	353.6	343.4	360.5	355.1
Jordan	26.9	23.3	26.5	24.8	29.4	30.1	39.1	31.6	37.9	37.9	42.1	37.1	32.6	31.6
Kuwait	56.5	64.5	71.8	62.7	72.1	80.5	77.2	75.2	88.0	71.0	68.7	59.3	54.1	53.0
Lebanon	52.9	53.5	44.4	52.2	47.9	58.0	65.3	65.5	74.6	69.6	63.2	63.2	64.9	61.2
Morocco	7.1	9.1	9.5	9.6	7.4	7.7	9.9	10.6	11.1	15.7	17.5	19.9	20.9	21.5
Oman	26.2	41.5	32.2	39.7	38.1	34.2	35.4	32.1	33.7	33.0	28.3	56.8	46.2	53.9
Qatar	33.4	66.8	78.1	74.9	77.5	101.6	105.7	101.4	71.6	64.6	68.7	67.6	71.7	68.8
SA	30.1	27.4	29.7	29.3	29.9	27.2	27.5	26.6	28.2	31.9	36.2	40.6	43.6	46.0
Syria	1.1	1.0	0.5	1.0	1.0	1.4	0.8	1.1	1.3	1.2	1.7	2.0	3.2	3.0
Tunisia	18.5	29.4	29.1	38.1	44.8	55.8	63.5	62.4	67.1	68.8	74.8	74.2	68.9	58.7
Turkey	49.7	63.2	80.9	95.2	106.2	124.5	123.8	128.3	128.7	137.9	138.3	141.1	153.8	162.3
UAE	29.8	34.9	27.3	32.4	27.8	28.1	31.6	22.3	25.2	23.5	22.6	24.8	23.6	24.5
Yemen	0.6	0.8	0.7	0.7	0.8	1.0	0.9	0.7	1.1	1.3	1.5	1.3	1.5	1.3
World	44.5	44.0	44.5	46.2	48.5	52.2	54.6	56.1	57.8	59.9	60.6	62.5	64.7	65.0

Source: National Science Foundation, National Center for Science and Engineering Statistics; Science and Engineering Indicators 2016.

Table 7.14. Number of Science & Engineering Articles in Other Life Sciences (Per Million Population) (2000–2013)

Country	2000	2001	2002	2003	2004	2005	2006	2007	2008	2009	2010	2011	2012	2013
Algeria	0.0	0.0	0.3	0.0	0.1	0.0	0.0	0.1	0.1	0.0	0.0	0.0	0.2	0.1
Bahrain	0.0	0.0	0.0	1.3	0.8	0.0	0.4	1.2	0.6	2.0	1.2	0.2	1.5	0.0
Cyprus	0.0	1.0	1.0	0.7	1.0	1.0	2.2	2.1	4.3	4.3	10.0	16.3	13.9	15.0
Egypt	0.0	0.0	0.0	0.0	0.0	0.0	0.0	0.1	0.1	0.1	0.2	0.2	0.2	0.2
Iran	0.0	0.0	0.1	0.1	0.2	0.2	0.4	0.6	0.8	1.1	1.0	1.7	2.3	2.0
Iraq	0.0	0.0	0.0	0.0	0.0	0.1	0.0	0.1	0.0	0.0	0.0	0.0	0.1	0.0
Israel	9.7	10.4	12.0	12.0	12.4	13.2	13.2	16.2	15.6	19.0	18.2	21.0	19.0	19.8
Jordan	1.5	1.3	1.2	1.0	1.9	3.1	1.9	3.0	3.3	5.0	3.8	6.0	4.7	5.1
Kuwait	0.1	0.1	0.5	1.3	0.9	1.8	1.2	1.6	2.3	2.5	2.1	0.8	0.6	1.4
Lebanon	0.2	0.5	0.3	1.1	1.4	1.7	1.6	3.0	2.0	2.5	4.3	2.6	3.5	3.5
Morocco	0.0	0.0	0.0	0.0	0.0	0.0	0.0	0.0	0.0	0.1	0.0	0.1	0.1	0.1
Oman	0.0	0.0	0.0	0.4	0.6	1.0	0.3	0.8	0.0	0.7	0.5	1.0	0.4	1.1
Qatar	0.0	0.0	0.0	0.0	0.0	0.0	0.8	0.8	0.4	1.1	3.0	1.9	0.9	3.4
SA	0.3	0.1	0.1	0.0	0.1	0.1	0.2	0.2	0.6	0.4	0.5	0.5	0.9	0.8
Syria	0.0	0.0	0.0	0.0	0.0	0.0	0.0	0.0	0.0	0.0	0.0	0.0	0.0	0.0
Tunisia	0.1	0.2	0.1	0.1	0.1	0.1	0.3	0.2	0.3	0.6	0.2	0.5	0.4	0.7
Turkey	0.4	0.4	0.3	0.7	1.1	1.2	1.5	1.9	2.0	2.3	3.1	2.2	3.0	2.6
UAE	0.6	0.9	0.9	1.0	1.0	0.5	1.0	0.5	0.3	0.8	0.9	0.8	1.1	1.1
Yemen	0.0	0.0	0.0	0.0	0.0	0.0	0.0	0.0	0.0	0.0	0.0	0.0	0.0	0.1
World	1.9	1.9	2.0	2.0	2.1	2.5	2.8	3.0	3.0	3.1	3.3	3.5	3.6	3.6

Source: National Science Foundation, National Center for Science and Engineering Statistics; Science and Engineering Indicators 2016.

Table 7.15. Number of Science & Engineering Articles in Physics (Per Million Population)

	(2000–2013)													
Country	2000	2001	2002	2003	2004	2005	2006	2007	2008	2009	2010	2011	2012	2013
Algeria	2.7	3.1	3.5	3.7	4.8	5.1	6.1	8.0	10.6	10.3	9.0	8.0	10.5	9.0
Bahrain	2.6	5.7	3.7	5.0	15.5	11.7	18.5	20.1	14.2	6.9	19.6	13.5	9.1	8.5
Cyprus	15.9	7.0	20.0	16.5	14.4	28.0	34.0	35.2	45.9	48.5	57.9	58.8	46.3	75.0
Egypt	3.7	4.3	4.2	4.6	4.4	4.9	5.0	5.7	5.4	6.3	5.8	5.3	5.3	5.6
Iran	2.4	2.6	4.0	4.3	6.1	7.8	10.9	13.4	18.8	22.0	24.5	28.7	30.4	31.7
Iraq	0.0	0.2	0.2	0.4	0.1	0.5	0.6	1.0	0.7	1.1	1.1	1.7	2.5	2.7
Israel	185.1	174.1	182.2	181.9	180.7	198.3	203.6	217.3	207.5	181.2	173.8	181.8	175.6	166.1
Jordan	8.5	5.0	10.0	8.3	10.0	9.0	9.1	8.8	10.4	9.7	9.4	9.5	9.2	7.5
Kuwait	10.6	7.3	7.0	4.1	8.3	6.0	11.2	8.8	9.9	11.5	7.0	8.1	7.4	8.5
Lebanon	6.3	5.1	5.2	2.5	4.9	5.2	5.0	8.0	6.6	7.2	8.2	6.9	6.4	6.0
Morocco	4.7	3.6	4.0	3.5	4.9	3.5	3.4	2.8	3.8	3.0	3.5	3.7	4.0	4.7
Oman	4.2	6.2	5.1	8.0	9.1	9.3	7.4	7.9	10.1	6.6	10.5	9.4	8.0	5.8
Qatar	0.2	2.3	3.1	6.4	3.2	4.5	7.8	8.7	9.6	8.2	7.9	11.8	12.0	15.8
SA	2.6	4.6	3.7	4.1	3.5	4.1	4.2	4.8	5.2	6.5	8.0	13.2	14.6	17.1
Syria	0.4	0.5	0.5	0.4	0.8	1.1	0.7	1.1	0.7	1.1	1.2	1.5	0.9	1.0
Tunisia	5.2	6.4	7.1	7.7	11.5	11.9	12.7	16.5	17.5	20.0	16.9	18.2	20.2	18.3
Turkey	5.9	7.3	8.8	9.8	11.4	12.0	13.7	19.5	15.3	17.6	16.1	17.0	19.7	18.2
UAE	3.2	5.2	6.3	6.7	5.2	6.8	5.8	7.0	5.0	6.8	5.5	5.8	9.4	9.1
Yemen	0.1	0.0	0.0	0.0	0.1	0.1	0.2	0.2	0.2	0.2	0.3	0.3	0.4	0.5
World	19.9	20.2	20.4	20.4	22.0	26.4	27.9	28.8	28.3	28.5	28.6	29.1	28.4	28.3

Source: National Science Foundation, National Center for Science and Engineering Statistics; Science and Engineering Indicators 2016.

year per million population. Cyprus has increased its scientific publications in physics and now ranks second place within MENA.

Table 7.16 presents the numbers of S&E articles per million population in psychology. Scientists from Israel have maintained the lead position within MENA in terms of the number of articles in psychology during the entire 2000–2013 period. Israel's publications ranged from 33 to 60 articles per year per million population. The world average ranged from 3 to 5 articles per year per million population. Cyprus is the only other MENA country with increased scientific publications in psychology and now ranks second place within MENA. The balance of MENA countries has yet to reach one article per year per million population.

Table 7.17 presents the numbers of S&E articles per million population in social sciences. Scientists from Israel have maintained the lead position within MENA in terms of the number of articles in social sciences during the entire 2000–2013 period. Israel's publications ranged from 51 to 115 articles per year per million population. The world average ranged from 4 to 14 articles per year per million population. Cyprus is the only other MENA country with increased scientific publications in social sciences and now ranks second place within MENA.

7.2. The Innovation Process within MENA

The statistical evidence on the outcome of a knowledge-based economy presented in the earlier section leaves open the question of why one set of countries are successful and others are not in producing knowledge. The development literature is quite certain that the dissemination and use of existing technologies are important determinants for economic and social development. Comin and Hobijn (2004), in a detailed study describing the dissemination of major global technologies, showed two key trends. First, the speed at which major innovations disseminate across countries has increased over time.[1] Second, the dissemination of technology to developing countries has increased, while dissemination within countries remains very slow.

The key innovation priority for developing countries is to acquire and use knowledge that already exists, which is less costly and less risky than

[1] Comin and Hobijn (2004) point out that while key innovations developed between 1750 and 1900 took, on average, slightly more than 100 years to disseminate to 80 percent of the countries surveyed, those developed between 1900 and 1950 took an average of 61 years; those developed between 1950 and 1975, an average of 24 years; and those developed between 1975 and 2000, an average of 16 years.

Table 7.16. Number of Science & Engineering Articles in Psychology (Per Million Population)

	(2000–2013)													
Country	2000	2001	2002	2003	2004	2005	2006	2007	2008	2009	2010	2011	2012	2013
Algeria	0.0	0.0	0.0	0.0	0.1	0.0	0.0	0.0	0.0	0.1	0.1	0.0	0.1	1.5
Bahrain	0.0	1.4	1.4	3.0	0.8	2.2	2.6	1.0	2.2	1.0	1.2	0.8	0.0	0.5
Cyprus	2.7	3.4	2.1	5.3	6.4	4.1	8.8	9.9	11.9	8.9	13.9	16.0	14.6	27.5
Egypt	0.0	0.1	0.0	0.0	0.1	0.0	0.0	0.1	0.1	0.1	0.2	0.1	0.1	0.2
Iran	0.1	0.1	0.1	0.2	0.2	0.3	0.4	0.5	0.6	0.5	0.6	0.8	0.8	0.9
Iraq	0.0	0.0	0.0	0.0	0.0	0.1	0.0	0.0	0.0	0.0	0.0	0.0	0.1	0.0
Israel	33.0	34.5	36.5	37.1	33.9	37.7	40.3	45.8	50.7	46.1	47.3	53.9	60.1	54.0
Jordan	1.6	1.2	0.5	0.8	0.5	1.1	1.0	1.0	0.3	0.9	1.4	0.9	1.0	1.9
Kuwait	2.8	4.3	6.4	8.0	9.0	9.8	12.9	6.8	7.8	5.0	3.9	3.6	5.0	3.3
Lebanon	0.7	1.1	1.6	0.2	0.6	2.5	1.6	2.6	2.3	0.8	2.1	2.0	1.7	2.0
Morocco	0.0	0.0	0.1	0.0	0.0	0.0	0.0	0.0	0.1	0.0	0.2	0.2	0.1	0.2
Oman	0.0	0.9	0.2	0.6	0.2	0.0	0.0	1.1	1.3	0.5	0.2	1.9	0.3	2.3
Qatar	0.0	0.0	0.0	0.0	1.3	1.7	2.0	1.6	1.8	0.3	1.4	1.1	4.1	2.4
SA	0.2	0.2	0.4	0.5	0.3	0.4	0.2	0.2	0.2	0.2	0.5	0.4	0.2	0.6
Syria	0.0	0.0	0.0	0.0	0.0	0.0	0.1	0.0	0.0	0.0	0.0	0.0	0.0	0.1
Tunisia	0.0	0.1	0.6	0.1	0.1	0.3	0.3	0.2	0.3	0.2	1.1	0.4	0.4	0.7
Turkey	0.6	0.6	0.8	1.0	1.1	1.4	1.5	1.8	2.0	2.6	2.1	2.1	2.2	2.6
UAE	1.4	1.4	2.8	1.7	2.0	1.4	0.5	0.7	1.2	0.8	1.8	1.6	1.8	2.1
Yemen	0.0	0.0	0.0	0.0	0.0	0.0	0.0	0.0	0.1	0.0	0.0	0.0	0.1	0.0
World	3.1	2.9	2.9	3.0	3.2	3.5	3.7	3.9	4.2	4.4	4.6	4.8	5.0	5.2

Source: National Science Foundation, National Center for Science and Engineering Statistics; Science and Engineering Indicators 2016.

Table 7.17. Number of Science & Engineering Articles in Social Sciences (Per Million Population)

(2000–2013)

Country	2000	2001	2002	2003	2004	2005	2006	2007	2008	2009	2010	2011	2012	2013
Algeria	0.1	0.2	0.2	0.1	0.3	0.2	0.3	0.4	0.5	0.6	0.2	0.6	0.5	0.7
Bahrain	4.5	3.6	3.1	1.9	3.5	1.7	5.5	1.0	4.2	3.4	2.8	6.6	3.0	5.5
Cyprus	8.0	10.7	21.6	19.9	22.4	20.9	23.7	27.4	41.3	44.2	44.3	66.3	61.4	81.8
Egypt	0.2	0.2	0.3	0.3	0.3	0.4	0.4	0.5	0.5	0.7	0.7	0.9	1.1	1.1
Iran	0.1	0.1	0.2	0.3	0.3	0.5	0.7	1.0	1.1	1.7	2.3	1.6	2.7	3.6
Iraq	0.0	0.0	0.0	0.0	0.2	0.1	0.1	0.1	0.2	0.3	0.1	0.2	0.2	0.2
Israel	51.9	51.5	74.3	76.4	81.4	73.6	85.3	85.0	91.4	103.3	103.6	101.7	108.2	115.1
Jordan	2.0	2.3	3.9	3.7	3.6	3.3	2.8	3.8	4.8	4.5	5.3	6.3	5.6	5.4
Kuwait	2.0	3.0	6.2	3.6	8.3	4.7	6.2	7.2	7.5	6.8	6.0	7.0	6.8	6.6
Lebanon	4.4	5.5	5.2	8.1	7.3	6.8	6.9	5.4	8.9	10.2	10.2	10.0	9.7	14.6
Morocco	0.2	0.2	0.4	0.3	0.6	0.5	0.5	0.2	0.7	0.9	0.5	0.7	0.9	1.1
Oman	2.2	2.6	1.3	1.3	1.0	1.4	1.3	0.6	2.0	4.3	3.1	5.3	2.7	4.9
Qatar	0.0	1.6	0.0	0.0	3.0	2.2	2.3	5.4	3.2	3.6	6.7	13.0	13.0	19.1
SA	0.4	0.8	0.4	0.4	0.7	0.6	0.5	0.7	0.5	1.0	1.0	1.5	1.8	2.0
Syria	0.0	0.1	0.1	0.0	0.1	0.2	0.2	0.2	0.2	0.2	0.4	0.5	0.3	0.5
Tunisia	0.7	0.6	0.7	1.5	1.2	2.4	2.1	2.9	3.7	5.0	5.6	6.8	7.7	8.7
Turkey	1.4	1.6	3.0	3.5	3.3	5.0	4.8	6.2	7.3	9.5	12.9	13.1	14.1	14.0
UAE	2.7	3.3	5.0	3.3	3.2	8.0	5.8	4.4	7.2	5.5	7.1	8.5	6.9	8.2
Yemen	0.0	0.0	0.1	0.0	0.1	0.1	0.0	0.0	0.1	0.1	0.1	0.1	0.1	0.1
World	4.4	4.7	6.3	6.7	7.1	7.7	8.2	8.7	9.6	10.6	11.8	12.5	13.2	13.8

Source: National Science Foundation, National Center for Science and Engineering Statistics; Science and Engineering Indicators 2016.

creating new knowledge. While some of this knowledge is protected by intellectual property rights and therefore would have to be purchased, an enormous amount is in the public domain. Therefore, policies that facilitate access to global knowledge are critical. How well developing countries use this form of innovation will depend not only on their policies but also on the support of the country's institutions and the effectiveness of those institutions and the people in them. Because productivity is dispersed within sectors, raising average productivity to local best practice (or, even better, to global best practice by acquiring more knowledge from abroad) can generate high returns.

Innovation policy when viewed from the paradigm of scientific ideology promoted the idea that technology derives naturally from science, so that governments need do no more than build a good science base. By contrast, innovation policy when interpreted in a market-based paradigm focuses on the process of innovation that occurs naturally when the institutional requirements are pro-business. Consequently, the role of the state is merely to assure that the environment is conducive to business activity, especially in maintaining an open, competitive environment. Furthermore, the state is expected to fund basic research, which in this paradigm is considered to be a public good.

The governing market paradigm in the 1960s and 1970s viewed a successful innovation process as one that concluded with a technological and industrial application. Modifications in the concept of the innovation process, introduced in the 1980s, included an interactive process of institutions and clusters. Government policies designed to facilitate market activity were no longer necessary and sufficient. The new innovation policy focused on facilitating interactions between universities, research laboratories, banks (for venture capital), and government agencies in charge of various sectors (industry, health and agriculture, for example) in order to facilitate a complex innovation.

A number of international agencies have attempted to formalize the complicated process of innovation dissemination from initial entry into a country to adoption. The latest such attempt was made in a recent report entitled *Innovation Policy: A Guide for Developing Countries* (World Bank, 2010, p. 59), where the specific features of innovation systems common to developing countries are presented. The construct begins with an innovation process where the innovation can originate from abroad or from other users in the same country, or it may be created by public or private R&D labs or firms in the same country. The innovation may be transferred in various ways, ranging from investment or formal purchases of technology, capital goods, components or products, to movement of people and informal sharing of information by people, or through information-enabled networks. It may be transferred to users: firms, government, public institutions, social organizations, or individuals. Dissemination occurs through market mechanisms such as the growth of more efficient firms, as well as through informal networks and special institutions or programs such as technological information centers and productivity and extension agencies.

A successful innovation strategy for economic development will therefore be associated with the ability of the country to create its own endogenous expertise (Segerstrom, 1991). Some like Archibugi and Pianta (1996), Patel and Pavitt (1991), Archibugi and Michie (1995, 1997), Archibugi *et al.* (1999), Pavitt and Patel (1999), Pianta and Tancioni (2008) and Gittleman and Wolff (2001) explore the conditions which allow nations to catch up in technological competence. The various components of technological competence requirements include not only general improvement in education, but also formal activities devoted to generate innovations, expertise in the capital goods sector, and a high level of international integration.

Gittleman and Wolff (2001) stress that each of these factors can play a different role depending on the nature of the technologies, industries and countries involved. Moreover, they argue that within the "restricted club of the industrial market economies", investment in formal R&D activities appears to be related to increasing growth rates. In developing countries, the role of education, well-functioning institutions, adequate capital stock, a productive infrastructure, etc., are more important at the initial stage of technological imitation. With time, imitative activities begin to resemble innovative activities. Without the initial conditions in place, developing countries will fail to couple imitation with innovation and will consequently jeopardize their long-term economic performance.

Pianta and Tancioni (2008) argue that technological change is a highly diversified phenomenon and the experience of developing countries is sufficiently diversified to bar simple generalizations. For some of these countries, the crucial source of growth has been intangible investment proxied by R&D expenditure, while for other countries the answer is increased gross fixed capital formation. Overall, the need is not so much to stimulate the innovation processes as it is to create receptive environments that will elicit the creativity of the other actors.

The latest UNESCO data presented in Table 7.18 lists current and capital expenditures for research and development (R&D) as a percent of GDP

Table 7.18. Research and Development Expenditure in MENA (% of GDP)

(2000–2015)

Country	2000	2001	2002	2003	2004	2005	2006	2007	2008	2009	2010	2011	2012	2013	2014	2015
Algeria	—	0.2	0.4	0.2	0.2	0.1	—	—	—	—	—	—	—	—	—	—
Bahrain	—	—	—	—	—	—	—	—	—	—	—	—	—	—	0.1	—
Cyprus	0.2	0.2	0.3	0.3	0.3	0.4	0.4	0.4	0.4	0.4	0.4	0.5	0.4	0.5	0.5	0.5
Egypt	0.2	—	—	—	0.3	0.2	0.3	0.3	0.3	0.4	0.4	0.5	0.5	0.6	0.6	0.7
Iran	—	0.5	0.5	0.6	0.5	0.6	0.6	—	0.7	0.3	0.3	—	0.3	—	—	—
Iraq	—	—	—	—	—	—	—	0.0	0.0	0.0	0.0	0.0	—	—	0.0	0.0
Israel	3.9	4.2	4.1	3.9	3.9	4.0	4.1	4.4	4.3	4.1	3.9	4.0	4.2	4.1	4.3	4.3
Jordan	—	—	0.3	—	—	—	—	—	0.4	—	—	—	—	—	—	—
Kuwait	0.1	0.2	0.2	0.1	0.1	0.1	0.1	0.1	0.1	0.1	0.1	0.1	0.1	0.3	—	—
Lebanon	—	—	—	—	—	—	—	—	—	—	—	—	—	—	—	—
Morocco	—	0.6	0.5	0.6	—	—	0.6	—	—	—	0.7	—	—	—	—	—
Oman	—	—	—	—	—	—	—	—	—	—	—	0.1	0.2	0.2	0.2	0.2
Qatar	—	—	—	—	—	—	—	—	—	—	—	—	0.5	—	—	—
SA	—	—	—	0.1	0.1	0.0	0.0	0.0	0.0	0.1	0.9	0.9	0.9	0.8	—	—
Syria	—	—	—	—	—	—	—	—	—	—	—	—	—	—	—	—
Tunisia	—	—	0.5	0.7	0.7	0.7	0.7	0.7	0.6	0.7	0.7	0.7	0.7	0.7	0.7	0.6
Turkey	0.5	0.5	0.5	0.5	0.5	0.6	0.6	0.7	0.7	0.8	0.8	0.9	0.9	0.9	1.0	—
UAE	—	—	—	—	—	—	—	—	—	—	—	0.5	—	—	0.7	0.9
Yemen	—	—	—	—	—	—	—	—	—	—	—	—	—	—	—	—
World	2.1	2.1	2.0	2.0	2.0	2.0	2.0	2.0	2.0	2.0	2.0	2.0	2.1	2.1	2.2	2.2

Source: United Nations Educational, Scientific, and Cultural Organization (UNESCO) Institute for Statistics.

for the period 2000–2015. R&D covers basic research, applied research, and experimental development. The data clearly indicates that within MENA only Israel is devoting a sizeable portion of their GDP to research and development. In fact, their expenditure is twice as large as that for the entire world. The Arab MENA countries, in contrast, spend less than 1 percent on research and development. This gap in funding R&D between Israel and the Arab MENA countries explains the general innovation and development gap between them.

In Chapter 4 we discussed the World Bank's KAM Knowledge Index (KI) which measures a country's ability to generate, adopt and diffuse knowledge. This is an indication of overall potential of knowledge development in a given country. The Knowledge Economy Index (KEI) takes into account whether the environment is conducive for knowledge to be used effectively for economic development. It is an aggregate index that represents the overall level of development of a country or region toward the Knowledge Economy. The KEI is calculated based on the average of the normalized performance scores of a country or region on all four pillars related to the knowledge economy — economic incentive and institutional regime, education and human resources, the innovation system, and ICT (World Bank, KAM).

The information presented in Chapter 4 included the KEI, the KI, and the Economy Incentive Index, the Innovation Index, the Education index, the ICT index and the country's rank as a knowledge economy. The data demonstrated that in the 21st century, few Arab MENA countries belong to the upper half of the world's countries on any of these indices. Only Israel and Cyprus have KEI and KI indices over 7 in 1995, 2000 and 2012. The overall knowledge ranking is 16 for Israel in 1995 dropping to 25 in 2012, 32 for Cyprus in 1995 dropping to 35 in 2012 and 36 for Bahrain in 1995 dropping to 43 in 2012. None of the other MENA countries had attained indices and ranks close to these three countries.

The assessment made by the UNDP (2009a, p. 184) which may well explain why science and technology policies within Arab MENA are ineffective is that these economies lack the "cultural, social, and economic environments that promote participation in a competitive economy and the presentation of outstanding products based upon the outcomes of scientific research." Without these minimal requirements, the "complementary relationship between innovation and development, allowing innovation to feed the development process and serve as a permanent source for regeneration and progress" will not occur. The UNDP (2009, pp. 184–185) sensibly concludes that "Creating policies that support science and technology is thus one of the most important steps that Arab MENA countries need to take in order to respond practically, competently, and seriously to the challenges of unemployment among youth, human capital flight, and the increasing drain of financial resources to the import and consumption of ready-made technical products."

This chapter has utilized the latest available statistics to explore the broad trends and the complexity of the global structure of R&D, science performance, invention and innovation. It has applied the accepted Western paradigm to evaluate MENA country performance in science, technology and innovation in a multidimensional process. The absolute importance of a significant globalization of R&D activity is found to be incontestable.

Implementing a knowledge-friendly set of institutions is the only way that a country within MENA can assure itself of an absolute growth of R&D and innovation-related activities. Furthermore, with globalization in the R&D activity, the performance of R&D in the services sector has improved, as has the growing focus on non-technological innovation and the widespread policy shifts toward fiscal incentives for R&D. Those economies within MENA (e.g., Israel and Cyprus) which are participating in the global economy of R&D and enhanced internationalization of the innovation process have also benefited from the enhanced mobility of highly skilled people, including greater participation of its women in the human resources for the science and technology labor force.

The evidence of such a positive externality is observed in Table 7.19 which lists the triadic patent families for the MENA countries between 1985 and 2015.[2] Clearly, underpinning the growth in triadic patent families has been the increasingly "knowledge-driven nature of innovation; the quickly changing organization of research, driven by informatics, collaboration and the sharing of knowledge; rapidly improving connectivity and the development of platform technologies and standards as globalization accelerates; and changes in markets, the competition environment and technology" (OECD, 2008a,b,c,d,e). The data on triadic patent families within MENA presented in Table 7.19 is very clear. Israel is the only member of MENA that is leading the drive to participate in a global innovation market and has been in this patent market since the mid-1980s. The 21st century

[2]Triadic patent families are patents filed at the European Patent Office (EPO), the US Patent and Trademark Office (USPTO) and the Japan Patent Office (JPO) that protect the same invention.

Table 7.19. Triadic Patent Families in MENA

(1985–2015)

	Cyprus	Israel	Saudi Arabia	Turkey
1985	0.0	52.3	0.0	1.0
1986	1.0	69.8	0.7	1.0
1987	0.0	72.8	1.0	0.1
1988	0.0	70.1	2.5	1.6
1989	0.0	90.2	0.0	1.3
1990	0.0	84.3	0.0	0.8
1991	2.0	113.6	0.0	0.5
1992	0.1	116.9	0.5	0.0
1993	0.4	124.9	2.0	2.5
1994	1.0	145.2	0.3	1.6
1995	0.2	165.6	1.5	1.9
1996	0.3	218.1	0.3	3.7
1997	0.3	299.2	1.8	4.7
1998	0.1	317.7	4.4	6.7
1999	2.8	300.8	4.6	3.4
2000	0.2	385.0	6.1	4.6
2001	0.3	381.6	7.1	12.1
2002	1.1	322.8	5.1	10.1
2003	2.4	361.8	4.9	10.6
2004	2.0	422.0	9.2	16.8
2005	3.7	501.2	14.7	15.5
2006	0.5	418.8	13.5	16.8
2007	3.4	350.0	12.0	9.0
2008	1.7	369.4	4.3	27.4
2009	2.7	375.9	14.6	27.9
2010	1.0	351.4	20.7	34.2
2011	1.3	368.7	76.9	41.0
2012	1.1	395.8	97.5	40.8
2013	1.7	411.6	98.9	45.0
2014	1.7	443.4	39.7	45.9
2015	1.7	462.9	38.5	49.7

Note: A triadic patent family is defined as a set of patents registered in various countries (i.e., patent offices) to protect the same invention. Triadic patent families are a set of patents filed at three of these major patent offices: the European Patent Office (EPO), the Japan Patent Office (JPO) and the United States Patent and Trademark Office (USPTO). Triadic patent family counts are attributed to the country of residence of the inventor and to the date when the patent was first registered. This indicator is measured as a number.
Source: World Bank. TC Data 360.

has also seen the inclusion of Saudi Arabia, Turkey and, to a limited extent, Cyprus in this global innovation market. The remaining members of MENA are not in this market nor will they be joining in the foreseeable future.

In Chapter 8, we focus on globalization away from science, technology and innovation to international trade flows in goods and services and the value-added chains that describes the 21st century international trade market.

Chapter 8

International Trade in MENA

When the MENA region was open to international trade and to the movement of factors of production, human capital, innovation and private business, it enjoyed a long period of prosperity. That period of prosperity was a long time before the current wave of globalization. Now that the world is enjoying the fruits of globalization, Arab MENA has fallen far behind. The non-Arab MENA, represented by Cyprus, Israel and Turkey, has not suffered the same fate. While the developed and developing world has experienced trade growth rates close to double digits, Arab MENA has only managed to experience growth in trade closer to 2 to 4 percent. As much of the developing world has assumed an active role in the innovation process as well as in the global production chain, Arab MENA continues to maintain its old economic links which depend on oil and natural resource exports, tourism and labor migration.

A review of the existing international trade volume of the MENA countries over the 2008–2016 period is presented in the next four tables. The overwhelming reality is that Arab MENA economies continue to be major non-participants in the global trading world. Table 8.1 presents MENA country exports to the world in millions of dollars and as a percent of world exports and as a percent of total MENA exports. Except for the oil-rich countries, none of the MENA country's exports represent the minimum threshold of 1 percent of world exports over the entire 2008–2016 period. When we measure MENA country exports relative to total MENA country exports, we get similar results where the oil-rich countries like Saudi Arabia and the UAE maintain an overly larger share of MENA exports. Among the non-oil countries, the exports of Iran, Israel, Kuwait and Turkey become slightly more interesting.

Table 8.1. MENA Country Exports to the World (Million US Dollars and Percent)

Exporters	2008	2009	2010	2011	2012	2013	2014	2015	2016
Algeria	79,298	45,194	57,051	73,436	71,866	65,998	60,388	34,796	29,992
% of World Exports	0.50	0.37	0.38	0.41	0.39	0.35	0.32	0.21	0.19
% of MENA Exports	7.60	6.39	6.29	6.35	4.60	4.27	4.05	3.38	2.90
Bahrain	13,803	8,384	16,059	22,562	16,621	20,036	23,746	16,684	12,892
% of World Exports	0.08	0.07	0.11	0.12	0.09	0.11	0.13	0.10	0.08
% of MENA Exports	1.25	1.18	1.77	1.95	1.06	1.30	1.59	1.62	1.25
Cyprus	1,713	1,351	1,506	1,955	1,826	2,134	1,924	1,935	1,920
% of World Exports	0.01	0.01	0.01	0.01	0.01	0.01	0.01	0.01	0.01
% of MENA Exports	0.16	0.19	0.17	0.17	0.12	0.14	0.13	0.19	0.19
Egypt	25,967	24,182	26,332	31,582	29,417	28,779	26,812	21,967	22,507
% of World Exports	0.16	0.20	0.17	0.17	0.16	0.15	0.14	0.13	0.14
% of MENA Exports	2.49	3.42	2.91	2.73	1.88	1.86	1.80	2.13	2.18
Iran	107,236	77,575	108,607	137,421	132,713	92,123	90,328	0	83,148
% of World Exports	0.67	0.63	0.72	0.76	0.72	0.49	0.48	0.00	0.52
% of MENA Exports	10.27	10.96	11.98	11.88	8.49	5.95	6.06	0.00	8.04
Israel	61,337	47,935	58,413	67,796	63,141	66,781	68,965	64,062	60,571
% of World Exports	0.38	0.39	0.39	0.37	0.34	0.35	0.37	0.39	0.38
% of MENA Exports	5.88	6.77	6.44	5.86	4.04	4.32	4.63	6.22	5.85
Jordan	7,782	6,366	7,023	7,963	7,877	7,920	8,385	7,833	7,509
% of World Exports	0.05	0.05	0.05	0.04	0.04	0.04	0.04	0.05	0.05
% of MENA Exports	0.75	0.90	0.77	0.69	0.50	0.51	0.56	0.76	0.73
Kuwait	87,457	51,960	62,698	102,696	114,536	114,125	101,132	55,162	46,242
% of World Exports	0.55	0.42	0.42	0.57	0.62	0.60	0.54	0.34	0.29
% of MENA Exports	8.38	7.34	6.92	8.88	7.33	7.38	6.79	5.35	4.47
Lebanon	3,478	3,484	4,254	4,267	4,446	3,937	3,312	2,952	2,977
% of World Exports	0.02	0.03	0.03	0.02	0.02	0.02	0.02	0.02	0.02
% of MENA Exports	0.33	0.49	0.47	0.37	0.28	0.25	0.22	0.29	0.29

(Continued)

Table 8.1. *(Continued)*

Exporters	2008	2009	2010	2011	2012	2013	2014	2015	2016
Libya	44,696	27,256	36,440	—	—	—	—	—	—
% of World Exports	0.28	0.22	0.24	—	—	—	—	—	—
% of MENA Exports	4.28	3.85	4.02	—	—	—	—	—	—
Morocco	20,306	14,069	17,765	21,650	21,417	21,965	23,816	22,037	22,858
% of World Exports	0.13	0.11	0.12	0.12	0.12	0.12	0.13	0.13	0.14
% of MENA Exports	1.95	1.99	1.96	1.87	1.37	1.42	1.60	2.14	2.21
Oman	37,719	27,651	36,600	47,092	52,138	55,497	50,718	31,927	24,455
% of World Exports	0.24	0.22	0.24	0.26	0.28	0.29	0.27	0.19	0.15
% of MENA Exports	3.61	3.91	4.04	4.07	3.34	3.59	3.40	3.10	2.36
Qatar	67,307	48,007	74,964	114,448	132,985	136,855	131,592	77,971	57,311
% of World Exports	0.42	0.39	0.50	0.63	0.72	0.72	0.70	0.48	0.36
% of MENA Exports	6.45	6.78	8.27	9.89	8.51	8.85	8.83	7.57	5.54
Saudi Arabia	312,999	191,810	250,577	364,139	387,374	375,361	341,947	201,492	207,572
% of World Exports	1.96	1.55	1.66	2.01	2.11	1.99	1.81	1.23	1.30
% of MENA Exports	29.99	27.10	27.65	31.48	24.78	24.26	22.95	19.55	20.06
Syria	14,380	9,694	11,353	—	—	—	—	—	—
% of World Exports	0.09	0.08	0.08	—	—	—	—	—	—
% of MENA Exports	1.38	1.37	1.25	—	—	—	—	—	—
Tunisia	19,320	14,445	16,427	17,847	17,007	17,060	16,760	14,073	13,575
% of World Exports	0.12	0.12	0.11	0.10	0.09	0.09	0.09	0.09	0.09
% of MENA Exports	1.85	2.04	1.81	1.54	1.09	1.10	1.12	1.37	1.31
Turkey	132,027	102,143	113,883	134,907	152,462	151,803	157,610	143,850	142,530
% of World Exports	0.83	0.83	0.75	0.75	0.83	0.80	0.84	0.88	0.89
% of MENA Exports	12.65	14.43	12.56	11.66	9.75	9.81	10.58	13.96	13.77
UAE	—	—	—	—	350,123	379,489	380,340	333,362	298,651
% of World Exports	—	—	—	—	1.90	2.01	2.02	2.03	1.87
% of MENA Exports	—	—	—	—	22.40	24.53	25.52	32.35	28.86
Yemen	7,584	6,259	6,437	6,948	7,062	7,130	2,417	510	0
% of World Exports	0.05	0.05	0.04	0.04	0.04	0.04	0.01	0.00	0.00
% of MENA Exports	0.73	0.88	0.71	0.60	0.45	0.46	0.16	0.05	0.00

Source: ITC calculations based on UN COMTRADE statistics.

In Table 8.2 we present the MENA country imports from the world in millions of dollars and as a percent of world imports and as a percent of total MENA imports. Turkey and the UAE attained the minimum threshold of 1 percent of world imports. When we measure MENA country imports relative to total MENA country imports, we get different results than we observed in MENA country exports. Countries in the 5 percent of MENA total imports included Egypt and Israel. The outliers were the oil- rich countries, Saudi Arabia and the UAE who maintained an overly larger share of MENA imports.

In Tables 8.3 and 8.4 we present the intra-MENA country trade in millions of dollars and as a percent of total MENA imports and exports. Overall, there is very little intra-MENA trade between the MENA countries. It appears that the UAE is the only country within MENA that has more than 1 percent of its exports and imports within this region.

The aggregate trade data points to countries that have not shifted into the global economy. Consequently, they cannot hope to utilize the value added associated with globalization to resolve Arab MENA's greatest challenge — job creation for its large and rapidly growing labor force. As noted in Chapter 5, for Arab MENA, unemployment among the young, educated and female population is very high and growing, and represents both an enormous waste of resources and a major threat to social and political stability.

The lack of Arab MENA's footprint in international trade reveals a complex reality of non-participation in the global economy. By contrast, in Israel the past 70 years has been characterized by a rising investment in ICT (information and communications technology), as well as investment in domestic education and human capital development. The outcome of these trends is observed in Israel's exports when they are measured in terms of value added. This result is in conformity with the general principals of "globalization," where what matters in a country's "competitiveness" is its ability to utilize intermediate goods and services from other countries without having to develop a whole integrated industry. As Baldwin (2009) and Baldwin and Venables (2010), have pointed out, what matters more today is "what you do" rather than "what you sell." In that vein, participating in a global network enhances competitiveness by providing access to cheaper, more differentiated, and better-quality inputs as well as technological spillovers.

The popular concept of "supply chains" in economics originates from the basic idea that today's goods and services do not have "parents" in the traditional country of origin definition (Pelzman and Shoham, 2010; Pelzman,

Table 8.2. MENA Country Imports from the World (Million US Dollars and Percent)

Exporters	2008	2009	2010	2011	2012	2013	2014	2015	2016
Algeria	39,475	39,258	41,000	47,220	50,369	54,910	58,618	51,803	47,091
% of World Imports	0.24	0.31	0.27	0.26	0.27	0.29	0.31	0.31	0.29
% of MENA Imports	4.17	6.31	5.66	5.73	4.50	4.60	4.85	4.87	4.62
Bahrain	18,415	11,993	16,002	17,643	14,249	18,618	20,074	16,378	14,749
% of World Imports	0.11	0.09	0.10	0.10	0.08	0.10	0.11	0.10	0.09
% of MENA Imports	1.95	1.93	2.21	2.14	1.27	1.56	1.66	1.54	1.45
Cyprus	10,849	7,933	8,645	8,789	7,377	6,418	6,829	5,699	6,604
% of World Imports	0.07	0.06	0.06	0.05	0.04	0.03	0.04	0.03	0.04
% of MENA Imports	1.15	1.28	1.19	1.07	0.66	0.54	0.57	0.54	0.65
Egypt	52,751	44,912	53,003	62,282	69,866	66,666	71,338	74,361	58,053
% of World Imports	0.32	0.36	0.35	0.34	0.38	0.35	0.38	0.45	0.36
% of MENA Imports	5.58	7.22	7.32	7.56	6.24	5.59	5.91	6.98	5.69
Iran	55,830	54,890	55,730	57,488	51,458	48,432	52,250	0	42,702
% of World Imports	0.34	0.43	0.36	0.31	0.28	0.26	0.28	0.00	0.27
% of MENA Imports	5.90	8.82	7.70	6.98	4.60	4.06	4.33	0.00	4.19
Israel	65,171	47,363	59,194	73,526	73,112	71,995	72,332	62,068	65,803
% of World Imports	0.40	0.38	0.39	0.40	0.40	0.38	0.38	0.37	0.41
% of MENA Imports	6.89	7.61	8.18	8.93	6.53	6.04	5.99	5.83	6.45
Jordan	16,872	14,075	15,262	18,301	20,691	21,549	22,740	20,475	19,207
% of World Imports	0.10	0.11	0.10	0.10	0.11	0.11	0.12	0.12	0.12
% of MENA Imports	1.78	2.26	2.11	2.22	1.85	1.81	1.88	1.92	1.88
Kuwait	24,840	19,906	22,691	25,142	27,264	29,299	31,489	31,909	30,826
% of World Imports	0.15	0.16	0.15	0.14	0.15	0.16	0.17	0.19	0.19
% of MENA Imports	2.63	3.20	3.14	3.05	2.44	2.46	2.61	3.00	3.02
Lebanon	16,136	16,232	17,970	20,163	21,147	21,234	20,487	18,069	18,705
% of World Imports	0.10	0.13	0.12	0.11	0.11	0.11	0.11	0.11	0.12
% of MENA Imports	1.71	2.61	2.48	2.45	1.89	1.78	1.70	1.70	1.83
Libya	9,116	12,859	17,674	—	—	—	—	—	—
% of World Imports	0.06	0.10	0.12	—	—	—	—	—	—

(Continued)

Table 8.2. *(Continued)*

Exporters	2008	2009	2010	2011	2012	2013	2014	2015	2016
% of MENA Imports	0.96	2.07	2.44	—	—	—	—	—	—
Morocco	42,322	32,882	35,379	44,263	44,790	45,186	46,192	37,546	41,696
% of World Imports	0.26	0.26	0.23	0.24	0.24	0.24	0.24	0.23	0.26
% of MENA Imports	4.48	5.28	4.89	5.37	4.00	3.79	3.82	3.53	4.09
Oman	22,925	17,851	19,775	23,619	28,118	34,331	29,303	29,007	23,260
% of World Imports	0.14	0.14	0.13	0.13	0.15	0.18	0.16	0.18	0.14
% of MENA Imports	2.42	2.87	2.73	2.87	2.51	2.88	2.43	2.72	2.28
Qatar	27,900	24,922	23,240	22,333	26,082	27,034	30,448	32,610	32,060
% of World Imports	0.17	0.20	0.15	0.12	0.14	0.14	0.16	0.20	0.20
% of MENA Imports	2.95	4.01	3.21	2.71	2.33	2.27	2.52	3.06	3.14
Saudi Arabia	112,273	92,457	103,622	127,963	151,260	163,013	168,240	163,821	129,796
% of World Imports	0.69	0.73	0.68	0.70	0.82	0.86	0.89	0.99	0.81
% of MENA Imports	11.87	14.86	14.32	15.54	13.52	13.67	13.93	15.39	12.73
Syria	18,105	15,443	17,562	—	—	—	—	—	—
% of World Imports	0.11	0.12	0.11	—	—	—	—	—	—
% of MENA Imports	1.91	2.48	2.43	—	—	—	—	—	—
Tunisia	24,638	19,096	22,215	23,952	24,471	24,266	24,793	20,223	19,487
% of World Imports	0.15	0.15	0.15	0.13	0.13	0.13	0.13	0.12	0.12
% of MENA Imports	2.61	3.07	3.07	2.91	2.19	2.03	2.05	1.90	1.91
Turkey	201,964	140,928	185,544	240,842	236,545	251,661	242,177	207,207	198,618
% of World Imports	1.24	1.12	1.21	1.32	1.28	1.33	1.28	1.25	1.24
% of MENA Imports	21.36	22.65	25.64	29.24	21.14	21.10	20.05	19.46	19.48
UAE	175,486	—	—	—	261,023	294,967	298,611	287,025	270,882
% of World Imports	1.07	—	—	—	1.41	1.56	1.58	1.73	1.69
% of MENA Imports	18.56	—	—	—	23.32	24.73	24.72	26.96	26.57
Yemen	10,546	9,185	9,255	10,034	11,260	13,273	12,042	6,573	0
% of World Imports	0.06	0.07	0.06	0.05	0.06	0.07	0.06	0.04	0.00
% of MENA Imports	1.12	1.48	1.28	1.22	1.01	1.11	1.00	0.62	0.00

Source: ITC calculations based on UN COMTRADE statistics.

Table 8.3. Intra — MENA Country Exports (Million US Dollars and Percent)

	2008	2009	2010	2011	2012	2013	2014	2015	2016
Algeria	5,348	3,412	4,592	4,862	5,558	6,196	5,996	3,886	2,871
% of MENA Exports	0.51	0.48	0.51	0.42	0.36	0.40	0.40	0.38	0.28
Bahrain	2,900	2,059	2,949	4,463	4,484	7,425	11,857	10,274	6,714
% of MENA Exports	0.28	0.29	0.33	0.39	0.29	0.48	0.80	1.00	0.65
Cyprus	227	229	229	258	311	351	350	473	527
% of MENA Exports	0.02	0.03	0.03	0.02	0.02	0.02	0.02	0.05	0.05
Egypt	6,936	8,410	8,791	10,202	10,370	10,834	10,473	8,942	10,676
% of MENA Exports	0.66	1.19	0.97	0.88	0.66	0.70	0.70	0.87	1.03
Iran	6,836	9,162	10,068	12,076	12,551	12,537	14,093	0	18,404
% of MENA Exports	0.66	1.29	1.11	1.04	0.80	0.81	0.95	0.00	1.78
Israel	2,984	2,064	2,429	3,294	2,749	3,938	3,973	2,354	1,777
% of MENA Exports	0.29	0.29	0.27	0.28	0.18	0.25	0.27	0.23	0.17
Jordan	3,509	3,297	3,427	3,711	3,829	4,004	4,195	3,730	3,342
% of MENA Exports	0.34	0.47	0.38	0.32	0.24	0.26	0.28	0.36	0.32
Kuwait	1,758	1,735	1,574	1,691	1,874	2,282	2,407	2,357	1,763
% of MENA Exports	0.17	0.25	0.17	0.15	0.12	0.15	0.16	0.23	0.17
Lebanon	1,944	1,692	1,995	1,794	1,867	2,200	1,875	1,673	1,381
% of MENA Exports	0.19	0.24	0.22	0.16	0.12	0.14	0.13	0.16	0.13
Libya	1,658	1,267	863	—	—	—	—	—	—
% of MENA Exports	0.16	0.18	0.10	—	—	—	—	—	—
Morocco	1,066	826	1,292	1,094	1,275	1,274	1,416	1,702	1,831
% of MENA Exports	0.10	0.12	0.14	0.09	0.08	0.08	0.10	0.17	0.18

(Continued)

Table 8.3. *(Continued)*

	2008	2009	2010	2011	2012	2013	2014	2015	2016
Oman	6,077	5,838	6,573	6,038	4,685	9,731	4,644	5,144	4,780
% of MENA Exports	0.58	0.82	0.73	0.52	0.30	0.63	0.31	0.50	0.46
Qatar	4,297	3,796	7,631	8,156	10,771	10,410	11,648	8,853	7,195
% of MENA Exports	0.41	0.54	0.84	0.71	0.69	0.67	0.78	0.86	0.70
Saudi Arabia	16,056	15,730	16,124	18,878	19,728	20,925	21,519	20,321	18,942
% of MENA Exports	1.54	2.22	1.78	1.63	1.26	1.35	1.44	1.97	1.83
Syria	8,224	5,786	5,516	—	—	—	—	—	—
% of MENA Exports	0.79	0.82	0.61	—	—	—	—	—	—
Tunisia	2,377	2,045	1,989	1,939	1,939	2,020	1,944	1,622	1,636
% of MENA Exports	0.23	0.29	0.22	0.17	0.12	0.13	0.13	0.16	0.16
Turkey	29,678	25,188	28,936	32,454	49,007	42,451	40,733	36,527	36,504
% of MENA Exports	2.84	3.56	3.19	2.81	3.14	2.74	2.73	3.54	3.53
UAE	22,531	—	—	—	67,784	79,665	80,172	46,657	38,661
% of MENA Exports	2.16	—	—	—	4.34	5.15	5.38	4.53	3.74
Yemen	985	693	695	691	406	1,170	794	295	—
% of MENA Exports	0.09	0.10	0.08	0.06	0.03	0.08	0.05	0.03	—

Source: ITC calculations based on UN COMTRADE statistics.

Table 8.4. Intra — MENA Country Imports (Million US Dollars and Percent)

	2008	2009	2010	2011	2012	2013	2014	2015	2016
Algeria	2,428	3,274	3,306	3,786	4,120	5,537	4,826	4,632	4,585
% of MENA Imports	0.26	0.53	0.46	0.46	0.37	0.46	0.40	0.44	0.45
Bahrain	2,123	1,383	1,389	9,133	2,232	10,906	10,315	6,609	1,717
% of MENA Imports	0.22	0.22	0.19	1.11	0.20	0..91	0.85	0.62	0.17
Cyprus	1,147	727	903	1,134	1,018	951	733	407	389
% of MENA Imports	0.12	0.12	0.12	0.14	0.09	0.08	0.06	0.04	0.04
Egypt	8,626	7,483	8,565	10,816	13,075	11,772	12,907	13,147	10,292
% of MENA Imports	0.91	1.20	1.18	1.31	1.17	0.99	1.07	1.23	1.01
Iran	16,315	19,258	19,957	21,576	14,957	15,345	15,898	0	8,699
% of MENA Imports	1.73	3.10	2.76	2.62	1.34	1.29	1.32	0.00	0.85
Israel	2,220	1,807	2,432	2,873	3,364	3,172	3,536	3,293	3,313
% of MENA Imports	0.23	0.29	0.34	0.35	0.30	0.27	0.29	0.31	0.32
Jordan	6,265	4,973	5,951	7,415	8,298	7,295	7,701	6,099	5,132
% of MENA Imports	0.66	0.80	0.82	0.90	0.74	0.61	0.64	0.57	0.50
Kuwait	4,028	3,267	3,704	4,832	5,142	6,110	6,988	7,082	6,495
% of MENA Imports	0.43	0.53	0.51	0.59	0.46	0.51	0.58	0.67	0.64
Lebanon	2,900	2,570	3,066	4,190	4,163	3,727	2,963	2,823	3,315
% of MENA Imports	0.31	0.41	0.42	0.51	0.37	0.31	0.25	0.27	0.33
Libya	1,086	2,327	3,214	—	—	—	—	—	—
% of MENA Imports	0.11	0.37	0.44	—	—	—	—	—	—
Morocco	7,655	4,616	5,760	7,923	7,850	8,128	7,888	5,133	4,762
% of MENA Imports	0.81	0.74	0.80	0.96	0.70	0.68	0.65	0.48	0.47

(Continued)

Table 8.4. *(Continued)*

	2008	2009	2010	2011	2012	2013	2014	2015	2016
Oman	7,879	5,756	7,239	9,116	9,156	15,430	12,512	13,266	13,030
% of MENA Imports	0.83	0.93	1.00	1.11	0.82	1.29	1.04	1.25	1.28
Qatar	5,620	4,903	4,612	4,651	5,039	4,906	5,950	6,387	6,407
% of MENA Imports	0.59	0.79	0.64	0.56	0.45	0.41	0.49	0.60	0.63
Saudi Arabia	10,352	9,114	11,460	14,594	17,644	20,098	19,712	19,969	16,543
% of MENA Imports	1.09	1.46	1.58	1.77	1.58	1.68	1.63	1.88	1.62
Syria	3,401	3,866	4,556	—	—	—	—	—	—
% of MENA Imports	0.36	0.62	0.63	—	—	—	—	—	—
Tunisia	3,449	2,191	2,213	2,258	2,912	3,227	3,416	2,348	2,364
% of MENA Imports	0.36	0.35	0.31	0.27	0.26	0.27	0.28	0.22	0.23
Turkey	15,844	8,987	15,621	23,286	24,273	25,252	23,389	16,123	16,467
% of MENA Imports	1.68	1.44	2.16	2.83	2.17	2.12	1.94	1.51	1.62
UAE	17,386	—	—	—	30,019	21,882	21,196	16,210	22,486
% of MENA Imports	1.84	—	—	—	2.68	1.83	1.75	1.52	2.21
Yemen	3,605	2,469	2,736	2,895	2,891	4,598	2,760	2,220	—
% of MENA Imports	0.38	0.40	0.38	0.35	0.26	O.39	0.23	0.21	—

Source: ITC calculations based on UN COMTRADE statistics.

2016). In a world where we have international production networks across firms, industries and countries, the reality of international trade is bound up in what Coe and Hess (2007) refer to as the international fragmentation of production. As Hudson (2004) points out, the shift in our understanding of "supply chains" as being "networks" represent the increasingly complex interactions among global producers and suppliers.

Historically there were two key drivers for this enormous flow of intermediate goods and services. The first of these was the drastic reduction in transaction costs. The cost of moving products across the many layers in intermediate producers — such as transport and port costs, freight and insurance costs, tariffs, costs associated with non-tariff measures, mark-ups by importers and wholesalers — all have dropped drastically. Add to that the continuous reduction in barriers to trade arising from successive rounds of global trade liberalization, and you have a clear cost incentive for entering the global production networks. (Grossman and Rossi-Hansberg, 2008; Baldwin, 2009). Liberalization of investment through multilateral and bilateral investment agreements (BIT) further spurred these interrelationships as firms use FDI to spread their production activities across many countries, thus leading to a further expansion of production networks.

The second driver to this expansion of production networks is less expensive and far more reliable telecommunications, information management software, and increasingly powerful computers (ICT). This second driver noted by Baldwin (2009) significantly decreased the cost of coordinating complex activities over long distances across global production networks. This has also transformed many non-tradable and tradable services. As the OECD has pointed out, despite the fact that distribution, sales and production activities were the first movers in these global production networks, they have led the way for R&D and decision-making activities to locate internationally. (OECD, 2011a, 2011b, 2011c).

To get a current picture of the supply chain for MENA, we look for trends using the database created at the OECD–WTO Trade in value added which links national I–O tables with bilateral trade data to develop inter-country I–O tables.

8.1. The Formal Model of the Value-Added Chain in International Trade

To better understand the tracking of international trade via value-added chains, we summarize the methodology applied by Koopman *et al.* (2010)

as it was implemented at the OECD–WTO–TVA database. The starting point for the conceptual framework is the standard 2×2 model, where each country produces differential tradable goods (i) ranging from 1 to N in T sectors.[1] Tradable goods include final, intermediate and raw material goods. Countries can treat these products as direct consumer goods or as intermediate inputs. For the database, it is assumed that each country exports both intermediate and final goods to the other.

In this framework, it is assumed that country ***j's*** output must be used as an intermediate good or a final good at home or abroad, or

$$X_j = A_{jj}X_j + A_{jk}X_k + Y_{jj} + Y_{jk} \quad j, k = 1, 2 \tag{8.1}$$

where X_j is the $N \times 1$ gross output vector of country $\boldsymbol{j}$, Y_{jk} is the $N \times 1$ final demand vector from country $\boldsymbol{k}$ for final goods produced in $\boldsymbol{j}$, and A_{jk} is the $N \times N$ IO coefficient matrix, giving intermediate use in $\boldsymbol{k}$ of goods produced in $\boldsymbol{j}$. The $2{\times}2$ production and trade relationship can be restated in matrix notation applied by the OECD–WTO–TVA:

$$\begin{bmatrix} X_1 \\ X_2 \end{bmatrix} = \begin{bmatrix} A_{11}A_{12} \\ A_{21}A_{22} \end{bmatrix} \begin{bmatrix} X_1 \\ X_2 \end{bmatrix} + \begin{bmatrix} Y_{11}Y_{12} \\ Y_{21}Y_{22} \end{bmatrix} \tag{8.2}$$

Rearranging terms, we have:

$$\begin{bmatrix} X_1 \\ X_2 \end{bmatrix} = \begin{bmatrix} I - A_{11} & -A_{12} \\ -A_{21} & I - A_{22} \end{bmatrix}^{-1} \begin{bmatrix} Y_{11} + Y_{12} \\ Y_{21} + Y_{22} \end{bmatrix} = \begin{bmatrix} B_{11}B_{12} \\ B_{21}Y_{22} \end{bmatrix} \begin{bmatrix} Y_1 \\ Y_2 \end{bmatrix} \tag{8.3}$$

where B_{kj} is the $N \times N$ Leontief inverse matrix, representing the total requirement matrix that gives the amount of gross output in producing country $\boldsymbol{k}$ required for a one-unit increase in final demand in country $\boldsymbol{j}$. Y_j is a $2N \times 1$ vector that gives the global use of ***j's*** final goods. That is:

$$X = (I - A)^{-1}Y = BY \tag{8.4}$$

where X and Y are $2N \times 1$ vectors, and A and B are $2N \times 2N$ matrices.

In order to decompose international trade into transactions in intermediate and final demands requires measuring domestic and foreign contents, first for production, and then for international trade. Let V_k be the $1 \times N$ direct value-added coefficient vector. Each element of Vs gives the share of direct domestic value added in total output. This is equal to one minus

[1]The rationale for adding the T sectors is that while trade occurs across N possible goods, the IO table is limited to only T sectors.

the intermediate input share from all countries (including domestically produced intermediates):

$$V_j \equiv u\left(I - \sum_k A_{kj}\right) \tag{8.5}$$

where u is a $1 \times N$ unity vector. One can consider V to be a $2 \times 2N$ matrix of direct domestic value added for both countries:

$$V \equiv \begin{bmatrix} V_1 & 0 \\ 0 & V_2 \end{bmatrix} \tag{8.6}$$

The unique contribution of the OECD–WTO–TVA database as explained by Koopman *et al.* (2011) is their creation of a "direct value-added share" (*VAS*) matrix by source:

$$VAS \equiv VB = \begin{bmatrix} V_1B_{11} & V_1B_{12} \\ V_2B_{21} & V_2B_{22} \end{bmatrix} \tag{8.7}$$

Within the *VAS* matrix, the individual elements represent domestic value-added share of domestically produced products in a particular sector at home. For example, V_2B_{21} denotes the share of country 2's value-added in a particular product. The first N columns in the *VAS* matrix includes all value-added, domestic and foreign, needed to produce one additional unit of domestic products in country 1. The second N columns present value-added shares for production in country 2. This matrix is expanded to $N \times N$ countries. Because all value-added must be either domestic or foreign, the sum along each column is one:

$$V_1B_{11} + V_2B_{21} = V_1B_{12} + V_2B_{22} = u \tag{8.8}$$

In order to link the value-added shares to exports the OECD–WTO–TVA database (Koopman *et. al.*, 2010) denote E_{jk} to represent an $N \times 1$ vector of gross exports from j to k.

$$E_{j*} = \sum_{k \neq j} E_{jk} = \sum_k (A_{jk}X_k + Y_{jk}) \quad j, k = 1, 2 \tag{8.9}$$

$$E = \begin{bmatrix} E_{1*} & 0 \\ 0 & E_{2*} \end{bmatrix} \tag{8.10}$$

and

$$\hat{E} = \begin{bmatrix} diag(E_{1*}) & 0 \\ 0 & diag(E_{2*}) \end{bmatrix} \tag{8.11}$$

where E is a $2N \times 2$ matrix and $\hat{E}$ is a $2N \times 2N$ diagonal matrix.

Combining the value-added share matrix and an export matrix as weights produces a $2 \times 2N$ matrix $VAS\_\hat{E}$ the sectoral measure of value-added share by source country:

$$VAS\_\hat{E} \equiv VB\hat{E} = \begin{bmatrix} V_1B_{11}\hat{E}_1 & V_1B_{12}\hat{E}_2 \\ V_2B_{21}\hat{E}_1 & V_2B_{22}\hat{E}_2 \end{bmatrix} \tag{8.12}$$

The elements of this matrix capture all upstream sectors' contributions to value added in a specific sector's exports.

Domestic and foreign content of exports and value-added exports are different concepts. Despite the fact that both concepts measure the value generated by factors employed in the producing country, domestic content of exports is independent of where that value is used. Value-added trade, on the other hand, depends on how a country's exports are used by importers. It is the value added generated by country 1 but absorbed by country 2. Consequently, the OECD–WTO–TVA database (Koopman *et al.*, 2010) define related measures of domestic and foreign contents in sector-level gross exports, not sector-level value-added exports. Because the later depends on who absorbs the value added it has to be defined in terms of final demand after zeroing its diagonal.

$$\hat{V}AT \equiv \hat{V}BY = \begin{bmatrix} \hat{V}_1 & 0 \\ 0 & \hat{V}_2 \end{bmatrix} \begin{bmatrix} B_{11} & B_{12} \\ B_{21} & B_{22} \end{bmatrix} \begin{bmatrix} Y_{11} & Y_{12} \\ Y_{21} & Y_{22} \end{bmatrix} \tag{8.13}$$

In equation (8.13), Y_{kj} is an N by 1 vector and Y is $2N$ by 2 final demand matrix. $\hat{V}_j$ is a N by N diagonal matrix with direct value-added coefficients along the diagonal. The resulting $\hat{V}AT$ is a $2N$ by 2 value-added production matrix, its diagonal elements represent each country's production of value added absorbed by itself while its off diagonal elements constitute the $2N \times 2$ bilateral value-added trade matrix. It excludes value added produced in the home country that returns home after processing abroad.

The aggregate (2×2) measure of value added by source in gross exports is given by:

$$VAS\_E \equiv VBE = \begin{bmatrix} V_1B_{11}E_{1*} & V_1B_{12}E_{2*} \\ V_2B_{21}E_{1*} & V_2B_{22}E_{2*} \end{bmatrix} \tag{8.14}$$

*VAS*_E represents the OECD–WTO–TVA database's (Koopman *et al.*, 2010) the value added by source measure. Diagonal elements of *VAS*_E define the domestic value added in each country's exports. Off-diagonal elements give the foreign value added embodied in each country's exports.

Gross exports are decomposed into foreign value added (FV) and domestic value added (DV) as follows:

$$DV = \begin{bmatrix} V_1 B_{11} E_{1*} \\ V_2 B_{22} E_{2*} \end{bmatrix} = \begin{bmatrix} V_1(I - A_{11} - A_{12}(I - A_{22})^{-1}A_{21})^{-1}E_{1*} \\ V_2(I - A_{22} - A_{21}(I - A_{11})^{-1}A_{12})^{-1}E_{1*} \end{bmatrix} \quad (8.15)$$

$$\begin{aligned} FV &= \begin{bmatrix} V_2 B_{21} E_{1*} \\ V_1 B_{12} E_{2*} \end{bmatrix} \\ &= \begin{bmatrix} u(A_{21} - A_{12}(I - A_{22})^{-1}A_{21})(I - A_{11} - A_{12}(I - A_{22})^{-1}A_{21})^{-1}E_{1*} \\ u(A_{12} - A_{21}(I - A_{11})^{-1}A_{12})(I - A_{22} - A_{21}(I - A_{11})^{-1}A_{12})^{-1}E_{2*} \end{bmatrix} \end{aligned} \quad (8.16)$$

The OECD–WTO–TVA database (Koopman *et al.*, 2010) accounts for a country importing its own value added, which has been exported but returns home after being processed abroad. *VAS_E* attributes foreign and domestic contents to multiple countries when intermediate products cross borders in the $N \times N$ cases.

In the $N \times N$ cases the OECD–WTO–TVA database (Koopman *et al.*, 2010) provide all value-added components despite the various complications. Production, value-added shares and sources of value added in gross exports are given by:

$$\begin{aligned} X &= (I - A)^{-1}Y = BY \\ VAS &= VB \\ VAS\_E &= VBE \end{aligned} \quad (8.17)$$

With N countries and N sectors, X and Y are $NN \times 1$ vectors; A and B are $NN \times NN$ matrices; V and VAS are $N \times NN$ matrices; E is a $NN \times N$ matrix; and VAS_E is a $N \times N$ matrix.

Summing over all trading partners for all goods, the OECD–WTO–TVA database (Koopman *et al.*, 2010) provides the key decomposition equation that states that a country's gross exports to the world is the sum of the following five broad terms:

$$\begin{aligned} E_{j*} &= DV_j + FV_j \\ &= V_j B_{jj} \sum_{k \neq j} Y_{jk} && \text{(a)} \\ &+ V_j B_{jj} \sum_{k \neq j} A_{jk} X_{kk} && \text{(b)} \end{aligned}$$

$$
\begin{aligned}
&+ V_j B_{jj} \sum_{k \neq j} \sum_{l \neq j,k} A_{jk} X_{kl} \quad && \text{(c)} \\
&+ V_j B_{jj} \sum_{k \neq j} A_{jk} X_{kj} && \text{(d)} \\
&+ FV_j && \text{(e)}
\end{aligned}
\tag{8.18}
$$

where (Koopman *et al.*, 2010, p. 14) notes that (a) Domestic value added embodied in the exports of final goods and services absorbed by the importer; (b) Domestic value added embodied in exports of intermediate inputs used by the importer to produce its domestically needed products; (c) Domestic value added embodied in intermediate exports used by the importer to produce goods for third countries ("indirect value-added exports') (d) Domestic value added embodied in intermediate exports used by the importer to produce goods shipped back to the source country ("reflected domestic value added") and (e) Value added from foreign countries embodied in gross exports ("foreign value added used in exports").

Summing (a), (b) and (c) generates each country's value-added exports to the world. Summing (a), (b), (c) and (d) generates domestic content in a country's gross exports. As such, the OECD–WTO–TVA database (Koopman *et al.*, 2010) captures only the direct effect and the first round of the indirect effect in the value chain stream. If the value-chain stream consists of multiple segmentations, then the only way to capture the full order of the decomposition is by using information on domestic final demand in the importing country to obtain domestic value added embodied in the intermediate goods used by direct importers to produce domestically needed final goods. This estimate is the best that can be provided by this data set. In that case, one can obtain a full-order decomposition, using the five value-added components to account for 100 percent of the country's gross exports only when trade values are summed over all sectors and all trading partners (total exports to the world).

8.2. The Value-Added Chain in MENA's International Trade: Looking Backward and Forward

In Table 8.5 we begin decomposing MENA's foreign trade in terms of value added. The first observation is that within MENA the only countries participating in global value-added chain are Israel, Turkey, Cyprus

Table 8.5. Foreign Value-Added Content of MENA's Exports by Major Categories as a Percent of Total Exports to the World (2000–2011)

	Total Exports				Total Manufactures				Chemicals and non-metallic mineral products				Electrical and optical equipment			
Year	Israel	Turkey	Cyprus	SA	Israel	Turkey	Cyprus	SA	Israel	Turkey	Cyprus	SA	Israel	Turkey	Cyprus	SA
2000	20.7	13.0	22.1	3.6	29.0	19.8	39.6	10.8	33.4	20.1	56.3	7.9	21.7	29.8	42.1	26.3
2001	21.7	15.1	22.8	3.7	30.3	22.5	40.1	10.6	34.7	22.0	57.0	7.5	24.1	29.3	41.4	25.0
2002	22.8	18.3	22.7	3.8	32.4	26.8	39.2	11.4	38.1	30.9	53.6	8.1	23.7	40.9	39.0	24.6
2003	24.6	19.6	22.6	3.7	34.3	27.8	39.0	14.0	37.8	31.3	55.4	9.7	22.5	39.5	37.0	25.1
2004	25.4	21.1	22.7	3.6	35.7	29.8	37.7	13.5	38.7	30.7	48.5	9.3	25.0	41.6	42.4	26.0
2005	25.8	20.9	22.0	3.7	36.4	29.3	39.0	16.5	37.2	30.2	38.6	13.7	27.3	38.2	52.5	24.6
2006	26.8	23.3	22.3	4.7	37.1	31.4	39.0	19.5	38.8	34.3	41.8	15.3	28.6	39.3	58.6	28.8
2007	27.4	24.1	23.6	4.5	37.6	32.2	40.4	17.5	39.0	34.0	39.8	11.9	28.8	39.1	62.9	29.6
2008	26.7	24.9	24.8	4.5	37.4	33.0	43.9	20.2	41.1	35.7	43.9	17.0	27.8	35.4	61.8	33.5
2009	21.7	21.5	21.6	4.6	30.6	29.6	38.3	16.4	32.9	29.5	39.4	12.5	23.6	32.5	53.4	28.5
2010	23.4	22.6	21.5	3.9	32.8	30.9	39.3	12.7	33.6	31.1	38.9	8.4	25.1	32.1	61.9	24.8
2011	25.0	25.7	21.4	3.3	35.1	35.2	38.5	12.2	35.7	31.6	39.9	8.4	26.2	37.2	59.2	25.2

Source: OECD–WTO Statistics on Trade in Value Added (TiVA).

and Saudi Arabia. The data shown in Table 8.5 is the foreign content of these four MENA country's exports by major categories over the 2000–2011 period. This represents looking backward along the value chain. The foreign content of these four MENA country's exports increased in total manufactures between 2000 and 2011. The foreign value-added content within chemical and non-metallic mineral products increased substantially for Turkey, dropping significantly for Cyprus, maintaining a status quo for Israel at 35 percent, and very minor position for Saudi Arabia, with 8.4 percent in 2011. For electrical and optical equipment, the foreign value-added content for Israel increased from 21.7 percent to 26.2 percent; the foreign value-added content for Turkey increased from 29.8 percent to 37.2 percent; the foreign value-added content for Cyprus increased from 42.1 percent to 59.2 percent; and the foreign value-added content for Saudi Arabia decreased from 26.3 percent to 25.2 percent.

The size of foreign value added in a country's total exports clearly depends on its size and patterns of specialization. Smaller economies tend to have higher shares of foreign value added embodied in their exports; larger economies have a wider variety of domestically sourced intermediate goods available and are therefore less reliant on foreign imports of intermediates. Countries with substantial natural resources, as Saudi Arabia, have lower ratios of foreign value added in exports as much of its oil activities require fewer intermediate goods in the production process.

The four MENA country exports are highly heterogeneous and therefore display varying degrees of foreign value-added content. This is not surprising given that variations in foreign value-added content of exports is determined by these country's economic structure and export composition. Moreover, the foreign value-added content is determined by technical characteristics of specific production functions and sophistication in support services which tend to facilitate the fragmentation and outsourcing that we observe in these MENA country exports.

Increased production standardization is a major factor explaining the increased foreign value added in exports. Van Assche and Gangnes (2007), Ma and Van Assche (2010) and Van Assche (2012) point out that when firms push the specialization envelope to its extreme form — referred to as "modulization" — the production process is compartmentalized into a very unique set of fixed I–O technical coefficients. Consequently, components can be brought in from a variety of sources if they meet the required technical specification. The more a product is standardized in this way, the easier it becomes to shift country of origin for many of the required components. Products that are composed of different "modules" can be assembled using components from other producers because the end product has a predetermined standard that has been codified with no room for improvising. This process of developing and accepting international standards for products is part of the process of "globalization" that the majority of MENA countries have not accepted. The major downside of this MENA policy has been the lack of codification of transactions and creation of new kinds of tradable services. Products that do not have this "modality" characteristic require components to be specifically adjusted to each other, thereby limiting the separability of production activities.

For the four MENA countries, the global value-added chain goes beyond the separability of the production function, it also involves extending its frontiers to include many of its European and Asian neighbors as part of its focus on integrating with its "normal trade partners." Table 8.6 presents the origin of these MENA country's total foreign value added in its exports. It is not surprising to find that the foreign value added of Israel's and Turkey's exports originate largely in neighboring Europe and the economies from the Asia-Pacific Economic Cooperation (APEC). For Cyprus, most of its exports over the period 2000–2011 embody intermediates sourced from within the EU. For Saudi Arabia, most of its exports over the period 2000–2011 embody intermediates sourced from the EU and APEC. The primary explanation for this geographical clustering is due to the importance of distance for general cost reduction in joint planning and inspection of production processes and the importance of distance to local transportation hubs.

As the four MENA countries grow more prosperous, wages rise, and we observe domestic production shifting offshore to other countries. Domestically produced inputs used in third country's exports reflect this 'forward' integration along the global value chain. The latter measured by summing over rows, excluding domestic industries, provides an estimate of the contribution of domestically produced intermediates to exports by third countries. The limited MENA country participation in this 'forward' global value chain is shown in Table 8.7. Over the period 2000 to 2011, forward participation for Israel has expanded from 16.5 to 19.6 across all categories. For Turkey, it has expanded from 14.8 percent to 15.4 percent. For Cyprus, forward participation has expanded from 14.3 percent to 17.1 percent. For Saudi Arabia, it has expanded from 35.0 percent to 42.4 percent.

Table 8.6. **Backward Participation: Origin of MENA Country Foreign Value-Added Content of Its Exports (2000–2011) (Percent)**

	2000	2001	2002	2003	2004	2005	2006	2007	2008	2009	2010	2011
Israel												
Total GVC Backward Participation	20.7	21.6	22.8	24.6	25.4	25.8	26.8	27.5	26.8	21.7	23.4	25.0
Asia-Pacific Economic Cooperation (APEC)	7.5	7.6	7.6	8.4	8.2	8.8	9.2	10.0	9.0	7.6	8.2	8.7
Association of South East Asian Nations (ASEAN)	0.5	0.5	0.5	0.5	0.4	0.6	0.6	0.7	0.8	0.7	0.7	0.7
Eastern Asia	1.9	1.9	1.8	2.2	2.3	2.5	2.8	3.1	2.9	2.5	3.0	3.0
European Union (15 countries)	7.0	7.9	8.4	8.7	9.0	8.9	8.7	8.9	8.1	7.0	6.8	7.2
European Union (28 countries)	7.4	8.3	9.0	9.3	9.6	9.6	9.6	9.6	8.8	7.7	7.5	7.8
Euro area (18 countries)	5.1	5.9	6.3	6.6	6.7	6.6	6.7	6.8	6.4	5.6	5.4	5.6
North American Free Trade Association (NAFTA)	4.4	4.6	4.5	4.7	4.7	4.8	4.6	4.9	4.2	3.7	3.6	4.1
Europe	8.6	9.7	10.5	11.2	11.2	11.3	11.4	11.5	10.8	9.1	9.0	9.5
East and South East Asia	2.4	2.4	2.4	2.8	2.7	3.0	3.4	3.8	3.7	3.1	3.6	3.7
South and Central America	0.2	0.2	0.3	0.3	0.3	0.5	0.6	0.6	0.5	0.2	0.2	0.3
Other regions	5.1	4.8	5.1	5.7	6.5	6.2	6.8	6.6	7.7	5.6	6.9	7.6
Turkey												
Total GVC Backward Participation	13.0	15.1	18.3	19.6	21.1	20.9	23.3	24.1	24.9	21.6	22.6	25.7
Asia-Pacific Economic Cooperation (APEC)	3.4	3.8	4.4	4.8	6.2	6.7	7.9	8.9	9.4	7.9	8.2	8.9
Association of South East Asian Nations (ASEAN)	0.2	0.2	0.2	0.3	0.4	0.4	0.5	0.5	0.5	0.5	0.5	0.6
Eastern Asia	0.9	1.0	1.2	1.4	1.8	1.9	2.2	2.4	2.4	2.2	2.4	2.8
European Union (15 countries)	5.1	5.3	6.8	7.8	8.3	7.4	7.8	7.8	7.2	6.9	6.8	8.0
European Union (28 countries)	5.5	5.7	7.5	8.6	9.3	8.4	9.0	9.1	8.4	8.1	8.1	9.5
Euro area (18 countries)	4.2	4.4	5.8	6.6	7.1	6.3	6.5	6.5	6.1	5.9	5.7	6.9
North American Free Trade Association (NAFTA)	1.2	1.2	1.5	1.4	1.5	1.5	1.5	1.6	1.9	1.8	1.8	2.4
Europe	6.7	7.2	9.4	10.7	12.2	11.5	12.9	13.6	13.2	11.7	11.8	12.6
East and South East Asia	1.1	1.3	1.4	1.7	2.2	2.3	2.6	2.9	2.9	2.7	2.9	3.5
South and Central America	0.2	0.2	0.2	0.3	0.3	0.5	0.5	0.4	0.4	0.5	0.5	0.7
Other regions	3.8	5.2	5.9	5.5	5.1	5.2	5.7	5.6	6.5	4.9	5.7	6.5

Cyprus												
Total GVC Backward Participation	22.1	22.8	22.7	22.6	22.7	22.0	22.3	23.6	24.7	21.6	21.5	21.4
Asia-Pacific Economic Cooperation (APEC)	5.7	5.5	5.6	6.0	5.7	4.9	5.2	4.4	5.2	4.1	4.4	4.4
Association of South East Asian Nations (ASEAN)	0.3	0.3	0.3	0.2	0.2	0.2	0.2	0.2	0.3	0.2	0.3	0.2
Eastern Asia	1.2	1.1	1.1	1.1	1.2	1.0	1.0	1.0	1.7	1.1	1.2	1.1
European Union (15 countries)	10.5	10.9	11.1	10.7	11.8	11.9	11.8	12.5	13.3	12.4	11.4	11.4
European Union (28 countries)	11.1	11.5	11.9	11.4	12.4	12.7	12.6	13.3	14.7	13.7	12.5	12.4
Euro area (18 countries)	7.9	8.4	8.7	8.4	9.4	9.7	9.5	9.3	10.3	9.6	8.7	8.7
North American Free Trade Association (NAFTA)	2.6	2.6	2.6	2.6	2.9	2.7	2.7	2.1	1.5	1.6	1.5	1.4
Europe	13.0	13.5	13.9	13.7	14.0	14.0	14.1	14.7	16.8	15.2	14.2	14.5
East and South East Asia	1.5	1.5	1.4	1.4	1.5	1.2	1.2	1.2	1.9	1.4	1.4	1.3
South and Central America	0.2	0.2	0.2	0.2	0.8	0.9	1.0	2.2	0.4	0.2	0.2	0.2
Other regions	4.8	5.0	4.6	4.7	3.5	3.2	3.4	3.3	4.2	3.3	4.2	4.0
Saudi Arabia												
Total GVC Backward Participation	3.6	3.7	3.8	3.7	3.6	3.7	4.7	4.5	4.5	4.6	3.9	3.3
Asia-Pacific Economic Cooperation (APEC)	1.7	1.7	1.7	1.5	1.3	1.1	1.5	1.5	1.4	1.6	1.3	1.1
Association of South East Asian Nations (ASEAN)	0.1	0.1	0.1	0.1	0.1	0.1	0.1	0.1	0.2	0.2	0.2	0.1
Eastern Asia	0.4	0.4	0.4	0.4	0.4	0.3	0.5	0.6	0.5	0.6	0.5	0.5
European Union (15 countries)	1.0	1.0	1.1	1.1	1.3	1.3	1.6	1.7	1.3	1.4	1.1	0.9
European Union (28 countries)	1.1	1.0	1.1	1.2	1.3	1.3	1.6	1.8	1.4	1.5	1.2	1.0
Euro area (18 countries)	0.6	0.6	0.7	0.7	0.6	0.6	0.9	1.1	0.8	0.9	0.7	0.5
North American Free Trade Association (NAFTA)	1.1	1.1	1.0	0.8	0.7	0.5	0.7	0.6	0.4	0.6	0.5	0.4
Europe	1.2	1.3	1.3	1.4	1.5	1.5	1.9	2.0	1.7	1.8	1.4	1.2
East and South East Asia	0.5	0.5	0.5	0.6	0.5	0.4	0.6	0.7	0.7	0.8	0.7	0.6
South and Central America	0.1	0.1	0.1	0.1	0.1	0.3	0.3	0.1	0.3	0.2	0.1	0.2
Other regions	0.7	0.8	0.9	0.9	0.9	1.1	1.3	1.1	1.4	1.3	1.2	1.0

Source: OECD–WTO Statistics on Trade in Value Added (TiVA).

Table 8.7. **Forward Participation in GVCs-Domestic MENA VA Embodied in Foreign Exports, as Percent of Total Gross Exports of the Source Country (Percent)**

	2000	2001	2002	2003	2004	2005	2006	2007	2008	2009	2010	2011
Israel												
Total GVC Farward Participation	16.5	16.5	15.0	15.6	16.8	16.5	16.4	17.3	18.7	17.9	19.1	19.6
Asia-Pacific Economic Cooperation (APEC)	8.2	7.9	7.3	7.7	8.6	8.6	8.8	9.2	9.5	9.8	10.4	10.4
Association of South East Asian Nations (ASEAN)	1.6	1.6	1.4	1.5	1.7	1.7	1.6	1.9	1.7	2.1	1.9	2.0
Eastern Asia	2.4	2.5	2.5	2.9	3.6	3.7	3.8	4.0	4.1	4.0	4.7	4.7
European Union (15 countries)	6.1	6.1	5.3	5.5	5.5	5.2	4.8	5.1	5.7	4.8	5.0	5.7
European Union (28 countries)	6.5	6.6	5.8	6.0	6.0	5.8	5.5	5.9	6.6	5.6	6.0	6.5
Euro area (15 countries)	5.0	5.1	4.5	4.7	4.7	4.5	4.1	4.5	5.0	4.1	4.1	4.4
North American Free Trade Association (NAFTA)	3.6	3.2	2.9	2.8	2.8	2.7	2.9	2.9	3.1	3.1	3.2	3.1
Europe	7.2	7.3	6.4	6.5	6.6	6.3	6.0	6.4	7.3	6.3	6.6	7.2
East and South East Asia	4.0	4.1	3.9	4.4	5.3	5.4	5.4	5.8	5.8	6.1	6.7	6.7
South and Central America	0.2	0.3	0.3	0.3	0.3	0.4	0.3	0.3	0.3	0.3	0.4	0.4
Other regions	1.5	1.6	1.5	1.6	1.8	1.7	1.7	1.8	2.3	2.1	2.3	2.2
Turkey												
Total GVC Farward Participation	14.8	13.7	12.4	12.6	13.8	14.0	14.7	15.2	15.2	13.5	14.6	15.4
Asia-Pacific Economic Cooperation (APEC)	4.6	3.5	3.3	2.8	3.5	3.5	3.3	3.3	3.6	3.4	3.9	4.3
Association of South East Asian Nations (ASEAN)	1.5	1.0	0.9	0.7	0.9	1.0	0.6	0.7	0.7	0.7	0.7	0.7
Eastern Asia	1.1	1.1	1.0	0.9	1.1	1.0	1.1	1.1	1.2	1.4	1.7	1.9
European Union (15 countries)	6.4	6.4	5.6	6.1	6.7	6.7	7.2	7.5	6.6	5.6	6.1	6.6
European Union (28 countries)	7.2	7.2	6.6	7.4	8.0	8.0	8.9	9.3	8.2	7.0	7.7	8.2
Euro area (18 countries)	5.6	5.7	5.0	5.5	6.0	5.9	6.4	6.7	6.0	4.9	5.3	5.8
North American Free Trade Association (NAFTA)	1.2	1.0	1.0	0.8	1.0	0.9	0.9	0.7	0.8	0.7	0.8	0.9
Europe	8.1	7.8	7.2	8.0	8.6	8.8	9.7	10.3	9.2	7.7	8.5	9.1
East and South East Asia	2.6	2.1	1.9	1.6	2.0	1.9	1.7	1.7	1.9	2.1	2.3	2.6
South and Central America	0.1	0.1	0.1	0.1	0.1	0.1	0.1	0.2	0.2	0.1	0.1	0.2
Other regions	2.8	2.7	2.3	2.2	2.1	2.3	2.3	2.4	3.1	2.9	2.8	2.6

Cyprus												
Total GVC Farward Participation	14.3	14.3	12.3	13.6	14.9	15.6	16.4	15.3	15.7	15.3	16.5	17.1
Asia-Pacific Economic Cooperation (APEC)	2.3	2.1	1.6	2.0	2.2	2.5	2.5	2.5	3.8	3.7	4.9	4.4
Association of South East Asian Nations (ASEAN)	0.4	0.3	0.3	0.4	0.5	0.5	0.5	0.4	0.3	0.4	0.4	0.5
Eastern Asia	0.4	0.3	0.3	0.5	0.6	0.6	0.7	0.8	1.5	1.0	0.9	0.9
European Union (15 countries)	9.3	9.4	8.6	9.2	9.6	9.9	9.8	9.9	8.2	8.0	7.0	7.9
European Union (28 countries)	9.8	9.8	9.0	9.8	10.4	10.8	11.4	11.3	10.3	9.9	9.7	10.8
Euro area (18 countries)	5.9	6.0	5.0	5.4	6.9	7.7	7.8	8.0	6.7	7.0	6.6	7.5
North American Free Trade Association (NAFTA)	0.6	0.6	0.5	0.6	0.7	0.6	0.5	0.5	0.3	0.3	0.3	0.3
Europe	11.1	11.0	9.7	10.8	11.7	12.3	13.0	12.4	12.2	12.2	13.3	13.7
East and South East Asia	0.8	0.7	0.6	0.8	1.0	1.1	1.2	1.1	1.8	1.4	1.2	1.4
South and Central America	0.0	0.0	0.0	0.1	0.1	0.0	0.1	0.0	0.1	0.0	0.0	0.0
Other regions	1.8	2.0	1.4	1.4	1.4	1.5	1.8	1.2	1.4	1.5	1.6	1.7
Saudi Arabia												
Total GVC farward Participation	35.0	33.7	31.4	32.6	35.6	37.8	39.0	39.4	40.3	36.0	39.3	42.4
Asia-Pacific Economic Cooperation (APEC)	20.8	20.5	19.2	19.3	21.9	25.1	25.8	26.7	27.7	25.0	27.7	28.9
Association of South East Asian Nations (ASEAN)	5.5	6.3	4.7	4.3	4.9	6.3	6.5	6.3	5.7	5.6	6.0	6.1
Eastern Asia	10.0	10.0	10.0	11.1	13.0	14.8	15.6	16.4	17.5	16.1	17.9	18.4
European Union (15 countries)	9.4	7.8	7.3	7.3	8.1	7.7	7.1	6.3	5.9	4.4	4.8	6.3
European Union (28 countries)	9.6	8.1	7.5	7.6	8.5	8.1	7.4	6.7	6.3	4.7	5.1	6.6
Euro area (18 countries)	8.7	7.1	6.9	6.9	7.6	7.2	6.7	5.9	5.5	4.0	4.4	5.8
North American Free Trade Association (NAFTA)	3.5	3.3	3.4	3.5	3.5	3.4	3.1	3.5	4.1	2.8	3.4	3.8
Europe	9.9	8.3	7.8	7.9	8.8	8.4	7.8	7.0	6.6	5.0	5.4	7.0
East and South East Asia	15.5	16.2	14.7	15.3	17.9	21.2	22.1	22.6	23.1	21.7	23.9	24.6
South and Central America	0.3	0.5	0.4	0.6	0.6	0.5	0.4	0.5	0.5	0.4	0.5	0.5
Other regions	5.8	5.3	5.2	5.4	4.9	4.4	5.6	5.9	5.9	6.1	6.2	6.6

Source: OECD–WTO Statistics on Trade in Value Added (TiVA).

It is not surprising to find that the forward participation for Israel is quite disaggregated. For Turkey its forward value added is concentrated in Europe. For Cyprus most of its forward participation is in Europe and the EU. For Saudi Arabia most of its forward participation is in APEC, Eastern Asia, and East and South East Asia.

8.3. Protectionism in MENA

The current paradigm in the trade and development literature is that free trade in goods and services generates positive consequences for economic growth. The OECD (1998, p. 36) states that: "More open and outward-oriented economies consistently outperform countries with restrictive trade and [foreign] investment regimes." The IMF (1997, p. 84) asserts that "Policies toward foreign trade are among the more important factors promoting economic growth and convergence in developing countries."

Within the academic literature, Fischer (2000) summarizes the accepted paradigm in the theoretical economic literature by noting that "Trade encourages specialization, increasing productivity and living standards, and providing consumers with access to a wider range of better-quality goods at lower prices. The argument for the free movement of capital is essentially the same: money can be channeled to more effcient uses, financing investment and giving savers better returns." Moreover, he concludes that "[i]ntegration into the world economy is the best way for countries to grow." This line has been shared by others in the discipline (Frankel and Romer, 1999; Dollar, 1992; Edwards, 1992, 1993, 1998; Krueger, 1998; Leamer, 1988; among others).

Rodriguez and Rodrik (2001, p. 264) reworded the relevant question for policymakers to: "Do countries with lower policy-induced barriers to international trade grow faster, once other relevant country characteristics are controlled for?" Furthermore, Rodriguez and Rodrik (2001, p. 266) state that the "bottom line is that the nature of the relationship between trade policy and economic growth remains very much an open question... [T]he relationship is a contingent one, dependent on a host of country and external characteristics." Rodriguez and Rodrik (2001, p. 318) conclude their argument by noting that while "the effects of trade liberalization may be on balance beneficial on standard comparative-advantage grounds,... the evidence provides no strong reason to dispute this."

Esfahani and Squire (2007) take up the challenge set by Rodriguez and Rodrik (2001) and investigate the different measures of protection in MENA. They conclude that despite the fact that none of the measures "is free of conceptual or data problems... they tell a broadly consistent story of increased protectionism in MENA countries relative to the rest of the developing world." At the beginning of the 21st century, "Arab MENA countries have liberalized relatively little and may even have increased protection at a time when other countries were rapidly liberalizing" (Esfahani and Squire, 2007, p. 671).

A conventional approach to measure the overall trade policy of a country is to create an index based on effective tariffs and quotas. However, as Rodriguez and Rodrik (2001) have pointed out, the problem with this approach is the patchy and unreliable nature of the available data. Moreover, as Pelzman and Shoham (2010) note, given the complexity of non-tariff measures, it is not easy to come up with appropriate weights for aggregation of various types of protection across all products. For example, effective rates of protection are often measured at the tariff line detail and weighted by the amount of imports. When barriers are very restrictive and reduce imports substantially, the weights used are biased toward zero.

An alternative to effective rates of protection is a trade policy index composed of various policy indicators. One such measure, developed by the Fraser Institute, which we present in Table 8.8 for the MENA countries, measures "freedom to trade internationally" ranging from 1 to 10. In order to get a high rating in this area, a country must have low tariffs, easy clearance and efficient administration of customs, a freely convertible currency, and few controls on the movement of capital.

Column (1) measures the amount of taxes on international trade as a share of exports and imports. Countries with no import taxes on international trade earn a perfect 10. As the revenues from these taxes rise toward 15 percent of international trade, ratings decline toward zero. During the 2010–2015 period, most of the MENA countries reduced their ad-valorem tariffs. Column (2) is an index based on un-weighted mean of tariff rates. The rating will decline toward zero as the mean tariff rate approaches 50 percent. Because tariff rates are not uniform, wide variation in tariff rates exerts a more restrictive impact on trade and, therefore, on economic freedom. Consequently, Column (3) presents a 1 to 10 ranking where countries with greater variation in their tariff rates have lower scores. Egypt is a case where the standard deviation of tariff rates increased toward 25 percent, forcing the index to decline to zero. By 2015, a large group of MENA countries had a large variation in tariffs. This may result from the fact that as tariffs have been reduced, the remaining tariff lines are concentrated in a smaller group of remaining sacred cows, and as NTBs are removed, their corresponding tariff rates are substantially higher than average. Column (4)

Table 8.8. Fraser Institute Index for Freedom to Trade Internationally for MENA (1 = Most Restrictive, 10 = Least Restrictive)

Year	Countries	Revenue from trade taxes (% of trade sector)	Mean tariff rate	Standard deviation of tariff rates	Tariffs	Non-tariff trade barriers	Compliance costs of importing and exporting	Regulatory trade barriers	Freedom to trade internationally
		(1)	(2)	(3)	(4)	(5)	(6)	(7)	(8)
2010	Algeria	8.61	6.28	5.83	6.91	4.73	7.05	5.89	5.79
2011	Algeria	8.48	6.28	5.83	6.86	3.39	7.05	5.22	5.69
2012	Algeria	8.48	6.28	5.83	6.86	4.05	7.05	5.55	5.31
2013	Algeria	8.48	6.28	5.83	6.86	4.51	7.12	5.81	4.87
2014	Algeria	8.48	6.24	5.79	6.84	5.95	0.00	2.97	4.66
2015	Algeria	8.48	6.24	5.79	6.84	4.29	0.00	2.14	4.01
2010	Bahrain	9.42	8.98	6.26	8.22	8.28	8.31	8.29	7.98
2011	Bahrain	9.51	8.98	6.67	8.39	7.26	8.31	7.78	7.89
2012	Bahrain	9.51	9.00	6.86	8.46	6.47	8.31	7.39	7.70
2013	Bahrain	9.48	9.06	7.10	8.55	6.45	8.31	7.38	7.66
2014	Bahrain	9.51	9.06	7.44	8.67	7.62	5.68	6.65	7.58
2015	Bahrain	9.48	9.06	7.29	8.61	6.71	5.88	6.30	7.43
2010	Cyprus	9.63	8.98	6.41	8.34	6.73	9.27	8.00	8.16
2011	Cyprus	9.66	8.94	6.23	8.27	6.43	9.27	7.85	8.11
2012	Cyprus	9.63	8.90	6.11	8.21	6.56	9.27	7.91	7.64
2013	Cyprus	9.64	8.90	6.22	8.25	6.72	9.27	7.99	7.54
2014	Cyprus	9.82	8.94	6.54	8.43	7.30	9.31	8.31	8.49
2015	Cyprus	9.10	8.98	7.00	8.36	6.18	9.31	7.75	8.22
2010	Egypt	8.29	6.60	0.00	4.96	5.09	8.41	6.75	6.32
2011	Egypt	8.51	6.64	0.00	5.05	4.49	8.35	6.42	6.24
2012	Egypt	8.55	6.64	0.00	5.06	4.37	8.22	6.30	6.15
2013	Egypt	8.51	6.64	0.00	5.05	4.87	8.22	6.55	6.45
2014	Egypt	8.55	6.64	0.00	5.06	4.79	2.41	3.60	5.91
2015	Egypt	8.28	6.64	0.00	4.97	5.03	2.02	3.53	5.60

2010	Iran	7.52	4.80	0.00	4.11	4.05	6.07	5.06	5.05
2011	Iran	7.52	4.68	0.00	4.07	4.44	6.07	5.25	5.09
2012	Iran	7.52	4.68	0.00	4.07	4.89	5.76	5.32	2.58
2013	Iran	7.52	4.68	0.00	4.07	4.87	5.76	5.31	4.12
2014	Iran	7.52	4.68	0.00	4.07	4.87	0.00	2.43	2.99
2015	Iran	7.52	4.68	0.00	4.07	5.30	0.00	2.65	4.53
2010	Israel	9.69	8.72	3.79	7.40	7.36	8.70	8.03	8.23
2011	Israel	9.70	8.72	3.79	7.40	6.08	8.70	7.39	7.95
2012	Israel	9.77	8.86	4.89	7.84	5.31	8.70	7.01	7.86
2013	Israel	9.77	9.08	5.99	8.28	5.33	8.70	7.02	7.91
2014	Israel	9.77	9.08	5.80	8.22	7.38	7.33	7.35	8.27
2015	Israel	9.72	9.10	5.91	8.24	5.94	7.33	6.63	8.11
2010	Jordan	9.13	8.00	3.72	6.95	5.61	8.14	6.87	7.89
2011	Jordan	9.22	8.00	3.80	7.01	5.77	8.14	6.95	7.90
2012	Jordan	9.27	7.82	4.07	7.05	5.74	8.14	6.94	7.90
2013	Jordan	9.21	8.10	4.00	7.10	5.48	8.22	6.85	7.89
2014	Jordan	9.21	7.96	4.08	7.08	6.02	7.38	6.70	7.89
2015	Jordan	9.15	8.00	4.00	7.05	5.11	7.20	6.15	7.63
2010	Kuwait	9.53	9.06	7.93	8.84	6.90	7.64	7.27	7.59
2011	Kuwait	9.65	9.06	7.93	8.88	6.00	7.64	6.82	7.46
2012	Kuwait	9.64	9.06	7.89	8.86	4.87	7.64	6.26	7.31
2013	Kuwait	9.62	9.06	7.89	8.86	4.56	7.66	6.11	7.27
2014	Kuwait	9.62	9.06	7.89	8.86	5.92	2.68	4.30	6.89
2015	Kuwait	9.62	9.06	7.89	8.86	5.26	2.77	4.01	6.76

(Continued)

Table 8.8. *(Continued)*

Year	Countries	Revenue from trade taxes (% of trade sector)	Mean tariff rate	Standard deviation of tariff rates	Tariffs	Non-tariff trade barriers	Compliance costs of importing and exporting	Regulatory trade barriers	Freedom to trade internationally
2010	Lebanon	8.67	8.74	3.88	7.09	5.80	6.32	6.06	7.16
2011	Lebanon	8.85	8.74	3.88	7.15	5.01	6.45	5.73	7.04
2012	Lebanon	8.95	8.74	3.88	7.19	5.39	6.45	5.92	7.06
2013	Lebanon	9.33	8.74	3.88	7.31	5.85	6.45	6.15	6.98
2014	Lebanon	9.33	8.86	5.35	7.85	5.85	2.24	4.05	6.77
2015	Lebanon	9.45	8.88	5.59	7.97	5.38	3.12	4.25	6.89
2010	Morocco	8.44	6.38	1.82	5.55	5.49	8.24	6.87	6.79
2011	Morocco	8.64	7.14	1.59	5.79	5.87	8.24	7.06	6.94
2012	Morocco	9.13	7.42	1.85	6.13	6.43	8.24	7.34	7.13
2013	Morocco	9.25	7.42	1.85	6.17	6.16	8.45	7.31	7.00
2014	Morocco	9.13	7.76	3.59	6.83	5.15	4.42	4.79	6.61
2015	Morocco	9.27	7.70	3.38	6.78	4.33	7.06	5.70	6.84
2010	Oman	9.41	8.90	5.44	7.92	6.51	8.76	7.64	8.05
2011	Oman	9.58	8.90	5.44	7.97	6.59	8.76	7.68	8.10
2012	Oman	9.43	9.06	7.14	8.55	6.74	8.76	7.75	8.27
2013	Oman	9.63	9.06	7.18	8.62	6.13	8.76	7.45	7.98
2014	Oman	9.63	9.06	7.61	8.77	7.31	6.77	7.04	8.05
2015	Oman	9.63	8.90	5.71	8.08	6.08	7.00	6.54	7.65
2010	Qatar	9.31	9.00	6.68	8.33	8.36	7.16	7.76	7.76
2011	Qatar	9.31	8.98	6.37	8.22	8.25	7.68	7.96	7.77
2012	Qatar	9.31	9.06	7.39	8.59	7.63	7.68	7.66	7.79
2013	Qatar	9.31	9.06	7.41	8.59	5.94	7.91	6.92	7.60
2014	Qatar	9.31	9.06	7.42	8.60	8.66	6.76	7.71	7.94
2015	Qatar	9.31	9.06	7.22	8.53	6.95	6.76	6.85	7.56

2010	Saudi Arabia		9.04	7.35	8.20	7.41	8.01	7.71	7.24
2011	Saudi Arabia		9.02	8.37	8.70	6.95	8.01	7.48	7.26
2012	Saudi Arabia		7.74	1.77	4.76	6.19	8.01	7.10	6.11
2013	Saudi Arabia		9.04	6.70	7.87	5.73	8.01	6.87	6.78
2014	Saudi Arabia		8.98	7.08	8.03	6.77	1.52	4.15	6.21
2015	Saudi Arabia		8.98	6.96	7.97	5.95	1.52	3.74	5.97
2010	Syria	8.37	7.16	3.18	6.24	4.64	7.60	6.12	5.98
2011	Syria	8.37	7.16	3.18	6.24	6.83	7.60	7.21	6.47
2012	Syria	8.37	7.16	3.18	6.24	6.55	6.86	6.71	4.62
2013	Syria	8.37	6.70	0.63	5.23	6.52	7.16	6.84	4.97
2014	Syria	8.37	6.70	0.63	5.23	5.24	2.82	4.03	4.51
2015	Syria	8.37	6.70	0.63	5.23	5.24	2.82	4.03	4.91
2010	Tunisia	8.86	6.70	5.18	6.91	5.77	8.01	6.89	6.44
2011	Tunisia	8.95	6.80	5.46	7.07	4.75	8.01	6.38	6.75
2012	Tunisia	8.83	6.90	5.16	6.97	5.13	8.01	6.57	7.06
2013	Tunisia	8.83	6.90	5.16	6.97	4.86	7.57	6.22	6.94
2014	Tunisia	8.83	7.18	5.54	7.19	6.18	7.26	6.72	7.34
2015	Tunisia	8.83	6.90	5.16	6.97	4.47	7.26	5.86	6.81
2010	Turkey	9.57	8.02	1.17	6.25	5.66	8.05	6.86	7.35
2011	Turkey	9.56	8.08	1.32	6.32	4.99	8.20	6.60	7.24
2012	Turkey	9.57	8.08	1.32	6.32	5.12	8.20	6.66	7.25
2013	Turkey	9.49	7.84	0.50	5.94	5.51	8.20	6.86	6.88
2014	Turkey	9.49	7.86	0.50	5.95	6.21	9.09	7.65	7.35
2015	Turkey	9.56	7.84	0.67	6.02	6.03	8.77	7.40	7.24

(Continued)

Table 8.8. *(Continued)*

Year	Countries	Revenue from trade taxes (% of trade sector)	Mean tariff rate	Standard deviation of tariff rates	Tariffs	Non-tariff trade barriers	Compliance costs of importing and exporting	Regulatory trade barriers	Freedom to trade internationally
2010	UAE	10.00	9.02	7.00	8.67	7.65	9.14	8.40	8.10
2011	UAE	10.00	9.02	6.94	8.65	7.49	9.14	8.31	8.12
2012	UAE	10.00	9.06	7.39	8.82	7.55	9.14	8.35	8.20
2013	UAE	9.99	9.06	7.37	8.81	7.52	9.14	8.33	8.26
2014	UAE	9.99	9.06	7.44	8.83	8.30	7.42	7.86	8.22
2015	UAE	9.99	9.06	7.16	8.74	7.45	8.30	7.87	8.22
2010	Yemen	8.98		8.12	8.55	6.17	6.34	6.25	7.08
2011	Yemen	8.82	8.58	8.13	8.51	5.03	6.17	5.60	6.92
2012	Yemen	8.92	8.50	8.20	8.54	4.18	6.17	5.18	6.82
2013	Yemen	8.92	8.50	7.90	8.44	4.71	6.05	5.38	6.88
2014	Yemen	8.92	8.50	7.90	8.44	4.71	5.76	5.23	6.86
2015	Yemen	8.92	8.50	7.87	8.43	4.44	10.00	7.22	7.31

Sources: Gwartney, James D. and Robert Lawson, Joshua C. Hall, et al. (2017), Economic Freedom of the World: 2017 Annual Report.

presents the overall index for the first three indexes. The results are not surprising — Bahrain, Cyprus, Israel, Kuwait, Oman, Qatar and the UAE had the least trade restrictions based on tariff policies.

The next three columns focus on non-tariff barriers. Column (5) is based on the World Economic Forum, Global Competitiveness Report survey question: "In your country, tariff and non-tariff barriers significantly reduce the ability of imported goods to compete in the domestic market." The least restrictive within MENA include Bahrain, Cyprus, Israel, Kuwait, and the UAE. Column (6) is based on the World Bank's *Doing Business* data on the time it takes (cost of procedures required) to export or import a full, 20-foot container of dry goods that contains no hazardous or military items. This index was constructed for: (i) the time cost to export a good (measured in number of calendar days required), and (ii) the time cost to import a good (measured in number of calendar days required). These two ratings were averaged to arrive at the final index.

The results in Columns (5) and (6) confirm the earlier results. Bahrain, Cyprus, Israel, Kuwait, and the UAE had the lowest NTBs and the lowest compliance costs. The resulting overall NTB measure in Column (7) combines the results of the partial indexes.

The final index reported in Column (8) is the overall "freedom to trade internationally" index. The leading countries include Bahrain, Cyprus, Israel, Jordan, Kuwait and the UAE. Hoekman and Messerlin (2002, p. 8) argue that such a short list is reasonable given that "the combination of small markets and high barriers has constrained the MENA region's growth opportunities, thereby freezing its trade structure, hindering economic diversification, and leading to overall rigidity in the economy that has constrained the development of modern industry."

To what extent is this observation correct?

In order to answer this question, the next section focuses on determining the export competitiveness of MENA countries.

8.4. MENA Country International Trade Competitiveness: An Assessment Based on Revealed Comparative Advantage (RCA) and Constant Market Share (CMS) Indexes

In the 21st century, a country's relative competitiveness has to be measured in an increasing internationalization of markets for goods and services, financial resources, corporations, industries and technology. While the trade literature points to a wide number of explanatory factors for the increased globalization of world markets, it is convenient to think of three major factors that have facilitated this increased globalization, which only a limited number of countries within MENA have relied on. First, the liberalization of capital movements and deregulation, of financial services in both market and non-market economies, has been a crucial lubricant. Second, the post Uruguay round liberalization of markets to trade and investment, spurred the growth of international competition. Third, as Baldwin (2011) has correctly pointed out, the continued globalization of the world economy and MENA's role in that globalization could not be accomplished without the pivotal role played by information and communication technologies (ICT) in MENA and its trade partners.

Within MENA, Israel is a major beneficiary of this new world economy where distances and national boundaries are far less important than in the period prior to GATT/WTO removal of most obstacles to market access. The production linkages between Israel and its Asian neighbors and the links to its markets in the OECD countries has changed the dynamics of trade, capital flows and transfer of technology. With the low cost of communication and network technology (ICT), transnational firms are organizing themselves into "transnational networks" in response to intense international competition and the increasing need for strategic interactions.

These changes have altered our concepts of "global competition." In this new environment, competitiveness increasingly depends on the utilization of a broad assortment of specialized industrial, financial, technological, commercial, administrative and cultural skills located in different countries. It is therefore not surprising to find that a growing number of Israeli, Cypriot and Turkish firms are competing in their own markets as well as in foreign ones, with new entrants from around the globe.

These increased dynamics in commercial activities between some within MENA and its competitors, places new demands on statistics and indicators designed to assess competitiveness. The traditional economic statistics and indicators were developed largely in an era where most economic activity, with the exception of trade, occurred domestically and trade in intermediate products was rare. Consequently, our discussion of MENA country relative competitiveness is based on a variety of measures. In the best-case scenario, MENA firm's competitiveness is affected by a number of factors including differentials in productivity, prices, quality of export products and delivery and service schedules. In the absence of analyzing price and non-price determinants of changes in competitiveness, the empirical trade literature has provided a number of statistical measures of trade performance to study the structure and competitiveness of MENA country's foreign trade. Within this class of indicators are indices of trade intensity, the most popular member of this family being the index of "revealed comparative advantage" (RCA). The form of each index and the interpretation given to their values have varied from author to author, but the empirical and theoretical literature appear to agree that a country reveals a comparative advantage (disadvantage) in a commodity if an index's value is greater (less) than one.

The classic RCA index is most often associated with the work of Balassa (1965). Very simply, the index compares a country's share of world exports in a sector to its share of total exports:

$$RCA_{ij} = \frac{X_{ij}/X_{wj}}{X_{it}/X_{wt}} \tag{8.19}$$

where X_{ij} and X_{wj} are exports of j by country i and the world w and X_{it} and X_{wt} represent the total exports of i and the world (w).

This index, in essence, applies a country's *ex post* specialization patterns to infer that a country's actual high specialization in a sector can be viewed as an indication that it has strong comparative advantage in that sector. The term "comparative advantage", as Bowen (1983) correctly points out, is misapplied in this literature since only exports are typically considered whereas comparative advantage is properly a net trade concept. While we use "Revealed Comparative Advantage" in our discussion here for consistency, the reader may wish to consider substituting "Revealed *Competitive* Advantage."

One can restate Balassa's RCA index into two related indices:

$$RCA_{ij} = \frac{X_{ij}/X_{wj}}{X_{it}/X_{wt}} = \frac{s_{ij}}{s_i} \tag{8.20}$$

or

$$RCA_{ij} = \frac{X_{ij}/X_{wi}}{X_{jt}/X_{wt}} = \frac{c_{ij}}{c_j} \tag{8.21}$$

where: $s_{ij} = \frac{X_{ij}}{X_{wj}}$ represents country i's share in export market j; $s_i = \frac{X_{it}}{X_{wt}}$ represents country i's share in the entire world export market; $c_{ij} = \frac{X_{ij}}{X_{wi}}$ measures country i's export specialization in product j; $c_j = \frac{X_{jt}}{X_{wt}}$ measures the world export specialization in product j.

From Bowen and Pelzman (1984) we can infer that when $RCA_{ij} > 1$ [Equation (8.20)] country i's competitiveness in product j (measured by

s_{ij}) is greater than its average competitiveness (measured by s_i). Furthermore, when $RCA_{ij} > 1$ [Equation (8.21)], country i's export specialization in product j (measured by c_{ij}) is higher than the world average export specialization in the product (measured by c_j). Overall, from both Equations (8.20) and (8.21) when $RCA_{ij} > 1$ it is inferred that country i has strong comparative advantage in product j. If we allow the RCA measure to reflect "competitiveness," then one can argue that trade-policy intervention may have created an outcome that some have incorrectly referred to as "comparative advantage." Furthermore, the concept of competitiveness is more appropriate to firms than to countries (Krugman, 1996). If a firm is not performing and its business position is unsustainable, i.e., if it is a 'non-performing asset,' it will eventually go bankrupt. It is far less likely that a country that is non-competitive will go bankrupt, although not impossible.

The decomposition of the Balassa RCA measure suggests that an alternative methodology to employ is one that decomposes a country's export growth based on departures from a steady-state world growth. The latter methodology is known as the Constant Market Share (CMS) methodology. The CMS model decomposes the actual growth of a country's exports into four components: world trade, commodity composition, market distribution, and (residual) competitiveness. Formally, the CMS identity for a change in total MENA exports can be written as:

$$X^{00} - X^{0} = rX^{0} + \sum_{i}(r_i - r)X_i^0 + \sum_{i}\sum_{j}(r_{ij} - r_i)X_{ij}^0 + \sum_{i}\sum_{j}(X_{ij}^{00} - X_i^0 - r_{ij}X_{ij}^0) \tag{8.22}$$

where X is total MENA country exports, X_{ij} is MENA country exports of commodity i to market j, X_j is total MENA country exports of commodity i, r is rate of growth of total world exports, $\mathrm{r_j}$ is rate of growth of total world exports of commodity i, r_{ij} is rate of growth of world exports of commodity i to market j, 0 is initial period and 00 is second period.

The first term in Equation (8.22) is the world-trade component and measures what MENA country exports would have been had they grown at the same rate as total world exports. The second term (commodity composition effect) measures whether MENA country export composition was skewed toward commodities whose rate of growth either exceeded or fell short of total world export growth. The third term (market distribution effect) measures whether MENA country exports were concentrated in markets where demand was growing either faster or slower than total world export demand in those markets. The fourth term (residual competitiveness) measures the difference between the actual increase in MENA country exports and the increase that would have occurred had the MENA countries maintained their export share in each market with respect to each commodity. In theory, an increase (decrease) in competitiveness is indicated by a positive (negative) value of the residual.

The application of the CMS procedure raises a number of questions concerning both measurement and aggregation. For example, what is the appropriate definition of the world market and regional markets in which the MENA countries compete? What is the appropriate level of commodity aggregation? Also, given a paucity of quantity data, value data are commonly used and thus price changes may hamper interpretation of the CMS estimates, especially if we use MENA country data. As Bowen and Pelzman (1984, p. 462) and Richardson (1971a, p. 231) noted, a positive commodity composition effect, normally taken to imply that a country's exports were concentrated in goods for which demand was growing rapidly, may instead be due to a country's exports being concentrated in goods whose (relative) price is rising. Such a price bias also applies to the competitive residual.

When data are in value terms, the competitive residual (CR) can be written as:

$$CR = \sum_i \sum_j V_{ij}^0[(\dot{X}_{ij} - \dot{X}_{ij}^w) + (\dot{P}_{ij} - \dot{P}_{ij}^w)] \tag{8.23}$$

where V_{ij}^0 is the value of MENA country exports of commodity i to market j and a dot over a variable denotes its rate of change. The first term in parentheses is the difference in the rates of growth of MENA country and the rest of world's quantity of exports of commodity i to market j. The second term is the difference in the rate of growth of MENA country and rest of world export price of commodity i in market j. The first term is the true competitive component, in that failure to maintain market share in quantity terms implies a negative value of this term. But with value data, a negative value of CR could also result from slower growth in MENA country export prices relative to the rest of the world's prices. These two forces are essentially in opposition, since a relative decline in MENA country export prices would be expected to result in a relative increase in MENA country exports. Ultimately, when value data are used, the sign of CR depends not only on differential growth in prices, but also on the elasticity of substitution in each market.

Although an interpretation of the sign of the competitive residual can be confounded by price movements when market shares are measured in value terms, the above does suggest that one can infer a failure to maintain quantity shares if, given a negative value of CR, one observes that a country's export prices increased relative to the export prices of the rest of the world.

In the case of most of the MENA countries, with distortionary trade policies and in some MENA countries an inconvertible currency, the distinction between value and quantity data for the MENA country measures may not be as important as the more fundamental flows. For our purposes, the RCA measures we report here are used for the descriptive purpose of identifying in which sectors MENA country exports, measured in value added terms or gross trade, are more or less than average. The comparison to world exports helps to 'normalize' the trade data for the sizes of sectors and countries, which otherwise might give misleading impressions of the importance of a sector and country in international trade.

We present both RCA and CMS measures as a guide to what causes actual trade patterns, whether these are driven by comparative advantage, strategic trade policy intervention or currency interventions. RCA and CMS indexes could be correlated with additional data on factor endowments and factor intensities to learn whether the Heckscher–Ohlin explanation of trade has significant explanatory power. This is done to a limited extent by analyzing for separate product aggregates classified according to the intensity with which they use unskilled labor, human capital or technology across a group of OECD and non-OECD countries.

To the extent that differences in total factor productivity can be measured, these could be related to RCA and CMS measures to see if a more strictly Ricardian explanation of trade patterns plays an important role.

In addition to the question of MENA country trade competitiveness, the question of commodity and country diversification is also addressed. The conventional development literature advocates export diversification as a mechanism by which to generate positive productivity and economic growth. Melitz (2003), Feenstra and Hiau (2008) and Feenstra (2010) argue that an increase in export variety — one of the sources of export diversification — can increase productivity given that exporters are more productive than non-exporters. It has also been argued that export diversification can reduce exposure to external shocks, reducing macroeconomic volatility and increasing economic growth. This argument is the reverse of the "Dutch Disease" argument applied to natural resource exporters. Lederman and Maloney (2003).

Despite the fact that the theoretical trade discussion is about "trade diversification," the indexes used empirically, most of them borrowed from the income-distribution literature, are about degree of concentration. The most frequently used concentration index is the Herfindahl index listed as Equation (8.24). The Herfindahl index of export concentration, (for country i) can be applied across categories (k) in order to measure product specific-concentration or across countries (n) for a specific commodity classification (k) in order to measure geographic concentration. The index is normalized to range between zero and one, where one implies complete concentration and the reverse to demonstrate complete diversification. For the MENA countries, we calculate both measures. Our discussion of RCA indexes will use geographic concentration. Our discussion of the CMS measures will present both geographic and product-level concentration.

$$H_i^k = \sum_{i=1}^{n} \left(\frac{X_i^k}{\sum_{i=1}^{n} X_i^k} \right)^2 \tag{8.24}$$

8.4.1. *Competitiveness Based on RCA and Herfindahl Indexes*

In order to assess the trade performance and specialization of the MENA countries, we begin by exploring the RCA indexes calculated in terms of MENA country's gross exports for five product groups. The product groups are capital goods, consumer goods, intermediate goods, raw materials, and manufactures. We are therefore able to differentiate between final goods and intermediate goods exports in the context of MENA country's revealed comparative advantage. The RCA calculations rely on COMTRADE trade statistics measured at the 6 digit HS nomenclature. The time frame for these indexes are over the period 2009 to 2015.

Table 8.9 presents the RCA indexes for all the MENA countries. These indexes are calculated using the "world" as the target market for MENA country exports. The RCA measures clearly separate out those MENA countries, like Algeria, Egypt, Jordan, Kuwait, Lebanon, Morocco, Oman, Qatar, Saudi Arabia, UAE and Yemen who have revealed comparative advantage that — an RCA above 1 — in raw materials. For capital goods, only Israel has an RCA greater than 1. For Consumer goods, Algeria, Bahrain, Cyprus, Egypt, Jordan, Lebanon, Morocco, Qatar, Tunisia, Turkey and Yemen had an RCA greater than 1. For intermediate

Table 8.9. Revealed Comparative Advantage (RCA) for MENA Country Exports by Major Product Group (2009–2015)

Country	Product Group	2009	2010	2011	2012	2013	2014	2015
Algeria	Capital goods	0.02	0.01	0.01	0.01	0.01	0	0.01
Algeria	Consumer goods	1.64	1.74	1.71	1.71	1.76	1.89	1.93
Algeria	Intermediate goods	0.07	0.08	0.05	0.06	0.05	0.1	0.16
Algeria	Raw materials	3.25	2.93	2.77	2.74	2.76	2.5	2.97
Algeria	Manufactures	0.03	0.04	0.02	0.02	0.02	0.03	—
Bahrain	Capital goods	0.11	0.08	0.08	0.19	0.24	0.09	0.15
Bahrain	Consumer goods	1.35	1.59	1.61	1.92	1.85	1.87	1.71
Bahrain	Intermediate good	1.89	1.63	1.64	1.28	1.43	1.74	1.82
Bahrain	Raw materials	0.35	0.57	0.39	0.33	0.37	0.16	0.2
Bahrain	Manufactures	0.38	0.35	0.38	0.33	0.36	0.34	—
Cyprus	Capital goods	1	0.85	0.84	0.52	0.49	0.7	0.59
Cyprus	Consumer goods	1.17	1.38	1.36	2.01	1.89	1.45	1.93
Cyprus	Intermediate goods	0.78	0.76	0.94	0.57	0.71	0.91	0.55
Cyprus	Raw materials	0.86	0.84	0.78	0.65	0.63	0.84	0.63
Cyprus	Manufactures	0.98	0.87	0.82	0.53	0.6	0.97	—
Egypt	Capital goods	0.13	0.09	0.07	0.07	0.07	0.07	0.1
Egypt	Consumer goods	1.58	1.49	1.25	1.29	1.22	1.16	1.23
Egypt	Intermediate goods	1.08	1.19	1.26	1.21	1.2	1.19	1.05
Egypt	Raw materials	1.6	1.64	1.86	1.88	2.11	2.33	2.9
Egypt	Manufactures	0.55	0.6	0.57	0.57	0.61	0.62	—
Iran	Capital goods	—	0.02	0.01	—	—	—	—
Iran	Consumer goods	—	0.26	0.18	—	—	—	—
Iran	Intermediate goods	—	0.51	0.44	—	—	—	—
Iran	Raw materials	—	4.66	4.34	—	—	—	—
Iran	Manufactures	—	0.15	0.14	—	—	—	—
Israel	Capital goods	1.02	0.82	0.73	0.79	0.81	0.83	0.87
Israel	Consumer goods	0.88	0.98	1.01	1	0.98	0.88	0.86
Israel	Intermediate goods	1.63	1.74	1.84	1.82	1.74	1.86	1.69
Israel	Raw materials	0.52	0.54	0.51	0.45	0.47	0.47	0.53
Israel	Manufactures	1.25	1.26	1.31	1.33	1.29	1.31	—
Jordan	Capital goods	0.15	0.14	0.11	0.14	0.17	0.22	0.17
Jordan	Consumer goods	1.26	1.32	1.12	1.16	1.38	1.33	1.53
Jordan	Intermediate goods	1.62	1.7	1.81	1.6	1.58	1.63	1.37
Jordan	Raw materials	1.1	0.94	1.23	1.49	1.18	1.08	1.38
Jordan	Manufactures	1.02	1.1	1.06	1.06	1.18	1.15	—
Kuwait	Capital goods	—	0.01	0.01	—	0	0.01	0.01
Kuwait	Consumer goods	—	0.81	0.81	—	0.75	0.79	0.82
Kuwait	Intermediate goods	—	0.29	0.24	—	0.27	0.27	0.37
Kuwait	Raw materials	—	4.38	4.05	—	4.3	4.42	5.4
Kuwait	Manufactures	—	0.11	0.09	—	0.09	0.1	—

(Continued)

Table 8.9. *(Continued)*

Country	Product Group	2009	2010	2011	2012	2013	2014	2015
Lebanon	Capital goods	0.49	0.48	0.86	0.43	0.53	0.52	—
Lebanon	Consumer goods	1.19	1.1	0.96	1.02	1.23	1.36	—
Lebanon	Intermediate goods	0.84	0.82	0.75	1.65	1.05	0.94	—
Lebanon	Raw materials	1.16	1.52	1.14	1.1	1.47	1.42	—
Lebanon	Manufactures	0.99	0.97	1.05	1	0.91	0.78	—
Libya	Capital goods	0	—	—	—	—	—	—
Libya	Consumer goods	0.59	0.5	—	—	—	—	—
Libya	Intermediate goods	0.12	0.12	—	—	—	—	—
Libya	Raw materials	5.32	5.16	—	—	—	—	—
Libya	Manufactures	0.03	0.04	—	—	—	—	—
Morocco	Capital goods	0.3	0.26	0.24	0.25	0.26	0.25	0.25
Morocco	Consumer goods	1.52	1.48	1.36	1.4	1.57	1.59	1.48
Morocco	Intermediate goods	1	1.15	1.29	1.35	1.15	1.1	1.13
Morocco	Raw materials	1.57	1.4	1.18	1.22	1.18	1.22	1.67
Morocco	Manufactures	0.93	0.93	0.99	1.02	1.02	1.04	—
Oman	Capital goods	0.02	0.02	0.01	0.02	0.03	0.03	0.03
Oman	Consumer goods	0.79	0.6	0.62	0.68	0.67	0.65	0.73
Oman	Intermediate goods	0.39	0.52	0.58	0.59	0.57	0.61	0.73
Oman	Raw materials	4.3	4.32	3.86	3.84	4.04	4.21	4.96
Oman	Manufactures	0.13	0.17	0.19	0.18	0.2	0.19	—
Qatar	Capital goods	—	0.01	—	—	0.01	0.01	0.01
Qatar	Consumer goods	—	1.67	—	—	1.94	1.91	1.99
Qatar	Intermediate goods	—	0.33	—	—	0.36	0.38	0.51
Qatar	Raw materials	—	2.7	—	—	1.96	2.01	2.16
Qatar	Manufactures	—	0.11	—	0.09	0.1	0.11	—
Saudi Arabia	Capital goods	0.01	0.01	0.01	0.01	0.01	0.01	0.03
Saudi Arabia	Consumer goods	0.36	0.32	0.28	0.29	0.27	0.32	0.51
Saudi Arabia	Intermediate goods	0.51	0.62	0.53	0.54	0.56	0.63	0.95
Saudi Arabia	Raw materials	5.27	4.87	4.62	4.61	4.83	4.89	5.11
Saudi Arabia	Manufactures	0.18	0.22	0.19	0.18	0.19	0.21	—
Syria	Capital goods	0.06	0.06	—	—	—	—	—
Syria	Consumer goods	0.78	0.77	—	—	—	—	—
Syria	Intermediate goods	0.6	0.56	—	—	—	—	—
Syria	Raw materials	4.11	3.99	—	—	—	—	—
Syria	Manufacture	0.27	0.28	—	—	—	—	—
Tunisia	Capital goods	0.62	0.62	0.67	0.6	0.61	0.66	0.65
Tunisia	Consumer goods	1.67	1.59	1.69	1.71	1.67	1.68	1.65
Tunisia	Intermediate goods	0.85	0.86	0.76	0.75	0.77	0.71	0.89
Tunisia	Raw materials	0.87	0.99	0.84	0.88	0.9	0.83	0.68
Tunisia	Manufactures	1.15	1.15	1.21	1.16	1.15	1.21	—
Turkey	Capital goods	0.63	0.63	0.72	0.66	0.72	0.68	0.64
Turkey	Consumer goods	1.46	1.53	1.49	1.44	1.47	1.48	1.43

(Continued)

Table 8.9. *(Continued)*

Country	Product Group	2009	2010	2011	2012	2013	2014	2015
Turkey	Intermediate goods	1.08	1.09	1.12	1.37	1.11	1.13	1.19
Turkey	Raw materials	0.7	0.62	0.51	0.45	0.62	0.61	0.69
Turkey	Manufactures	1.17	1.2	1.26	1.25	1.22	1.2	—
UAE	Capital goods	—	—	—	0.13	0.16	0.16	0.16
UAE	Consumer goods	—	—	—	0.79	0.79	0.89	0.92
UAE	Intermediate goods	—	—	—	1.13	0.99	0.9	1.19
UAE	Raw materials	—	—	—	2.76	2.98	3.09	3.24
UAE	Manufactmes	0.32	0.45	0.39	0.31	0.31	0.31	—
Yemen	Capital goods	0.02	0	0.01	0.01	0	0	0.02
Yemen	Consumer goods	0.23	0.67	1.11	1.07	1.49	1.87	1.41
Yemen	Intermediate goods	0.08	0.07	0.06	0.19	0.09	0.08	0.17
Yemen	Raw materials	5.59	4.78	3.72	3.69	3.21	2.57	4.25
Yemen	Manufactures	0.02	0.01	0.02	0.02	0.02	0.02	—

Source: UN COMTRADE Database.

goods Bahrain, Egypt, Israel, Jordan, Morocco and Turkey had an RCA greater than 1. For manufactures Israel, Jordan, Tunisia and Turkey had an RCA greater than 1.

In Table 8.10 we present the Herfindahl index of geographic concentration. This indicator is a measure of the dispersion of trade value across an exporter's partners. A county with a preponderance of trade value concentrated in a very few markets will have an index value close to 1, whereas a country trading equally with all partners will have an index close to 0. A low index may not, however, be a true indicator of a broad partner base if the number of partners is low: it simply implies that it trades with each of them equally. The data in Table 8.10 present a low concentration index primarily because the MENA countries have limited trade partners. Apart from Israel, Turkey and the UAE who had more than 210 trade partners, the balance of MENA countries have, on average, 150 trade partners.

8.4.2. *Competitiveness Based on CMS Decompositions*

The Constant Market Share (CMS) decomposition of MENA country export growth stresses the importance of the competitiveness effect as the predominant explanation behind the changes in the MENA country exports over the period 2012 to 2016. Table 8.11 presents the estimates of the source of growth in MENA country exports calculated at the 6-digit HS classification and presented for the aggregate HS categories.

Table 8.10. **Herfindahl Market Concentration Index (2000–2016)**

Country	2000	2001	2002	2003	2004	2005	2006	2007	2008	2009	2010	2011	2012	2013	2014	2015	2016
Algeria	0.09	0.10	0.09	0.11	0.11	0.11	0.14	0.14	0.12	0.11	0.12	0.09	0.08	0.08	0.08	0.08	0.09
Bahrain	0.04	0.04	0.04	0.04	0.04	0.04	0.04	0.04	0.05	0.06	0.04	0.04	0.04	0.04	0.06	0.07	0.06
Cyprus	0.09	0.08	0.07	0.06	0.07	0.08	0.30	0.08	0.09	0.11	0.07	0.06	0.08	0.08	0.05	0.05	0.06
Egypt	0.07	0.07	0.08	0.06	0.05	0.05	0.05	0.04	0.04	0.04	0.03	0.04	0.04	0.04	0.04	0.04	0.04
Iran	0.07	0.09	0.09	0.10	0.08	0.09	0.08	—	—	—	0.09	0.11	—	—	—	—	—
Israel	0.19	0.18	0.20	0.19	0.17	0.18	0.19	0.16	0.14	0.15	0.14	0.13	0.13	0.12	0.13	0.17	0.18
Jordan	0.07	0.07	0.08	0.11	0.14	0.16	0.17	0.12	0.13	0.10	0.08	0.09	0.09	0.08	0.08	0.09	0.14
Kuwait	0.12	0.12	0.12	0.11	0.10	—	0.09	0.09	0.09	—	0.09	0.09	—	0.09	0.09	0.08	—
Lebanon	0.05	0.06	0.09	0.08	0.09	0.05	0.05	0.04	0.04	0.05	0.04	0.07	0.09	0.06	0.05	—	—
Libya	—	—	—	—	—	—	—	0.16	0.15	0.16	0.14	—	—	—	—	—	—
Morocco	0.11	0.11	0.11	0.12	0.12	0.11	0.10	0.11	0.08	0.11	0.09	0.08	0.07	0.08	0.09	0.09	0.11
Oman	0.18	0.15	0.13	0.16	0.19	0.16	0.16	0.16	0.18	0.12	0.15	0.15	0.16	0.18	0.25	0.24	0.26
Qatar	0.30	0.31	0.27	0.27	0.23	0.23	0.23	0.23	0.21	—	0.15	—	0.14	0.14	0.14	0.11	0.11
Saudi Arabia	0.09	0.09	0.09	0.09	0.08	0.08	0.08	0.08	0.08	0.08	0.08	0.08	0.08	0.08	0.08	0.07	—
Syria	—	0.10	0.08	0.09	0.09	0.10	0.10	0.10	0.09	0.07	0.08	—	—	—	—	—	—
Tunisia	0.16	0.17	0.18	0.19	0.19	0.18	0.17	0.18	0.14	0.13	0.13	0.16	0.13	0.13	0.15	0.14	0.17
Turkey	0.08	0.07	0.07	0.06	0.06	0.05	0.05	0.04	0.04	0.04	0.04	0.04	0.04	0.03	0.04	0.04	0.04
UAE	0.19	0.16	0.14	0.12	0.11	0.12	0.13	0.11	0.12	0.10	0.09	0.08	0.08	0.07	0.07	0.06	0.07
Yemen	—	—	—	—	0.24	0.27	0.18	0.16	0.22	0.14	0.20	0.15	0.23	0.16	0.19	0.24	—

Source: UN COMTRADE Databases.

Table 8.11. Decomposition of Changes in MENA Country Exports into CMS Components (2012–2016 and Percent)

Sectors	Relative change of world market share (%)	Competitiveness effect (%)	Initial geographic specialisation (%)	Initial product specialisation (%)	Adaptation effect (%)
		(a)	(b)	(c)	(d)
Algeria					
Fresh food	8.35	6.66	0.34	4.56	−3.21
Processed food	0.10	4.16	−2.46	−6.29	4.70
Wood products	5.46	7.31	0.54	−0.26	−2.12
Textiles	6.97	6.70	−1.45	6.09	−4.38
Chemicals	17.24	41.22	−0.46	−7.54	−15.98
Leather products	−11.60	−8.59	−1.02	−5.44	3.45
Basic manufactures	−13.42	−14.82	1.53	−0.38	0.25
Non-electronic machinery	−0.86	−8.18	0.17	−1.85	9.01
IT & Consumer electronics	—	—	—	—	—
Electronic components	323.96	266.81	−1.61	−0.13	58.90
Transport equipment	−4.39	246.14	49.34	−40.72	−259.15
Clothing	3.39	3.31	−1.67	6.25	−4.49
Miscellaneous manufacturing	−3.35	−1.81	1.56	1.33	−4.43
Minerals	−3.85	−1.38	0.24	−1.37	−1.34
Bahrain					
Fresh food	0.06	3.18	5.58	6.16	−14.86
Processed food	−4.69	−5.81	3.07	−0.52	−1.44
Wood products	−8.21	−12.17	−1.47	−5.16	10.60
Textiles	13.25	15.09	−0.35	1.54	−3.03
Chemicals	−1.54	3.87	0.97	−4.61	−1.78
Leather products	164.00	133.24	0.88	−4.33	34.20
Basic manufactures	4.59	−1.82	−0.22	−3.20	9.83
Non-electronic machinery	10.69	9.56	−0.98	0.30	1.81
IT & Consumer electronics	−0.91	31.00	−8.74	−1.45	−21.72
Electronic components	10.46	14.58	−1.24	−2.25	−0.63
Transport equipment	−0.99	4.77	−1.25	−5.12	0.61
Clothing	41.10	23.17	2.74	−1.37	16.56
Miscellaneous manufacturing	21.21	29.93	−0.95	1.57	−9.35
Minerals	4.52	−1.70	3.74	−3.77	6.24
Cyprus					
Fresh food	−0.49	−2.06	−0.71	4.12	−1.83
Processed food	7.58	8.19	0.37	−0.30	−0.69
Wood products	−5.74	−5.29	0.73	−1.71	0.53

(Continued)

Table 8.11. *(Continued)*

Sectors	Relative change of world market share (%)	Competitiveness effect (%)	Initial geographic specialisation (%)	Initial product specialisation (%)	Adaptation effect (%)
		(a)	(b)	(c)	(d)
Textiles	−9.75	−4.11	0.92	0.25	−6.82
Chemicals	−1.97	−2.41	−0.37	1.87	−1.06
Leather products	−7.42	−9.55	2.60	0.88	−1.35
Basic manufactures	10.58	−0.09	−0.32	−0.36	11.35
Non-electronic machinery	1.70	−0.19	1.13	1.09	−0.33
IT & Consumer electronics	57.85	37.44	1.86	−0.36	18.91
Electronic components	−4.17	−3.05	−4.11	3.87	−0.87
Transport equipment	−7.74	−9.00	2.07	6.99	−7.79
Clothing	−7.24	−6.02	0.65	0.44	−2.32
Miscellaneous manufacturing	−2.67	−1.95	−0.27	0.63	−1.08
Minerals	68.26	75.23	2.20	−1.91	−7.25
Egypt					
Fresh food	2.02	1.25	−0.73	0.99	0.51
Processed food	2.31	0.86	−1.13	2.49	0.09
Wood products	−4.67	−5.88	−0.38	3.53	−1.94
Textiles	−3.09	−1.57	−0.44	−1.74	0.67
Chemicals	−4.24	−1.64	−0.80	−3.04	1.24
Leather products	0.64	4.57	0.60	−5.61	1.08
Basic manufactures	−5.83	−2.12	−2.78	−0.78	−0.13
Non-electronic machinery	−7.96	−8.63	−1.79	−1.27	3.72
IT & Consumer electronics	154.28	219.08	−8.60	2.60	−58.79
Electronic components	−3.66	−0.61	−1.38	−2.93	1.26
Transport equipment	0.61	−3.33	−1.24	−0.56	5.75
Clothing	−3.64	−2.73	3.55	−2.76	−1.70
Miscellaneous manufacturing	1.96	−2.20	−0.41	2.10	−1.45
Minerals	−5.25	−7.27	4.18	4.21	−6.38
Iran					
Fresh food	−4.28	−4.17	−0.37	0.18	0.08
Processed food	−12.53	−12.46	−1.56	−1.85	3.34
Wood products	−12.48	−1.57	0.55	3.98	−15.45
Textiles	−4.39	0.28	−1.02	−4.08	0.42
Chemicals	−4.67	−3.57	0.02	−1.90	0.77
Leather products	−10.10	−4.48	−2.40	−8.01	4.79
Basic manufactures	1.68	5.29	−1.13	−2.24	−0.24
Non-electronic machinery	−10.56	−9.64	−5.93	−1.94	6.95
IT & Consumer electronics	−12.98	−11.40	0.05	−0.29	−1.35
Electronic components	−13.06	−11.34	1.99	−9.92	6.21

(Continued)

Table 8.11. *(Continued)*

Sectors	Relative change of world market share (%)	Competitiveness effect (%)	Initial geographic specialisation (%)	Initial product specialisation (%)	Adaptation effect (%)
		(a)	(b)	(c)	(d)
Transport equipment	−7.89	−10.99	−2.69	−0.34	6.14
Clothing	−12.14	−10.70	2.73	6.55	−10.72
Miscellaneous manufacturing	−16.36	−17.36	−4.51	−2.47	7.98
Minerals	0.81	−4.79	8.40	2.87	−5.66
Israel					
Fresh food	−1.12	−0.01	−0.76	3.06	−3.42
Processed food	−2.98	−2.98	0.22	0.85	−1.07
Wood products	−1.45	−2.30	−0.02	−2.38	3.25
Textiles	−0.29	−2.22	0.11	−3.71	5.54
Chemicals	−1.57	−3.52	−0.10	4.03	−1.98
Leather products	−2.98	12.61	0.81	0.29	−16.68
Basic manufactures	6.22	0.78	0.11	5.17	0.17
Noil-electronic machinery	1.24	−0.28	0.74	0.30	0.49
IT & Consumer electronics	−2.45	−3.21	−0.07	1.48	−0.65
Electronic components	2.06	1.44	1.45	−1.47	0.64
Transport equipment	8.88	3.92	8.93	6.04	−10.00
Clothing	−1.57	−3.51	0.22	2.85	−1.13
Miscellaneous manufacturing	3.36	1.45	1.16	0.84	−0.09
Minerals	15.32	−0.85	5.09	13.92	−2.83
Jordan					
Fresh food	−1.14	−3.59	−2.07	1.33	3.19
Processed food	−0.52	6.93	−1.86	4.03	−9.63
Wood products	−6.76	−8.34	2.13	−2.64	2.09
Textiles	−6.50	−5.68	−1.92	−1.85	2.95
Chemicals	−2.24	−1.17	−0.12	−1.65	0.69
Leather products	−14.93	−8.13	−4.38	−6.34	3.93
Basic manufactures	0.46	−1.29	−4.68	8.25	−1.82
Non-electronic machinery	0.75	14.83	−3.90	2.41	−12.59
IT & Consumer electronics	9.33	288.08	−8.65	1.84	−271.94
Electronic components	−2.26	−1.48	−6.70	−2.73	8.64
Transport equipment	50.36	58.11	−8.88	2.63	−1.50
Clothing	4.93	2.15	1.00	2.28	−0.51
Miscellaneous manufacturing	−2.81	−3.37	0.01	0.20	0.35
Minerals	8.38	−0.30	10.24	−2.37	0.81
Kuwait					
Fresh food	28.37	60.45	−0.50	10.51	−42.08
Processed food	14.95	4.83	2.41	6.55	1.16
Wood products	3.99	10.58	0.67	−3.45	−3.81
Textiles	−0.19	3.41	−1.67	3.15	−5.08

(Continued)

Table 8.11. (Continued)

Sectors	Relative change of world market share (%)	Competi-tiveness effect (%)	Initial geographic speciali-sation (%)	Initial product speciali-sation (%)	Adaptation effect (%)
		(a)	(b)	(c)	(d)
Chemicals	−6.99	−5.89	0.41	−4.43	2.93
Leather products	8.32	39.60	−1.17	−3.02	−27.10
Basic manufactures	−0.01	0.40	−1.39	3.44	−2.46
Non-electronic machinery	3.11	10.05	−1.09	0.43	−6.28
IT & Consumer electronics	0.58	7.22	−3.93	1.51	−4.22
Electronic components	−11.54	−6.49	−2.39	−4.45	1.79
Transport equipment	2.41	42.77	−4.46	−3.57	−32.34
Clothing	34.54	34.59	0.66	4.85	−5.55
Miscellaneous manufacturing	0.82	3.58	−3.31	−0.74	1.30
Minerals	−4.76	−8.87	2.87	4.99	−3.75
Lebanon					
Fresh food	2.94	3.96	−1.31	7.04	−6.75
Processed food	3.28	10.87	−0.39	5.07	−12.27
Wood products	−6.24	−1.01	−2.58	4.00	−6.65
Textiles	−4.73	−2.43	−2.66	5.13	−4.77
Chemicals	−1.20	4.12	−0.32	−0.35	−4.66
Leather products	−9.92	−7.27	0.23	−1.61	−1.26
Basic manufactures	−5.73	−0.80	−2.43	5.56	−8.06
Non-electronic machinery	−1.38	5.93	−3.31	0.85	−4.85
IT & Consumer electronics	−5.37	9.69	−4.61	1.58	−12.04
Electronic components	−8.75	−0.78	−3.61	−1.17	−3.19
Transport equipment	−11.45	−5.22	−7.00	−1.50	2.27
Clothing	−6.20	−3.87	3.10	5.05	−10.48
Miscellaneous manufacturing	−4.23	0.03	−1.64	0.83	−3.45
Minerals	−5.76	−5.35	1.77	7.06	−9.23
Libya					
Fresh food	15.47	10.05	0.98	6.70	−2.25
Processed food	—	—	—	—	—
Wood products	—	—	—	—	—
Textiles	—	—	—	—	—
Chemicals	15.98	32.23	−0.82	−6.70	−8.73
Leather products	—	—	—	—	—
Basic manufactures	−5.67	−10.23	0.81	68.99	−65.24
Non-electronic machinery	−3.83	−6.93	2.21	−4.69	5.58
IT & Consumer electronics	—	—	—	—	—
Electronic components	52.29	28.77	−2.18	−1.17	27.41
Transport equipment	−3.85	−9.40	−5.34	2.69	8.19
Clothing	—	—	—	—	—

(Continued)

Table 8.11. *(Continued)*

Sectors	Relative change of world market share (%)	Competitiveness effect (%)	Initial geographic specialisation (%)	Initial product specialisation (%)	Adaptation effect (%)
		(a)	(b)	(c)	(d)
Miscellaneous manufacturing	−14.02	−10.21	−3.18	−2.40	1.77
Minerals	−15.62	−14.31	0.20	−1.49	−0.02
Morocco					
Fresh food	7.63	5.39	−0.25	3.27	−0.77
Processed food	6.03	6.25	−0.75	0.63	−0.09
Wood products	−4.69	−6.71	−0.91	−0.75	3.68
Textiles	5.51	−1.91	0.44	−1.93	8.92
Chemicals	−1.99	−0.89	−0.01	−3.74	2.65
Leather products	−2.17	0.23	0.29	−1.89	−0.80
Basic manufactures	0.15	3.28	−0.35	−2.22	−0.55
Non-electronic machinery	6.81	8.03	0.40	0.01	−1.63
IT & Consumer electronics	−6.49	−4.75	−1.49	3.44	−3.68
Electronic components	5.33	2.75	−0.85	2.78	0.65
Transport equipment	32.62	19.15	2.18	1.01	10.29
Clothing	−2.80	−4.52	1.18	−0.17	0.71
Miscellaneous manufacturing	2.73	0.69	1.30	1.09	−0.34
Minerals	−3.16	−4.71	4.11	−3.46	0.90
Oman					
Fresh food	13.79	12.02	4.97	9.54	−12.74
Processed food	1.64	17.43	−0.61	−0.76	−14.43
Wood products	8.32	11.11	1.06	3.44	−7.29
Textiles	−3.14	−2.23	0.50	1.14	−2.55
Chemicals	−8.07	−5.96	0.77	−5.11	2.22
Leather products	−14.51	−13.96	26.04	−0.73	−25.86
Basic manufactures	−0.05	7.59	1.21	0.11	−8.96
Non-electronic machinery	—	—	—	—	—
IT & Consumer electronics	—	—	—	—	—
Electronic components	−1.41	1.39	−1.61	−0.18	−1.01
Transport equipment	6.67	14.39	0.08	6.03	−13.83
Clothing	−7.36	−5.80	5.77	2.70	−10.02
Miscellaneous manufacturing	7.71	12.90	−2.39	7.90	−10.70
Minerals	−4.40	−8.54	4.23	4.92	−5.01
Qatar					
Fresh food	—	—	—	—	—
Processed food	9.64	−2.83	2.92	7.46	2.09
Wood products	−12.80	−12.97	0.46	−0.94	0.65
Textiles	—	—	—	—	—

(Continued)

Table 8.11. *(Continued)*

Sectors	Relative change of world market share (%)	Competitiveness effect (%)	Initial geographic specialisation (%)	Initial product specialisation (%)	Adaptation effect (%)
		(a)	(b)	(c)	(d)
Chemicals	493.41	430.53	−0.15	−5.88	68.91
Leather products	—	—	—	—	—
Basic manufactures	17.62	15.42	0.51	−15.65	17.34
Non-electronic machinery	—	—	—	—	—
IT & Consumer electronics	—	—	—	—	—
Electronic components	—	—	—	—	—
Transport equipment	−16.05	−18.08	−1.44	2.88	0.59
Clothing	—	—	—	—	—
Miscellaneous manufacturing	32.60	15.51	0.93	1.09	15.06
Minerals	33.20	6.99	7.78	−1.43	19.86
Saudi Arabia					
Fresh food	0.63	7.70	1.07	−1.32	−6.82
Processed food	1.90	1.13	1.21	0.21	−0.65
Wood products	−4.25	−4.58	−0.89	−3.33	4.56
Textiles	−1.35	−0.15	0.12	−2.34	1.02
Chemicals	−3.19	−2.96	−0.21	−2.91	2.89
Leather products	−8.32	4.40	4.15	−13.56	−3.32
Basic manufactures	8.84	9.00	2.72	−3.84	0.95
Non-electronic machinery	2.48	6.72	0.76	−1.89	−3.11
IT & Consumer electronics	−7.94	6.60	−4.16	0.43	−10.81
Electronic components	−1.53	5.76	−0.92	−0.70	−5.67
Transport equipment	5.21	0.15	−0.12	4.36	0.82
Clothing	−1.64	2.05	3.15	−4.78	−2.06
Miscellaneous manufacturing	−4.99	−3.42	−1.56	0.50	−0.50
Minerals	−0.55	−6.29	−18.50	0.33	23.91
Syria					
Fresh food	−6.58	−9.10	0.03	4.99	−2.50
Processed food	−6.64	−10.30	0.28	1.30	2.08
Wood products	−17.72	−17.04	−2.24	1.09	0.47
Textiles	−18.11	−16.99	−1.59	−3.08	3.55
Chemicals	−15.68	−16.64	−0.70	0.58	1.09
Leather products	−14.75	−10.86	−1.19	4.05	−6.75
Basic manufactures	−13.44	−14.86	−1.37	13.17	−10.38
Non-electronic machinery	−18.33	−18.19	−0.24	3.29	−3.19
IT & Consumer electronics	—	—	—	—	—
Electronic components	—	—	—	—	—
Transport equipment	—	—	—	—	—
Clothing	−14.76	−15.55	0.16	2.74	−2.12

(Continued)

Table 8.11. *(Continued)*

Sectors	Relative change of world market share (%)	Competitiveness effect (%)	Initial geographic specialisation (%)	Initial product specialisation (%)	Adaptation effect (%)
		(a)	(b)	(c)	(d)
Miscellaneous manufacturing	−16.75	−17.00	−0.20	2.14	−1.68
Minerals	−19.37	−19.10	7.82	−7.98	−0.10
Tunisia					
Fresh food	1.20	−3.81	−0.63	3.82	1.83
Processed food	−6.96	−10.29	−2.27	1.44	4.16
Wood products	−9.46	−9.69	−5.34	2.38	3.19
Textiles	−5.08	−6.32	−3.46	1.36	3.34
Chemicals	−7.97	−7.81	−0.58	−4.00	4.42
Leather products	0.88	0.94	−1.11	−1.65	2.70
Basic manufactures	−2.36	−4.54	−1.31	0.47	3.02
Non-electronic machinery	0.29	−0.89	1.25	0.04	−0.10
IT & Consumer electronics	−3.12	−4.27	−1.12	2.52	−0.25
Electronic components	−1.45	−2.15	−2.03	−1.00	3.73
Transport equipment	4.63	1.48	0.59	2.72	−0.16
Clothing	0.04	0.35	−0.20	−3.64	3.53
Miscellaneous manufacturing	1.96	−1.90	0.30	−1.20	4.76
Minerals	−7.92	−7.23	−0.99	−3.19	3.49
Turkey					
Fresh food	2.04	2.00	−2.09	3.41	−1.28
Processed food	2.39	2.24	−2.46	3.27	−0.66
Wood products	3.83	3.37	−0.82	1.48	−0.19
Textiles	0.07	0.12	−1.39	0.82	0.51
Chemicals	0.90	1.25	−0.83	−0.03	0.51
Leather products	−0.56	7.21	1.04	9.11	−17.92
Basic manufactures	−2.58	0.01	−1.88	−1.21	0.50
Non-electronic machinery	2.46	3.98	−0.64	2.25	−3.14
IT & Consumer electronics	−4.98	2.96	−1.01	−3.01	−3.92
Electronic components	−2.45	0.99	−2.65	−0.10	−0.69
Transport equipment	5.53	3.33	0.85	3.73	−2.38
Clothing	−0.60	−1.28	1.15	1.72	−2.20
Miscellaneous manufacturing	4.09	15.75	−1.55	0.38	−10.50
Minerals	1.82	−1.63	5.42	2.45	−4.42
UAE					
Fresh food	−1.12	−8.45	−0.30	0.78	6.86
Processed food	−5.73	−10.35	−2.02	−5.04	11.67
Wood products	−2.64	−6.01	1.14	−1.17	3.40
Textiles	−14.19	−15.66	0.76	−3.53	4.24
Chemicals	−0.48	−2.55	0.05	−1.93	3.95

(Continued)

Table 8.11. *(Continued)*

Sectors	Relative change of world market share (%)	Competi-tiveness effect (%)	Initial geographic speciali-sation (%)	Initial product speciali-sation (%)	Adaptation effect (%)
		(a)	(b)	(c)	(d)
Leather products	−16.74	−15.59	1.01	0.70	−2.85
Basic manufactures	7.90	1.04	0.02	0.76	6.07
Non-electronic machinery	−12.67	−13.92	−1.25	−2.96	5.45
IT & Consumer electronics	−18.84	−18.62	−9.50	−2.00	11.28
Electronic components	−10.98	−12.27	−2.14	−1.32	4.75
Transport equipment	−17.68	−15.05	−6.15	−0.25	3.76
Clothing	−15.71	−16.44	4.21	−1.37	−2.11
Miscellaneous manufacturing	−14.86	−15.16	−3.72	−5.73	9.74
Minerals	4.08	−6.06	−14.18	0.51	23.81
Yemen					
Fresh food	−10.59	−13.94	3.56	−2.60	2.39
Processed food	−11.94	−12.85	1.14	−1.37	1.15
Wood products	—	—	—	—	—
Textiles	—	—	—	—	—
Chemicals	−13.56	−9.29	−2.39	−0.85	−1.04
Leather products	−18.01	−4.06	2.83	−2.18	−14.60
Basic manufactures	−14.89	−16.03	−3.14	−8.03	12.32
Non-electronic machinery	—	—	—	—	—
IT & Consumer electronics	—	—	—	—	—
Electronic components	—	—	—	—	—
Transport equipment	−18.10	−19.62	5.78	−11.75	7.48
Clothing	—	—	—	—	—
Miscellaneous manufacturing	−2.86	−2.43	0.97	2.92	−4.33
Minerals	−18.82	−19.20	11.44	9.71	−20.77

Source: COMTRADE Databases.

The first column represents the overall percentage change in MENA country exports to the world market, measured in terms of their changes in market share. The percentage change in the first column is calculated as:

$$\left(\frac{X_{ik}^{t_n}}{X_{wk}^{t_n}}\right) - \left(\frac{X_{ik}^{t_o}}{X_{wk}^{t_o}}\right) = \sum_j \left[\left(\frac{X_{ik}^{t_n}}{X_{jk}^{t_n}}\right)\left(\frac{X_{jk}^{t_n}}{X_{wk}^{t_n}}\right) - \left(\frac{X_{ik}^{t_o}}{X_{jk}^{t_o}}\right)\left(\frac{X_{jk}^{t_o}}{X_{wk}^{t_o}}\right)\right] \tag{8.25}$$

where: t_o = first period considered; t_n = end period considered; i = the MENA country; k = the HS sector; w = are the world exports; j = importers.

Consequently,

$\left(\frac{X_{ik}^{t_n}}{X_{jk}^{t_n}}\right)$ is the MENA country market share on all import markets for end period t_n;

$\left(\frac{X_{jk}^{t_n}}{X_{wk}^{t_n}}\right)$ is the share of import markets in world imports in t_n;

$\left(\frac{X_{ik}^{t_o}}{X_{jk}^{t_o}}\right)$ is the MENA country market share on all import markets for the initial period t_o;

$\left(\frac{X_{jk}^{t_o}}{X_{wk}^{t_o}}\right)$ is the share of import markets in world imports in t_o;

The second column, marked as Column (a) is labeled the competitiveness effect. It is expressed in percent and represents a residual hypothetical gain (or loss) of the MENA country's aggregate market share that would occur if changes were only due to variations in the individual country's market share in import markets (demand side), regardless of the structure of the MENA country exports. The percentage change in Column (a) is calculated as:

$$\sum_j \left(\frac{X_{ijk}^{t_n}}{X_{jk}^{t_n}} - \frac{X_{ijk}^{t_o}}{X_{jk}^{t_o}}\right)\left(\frac{X_{jk}^{t_o}}{X_{wk}^{t_o}}\right) \tag{8.26}$$

where:

$\left(\frac{X_{ijk}^{t_n}}{X_{jk}^{t_n}} - \frac{X_{ijk}^{t_o}}{X_{jk}^{t_o}}\right)$ is the variations in the MENA country's market share in its import markets;

$\left(\frac{X_{jk}^{t_o}}{X_{wk}^{t_o}}\right)$ is the initial share of world markets in world imports.

The third column, marked as Column (b) is labeled as the initial geographic specialization effect. It represents the degree to which the initial country distribution of each MENA country exports were helpful to their export growth. For each MENA country with the exception of Israel, their export pattern was more characteristic of developing country exporters than developed or newly industrialized economy exporters. The percentage change in Column (b) is calculated as:

$$\sum_j \left(\frac{X_{ijk}^{t_o}}{X_{jk}^{t_o}}\right)\left(\frac{X_{jk}^{t_n}}{X_{wk}^{t_n}} - \frac{X_{jk}^{t_o}}{X_{wk}^{t_o}}\right) \tag{8.27}$$

where:

$\left(\frac{X_{ijk}^{t_o}}{X_{jk}^{t_o}}\right)$ is the MENA country's initial export share in the partner country's imports;

$\left(\frac{X_{jk}^{t_n}}{X_{wk}^{t_n}} - \frac{X_{jk}^{t_o}}{X_{wk}^{t_o}}\right)$ is the geographic variation in each MENA country's export destination.

With the exception of the anti-Israel bias and boycott from most of the Arab MENA countries, we turn to the fourth column, marked as Column (c) which is labeled as the initial product specialization effect. This calculation reflects trade impact of commodity concentration. Were MENA country exports in those commodities where there was 'dynamic demand?' In majority of HS categories, over the 2012–2016 time band, MENA country exports were concentrated in those areas where there was 'dynamic demand.' The percentage change in Column (c) is calculated as:

$$\sum_j \left(\frac{X_{ijk}^{t_o}}{X_{jk}^{t_o}} - \frac{X_{ij}^{t_o}}{X_j^{t_o}}\right)\left(\frac{X_{jk}^{t_n}}{X_w^{t_n}} - \frac{X_{jk}^{t_o}}{X_w^{t_o}}\right) \tag{8.28}$$

where:

$\left(\frac{X_{ijk}^{t_o}}{X_{jk}^{t_o}} - \frac{X_{ij}^{t_o}}{X_j^{t_o}}\right)$ is the difference between MENA country's initial market share in import markets and the MENA country's initial market share in the partner country's total imports.

$\left(\frac{X_{jk}^{t_n}}{X_w^{t_n}} - \frac{X_{jk}^{t_o}}{X_w^{t_o}}\right)$ is the shift in product specialization.

The fifth column, marked as Column (d) is labeled as the adaptation effect. This calculation reflects the MENA country's ability to respond to shifts in world demand. The percentage change in Column (d) is calculated as:

$$\sum_j \left(\frac{X_{ijk}^{t_n}}{X_{jk}^{t_n}} - \frac{X_{ijk}^{t_o}}{X_{jk}^{t_o}}\right)\left(\frac{X_{jk}^{t_n}}{X_w^{t_n}} - \frac{X_{jk}^{t_o}}{X_w^{t_o}}\right) \tag{8.29}$$

where:

$\left(\frac{X_{ijk}^{t_n}}{X_{jk}^{t_n}} - \frac{X_{ijk}^{t_o}}{X_{jk}^{t_o}}\right)$ is the variation in MENA country's market share in import markets.

$\left(\frac{X_{jk}^{t_n}}{X_w^{t_n}} - \frac{X_{jk}^{t_o}}{X_w^{t_o}}\right)$ is the variation in the share of import market in world imports.

The CMS decomposition suggest that during the 2012–2016 period, a major factor accounting for increases in MENA country exports was the competitiveness effect. For Algeria this was true for electronic components, transport equipment, chemicals, wood products and processed food exports. For Bahrain the competitiveness effect was a major explanatory factor in leather products, IT and consumer electronics, clothing and miscellaneous manufacturing exports. For Cyprus the only sector where competitiveness effect was a major explanatory factor was in the exports of minerals. For Egypt, the only competitiveness effect was in the exports of IT and consumer electronics. For Iran the negative competitiveness effect was the consistent explanation of the decline in Iran's exports to the world. These results for Iran may also be affected by the general worldwide set of sanctions imposed against Iran. For Israel, the competitiveness effect was a major explanatory factor in both positive and negative exports over this period. For Jordan the competitiveness effect was a major explanatory factor in the exports of IT and consumer electronics and transport equipment. Kuwait's and Lebanon's exports were all positively affected by the competitiveness effect. For Oman, the competitiveness effect along with the initial product specialization and adaptation effect were major factors explaining the decline in the exports of leather products. For Qatar the competitiveness effect was a major explanatory factor in the exports chemicals. For Saudi Arabia, the competitiveness effect was a major explanatory factor in both positive and negative exports over this period.

One should observe, however, that a wide range of economic aspects affect the competitiveness of MENA country exports in the world market. A change in competitiveness reflects changes in non-tariff barriers, shifts in competing sources and tastes and changes in technology of both exporting and consuming industries. The most noteworthy factor however, is the change in relative prices. The fact that many MENA countries continue to have non-convertible currencies, may explain the latitude that MENA country exporters have to "price to market" with much higher degrees of freedom then for market economy exporters like Israel with convertible currencies.

8.5. Regional Trade Agreements and MENA

Historically, the post-WWII period has seen a dramatic reduction in tariff barriers across the world. With the evolution of the GATT to the new

World Trade Organization (WTO) in 1994, a new "rules-based" system was created in order to tackle the various non-tariff barriers and to assure that the key pillar of the multilateral trading system was to rely on non-discrimination among trading partners (Pelzman and Shoham, 2007, 2009). Given the very disappointing results of the Doha Round, a growing number of countries have shifted their interest toward regional and bilateral trade agreements (RTAs) that reduce barriers to trade on a reciprocal and preferential basis for those in the group (Pelzman and Shoham, 2011). Table 8.12 lists a number of the better known of these RTAs. According to the WTO, close to 50 percent of total global trade is between the RTA members. While the tariff levels have been reduced across the board, the proliferation of RTAs has created a new set of product exclusions and restrictive rules of origin, eliminating much of the gains of trade-expanding effects of RTAs (Pelzman and Shoham, 2010). The end result of this RTA proliferation is an increasingly complex global trading system where different countries' access to a given market is often governed by very different sets of country-of-origin rules.

The research on RTAs has concluded that regional preferential trading arrangements followed rather than preceded regional integration. In cases where there is no regional trade expansion, the proliferations of RTAs have not created any positive spillover effects. The two regions which are characteristic of this conclusion are the Arab MENA and Sub-Saharan Africa (Frankel *et al.*, 1996; Robinson and Thierfelder, 2002; and Schiff and Winters, 2003).

The potential costs and benefits to Arab MENA of integration with Europe have been widely discussed (Galal and Hoekman, 1997; Page and Underwood, 1997). Existing studies of regional integration in Arab MENA have emphasized the importance of labor and capital as opposed to product flows (Shafik, 1992, 1995; Fischer, 1993), Arab MENA's low levels of trade in general (World Bank, 1995) and the potential for greater integration on the basis of well-established trade links, commonality of language and cultural affinity (El-Erian and Fischer, 1996).

Rutherford *et al.* (1993) point out that an Arab MENA integration agreement has the potential to increase member country growth rates depending on the major structural and cultural attitudes toward trade. First, to the extent that an Arab MENA free trade area offers the potential for trade creation, it can provide a mechanism for "learning by exporting." Second, integration within Arab MENA must embrace the harmonization of

Table 8.12. Leading Regional Trading Agreements

Agreement	Full Name	Members
AFTA	ASEAN Free Trade Area	Brunei Darussalam, Cambodia, Indonesia, Lao People's Democratic Republic, Malaysia, Myanmar, Philippines, Singapore, Thailand, Vietnam
APEC	Asia Pacific Economic Cooperation	Australia, Brunei, Canada, Chile, China, Hong Kong (China), Indonesia, Japan, Korea, Malaysia, Mexico, New Zealand, Papua New Guinea, Peru, Philippines, Russia, Singapore, Taiwan (China), Thailand, United States, Vietnam
CACM	Central American Common Market	Costa Rica, El Salvador, Guatemala, Honduras, Nicaragua
CAFTA	Central America Free Trade Area	United States, Costa Rica, El Salvador, Guatemala, Honduras, Nicaragua, Dominican Republic
CAN	Andean Community	Bolivia, Colombia, Ecuador, Peru, República Bolivariana de Venezuela
CARICOM	Caribbean Community and Common Market	Antigua and Barbuda, Bahamas, Barbados, Belize, Dominica, Grenada, Guyana, Haiti, Jamaica, Monserrat, Trinidad and Tobago, St. Kitts and Nevis, St. Lucia, St. Vincent and the Grenadines, Suriname
CEFTA	Central European Free Trade Agreement	Bulgaria, Czech Republic, Hungary, Poland, Romania, Slovak Republic, Slovenia
CEMAC	Economic and Monetary Community of Central Africa	Cameroon, Central African Republic, Chad, Republic of Congo, Equatorial Guinea, Gabon
CER (ANZCERTA)	Closer Economic Relations Trade Agreement	Australia, New Zealand
CIS	Commonwealth of Independent States	Azerbaijan, Armenia, Belarus, Georgia, Moldova, Kazakhstan, Russian Federation, Ukraine, Uzbekistan, Tajikistan, Kyrgyz Republic
COMESA	Common Market for Eastern and Southern Africa	Angola, Burundi, Comoros, Democratic Republic of Congo, Djibouti, Arab Republic of Egypt, Eritrea, Ethiopia, Kenya, Madagascar, Malawi, Mauritius, Namibia, Rwanda, Seychelles, Sudan, Swaziland, Uganda, Zambia, Zimbabwe
EAC	East African Community	Kenya, Tanzania, Uganda

(*Continued*)

Table 8.12. (*Continued*)

Agreement	Full Name	Members
ECOWAS	Economic Community of West African States	Benin, Burkina Faso, Cape Verde, Gambia, Ghana, Guinea, Guinea-Bissau, Côte d'Ivoire, Liberia, Mali, Niger, Nigeria, Senegal, Sierra Leone, Togo
EEA	European EU Economic Area	Iceland, Liechtenstein, Norway
EFTA	European Free Trade Association	Iceland, Liechtenstein, Norway, Switzerland
EMFTA	Euro-Mediterranean Free Trade Area	EU, Algeria, Cyprus, Egypt, Israel, Jordan, Lebanon, Malta, Morocco, Syrian Arab Republic, Tunisia, Turkey, Palestinian Authority
FTAA	Free Trade Area of the Americas	Antigua and Barbuda, Argentina, Bahamas, Barbados, Belize, Bolivia, Brazil, Canada, Chile, Colombia, Costa Rica, Dominica, Dominican Republic, Ecuador, El Salvador, Grenada, Guatemala, Guyana, Haiti, Honduras, Jamaica, Mexico, Nicaragua, Panama, Paraguay, Peru, St. Kitts and Nevis, St. Lucia, St. Vincent and the Grenadines, Suriname, Trinidad and Tobago, United States, Uruguay, Venezuela
GAFTA	Greater Arab Free Trade Area	Bahrain, Egypt, Iraq, Jordan, Kuwait, Lebanon, Libya, Morocco, Oman, Palestine, Qatar, Saudi Arabia, Somalia, Sudan, Syria, Tunisia, United Arab Emirates, Yemen
GCC	Gulf Cooperation Council	Bahrain, Kuwait, Oman, Qatar, Saudi Arabia, United Arab Emirates
MERCOSUR	Southern Common Market	Argentina, Brazil, Paraguay, Uruguay
NAFTA	North American Free Trade Agreement	Canada, Mexico, United States
SACU	Southern African Customs Union	South Africa, Botswana, Lesotho, Swaziland, Namibia
SADC	Southern African Development Community	Angola, Botswana, Democratic Republic of Congo, Lesotho, Malawi, Mauritius, Mozambique, Namibia, South Africa, Swaziland, Seychelles, Tanzania, Zambia, Zimbabwe
SAFTA	South Asian Free Trade Area	Bangladesh, Bhutan, India, Maldives, Nepal, Pakistan, Sri Lanka
SAPTA	South Asian Preferential Trade Arrangement	Bangladesh, Bhutan, India, Maldives, Nepal, Pakistan, Sri Lanka
WAEMU	West African Economic and Monetary Union	Benin, Burkina Faso, Côte d'Ivoire, Guinea Bissau, Mali, Niger, Senegal, Togo

Source: WTO.

standards, improvements in trade facilitation, reductions in barriers to the movement of technical and professional manpower, and the development of trade-related infrastructure.

The proliferation of RTAs as a policy alternative within Arab MENA in the 21st century suggests that a number of countries in the region are looking for a new source of global comparative advantage. However, an RTA-based solution will work only if Arab MENA commits to gradual liberalization of their economies. Given the history of failed attempts at Arab MENA integration, the probability that these economies will embrace globalization is not very high. Thus far, Arab MENA's RTAs do not go far enough in terms of liberalization, the harmonization of product standards, information exchange and factor mobility.

Chapter 9

Conclusions and Prospects for MENA

The main conclusion of the 2nd edition of this volume is that without accepting the principle of free trade in goods, services and factors of production, the Arab MENA countries will become more vulnerable to their own excess supply of labor and the resulting political instability. The empirical observations presented in this volume make it patently obvious that Arab MENA countries are already crowded out in manufacturing in both labor-intensive and skill-intensive products because of intense competition from countries with greater comparative advantages in these areas in the non-Arab MENA, South East Asia and China. When you add the displacement that will come from robotics, the picture for the Arab youth in MENA becomes ever more dismal. The only way to reverse these outcomes is by increasing investment in human capital and by introducing knowledge economy-friendly policies. Improvements in human capital formation and broader improvements in governance and gender equality will be essential to enable shifts to more knowledge-based activities.

Without these policy shifts, closer trade and investment links with Europe and other trading partners will not alter Arab MENA's aversion to major structural reforms. The notion that membership in RTAs and the WTO will help to induce domestic constituencies to support major reforms and to strengthen the credibility and commitment to reform generally, is very unrealistic. The devastating effect of xenophobia, religious intolerance, aversion to globalization, and endless conflicts with the only democracy in MENA — Israel — has been astronomical. The only realistic alternative is to discard the old business model of hate and xenophobia and create a new business model of mutual welfare improving co-operation. It has been argued that to depart from the old business model will take many centuries.

The technology gap between Arab MENA and Israel and the rest of the world will never be closed unless Arab MENA departs from their old business model. While many would like to think that the Arab MENA countries are no different from the rest of the world in terms of the impact of poor economic policies on local performance, the incentives to the ruling autocracies to improve the quality of their citizens' welfare do not exist. Why would this ruling elite support a private market response, as compared to a time-honored tradition to depend on the public sector as the solution? To be effective, Arab MENA reforms must widen the domain of liberalization so that more sectors and groups perceive the benefits of liberalization.

Thus far, a number of small resource-rich countries in the Gulf region are the only test cases of trade and structural reforms. They have an active GCC customs union; are liberalizing private entry in power, water, real estate and other previously protected sectors; and are reforming banking and financial regulations. These countries have sector-specific strategies for such niche areas as tourism, information technology, and the media. Despite these changes, the wealthy countries within the GCC have not fully implemented privatization and financial sector regulation, and reforms in the labor markets. Building pyramids in the desert will not postpone the major overhaul of the economic infrastructure that will be needed to compete in the 21st century.

Data Appendix

Agriculture, value added (% of GDP) Agriculture corresponds to ISIC divisions 1–5 and includes forestry, hunting and fishing, as well as cultivation of crops and livestock production. Value added is the net output of a sector after adding up all outputs and subtracting intermediate inputs. It is calculated without making deductions for depreciation of fabricated assets or depletion and degradation of natural resources. The origin of value added is determined by the International Standard Industrial Classification (ISIC), revision 3.

Industry, value added (% of GDP) Industry corresponds to ISIC divisions 10–45 and includes manufacturing (ISIC divisions 15–37). It comprises value added in mining, manufacturing (also reported as a separate subgroup), construction, electricity, water, and gas. Value added is the net output of a sector after adding up all outputs and subtracting intermediate inputs. It is calculated without making deductions for depreciation of fabricated assets or depletion and degradation of natural resources. The origin of value added is determined by the International Standard Industrial Classification (ISIC), revision 3.

Manufacturing, value added (% of GDP) Manufacturing refers to industries belonging to ISIC divisions 15–37. Value added is the net output of a sector after adding up all outputs and subtracting intermediate inputs. It is calculated without making deductions for depreciation of fabricated assets or depletion and degradation of natural resources. The industrial origin of value added is determined by the International Standard Industrial Classification (ISIC), revision 2.

Services, etc., value added (% of GDP) Services correspond to ISIC divisions 50–99 and they include value added in wholesale and retail trade (including hotels and restaurants), transport, and government, financial, professional, and personal services such as education, health care, and real estate services. Also included are imputed bank service charges, import duties, and any statistical discrepancies noted by national compilers as well as discrepancies arising from rescaling. Value added is the net output of a sector after adding up all outputs and subtracting intermediate inputs. It is calculated without making deductions for depreciation of fabricated assets or depletion and degradation of natural resources. The industrial origin of value added is determined by the International Standard Industrial Classification (ISIC), revision 3.

External balance on goods and services (% of GDP) External balance on goods and services (formerly resource balance) equals exports of goods and services minus imports of goods and services (previously non-factor services).

Current account balance (% of GDP) Current account balance is the sum of net exports of goods and services, income, and current transfers.

Current revenue, excluding grants (% of GDP) Current revenue includes all revenue from taxes and non-repayable receipts (other than grants) from the sale of land, intangible assets, government stocks, or fixed capital assets, or from capital transfers from non-governmental sources. It also includes fines, fees, recoveries, inheritance taxes, and non-recurrent levies on capital. Data are shown for central government only.

Exports of goods and services (% of GDP) Exports of goods and services represent the value of all goods and other market services provided to the rest of the world. They include the value of merchandise, freight, insurance, transport, travel, royalties, license fees, and other services such as communication, construction, financial, information, business, personal, and government services. They exclude compensation of employees and investment income (formerly called factor services) and transfer payments.

Imports of goods and services (% of GDP) Imports of goods and services represent the value of all goods and other market services received from the rest of the world. They include the value of merchandise, freight, insurance, transport, travel, royalties, license fees, and other services such as communication, construction, financial, information, business, personal, and government services. They exclude compensation of employees and investment income (formerly called factor services) and transfer payments.

Merchandise trade (% of GDP) Merchandise trade as a share of GDP is the sum of merchandise exports and imports divided by the value of GDP, all in current US dollars.

Trade (% of GDP) Trade is the sum of exports and imports of goods and services measured as a share of gross domestic product.

Trade in services (% of GDP) Trade in services is the sum of service exports and imports divided by the value of GDP, all in current US dollars.

Computer, communications and other services (% of commercial service imports) include such activities as international telecommunications, and postal and courier services; computer data; news-related service transactions between residents and non-residents; construction services; royalties and license fees; miscellaneous business, professional, and technical services; and personal, cultural, and recreational services.

Computer, communications and other services (% of commercial service exports) include such activities as international telecommunications, and postal and courier services; computer data; news-related service transactions between residents and non-residents; construction services; royalties and license fees; miscellaneous business, professional, and technical services; and personal, cultural, and recreational services.

Communications, computer, etc. (% of service exports) Communications, computer, information, and other services cover international telecommunications and postal and courier services; computer data; news-related service transactions between residents and non-residents; construction services; royalties and license fees; miscellaneous business, professional, and technical services; personal, cultural, and recreational services; and government services not included elsewhere. Service exports refer to economic output of intangible commodities that may be produced, transferred, and consumed at the same time. International transactions in services are defined by the IMF's Balance of Payments Manual (1993), but definitions may nevertheless vary among reporting economies.

Communications, computer, etc. (% of service imports) Communications, computer, information, and other services cover international telecommunications and postal and courier services; computer data; news-related service transactions between residents and non-residents; construction services; royalties and license fees; miscellaneous business, professional, and technical services; personal, cultural, and recreational services; and government services not included elsewhere. Service imports refer to economic output of intangible commodities that may be produced, transferred, and consumed at the same time. International transactions in services are defined by the International Monetary Fund's (IMF) Balance of Payments Manual (1993), but definitions may nevertheless vary among reporting economies.

Food exports (% of merchandise exports) Food comprises the commodities in SITC sections 0 (food and live animals), 1 (beverages and tobacco), and 4 (animal and vegetable oils and fats) and SITC division 22 (oil seeds, oil nuts, and oil kernels).

Food imports (% of merchandise imports) Food comprises the commodities in SITC sections 0 (food and live animals), 1 (beverages and tobacco), and 4 (animal and vegetable oils and fats) and SITC division 22 (oil seeds, oil nuts, and oil kernels).

Fuel exports (% of merchandise exports) Fuels comprise SITC section 3 (mineral fuels).

Fuel imports (% of merchandise imports) Fuels comprise the commodities in SITC section 3 (mineral fuels).

High-technology exports (% of manufactured exports) High-technology exports are products with high R&D intensity, such as in aerospace, computers, pharmaceuticals, scientific instruments, and electrical machinery.

Insurance and financial services (% of commercial service exports) Insurance and financial services cover freight insurance on goods exported and other direct insurance such as life insurance; financial intermediation services such as commissions, foreign exchange transactions, and brokerage services; and auxiliary services such as financial market operational and regulatory services.

Insurance and financial services (% of commercial service imports) Insurance and financial services cover freight insurance on goods imported and other direct insurance such as life insurance; financial intermediation services such as commissions, foreign exchange transactions, and brokerage services; and auxiliary services such as financial market operational and regulatory services.

Insurance and financial services (% of service exports, BoP) cover various types of insurance provided to non-residents by resident insurance enterprises and vice versa, and financial intermediary and auxiliary services (except those of insurance enterprises and pension funds) exchanged between residents and non-residents. Service exports refer to economic output of intangible commodities that may be produced, transferred, and consumed at the same time. International transactions in services are defined by the IMF's Balance of Payments Manual (1993), but definitions may nevertheless vary among reporting economies.

Insurance and financial services (% of service imports, BoP) cover various types of insurance provided to non-residents by resident insurance enterprises and vice versa, and financial intermediary and auxiliary services (except those of insurance enterprises and pension funds) exchanged between residents and non-residents. Service imports refer to economic output of intangible commodities that may be produced, transferred, and consumed at the same time. International transactions in services are defined by the International Monetary Fund's (IMF) Balance of Payments Manual (1993), but definitions may nevertheless vary among reporting economies.

International tourism, expenditures (% of total imports) International tourism expenditures are expenditures of international outbound visitors in other countries, including payments to foreign carriers for international transport. These expenditures may include those by residents traveling abroad as same-day visitors, except in cases where these are important enough to justify separate classification. Some countries do not include expenditures for passenger transport items. Their share in imports is calculated as a ratio to imports of goods and services, which comprise all transactions between residents of a country and the rest of the world involving a change of ownership from non-residents to residents of general merchandise, goods sent for processing and repairs, non-monetary gold, and services.

International tourism, receipts (% of total exports) International tourism receipts are expenditures by international inbound visitors, including payments to national carriers for international transport. These receipts include any other prepayment made for goods or services received in the destination country. They also may include receipts from same-day visitors, except when these are important enough to justify separate classification. Some countries do not include receipts for passenger transport items. Their share in exports is calculated as a ratio to exports of goods and services, which comprise all transactions between residents of a country and the rest of the world involving a change of ownership from residents to non-residents of general merchandise, goods sent for processing and repairs, non-monetary gold, and services.

Manufactures exports (% of merchandise exports) Manufactures comprise commodities in SITC sections 5 (chemicals), 6 (basic manufactures), 7 (machinery and transport equipment), and 8 (miscellaneous manufactured goods), excluding division 68 (non-ferrous metals).

Manufactures imports (% of merchandise imports) Manufactures comprise the commodities in SITC sections 5 (chemicals), 6 (basic manufactures), 7 (machinery and transport equipment), and 8 (miscellaneous manufactured goods), excluding division 68 (non-ferrous metals).

Travel services (% of commercial service exports) cover goods and services acquired from an economy by travelers in that economy for their own use during visits of less than one year for business or personal purposes. Travel services include the goods and services consumed by travelers, such as lodging and meals and transport (within the economy visited).

Travel services (% of commercial service imports) cover goods and services acquired from an economy by travelers in that economy for their own use during visits of less than one year for business or personal purposes. Travel services include the goods and services consumed by travelers, such as lodging, meals, and transport (within the economy visited).

Quasi-liquid liabilities (% of GDP) Quasi-liquid liabilities are the sum of currency and deposits in the central bank (M0), plus time and savings deposits, foreign currency transferable deposits, certificates of deposit, and securities repurchase agreements, plus traveler's checks, foreign currency time deposits, commercial paper, and shares of mutual funds or market funds held by residents. They equal the M3 money supply less transferable deposits and electronic currency (M1).

Final consumption expenditure, etc. (% of GDP) Final consumption expenditure (formerly total consumption) is the sum of household final consumption expenditure (private consumption) and general government final consumption expenditure (general government consumption). This estimate includes any statistical discrepancy in the use of resources relative to the supply of resources.

General government final consumption expenditure (% of GDP) General government final consumption expenditure (formerly general government consumption) includes all government current expenditures for purchases of goods and services (including compensation of employees). It also includes most expenditures on national defense and security, but excludes government military expenditures that are part of government capital formation.

Household final consumption expenditure, etc. (% of GDP) Household final consumption expenditure (formerly private consumption) is the market value of all goods and services, including durable products (such as cars, washing machines and home computers), purchased by households. It excludes purchases of dwellings but includes imputed rent for owner-occupied dwellings. It also includes payments and fees to governments to obtain permits and licenses. Here, household consumption expenditure includes the expenditures of non-profit institutions serving households, even when reported separately by the country. This item also includes any statistical discrepancy in the use of resources relative to the supply of resources.

Financing via international capital markets (gross inflows, % of GDP) Financing via international capital markets is the sum of gross bond issuance, bank lending and new equity placement. Bond issuance is the notional amount of bond issuance by government, public and private sector borrowers in international capital markets. Bank lending is the committed amount of funds raised by government, public and private sector borrowers via international syndicated lending. Equity placement is the notional amount of cross-border equity placement.

Foreign direct investment, net inflows (% of GDP) Foreign direct investment is the net inflow of investment to acquire a lasting management interest (10 percent or more of voting stock) in an enterprise operating in an economy other than that of the investor. It is the sum of equity capital, reinvestment of earnings, other long-term capital, and short-term capital as shown in the balance of payments. This series shows net inflows (new investment inflows less disinvestment) in the reporting economy from foreign investors, and is divided by GDP.

Foreign direct investment, net outflows (% of GDP) Foreign direct investment is the net inflow of investment to acquire a lasting management interest (10 percent or more of voting stock) in an enterprise operating in an economy other than that of the investor. It is the sum of equity capital, reinvestment of earnings, other long-term capital, and short-term capital as shown in the balance of payments. This series shows net outflows of investment from the reporting economy to the rest of the world, and is divided by GDP.

Gross capital formation (% of GDP) Gross capital formation (formerly gross domestic investment) consists of outlays on additions to the fixed assets of the economy plus net changes in the level of inventories. Fixed assets include land improvements (fences, ditches, drains, and so on); plant, machinery, and equipment purchases; and the construction of roads, railways, and the like, including schools, offices, hospitals, private residential dwellings, and commercial and industrial buildings. Inventories are stocks of goods held by firms to meet temporary or unexpected fluctuations in production or sales, and "work in progress." According to the 1993 SNA, net acquisitions of valuables are also considered capital formation.

Gross domestic savings (% of GDP) Gross domestic savings are calculated as GDP less final consumption expenditure (total consumption).

Gross fixed capital formation (% of GDP) Gross fixed capital formation (formerly gross domestic fixed investment) includes land improvements (fences, ditches, drains, and so on); plant, machinery, and equipment purchases; and the construction of roads, railways, and the like, including schools, offices, hospitals, private residential dwellings, and commercial and industrial buildings. According to the 1993 SNA, net acquisitions of valuables are also considered capital formation.

Gross national expenditure (% of GDP) Gross national expenditure (formerly domestic absorption) is the sum of household final consumption expenditure (formerly private consumption), general government final consumption expenditure (formerly general government consumption), and gross capital formation (formerly gross domestic investment).

Gross savings (% of GDP) Gross savings are calculated as gross national income less total consumption, plus net transfers.

Military expenditure (% of GDP) Military expenditures data from SIPRI are derived from the NATO definition, which includes all current and capital expenditures on the armed forces, including peacekeeping forces; defense ministries and other government agencies engaged in defense projects; paramilitary forces, if these are judged to be trained and equipped for military operations; and military space activities. Such expenditures include military and civil personnel, including retirement pensions of military personnel and social services for personnel; operation and maintenance;

procurement; military research and development; and military aid (in the military expenditures of the donor country). Excluded are civil defense and current expenditures for previous military activities, such as for veterans' benefits, demobilization, conversion, and destruction of weapons. This definition cannot be applied for all countries, however, since that would require much more detailed information than is available about what is included in military budgets and off-budget military expenditure items. (For example, military budgets might or might not cover civil defense, reserves and auxiliary forces, police and paramilitary forces, dual-purpose forces such as military and civilian police, military grants in kind, pensions for military personnel, and social security contributions paid by one part of government to another.)

Military expenditure (% of central government expenditure) Military expenditures data from SIPRI are derived from the NATO definition, which includes all current and capital expenditures on the armed forces, including peacekeeping forces; defense ministries and other government agencies engaged in defense projects; paramilitary forces, if these are judged to be trained and equipped for military operations; and military space activities. Such expenditures include military and civil personnel, including retirement pensions of military personnel and social services for personnel; operation and maintenance; procurement; military research and development; and military aid (in the military expenditures of the donor country). Excluded are civil defense and current expenditures for previous military activities, such as for veterans' benefits, demobilization, conversion, and destruction of weapons. This definition cannot be applied for all countries, however, since that would require much more detailed information than is available about what is included in military budgets and off-budget military expenditure items. (For example, military budgets might or might not cover civil defense, reserves and auxiliary forces, police and paramilitary forces, dual-purpose forces such as military and civilian police, military grants in kind, pensions for military personnel, and social security contributions paid by one part of government to another.)

Cash surplus/deficit (% of GDP) Cash surplus or deficit is revenue (including grants) minus expense, minus net acquisition of non-financial assets. In the 1986 GFS manual, non-financial assets were included under revenue and expenditure in gross terms. This cash surplus or deficit is closest to the earlier overall budget balance (still missing is lending minus repayments, which are now a financing item under net acquisition of financial assets).

Central government debt, total (% of GDP) Debt is the entire stock of direct government fixed-term contractual obligations to others outstanding on a particular date. It includes domestic and foreign liabilities such as currency and money deposits, securities other than shares, and loans. It is the gross amount of government liabilities reduced by the amount of equity and financial derivatives held by the government. Because debt is a stock rather than a flow, it is measured as of a given date, usually the last day of the fiscal year.

Domestic credit provided by banking sector (% of GDP) Domestic credit provided by the banking sector includes all credit to various sectors on a gross basis, with the exception of credit to the central government, which is net. The banking sector includes monetary authorities and deposit money banks, as well as other banking institutions where data are available (including institutions that do not accept transferable deposits but do incur such liabilities as time and savings deposits). Examples of other banking institutions are savings and mortgage loan institutions and building and loan associations.

Domestic credit to private sector (% of GDP) Domestic credit to private sector refers to financial resources provided to the private sector, such as through loans, purchases of non-equity securities, and trade credits and other accounts receivable, that establish a claim for repayment. For some countries, these claims include credit to public enterprises.

Expense (% of GDP) Expense is cash payments for operating activities of the government in providing goods and services. It includes compensation of employees (such as wages and salaries), interest and subsidies, grants, social benefits, and other expenses such as rent and dividends.

Taxes on income, profits and capital gains (% of total taxes) Taxes on income, profits and capital gains are levied on the actual or presumptive net income of individuals, on the profits of corporations and enterprises, and on capital gains, whether realized or not, on land, securities, and other assets. Intra-governmental payments are eliminated in consolidation.

Revenue, excluding grants (% of GDP) Revenue is cash receipts from taxes, social contributions, and other revenues such as fines, fees, rent, and income from property or sales. Grants are also considered as revenue but are excluded here.

Tax revenue (% of GDP) Tax revenue refers to compulsory transfers to the central government for public purposes. Certain compulsory transfers such as fines, penalties, and most social security contributions are excluded. Refunds and corrections of erroneously collected tax revenue are treated as negative revenue.

Taxes on goods and services (% of revenue) Taxes on goods and services include general sales and turnover or value added taxes, selective excises on goods, selective taxes on services, taxes on the use of goods or property, taxes on extraction and production of minerals, and profits of fiscal monopolies.

Taxes on income, profits and capital gains (% of revenue) Taxes on income, profits and capital gains are levied on the actual or presumptive net income of individuals, on the profits of corporations and enterprises, and on capital gains, whether realized or not, on land, securities, and other assets. Intra-governmental payments are eliminated in consolidation.

Taxes on international trade (% of revenue) Taxes on international trade include import duties, export duties, profits of export or import monopolies, exchange profits, and exchange taxes.

Grants and other revenue (% of revenue) Grants and other revenue include grants from other foreign governments, international organizations, and other government units; interest; dividends; rent; requited, non-repayable receipts for public purposes (such as fines, administrative fees, and entrepreneurial income from government ownership of property); and voluntary, unrequited, non-repayable receipts other than grants.

Internet users (per 100 people) Internet users are people with access to the worldwide network.

Researchers in R&D (per million people) Researchers in R&D are professionals engaged in the conception or creation of new knowledge, products, processes, methods or systems, and in the management of the projects concerned. Postgraduate PhD students (ISCED97 level 6) engaged in R&D are included.

Technicians in R&D (per million people) Technicians in R&D and equivalent staff are people whose main tasks require technical knowledge and experience in engineering, physical and life sciences (technicians), or social sciences and humanities (equivalent staff). They participate in R&D by performing scientific and technical tasks involving the application of concepts and operational methods, normally under the supervision of researchers.

Research and development expenditure (% of GDP) Expenditures for research and development are current and capital expenditures (both public and private) on creative work undertaken systematically to increase knowledge, including knowledge of humanity, culture, and society, and the use of knowledge for new applications. R&D covers basic research, applied research, and experimental development.

Scientific and technical journal articles Scientific and technical journal articles refer to the number of scientific and engineering articles published in the following fields: physics, biology, chemistry, mathematics, clinical medicine, biomedical research, engineering and technology, and earth and space sciences.

Information and communication technology expenditure (% of GDP) Information and communications technology expenditures include computer hardware (computers, storage devices, printers, and other peripherals); computer software (operating systems, programming tools, utilities, applications, and internal software development); computer services (information technology consulting, computer and network systems integration, Web hosting, data processing services, and other services); and communications services (voice and data communications services) and wired and wireless communications equipment.

Market capitalization of listed companies (% of GDP) Market capitalization (also known as market value) is the share price times the number of shares outstanding. Listed domestic companies are the domestically incorporated companies listed on the country's stock exchanges at the end of the year. Listed companies do not include investment companies, mutual funds, or other collective investment vehicles.

Literacy rate, adult female (% of females ages 15 and above) Adult literacy rate is the percentage of people ages 15 and above who can, with understanding, read and write a short, simple statement on their everyday life.

Literacy rate, adult male (% of males ages 15 and above) Adult literacy rate is the percentage of people ages 15 and above who can, with understanding, read and write a short, simple statement on their everyday life.

Literacy rate, adult total (% of people ages 15 and above) Adult literacy rate is the percentage of people ages 15 and above who can, with understanding, read and write a short, simple statement on their everyday life.

Literacy rate, youth female (% of females ages 15–24) Youth literacy rate is the percentage of people ages 15–24 who can, with understanding, read and write a short, simple statement on their everyday life.

Literacy rate, youth male (% of males ages 15–24) Youth literacy rate is the percentage of people ages 15–24 who can, with understanding, read and write a short, simple statement on their everyday life.

Literacy rate, youth total (% of people ages 15–24) Youth literacy rate is the percentage of people ages 15–24 who can, with understanding, read and write a short, simple statement on their everyday life.

Expenditure per student, primary (% of GDP per capita) Public expenditure per student is the public current spending on education divided by the total number of students by level, as a percentage of GDP per capita. Public expenditure (current and capital) includes government spending on educational institutions (both public and private), education administration as well as subsidies for private entities (students/households and other private entities).

Expenditure per student, secondary (% of GDP per capita) Public expenditure per student is the public current spending on education divided by the total number of students by level, as a percentage of GDP per capita. Public expenditure (current and capital) includes government spending on educational institutions (both public and private), education administration as well as subsidies for private entities (students/households and other private entities).

Expenditure per student, tertiary (% of GDP per capita) Public expenditure per student is the public current spending on education divided by the total number of students by level, as a percentage of GDP per capita. Public expenditure (current and capital) includes government spending on educational institutions (both public and private), education administration as well as subsidies for private entities (students/households and other private entities).

Public spending on education, total (% of GDP) Public expenditure (current and capital) on education includes government spending on educational institutions (both public and private), education administration as well as subsidies for private entities (students/households and other private entities).

Health expenditure, private (% of GDP) Private health expenditure includes direct household (out-of-pocket) spending, private insurance, charitable donations, and direct service payments by private corporations.

Health expenditure, public (% of GDP) Public health expenditure consists of recurrent and capital spending from government (central and local) budgets, external borrowings and grants (including donations from international agencies and non-governmental organizations), and social (or compulsory) health insurance funds.

Health expenditure, total (% of GDP) Total health expenditure is the sum of public and private health expenditure. It covers the provision of health services (preventive and curative), family planning activities, nutrition activities, and emergency aid designated for health, but does not include provision of water and sanitation.

Health expenditure, public (% of government expenditure) Public health expenditure consists of recurrent and capital spending from government (central and local) budgets, external borrowings and grants (including donations from international agencies and non-governmental organizations), and social (or compulsory) health insurance funds.

Health expenditure, public (% of total health expenditure) Public health expenditure consists of recurrent and capital spending from government (central and local) budgets, external borrowings and grants (including donations from international agencies and non-governmental organizations), and social (or compulsory) health insurance funds. Total health expenditure is the sum of public and private health expenditure. It covers the provision of health services (preventive and curative), family planning activities, nutrition activities, and emergency aid designated for health, but does not include provision of water and sanitation.

Life expectancy at birth, female (years) Life expectancy at birth indicates the number of years a newborn infant would live if prevailing patterns of mortality at the time of its birth were to stay the same throughout its life.

Life expectancy at birth, male (years) Life expectancy at birth indicates the number of years a newborn infant would live if prevailing patterns of mortality at the time of its birth were to stay the same throughout its life.

Life expectancy at birth, total (years) Life expectancy at birth indicates the number of years a newborn infant would live if prevailing patterns of mortality at the time of its birth were to stay the same throughout its life.

Labor force, total (thousands) Total labor force comprises people ages 15 and older who meet the International Labor Organization definition of the economically active population: all people who supply labor for the production of goods and services during a specified period. It includes both the employed and the unemployed. While national practices vary in the treatment of such groups as the armed forces and seasonal or part-time workers, in general the labor force includes the armed forces, the unemployed, and first-time job-seekers, but excludes homemakers and other unpaid caregivers and workers in the informal sector.

Labor participation rate, female (% of female population ages 15+) Labor force participation rate is the proportion of the population ages 15 and older that is economically active: all people who supply labor for the production of goods and services during a specified period.

Labor participation rate, male (% of male population ages 15+) Labor force participation rate is the proportion of the population ages 15 and older that is economically active: all people who supply labor for the production of goods and services during a specified period.

Labor participation rate, total (% of total population ages 15+) Labor force participation rate is the proportion of the population ages 15 and older that is economically active: all people who supply labor for the production of goods and services during a specified period.

Population ages 0–14 (% of total) Population between the ages 0 to 14 as a percentage of the total population. Population is based on the de facto definition of population.

Population ages 15–64 (% of total) Population between the ages 15 to 64 as a percentage of the total population. Population is based on the de facto definition of population.

Population ages 65 and above (% of total) Population ages 65 and above as a percentage of the total population. Population is based on the de facto definition of population.

Population, female (% of total) Female population as a percentage of the total population. Population is based on the de facto definition of population.

Urban population (% of total) Urban population refers to people living in urban areas as defined by national statistical offices. It is calculated using World Bank population estimates and urban ratios from the United Nations World Urbanization Prospects.

Merchandise exports to developing economies in East Asia & Pacific (% of total merchandise exports) Merchandise exports to developing economies in East Asia and Pacific are the sum of merchandise exports from the reporting economy to developing economies in the East Asia and Pacific region according to World Bank classification of economies as of July 1, 2009. Data are expressed as a percentage of total merchandise exports by the economy. Data are computed only if at least half of the economies in the partner country group had non-missing data.

Merchandise exports to developing economies in Europe & Central Asia (% of total merchandise exports) Merchandise exports to developing economies in Europe and Central Asia are the sum of merchandise exports from the reporting economy to developing economies in the Europe and Central Asia region according to World Bank classification of economies as of July 1, 2009. Data are as a percentage of total merchandise exports by the economy. Data are computed only if at least half of the economies in the partner country group had non-missing data.

Merchandise exports to developing economies in Latin America & the Caribbean (% of total merchandise exports) Merchandise exports to developing economies in Latin America and the Caribbean are the sum of merchandise exports from the reporting economy to developing economies in the Latin America and the Caribbean region according to World Bank classification of economies as of July 1, 2009. Data are as a percentage of total merchandise exports by the economy. Data are computed only if at least half of the economies in the partner country group had non-missing data.

Merchandise exports to developing economies in Middle East & North Africa (% of total merchandise exports) Merchandise exports to developing economies in Middle East and North Africa are the sum of merchandise exports from the reporting economy to developing economies in the Middle East and North Africa region according to World Bank classification of economies as of July 1, 2009. Data are as a percentage of total merchandise exports by the economy. Data are computed only if at least half of the economies in the partner country group had non-missing data.

Merchandise exports to developing economies in South Asia (% of total merchandise exports) Merchandise exports to developing economies in South Asia are the sum of merchandise exports from the reporting economy to developing economies in the South Asia region according to World Bank classification of economies as of July 1, 2009. Data are as a percentage of total merchandise exports by the economy. Data are computed only if at least half of the economies in the partner country group had non-missing data.

Merchandise exports to developing economies in Sub-Saharan Africa (% of total merchandise exports) Merchandise exports to developing economies in Sub-Saharan Africa are the sum of merchandise exports from the reporting economy to developing economies in the Sub-Saharan Africa region according to World Bank classification of economies as of July 1, 2009. Data are as a percentage of total merchandise exports by the economy. Data are computed only if at least half of the economies in the partner country group had non-missing data.

Merchandise exports to developing economies outside region (% of total merchandise exports) Merchandise exports to developing economies outside region are the sum of merchandise exports from the reporting economy to other developing economies in other World Bank regions according to the World Bank classification of economies as of July 1, 2009. Data are expressed as a percentage of total merchandise exports by the economy. Data are computed only if at least half of the economies in the partner country group had non-missing data.

Merchandise exports to developing economies within region (% of total merchandise exports) Merchandise exports to developing economies within region are the sum of merchandise exports from the reporting economy to other developing economies in the same World Bank region, expressed as a percentage of total merchandise exports by the economy. Data are computed only if at least half of the economies in the partner country group had non-missing data. No figures are shown for high-income economies, because they are a separate category in the World Bank classification of economies.

Merchandise exports to high-income economies (% of total merchandise exports) Merchandise exports to high-income economies are the sum of merchandise exports from the reporting economy to high-income economies according to the World Bank classification of economies as of July 1, 2009. Data are expressed as a percentage of total merchandise exports by the economy. Data are computed only if at least half of the economies in the partner country group had non-missing data.

Merchandise imports from developing economies in East Asia & Pacific (% of total merchandise imports) Merchandise imports from developing economies in East Asia and Pacific are the sum of merchandise imports by the reporting economy from developing economies in the East Asia and Pacific region according to the World Bank classification of economies as of July 1, 2009. Data are expressed as a percentage of total merchandise imports by the economy. Data are computed only if at least half of the economies in the partner country group had non-missing data.

Merchandise imports from developing economies in Europe & Central Asia (% of total merchandise imports) Merchandise imports from developing economies in Europe and Central Asia are the sum of merchandise imports by the reporting economy from developing economies in the Europe and Central Asia region according to the World Bank classification of economies as of July 1, 2009. Data are expressed as a percentage of total merchandise imports by the economy. Data are computed only if at least half of the economies in the partner country group had non-missing data.

Merchandise imports from developing economies in Latin America & the Caribbean (% of total merchandise imports) Merchandise imports from developing economies in Latin America and the Caribbean are the sum of merchandise imports by the reporting economy from developing economies in the Latin America and the Caribbean region according to the World Bank classification of economies as of July 1, 2009. Data are expressed as a percentage of total merchandise imports by the economy. Data are computed only if at least half of the economies in the partner country group had non-missing data.

Merchandise imports from developing economies in Middle East & North Africa (% of total merchandise imports) Merchandise imports from developing economies in Middle East and North Africa are the sum of merchandise imports by the reporting economy from developing economies in the Middle East and North Africa region according to the World Bank classification of economies as of July 1, 2009. Data are expressed as a percentage of total merchandise imports by the economy. Data are computed only if at least half of the economies in the partner country group had non-missing data.

Merchandise imports from developing economies in South Asia (% of total merchandise imports) Merchandise imports from developing economies in South Asia are the sum of merchandise imports by the reporting economy from developing economies in the South Asia region according to the World Bank classification of economies as of July 1, 2009. Data are expressed as a percentage of total merchandise imports by the economy. Data are computed only if at least half of the economies in the partner country group had non-missing data.

Merchandise imports from developing economies in Sub-Saharan Africa (% of total merchandise imports) Merchandise imports from developing economies in Sub-Saharan Africa are the sum of merchandise imports by the reporting economy from developing economies in the Sub-Saharan Africa region according to the World Bank classification of economies as of July 1, 2009. Data are expressed as a percentage of total merchandise imports by the economy. Data are computed only if at least half of the economies in the partner country group had non-missing data.

Merchandise imports from developing economies outside region (% of total merchandise imports) Merchandise imports from developing economies outside region are the sum of merchandise imports by the reporting economy from other developing economies in other World Bank regions according to the World Bank classification of economies as of July 1, 2009. Data are as a percentage of total merchandise imports by the economy. Data are computed only if at least half of the economies in the partner country group had non-missing data.

Merchandise imports from developing economies within region (% of total merchandise imports) Merchandise imports from developing economies within region are the sum of merchandise imports by the reporting economy from other developing economies in the same World

Bank region according to the World Bank classification of economies as of July 1, 2009. Data are expressed as a percentage of total merchandise imports by the economy. Data are computed only if at least half of the economies in the partner country group had non-missing data. No figures are shown for high-income economies, because they are a separate category in the World Bank classification of economies.

Merchandise imports from high-income economies (% of total merchandise imports) Merchandise imports from high-income economies are the sum of merchandise imports by the reporting economy from high-income economies according to the World Bank classification of economies as of July 1, 2009. Data are expressed as a percentage of total merchandise imports by the economy. Data are computed only if at least half of the economies in the partner country group had non-missing data.

Definition of Sectors for CMS Analysis

1 Fresh food and raw agro-based products			
001	LIVE ANIMALS	075	SPICES
011	BOVINE MEAT	121	TOBACCO, UNMANUFACTURED
012	OTHER MEAT, MEAT OFFAL	211	HIDES, SKINS (EX. FURS), RAW
034	FISH, FRESH, CHILLED, FROZEN	212	FURSKINS, RAW
036	CRUSTACEANS, MOLLUSCS, ETC.	222	OILSEED (SFT. FIX VEG. OIL)
041	WHEAT, MESLIN, UNMILLED	223	OILSEED (OTH. FIX VEG. OIL)
0421	RICE	231	NATURAL RUBBER, ETC.
043	BARLEY, UNMILLED	261	SILK
044	MAIZE, UNMILLED	263	COTTON
045	OTHER CEREALS, UNMILLED	264	JUTE, OTH. TXTL. BAST FIBR
054	VEGETABLES	265	VEGETABLE TEXTILE: FIBRES
057	FRUIT, NUTS, EXCL. OILNUTS	268	WOOL, OTHER ANIMAL HAIR
071	COFFEE, COFFEE SUBSTITUTE	291	CRUDE ANIMAL MATERLS, NES
072	COCOA	292	CRUDE VEG. MATERIALS, NES
074	TEA AND MATE		
2 Processed food and agro-based products			
016	MEAT, ED. OFFL, DRY, SLT, SMK	059	FRUIT, VEGETABLE JUICES
017	MEAT, OFFL, PRSVD, NES	061	SUGARS, MOLASSES, HONEY
022	MILK AND CREAM	062	SUGAR CONFECTIONERY
023	BUTTER, OTHER FAT OF MILK	073	CHOCOLATE, OTH. COCOA PREP

(*Continued*)

(*Continued*)

024	CHEESE AND CURD	081	ANIMAL FEED STUFF
025	EGGS, BIRDS, YOLKS, ALBUMIN	091	MARGARINE AND SHORTENING
035	FISH, DRIED, SALTED, SMOKED	098	EDIBLE PROD. PREPRTNS, NES
037	FISH, ETC., PREPD, PRSVD, NES	111	NON-ALCOHOL BEVERAGES, NES
0422	RICE	112	ALCOHOLIC BEVERAGES, NES
0423	RICE	122	TOBACCO, MANUFACTURED
046	MEAL, FLOUR OF WHEAT, MSLN	411	ANIMAL OILS AND FATS
047	OTHER CEREAL MEAL., FLOURS	421	FIXED VEG. FAT, OILS, SOFI'
048	CEREAL PREPARATIONS	422	FIXED VEG. FAT, OILS, OTHER
056	VEGETABLES, PRPD, PRSVD, NES	431	ANIMAL VEG. FATS, OILS, NES
058	FRUIT, PRESERVED, PREPARED	551	ESSNTL. OIL. PERFUME, FLAVR
3 Wood, wood products and paper			
244	CORK, NATURAL, RAW, WASTE	633	CORK MANUFACTURES
245	FUEL WOOD, WOOD CHARCOAL	634	VENEERS PLYWOOD, ETC.
246	WOOD IN CHIPS, PARTICLES	635	WOOD MANUFACTURES, NES
247	WOOD ROUGH, ROUGH SQUARED	641	PAPER AND PAPERBOARD
248	WOOD, SIMPLY WORKED	642	PAPER, PAPERBOARD, CUT, ETC.
251	PULP AND WASTE PAPER	8215	WOODEN FURNITURE
4 Yarn, fabrics and textiles			
651	TEXTILE YARN	656	TULLE, LACE, EMBROIDERY, ETC.
652	COTTON FABRICS, WOVEN	657	SPECIAL. YARN, TXTL. FABRIC
653	FABRICS, MAN-MADE FIBRES	658	TEXTILE ARTICLES, NES
654	OTH. TEXTILE FABRIC, WOVEN	659	FLOOR COVERINGS, ETC.
655	KNIT, CROCHET FABRIC, NES		
5 Chemicals			
232	SYNTHETIC RUBBER, ETC.	554	SOAP, CLEANERS, POLISH, ETC.
266	SYNTHETIC FIBRES	562	FERTILIZER, EXCEPT GRP272
267	OTHER MAN-MADE FIBRES	571	POLYMERS OF ETHYLENE
511	HYDROCARBONS, NES, DERIVTS	572	POLYMERS OF STYRENE

(*Continued*)

(Continued)

512	ALCOHOL, PHENOL, ETC., DERIV	573	POLYMERS, VINYL, CHLORIDE
513	CARBOXYLIC ACIDS, DERIVTS	574	POLYACETAL, POLYCARBONATE
514	NITROGEN-FUNCT. COMPOUNDS	575	OTH. PLASTIC, PRIMARY FORM
515	ORGANO-INORGANIC COMPOUNDS	579	PLASTIC WASTE, SCRAP, ETC.
516	OTHER ORGANIC CHEMICALS	581	PLASTIC TUBE PIPE HOSE
522	INORGANIC CHEM. ELEMENTS	582	PLASTIC PLATE, SHEETS, ETC.
523	METAL SALTS INORGAN. ACID	583	MONOFILAMENT OF PLASTICS
524	OTHER CHEMICAL COMPOUNDS	591	INSECTICIDES, ETC.
525	RADIOACTIVE MATERIALS	592	STARCHES, INULIN, ETC.
531	SYNTH. COLOURS, LAKES, ETC.	593	EXPLOSIVES, PYROTECHNICS
532	DYEING, TANNING, MATERIALS	597	PREPRD ADDITIVES, LIQUIDS
533	PIGMENTS, PAINTS, ETC.	598	MISC. CHEMICAL PRODTS., NES
541	MEDICINES, ETC., EXC. GRP542	621	MATERIALS OF RUBBER
542	MEDICAMENTS	625	RUBBER TYRES, TUBES, ETC.
553	PERFUMERY, COSMETICS, ETC.	629	ARTICLES OF RUBBER, NES
6 Leather and leather products			
611	LEATHERS	831	TRUNK, SUITCASES, BAG, ETC.
612	MANUFACT. LEATHER, ETC., NES	851	FOOTWEAR
613	FURSKINS, TANNED, DRESSED		
7 Metal and other basic manufacturing			
661	LIME, CEMENT, CONSTR. MATRL	681	SILVER, PLATINUM, ETC.
662	CLAY, REFRCT. CONSTR. MATRL	682	COPPER
663	MINERAL MANUFACTURES, NES	683	NICKEL
664	GLASS	684	ALUMINIUM
665	GLASSWARE	685	LEAD
666	POTTERY	686	ZINC
670	REST OF 67 NOT DEFINED	687	TIN
671	PIG IRON, SPIEGELEISN, ETC.	689	MISC. NON-FERR. BASE METAL

(Continued)

(*Continued*)

672	INGOTS, ETC., IRON OR STEEL	691	METALLIC STRUCTURES, NES
673	FLAT-ROLLED IRON, ETC.	692	CONTAINERS, STORAGE, TRNSP
674	FLAT-ROLLED PLATED IRON	693	WIRE PRODUCTS EXCL. ELECT.
675	FLAT-ROLLED ALLOY STEEL	694	NAILS, SCREWS, NUTS, ETC.
676	IRON, STL. BAR, SHAPES, ETC.	695	TOOLS
677	RAILWAY TRACK IRON STEEL	696	CUTLERY
678	WIRE OF IRON OR STEEL	697	HOUSEHOLD EQUIPMENT, NES
679	TUBES, PIPES, ETC., IRON OR STL	699	MANUFACTS. BASE METAL, NES
8 Non-electric machinery			
711	STEAM GENER. BOILERS, ETC.	731	METAL REMOVAL WORK TOOLS
712	STEAM TURBINES	733	MACH-TOOLS METAL WORKING
713	INTRNL COMBUS. PSTN ENGINE	735	PARTS, NES, FOR MACH TOOLS
714	ENGINES, MOTORS, NON-ELECT.	737	METAL-WORKING MACHINERY, NES
716	ROTATING ELECTRIC PLANT	741	HEATING COOLNG EQUIP, PARTS
718	OTH. POWER-GENRTNG MACHNRY	742	PUMPS FOR LIQUIDS, PARTS
721	AGRIC. MACHINES, EX. TRACTR	743	PUMPS, NES, CENTRIFUGS, ETC.
722	TRACTORS	744	MECHANICAL HANDLNG EQUIP
723	CIVIL ENGINEERING EQUIPT	745	OTH. NON-ELEC. MCH, TOOL, NES
724	TEXTILE, LEATHER MACHINES	746	BALL OR ROLLER BEARINGS
725	PAPER, PULP MILL MACHINES	747	TAPS, COCKS, VALVES, ETC.
726	PRINTNG, BOOKBING MCHS	748	TRANSMISSIONS SHAFTS, ETC.
727	FOOD-PROCESS MCH. NON. DOM	749	NON-ELECT. MACH, PARTS, ETC.
728	OTH. MACH, PTS, SPCL INDUST		
9 Computers, telecommunications and electronics			
751	OFFICE MACHINES		
752	AUTOMATIC DATA PROC. EQUIP.	762	RADIO-BROADCAST RECEIVER

(*Continued*)

(Continued)

759	PARTS FOR OFFICE MACHINS	763	SOUND RECORDER, PHONOGRPH
761	TELEVISION RECEIVERS, ETC.	764	TELECOMM. EQUIP, PARTS, NES
10 Electronic components			
771	ELECT. POWER MACHNY, PARTS		
772	ELEC. SWITCH, RELAY, CIRCUIT	775	DOM. ELEC., NON-ELEC. EQUIPT
773	ELECTR. DISTRIBT. EQPT, NES	776	TRANSISTORS, VALVES, ETC.
774	ELECTRO-MEDCL, XRAY EQUIP	778	ELECTRIC MACH APPART., NES
11 Transport equipment			
781	PASS. MOTOR VEHCLS., EX. BUS		
782	GOODS, SPCL TRANSPORT VEH	786	TRAILERS, SEMI-TRAILR, ETC.
783	ROAD MOTOR VEHICLES, NES	791	RAILWAY VEHICLES EQUIPNT
784	PARTS, TRACTORS, MOTOR VEH	792	AIRCRAFT, ASSOCTD. EQUIPNT
785	CYCLES, MOTORCYCLES, ETC.	793	SHIP, BOAT, FLOAT, STRUCTRS
12 Clothing			
841	MENS, BOYS CLOTHNG, X-KNIT		
842	WOMEN, GIRLS CLOTHNG, X-KNIT	845	OTHR TEXTILE APPAREL, NES
843	MENS, BOYS CLOTHING, KNIT	846	CLOTHING ACCESSRS, FABRIC
844	WOMEN, GIRLS CLOTHING, KNIT	848	CLOTHNG, NON-TXTL, HEADGEAR
13 Misc. manufacturing			
811	PREFABRICATED BUILDINGS	885	WATCHES AND CLOCKS
812	PLUMBNG, SANITRY, EQPT, ETC.	891	ARMS AND AMMUNITION
813	LIGHTNG FIXTURES, ETC., NES	892	PRINTED MATTER
871	OPTICAL INSTRUMENTS, NES	893	ARTICLES, NES, OF PLASTICS
872	MEDICAL INSTRUMENTS, NES	894	BABY CARRIAGE, TOYS, GAMES
873	METERS, COUNTERS, NES	895	OFFICE, STATIONERY SUPPLY
874	MEASURE, CONTROL INSTRMNT	896	WORKS OF ART, ANTIQUE, ETC.

(Continued)

(*Continued*)

881	PHOTOGRAPH APPAR., ETC., NES	897	GOLD, SILVERWARE, JEWL, NES
882	PHOTO CINEMATOGRPH. SUPPL	898	MUSICAL INSTRUMENTS, ETC.
883	CINE. FILM. EXPOSD, DEVELOPD	899	MISC. MANUFCTRD GOODS, NES
884	OPTICAL GOODS, NES		
14 Minerals to be excluded			
272	FERTILIZERS, CRUDE	289	PREC. METAL ORES, CONCTRTS
273	STONE, SAND AND GRAVEL	321	COAL, NOT AGGLOMERATED
274	SULPHUR, UNRSTD. IRON PYRS	322	BRIQUETTES, LIGNITE, PEAT
277	NATURAL ABRASIVES, NES	325	COKE, SEMI-COKE, RET. CARBN
278	OTHER CRUDE MINERALS	333	PETROLEUM OILS, CRUDE
281	IRON ORE, CONCENTRATES	334	PETROLEUM PRODUCTS
282	FERROUS WASTE AND SCRAP	335	RESIDUAL PETROL PRODUCTS
283	COPPER ORES, CONCENTRATES	342	LIQUEFIED PROPANE, BUTANE
284	NICKEL ORES, CONCTR, MATTE	343	NATURAL GAS
285	ALUMINIUM ORE, CONCTR, ETC.	344	PETROLEUM GASES, NES
286	URANIUM, THORIUM ORES, ETC.	345	CAL, GAS, WATER, GAS, ETC.
287	ORE, CONCENTR, BASE, METALS	351	ELECTRIC: CURRENT'
288	NON-FERROUS WASTE, SCRAP	667	PEARLS, PRECIOUS STONES

References

Abed, G.T. and H.R. Davoodi (2003). *Challenges of Growth and Globalization in the Middle East and North Africa.* IMF, USA.

Agénor, P.-R., M.K. Nabli, T. Yousef and H.T. Jensen (2007). "Labor Market Reforms, Growth, and Unemployment in Labor-exporting Countries in the Middle East and North Africa." *Journal of Policy Modeling* 29, pp. 277–309.

Aggarwal, R.K. and T. Yousef (2000). "Islamic Banks and Investment Financing." *Journal of Money, Credit and Banking* 32:1, pp. 93–120.

Aghion, P. and P. Howitt (1998). *Endogenous Growth Theory.* Cambridge, MA: MIT Press.

Aghion, P. *et al.* (2012). "Industrial Policy and Competition." Harvard University, Working Paper.

Ahmad, Z. (1995). *Islamic Banking: State of the Art.* Islamic Development Bank.

Ambinder, L.P., N. de Silva and J. Dewar (2001). "The Mirage Becomes Reality: Privatization and Project Finance Developments in The Middle East Power Market." *Fordham International Law Journal* 24, pp. 1029–1051.

Amnesty International Secretariat (2008). *Challenging Repression: Human Rights Defenders in the Middle East and North Africa.*

Archibugi, D. and J. Michie (1995). "The Globalization of Technology — A New Taxonomy." *Cambridge Journal of Economics* 19:1, pp. 121–140.

Archibugi, D. and J. Michie (1997)."Technological Globalization or National Systems of Innovation?" *Futures* 29:2, pp. 121–137.

Archibugi, D. and M. Pianta (1996). "Innovation Surveys and Patents as Technology Indicators: The State of the Art." In *Innovation Patents, and Technological Strategies.* OECD, Paris, pp. 17–56.

Archibugi, D., J. Howells, *et al.* (1999). "Innovation Systems in a Global Economy." *Technology Analysis and Strategic Management* 11:4, pp. 527–539.

Atkinson, G. and K. Hamilton (2003). "Savings, Growth and the Resource Curse Hypothesis." *World Development* 31, pp. 1793–1807.

Auty, R. M. (1993). *Sustaining Development in Mineral Economies: The Resource Curse Thesis.* London and New York: Rutledge.

Auty, R.M. (2000). "How Natural Resources Affect Economic Development." *Development Policy Review* 18:4, pp. 347–364.

Auty, R.M. (ed.), (2001a). *Resource Abundance and Economic Development.* Oxford: Oxford University Press.

Auty, R.M. (2001b). "The Political Economy of Resource-Driven Growth." *European Economic Review* 45:4–6, pp. 839–846.

Auty, R.M. (2006). "Patterns of Rent-Extraction and Deployment in Developing Countries: Implications for Governance, Economic Policy, and Performance." WIDER research paper 2006/16. Helsinki: United Nations University, World Institute for Development Economics Research.

Azam, J.P. (2001). "The Redistributive State and Conflicts in Africa." *Journal of Peace Research* 38:4, pp. 429–444.

Badr, G.M. (1978). "Islamic Law: Its Relation to Other Legal Systems." *The American Journal of Comparative Law* 26:2, pp. 187–198.

Balassa, B. (1965). "Trade Liberalization and Revealed Comparative Advantage." The Manchester School of Economic and Social Studies, 33, pp. 92–123.

Baldwin, R. (2009). "The Great Trade Collapse: What Caused it and What Does it Mean?" In R. Baldwin (ed.), *The Great Trade Collapse: Causes, Consequences and Prospects.* Available at: www.vox.eu.org.

Baldwin, R. and A. Venables (2010). "Spiders and Snakes: Offshoring and Agglomeration in the Global Economy." NBER Working Paper Series, No. 16611, Cambridge, MA.

Baldwin, R. (2011). "Trade and Industrialization after Globalization's 2nd Unbundling: How Building and Joining a Supply Chain are Different and Why It Matters," NBER Working Paper Series, No. 17716, Cambridge, MA.

Barro, R. and J.-W. Lee (2013). "A New Data Set of Educational Attainment in the World, 1950–2010." *Journal of Development Economics*, 104, pp. 184–198.

Beck, T., D-K. Asli and M. Ouarda (2013). "Islamic vs. conventional banking: Business model, efficiency and stability." *Journal of Banking & Finance* 37, pp. 433–447.

Benhabib, J. and M.M. Spiegel (1994). "The Role of Human Capital in Economic Development: Evidence from Aggregate Cross-Country Data." *Journal of Monetary Economics* 34, pp. 143–173.

Bergsten, C.F. (2004). "The G-20 and the World Economy." Speech to the Deputies of the G-20, Leipzig, Germany, March 4.

Bernheim, B.D. and M. Whinston (1986)."Menu Actions, Resource Allocation and Economic Influence." *Quarterly Journal of Economics* 101, pp. 1–31.

Berthelemy, J.C., C.A. Pissarides and A. Varoudakis (1999). "Human Capital and Growth: The Cost of Rent-Seeking Activities." In T. De Ruyter van Steveninck (ed.), *Economic Growth and Its Determinants* Dordrecht: Kluwer Academic Publishers.

Birdsall, N. and A. de la Torre (2001). *Washington Contentious: Economic Policies for Social Equality in Latin America.* Carnegie Endowment for International Peace and Inter-American Dialogue, USA.

Bond, E. (2001). "Trade Structure and Development: The Role of Logistics Costs in Latin American Countries." Department of Economics, Penn State University. University Park, Penn. Processed.

Bonner, M. (2005). "Poverty and Economics in the Koran." *Journal of Interdisciplinary History* 35, pp. 391–406.

Bosworth, B.P. and S.M. Collins (2003). "The Empirics of Growth: An Update." *Brookings Papers on Economic Activity* 2, pp. 113–206.

Bowen, H. (1983). "On the Theoretical Interpretation of Indices of Trade Intensity and Revealed Comparative Advantage." *Weltwirtschaftliches Archiv*, 119, pp. 464–472.

Bowen, H. and J. Pelzman, (1984). "US Export Competitiveness: 1962–1977." *Applied Economics* 16, pp. 461–473.

Bulte, E. and R. Damania (2008). "Resources for Sale: Corruption, Democracy and the Natural Resource Curse." *BE. Journal of Economic Analysis and Policy* 8:1, Article 5.

Chen, H.C. Derek and C.J. Dahlman (2006). "The Knowledge Economy, the KAM Methodology, and World Bank Operations." *World Bank Institute*. Washington DC.

Chong, Beng Soon and Ming-Hua Liu (2009). "Islamic Banking: Interest-free or Interest-based?" *Pacific-Basin Finance Journal* 17, pp. 125–144.

Coe, N.M. and M. Hess (2007). "Global Production Networks: Debates and Challenges." Paper prepared for the GPERG Workshop, University of Manchester, England.

Comin, D. and B. Hobijn (2004). "Cross-Country Technology Adoption: Making the Theory Face the Facts." *Journal of Monetary Economics* 51:1, pp. 39–83.

Commission on Growth and Development (2008). *The Growth Report: Strategies for Sustained Growth and Inclusive Development.* Washington, DC: World Bank.

Corden, W.M. (1984). "Booming Sector and Dutch Disease Economics: Survey and Consolidation." *Oxford Economic Papers* 36:3, pp. 359–380.

Corden, W.M. and J.P. Neary (1982). "Booming Sector and De-Industrialization in a Small Open Economy." *The Economic Journal* 92, pp. 825–848.

Coulson, N. (1964). *A History of Islamic Law.* Edinburgh.

Credit Suisse (2016). Global Wealth Data Book, 2016. Zurich: Credit Suisse Research Institute.

Dasgupta, P. and M. Weale (1992), "On Measuring the Quality of Life." *World Development* 20:1, pp. 119–131.

Davis, G. (1995). "Learning to Love the Dutch Disease: Evidence from the Mineral Economies." *World Development* 23:10, pp. 1765–1779.

de Soto, H. (2000). *The Mystery of Capital: Why Capitalism Triumphs in the West and Fails Everywhere Else.* New York: Basic Books.

Djankov, S., R. La Porta, F. Lopez-de-Silanes and A. Shleifer (2003). "Courts." *Quarterly Journal of Economics* 118:2, pp. 453–517.

Djankov, S., R. La Porta, F. Lopez-de-Silanes and A. Shleifer (2008). "The Law and Economics of Self-Dealing." *Journal of Financial Economics* 88:3, pp. 430–465.

Djankov, S., T. Ganser, C. McLiesh, R. Ramalho and A. Shleifer (forthcoming). "The Effect of Corporate Taxes on Investment and Entrepreneurship." *American Economic Journal: Macroeconomics.*

Dollar, D. (1992). "Outward-Oriented Developing Economies Really Do Grow More Rapidly: Evidence from 95 LDCs, 1976–1985." *Economic Development and Cultural Change* 40:3, pp. 523–544.

Easterly, W. (2001). *The Elusive Quest for Growth.* USA: MIT University Press.

Easterly, W. (2005). "National Policies and Economic Growth: A Reappraisal." In Philippe Aghion and Steven N. Durlauf (eds.), *Handbook of Economic Growth*, Volume 1A. Elsevier B.V., Chapter 15.

Ebrahim, M.S. and S. Rahman (2005). "On the Pareto-optimality of Futures Contracts over Islamic Forward Contracts: Implications for the Emerging Muslim Economies." *Journal of Economic Behavior & Organization* 56, pp. 273–295.

Edwards, S. (1992). "Trade Orientation, Distortions, and Growth in Developing Countries." *Journal of Development Economics* 39:1, pp. 31–57.

Edwards, S. (1993). "Openness, Trade Liberalization, and Growth in Developing Countries." *Journal of Economic Literature* 31:3, pp. 1358–1393.

Edwards, S. (1998). "Openness, Productivity and Growth: What Do We Really Know?" *Economic Journal* 108, pp. 383–398.

El-Erian, M. and S. Fischer (1996). "Is MENA a Region?" IMF Working Paper 96/30, International Monetary Fund, Washington, D.C.

El-Gamal, M.A. (2000). *A Basic Guide to Contemporary Islamic Banking and Finance.* ISNA Islamic banking & finance series.

El-Gamal, M.A. (2003). " 'Interest' and the Paradox of Contemporary Islamic Law and Finance." *Fordham International Law Journal* 27, pp. 108–149.

Esfahani, H.S. and L. Squire (2007). "Explaining Trade Policy in the Middle East and North Africa." *The Quarterly Review of Economics and Finance* 46, pp. 660–684.

Falkingham, J. (2004). "Poverty, Out-of-Pocket Payments and Access to Health Care: Evidence from Tajikistan." *Social Science & Medicine* 58:2, pp. 247–258.

Feenstra, R.C. and L.K. Hiau (2008). "Export Variety and Country Productivity: Estimating the Monopolistic Competition Model with Endogenous Productivity." *Journal of International Economics* 74, pp. 500–514.

Feenstra, R.C. (2010). "Measuring the Gains from Trade under Monopolistic Competition." *The Canadian Journal of Economics* 43:1, pp. 1–28.

Findlay, R. and R.W. Jones (2001). "Input Trade and the Location of Production." *American Economic Review* 91, pp. 29–33.

Fischer, S. (1993). "Prospects for Regional Integration in the Middle East." In J. De Melo and A. Panagariya (eds.), *New Dimensions in Regional Integration* Cambridge: CEPR, Cambridge University Press.

Fischer, S. (2000). Lunch address given at the conference on "Promoting Dialogue: Global Challenges and Global Institutions." Washington, American University.

François, J. (1997). "External Bindings and the Credibility of Reform." In A. Galal and B. Hoekman (eds.), *Regional Partners in Global Markets: Limits and Possibilities of the Euro-Med Agreements* CEPR, London and ECES, Cairo.

Frankel, J.A. and D. Romer (1999). "Does Trade Cause Growth?" *American Economic Review* 89:3, pp. 379–399.

Frankel, J.A., E. Stein and S.-J. Wei (1996). "Regional Trading Arrangements: Natural or Supernatural?" *American Economic Review* 86:2, pp. 52–56.

Galal, A. and B. Hoekman (1997). *Regional Partners in Global Markets: Limits and Possibilities of the Euro-Med Agreements.* CEPR, London and ECES, Cairo.

Gelb, A., J.B. Knight and R.H. Sabot (1991). "Public Sector Employment, Rent Seeking and Economic Growth." *Economic Journal* 101, pp. 1186–1199.

Gittleman, M. and E.N. Wolff (2001). "R&D Activity and Economic Development." *International Journal of Public Administration* 24:10, pp. 1061–1081.

Gollin, D. (2002). "Getting Income Shares Right." *Journal of Political Economy* 110:2, pp. 458–474.

Grossman, G.M. and E. Helpman (1991). *Innovation and Growth in the Global Economy.* Cambridge, MA: MIT Press.

Grossman, G.M. and E. Helpman (1994). "Protection for Sale." *American Economic Review* 84:4, pp. 833–850.

Grossman, G. and E. Rossi-Hansberg (2008). "Trading Tasks: A Simple Theory of Offshoring." *American Economic Review* 98:5, pp. 1978–1997.

Gylfason, T. (2001). "Natural Resources, Education, and Economic Development." *European Economic Review* 45:4–6, pp. 847–859.

Gylfason, T., T.T. Herbertsson and G. Zoega (1999). "A Mixed Blessing: Natural Resources and Economic Growth." *Macroeconomic Dynamics* 3:2, pp. 204–225.

Hagedoorn, John and Geert Duysters (2002). "External Sources of Innovative Capabilities: The Preference for Strategic Alliances or Mergers and Acquisitions," *Journal of Management Studies* 39:2 (March) pp. 167–188.

Hakura, D.S. (2001). "Why Does HOV Fail? The Role of Technological Differences within the EC." *Journal of International Economics* 54, pp. 361–382.

Hall, R. and C.I. Jones (1999). "Why Do Some Countries Produce So Much More Output per Worker than Others?" *Quarterly Journal of Economics* 114:1, pp. 83–116.

Hanushek, E.A. and L. Woessmann (2010). "The Economics of International Differences in Educational Achievement." Paper presented at Handbook of the Economics of Education conference at CESifo in Munich.

Hanushek, E.A., P.E. Peterson and L. Woessmann (2013). "Human Capital and Economic Prosperity." In Hanushek, Eric A., Paul E. Peterson and Ludger Woessmann (eds.), *Endangering Prosperity.* Washington: Brookings Institution Press.

Harrison, A. and A. Rodríguez-Clare (2010). Trade, "Foreign Investment, and Industrial Policy for Developing Countries." *Handbook of Development Economics* 5, 4039–4214.

Hasan, Z. (2016). "Nature and Significance of Islamic Economics." *Journal of Economic and Social Thought* 3:3, 400–416.

Hausmann, R. and D. Rodrik (2003). "Economic Development as Self-discovery." *Journal of Development Economics* 72: 603–633.

Hoekman, B. and P. Messerlin (2002). *Harnessing Trade for Development and Growth in the Middle East* The Council on Foreign Relations.

Homer, S. and R. Sylla (1996). *A History of Interest Rates*, 3rd edn. New Brunswick, NJ: Rutgers University Press.

Houston, J., Chen Lin, Ping Lin and Yue Ma (2010). "Creditor Rights, Information Sharing, and Bank Risk Taking." *Journal of Financial Economics*, forthcoming.

Hsieh, Chang-Tai and Peter J. Klenow (2009), "Misallocation and Manufacturing TFP in China and India." *Quarterly Journal of Economics* 124(4): 1403–1448.

Hudson, R. (2004). "Conceptualizing Economies and their Geographies: Spaces, Flows and Circuits." *Progress in Human Geography* 28, pp. 447–471.

Hulten, C.R. and A. Isaksson (2007). "Why Development Levels Differ: The Sources of Differential Economic Growth in a Panel of High and Low Income Countries." *NBER Working Paper No. 13469.* (October) Washington.

Humphreys, M., J.D. Sachs and J.E. Stiglitz (eds.), (2007). *Escaping the Resource Curse.* Columbia University Press.

Huntington, S. (1991). *The Third Wave: Democratization in the Late Twentieth Century.* Norman, Oklahoma: University of Oklahoma Press.

ILO (2012). International Standard Classification of Occupations, Volume 1. Geneva.

ILO (2015a). *Global Employment Trends for Youth 2015: Scaling up investments in decent jobs for youth.* Geneva.

ILO (2015b). *Synthesis Review of ILO Experience in Youth and Women's Employment in the MENA Region: Summary Version:* Geneva

IMF (1997). *World Economic Outlook*, Washington.

IMF (2017). *Government Finance Statistics* (GFS), Washington DC.

Isaksson, Anders (2007). "Determinants of Total Factor Productivity: A Literature Review." UNIDO. July.

Islamic Financial Services Board (2013). "Islamic Financial Services Industry Stability Report," IFSB Bank Negara Malaysia: Kuala Lumpur.

Iqbal, M. (2005). *Islamic Perspectives on Sustainable Development.* London: Macmillan-Palgrave.

Jamison, E.A., D.T. Jamison and E.A. Hanushek (2006). "The Effects of Education Quality on Mortality Decline and Income Growth." Paper presented at the International Conference on the Economics of Education "How Do Recent Advances in Economic Thinking Contribute to the Major Challenges Faced by Education?" Dijon, France, June 20–23.

Jensen, N. and L. Wantchekon (2004)."Resource Wealth and Political Regimes in Africa." *Comparative Political Studies* 37, pp. 816–841.

Jones, R.W. (1965). "The Structure of Simple General Equilibrium Models" *Journal of Political Economy* Vol. 73, No. 6 (Dec., 1965), pp. 557–572.

Jones, R.W. (2000). *Globalization and the Theory of Input Trade.* Cambridge, MA: MIT Press.

Kabir, M. (2008). "Determinants of Life Expectancy in Developing Countries." *The Journal of Developing Areas* 41:2, pp. 185–204.

Karl, T. (1997). *The Paradox of Plenty: Oil Booms and Petro-States.* Berkeley, CA: University of California Press.

Kaufmann, D. (2002). *Rethinking Governance* World Bank Institute, World Bank, USA.

Kaufmann, D., A. Kraay and M. Mastruzzi (2010). "The Worldwide Governance Indicators: A Summary of Methodology, Data and Analytical Issues." World Bank Policy Research Working Paper No. 5430.

Keller, J. and M.K. Nabli (2007). "The Macroeconomics of Labor Market Outcomes in MENA: How Growth Has Failed to Keep Pace with a Burgeoning Labor Market." In *Breaking the Barriers to Higher Economic Growth: Better Governance and Deeper Reforms in the Middle East and North Africa.* World Bank, USA, pp. 169–201.

Khan, F. (2010). "How 'Islamic' is Islamic banking?" *Journal of Economic Behavior and Organization* 76, pp. 805–820.

Klenow, P. and A. Rodriguez-Clare (2005). "Externalities and Growth." In P. Aghion and S. Durlauf (eds.), *Handbook of Economic Growth,* Volume 1A. Amsterdam, The Netherlands: North-Holland.

Koopman, R., W. Powers, Z. Wang and S.-J. Wei (2011). "Give Credit Where Credit is Due: Tracing Value Added in Global Production Chains." NBER Working Paper Series No. 16426, September 2010, Revised September 2011. Cambridge, MA.

Krämer, G. (2008). *A History of Palestine: From the Ottoman Conquest to the Founding of the State of Israel,* translated by Gudrun Krämer and Graham Harman. USA: Princeton University Press.

Krueger, A.O. (1998). "Why Trade Liberalization is Good for Growth." *The Economic Journal* 108, pp. 1513–1522.

Krugman, P. (1979). "Increasing Returns, Monopolistic Competition and International Trade." *Journal of International Economics* 9, pp. 469–479.

Krugman, P. (1995). "Dutch Tulips and Emerging Markets." *Foreign Affairs* 74:4, pp. 28–44.

Krugman, P. (1996). *Pop Internationalism.* Cambridge, MA: MIT Press.

Kuczynski, P.-P. and J. Williamson (eds.), (2003). *After the Washington Consensus: Restarting Growth and Reform in Latin America.* Institute for International Economics, USA.

Kuran, T. (1995). "Islamic Economics and the Islamic Subeconomy," *Journal of Economic Perspectives* 9:4, pp. 155–173.

Kuran, T. (1997). "The Genesis of Islamic Economics: A Chapter in the Politics of Muslim Identity." *Social Research* 64:2, pp. 301–338.

Kuran, T. (2004). "Why the Middle East Is Economically Underdeveloped: Historical Mechanisms of Institutional Stagnation." *The Journal of Economic Perspectives* 18:3, pp. 71–90.

Kuran, T. (2005). "The Logic of Financial Westernization in the Middle East." *Journal of Economic Behavior and Organization* 56, pp. 593–615.

Kuran, T. (2007). "Modern Islam and Economy." In M. Cook and R. Hefner (eds.), *New Cambridge History of Islam,* Vol. 6. Cambridge, MA: Cambridge University Press.

Leamer, E.E. (1984). *Sources of International Comparative Advantage: Theory and Evidence.* Cambridge, MA: MIT Press.

Leamer, E.E. (1988). "Measures of Openness." In R. Baldwin (ed.), *Trade Policy and Empirical Analysis* Chicago: University of Chicago Press.

Lederman, D. and W.F. Maloney (2003). "Trade Structure and Growth." Policy Research Working Paper No. 3025, World Bank, Washington, DC.

Lucas, R.E. (1988). "On the Mechanics of Economic Development." *Journal of Monetary Economics* 22, pp. 3–42.

Luciani, G. (1987). "Allocation versus Production States: A Theoretical Framework." In Hazem Beblawi and Giacomo Luciani (eds.), *The Rentier State* New York: Croom Helm.

Ma, A. and A. Van Assche (2010). "The Role of Trade Costs in Global Production Networks — Evidence from China's Processing Trade Regime." Policy Research Working Paper No. 5490, The World Bank, Washington, DC.

Mahdavy, H. (1970). "The Patterns and Problems of Economic Development in Rentier States: The Case of Iran." In M.A. Cook (ed.), *Studies in the Economic History of the Middle East.* London: Oxford University Press.

Mallat, C. (2003). "From Islamic to Middle Eastern Law: A Restatement of the Field (Part I)." *The American Journal of Comparative Law* 51:4, pp. 699–750.

Mallat, C. (2004). "From Islamic to Middle Eastern Law: A Restatement of the Field (Part II)." *The American Journal of Comparative Law* 52:1, pp. 209–286.

Mankiw, G., D. Romer and D. Weil (1992). "A Contribution to the Empirics of Economic Growth." *Quarterly Journal of Economics* 107:2, pp. 407–437.

McMillen, M.J.T. (2001). "Islamic Shari'ah-Compliant Project Finance: Collateral Security and Financing Structure Case Studies." *Fordham International Law Journal* 24, pp. 1184–1262.

Mehlum, H., K. Moene and R. Torvik (2006). "Institutions and the Resource Curse." *Economic Journal* 116:508, pp. 1–20.

Melitz, M.J. (2003). "The Impact of Trade on Intra-Industry Reallocations and Aggregate Industry Productivity." *Econometrica* 71, pp. 1695–1725.

Murray, C.J.L., S.C. Kulkarni, C. Michaud, N. Tomijima, M.T. Bulzacchelli, T.J. Iandiorio and M. Ezzati (2006). "Eight Americas: Investigating Mortality Disparities Across Races, Counties, and Race-Counties in the United States." *PLoS Medicine* 3:9, p. e260. Available at: http://dx.doi.org/10.1371/journal.pmed.0030260.

Naim, M. (2000). "Fads and Fashion in Economic Reforms: Washington Consensus or Washington Confusion?" *Third World Quarterly* 21:3, pp. 505–528.

Neumayer, E. (2004). "Does the 'Resource Curse' Hold for Growth in Genuine Income as Well?" *World Development* 32:10, pp. 1627–1640.

Noland, M. and H. Pack (2007). *Arab Economies in a Changing World.* Peterson Institute for International Economics, USA.

North, D. (1990). *Institutions Institutional Change and Economic Performance.* Cambridge: Cambridge University Press.

Norton Rose (2008, June). "Islamic Finance Structures" [hereinafter "Islamic Financial Structures"]. Available at: http://www.nortonrose.com/knowledge/publications/2008/pub15418.aspx?lang=en-gb&page=all.

OECD (1998). *Open Markets Matter: The Benefits of Trade and Investment Liberalization.* OECD, Paris.

OECD (2006a). "The Internationalization of R&D." In *Science Technology and Industry: Outlook 2006* OECD, Paris, pp. 121–148.

OECD (2008a). *The Internationalization of Business R&D: Evidence Impacts and Implications.* OECD, Paris.

OECD (2008b). *The Global Competition for Talent: Mobility for the Highly Educated.* OECD, Paris.

OECD (2008c). *Information Technology Outlook.* OECD, Paris.

OECD (2008d). *Intellectual Assets and Value Creation: Synthesis Report.* Available at: www.oecd.org/dataoecd/36/35/40637101.pdf.

OECD (2008e). *Science Technology and Industry: Outlook 2008.* OECD, Paris.

OECD (2011a). *Agricultural Policy Monitoring and Evaluation 2011.* OECD, Paris.

OECD (2011b). *Attractiveness for Innovation: Location Factors for International Investment.* OECD Publishing.

OECD (2011c). *OECD Science, Technology and Industry Scoreboard 2011.* OECD Publishing.

Page, J. and J. Underwood (1997). "Growth, the Maghreb and Free Trade with the European Union." In A. Galal and B. Hoekman (eds.), *Regional Partners in Global Markets: Limits and Possibilities of the Euro-Med Agreements.* CEPR, London and ECES, Cairo.

Pamuk, S. (2000). *A Monetary History of Ottoman Empire.* Cambridge University Press.

Papyrakis, E. and R. Gerlagh (2004)."The Resource Curse Hypothesis and Its Transmission Channels." *Journal of Comparative Economics* 32:1, pp. 181–193.

Patel, P. and K. Pavitt (1991)."Large Firms in the Production of the World Technology: An Important Case of 'Non-Globalization,'" *Journal of International Business Studies* 22:1, pp. 1–21.

Pavitt, K. and P. Patel (1999)."Global Corporations and National Systems of Innovation: Who Dominates Whom?" In D. Archibugi, J. Howells and J. Michie (eds.), *Innovation Policy in a Global Economy.* Cambridge: Cambridge University Press, pp. 94–119 (Chapter 6).

Pecorino, P. (1992). "Rent Seeking and Growth: The Case of Growth Through Human Capital Accumulation." *Canadian Journal of Economics* 25:4, pp. 944–956.

Pelzman, J. and A. Shoham (2007). "WTO Enforcement Issues." *The Global Economy Journal* 7:1.

Pelzman, J. and A. Shoham (2009). "WTO DSU — Enforcement Issues." In James Hartigan (ed.), Frontiers of Economics and Globalization, Vol. 6, *Trade Disputes and the Dispute Settlement Understanding of the WTO:*

An Interdisciplinary Assessment. London: Emerald Group Publishing Ltd., pp. 369–395.

Pelzman, J. and A. Shoham (2010). "Measuring the Welfare Effects of Country of Origin Rules: A Suggested Methodology." *The Global Economy Journal* 10:1.

Pelzman, J. and A. Shoham (2011). "US-Regional Agreements with Latin America — The Saga of CAFTA and the FTAA." In process.

Pelzman, J. (2016). *Spillover Effects of China Going Global.* London: World Scientific Press.

Pelzman, J. (2018). "Accounting for Digital Assets in International Trade Agreements." Paper presented at the ASSA 2018 Annual Meetings. International Trade and Finance Association session on The Impact of the Digital Economy, Philadelphia, PA, January 5, 2018.

Pianta, M. and M. Tancioni (2008). "Innovations, Profits and Wages." *Journal of Post-Keynesian Economics* 31:1, pp. 103–125.

Posner, R.A. (1980). "A Theory of Primitive Society, with Special Reference to Law." *Journal of Law and Economics* 23:1, pp. 1–53.

Pritchett, L. (2006). "Does Learning to Add Up Add Up? The Returns to Schooling in Aggregate Data." In Eric A. Hanushek and Finis Welch (eds.), *Handbook of the Economics of Education.* Amsterdam: North Holland, pp. 635–695.

Psacharopoulos, G. (1994). "Returns to Investment in Education: A Global Update" *World Development* 22:9, pp. 1325–1343.

Qureshi, A. (1990). *Islam and the Theory of Interest*, 4th edn. Lahore: Ashraf.

Richards, A. and J. Waterbury (2007). *A Political Economy of the Middle East*, 3rd edn. Perseus Press.

Richardson, J.D. (1971a). "Constant-Market-Shares Analysis of Export Growth." *Journal of International Economics* 1, pp. 227–239.

Robinson, J.A. and R. Torvik (2005). "White Elephants." *Journal of Public Economics* 89, pp. 197–210.

Robinson, J.A., R. Torvik and T. Verdier (2006). "Political Foundations of the Resource Curse." *Journal of Development Economics* 79:2, pp. 447–468.

Robinson, S. and K. Thierfelder (2002). "Trade Liberalization and Regional Integration: The Search for Large Numbers." *Australian Journal of Agricultural and Resource Economics* 46:4, pp. 585–604.

Rodriguez, F. and D. Rodrik (2001). "Trade Policy and Economic Growth: A Skeptic's Guide to the Cross-National Literature." In Ben S. Bernanke and Kenneth Rogoff (eds.), *NBER Macroeconomics Annual 2000.* pp. 261–338.

Rodrik, D. (2000)."What Drives Public Employment in Developing Countries?" *Review of Development Economics* 4, pp. 229–243.

Rodrik, D. (2005). "Growth Strategies." In Philippe Aghion and Steven N. Durlauf (eds.), *Handbook of Economic Growth*, Volume 1A. Elsevier B.V., pp. 967–1010.

Romer, P.M. (1986). "Increasing Returns and Long-Run Growth." *Journal of Political Economy* 94, pp. 500–521.

Romer, P.M. (1990). "Endogenous Technological Change." *Journal of Political Economy* 98:5, Part 2, pp. S71–S102.

Rosenzweig, M. (1988). "Labour Markets in Low-Income Countries." In Hollis Chenery and T.N. Srinivasan (eds.), *Handbook of Development Economics*, Vol. I. Amsterdam: North Holland.

Ross, M.L. (2001a). "Does Oil Hinder Democracy?" *World Politics* 53:3, pp. 325–361.

Ross, M.L. (2001b). *Timber Booms and Institutional Breakdown in Southeast Asia*. Cambridge, UK.

Ross, M.L. (2008b). "Oil, Islam and Women." *American Political Science Review* 102:1, pp. 107–123.

Roy, O. (1994). *The Failure of Political Islam*. USA: Harvard University Press.

Ruffin, R.J. (1999)."The Nature and Significance of Intra-Industry Trade." *Economic and Financial Review*, Federal Reserve Bank of Dallas Q4, pp. 2–9.

Rutherford, T., E. Ruström and D. Tarr (1993). "Morocco's Free Trade Agreement with the European Community." Policy Research Working Paper 1173, World Bank, Washington, DC.

Sabahi, B. (2004). "Islamic Financial Structures as Alternatives to International Loan Agreements: Challenges for American Financial Institutions." *BE Press Legal Series*, Paper No. 385.

Sachs, J.D. and A.M. Warner (1995a). "Economic Reform and the Process of Global Integration." *Brookings Papers on Economic Activity* 1, pp. 1–95.

Sachs, J.D. and A.M. Warner (1995b). "Natural Resource Abundance and Economic Growth." Working Paper 5398, National Bureau of Economic Research, Cambridge, MA.

Sachs, J.D. and A.M. Warner (1997a). "Natural Resource Abundance and Economic Growth — Revised." Harvard Institute for International Development Discussion Paper, Cambridge.

Sachs, J.D. and A.M. Warner (1997b). "Fundamental Sources of Long-Run Growth." *American Economic Review* 87:2, pp. 184–188.

Sachs, J.D. and A.M. Warner (1999). "The Big Push, Natural Resource Booms, and Growth." *Journal of Development Economics* 59:1, pp. 43–76.

Sachs, J.D. and A.M. Warner (2001) "The Curse of Natural Resources." *European Economic Review* 45, pp. 827–838.

Schacht, J. (1964). *An Introduction to Islamic Law*. Oxford.

Schiff, M. and L.A. Winters (2003). *Regional Integration and Development*. Washington, DC: World Bank.

Schultz, T.P. (1993). *Origins of Increasing Returns*. Oxford.

Segerstrom, P.S. (1991). "Innovation, Imitation, and Economic Growth." *Journal of Political Economy* 99:4, pp. 807–827.

Senor, D. and S. Singer (2009). *Start-Up Nation: The Story of Israel's Economic Miracle*. A Council on Foreign Relations Book, New York.

Shafik, N. (1992). "Has Labor Migration Promoted Economic Integration in the Middle East?" Mimeo, World Bank, Washington, DC.

Shafik, N. (1995). "Learning from Doers: Lessons on Regional Integration for the Middle East." In H. Kheir-El-Din (ed.), *Economic Cooperation in the Middle East: Prospects and Challenges.* Dar Al Mostaqbal Al Arabi, Cairo.

Silverberg, G., G. Dosi and L. Orsenigo (1988). "Innovation, Diversity and Diffusion: A Self-Organization Model." *The Economic Journal* 98, pp. 1032–1054.

Smith, A. [1776 (1976)]. *An Inquiry into the Nature and Causes of the Wealth of Nations.* Oxford.

Stiglitz, J.E. (1998). *More Instruments and Broader Goals Moving Toward the Post-Washington Consensus.* United Nations University/WIDER, Helsinki.

Tansel, A. (2000). "Wage Earners, Self-Employed and Gender in the Informal Sector in Turkey." Unpublished, Middle East Technical University.

Taqi Usmani, M. (1998). *An Introduction to Islamic Finance.* Arab & Islamic Laws Series.

The Economist (2014). "Islamic Finance, Big Interest, No Interest." 412 (8904) September 13, pp. 75–76.

The Gutnick Edition (2006). *Chumash: With commentary from Classic Rabbinic Texts and the Lubavitcher Rebbe.* New York: Kol Menachem Publisher.

Topel, R. (1999). "Labor Markets and Economic Growth." In O.C. Ashenfelter and D. Card (eds.), *Handbook of Labor Economics* Amsterdam: North-Holland.

Tornell, A. and P. Lane (1999)."The Voracity Effect." *American Economic Review* 89, pp. 22–46.

Torvik, R. (2002). "Natural Resources, Rent Seeking and Welfare." *Journal of Development Economics* 67, pp. 455–470.

Trefler, D (1995). "The Case of the Missing Trade and Other HOV Mysteries." *American Economic Review* 85:5, pp. 1029–1046.

Tunali, I. (2003). "Background Study on Labour Market and Employment in Turkey." European Training Foundation, Torino.

UNDP (2002). *Arab Human Development Report: Creating Opportunities for Future Generations.* New York.

UNDP (2003). *Arab Human Development Report: Building a Knowledge Society.* New York.

UNDP (2004). *Arab Human Development Report: Towards Freedom in the Arab World.* New York.

UNDP (2005). *Arab Human Development Report: Towards the Rise of Women in the Arab World.* New York.

UNDP (2009a). *Arab Human Development Report: Challenges to Human Security in the Arab Countries.* New York.

UNDP (2016a). *Arab Human Development Report: Youth and the Prospects for Human Development in a Changing Reality.* New York.

UNDP (2016b). *Human Development Report 2016.* New York.

UNDP (2009b). *Arab Knowledge Report.* New York.

UNESCO (2009). *Education for All: Meeting Our Collective Commitments.* UNESCO Publishing.

UNESCO (2017). *Accountability in Education: Meeting our Commitments.* UNESCO Publishing.

USAID (2004). "Strengthening Education in the Muslim World Country Profiles and Analysis." Washington, USA.

Van Assche, A. (2012). *Global Value Chains and Canada's Trade Policy: Business as Usual or Paradigm Shift*, IRRP Study, No. 32. Available at: www.irp.org.

Van Assche, A. and B. Gangnes (2007). *Electronics Production Upgrading: Is China Exceptional?* CIRANO Scientific Series, 2007s-16.

Vandewalle, D. (1998). *Libya Since Independence: Oil and StateBuilding* Ithaca, NY: Cornell University Press.

Venables, A.J. (2001). "Trade, Location, and Development: An Overview of Theory." London School of Economics and CEPR/World Bank, Washington, DC. Processed.

Williamson, J. (1990). "What Washington Means by Policy Reform." In J. Williamson (ed.), *Latin American Adjustment: How Much Has Happened?* Institute for International Economics, USA.

World Economic Forum (WEF) (2016). *The Global Information Technology Report 2016: Innovating in the Digital Economy.* Geneva: World Economic Forum.

World Bank (1995). *Claiming the Future: Choosing Prosperity in the Middle East/North Africa Region.* Washington, DC.

World Bank (1998). *Beyond the Washington Consensus: Institutions Matter.* Washington, USA.

World Bank (2004a). *Unlocking the Employment Potential in the Middle East and North Africa: Toward a New Social Contract.* Washington, USA.

World Bank (2004b). *Innovation Systems: World Bank Support of Science and Technology Development* Washington, USA.

World Bank (2007). *Breaking the Barriers to Higher Economic Growth: Better Governance and Deeper Reforms in the Middle East and North Africa.* Washington, USA.

World Bank (2008).*The Road Not Traveled — Education Reform in the Middle East and North Africa.* Washington, USA.

World Bank (2010). *Innovation Policy: A Guide for Developing Countries.* Washington, USA.

World Bank (2015). *Jobs or Privileges: Unleashing the Employment Potential of the Middle East and North Africa.* Washington, USA.

World Bank (2016a). *What's Holding Back the Private Sector In MENA? Lessons From The Enterprise Survey.* Jointly published with the European Bank for Reconstruction and Development (EBRD) and the European Investment Bank (EIB). Washington, USA.

World Bank (2016b). *Middle East and North Africa Public Employment and Governance in MENA.* Washington, USA.

World Bank (2017). *Doing Business 2017: Equal Opportunity for All.* Washington, USA.

World Bank (2018). *Doing Business 2018: Reforming to Create Jobs.* Washington, USA.

World Economic Forum (2007). *The Global Competitiveness Report 2007–2008.* New York: Palgrave Macmillan.

World Economic Forum (2008). *The Global Competitiveness Report 2008–2009*. New York: Palgrave Macmillan.

World Economic Forum (2009). *The Global Competitiveness Report 2009–2010*. Geneva: World Economic Forum.

Zwaini, L. and R. Peters (1994). *A Bibliography of Islamic Law 1980–1993*. Leiden.

Index

Abed and Davoodi, 17
Adam Smith, 335
Agénor, 231
Aggarwal and Yousef, 175
Aghion, 30
Aghion and Howitt, 231
Ahmad, 168
Ambinder, de Silva and Dewar, 174
Arab Spring, 1, 29, 33, 124
Arab youth, 31, 32, 34, 465
Archibugi *et al.*, 402
Archibugi and Michie, 402
Archibugi and Pianta, 402
Atkinson and Hamilton, 349
Auty, 124, 340
Azam, 341

Badr, 168, 169
Balassa, 441, 442
Baldwin, 412, 419, 440
Baldwin and Venables, 412
Barro and Lee, 232, 268
Beck *et al.*, 176
Benhabib and Spiegel, 231
Bergsten, 18
Bernheim and Whinston, 366
Berthelemy *et al.*, 307
Birdsall and de la Torre, 15
Bond, 335
Bonner, 168
Bosworth and Collins, 83
Bowen, 441
Bowen and Pelzman, 441, 443
Bulte and Damania, 366

Chen and Dahlman, 370, 371, 373
Chong and Liu, 175, 176
Coe and Hess, 419
Comin and Hobijn, 398
control of corruption, 4, 6
Corden, 337–339, 341
Corden and Neary, 337, 338, 340, 341
Coulson, 168
Credit Suisse, 175

Dasgupta and Weale, 52
Davis, 340
De Soto, 142
de-globalization, 18
Djankov *et al.*, 147, 150, 158
Dollar, 432

Easterly, 14, 271
Ebrahim and Rahman, 173
Edwards, 432
El-Erian and Fischer, 461
El-Gamal, 168, 170–173, 175
ensen and Wantchekon, 341
Esfahani and Squire, 432, 433

Falkingham, 52
Feenstra, 444
Feenstra and Hiau, 444
Findlay and Jones, 335

Fischer, 432, 461
François, 97
Frankel, 461
Frankel and Romer, 432

Galal and Hoekman, 461
Gelb, Knight and Sabot, 277
gender equality, 2, 3, 31, 36, 37, 163, 341, 465
gender inequality, 36
Gittleman and Wolff, 402
globalization, 17, 20, 30, 40, 52, 83, 209, 369, 372, 405, 407, 409, 427, 440, 465
Gollin, 272
Government Effectiveness, 6
Grossman and Helpman, 335, 366
Grossman and Rossi-Hansberg, 419
Growth Commission Report, 373
Gylfason, 340, 342

Hagedoorn and Duysters, 375
Hakura, 335
Hall and Jones, 232
Hanushek and Woessmann, 271
Hanushek, Peterson and Woessmann, 270
Harrison and Rodriguez-Clare, 30
Hasan, 163
Hausmann and Rodrik, 30
Hoekman and Messerlin, 439
Homer and Sylla, 168
Hsieh and Klenow, 179
Hudson, 419
Hulten and Isaksson, 373
human capital, 1, 14, 18, 19, 40, 52, 67, 68, 81, 83, 122, 163, 180–183, 185, 210, 215, 229, 231, 232, 269–272, 276, 334, 335, 341, 370, 372, 383, 405, 409, 412, 444
human capital-augmented, 274
Human Development Indicator, 40
Humphreys *et al.*, 341
Huntington, 367

ILO, 36, 37, 307, 332
IMF, 2, 14, 33, 84, 124, 432
Iqbal, 168
Isaksson, 372
Islamic Financial Services Board, 174

Jamison *et al.*, 270, 271
Jones, 335, 337

Kabir, 52
Karl, 341, 349
Kaufmann, 15, 349, 365, 366
Keller and Nabli, 274, 276
Khan, 176
Klenow and Rodríguez-Clare, 272
Knowledge Economy Index, 19, 210, 404
Knowledge Index, 19, 210, 404
Koopman, 419, 421–424
Krueger, 432
Krugman, 15, 335, 442
Kuczynski and Williamson, 15
Kuran, 163–165, 168

Leamer, 333, 334, 432
Lederman and Maloney, 444
Lucas, 179, 232
Luciani, 367

Ma and Van Assche, 426
Mahdavy, 367
Mallat, 169
Mankiw, 232
McMillen, 173
Mehlum, 340, 342, 349
Melitz, 444
Murray *et al.*, 52

Naim, 15
Neumayer, 340
Noland and Pack, 18
North, 97
Norton Rose, 173, 174

OECD, 14, 29, 31, 32, 34, 42, 52

Page and Underwood, 461
Palestine, 2, 82
Pamuk, 168
Papyrakis and Gerlagh, 342
Patel and Pavitt, 402
Pavitt and Patel, 402
Pecorino, 231
Pelzman, 30, 369, 412
Pelzman and Shoham, 412, 433, 461
Pianta and Tancioni, 402
Political Stability and Absence of Violence/Terrorism, 6
Posner, 83, 168
Pritchett, 271
private sector employment, 32, 33
Psacharopoulos, 232
public sector, 33, 150, 163, 231, 276, 277, 305, 307, 332, 349, 367, 466

Qur'an, 168
Qureshi, 168

Regulatory Quality, 6, 342, 365, 366
Richards and Waterbury, 29
Richardson, 443
Robinson, 342, 349
Robinson and Thierfelder, 461
Robinson and Torvik, 341
Robinson *et al.*, 341
Rodriguez and Rodrik, 432, 433
Rodrik, 15, 16, 277
Romer, 179, 180, 372
Rosenzweig, 276
Ross, 341
Roy, 168
Ruffin, 335
Rule of Law, 6, 11, 83, 342, 349, 350, 365, 368, 372, 373
Rutherford, 461

Sabahi, 170–172
Sachs and Warner, 124, 340, 341
Schacht, 168
Schiff and Winters, 461
Schultz, 271
Segerstrom, 402
Senor and Singer, 367
Shafik, 461
Silverberg, 369
Stiglitz, 15
Sukuk, 174

Takaful, 174
Tansel, 276
Taqi Usmani, 172
The Gutnick Edition of the Chumash, 169
Topel, 231
Torah, 1, 2, 169
Tornell and Lane, 349
total factor productivity, 19, 166, 179, 180, 183, 272, 276, 372, 444
Trefler, 335
Tunali, 276

UN, 2, 14, 32, 36, 163, 183–185, 208
UNDP, 31, 32, 36, 37, 40, 81, 82, 122, 124, 125, 183–185, 215, 229, 342, 367, 370, 383, 404
UNESCO, 228, 268, 270, 402
UNIDO, 373
USAID, 270

Van Assche, 426
Van Assche and Gangnes, 426
Vandewalle, 367
Venables, 335
Voice and Accountability, 11, 365

Washington Consensus, 3, 14–16, 163, 179, 180
WEF, 369
Williamson, 14, 15
World Bank, 2, 14, 19, 32–34, 36, 123–126, 209, 210, 215, 228, 229, 232, 270, 274, 307, 332, 370, 371, 374, 401, 404, 439, 461
World Economic Forum, 150, 439

Zwaini and Peters, 168

Printed in the United States
By Bookmasters